CHELSEA

A COMPLETE RECORD
1905-1991

CHELSEA

A COMPLETE RECORD
1905-1991

SCOTT
CHESHIRE

BREEDON
BOOKS
SPORT

First published in Great Britain by
The Breedon Books Publishing Company Limited
44 Friar Gate, Derby DE1 1DA
1991

ISBN 0 907969 87 9

Printed and bound in Great Britain by Bath Press, Bath and London.
Jacket printed by The Nuffield Press, Cowley, Oxford.

Contents

Foreword

AS THE Chelsea story joins the celebrated Breedon Books Complete Record series, the thought occurs that if any of the books already published in this series was the work of a more devoted follower of his club than Scott Cheshire, then *This is Your Life* should know about him.

Being born within shouting distance of Stamford Bridge, Scottie was always going to be right for Chelsea. He was first brought to see the Blues, or rather the Pensioners as they were then, by his father as a Christmas treat in 1933. The team responded with a 4-0 win against Sunderland, and a wide-eyed boy became an instant fan.

Those were the days when George Mills was scoring at one end and Vic Woodley was keeping them out at the other . . .when football's record transfer fee was £10,000 . . .when the game's top stars were earning £8 a week in the winter, £6 in the summer.

It is the safest of football wagers that Scott Cheshire has now seen more Chelsea matches than anyone else on earth. For the last 16 years, every game at Stamford Bridge has meant a 300-mile round trip from his home near Stoke, and he still attends many more away games than he misses.

Within these covers, the Chelsea story, year by year from Day One, is told comprehensively in words, figures and photographs. To the Chelsea-minded, it will be welcomed like the coming of a new star to the team.

Talking of Chelsea players, isn't it time they stopped selling Scottie — and every other supporter of this club — short in the matter of prizes won?

For a club of Chelsea's eminence and durability, the list of major honours brought to Stamford Bridge is a pitiful reward for more than 80 years of trying, whilst all the time they have been building bigger trophy rooms at Highbury, Anfield, White Hart Lane and Old Trafford.

How about it fellows, under your new manager in season 1991-2?

I shall add this tome to my football library with pride. Would that such an outstanding reference book had been at hand through the 25 seasons I was privileged to edit the Chelsea programme, and subsequently as a contributor to both programme and club newspaper.

Here's to every success, Scottie, with your latest Chelsea creation.

Albert Sewell

Introduction
and Acknowledgements

IT WAS in 1985 that Ron Hockings and I compiled and published the *Chelsea Football Club Full Statistical Story* and this new volume inevitably draws heavily upon much of the research which went into that book and its two subsequent 'update' editions. My thanks are therefore due to Ron for the many hours' labour which went into producing especially the 'season-by-season' section.

In addition, I owe an enormous debt to Jim Creasey, who has spent endless time uncovering numerous factual items for the *Chelsea Who's Who* pages in this new book, which would be so much less complete but for his labours and those of his helpers, Mike Davage, Ian Garland and John Blackmore. Colm Kerrigan also produced much valuable material for the early years, as did Robert Randall whose diligent researches brought to light many slips in the earlier Chelsea books. And, as always, Albert Sewell has been at hand to help and offer professional advice.

It is also right and proper to recognize the vital and varied contributions made by the Association of Football Statisticians over the years, many of which, I fear, are taken on board without acknowledgements. I venture to suggest that no book of this type could be anywhere near as complete without AFS members.

Finally, and not least, I also owe much to Anton Rippon and his admirable staff at Breedon Books for being so patient and tolerant, especially in adapting and transferring material from the earlier Chelsea tomes into the present volume. What I thought would be 'short-cuts' often turned out to create considerable problems, all of which were uncomplainingly overcome.

As anyone who has attempted to produce any similar work well knows, one's labours can never be considered completed and I would be grateful to receive further information through Breedon Books, particularly additional biographical details of former Chelsea players.

All statistics, including international appearances, are up to and including the last day of the 1990-91 Football League season. League figures include play-off matches.

Scott Cheshire
May 1991

Photographic acknowledgements

Photographs have been supplied by Scott Cheshire, Albert Sewell, Action Images, Empics, the *Bolton Evening News* and the *Grimsby Evening Telegraph*.

The Chelsea Story

FEW of England's Football League clubs came into existence in such a strange and fortuitous manner as Chelsea in the early months of 1905. Nine years before, the well-known London building contractor, H.A. ('Gus') Mears, and his brother, J.T.Mears, had the foresight to purchase, first, the Stamford Bridge Athletic Grounds and, soon afterwards, a large area of market garden immediately adjoining that property to lay the foundations for the football stadium 'Gus' Mears had set his sights on building.

Yet, almost certainly, such ambitions would have foundered but for the historic meeting which took place on the ground one Sunday morning between Gus Mears and F.W.Parker, a well-known financier. Mears was on the point of accepting an attractive offer from the Great Western Railway Company for the whole site to be developed as a coal and goods siding. Confiding in his friend that unfortunately 'no one would come in with him', he had decided to sell. Suddenly, Parker was savagely attacked and bitten by Mears' dog, an Aberdeen terrier. With blood flowing from the wound, Mears calmly observed, "Scotch Terrier, always bites before he speaks." Then, slapping his friend on the back, he added, "You took that damned well; most men would have kicked up hell about it. Look here, I'll stand on you. Go to the chemist and get that bite seen to and we'll meet here tomorrow morning and get busy."

Chelsea line-up in 1905. Left to right: Watson, McRoberts, Key, Windridge, Mackie, Foulke, Copeland, J.T.Robertson, McEwan, Moran, Kirwan.

Within days, a meeting with the famous football stand architect, Archibald Leitch, was arranged, with Mears and Parker travelling to Glasgow to inspect football stadiums, including Hampden Park, Ibrox and Celtic Park. Mears' dog had certainly set the wheels in motion and, indeed, might have made a more suitable emblem on the Chelsea club's badge than the famous Pensioner.

Even then, there was no thought of forming a new football club. Rather, the stadium was offered to John Dean of Fulham FC for 'their club matches only', at a suggested fee of £1,500 per annum, with Mears retaining the right to stage 'extraneous matches' at the ground. Dean, however, was overruled by another director of Fulham, H.G.Norris, who considered the sum involved too high.

Whereupon, Parker again intervened. "You have the finest ground in the kingdom," he told Mears. "If they won't come to terms, then tell them we'll start a new club that is bound to become one of the best in the country." And so the seed of what was to emerge as Chelsea Football Club was sown.

Application to join the Southern League was made but met with opposition from other London clubs, Fulham and Tottenham Hotspur included. As a result, the decision to test certain clubs in the Football League for their reaction was made. Again, Parker was much involved and, writing some 30 years later, he justifiably stated, "Mr Mears was truly the Father of the Club but I can claim to be its Godfather."

Parker, too, was responsible for the club's name. Stamford Bridge had been suggested. But, apart from its Yorkshire connections, try shouting, "Play up Stamford Bridge", Parker sensibly queried. So Chelsea it was.

The first meeting of Chelsea FC took place at 7.30pm on 14 March 1905. Claude

9

Kirby was appointed chairman, and canvassing for election to the Football League began in earnest a month later, on 19 April, by which time John Tait Robertson, the Scottish international half-back had been appointed player-manager.

Parker and Robertson visited the four Manchester and Liverpool clubs before going on to others in the North and Midlands. At Lytham they met the president of the Football League, J.J.Bentley, who demanded to know, "Which are you really trying for, the Southern League or us?"

That was enough for Parker. Leaving the meeting, he immediately went to his hotel to telephone the London Press Agency, announcing that Chelsea were not applying for election to the Southern League but to the 'Football League only'. And to prove that the club meant business players were signed up straight away. From Small Heath came Bob McRoberts and James Robertson, for £150, and, a day later, Jimmy Windridge was added to the list, for £190. Within a month, the already legendary Willie Foulke, Sheffield United's 22-stone goalkeeper, was enlisted along with full-backs Tommy Miller, Marshall McEwan and Bob Mackie, and Tottenham's left-wing pair, Johnny Kirwan and David Copeland.

Seldom in football can such acts of faith have occurred, for Chelsea's election to the League was still far from certain.

On 29 May, the decisive annual general meeting of the Football League was held in the Tavistock Hotel in London with a bevy of other clubs equally intent on 'pushing their boats out'. The night before, and well into the early hours of the morning canvassing continued. Years later, Parker again revealed his resourcefulness. Writing to a friend he admitted, "I took the precaution to bribe the girl behind the bar that night, so that whenever I called for so many 'Scotch and Pollies' the glass on the extreme left should always be a Ross's Dry Ginger. So I was able to keep my head clear."

His confidence, too, was typical of the man. Despite considerable opposition from several managers, he took bets with both Kirby and Jackie Robertson — "Five bob we do get elected." Then, being informed at short notice by his chairman that he would be making the speech on behalf of Chelsea, he walked into the meeting 'whistling and humming'. Making his points with simplicity and clarity, he emphasized the stability of Chelsea's financial position, and the ground and accommodation facilities which, although unfinished, would 'bear comparison with any in the League'. Over-running his alloted three minutes, he read out a list of the players already

Action from Chelsea's first season. Manchester United on the attack at Stamford Bridge in April 1906.

signed, before concluding, "I thank you all for listening so attentively to me and will not trespass on you further beyond suggesting that when you consider the points that I have made you will come to the conclusion that you cannot really refuse us!"

In view of such oratory, perhaps not surprisingly, Chelsea were duly elected. And without ever having kicked a ball!

Despite starting their League career with a single goal defeat, at Stockport on 2 September 1905, Chelsea immediately demonstrated their right to compete in the Football League. Moreover, great crowds attended their games up and down the country, their arrival in midland and northern towns often being greeted by large numbers of opposing supporters at the railway stations. 67,000 packed into Stamford Bridge for the Good Friday fixture against Manchester United, with both clubs challenging strongly for promotion.

Finishing their first season in third place, nine points behind promoted United, was a marvellous beginning and no club in the division bettered their 90 goals. A year later, promotion to the First Division was celebrated, as only one of 19 League fixtures at Stamford Bridge failed to result in victory.

The arrival of the first in a long line of outstanding Chelsea marksmen was probably the key factor. George Hilsdon, a 20-year-old forward from West Ham United, had been signed by Robertson after he had set out to watch another player appearing in the Hammers' reserve team. Scoring five goals in his first match for Chelsea (against Glossop), for five seasons, apart from one short break, 'Gatling Gun George' was a consistent goalscorer, respected and feared by opponents everywhere.

Promotion had been achieved with a comfortable nine-point margin, exceeding even the hopes of the fondest optimist. Life in Division One, however, in only the third season, was never easy. David Calderhead ('the Sphinx') had taken over the managership from Jackie Robertson, knowing only too well that new blood was required. The 9-1 win over Worksop Town in the FA Cup (a club record still standing today) was the highlight in an otherwise uphill struggle.

Prominent newcomers included Fred Rouse from Stoke (Chelsea's first 'four-figure' signing). And another important addition, from Derby County, was Ben Warren,

Chelsea before the start of the 1908-09 season. Back row (left to right): Moir (assistant trainer), Reilly, Cane, Cartwright, Cameron, Kennedy, Harding, H.Ransom (trainer). Second row: Miller, A.J.Palmer (assistant secretary), David Calderhead (secretary-manager), Henderson, Warren, Robinson, Brawn, Douglas, Dolby, Whitley, Birnie, McKenzie, Key. Seated: Directors G.Schomberg, J.H.Maltby, H.A.Mears, W.C.Kirby (chairman), J.T.Mears, F.W.Parker, T.L.Kinton, E.H.Janes. On ground: Walton, Freeman, Rouse, Hilsdon, McRoberts (captain), Windridge, Humphreys, Bridgeman, Fairgray.

already an England international half-back, whose career was shortly to be terminated by illness, prior to his death at the age of 38. In the circumstances, a final placing of 13th was creditable.

So, too, was 11th in the 1908-09 season. Relegation, 12 months later, was Chelsea's first major set-back. Hilsdon missed nearly half the season through injury, and 34 players were tried as Calderhead failed to hit on a winning combination. But on the credit side, the great Corinthian amateur, Vivian ('V.J.') Woodward, began his association with the club and defenders Walter Bettridge, Fred Taylor and Alec Ormiston were others destined to play major parts in Chelsea's future, along with inside-forward Bob Whittingham, another son of the Potteries.

Desperate to avoid the 'big drop', it was the signing of five players, at a cost of £3,575, during the closing weeks of that season which led to the Football League introducing their 16 March transfer 'deadline', after which date players could only represent their new clubs with the consent of the management committee. Chelsea were already making their mark, although, in the event, this desperate effort failed, with Tottenham winning the vital last game, 2-1 at White Hart Lane, the deciding goal coming from Percy Humphreys, whom Chelsea had transferred to Spurs only months before.

Yet, still the crowds kept pouring into Stamford Bridge. The 70,000 watching the Newcastle United game in December 1909 was the largest to attend any Football League match up to that time.

Third in the Second Division in 1910-11, with Whittingham (38 goals) and Hilsdon (18) forming a lethal spearhead was not enough to win promotion. Another new Stamford Bridge 'gate' record saw 77,952 watching an FA Cup tie with Swindon Town.

History repeated itself, however, when promotion followed at the second attempt, 12 months later. This time the struggle went to the final day when a goal from Charlie Freeman, never a regular first-teamer but to serve Chelsea in various capacities for 46 years, scored the only goals of the match against Bradford at The Bridge. By then three others destined to match Freeman's loyalty had arrived. Full-back Jack Harrow, from Croydon Common, began his 15-year playing stint, to be followed by almost equally lengthy service as a member of the training staff. And Jim ('Moly') Molyneux was to guard Chelsea's net for a dozen seasons, including World War One, while his goalkeeping deputy, Jack Whitley, stayed for 32 years, the majority of them as first-team trainer.

Calderhead had, arguably, built Chelsea's strongest squad up to that time, a claim unfortunately not borne out by the results which followed. Hilsdon had returned to West Ham; Whittingham found First Division defences harder to unlock; while, at the other end of the field, only relegated Woolwich Arsenal conceded more goals.

A year later, however, the story was happier as Chelsea ended 1913-14 in the top half of the Championship for the first time. Harold Halse, from Aston Villa, added skill and finesse at inside-forward. Tommy Logan, from Scotland, and the 'Great Dane', Nils Middelboe bolstered the defence.

So far, apart from a lone appearance in the FA Cup semi-final against Newcastle United at Birmingham in March 1911, success had eluded Chelsea in knock-out football. In the final season before World War One caused a four-year interruption of the League and Cup, however, Chelsea went one better. Along their path to the Final, their victims included Woolwich Arsenal, Manchester City, Newcastle United and Everton, in a Villa Park semi-final. With war already in progress and teams decimated by players away on more urgent matters, the venue of the Final was switched from London to Manchester, for security reasons.

Travel was difficult and few supporters made the journey north on 24 April 1915 to see Sheffield United, cheered on by the majority of the 50,000 present, in what proved a depressingly one-sided contest. Lt V.J.Woodward, home on leave from France, could not be persuaded to take over regular Bob Thomson's place in the forward line, and, in a somewhat unrealistic atmosphere the Blades cantered to a 3-0 victory.

Worse followed four days later, when defeat in the League fixture against Notts County apparently doomed Chelsea to relegation for the third time in ten seasons. Luck, however, was later to intervene. By the time hostilities had ended, four years on, not only had the Football League decided to extend the First Division from 20 to 22 clubs, but also, after a somewhat complicated inquiry involving players of Liverpool and Manchester United in a result proved to have been 'fixed', Chelsea were duly reinstated in the top class.

When normal football resumed, on 1 September 1919, most of the pre-war team were available, but, within weeks, Jack Cock had arrived from Huddersfield Town to strengthen the attack. His 21 goals from 25 games tells its own story. Indeed, had he been at Chelsea from the beginning of the season, he could well have made the team into serious Championship contenders. As it was, a final placing of third and another FA Cup semi-final appearance — Aston Villa winning 3-1 at Bramall Lane — put Chelsea among the top clubs in the country for the first time.

However, the side was ageing and 11 newcomers, among them wing-half Tommy Meehan, moved in. Meehan, a gifted and most stylish performer from Manchester United, was all too soon to contract the illness which brought about his premature death in the summer of 1924, when still at the height of his career. From a playing staff of 36, the right blend was never achieved and for the next four seasons merely maintaining a First Division place again became the main concern.

Over this period the loss of such stalwarts as Molyneux, Bettridge, Halse, Thomson, Logan and Croal proved insurmountable, as replacements failed to measure up to their standards. Only the arrival of goalkeeper Benjamin Howard Baker, athlete and all-rounder extraordinary, brightened the scene. When not keeping goal for the Corinthians, or representing Great Britain in the Olympics and in other athletic meetings, he was Chelsea's first choice between the posts for five seasons. Like Foulke before him, his spectacular feats pulled in the crowds and he would certainly have won more full international caps had he been able to concentrate solely on football.

Meehan played his last game for Chelsea in March 1924 and, within six weeks, the club again returned to Division Two. And this time there was to be no quick comeback. Final positions of fifth, third, fourth, third and ninth bred considerable frustration, not helped by an inability to make any notable progress in the FA Cup competition during those years. At least a better vintage of players had arrived. Simeon ('Sam') Millington was a dependable goalkeeper. George Smith and Tommy Law established their distinguished full-back partnership. Smith's 370 first-team games was unequalled in Chelsea history, until the 1950s, and Law could well have exceeded those figures but for several injuries during his 13-year spell on the staff. A familiar figure at The Bridge long after his playing career had finished, this member of the Scottish 1928 'Wembley Wizards' was one of the best-loved of all Chelsea's many star players.

During this span and, for the first time, Chelsea failed to unearth a genuine goalscorer. Bobby McNeil (the final survivor from pre-war days), Jackie Crawford and George Pearson were sparkling wingers. Willie Ferguson, Harold Miller and Andy Wilson notable inside-forwards. Wilson, in particular, was a supreme artist, who played for Scotland 12 times when international matches were much rarer events than in modern times and 'Anglos' were not exactly welcomed by the Scottish selectors. Yet only Bob Turnbull, for two seasons, and Jimmy Thomson for one, found the net with any consistency.

Not until Christmas 1929, when Chelsea noticed a gangling youngster playing amateur football for Bromley on Saturdays and working at a City desk during the rest of the week, did a worthy long-term successor to Hilsdon and Cock emerge. George Mills' 14 goals in 20 matches before the end of that season was a vital factor in clinching promotion, greatly contributing to a sequence of 25 points from 17 games up to the beginning of April. Even so, the promotion battle went to the last ditch, at Bury's Gigg Lane. A tense and agonizingly close contest was won by the Lancastrians' single goal, the resultant depression being dispelled only by the news of Oldham Athletic's defeat across the Pennines at Barnsley, which was enough to give Chelsea the vital runner's-up position.

The nine seasons leading up to the outbreak of World War Two followed a pattern. Only twice did the team finish above the half-way mark, and twice relegation was avoided by a whisker. Brilliance one week would be followed by incompetence the next, to fuel the repertoires of music-hall artists up and down the land. Yet, no expense was spared to bring top players to Stamford Bridge who, if they failed to bring the required results, at least continued to attract large crowds through the turnstiles, at a time when Arsenal were carrying all before them in North London, with their three consecutive Championship titles.

In 1933, David Calderhead's 26-year reign as manager at last came to an end when he was succeeded by Leslie Knighton, whose previous experience in this field

Chelsea goalkeeper B. Howard Baker punches clear from a Bradford City forward at Stamford Bridge at the start of the 1925-6 season. A. G. Bower, another famous amateur, covers the goalmouth.

had included six years in charge of Arsenal. But the change signalled no shift of boardroom policy, and continued 'chequebook' management brought no greater degree of success on the field.

Twenty-one internationals wore the blue shirt during this time, of whom only three (Mills, Vic Woodley and Peter Buchanan — one Scottish cap) did not involve transfer fees. Another semi-final appearance, this time at Huddersfield, against Newcastle United, was an isolated pinnacle of the 1930s, even then the 'Geordies' winning 2-1.

Competition for places was greater than ever before, undoubtedly a contributory factor to the frequent lack of harmony in the dressing-room. Woodley (England) and Jackson (Scotland) were two of the finest 'keepers in Britain and both represented their countries. Indeed, Woodley won 19 international caps in succession, a sequence broken only by the outbreak of World War Two. In 1934-5, Scotland's Hughie Gallacher, Ireland's Joe Bambrick and Mills, to play for England in the near future, jostled for the centre-forward position. For a time, internationals Allan Craig and Peter O'Dowd were rivals for selection at centre-half. Seemingly little thought went into building a team and the theory that the assembling of talent was all that was needed to ensure success was continually being disproved.

A further unsettling factor was the approach to Chelsea players from overseas clubs. At a time of the £8-a-week maximum wage, such as Alex Cheyne and Wilson

15

Chelsea appeal but the referee allows this West Brom goal during an FA Cup tie at Stamford Bridge in January 1934. The Chelsea players are (left to right) Barber, Allum, Woodley and Law.

Jimmy Argue saves Chelsea a point when he heads home against Aston Villa at Stamford Bridge in March 1939. George Barber challenges Villa goalkeeper Biddlestone as Dick Spence waits hopefully.

received offers from French club, Nimes, and O'Dowd from Valenciennes. Alex Jackson, the 'Gay Cavalier', walked out of League football at the age of 28 in search of greater financial reward, and Tom Priestley was so disenchanted with life at The Bridge that he returned home to Ireland after one season, refusing to re-sign, and dropped out of the English game forever.

From this galaxy four stars stood out. Law was one of the best full-backs in the Football League. For three seasons O'Dowd was arguably the outstanding footballing centre-half in the game. And, of course, Gallacher was already a legend when he came down the Fulham Road. Of excitable temperament and an extravagant drinker, he, nevertheless, possessed such talent that many rated him the best centre-forward to have played football up to that time. And this despite standing only 5ft 5in, a handicap for which his ball-skills more than adequately compensated. From Chelsea's point of view, however, their 'Player of the 1930s' was unquestionably Woodley. For nearly eight seasons his consistently fine goalkeeping kept the club in the First Division. Possessing a wonderful positional sense and a marvellously safe pair of hands, it is not always appreciated that his England caps were won in the face of competition from such as Harry Hibbs, Frank Swift (then in his prime) and a young Sam Bartram.

Nevertheless, it was mainly from the less expensive, but infinitely more dependable, players that Chelsea obtained value and loyalty. George Barber and Craig, in defence, terrier Billy Mitchell and the elegant Sam Weaver at wing-half, Jimmy Argue, Harry Burgess and Dick Spence in attack were the ones who performed reliably week in, week out.

In April 1939, Knighton was replaced by Billy Birrell, a likeable Scot, who had had considerable experience of English football with Middlesbrough as a player, and with Queens Park Rangers as manager. Years later the outgoing incumbent was to write, "In a lifetime of football management I have never handled a more intriguing side than Chelsea . . .if my hair is grey, there is a reason for it."

Before Birrell, could get to grips with Chelsea's problems, World War Two had begun and an already difficult task was considerably greater when normal football resumed seven years later. Of his first team which met Bolton Wanderers in August 1939, only one — Dick Spence — survived. Of the remainder all but Woodley, first with Bath City and later with Derby County, Weaver, who made two post-war appearances for Stockport County, and Joe Payne, a handful of games with West Ham United, had retired.

Fortunately, the new manager had already been planning ahead. Flourishing the chequebook in best Chelsea traditions, Danny Winter and John Harris had been signed, cheaply in fact, after several seasons of wartime football at Stamford Bridge. More notably, the international trio of Tommy Lawton, indisputably England's top centre-forward of the day, and veteran inside-forwards, Len Goulden (England) and Tommy Walker (Scotland) also arrived, at a total outlay of some £30,000.

Long-term rebuilding proved more difficult. Never once in his six seasons in control after the war was Birrell able to steer his teams into the top half of the table. Twice relegation was avoided by narrow margins. Indeed, in 1950-51, it had already been accepted as a certainty when Liverpool arrived down the Fulham Road on 21 April, with Chelsea (14 games without a win) six points adrift of Everton in 20th place in the table. Not only was that game won but, in turn, Wolverhampton Wanderers, Fulham and Bolton Wanderers were also beaten and Chelsea had accomplished one of football's greatest 'Houdini' acts, clinging to their First Division place by 0.044 of a goal!

Apart from two further semi-final appearances, both against Arsenal at White Hart Lane and both requiring replays on the same ground, Birrell's main achievement was the launching of the Chelsea youth scheme which was to pay such rich dividends.

Above: Jimmy Payne's shot spins out of goalkeeper Bill Robertson's hands at Anfield during the game against Liverpool in December 1951. Opposite: Arsenal goalkeeper George Swindin punches clear at White Hart Lane in the 1952 FA Cup semi-final. Roy Bentley (10) is the Chelsea forward.

On 7 February 1948, under the name 'Tudor Rose', a Chelsea Junior side played its inaugural fixture and a new era in the Chelsea story had begun.

In the senior teams, however, new faces had begun to emerge. Ken Armstrong had been spotted playing in Army football, Jimmy Bowie was recruited from the Royal Navy, while relatively modest transfer fees obtained the service of Harry Medhurst to keep goal, full-backs Billy Hughes and Stan Willemse, wingers Bobby Campbell and Billy Gray and, most notable of all, Roy Bentley, about to be converted from inside-forward to a new-style 'roving' centre-forward.

An equally influential 'newcomer', and also a centre-forward — if one from the past — was Ted Drake. In the spring of 1952 he was appointed to succeed Birrell as manager. Reared on success as a player with Arsenal, he at once banished the Chelsea Pensioner from the club badge, as he set about ridding the club of its music-hall image. However much an endearing emblem, it was one scarcely likely to promote success. And, within three years he had brought the Football League Championship trophy to Stamford Bridge.

Positive and aggressive on the field as a player, he introduced similar qualities to his role as manager. After dangerously flirting with relegation in his first season, within 12 months he had turned things around with shrewd additions to the playing staff, as Chelsea's 14-match unbeaten spell in the 1953-4 mid-season set a new club record.

Drawing on his knowledge of the lower divisions of the Football League, gleaned from his time in charge of Reading, Peter Sillett (Southampton), Ron Greenwood (Brentford) who had started his career as a Chelsea 'apprentice' in 1940, Les Stubbs (Southend United), John McNichol (Brighton), Frank Blunstone (Crewe Alexandra) and Stan Wicks (Reading) all moved in. So, too, did amateurs Derek Saunders and Jim Lewis. Only Eric Parsons, a flying winger from West Ham United, at £23,000, cost more than a relatively modest sum.

On 23 April 1955, the Championship title was won in Chelsea's Golden Jubilee year. From an anonymous mid-table berth in November, the final 24 games included 15 wins and six draws and this greatest day in the club's history was duly celebrated

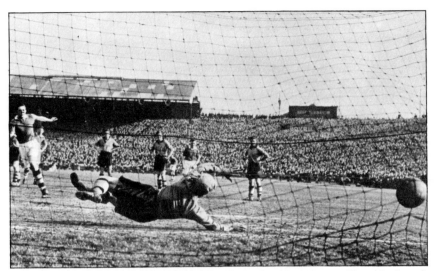

Peter Sillett scores the only goal of the Chelsea-Wolves game from the penalty spot. The result effectively ruled Wolves out of the 1955 Championship race.

The Chelsea team that won the only Football League Championship title in the club's history. Back row (left to right): Armstrong, Harris, Robertson, Saunders, Willemse, Greenwood. Front row: Parsons, McNichol, Bentley, Stubbs, Lewis.

by scenes of emotion and excitement after Sheffield Wednesday were beaten by three clear goals in the penultimate fixture, at The Bridge.

Bentley, the captain, led the attack superbly with tremendous flair, scoring 21 goals. Parsons (11 goals) was a dashing cavalier down the right flank, with Blunstone's trickery or Lewis's more direct approach a nice contrast on the opposite side. McNichol, Stubbs, and another amateur, Seamus O'Connell, better known in Carlisle and Bishop Auckland, added 26 goals from inside-forward. Greenwood and Wicks shared the centre-half position, flanked by Armstrong's stylish constructive play on the right and Saunders' waspish tackling and clever distribution on the left. Goalkeeper Bill Robertson, or his deputy 'Chick' Thomson, played behind Harris (now at full-back and nearing the end of his long and honourable playing career), the young Sillett and Willemse, with his endless enthusiasm and energy. Individually there may have been weaknesses, and many critics were grudging in acknowledging Chelsea's feat, but no one could deny the indomitable spirit which ran through the whole team, the very ingredient which had so often been lacking in many Chelsea teams of greater ability in the past.

As a result of being Champions of England, Chelsea had qualified for the first-ever European Cup competition, but, on the advice of the Football League, they declined the offer to take part. An extraordinarily ill-judged and timid decision.

The Championship side disintegrated quickly — six were already past their 30th birthdays — and their replacements were men of lesser pedigree and resolve. Exceptions were Reg Matthews, already an England goalkeeper, who never produced his best at Chelsea, craggy centre-half John Mortimore (yet another of Drake's acquisitions from amateur football), and three products from the Juniors, Peter Brabrook, Ron Tindall and Barry Bridges.

But if the crown was fading, one new jewel had arrived in the shape of Jimmy Greaves, bursting on to the scene after prodigious scoring feats as a junior. Within months of his senior debut, marked by a goal at Tottenham, he was rattling four into the Portsmouth net at Stamford Bridge on the morning of Christmas Day 1957. He went on to notch 132 goals from 169 senior games, a strike-rate unparalleled in the club's history. His departure to Italian football, after marking his last game at The Bridge with another four goals, was a hard blow for supporters to take.

Drake had been unable to sustain his earlier success and parted company with Chelsea in September 1961, to be replaced by his chief coach, Tommy Docherty, who then appointed Dave Sexton as his right-hand man.

He had left behind a good reservoir of talent. Peter Bonetti had begun his long tenancy of the goalkeeping position, and Terry Venables and Bobby Tambling had already a season of first-team experience. Blunstone, Brabrook and Bridges were established, and the youth scheme was in full production, with such as Ken Shellito, Bert Murray and the brothers Harris, Allan and Ron, waiting in the wings.

Relegation at the end of Docherty's first season was probably inevitable, and even a disguised blessing. It enabled young men to find their feet on a less demanding stage and to build up confidence in a winning team. And Docherty's frequent excursions into the transfer market, by no means always successful, included a bargain in Scottish full-back Eddie McCreadie and useful additions to the staff in Frank Upton and, more permanently, Marvin Hinton.

In August 1962, in Division Two for the first time since 1930, Chelsea were enjoying themselves and apparently romping away with the title. The club's best-ever unbeaten sequence, involving ten wins from 11 matches opened up a six-point advantage by the end of the year. Then snow and ice caused a virtual shut-down for two months, whereupon four defeats in March drastically changed matters. In the end, a crucial single-goal victory over Sunderland at Roker (the ball cannoning off Tommy Harmer's thigh into the net for the only goal of the game), and a spectacular

Chelsea outside-right Bert Murray (arms raised) scores his side's second goal against Stoke City at Stamford Bridge in October 1964.

seven-goal win against Portsmouth in the final game of the season at Stamford Bridge was enough to squeeze into the second promotion spot — by 0.401 of a goal.

The quality of the playing staff, not least in its depth, was probably now better than at any time in the club's history. Ten years of sustained success were to make the period from 1962 Chelsea's 'Golden Years'. Bonetti, Ron Harris, Mortimore and McCreadie presented a strong defensive barrier. Venables, playing possibly the best football of his career, was a marvellously creative figure in midfield. And Tambling, on his way to becoming the heaviest scorer in the club's history, had admirable support from Murray, Bridges, and the evergreen Blunstone.

In Docherty's exciting, and at times turbulent, reign League positions of fifth, third, fifth and ninth were accompanied by four FA Cup semi-finals, one of them leading to a first peacetime Wembley appearance in 1967. Disappointingly, Tottenham won the Final, 2-1, as Chelsea utterly failed to meet the occasion.

Two years earlier, the Football League Cup had been won, with Leicester City going under in a two-leg Final, so qualifying Chelsea for a bite of European football for the second time (they had appeared briefly and unsuccessfully in the Inter-Cities Fairs' Cup in 1958-9).

This time, in the same competition, in some memorable encounters they defeated, in turn, AS Roma, SK Weiner (Austria), AC Milan (winning the play-off third game in Milan on the toss of a coin) and Munich 1860, before bowing out to CF Barcelona in the semi-final. Once again a third game was required, after the first two ties had seen the teams locked together, 2-2 on aggregate. Penalty deciders had not cast their ugly shadow over the game in those days. There were nights of scintillating football, as well as some very ugly scenes, both on and off the field, on a sad October evening in Rome.

By now, John Hollins, Peter Osgood and, too briefly, George Graham had arrived on the scene. Successful though Docherty had been, his teams were prone to fall

Dave Mackay clears from Bobby Tambling during the 1967 FA Cup Final at Wembley.

at the final hurdle, as four semi-final failures and some relatively near-misses in the League suggest. Restlessly and impetuously, he sought to guide Chelsea to the top, but it was a bad day for the club when differences between manager and player led to the departure of Venables, despite it making way for the entry of Charlie Cooke.

The summer of 1966 had brought tragedy to Chelsea. Chairman Joe Mears died suddenly. President of the Football Association, he was an experienced and wise counsellor, and his relationship with the often unpredictable Docherty was a crucial one. Within months of Mears' death, rifts between board and manager were surfacing, confidence and respect lost on both sides. On 6 October 1967, Docherty resigned, his departure from the club coinciding with the Football Association imposing a month's suspension following incidents on Chelsea's summer tour of Bermuda.

Three weeks later, David Sexton, who three seasons earlier had left Chelsea, first to manage Orient and then to move on to coach, in turn, Fulham and Arsenal, was appointed as Docherty's successor. He was warmly welcomed by the playing staff, who, indeed, had been instrumental in getting him appointed.

Dressing-room morale, which had declined alarmingly, was restored and from

23

Chelsea's 1970 team. Back row (left to right): Hinton, Hutchinson, Webb, Hughes, Bonetti, Dempsey, McCreadie, Hollins. Front row: Birchenall, Cooke, Hudson, Boyle, Harris, Houseman, Osgood, Baldwin, Tambling.

Peter Bonetti can only watch as Mick Jones' effort for Leeds squeezes in at the post during the 1970 FA Cup Final at Wembley.

a position of 18th in the table at Christmas, the team rose to sixth by the end of the term, enough to qualify for Europe again. Alan Birchenall and David Webb were the only newcomers of note, but Osgood, out for nearly a whole season with a broken leg, returned, allowing his one-season replacement, Tony Hateley, to move on to Liverpool.

Stability and harmony did not bring immediate success. Fifth in the final table of 1968-9 was not accompanied by notable success in the three Cup competitions. Tambling played his last full season, and Shellito's five-year struggle against injury ended with his enforced retirement from the game. Ian Hutchinson, hitherto unknown on the League circuit, arrived with his giant 100ft throw-in, and centre-half John Dempsey was signed from Fulham.

But glory was at hand. Sexton's second full season in charge brought Chelsea their third major trophy in 65 years when Leeds United were beaten in a dramatic FA Cup Final replay at Old Trafford, 2-1 in extra-time after a 2-2 draw at Wembley 18 days earlier. Finishing third in the Championship almost went unnoticed, despite the fact that it had only once been bettered, in the title-winning season. A strong squad of 14 players meant that a settled team (not a common feature of Chelsea's history) was able to provide the springboard for success.

Sexton had, of course, been lucky in finding such a rich vein of talent when he arrived. But his clever and wide tactical knowledge was also of enormous significance. He had won the respect and confidence of his potentially temperamental pupils, one of whom, Alan Hudson, whose mature midfield generalship was a vital factor in the scheme of things, sadly, was forced to miss the FA Cup Final through injury.

Thirteen months later, in May 1971, the scene shifted from Manchester to the more exotic Karaiskaki Stadium in Athens. This time it was the European Cup-winners' Cup Final and again a second bite was required to overcome the original 'Kings of Europe', Real Madrid. Two days after a 1-1 draw, at the same venue, a rare goal from Dempsey and another from Osgood proved too great a leeway for Real to make up, despite their late challenge, Chelsea winning 2-1. Again, Sexton's shrewd planning was in evidence. In the short interval between the two games, as a result of injury to Hollins in the first contest, he redrafted his tactical plan by introducing Tommy Baldwin as a 'support' striker for Osgood in a reformed '4-2-4' formation. Returning to the Kings Road, captain Ron Harris proclaimed, "We are the Kings of Europe."

And so it was. Deprived of the services of McCreadie and Hutchinson through injury, Irishman Paddy Mulligan and Millwall's Keith Weller had joined the senior squad. Yet the golden years were to end all too soon, and for reasons which should have been avoided.

At first in the following season, even though Atvidaberg, an almost unknown Swedish club, had bundled Chelsea out of the Cup-winners' Cup, and lowly Orient had likewise eliminated the team in the FA Cup, matters did not seem too serious. But then Stoke City emphasized a rapidly deteriorating situation by winning the 1972 Football League Cup Final at Wembley, after Osgood had equalized an early goal, only for George Eastham, an infrequent scorer, to get the winner and, as one critic put it, 'knock logic sideways'.

What had appeared to be hairline cracks in the dressing-room harmony now opened up alarmingly. Seventh was the lowest finishing place in the League for five years. A year later, in 1972-3, it was 12th with a semi-final appearance in the Football League Cup, small beer compared with what had gone before. The side was breaking up as Sexton faced a situation now beyond reprieve. Cooke and Mulligan had already gone, soon to be followed by Hudson, Osgood and Webb.

The rift between manager and senior staff was irreconcilable. Some of the very players who had canvassed the board for Sexton's appointment were now demanding his removal. By the spring of 1974, avoiding relegation had become the main incentive, since elimination from both domestic Cup competitions had occurred at the first hurdle. Moreover, all this had happened in the ever-lengthening shadow of the new giant East Stand now in the course of erection. Undoubtedly, bad planning mistakes were made by new chairman Brian Mears and his directors in commiting Chelsea to an outlay of more than £3 million in rebuilding the stadium, but a soaring rate of inflation and industrial action in the steel industry compounded a rapidly worsening financial crisis. Money could not be found to rebuild a team now in tatters.

On 3 October 1974, Sexton left the club after seven years. He had given Chelsea their greatest days, but his intransigence and inability to communicate with temperamental players brought his downfall. Briefly under the control of Ron Suart, and then with Eddie McCreadie as team manager, relegation to the Second Division was confirmed in the spring of 1975, when the final six games of the season failed to produce a single victory.

Of the 'old guard', only faithful Ron Harris, Peter Houseman, Hollins, Cooke (back at The Bridge after a sojourn with Crystal Palace) and a never fully fit Hutchinson remained. Despite the income generated by the constant sale of players, financial problems were still present. And that eternal provider of talent, the Chelsea youth scheme, was unable to produce the quality most needed, experience. Gary Locke, Micky Droy and Ray Wilkins had appeared but, for varying reasons, fees paid out for David Hay, Chris Garland, Bill Garner and John Sissons were never justified by performances on the field.

McCreadie brought the enthusiasm he had shown in his playing days into the manager's chair. Well-supported by his staff, dressing-room morale rose once more and a final place of 11th in the Second Division in 1975-6 could have been worse, even though it was the lowest in Chelsea's history. A year later, with no transfer

Paul Mariner scores for Plymouth Argyle at Home Park in September 1976. Chelsea, however, won the game 3-2 and at the end of the season had regained their First Division place. Steve Wicks and Peter Bonetti are powerless to intervene.

26

fee being paid out for any player, amazingly, promotion was celebrated, a considerable feat in such difficult circumstances. A rare bonus was the return of Bonetti, already bracketed with Woodley as the greatest of Chelsea's goalkeepers, after a brief spell in North American football.

The season had begun with the news that Chelsea's debts now amounted to £3.4 million. A firm of leading accountants were called in and creditors agreed to a one-year moratorium, albeit somewhat reluctantly. The training ground at Mitcham was sold. This at least meant Chelsea Football Club was still alive. But it had been a close thing.

First Division football, back at The Bridge again in August 1977, was never going to be easy. Fortunately, a cluster of talented youngsters in the shape of Kenny Swain, Steve Finnieston, Ian Britton, Steve Wicks and Garry Stanley had emerged from the junior ranks. But a stunning blow to the club's hopes of re-establishing itself as a playing force came with the resignation of McCreadie, over a relatively trivial dispute regarding his new contract. Hurriedly, Ken Shellito was promoted from his post as youth team coach, and a 16th final placing was acceptable in the circumstances.

A year later, however, there was no escape. The lowest-ever points total (20) inevitably once again brought descent to a lower division. Shellito resigned and Danny Blanchflower was appointed in his stead on a 'month-to-month' basis. A limited amount of cash was made available and Duncan McKenzie (Everton), Eamonn Bannon (Heart of Midlothian), and Petar Borota, a Yugoslav international goalkeeper, moved in, as Bonetti at last ended his long and distinguished playing career, at the age of 38 and with 729 first-team games under his belt.

Blanchflower, outstanding as he had been as a player, was unhappily a misfit in the office of manager, lasting a mere eight months before a new take-over saw England's World Cup hero, Geoff Hurst, and Bobby Gould move in. Finishing fourth in the Second Division was a promising beginning for them and a good deal better than could have been anticipated. Survivor Harris, together with Locke, Droy and the erratic showman Borota, formed a reasonably solid defence. In front of them the greater mobility of Britton, Gary Chivers, and a youthful John Bumstead, allied to the varying skills and enthusiasm of Mike Fillery, speedy Clive Walker and Tommy Langley, completed at least a competent line-up.

Nevertheless, the slide to 12th in 1980-81 was disappointing, and enough to trigger off yet another change at the helm. This time the board sought an experienced hand in the shape of John Neal, with 12 years experience in charge of Wrexham and Middlesbrough. Almost immediately, Brian Mears resigned the chairmanship. That he made errors in judgement has already been acknowledged. But, equally, it must be remembered that luck was seldom on his side and he just did not possess the necessary muscle to cope with a situation which escalated alarmingly before it ran out of his control. Nor did his colleagues on the board offer expertise or business acumen, rather regarding their position as a hobby.

The new regime, with Viscount Chelsea presiding as chairman, produced no immediate miracles. Steve Francis and Colin Pates became established first-team players and Neal soon showed his skill in the transfer market by bringing in David Speedie, then almost unknown, and signing Joey Jones, an experienced defender. The side were never in serious trouble in the League and a place in the last eight in the FA Cup was a welcome bonus for the long-suffering fans.

An event of much greater significance, however, took place on 2 April 1982 when Kenneth Bates, who had had previous experience in the world of football as chairman of Oldham Athletic in the 1960s, purchased Chelsea Football Club. If Gus Mears was the founder of the club, then Bates can rightly claim to be its saviour. Without his timely intervention it is at least possible the Chelsea club could not have survived.

As Ted Drake changed the image of Chelsea some 30 years earlier, so now again did the new owner, shortly to become chairman as well, bring about equally far-reaching reforms. In 18 months the final connections with the Mears family had been severed with the last survivor, David, leaving in unhappy circumstances. A vastly more professional and businesslike approach, if necessarily ruthless at times, set the club on the road to recovery.

But, first another crisis of a different kind was averted almost at the last gasp. In Bates' first season in control, it needed a spectacular and, let it be said, somewhat fortuitous goal from Clive Walker, on a miserable and gloomy afternoon at Bolton in May 1983, to stave off almost certain relegation to Division Three. Not only was his goal enough to ensure victory, it also condemned the Trotters to relegation. The lowest point in Chelsea's history had passed.

This indignity avoided, chairman and manager acted swiftly during the summer of 1983 to ensure nothing similar should occur again. Seven new players were signed and eight others moved out. Among the newcomers were goalkeeper Eddie Niedzwiecki, commanding centre-half Joe McLaughlin, midfielder Nigel Spackman, an old-fashioned touch-line-hugging winger, Pat Nevin, and Kerry Dixon with an impressive goalscoring record at Reading already behind him. In addition, new 'old friends', John Hollins (as player-coach) and Alan Hudson returned to the fold.

Kicking off with a 5-0 home win over Derby County, the team gathered momentum, were never out of the top six in the table and, with a final sprint bringing maximum points from the last four fixtures, won the Second Division championship for the first time, on goal-difference from Sheffield Wednesday. Between them Dixon, Speedie and Nevin scored 55 goals.

Back in the top class, sixth place was accompanied by progress to the semi-final of the League Cup. Included in this was an astonishing recovery from a three-goal half-time deficit at Hillsborough against Sheffield Wednesday. So great was

Chelsea celebrate their first senior honour for some years, the newly-created Full Members' Cup which they won by beating Manchester City 5-4 at Wembley in 1986.

the transformation that, with minutes to go, Chelsea were leading 4-3 before a last-gasp penalty gave Wednesday a temporary reprieve, with Chelsea going on to win the replay. Losing both legs of the semi-final to Sunderland was an unworthy end to a fine Cup run, and included some ugly crowd scenes in the game at Stamford Bridge.

With John Neal being elevated to the Board, John Hollins was promoted to manager before the start of the 1985-6 campaign. Chelsea repeated their finishing spot of sixth, as well as becoming holders of the newly-created Full Members' Cup, winning an exciting Final at Wembley with Manchester City, 5-4.

Success at top level once more seemed within grasp, but a thoroughly anonymous season — 14th in the Championship and two early Cup exits — followed to dampen such optimism. Gordon Durie, from Scotland, and Tottenham's Micky Hazard strengthened a squad which consistently under-performed. But worse was to follow.

Dressing-room discontent again began to cause problems early in the 1987-8 season and, after weeks of speculation, John Hollins left Chelsea with results on the field never reflecting the ability of his players. A sad parting for one of the outstanding figures in Chelsea's history. Bobby Campbell, who had arrived as coach a few weeks earlier took over, first temporarily, with a long record of coaching and management behind him, but too late to prevent inevitable relegation. Chelsea's fate was sealed by defeat in the 'play-off' Final against Middlesbrough at Stamford Bridge. At the

Kerry Dixon gets his head to the ball during the play-off game against Middlesbrough at Stamford Bridge in May 1988.

conclusion of that match, scenes of crowd disorder — which were to have repercussions as the FA ordered the Stamford Bridge terraces to be closed for the first six games of the following season — put the seal on a dispiriting final six months.

With cash available to bolster an already healthy playing staff, Chelsea bounced straight back again. Colin Pates, still going strong after ten seasons, McLaughlin and Dixon remained from John Neal's squad. John Hollins had signed full-backs Steve Clarke and Tony Dorigo, midfielder Clive Wilson and striker Kevin Wilson. Now Campbell added to this strong background by signing experienced battlers and internationals Graham Roberts and Peter Nicholas, along with goalkeeper Dave Beasant, at a then record fee for a Chelsea player of £725,000.

Taking over the leadership of the division on Boxing Day, Chelsea won the 1989 Second Division title in a canter, finishing 17 points clear of runners-up, Manchester City. Exciting as all this was, it nevertheless emphasized the unnecessary futility of relegation 12 months earlier, a fact further underlined by the ease with which largely the same players coped comfortably enough on their return to the top class.

By then Ken Monkou had been plucked from Dutch football at a bargain fee, later to be joined in central defence by Norwegian Erland Johnsen from Bayern

Celebrations in the Zenith Data Systems Cup Final as colleagues congratulate Tony Dorigo for his goal (left) and the scorer himself (right) with the trophy.

Munich. Fifth in the final table was satisfactory and if success in the major knock-out competitions continued to prove elusive, at least the Full Members' Cup (now in the guise of its Zenith Data sponsors) was won, for the second time in four seasons, when Middlesbrough were beaten 1-0 at Wembley.

Twelve months later, the picture had changed once again. Having paid out £2.8 million for Andy Townsend and Dennis Wise in the 1990 close season, Chelsea proceeded once more to strain the loyalty of their supporters with a maddening inconsistency, never exceeded even in the 1930s. Victories over Arsenal (inflicting the only League defeat of the season on the Champions), Liverpool, Manchester United (twice) and Tottenham Hotspur (twice) counted for little when placed alongside ignominious reverses in the three senior Cup competitions, at the hands of Oxford United, Luton Town and Sheffield Wednesday.

Indeed, one would be hard-pressed to recall a more dispiriting performance than that on a bleak Sunday morning in February when the Hillsborough club's immeasurably greater commitment and endeavour saw them take a controlling lead in the first leg of the Rumbelows Cup semi-final. Two months later, a 7-0 drubbing at the hands of Nottingham Forest confirmed that remedial work was urgently required.

A final mid-table standing in the First Division was totally unacceptable in view of the ability and depth of the first-team squad and it came as little surprise when Bobby Campbell stood down as manager four days before the final fixture. Once more, Chelsea found themselves, as so often, standing at the crossroads. This time, however, they at least have a club chairman who is determined to take the correct turn — as Mr Bates made abundantly clear in his final club programme column of the 1990-91 season.

Kerry Dixon gets the better of England centre-half Mark Wright during the 6-4 thriller at Derby in December 1990.

31

The Stamford Bridge Story

FEW clubs in the history of British football can have had their destiny controlled by their ground to the extent that Stamford Bridge has governed the fortunes of Chelsea Football Club. Indeed, it is safe to say that the club would have never come into being, had not this large, under-used, and partly derelict area not been available and crying out for development at the turn of this century.

Stamford Bridge was opened on Sunday, 28 April 1877 to provide a home for athletics in London. The site, within easy reach of the centre of the capital, was ideal. The adjacent sports ground at Lillie Bridge, which had been the home of the London Athletic Club (and where the FA Cup Final was staged in 1873) was proving inadequate to meet the expanding need of both sports.

As a result, for the sum of £2,899, this eight-and-a-half acre market-garden site was acquired on behalf of the London Athletic Club — and Stamford Bridge Stadium was born.

Two stands, one occupying the east side and another in the south-west corner, overlooked the running track. And, within a month of the opening, the first of many international athletic events had taken place.

It was almost 20 years later, however, before thought was given to the staging of football matches. The original idea came from Frederick Parker who, having held an official post as starter with the LAC, had the vision to recognize the enormous potential of the site.

This, together with Parker's friendship with H.A. ('Gus') Mears and his brother, J.T.Mears, provided the seed from which Chelsea Football Club was to emerge.

The Mears family was the owner of a well-established and wealthy firm of building contractors. The two brothers were keen sportsmen and football, particularly, had been their main outlet in this direction.

Difficulties in effecting the purchase of the grounds in order to obtain the freehold were swept aside as Gus Mears pursued his vision of turning Stamford Bridge into England's premier sporting arena.

On 25 September 1904, the deeds were signed and discussions with Fulham Football Club were begun, the original plan being that the Southern League club should move from their Craven Cottage headquarters to lease Stamford Bridge at an annual rental of £1,500. For financial reasons the negotiations broke down but, far from being discouraged, Mears decided instead to form a new club.

With Parker's financial backing and drive, the dream became reality within six months and, more incredibly still, the new Chelsea Football Club had not only been founded but had gained election to the Football League as well.

Two months earlier, in Feburary 1905, the famous Archibald Leitch, architect supreme of football club grandstands the length and breadth of Britain, had been commissioned to design a new stand, 120 yards long and occupying the length of the touch-line along the eastern side of the ground, to accommodate 5,000 spectators.

On the other three sides of the stadium almost unlimited material for building up vast terracing became available from the excavation of the new Piccadilly underground railway line, as well as from the Kingsway tramway tunnel then being built. The capacity of the ground was envisaged as being 100,000.

Unquestionably, the biggest asset of the new stadium, however, was its position

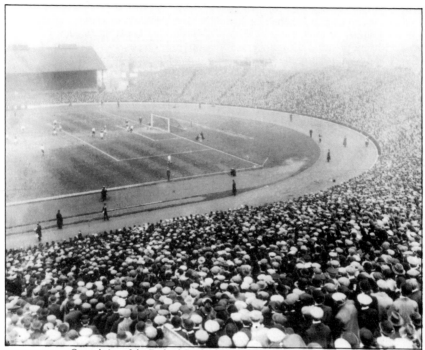

General view of the England-Scotland game at Stamford Bridge in 1913.

in London. As motor transport developed, men could move from an office in the City to 'The Bridge' within minutes and, not surprisingly therefore, large crowds for sporting fixtures were attracted from the beginning.

As a result, other contests were soon being held. Athletic meetings continued to be regular events. The first of four international football fixtures was played on 5 April 1913, when England beat Scotland 1-0 to win the Home International Championship in front of a crowd of 52,000. Sixteen years later, England beat Wales 6-0 and, in December 1932, Austria by 4-3. Finally, in May 1946, on the last occasion Stamford Bridge was used for a 'full' international, England beat Switzerland 4-1.

For three seasons, too, immediately before the opening of the Empire Stadium at Wembley, the FA Cup Final was staged on the ground. In 1920, Aston Villa beat Huddersfield 1-0 in front of 72,000 spectators; 12 months later Tottenham Hotspur overcame Wolverhampton Wanderers by a similar margin; and, in April 1922, a single goal was enough to bring Huddersfield Town victory over Preston North End.

In addition to these top 'box-office' attractions, Stamford Bridge also housed four inter-League fixtures, two amateur internationals, four FA Amateur Cup Finals and ten FA Charity Shield matches.

Nor was the use of the arena by any means confined to football and athletics. On 8 Feburary 1908, a Rugby League 'Test match' between what was then known as the 'Northern Union' and New Zealand was staged, the visitors winning 18-6.

Baseball made its bow when the New York Giants faced the Chicago White Sox on 26 February 1914. And, for two seasons from 1923 to 1925, baseball matches in the American Legion Baseball League took place regularly on Sunday afternoons.

In the summer of 1948, midget car racing was another experiment. This, however, failed to bring in sufficient numbers. Rifle-shooting was also tried briefly. Cricket fixtures against other London football clubs took place both before and after World War One, but easily the most notable of all such matches was staged on 14 August 1980, when Essex beat the West Indian tourists (on faster scoring rate) in a most spectacular evening's entertainment. Some 450 runs were scored in 68 overs, before rain brought a halt to the proceedings.

The name of Malcolm Campbell also has its niche in Stamford Bridge history. On 5 May 1928 he opened a track for motorcycle speedway racing, meetings subsequently being held on Wednesday and Saturday nights. A year later, a Stamford Bridge team (whose colours, of course, were blue and white) entered the National League, winning the title in 1932. Speedway 'Test matches' between England and Australia were held in 1930 and 1931.

Better remembered are the regular greyhound racing meetings which took place twice-weekly from 1933 until 1968. It was this venture which brought about the formation of Stamford Bridge Stadium Limited. Indeed, it was the Greyhound Racing Association which was responsible for the erection of the cover built over the back of the terracing at the southern end of the ground early in the 1930s, later affectionately to be christened 'The Shed'.

But the marriage between Chelsea Football Club and Stamford Bridge Stadium was never an easy one and was marked by much haggling over such matters as leasing and rentals. At a time when both Arsenal and Tottenham Hotspur were leading the way in stadium developments, this disharmony undoubtedly contributed to Highbury Stadium and White Hart Lane outstripping Stamford Bridge so far as spectator facilities were concerned.

Gus Mears would have been shocked that his descendants could do no more than add a relatively small extension to the terracing, in 1920, then allow another company to construct meagre cover for a few thousand standing customers some ten years later, before embarking on the building of a North Stand in the summer of 1939. At one time it was intended that this should later be extended to provide an upper deck over the original East Stand but, not only did this never happen, as a result of the outbreak of World War Two, even the first stage of the new structure was never entirely finished.

For 60 years Stamford Bridge was allowed to stagnate for reasons of internal politics, allied to lack of ambition.

Not until 1965 was the appearance of the ground materially altered when the building of a stand on the west side was undertaken. Providing 6,300 seats, it was achieved only at the expense of more than 20,000 standing places on the most awe-inspiring terrace in Britain. Because of constructional problems, a cantilever stand was ruled out and, at a cost of £150,000, the new stand consisted of seats fixed into the remodelled terracing in front of six executive boxes. A decision to install bench-seats at the front of the stand (and open to the elements) was much criticized, removing, as it did, the chance for standing customers to watch games from the side of the ground.

Belatedly, more adventurous plans were in the pipeline. In 1970, a 'blue-print' for the phased-construction of a completely newly-developed Stamford Bridge was announced as, at long last, Chelsea showed initiative by moving ahead of their rivals to produce a 'stadium for the 21st century'.

This envisaged seating for every spectator, with a total capacity of 60,000 capable, if necessary, of being enlarged at a later date to accommodate 80,000.

A direct link into the ground from Fulham Broadway underground station was

34

included. A new British Rail station would be opened close to the site of the previous Chelsea and Fulham station, closed in 1940, and only 100 yards from the main entrance to the ground. Other modern facilities encompassed 156 private boxes, a public restaurant, and an indoor practice playing area.

In the event, only one phase of this scheme was ever carried out, and even that was not fully completed. Unwise decisions were undoubtedly made. But sympathy for Brian Mears (the great-grandson of Gus) and his board of directors is also in order.

Contractors failed to meet deadlines. Soaring inflation (impossible to foresee when the plans were drawn up) caused financial problems to escalate alarmingly. And industrial action in the steel industry was another setback for which the directors could not be held responsible.

In any event, and for whatever reasons, Chelsea Football Club was brought to the brink of financial disaster. Repercussions were felt throughout the City, and even in Parliament, as debts could not be met and creditors became ever-more vociferous in their demands.

Finally, in June 1976, a 12-month moratorium with creditors was agreed on the recommendation of Martin Spencer, a chartered accountant and later to become the club's chief executive. Valuable time had been bought and the immediate crisis averted, if only temporarily.

Soon another had arrived in the shape of the Safety of Sports Ground Act, necessitating a further outlay of more than half a million pounds in order to meet the requirements of the Greater London Council.

In fact, from 1976 to 1982, financial disaster was never far distant, with the club's bankers increasingly making clear that the situation could not continue indefinitely. On 2 June 1981, Brian Mears resigned as chairman of Chelsea FC, and a new holding company, the Stamford Bridge Property Company, was formed, giving them the right to nominate two directors to the Football Club board.

How long, or how easily, such an uneasy partnership would have survived, or whether Chelsea could have remained at Stamford Bridge under such an unsatisfactory arrangement, will never be known for, on 2 April 1982, the football club was purchased by Kenneth Bates, a former chairman of Oldham Athletic.

Now came the firm guiding hand which had been missing for so long. Much-needed strong, and at times ruthless, decisions were taken. By the end of that first month, Bates had requested the resignations of his fellow directors, although Viscount Chelsea and David Mears remained as the two SB Property nominees.

At best harmony was uneasy and, in January 1984, the situation deteriorated when David Mears sold his 40 per cent SB Property holding to Marler Estates, thereby putting Chelsea Football Club at the mercy of a firm of property speculators whose sole aim was to evict the club and develop a site of enormous potential. It was an unhappy ending to a connection with the Mears family which had endured through four generations, for almost 80 years.

Fortunately, Chelsea had a further seven-year tenure of Stamford Bridge before their lease terminated in 1989, with an option to buy the freehold in August 1988, at Marler's suggested price of £40 million, a figure regarded as unrealistic by Chelsea.

However unpromising, this interval at least provided a potential lifeline, and in April 1987 a 'Save the Bridge' appeal was launched to raise a projected £15 million to buy Stamford Bridge, redevelop six acres of the area and build a completely new football ground on the remaining part of the property, with a 40,000 capacity.

Objections were raised initially by the Hammersmith and Fulham planning authority, but an oversight on the part of Marler Estates allowed their own application to lapse and, subsequently, Chelsea were given planning consent to build three new stands (seating 24,000) to go alongside the present East Stand. In addition, the

provision also included a 160-bedroom hotel and 264 flats with penthouse suites and service apartments.

In February 1991, Cabra Estates Plc (who had acquired Marler Estates) at last conceded Chelsea's option to buy the ground 'at a fair price'. However, on this question of valuation, both parties still appeared poles apart and resort to independent arbitration seemed the only solution, inevitably causing further delay and expense.

Meanwhile, in May, a start was made on major refurbishment work of the East Stand, never completed in the 1970s through lack of funds. Subsequently, the work on the total reconstruction of the other three sides of the ground will be phased

over three or four years, in order to enable Chelsea to continue to play football
at The Bridge during that period.

The Taylor Report recommendations will, of course, be implemented in full and,
at long last, provide Chelsea FC with a home which will compare favourably with
any ground in the country — and certainly one to qualify for 'Super League' status.
So, the future of Stamford Bridge remains as exciting in 1991 as it was when 'Gus'
Mears and Frederick Parker met on the famous turf on that eventful Sunday morning
86 years ago.

Attendances

Over 70,000 at Stamford Bridge:

82,905 (ground record) v Arsenal *Division One, 12 October 1935.*
77,952 v Swindon Town *FA Cup 4th round, 13 March 1911.*
77,696 v Blackpool *Division One, 16 October 1948.*
76,000 *(E)* v Tottenham Hotspur *Football League, Division One, 16 October 1920.*
75,952 v Arsenal *Division One, 9 October 1937.*
75,334 v Arsenal *Division One, 29 November 1930.*
75,043 v Wolverhampton Wanderers *Division One, 9 April 1955.*
75,000 *(E)* England v Switzerland *Full International, 11 May 1946.*
74,667 v Arsenal *Division One, 29 November 1930.*
74,496 v Dinamo Moscow *Friendly, 13 November 1945.*
74,365 v Birmingham *FA Cup 6th round replay, 4 March 1931.*
74,190 v Arsenal *Division One, 22 April 1933.*
72,805 Tottenham Hotspur v Wolverhampton Wanderers *FA Cup Final, 23 March 1921.*
72,614 v Arsenal *Division One, 3 April 1953.*
70,362 v Manchester United *FA Cup 6th round, 4 March 1950.*
70,257 v Arsenal *FA Cup 3rd round, 11 January 1947.*
70,184 v Cardiff City *FA Cup 6th round, 5 March 1927.*
70,123 v Tottenham Hotspur *FA Cup 3rd round replay, 8 January 1964.*
70,000 *(E)* v Newcastle United *Division One, 27 December 1909.*
70,000 *(E)* v Aston Villa *Division One, 2 April 1920.*
(E) – Estimated attendance.

43,330 *(A)* v Tottenham Hotspur *Football League Cup semi-final, 1st leg, 22 December 1971.*
59,541 *(B)* v AC Milan *Inter-Cities' Fairs Cup 3rd round, 16 February 1966.*
(A) – Highest home attendance at any Football League Cup tie.
(B) – Highest home attendance at any European tie.

When Chelsea met Dinamo Moscow on 13 November 1945, many thousands obtained admission illegally after all entrance gates had been closed. Estimates of the number gaining entry in this way vary, but the number who watched the match is thought to be about 100,000.

Big Attendances At Chelsea Matches On Other Grounds

100,000 v Tottenham Hotspur at Wembley Stadium *FA Cup Final, 20 May 1967.*
100,000 v Leeds United at Wembley Stadium *FA Cup Final, 11 April 1970.*
100,000 v Stoke City at Wembley Stadium *Football League Cup Final, 4 March 1972.*
90,000 v Millwall at Wembley Stadium *Football League Cup South Final, 7 April 1945.*
85,000 v Charlton Athletic at Wembley Stadium *Football League Cup South Final, 15 April 1944.*
76,369 v Middlesbrough at Wembley Stadium *Full Members' Cup Final, 25 March 1990.*
70,000 v CF Barcelona at Barcelona *Inter-Cities' Fairs' Cup semi-final 1st leg, 27 April 1966.*
68,386 *(A)* v Newcastle United at St James' Park *Division One, 3 September 1930.*

68,084 *(B)* v Arsenal at White Hart Lane *FA Cup semi-final, 5 April 1952.*
52,755 *(C)* v Tottenham Hotspur at White Hart Lane *Football League Cup semi-final 2nd leg, 5 January 1972.*
(A) – Highest away attendance at any Football League match.
(B) – Highest away attendance at any FA Cup tie (other than the Final).
(C) – Highest away attendance at any Football League Cup tie (other than the Final tie).

Smallest Attendances

League (home) — 3,000 v Lincoln City, *Division Two, 17 Feb 1906.*
Post-war — 6,009 v Orient *Division Two, 5 May 1982.*
League (away) — 3,000 *on five occasions 1905-1912*
Post-war — 3,935 v Wrexham *Division Two, 27 February 1982.*
FA Cup (home) — 5,000 v 1st Battalion, Grenadier Guards *Preliminary round, 7 October 1905.*
FA Cup (away) — 3,000 v Crystal Palace *Preliminary round, 18 November 1905.*
Football League Cup (home) — 5,630 v Workington, *2nd round, 24 October 1960.*
Football League Cup (away) — 4,579 v Tranmere Rovers, *2nd round 1st leg, 28 October 1982.*
European Cups (home) — 13,104 v Frem (Copenhagen) *Fairs Cup 1st round 2nd leg, 4 November 1958.*
European Cups (away) — 4,000 Wiener SK *Fairs Cup, 2nd round 1st leg, 17 November 1965.*
Full Members' Cup (home) — 4,767 v Plymouth Argyle *1st round, 9 November 1988.*
Full Members' Cup (away) — 3,714 v Charlton Athletic *Southern Group match, 23 October 1985.*

Record Receipts at Stamford Bridge

Football League — £257,646, Chelsea v Tottenham Hotspur, *Division One, December 1990,* (excluding season-ticket holders and executive box returns).
FA Cup — £158,227.50, Chelsea v Tottenham Hotspur *6th Round, 6 March 1982.*
Football League Cup — £160,640, Chelsea v Sunderland *semi-final, 4 March 1985.*
Neutral Match — £147,225, Orient v Arsenal *FA Cup semi-final, 8 April 1978.*
Highest for any Chelsea match — £1,170,000, Chelsea v Middlesbrough, *Full Members' Cup Final, 25 March 1990 (at Wembley).*

A precarious perch at Stamford Bridge for Chelsea's match against Spurs in 1913.

Chelsea Managers

John Tait Robertson
April 1905-October 1906

IT was never likely, or intended, that Jackie Robertson's stay at Stamford Bridge would be a lengthy one. He was already approaching the age of 30, with a long and distinguished playing career behind him, when he was appointed Chelsea's player-manager.

Acknowledged to be a shrewd judge of footballing talent, his main task was to sign up a professional staff which could establish Chelsea as a force in the Football League. Supported by his chairman, Mr H.A.Mears, he lost no time in enticing a series of well-known, and proven, players to the Fulham Road.

As a stylish wing-half, Robertson had played most of his football north of the border and his 16 full international caps had been acquired over a period of seven years. Strangely, his career as a young man had taken him as far afield as Everton and Southampton before he returned home to serve Glasgow Rangers for six seasons immediately prior to coming to London.

That he succeeded in justifying himself as a manager cannot be doubted. Quickly, he moulded a squad of complete strangers into a team, which not only attracted large crowds by their entertaining performances, but also might well have won promotion in their first season. Admittedly, he was fortunate in having ready money available to buy players, but, in almost every case, his signings justified the outlay involved. And it was essentially Jackie Robertson's team which won promotion in April 1907.

After Robertson's move to Glossop in the autumn of Chelsea's second season, William Lewis, the club secretary, took over the managing of the team for six months in a 'caretaker' capacity.

David Calderhead
August 1907-May 1933

IN January 1907, Chelsea were drawn against Lincoln City in the first round of the FA Cup, losing by a single goal in a replay at Stamford Bridge after a 2-2 draw at Sincil Bank four days earlier. The two games aroused little comment at the time, as Chelsea's eyes were largely focussed on winning promotion.

But those two games were to have an important spin-off. The Lincoln manager, David Calderhead, a Scotsman who had won an international cap against Ireland in 1887, obviously impressed the Chelsea directors enough for them to lure him to Stamford Bridge a few months later, where he was to remain as manager for more than a quarter of a century.

A distinguished centre-half in his playing days, he was a man of few words. Those outside the club were scarcely aware of his presence. Not for him rash predictions, revealing Press conferences or controversial columns in programme or newspapers.

But he was certainly a man of action. Few of his contemporary managers were more active in the transfer market and, like his predecessor, he produced teams that drew large numbers of spectators through the turnstiles. He continued to maintain close associations with Scottish football and pulled in players from a wide catchment area in times when many clubs relied predominantly on local talent.

Twice he guided Chelsea to promotion from Division Two; twice his teams suffered relegation, avoiding a third descent in 1919 only when two additional clubs were elected to the First Division. He was at the helm when Chelsea made their first FA Cup Final appearance, and steered the club as far as the semi-finals on three other occasions.

Yet, in retrospect, given the sums of money at his disposal, he might have achieved rather more. Like others after him in Chelsea's managerial chair, he found inconsistency in the club's performances a difficult hurdle to surmount. Nevertheless, the 'Chelsea Sphinx', as he was known, was highly regarded throughout the game and few managers in its history can equal his 26-year stint in control at one club. He died in 1938.

Leslie Knighton
May 1933-April 1939

LESLIE Knighton came to Stamford Bridge with the prime object of moulding some of the most exciting talent in the game into a coherent unit and, above all, into a winning team. With Chelsea having won promotion three years earlier, the directors were always prepared to make money available to achieve long-awaited success. Indeed, his first Chelsea side to take the field, on 26 August 1933, contained six full internationals.

Mr Knighton well fitted the image of the football manager of his time. Invariably in his dark suit and hat, he controlled affairs from his office desk. Like his immediate predecessor he was also secretary and, as such, performed a range of administrative duties long since discarded by modern managers. A contemporary player once said of him: "We seldom saw Mr Knighton during the week as Jack Whitley, the trainer, supervised our fitness and tactical training; but he was a most kind man whom we respected. A real gentleman."

His six seasons in charge of Chelsea brought many problems. For the first time, Continental teams, already able to offer much larger cash incentives, were 'tapping' English professionals. Two international stars at Stamford Bridge succumbed to the temptation, and others became unsettled as a result of these approaches. As newspapers widened their scope and coverage of the game, eruptions of internal discipline also surfaced. Inside and outside the game things were changing.

Be that as it may, Knighton, despite his long managerial experience with Huddersfield Town, Manchester City, Arsenal, Bournemouth and Birmingham, failed to solve the riddle of Chelsea's lack of success, more often being forced to devote his energies to avoiding relegation than with winning championships and cups and, after

six years, it was clearly time for him to move on, and to make way for a younger man, more in touch with the climate and atmosphere in the dressing-room.

Billy Birrell
May 1939-May 1952

OF all Chelsea managers down the years, Billy Birrell is the one most deserving of sympathy and understanding. He arrived after a relatively successful spell in the managerial chair at Queen's Park Rangers, with war clouds already gathering. Once again, Chelsea had been flirting with relegation for most of that last full peacetime season of 1938-9 and, most ominously, with a team shorn of much of its glamour and with many members already well into the latter parts of their playing careers.

Such as Peter O'Dowd, Hughie Gallacher, Alex Jackson, Joe Bambrick had gone. Tommy Law and Allan Craig had retired in the spring of that 1939. The reserve team contained little either in the way of youthful promise or proven talent.

Before Birrell had a chance to show his hand ,World War Two had begun and for

seven years he managed teams of ever-changing personnel including many 'outsiders' who, if lucky, might get together for an hour or so before each fixture. Success, or failure, in such times meant relatively little in the medium, or long-term.

As the skies began to clear, in the winter of 1944-5, he started to plan ahead, realizing only too well that he would soon be faced

42

with having to construct a completely new team. Fortune smiled on him to the extent that he had been able to acquire the temporary services of several guest players of true quality who had put down firm roots during their stay at Stamford Bridge. Thus, such as Danny Winter (Bolton Wanderers), John Harris (Wolves), Bobby Russell (Airdrieonians), Johnny Galloway (Glasgow Rangers) and Tommy Walker (Hearts) had all been signed on a permanent basis by September 1946.

Inevitably, his horizons were narrow and ambitions limited to keeping Chelsea in the top division. Fortunately, others were in a similar quandary. In his six 'normal' seasons in charge, he twice steered Chelsea as high as 13th in the final table. Twice he was happy merely to avoid relegation. Twice, too, he took his team into FA Cup semi-finals, and on the first of these occasions was robbed of a Wembley appearance more by ill-fortune than anything else.

Then, before he had had a real chance to come to grips with longer term planning, he had slipped quietly into retirement. As a player with Raith Rovers and, more permanently, Middlesbrough, he had shown the traditional intricate ball-skills of the Scotsman. As manager, too, he was a clever and canny operator in the transfer market. Never one to seek the limelight, he was both universally liked and respected throughout football. Easily approachable by everyone in whatever capacity, down to the most casual supporter, he made no enemies. He probably lacked the drive and purpose necessary to become a really top-class, successful manager. But he achieved much in his days at Chelsea on which he could look back with satisfaction.

Ted Drake
May 1952-September 1961

TED Drake had been a fearless, forthright, and positive centre-forward in the great Arsenal days of the 1930s, his five England international caps being won in the face of stiff competition for his position. At Reading after the war, he had learned his trade as a manager and it was to him that the Chelsea directors turned after Billy Birrell had negotiated the difficult immediate post-war years.

From his first day in office he set about blowing away cobwebs which had hung around Stamford Bridge for years. For a

start the Chelsea Pensioner was banished from the club badge, soon to be followed by the equally enduring 'music-hall' image. His track suit replaced the lounge suit of his predecessors, as he largely foresook the office for the training ground. No longer did his title include the prefix 'secretary'.

At least he had some foundations on which to build. Such sturdy first-team performers as Bill Robertson, Stan Willemse, John Harris, Ken Armstrong and Roy Bentley still had a few more seasons of service to offer. The Chelsea youth scheme was beginning to gain momentum and produce players of the future. And Stamford Bridge, raw and undeveloped as it still was, was rich in potential for supporting a successful club.

His knowledge of the lower divisions was quickly turned to advantage. From Brighton came John McNichol; Leslie Stubbs also arrived from the seaside, via Southend United; Ron Greenwood from Brentford; Peter Sillett from Southampton, where Drake had played with the powerful full-back's father in pre-war days; and, soon and brightest of all, Frank Blunstone of Crewe Alexandra appeared as a raw unknown.

More important than such details, however, was the noticeable change of attitude around the place. Team spirit and total commitment were factors close to Drake's heart. No cause was ever to be considered lost. In short, he expected his players to approach their profession in the positive manner he, himself, had done in his own highly successful career. A great motivator, he sent teams on to the field expecting to win.

Not surprisingly, things did not happen all at once and, after a rumbustious start, the team was only one point clear of relegation at the end of his first season. But he knew what he was doing and where he was going. His second campaign contained a sequence of 24 games with only three defeats. "I am confident that we have broken the barrier," said Drake. And so he had.

The winning of the Football League Championship was, of course, his pinnacle, achieved at the end of his third season. From that moment, strangely, things went downhill. More than half his title-winning team were past their best. Highly promising youngsters from the youth scheme, Jimmy Greaves included, lacked the necessary consistency to carry on what Drake had started in terms of results. In several cases potential went unfulfilled. Once more Chelsea seemed to be going nowhere.

The difference now was that the directors, having tasted success, were not prepared for mediocrity to continue and, another indifferent start to Drake's tenth season at the helm, brought about his dismissal. At least he walked away having given the club a taste of the success which had eluded it for nearly half a century prior to his arrival and with the base for future prosperity firmly laid.

Tommy Docherty
January 1962-October 1967

AS long as football is played, the name of Tommy Docherty will be remembered in a myriad of ways, and in association with countless football clubs in various different parts of the world.

Originally he arrived at Stamford Bridge from Arsenal, in September 1961, his playing career virtually at an end, as assistant coach under the watchful eye of manager Ted Drake. In the event, he turned out for Chelsea in four League fixtures that autumn before finding himself catapulted into the hot seat first as chief coach, in October, and as manager three months later, after Drake had left Stamford Bridge.

Despite the fact that Chelsea were en route to the Second Division, in many ways the situation was made for Docherty. Suddenly he found himself in charge of one of the biggest clubs in the land with a whole crop of youngsters, largely untried, rolling off the youth-team conveyor belt and hungry to succeed. At once susceptible to Docherty's infectious drivings and enthusiasm, these 'ducklings' quickly took to the water, and, when Dave Sexton moved in as coach almost immediately, the two men forged a partnership which was to take Chelsea to the very brink of success on several occasions.

The young manager's impetuosity and unpredictable words and actions often created problems which, later in his career, frequently led to a parting of the ways with other clubs. But at Chelsea he was fortunate enough to be guided by his chairman, Joe

Mears, a father figure enormously respected by Docherty, who was invariably at hand to curb the more outrageous of his excesses and keep a strong hand on the tiller.

If his excursions into the transfer market were by no means always successful, the younger players revelled in the climate created by Docherty and Sexton. The youngest team in club history, having won promotion at the first attempt, romped up the First Division table the following season to finish fifth. Then, the next year, they won the Football League Cup, reached the semi-final of the FA Cup and ended in third spot in the League. This was followed by two further major Cup semi-finals and again, fifth place in the table in 1965-6, and Chelsea's first Wembley FA Cup Final 12 months on. Everything was happening at breakneck speed.

Already the comment was frequently made, however, that Chelsea were continually falling at the final hurdle; bridesmaid but never bride. As a result,

Docherty became still more restless in his pursuit for success. But two events had already cast a shadow. In January 1965, Dave Sexton left to take over as manager of Leyton Orient. And, tragically, on 1 July 1966, chairman Joe Mears collapsed and died whilst walking in a Scandinavian park during the World Cup in Sweden. In 18 months, Docherty had lost his right-hand man and, still more seriously, his sage and mentor.

A month's suspension by the Football Association, following incidents on Chelsea's 1967 summer tour of Bermuda may have precipitated a crisis now unravelling almost daily. Docherty had lost any respect for his new chairman, Mr Charles Pratt, and the Board could no longer allow the manager to ride rough-shod over their directions and wishes. As a result, he resigned on 6 October 1967, and an exciting, breathless, era in the Chelsea saga was at an end.

Dave Sexton
October 1967-October 1975

DAVE Sexton was already a well-known face in the Chelsea dressing-room when he succeeded Tommy Docherty, 17 days after his predecessor had moved out. Indeed, it is no exaggeration to say that the players themselves exerted considerable pressure on the Board to appoint Sexton. For more than three years as Docherty's assistant coach, he had won the respect and confidence of everyone at Stamford Bridge and, accordingly, was hailed with great enthusiasm on his return.

He was, of course, fortunate in a number of respects. The playing staff was strong, and contained great potential. Money was available, if required, to strengthen the squad. And a further factor, not always to the fore in Chelsea's history, was that there was a burning desire for success at every level within the club. Morale, which had taken a bit of battering (Chelsea had just returned from Elland Road with a 7-0 beating at the hands of Leeds United), recovered immediately.

Sexton had pulled up few trees during his playing career. From Chelmsford City and Luton Town in the 1950s, his best spell was with West Ham United (qualifying therefore as a member of the Upton Park ex-players' 'Managers Academy') before running down at Leyton Orient, Brighton and Crystal Palace.

However, it was obvious that his real forté was coaching. The number two job at Chelsea was never going to be attractive enough to detain him for long. Soon he had moved into managership with Leyton Orient before returning to a coaching role with, first, Fulham and then Arsenal.

Back at Stamford Bridge, success was not immediate, although it was at once clear he was steering his ship in the right direction. Runners-up in the League and two points behind champions Wolverhampton Wanderers at the end of his first full season in charge, in April 1969, was a foretaste of what was to follow. That his successes were to be largely in Cup football is not, perhaps, surprising. At Chelsea he had players of skill and ability, with more than a touch of genius in one or two places. But genius can be wayward at times. Winter afternoons on windswept, sparsely populated, grounds in the north of England did not always draw the same response as the more glamorous occasions, with their self-motivating atmosphere in a packed stadium.

The FA Cup victory in 1970 against Leeds United, probably the best team in England at the time, was Sexton's first peak. The second, 12 months later, was in Athens when Real Madrid were beaten in the European Cup-winners' Cup. Banners lined the Fulham Road on the team's homecoming, proclaiming them the 'King's of Europe'. The future seemed limitless in possibility, as the directors planned a stadium to match such stirring deeds on the field of play.

Under the surface, nevertheless, all was not what it seemed to be. Maybe one or two players were enjoying success too extravagantly? Or merely taking it for granted? Discipline needed tightening and when Sexton, alive to his problems, cracked his whip he encountered resistance. Out went Chelsea to an enthusiastic bunch of amateurs in the Cup-winners' Cup early in 1971-2; in eight days Leyton Orient and Stoke City ejected the club from the two domestic Cup competitions — Stoke in the League Cup Final at Wembley, when Chelsea were the hottest favourites in years.

Man management and communication were never Sexton's strongest points and the increasingly rebel element in the dressing-room was never quelled. His directors supported him initially, but at the expense of several players being allowed to leave. Then, as the situation deteriorated, they switched allegiance early in the 1974-5 season and Sexton, himself, was dismissed. By then the club had tumbled from its place near the very top of the football tree, falling to earth between two stools. The exciting party and Chelsea's 'Golden Years' were over.

Ron Suart
October 1974-April 1975

RON Suart, scholarly in appearance and a deep thinker about the game, was Chelsea's shortest-serving manager. Nor was it ever intended that his appointment should be much more than in a caretaker capacity. For seven years previously he had been, in turn, both assistant to Tommy Docherty and Dave Sexton and on his elevation to the full managerial post he was given Eddie McCreadie as his right-hand man.

Few envied him his task in picking up the pieces after Sexton left. Already the playing staff had been weakened by the departure of such as Peter Osgood, Alan Hudson and David Webb. Others were openly unhappy at the way problems had been allowed to escalate and, with the team already embedded in the nether regions of the First Division, ambition centred merely on holding on to a place in the top drawer.

Relying on his experience as a player with Blackpool and Blackburn Rovers and, perhaps more importantly, as manager with Scunthorpe United and, for nine years, Blackpool, Suart concentrated mainly on team affairs off the field, leaving McCreadie to attend to the day-to-day training and handling of the team. Cash was now in very short supply and the money spent on David Hay, Celtic's Scottish international, and John Sissons, from West Ham United, did not bring the dividends expected, for entirely different reasons.

For seven months the team struggled on, just occasionally raising hopes that First Division status could be preserved. Throughout it all Ron Suart never panicked, and remained philosophical, retaining everyone's respect. But it was, unhappily, not enough.

Eddie McCreadie
April 1975-July 1977

WITH three fixtures of the 1974-5 season remaining, and with a only slim chance of avoiding relegation to Division Two, Eddie McCreadie found himself propelled from first-team coach into the team manager's chair. It was a desperate gamble which failed in the short-term, but was soon to pay off handsomely.

As a player, McCreadie was an all-action, enthusiastic full-back never willing even to contemplate defeat. A gambler on the field, no situation was too daunting and the tougher the going, the more belligerent was his response. And so he was as a manager.

Like Ron Suart before him, he had to rely on his existing playing staff, reinforced by whatever the youth scheme could throw up, with some occasional 'wheeler-dealing' in the transfer market. At least such as the enduring Peter Bonetti, John Dempsey, Micky Droy and the indestructible Ron Harris provided the framework of a defence. Gary Stanley and Ray Wilkins, in constrasting styles, brought youthful promise into midfield, whilst Steve Finnieston and Tommy Langley beavered away up front. Skill may not always have been of the highest in every case, but rarely could effort be faulted.

For a season the team were allowed to find their bearings on a less demanding, but intensely competitive, stage. There were a few high spots — and rather more disappointments. Yet, finishing in a half-way placing was progress. Then, without a single fee being paid for a new player, the team took off in the 1976-7 season. Only two matches were lost before the beginning of December, by which time Chelsea were six points ahead of their nearest rivals. Of equal importance was the fact that the side were playing exciting football which drew in the fans — 55,000 of them to watch the local derby against Fulham on Boxing Day. And, if in the end Chelsea had to make do with the second promotion place, no one could quibble. McCreadie, given his limited resources, had performed a miracle.

As the crowd filed out of the ground after the final fixture, once more the future could be faced with at least guarded optimism. Even if there was no cash available for new players, the existing team could surely be relied upon to keep their heads above water in the First Division whilst their football education continued.

When Eddie McCreadie announced his resignation on 1 July 1977, the shock waves spread far beyond the boundaries of Chelsea and Fulham. A dispute over contract between chairman and manager proved irreconcilable and before either party had time for second thoughts, or compromise, McCreadie was seeking a new future on the other side of the Atlantic. Speculation is pointless, yet one still wonders what he might have achieved at Stamford Bridge, had tempers cooled and common sense prevailed.

Ken Shellito
July 1977-December 1978

KEN Shellito was a Chelsea man through and through. Born in East Ham, he arrived at Stamford Bridge as a 15-year old schoolboy and through 23 years he progressed, first to professional status as a player and, when his playing career was cruelly truncated by injury, he moved easily on to the coaching staff and became 'manager of the youth section'.

Football dealt him a harsh hand. Capped by England in his early 20s, it seemed almost formality that he would be an automatic choice for the right-back position in the national side for some years. But his left knee, on which four operations were performed, gave way and, although he struggled on bravely for seven seasons to make more than 100 first-team appearances for Chelsea, it was a battle he could never win.

Coaching young players was his forté. His experience in the game and his reputation as a player won him great respect. He was a good communicator, and at Chelsea he had fertile ground in which to work. So, when his full-back partner of earlier days, Eddie McCreadie, resigned as manager at short notice he seemed well-equipped to take over.

In this situation Shellito found himself in charge of a band of players which had, against expectation, just fought their way out of the Second Division with tremendous spirit. There was experience; a fair measure of ability; and there was the promise of youth. Had money been available, two, or perhaps three, signings could have concealed obvious weaknesses. In the event, and without recourse to the chequebook, Shellito did well to keep his team afloat in the top class. In this respect, his deep knowledge of the majority of his wards who had grown up under his tutelage, was a great asset.

But time and circumstances were against him, and a wretched start to his second season of 1978-9 sealed his fate. Understandably, the directors were desperate to take any measures which would avoid a return to the Second Division, and Shellito was unfeelingly cast aside. However sad the parting, at least he could walk away with head held high and in the knowledge that the service he had given to the club was both long and honourable and that, in such an impossible situation, no one could reasonably have been expected to do more.

Danny Blanchflower
December 1978-September 1979

WHEN Danny Blanchflower arrived to take over as manager, Chelsea were in very low water. Two months earlier, protracted negotiations had taken place with the famous Yugoslav coach, Miljan Miljanic, who, after observing the running of the club at close quarters for ten days, decided he could not accept the post of 'technical director'.

So, in desperation, and with matters deteriorating rapidly on the field, the directors decided that the famous Tottenham Hotspur and Northern Ireland international wing-half was the man for Chelsea. At the age of 52, he had been out of regular day-to-day contact with football for 15 years. Further, his appointment on a 'month-to-month' basis scarcely suggested permanence at Stamford Bridge.

While it is probably fair to say that Blanchflower was never cut out to be a manager, it is undoubtedly true to point out that Chelsea needed a person of experience in this field and with an intimate working knowledge of the current state of English football. Never at any time did Chelsea's fifth holder of the office in as many years suggest that he had the equipment to climb this mountain.

Some of the playing staff were past their best. More were, frankly, never First Division quality. Others of promise were thrown into the bullring too soon. No fewer than 31 were given their chance in a first team that had become companions of defeat during that 1978-9 season.

Blanchflower cajoled and encouraged. He experimented and theorized. But, as one senior player confided: "He is fascinating to listen to, but we're never quite sure what he's trying to say." Happily for all concerned, in less than a year both employers and employee realized it could never work.

Geoff Hurst
October 1979-April 1981

GEOFF Hurst became the fourth Chelsea manager in succession to be appointed to his post without any similar previous experience in League football. Two and a half years in charge of Southern League Telford United was undoubtedly of some value by way of preparation, but scarcely enough to equip him for coping with the many-sided problems besetting Chelsea at that time. For four months prior to his appointment he had been Danny Blanchflower's right-hand man, as coach, so was under no illusion as to what was required.

With Bobby Gould moving from Hereford United as his assistant, he quickly transformed a team which had made a hesitant, stuttering start to the 1979-80 season on their return to the Second Division. By the beginning of December he had steered Chelsea to the top of the table, a position they were still clinging to four months later. Then, three Easter fixtures produced only a single point and the chance of promotion had flown out of the window.

Yet, it seemed that Hurst had built the basis for success. The unwieldy professional staff of 33 had sensibly been trimmed. Much-needed experience had arrived with the signings of Dennis Rofe and Colin Viljoen. Colin Lee, too, looked a useful asset. And a crop of younger players had advanced noticeably. The traumas of the past three years had apparently receded, a view that the autumn of 1980 seemed to confirm.

At the half-way stage, Chelsea were in second place in the table, one point behind West Ham United, and apparently going hot-foot towards promotion. No one, however, could have foreseen what was to follow. Six games failed to produce a single victory and, more catastrophically still, starting in early February, a sequence of 13 fixtures saw the team fail to score, apart from a lone two-goal victory in early March. Nine consecutive games passed without Chelsea finding the net. With one exception the team that had started out confidently the previous August had totally collapsed.

Once again, the directors, with Ken Bates now a member of the Board, decided a change was required. Hurst, sadder and wiser, moved out of Stamford Bridge — and out of football altogether.

John Neal
May 1981-June 1985

EVER since the departure of Ron Suart in 1975, Chelsea had been lacking in experienced management. At any time the First Division is a harsh environment in which to learn this trade. And when the club concerned is beset by mountainous financial problems and other upheavals behind the scenes, then it becomes well-nigh impossible. Shellito, Blanchflower and Hurst were all written-off as failures. Yet, the circumstances under which they operated would have taxed men of far greater experience. They deserve every sympathy.

Next to try his luck was John Neal. And he proved an inspired appointment. Twelve years in charge of Wrexham and, then, Middlesbrough was a sound preparation for what was required. To succeed he was going to need some breaks and, within a year of arriving at Stamford Bridge, he had his first stroke of luck. Brian Mears, wearied and depressed by Chelsea's steep decline, resigned after 12 years as chairman and, after a short spell with Viscount Chelsea at the helm, was replaced by the club's new owner, Ken Bates.

At once the impact of the new leader became apparent. Determination to find a solution to each and every problem, a necessarily ruthless approach to bring in long-needed reforms, and burning ambition to make Chelsea, once more, one of the country's top teams swept through the place. And, not least, if to a limited degree only, Chelsea would again be able to compete in the transfer market.

Neal's first season, under the old regime, was undistinguished. The team ended, as it had done under Hurst 12 months before, in 12th place in the Second Division. Liverpool, however, were beaten in a memorable fifth-round FA Cup-tie and, in the quarter-final, Spurs were made to fight all the way. Over 80,000 fans watched the two ties at Stamford Bridge.

Darkness, however, was to come before the dawn. The 1982-3 campaign marked the lowest point in Chelsea's entire history. Relegation to Division Three was a distinct possibility until the first week of May, and Neal's earlier promise to supporters that he would 'work hard to put us into a position where we would be eager for the start of the new season', raised smiles of cynicism rather than expectation.

But August 1983 saw that promise fulfilled, and a transformation, indeed. Eight of the 'old guard' had moved out to be replaced by seven newcomers, including former heroes, John Hollins and Alan Hudson. Despite warnings that it would take time for the team to settle down as 'strangers' became acquainted, Chelsea started with a 5-0 defeat of Derby County and swept all before them, triumphantly clinching the Second Division championship on the final day of the season. The Bridge was a 'bridge of smiles' once more.

And, if anything the next year was even better. A finishing place of fifth in the First Division, ahead of such as Arsenal and Nottingham Forest, and a League Cup semi-final appearance reflected enormous credit on John Neal's shrewd and unostentatious methods of building a side for the future. More and more John Hollins was now confining his activity to his duties as club coach, with assistant manager Ian McNeil also an able lieutenant.

It was, nevertheless, a shock when it was announced in the summer of 1985 that Hollins was to take over the managership of Chelsea immediately and that John Neal had been appointed to the Board. Neal had undergone heart surgery 12 months earlier and that, possibly, had been a factor. Mr Bates had already said that Hollins was being groomed for the job and would be Chelsea's 'next manager'. It was just that things seemed to have been hurried along more than was expedient and that Neal's move 'upstairs' was, perhaps, a little premature.

John Hollins
June 1985-March 1988

DOWN the years, there have been few more popular, or more respected, players in the Chelsea story than John Hollins. Only Ron Harris and Peter Bonetti can better his number of first-team appearances, and one full international cap for England does little justice to his skill and ability on the field.

He was 37 when he returned to the Stamford Bridge fold after nearly eight years away at Queen's Park Rangers and Arsenal. And it was obviously mainly with coaching and management in mind that he had been signed. After a final, and most influential, season at right-back, he was made 'club coach', and, in partnership with John Neal, the renaissance of Chelsea FC continued. Twelve months later, he found himself in full control as manager.

Unlike any of his predecessors in this office, Hollins took over a successful ship that, having been on the rocks, was now once more proceeding full steam ahead. Everything seemed made for him to capitalize on the outstanding progress already made. And, if his first season did not actually show any such advance, it repeated the considerable achievement of finishing sixth in Division One, and put another trophy in the cabinet in the shape of the newly-inaugurated Full Members' Cup, a minor tournament maybe, but still one which attracted nearly 70,000 spectators to Wembley for the Final with Manchester City.

It was in the autumn of 1987 that things started to go awry. Lying in second position behind Queen's Park Rangers at the end of September raised further exciting possibilities. The suddeness of the decline, when it came, was alarming. Oxford United were beaten 2-1 on the last day of October, but another twenty-two matches were to pass before the next victory was chalked up, in early April. By that time relegation was looming, and Hollins had gone.

His departure had been preceded by weeks of rumour and speculation. Individuals were performing way below their ability, and players were openly expressing dissatisfaction with methods of coaching. Despite frequent denials, morale had plummeted and discontent was surfacing everywhere. And when Bobby Campbell replaced Ernie Walley as coach, seemingly without Hollins' blessing, the manager's days were numbered. In fact, the new and uneasy partnership survived fractionally over one month, before Hollins walked away a sad and disillusioned figure.

Like others before him, he had learned the hard way that coaching and management are poles apart and require totally different skills. But that this should happen to such a likeable and distinguished Chelsea figure was all the more sad.

Bobby Campbell
May 1988-May 1991

AFTER four of the five previous incumbents had failed to make a successful

mark in the highly specialized career of football management at Stamford Bridge, it was back again to an experienced hand, when Bobby Campbell took over in the closing weeks of the 1987-8 season. First arriving as coach, then graduating to acting manager on Hollins' departure, his appointment was confirmed on a permanent basis before the play-offs doomed Chelsea once more to relegation.

He had previously been in charge at both Fulham (1976-80) and Portsmouth (1982-84), after cutting his teeth as assistant manager at Aldershot, and had also had spells of coaching Queen's Park Rangers (twice), Arsenal and Fulham. If his track record was not an outstanding one, at least it was respectable and he had been in close enough touch with the Stamford Bridge scene for some time to know what had to be done, and what would be demanded.

He inherited a good squad of players who had already proved themselves in top company before unaccountably, losing their way. Major surgery was certainly not one of the measures required. Rather the team needed a steady, guiding hand, and a man who could bring out the potential of some highly talented performers. Apart from international defenders Peter Nicholas and Graham Roberts, there were no notable newcomers during his first season when, most satisfactorily, the Second Division championship was won by a 17-point margin and with one or two records being chalked up along the way.

Only then did Campbell shell out big money. Alan Dickens arrived in June 1989 at a cost of £650,000, and a further £2.8 million was spent on strengthening the staff during the summer of 1990. Campbell was fortunate, too, in finding that talent was emerging from the junior club ranks once again, after a comparatively barren interval. Five, and even six, of the team had been 'educated' at The Bridge.

However, despite these substantial amounts paid out for new blood, results in the 1990-91 season deteriorated alarmingly, after an encouraging start.

An 11-match spell, beginning with two abysmal League Cup semi-final defeats at the end of February, brought only one victory and it came as no suprise when Bobby Campbell's three-year stint as Chelsea manager was terminated in the final week of the season.

Ian Porterfield
June 1991-

WHEN Ian Porterfield was appointed Chelsea's ninth manager in 17 years, he was not their first choice. At least two other managers from the lower echelons of the Football League had resisted the chairman's highly lucrative overtures.

Porterfield, however, had much to commend him. From August 1988 to November 1989, he was assistant to Bobby Campbell at Stamford Bridge and the players respected his deep knowledge of the game. His departure for Reading might have accounted for a pronounced decline in Chelsea's playing fortunes as they slumped from top of the First Division to mid-table three months later.

Born in Dunfermline in 1946, Porterfield became a national figure by netting the only goal of the 1973 FA Cup Final, when Second Division Sunderland scored a sensational victory over Leeds, although he was never a prolific scorer in some 300 League games with Sunderland and Sheffield Wednesday.

After his career was badly interrupted and scarred by a serious road accident soon after that Cup Final, he managed Rotherham United from the brink of relegation to the Third Division championship, then in five years at Bramall Lane piloted Sheffield United from Division Four to a highly-placed spot in Division Two. In 1986, he succeeded Alex Ferguson at Aberdeen and took them to the Scottish League Cup Final, where Rangers won a penalty 'shoot-out'. His overall record of only 12 defeats from 98 games needs no elaboration.

The move to Reading from Stamford Bridge coincided with difficult times for the Berkshire club and involved a change of ownership.

At Chelsea he meets a familiar challenge: how to harness great ability, so often wayward, into success and consistency. He said on his appointment: "We have a good squad and don't need an awful lot to be a successful side."

Chelsea Who's Who

ABRAMS*, Robert Lawrence (1914-1920) Wing-half
Born: Banks, 14 May 1889; Died: Southport, 20 March 1966.
5ft 9½in; 12st 12lb.
Career: Southport Central (1905), Colne (June 1907), Stockport County (cs 1907), Heart of Midlothian, Chelsea (June 1914), Cardiff City (May 1920), Southport (June 1921), Retired (February 1923).
Chelsea debut: 5 September 1914. Appearances: League 44, FA Cup 5; Goals: League 7.
One of the many players whose career was badly interrupted by World War One, Abrams established himself at left-half in the first team soon after his arrival at Stamford Bridge. However, after a few games at outside-left, following the resumption of normal football five years later, he was unable to hold his place. Powerfully built, he was noted for his strong tackling and was most unlucky not to be selected to play for Chelsea in the 1915 FA Cup Final. He played for England against Scotland in a Military international during World War One.
*Although known throughout his football career as Abrams, his surname on both birth and death certificates was registered as Abram.

ALEXANDER, David B. (1939-1945)   Wing-half
Born: Glasgow.
Career: Clydebank, Lancs football, Chelsea (1939-45).
Chelsea debut: 7 April 1939. Appearances: League 1.
A signing from Lancastrian football in the early months of 1939, Alexander made his first-team debut on Good Friday, against Charlton Athletic at The Valley, and became a regular member of the side in the first season of wartime regional football. An athletically built and skilful player, his promising career was ended prematurely by a motor-cycle accident during his Army service and he was invalided out the forces.

ALLEN, Leslie William (1954-1959)   Forward
Born: Dagenham, 4 September 1937.
5ft 8in; 10st.
Career: Briggs Sports, Chelsea (September 1954), Tottenham Hotspur (December 1959, exchange Johnny Brooks), Queen's Park Rangers (July 1965).
Honours: England Under-23 international (1 cap), Football League Championship medal 1961, FA Cup winners' medal 1961.
Chelsea debut: 1 September 1956. Appearances: League 44, FA Cup 2, League Cup 3; Goals: League 11.
One of manager Ted Drake's many young signings, Allen's opportunities at Stamford Bridge were reduced by the keen competition for first-team places at that time and he was allowed to move to Tottenham Hotspur (in exchange for Johnny Brooks), where he became an integral part of Spurs' famous 1960-61 League and FA Cup double team, playing in every League game and scoring 23 goals. A neat, ball-playing inside or

centre-forward, he later managed QPR (from December 1968) and Swindon Town (1971). Father of England international Clive Allen.

ALLISTER, John G. (1949-1952)   Wing-half
Born: Edinburgh, 30 June 1927.
5ft 9in; 11st 2lb.
Career: Tranent Juniors, Chelsea (July 1949), Aberdeen (July 1952, £4,000). Chesterfield (June 1958).
Chelsea debut: 12 March 1952. Appearances: League 4; Goals: League 1.
A strong, forceful, attacking wing-half who could also perform adequately at centre-forward, Allister was unable to establish a first-team place at Chelsea but, on returning north of the border, was a member of Aberdeen's Scottish First Division team for some six seasons.

ALLUM, Leonard Hector (1932-1939)   Wing-half
Born: Reading, July 1907; Died: Reading 9 May 1980.
5ft 9in; 9st 12lb.
Career: Maidenhead United, Fulham (amateur) (August 1929), Chelsea (May 1932), Clapton Orient (May 1939).
Chelsea debut: 29 October 1932. Appearances: League 93, FA Cup 9; Goals: League 2.
A slim, lightweight wing-half with considerable skill

on the ball, Allum proved a most dependable reserve for the seven seasons leading up to World War Two. Having won amateur representative honours with Maidenhead United, he was unable to establish himself fully at Stamford Bridge. Moving to Clapton Orient, he played many games for the East London club in regional football throughout the war.

ANDERSON, George Russell (1927-1929) Centre-forward
Born: Saltcoats, 29 October 1904; Died: 9 November 1974.
Career: Dalry Thistle, Airdrieonians (cs 1925), Brentford (May 1926), Chelsea (May 1927), Norwich City (May 1929), Carlisle United (August 1930), Gillingham (cs 1930), Cowdenbeath (October 1931), Yeovil & Petter's United (July 1932), Bury (non-contract June 1933), Huddersfield Town (November 1934), Mansfield Town (January 1936 cs 1937).
Chelsea debut: 4 February 1928. Appearances: League 9.
Anderson began his career at Airdrie, where he was deputy to Hughie Gallacher, the Scottish international centre-forward, who was later to play for Chelsea. At Stamford Bridge, Anderson was given several opportunities to establish himself in the first team but was unable to adapt himself to the faster pace of English First Division football.

ANDERTON, Sylvan James (1959-1962) Wing-half
Born: Reading, 23 November 1934.
5ft 9in; 12st.
Career: Reading (June 1951), Chelsea (March 1959, £10,000), Queen's Park Rangers (January 1962, £5,000).
Chelsea debut: 28 March 1959. Appearances: League 76, FA Cup 3, League Cup 1, Fairs Cup 2; Goals: League 2.
After nearly 200 first-team games for Reading, Anderton spent more than three years at Chelsea, mostly in the senior side. He was a strongly-built, hard-tackling and constructive wing-half but the arrival of Andy Malcolm, from West Ham United, signalled the end of his days at The Bridge.

ARGUE, James (1933-1947) Inside-forward
Born: Glasgow, 26 November 1911; Died: Lennoxtown, 11 April 1978.
5ft 11in; 11st 11lb.
Career: St Roch's Juniors (Glasgow), Birmingham (December 1931), Chelsea (May 1933, free transfer), Shrewsbury Town (1947).
Chelsea debut: 9 December 1933. Appearances: League 118, FA Cup 7; Goals: League 30, FA Cup 5.
Argue was Leslie Knighton's first signing after the manager's appointment in 1933, rejoining his boss from Birmingham. A strongly-built, tough and aggressive inside-forward with a flair for scoring vital goals, Argue was easily identified by his shock of red hair. He became an integral member of the team in the immediate pre-war period, despite missing many games through injury. He was captain of the reserve team in 1946-7 before moving, briefly, to Shrewsbury Town. His son played for St Johnstone in Scottish League football.

ARMSTRONG, James William (1922-1927) Centre-forward
Born: Newcastle upon Tyne, 6 September 1901; Died: Gateshead, August 1977.

5ft 8in; 10st.
Career: Spen Black and White, Chelsea (January 1922), Tottenham Hotspur (May 1927), Luton Town (July 1930), Bristol Rovers (March 1931).
Chelsea debut: 23 December 1922. Appearances: 29 League, 2 FA Cup; Goals: League 9, FA Cup 1.
After a promising start to his Chelsea career — he scored on his debut, at White Hart Lane — Armstrong never fulfilled his potential, largely because of a somewhat frail physique.

ARMSTRONG, Kenneth (1946-1957) Wing-half
Born: Bradford, 3 June 1924; Died: New Zealand, June 1984.
5ft 8in; 11st.
Career: Bradford Rovers, Chelsea (December 1946), Eastern Union (NZ), Gisborne (NZ).
Honours: England international (1 cap), England 'B' (3 caps), Football League XI, Football League Championship medal 1955. Also 1 FA Charity Shield appearance 1955.
Chelsea debut: 23 August 1947. Appearances: League 362, FA Cup 39; Goals: League 25, FA Cup 5.
One of Chelsea's most popular and most consistent players, Ken Armstrong joined the club from Army football in December 1946 and acclimatized easily to the demands of professional football. For ten seasons he was a permanent fixture in the first team, usually at right-half but, on occasions, in the forward line. Indeed, in 1947-8 he was top scorer after he had temporarily taken over the centre-forward spot from Tommy Lawton. A polished and artistic performer, he deserved more than the one full international cap which came his way, against Scotland at Wembley in 1955, when England won 7-2. He held Chelsea's all-time record of League appearances until Peter Bonetti overtook his total in 1969. Having been granted a testimonial, Armstrong went to live in New Zealand where he became national coach. After his death, his ashes were strewn on the Stamford Bridge pitch.

ASHFORD, James William (1920-1925) Full-back
Born: Barnborough, near Doncaster, 24 May 1987; Died: Poole, 1970.
5ft 8in; 9st 7lb.
Career: Ebbw Vale (October 1919), Chelsea (March 1920), Doncaster Rovers (cs 1925), Bristol Rovers (August 1926), Scunthorpe United (August 1928).
Chelsea debut: 23 April 1921. Appearances: 8 League.
Ashford was a lightweight full-back who made occasional first-team appearances during his five seasons on the staff, deputizing for Walter Bettridge, Jack Harrow or George Smith.

AYLOTT, Trevor Keith Charles (1975-1979) Striker
Born: Bermondsey, 26 November 1957.
6ft 1in; 13st 10lb.
Career: Chelsea (November 1975), Queen's Park Rangers (loan), Barnsley (November 1979, £50,000), Millwall (August 1982), Luton Town (March 1983), Crystal Palace (June 1984), Barnsley (loan), AFC Bournemouth (August 1986), Birmingham City (October 1990).
Chelsea debut: 22 October 1977. Appearances: League 26(3), FA Cup 1; Goals: League 2.
A heavily-built striker who graduated to full professional status from the Chelsea Juniors without ever

establishing himself in the first team, Aylott lacked the finesse to break down First Division defences.

BAIN, James A. (1945-1947)   **Outside-left**
Born: Blairgowrie, 14 December 1919.
5ft 8in; 10st.
Career: Gillingham, Chelsea (May 1945), Swindon Town (May 1947).
Chelsea debut: 5 January 1946. Appearances: League 9, FA Cup 5; Goals: League 1.
Bain had the distinction of being Chelsea's first full-time professional after the end of World War Two. Lightly-built, he was unable to establish a regular first-team place but went on to play more than 250 first-team games for Swindon Town before retiring in 1953.

BAKER, Benjamin Howard (1921-1926)   **Goalkeeper**
Born: Liverpool, 12 January 1892; Died: Warminster, 10 September 1987.
5ft 11in; 12st.
Career: Old Marlburians, Liverpool Balmoral, Preston North End (December 1919), Corinthians, Liverpool (March 1920), Everton (November 1920), Chelsea (October 1921), Everton (August 1926), Oldham Athletic (March 1929).
Honours: England international (2 caps), Football League XI, England Amateur international (10 caps), Welsh Amateur Cup winner 1921.
Chelsea debut: 15 October 1921. Appearances: League 92, FA Cup 1; Goals: League 1.

One of football's legendary names, Baker was also British high-jump champion —setting a British record of 6ft 5in on 5 June 1921 — and excelled at high-diving, water polo and lawn tennis. He was a distinguished and colourful personality who retained his amateur status throughout his playing career. A famous Corinthian footballer — he was their goalkeeper at a time when they consistently challenged the best professional teams in the land in the FA Cup competition — he played for Chelsea, whenever available, for five seasons. His unorthodox methods made him a star attraction wherever he played. The length of his goalkicking, his dashes into midfield and his taking of penalty-kicks were all part of his remarkable repertoire.

BALDWIN, Thomas (1966-1974)   **Striker**
Born: Gateshead, 10 June 1945.
5ft 9½in; 12st.
Career: Wrekenton Juniors, Arsenal (December 1962), Chelsea (September 1966), Millwall (November 1974), Manchester United (loan), Gravesend & Northfleet, Brentford (October 1977 player-coach).
Honours: England Under-23 international (2 caps), FA Cup winners' medal 1970, runners-up medal 1967.
Chelsea debut: 1 October 1966. Appearances: League 182(5), FA Cup 21, League Cup 14(3), Fairs Cup 4, European Cup-winners' Cup 7(3); Goals: League 74, FA Cup 5, League Cup 6, Fairs Cup 1, European Cup-winners' Cup 6.
Known as the 'sponge' for his ability to retain the ball under pressure and skilfully shield it from opponents while seeking an opening to set up an attack, Baldwin was a regular goalscorer, especially in his early days at The Bridge. Whilst lacking the flair of some of his colleagues he was, nevertheless, a vital cog in the team which made four Cup Final appearances between 1967 and 1972. He was coach at Brentford for a period after his playing career ended.

BAMBRICK, James (1934-1938)   **Centre-forward**
Born: Belfast, 3 November 1907; Died: 27 November 1983.
5ft 11in; 11st 2lb.
Career: Rockville, Ulster Rangers, Bridgemount Ards, Glentoran, Linfield (August 1927), Chelsea (December 1934, £2,000), Walsall (March 1938, £2,500).
Honours: Northern Ireland international (11 caps).
Chelsea debut: 25 December 1934. Appearances: League 59, FA Cup 7; Goals: League 33, FA Cup 4.
'Joe' Bambrick was a prolific scorer whose six goals for Northern Ireland against Wales at Celtic Park, Belfast, in February 1930 is still a record. At Linfield he once scored 94 goals in a season and he scored over 600 goals during his career in senior football. In English football he found the competition a good deal more intense and at Chelsea he contested the centre-forward spot with George Mills. Strongly built, he was a highly intelligent player, a powerful header of the ball and had clever control on the ground.

BANNON, Eamonn John (1979)   **Midfield**
Born: Edinburgh, 18 April 1958.
5ft 10in; 11st 7lb.
Career: Links Boys' Club (Edinburgh), Heart of Midlothian (1976), Chelsea (January 1979, £200,000), Dundee United (November 1979, £170,000), Heart of Midlothian (cs 1988).
Honours: Scotland international (11 caps), Scotland Under-21 (7 caps), Scotland Schoolboys, Scottish League XI (1 appearance), Scottish FA Cup runners-up medals 1981, 1985, Scottish League Cup winners' medals 1980, 1981, runners-up medals 1982, 1985, Scottish League Championship medal 1983.
Chelsea debut: 3 February 1979. Appearances: League 25, League Cup 2; Goals: League 1.
Manager Danny Blanchflower's first signing for Chelsea, Bannon was a most talented midfield player who was unable to settle into English football at a time when Chelsea were in the throes of relegation from Division One and in dire financial straits. On his return north of the border, he rapidly developed into one of his country's outstanding players.

BARBER, George Frederick (1930-1941)   **Full-back**
Born: West Ham, 1 August 1908; Died: Ilford, 7 July 1974.
6ft 1in; 10st 13lb.
Career: Fairnburn House Lads, Redhill, Luton Town (October 1929), Chelsea (May 1930, free transfer). Retired (September 1941).
Chelsea debut: 26 December 1930. Appearances: League 262, FA Cup 32; Goals: FA Cup 1.
Barber was one of the best bargain signings ever made by Chelsea. At a time when the club was paying large sums of money for star players of proven reputation, he was obtained on a free transfer and went on to become a reliable pillar of the defence for a decade. Tutored by Scottish international Tommy Law, he was surprisingly light on his feet for such a big man. At home on either right or left, he is perhaps best recalled for his sliding tackle which dispossessed many a startled opponent. Barber also had cricket trials with Essex and later ran a hairdressing business.

BARKAS, Edward (1937-1939)   **Full-back**
Born: Wardley Colliery, 21 November 1902; Died: Little Bromwich, 4 April 1962.
5ft 7½in; 12st 12lb.
Career: St Hilda OB, Bedlington United, South Shields, Hebburn Colliery, Norwich City (amateur, October 1920), Bedlington United, Huddersfield Town (January 1921), Birmingham (December 1928), Chelsea (May 1937), Solihull Town (player-manager), Wilmot Breedon, Nuffield Mechanisations.
Honours: Football League Championship medals 1925, 1926, FA Cup runners-up medal 1931, Toured Canada with FA 1928.
Chelsea debut: 1 January 1938. Appearances: League 27, FA Cup 1.
'Ned' Barkas, cousin of England player William Felton, was signed by manager Leslie Knighton, under whom he had played at Birmingham, in the twilight of his distinguished career. After 16 years as a League player, he was, not surprisingly, lacking in pace, but played regularly during the second half of 1937-8. Well remembered for his robust shoulder-charges, he was a most likeable personality whose three brothers also played League football, Sam winning five full caps for England.

BARRACLOUGH, William (1934-1937) Outside-left
Born: Hull, 4 January 1909; Died: Hull, 6 August 1969.
5ft 4in; 9st 10lb.
Career: Bridlington Town, Hull City (amateur, January 1928), Wolverhampton Wanderers (October 1928), Chelsea (October 1934), Colchester Town (August 1937), Doncaster Rovers (August 1938).
Honours: Second Division championship medal 1932.
Chelsea debut: 3 November 1934. Appearances: League 74, FA Cup 7; Goals: League 8, FA Cup 3.
Barraclough was a clever winger whose intricate ball skills were sometimes displayed at the cost of directness, a fact which did not make him popular with the Stamford Bridge fans and he became a target for barracking from a section of the crowd. Barraclough an ex-clerk in Hull Docks, later worked in a fruit merchants.

BARRETT, Frederick (1920-1927)   **Full-back**
Born: Kent, 12 April 1896.

5ft 9in; 12st 7lb.
Career: Belfast Celtic, Chelsea (June 1920), Dundalk (cs 1927).
Honours: Irish League XI.
Chelsea debut: 18 September 1920. Appearances: League 64, FA Cup 6; Goals: League 6.
Barrett, an ex-soldier with the Norfolk Regiment, had six seasons of first-team experience with Belfast Celtic before he signed for Chelsea. Apart from one season, his time at Stamford Bridge was spent mainly in the reserve team. Noted for his long kicking, most of his goals came from set-pieces — he once scored two against Darlington, both from free-kicks.

BARRON, James (1965-1966)   **Goalkeeper**
Born: Tantobie, Co Durham, 19 October 1943.
5ft 11in; 11st 12lb.
Career: Newcastle West End, Wolverhampton Wanderers (November 1961), Chelsea (April 1965, £5,000), Oxford United (March 1966), Nottingham Forest, Swindon Town, Peterborough United.
Chelsea debut: 1 September 1965. Appearances: League 1.
Barron was one of several goalkeepers who had the thankless task of understudying Peter Bonetti. He later went on to make some 400 League appearances, most of them at Oxford and Forest, and was also Wolves' assistant manager for a time. He was the son of Jim Barron who played for Darlington.

BASON, Brian (1972-1977)   **Midfield**
Born: Epsom, 3 September 1955.
5ft 9in; 11st 11lb.
Career: Chelsea (September 1972), Plymouth Argyle (September 1977, £30,000), Crystal Palace (March 1981), Portsmouth (loan), Reading (August 1982).
Honours: England Schoolboy international (15 caps).
Chelsea debut: 16 September 1972. Appearances: League 18(1), League Cup 2(1); Goals: League 1.
Making his first-team debut while still an apprentice, Bason was later converted from striker to midfield player. He was strong in the tackle and ever willing to move forward on to attack but his Chelsea career was held back by a double fracture of the right shin in a League Cup tie at Arsenal, just when he seemed likely to establish a regular place in the senior side.

BATHGATE, Sydney (1946-1953)   **Full-back**
Born: Aberdeen, 20 December 1919; Died: 1963.
5ft 8in; 11st 6lb.
Career: Parkvale Juniors (Aberdeen), Chelsea (September 1946), Hamilton Academical (July 1953).
Chelsea debut: 4 January 1947. Appearances: League 135, FA Cup 12.
Having lost important seasons of his playing career during World War Two, Bathgate joined Chelsea on demobilization from the RAF. Stockily built, he gave loyal service to the club, although he was often unsure of a regular first-team spot with competition from Welsh internationals Billy Hughes and Danny Winter. A good tackler with a sound positional sense, if a little short of pace, he was a defender of the old school.

BAXTER, Thomas James C. (1919-1920) Centre-half
Born: Wandsworth, October 1893.
5ft 9½in; 12st.
Career: Army football with the Salonika Expeditionary

Force, Chelsea (September 1919), Gillingham (May 1920, free transfer)
Chelsea debut: 27 September 1919. Appearances: League 1.
Although he was a regular member of the London Combination side in the first season after World War One, Baxter was unable establish himself in the first team.

BEASANT, David John (1989-)   **Goalkeeper**
Born: Willesden, 20 March 1959.
6ft 3in; 13st.
Career: Edgware Town, Wimbledon (July 1979), Newcastle United (June 1988), Chelsea (January 1989, £725,000).
Honours: England international (2 caps), England 'B' (7 caps), Fourth Division championship medal 1983, FA Cup winners' medal 1988, Second Division championship medal 1989, Full Members' Cup winners' medal 1990.
Chelsea debut: 14 January 1989. Appearances: League 95, FA Cup 4, League Cup 10, Full Members Cup 8.

Chelsea paid what was then a club record fee for Beasant, who earlier in his career had been one of the cornerstones of Wimbledon's rise from non-League obscurity to FA Cup winners in the space of 12 seasons. At his best he is a fine, commanding 'keeper, renowned not only for the length of his kicking but also for the accuracy of his distribution, which launches many a swift counter-attack. His massive frame reduces the size of the target offered to opposing strikers, whilst his penalty-kick save in the 1988 FA Cup Final assured him of a place in the game's history.

BELL, Dr John Barr (1920-1923)   **Outside-right**
Born: Barrow-in-Furness, 5 April 1901.
5ft 8½in; 11st 10lb.

Career: Queen's Park, Chelsea (amateur, August 1920; professional, July 1921), Hamilton Academical (cs 1924).
Chelsea debut: 11 September 1920. Appearances: League 42, FA Cup 2; Goals: League 9, FA Cup 1.

Bell arrived at Chelsea with the reputation of being the fastest player in the Scottish League. After one season he signed professional forms but was never a great favourite with the Stamford Bridge crowd, although he continued his association with the club and signed professional whilst still fulfilling his medical duties, at Guy's Hospital.

BELLETT, Walter Ronald (1954-1958)   **Full-back**
Born: Stratford (London), 14 November 1933.
5ft 9in; 11st 10lb.
Career: Barking Town, Chelsea (September 1954), Plymouth Argyle (December 1958, combined fee of £12,000 with Len Casey), Leyton Orient (January 1961), Chester (July 1961), Wrexham (July 1962), Tranmere Rovers (July 1963).
Chelsea debut: 11 February 1956. Appearances: League 35; Goals: League 1.
Hard tackling and quick off the mark, the rugged Bellett was a contemporary of the brothers Sillett and, apart from one extended run in the first team, was unable to claim a regular place.

BENNETT, Walter R. (1922-1924)   **Centre-half**
Born: Sheffield, 1901.
5ft 9in; 11st 6lb.
Career: Birmingham (Trialist February 1922), Chelsea (October 1922), Southend United (May 1924), Doncaster Rovers (August 1925), Wombwell Town (October 1925), Portsmouth (May 1926), Gainsborough Trinity (May 1927), Bristol City (May 1928), Ballymena United (June 1931), Weymouth Town (August 1933).
Chelsea debut: 18 November 1922. Appearances: League 5.
Bennett was on the staff for almost two seasons, playing mostly in the reserve team at a time when Jack Priestley,

59

Tommy Meehan and Harold Wilding were the recognized choices for the half-back positions.

BENTLEY, Roy Thomas Frank (1948-1956)   **Centre-forward**
Born: Bristol, 17 May 1924.
5ft 10in; 12st.
Career: Portway School, Bristol Rovers (1937), Bristol City (1938), Newcastle United (June 1946), Chelsea (January 1948, £11,000), Fulham (August 1956, £8,500), Queen's Park Rangers (May 1961), Retired (January 1963).
Honours: England international (12 caps), England 'B' (1 cap), Football League XI (3 appearances), Football League Championship medal 1955. Also 1 FA Charity Shield appearance and 1 goal 1955.
Chelsea debut: 17 January 1948. Appearances: League 324, FA Cup 42; Goals: League 128, FA Cup 21.

Roy Bentley, who captained the 1955 Football League Championship winning team, was one of the outstanding players in Chelsea's history. Signed as an inside-forward, he was soon converted into a goalscoring centre-forward of somewhat unorthodox method for those days, employing a degree of mobility which frequently saw him raiding down the flanks. A superb header of the ball, he was Chelsea's leading scorer for eight consecutive seasons. He finished his career with Fulham and Queen's Park Rangers, for which clubs he played more than 200 first-team games, mostly at centre-half. After retiring as a player he managed Reading (1963-69)and Swansea Town (1969-72) for a spell, was a scout for Bradford City and subsequently became secretary, first at Reading (1977-84) and later with Aldershot (1984).

BERRY, Paul (1953-1960)   **Centre-half**
Born: Chadwell St Mary, Essex, 15 November 1935.
6ft; 11st 9lb.

Career: Chelsea (April 1953), Tonbridge (summer 1960).
Chelsea debut: 9 March 1957. Appearances: League 3.
A product of the Chelsea Juniors, this tall defender spent nine years on the staff playing almost entirely in the Reserves and 'A' team.

BETTRIDGE, Walter (1909-1922)   **Full-back**
Born: Oakthorpe (Leicestershire), October 1886; Died: Measham, Leicestershire, 23 December 1931.
5ft 8in; 10st 3lb.
Career: Worksop, Burton United, Chelsea (May 1909), Gillingham (November 1922).
Honours: FA Cup runners-up medal 1915.
Chelsea debut: 16 October 1909. Appearances: League 224, FA Cup 31.
One of the famous names in Chelsea's history, Bettridge was a stalwart full-back who played regularly in the first team for 11 seasons (apart from one year during World War One when he was not available). Spotted whilst playing junior football in the Burton upon Trent area, he was one of the first defenders to recognize the advantage of adopting an attacking role. He was also renowned for his consistency and length of kicking. He partnered Jock Cameron in the promotion season of 1911-12 and Jack Harrow in 1914-15, when Chelsea made their first FA Cup Final appearance. Bettridge was mine host of the Bird-in-Hand at Measham at the time of his death.

BIDEWELL, Sidney Henry (1937-1946)   **Centre-forward**
Born: Watford, 6 June 1918.
Career: Wealdstone, Chelsea (May 1937). Gravesend and Northfleet (cs 1946).
Chelsea debut: 4 December 1937. Appearances: League 4; Goals: League 2.
Any chance this forceful attacker had of establishing himself in the senior side was ruined by the outbreak of World War Two. Bidewell made a sensational debut against Huddersfield Town by scoring two goals but the competition for his position was stiff and he could not sustain his success. He served in the Army during the war.

BILLINGTON, Hugh John R. (1948-1951)
Centre/Inside-forward
Born: Ampthill, 24 February 1916; Died: Luton, 1988.
5ft 8½in; 12st 7lb.
Career: Waterlows, Luton Town (May 1938), Chelsea (March 1948, £8,000), Worcester City (August 1951).
Honours: Third Division North championship medal 1937.
Chelsea debut: 13 March 1948. Appearances: League 83, FA Cup 7; Goals: League 28, FA Cup 4.
Billington came to Chelsea towards the end of a long and honourable career spent until then entirely with Luton Town. Thus, at the age of 33, he experienced his first complete season of First Division football, ending up joint leading goalscorer with Roy Bentley. Powerfully built, he possessed a strong shot in either foot and many of his goals came from long-range efforts.

BIRCHENHALL, Alan John (1967-1970)   **Striker**
Born: East Ham, 22 August 1945.
5ft 11½in; 13st 1lb.
Career: Thorneywood Thistle, Sheffield United (June 1963), Chelsea (November 1967, £100,000), Crystal

Palace (June 1970, £100,000), Leicester City (September 1971), Notts County (loan), San Jose Earthquakes (1977), Notts County (September 1977), Memphis Rogues (1978), Blackburn Rovers (September 1978), Luton Town (March 1979), Hereford United (October 1979), Trowbridge Town (player-manager, cs 1980).
Honours: England Under-23 international (4 caps).
Chelsea debut: 2 December 1967. Appearances: League 74(1), FA Cup 10, League Cup 7, Fairs Cup 4; Goals: League 20, FA Cup 3, League Cup 3, Fairs Cup 2.
This tall, blond striker was manager Dave Sexton's first major signing for Chelsea. Birchenall lost his place to Ian Hutchinson early in the 1969-70 season, transferring to Crystal Palace at the end of that campaign to become one of soccer's nomads. After moving into midfield in the later part of his career, he became PRO with Leicester City when his playing days ended.

BIRNIE, Edward Lawson (1906-1910)   Centre/Wing-half
Born: Sunderland, 25 August 1878; Died: Southend, 21 December 1935.
Career: Sunderland Seaburn, Newcastle United (June 1898), Crystal Palace (cs 1905), Chelsea (August 1906), Spurs (July 1910).
Chelsea debut: 8 September 1906. Appearances: League 101, FA Cup 7; Goals League 3.
A fine commanding defender, Ted Birnie played most of his football for Chelsea at left-half where his speed, heading ability and intelligent reading of the game

made him a tremendous asset in the first promotion side of 1906-07. After his playing career ended, he became player-coach with Mulheim in Germany, and later assistant trainer at Sunderland, and manager of Southend United from 1922-34.

BISHOP, Sidney Macdonald (1928-1933)   Wing-half
Born: Stepney, 10 February 1900; Died: Chelsea, 4 April 1949.
6ft; 10st 11lb.
Career: Ilford, Crystal Palace (trialist), West Ham United (May 1920), Leicester City (November 1926), Chelsea (June 1928, £4,500), Retired (May 1933).
Honours: England international (4 caps), Football League XI, FA Cup runners-up medal 1923.
Chelsea debut: 25 August 1928. Appearances: League 103, FA Cup 6; Goals: League 5, FA Cup 1.
A cultured and highly skilled half-back, Bishop came to Chelsea in his days as a respected and fine professional footballer. He played a crucial part in gaining promotion from the Second Division in the spring of 1930. He had first been noticed playing for the RAF and was recruited by West Ham from amateur football. Having left the East Enders in November 1926, he spent 18 months with Leicester City but failed to settle in the Midlands.

BISWELL, George William (1928-1929)
Inside-forward/Wing-half
Born: Watford, 1 September 1907.
5ft 8½in; 11st 2lb.
Career: Villa Juniors, St Albans City, Watford (amateur), Charlton Athletic (September 1924), Chelsea (January 1928, £3,250), Ards, Chester (September 1930), Charlton Athletic (August 1931), Retired (cs 1934).
Chelsea debut: 28 January 1928. Appearances: League 24, FA Cup 1; Goals: League 10.
Something of a utility player, Biswell played for Chelsea mostly in the forward line, but, especially later in his career, was looked upon mainly as a wing-half. Unable to tie down a regular first-team place at Stamford Bridge, he was on the staff for just over a year. Biswell was also a fine golfer.

BLOCK, Michael J. (1957-1962)   Outside-right
Born: Ipswich, 28 January 1940.
5ft 11in; 12st 7lb.
Career: Chelsea (February 1957), Brentford (January 1962, £5,000), Watford (September 1966), Chelmsford City (July 1967).
Chelsea debut: 11 September 1957. Appearances: League 37, FA Cup 2, Fairs Cup 1; Goals: League 6.
Block was a product of the Chelsea youth scheme but never quite fulfilled his early promise. Speedy, despite his stocky build, he was unble to displace Peter Brabrook and Frank Blunstone from the wing positions in the first team but moved on to become a regular in the Brentford side for five seasons.

BLUNSTONE, Frank (1953-1964)   Outside-left
Born: Crewe, 17 October 1934.
5ft 6in; 11st 6lb.
Career: Crewe Alexandra (January 1952), Chelsea (February 1953, £7,000), Retired (June 1964).
Honours: England international (5 caps), England Under-23 (5 caps), England Youth, Football League

XI (2 appearances), Football League Championship medal 1955. Also 1 FA Charity Shield appearance and 1 goal 1955.
Chelsea debut: 14 March 1953. Appearances: League 317, FA Cup 24, League Cup 3, Fairs Cup 2; Goals: League 47, FA Cup 4, League Cup 2.

Frank Blunstone was one of Chelsea's best-ever bargain buys. Despite twice breaking his leg and being forced to miss the whole of the 1957-8 season, his career was a most distinguished one. A close-dribbling ball player, he was a member of both the 1954-5 Championship team (sharing the outside-left berth with Jim Lewis) and the 1962-3 Second Division promotion team. Injury on Chelsea's Caribbean tour in the summer of 1964 finally forced his premature retirement and he became youth-team coach before being appointed manager of Brentford in December 1969. He was subsequently associated with Manchester United, Derby County and Sheffield Wednesday in either managerial or coaching duties.

BODLEY, Michael (1985-1989)   **Defender**
Born: Hayes (Middlesex) 14 September 1967.
5ft 11in; 12st.
Career: Chelsea (September 1985), Northampton Town (January 1989, £50,000), Barnet.
Chelsea debut: 19 September 1987. Appearances: League 6, League Cup 1, Full Members' Cup 1; Goals: League 1.
A strongly-built central defender, Bodley graduated to the first team via the junior and reserve sides but was unable to establish a regular place in the League team.

BOLLAND, Gordon Edward (1960-1962) Inside-forward
Born: Boston, 12 August 1943.
5ft 10½in; 11st 3lb.
Career: Boston United (amateur), Chelsea (August 1960), Leyton Orient (March 1962, £8,000), Norwich City (March 1964), Charlton Athletic (November 1967), Millwall (October 1968), Boston United (June 1975), Retired (1977).
Chelsea debut: 9 December 1961. Appearances: League 2.
Bolland joined Chelsea Juniors in February 1959 and turned professional 18 months later. Unable to win a first-team place at Stamford Bridge he, nevertheless, went on to play more than 400 League games with four other clubs, notching up a century of goals.

BONETTI, Peter Phillip (1959-1975 & 1975-1979) Goalkeeper
Born: Putney, 27 September 1941.
5ft 10½in; 10st 12lb.
Career: Worthing RC Youth Club, Chelsea (April 1959), not retained May 1975, St Louis Stars 1975, re-signed for Chelsea (October 1975), Dundee United (July 1979) Retired (1980).
Honours: England international (7 caps), England Under-23 (12 caps), Football League XI (4 appearances), FA Cup winners' medal 1970, runners-up medal

62

1967, Football League Cup winners' medal 1966, runners-up medal 1972, European Cup-winners' Cup winners' medal 1971, FA Youth Cup winners' medal 1960. Also 1 FA Charity Shield appearance 1969. *Chelsea debut: 2 April 1960. Appearances: League 600, FA Cup 57, League Cup 45, European Cup-winners' Cup 10. Fairs Cup 16.*

Peter Bonetti was a brilliant goalkeeper whose Chelsea career exceeded that of any player in the club's history by extending over 20 seasons. Known as 'the Cat', his wonderful agility and safe handling played a vital part in the four Cup-winning sides between 1966 and 1971. Contemporary with Gordon Banks, his extraordinary talent never received the recognition due at international level. Having not been retained at the end of the 1974-5 season, he spent the summer in the North American Soccer League before being hastily recalled within weeks of the following campaign starting. He went on to add a further century of League appearances to his total. After having moved to the Isle of Mull in 1979, he then returned to London and joined the Stamford Bridge coaching staff to maintain an association lasting over a quarter of a century, still making occasional appearances in Chelsea reserve team and, on one occasion, for Woking.

BOROTA, Petar (1979-1982) Goalkeeper
Born: Belgrade, 5 March 1952.
6ft; 12st 7lb.
Career: Partizan Belgrade, Chelsea (March 1979, £70,000), Brentford, Benfica (Portugal), FC Porto (Portugal).
Honours: Yugoslavia international (14 caps).
Chelsea debut: 3 March 1979. Appearances: League 107, FA Cup 2, League Cup 5.
Borota was an eccentric goalkeeper who endeared himself to Chelsea supporters through his flamboyant and spectacular style. His 'keeping alternated between brilliance and uncertainty — but was never predictable. Never one to be restricted to the confines of his own penalty area, his excursions upfield delighted spectators and opponents, if not his own colleagues.

BOWER, Alfred George ('Baishe') (1924-1925) Full-back
Born: Bromley, 10 November 1895; Died: 30 June 1970.
Career: Charterhouse School, Old Carthusians, Corinthians (1919-1930), Casuals, Chelsea (February 1924 to October 1925).
Honours: England international (5 caps), England Amateur international (13 caps).
Chelsea debut: 1 March 1924. Appearances: League 9.
Bower was one of several fine players from the famous amateur team, Corinthians, who played for Chelsea. A fine, stylish defender, it was a matter of regret that he was not more regularly available. FA Council member (1928-1933).

BOWIE, James Duncan (1944-1951) Inside-forward
Born: Aberdeen, 9 August 1924.
5ft 6in; 10st 5lb.
Career: Park Vale Juniors, Chelsea (January 1944, £25), Fulham (January 1951, £20,000), Brentford (March 1956), Watford (July 1952), Bedford Town (January 1956), March Town, Wisbech Town.
Chelsea debut: 17 September 1947. Appearances: League 76, FA Cup 8; Goals: League 18, FA Cup 4.
Bowie first came to Chelsea's notice when he was a

Naval rating in 1944 and that year he played at Wembley in the wartime Cup Final against Charlton Athletic. A ball-playing inside-forward with clever skills and close control, he was also a strong finisher.

BOWMAN, Andrew (1951-1955) Wing-half
Born: Pittenweem (Fifeshire), 7 March 1934.
5ft 8in; 11st.
Career: Chelsea (June 1951), Heart of Midlothian (summer 1955), Newport County (August 1961).
Honours: Scotland Schoolboy international.
Chelsea debut: 17 October 1953. Appearances: League 1.
One of the earliest products of the Chelsea youth scheme, Bowman signed professional forms after two years on the groundstaff. The auburn-haired wing-half was unable to win a first-team place from Ken Armstrong or Derek Saunders, the regular wing-halves at the time.

BOYLE, John (1964-1973) Midfield/Defender
Born: Motherwell, 25 December 1946.
5ft 8in; 11st 10lb.
Career: Chelsea (August 1964), Brighton & Hove Albion (September 1973, 'nominal'), Orient (December 1973). Tampa Bay Rowdies (1975).
Honours: European Cup-winners' Cup winners' medal 1971, FA Cup runners-up medal 1967, Football League Cup winners' medal 1966.
Chelsea debut: 20 January 1965. Appearances: League 188(10), FA Cup 24(1), League Cup 21, Fairs Cup 11, European Cup-winners' Cup 9(2); Goals: League 10, League Cup 1, Fairs Cup 1.
A hard-tackling, tenacious midfielder or defender, Boyle was either in, or on the verge of, the first-team for ten seasons, playing in all three of Chelsea's Cup-winning teams of that period. He first signed for the club after walking into the Stamford Bridge ground, unannounced, while in London on holiday at the age of 15.

BRABROOK, Peter (1955-1962) Winger
Born: Greenwich, 8 November 1937.
5ft 8in; 10st 4lb.
Career: Chelsea (March 1955), West Ham United

(October 1962, £35,000), Orient (July 1968), Romford (August 1971), Woodford Town.
Honours: England international (3 caps), England Under-23 (9 caps), Football League XI (3 appearances) FA Cup winners' medal 1964. Third Division championship medal 1970. Football League Cup runners-up medal 1966. Also 1 FA Charity Shield appearance 1955.
Chelsea debut: 29 March 1955. Appearances: League 251, FA Cup 12, League Cup 4, Fairs Cup 3; Goals: League 47, FA Cup 4, League Cup 4, Fairs Cup 2.
A fast and most skilful winger, Brabrook joined the Chelsea groundstaff at Easter 1953, signing professional forms two years later. He played three games in the 1954-5 Championship winning team and went on to become a permanent fixture on the right wing for the next seven seasons. Possessing intricate footwork, he was also extremely fast and liked to move direct towards goal. Later manager of Tilbury FC, and coach to Ford United.

BRADBURY, Terry E. (1957-1962)   **Wing-half**
Born: London, 15 November 1939.
5ft 11in; 11st 6lb.
Career: Chelsea (July 1957), Southend United (September 1962, £4,500), Leyton Orient (June 1966), Wrexham (June 1967), Chester (June 1969).
Honours: England Schoolboy international.
Chelsea debut: 20 August 1960. Appearances: League 29; Goals: League 1.
Bradbury was a strongly-built wing-half who was on the verge of the first team for two seasons at a time when the club were very much in a transitional stage. The emergence of Terry Venables and the signing of Frank Upton effectively ended his chances of becoming a regular.

BRADSHAW, Joseph (1909-1910)   Inside-forward
Born: Burnley.
5ft 7in; 10st 6lb.
Career: Woolwich Polytechnic, Woolwich Arsenal (amateur), West Norwood, Fulham (March 1904), Chelsea (May 1909), Queen's Park Rangers (cs 1910), Southampton.
Chelsea debut: 4 December 1909. Appearances: League 6; Goals: League 3.
Bradshaw is one of Chelsea's more mysterious players. He burst on the scene by scoring a fine goal on his debut for the club and followed this up with two more in the next two games, attracting much favourable comment in the process. Then, after three more outings, he disappeared from the scene and never played for the club again. Later he became manager of Southend United, Swansea Town, Fulham and Bristol City. His father, Harry, was at one time also manager of Arsenal, Fulham, and secretary of the Southern League.

BRAWN, William Frederick (1907-1911)   Outside-right
Born: Wellingborough, 1 August 1878; Died: Brentford, 18 August 1932.
6ft 2½in; 13st 5lb.
Career: Wellingborough Town, Northampton Town (1898), Sheffield United (January 1900), Aston Villa (December 1901), Middlesbrough (March 1906), Chelsea (November 1907), Brentford (cs 1911), Retired (1913).
Honours: England international (2 caps), FA Cup

winners' medal 1905.
Chelsea debut: 23 November 1907. Appearances: League 93, FA Cup 6; Goals: League 10, FA Cup 1.
Described as 'one of the most dangerous outside-rights in the kingdom', Billy Brawn, although tall for a winger, was renowned for his speed. In three seasons with Chelsea he lived up to this reputation and was a prominent member of the side which established itself in the First Division for the first time. Brawn ended his career at Brentford, where he subsequently became a director.

BREBNER, Ronald Gilchrist (1906-1907 & 1912-1913) Goalkeeper
Born: Darlington, 23 September 1881; Died: 11 November 1914.
5ft 11in; 11st 7lb.
Career: Edinburgh University, Sunderland (amateur cs 1905, Glasgow Rangers (February 1906), Chelsea Amateur (October 1906), Queen's Park, London Caledonians, Northern Nomads, Wanderers, Darlington (amateur), Stockton (amateur), Huddersfield Town (amateur August 1911), Chelsea (amateur August 1912-January 1913), Leicester Fosse (May 1913).
Honours: England Amateur international (23 caps), Great Britain Olympic Football gold medal.
Chelsea debut: 27 October 1906. Appearances: League 18, FA Cup 1.
A true amateur throughout his career, Brebner was a dental surgeon by profession and widely recognized as one of the finest goalkeepers of his day. He played for a large number of clubs and for the first part of the 1912-13 season was undisputed first choice at Chelsea, gaining preference ahead of both Jim Molineux and Jack Whitley. His death occurred as a result of an injury sustained whilst playing football.

BRIDGEMAN, William Walter (1906-1919)
Winger/Inside-forward
Born: Bromley (Kent), 12 December 1883.
5ft 7in; 12st 1lb.
Career: West Ham United (1903), Chelsea (November 1906), Southend United (July 1919).
Chelsea debut: 1 December 1906. Appearances: League 147, FA Cup 13; Goals: League 20, FA Cup 2.
Bridgeman was a fast, dashing winger who learnt his football in the East End of London as a schoolboy, at the same school as George Hilsdon. After beginning his Chelsea career at inside-right, thereafter he played almost entirely at outside-left. Fearless and with the reputation for being a hard worker, he laid on many scoring opportunities for others. He received a joint-benefit (with George Hilsdon) on Easter Monday 1912 (receipts £180). Despite often not being an automatic choice, he played first-team football for 13 consecutive seasons , including the wartime years.

BRIDGES, Barry John (1958-1966)   Striker
Born: Horsford (nr Norwich), 29 April 1941.
5ft 10in; 11st 13lb.
Career: Chelsea (May 1958), Birmingham City (May 1966, £55,000), Queen's Park Rangers (August 1968), Millwall (September 1970), Brighton & Hove Albion (August 1971). Highland Park (SA) (cs 1974).
Honours: England international (4 caps), England Youth, England Schoolboys, Football League XI, Football League Cup winners' medal 1965.

Chelsea debut: 7 February 1959. Appearances: League 174(2), FA Cup 17, League Cup 5, Fairs Cup 7; Goals: League 80, FA Cup 9, League Cup 3, Fairs Cup 1.
Bridges was one of the earliest products of the Chelsea youth scheme to play for England. He made a sensational debut whilst still a junior, at the age of 16, with Bobby Tambling (also 16), each of them scoring in the 3-2 home win over West Ham United.

A striking forward, either in the centre or down the flanks, with a devastating burst of speed, he left Chelsea after the arrival of Peter Osgood and went on to score over 200 League goals in his career with five clubs over 14 years. He was in turn manager of St Patrick's Athletic (Republic if Ireland), Sligo Rovers, Dereham Town, King's Lynn and Horsford (Anglian Combination) after his playing days ended.

BRITTAN, Harold Pemberton (1913-1920) Inside-forward
Born: Derby, 1894.
5ft 8in; 11st 3lb.
Career: Ilkeston United, Chelsea (cs 1913), free transfer (May 1920), USA football.
Chelsea debut: 18 April 1914. Appearances: League 24; Goals: League 7.
Brittan's career, so promising at the outset, was marred by illness and the outbreak World War One. Failing to establish himself as a first-team regular, he left Stamford Bridge in the summer of 1920 to play in the USA.

BRITTON, Ian (1971-1982) Midfield
Born: Dundee, 19 May 1954.
5ft 5in; 9st 7lb.
Career: Hillside Rangers, Chelsea (July 1971), Dundee United (August 1982), Blackpool (December 1983), Burnley (August 1986).
Chelsea debut: 30 December 1972. Appearances: League 253(10), FA Cup 15, League Cup 11; Goals: League 33, League Cup 1.
Britton was a dynamic non-stop runner whose enthusiasm and skill with the ball kept him in, or on the fringe of, the first team for more than ten years, although his lack of physical strength prevented him from becoming a controlling force in midfield. Sadly, his Chelsea days coincided with a barren period for the club but he never failed to make a wholehearted contribution, however depressing the circumstances.

BROLLY, Michael Joseph (1971-1974) Midfield
Born: Kilmarnock, 6 October 1954.
5ft 8in; 10st 12lb.
Career: Chelsea (November 1971), Bristol City (June 1974), Grimsby Town (September 1976), Derby County (August 1981), Scunthorpe United (August 1983), Scarborough, Goole Town, Boston United.
Honours: Scotland Schoolboy international. Third Division championship medal 1980.
Chelsea debut: 3 April 1973. Appearances: League 7(1), FA Cup 1; Goals: League 1.
Brolly signed professional after graduating from the Juniors and, although opportunities were limited for him at Stamford Bridge, he went on to a fruitful career comprising some 500 senior games for his five League clubs, developing into a skilful and highly respected midfield player.

BROOKS, John (1959-1961) Inside-forward
Born: Reading, 23 December 1931.
5ft 9½in; 11st 10lb.
Career: Coley Boys' Club, Reading (April 1949), Tottenham Hotspur (February 1953), Chelsea (December 1959, exchange Les Allen), Brentford (September 1961), Crystal Palace (January 1964), Stevenage Town, Canadian football, Knebworth.
Honours: England international (3 caps). Fourth Division championship medal 1963.
Chelsea debut: 12 December 1959. Appearances: League 46, FA Cup 2, League Cup 4; Goals: League 6, League Cup 1.
Brooks arrived from Tottenham with a big reputation and high hopes but never did himself justice at Chelsea. He was a well-built, forceful inside-forward whose son, Shaun, also played professional football for Crystal Palace and Orient.

BROWN, Dennis J. (1962-1964) Inside-forward
Born: Reading, 8 February 1944.
5ft 7½in; 10st 10lb.
Career: Chelsea (June 1962), Swindon Town (November 1964, £17,000), Northampton Town (February 1967), Aldershot (July 1969).
Chelsea debut: 25 September 1963. Appearances: League 10, FA Cup 1, League Cup 2; Goals: League 1, League Cup 1.
Brown was another of those who reached the professional ranks via Chelsea Juniors. Possessing a powerful shot — hence his nickname of 'Bullets' —

65

he failed to oust such as Bobby Tambling and George Graham from the senior side and moved into a lower division to further his career which ended with nearly 400 League games and over a century of goals.

BROWN, John A. (1912-1915) **Winger**
Born: Cowdenbeath.
5ft 11in; 12st 3lb.
Career: Glasgow Celtic, Chelsea (December 1912).
Chelsea debut: 26 December 1912. Appearances: League 16; Goals: League 5.
After having a spell in the first team shortly after coming to England from Scottish football he played mostly for the reserves and did not resume his career after World War One ended.

BROWN, William (1924-1929) **Inside-forward**
Born: Fence Houses (Co Durham), 22 August 1900; Died: Easington (Co Durham), January 1985.
5ft 7½in; 11st 6lb.
Career: Hetton (Co Durham), West Ham United, Chelsea (February 1924), Fulham (May 1929), Stockport County (July 1930), Hartlepools United (September 1931).
Honours: England international (1 cap), FA Cup runners-up medal 1923.
Chelsea debut: 1 March 1924. Appearances: League 54, FA Cup 3; Goals: League 20, FA Cup 1.
Signed in an unsuccessful attempt to stave off relegation from Division Two, this thrustful inside-forward never succeeded in establishing a regular first-team place — this despite an impressive 'striking ratio'. Previously he had scored two goals for West Ham against Derby County in an FA Cup semi-final at Stamford Bridge and had gone on to play in the first Wembley Final. He was noted for his accurate shooting and skilful ball-control.

BROWN, William Young (1911-1913) **Inside-forward**
Born: Dysart (Fifeshire).
5ft 11in; 12st 3lb.
Career: Kettering Town, Queen's Park Rangers (cs 1910), Chelsea (July 1911), Bristol City (November 1913), Swansea Town (September 1919).
Chelsea debut: 9 September 1911. Appearances: League 9, FA Cup 1; Goals: League 2.
Brown was a Scottish inside-forward who was a regular scorer of goals in the Combination team but who failed to establish himself in the first team and became the butt for much barracking from the terraces. He later played for Swansea Town and was wounded during World War One, during which he also played for Queen's Park Rangers.

BROWNING, John (1919-1920) **Outside-left**
Born: Dumbarton, 29 January 1888.
5ft 6½in; 11st 8lb.
Career: Bonhill Hibs, Vale of Leven, Dumbarton Harp, Glasgow Celtic (1912), Chelsea (June 1919), Vale of Leven (June 1920), Dumbarton (September 1920).
Honours: Scotland international (1 cap), Scottish League XI (2 appearances), Scottish FA Cup winners' medal 1914.
Chelsea debut: 20 August 1919. Appearances: League 5, FA Cup 1; Goals: League 1, FA Cup 1.
Browning arrived with a reputation of being one of the best players in Scottish football but failed to justify

this assertion and was soon replaced in the first team by Bobby McNeil. A stocky winger, his son (also John) was with Liverpool from 1934-39.

BUCHANAN, Peter Symington (1935-1946) **Winger**
Born: Glasgow, 13 October 1915.
5ft 10in; 10st 7lb.
Career: St Mungo (Glasgow), Wishaw Juniors, Chelsea (November 1935), Fulham (July 1946), Brentford (August 1947), Headington United (cs 1949).
Honours: Scotland international (1 cap).
Chelsea debut: 13 February 1937. Appearances: League 39, FA Cup 1; Goals: League 6.

Buchanan was a highly talented, if rather unpredictable and mercurial, performer. He first came to Chelsea in 1933 as an apprentice on the groundstaff but failed to settle down in London. However, he was signed on a permanent basis two years later and went on to win an international cap, against Czechoslovakia, within months of making his League debut. Vying with Dick Spence for the outside-right position, he had only one full season as first choice before his promising career was further hampered by the outbreak of war. Strongly built he was very fast with good ball-control. Poised and confident he never quite did justice to his great ability. During the war he 'guested' for no fewer than eight clubs in the South of England.

BUCHANAN, Robert (1911-1913)   **Full-back**
Born: Bellshill.
5ft 8½in; 11st 4lb.
Career: Bellshill, Leyton (cs 1910), Chelsea (May 1911), Southend United (summer 1913).
Chelsea debut: 21 October 1911. Appearances: League 3.
He was on the Chelsea staff for two seasons, playing regularly in the Combination team as deputy to Walter Bettridge. His elder brother, David, managed Clapton Orient for a spell.

BUMSTEAD, John (1976-1991)   **Midfield**
Born: Rotherhithe, 27 November 1958.
5ft 7in; 10st 5lb.
Career: Chelsea (December 1976), not retained (April 1991).
Honours: Second Division championship medals 1984, 1989, Full Members' Cup winners' medals 1986, 1990.
Chelsea debut: 22 November 1978. Appearances: League 318(24), FA Cup 20(1), League Cup 29(5), Full Members' Cup 12, Goals: League 38, FA Cup 3, League Cup 1, Full Members' Cup 2.

A strong-running, hard-tackling midfielder, Bumstead made the step up from reserve-team football in 1978-9, having first joined Chelsea as a 13-year-old schoolboy. He signed apprentice forms in July 1975 and turned professional 18 months later. A powerful defender and forceful attacker with good shooting ability, he played a notable part in the 1983-4 Second Division promotion team, several of his seven goals coming from direct free-kicks.

BURGESS, Harry (1935-1945)   **Inside-forward**
Born: Alderley Edge (Cheshire), 20 August 1904; Died: Northwich 1968.
5ft 8in; 11st 10lb.
Career: Alderley Edge, Stockport County (March 1926), Sandbach Ramblers (loan), Sheffield Wednesday (June 1929), Chelsea (March 1935), Retired (1945).
Honours: England international (4 caps), Football League Championship medal 1930.
Chelsea debut: 16 March 1935. Appearances: League 142, FA Cup 13; Goals: League 33, FA Cup 4.
Burgess, a long-striding, forceful inside-forward, came to Chelsea after an already distinguished career during which he had played for England four times. For the five seasons leading up to the outbreak of World War Two he was a vital pillar of a team, often struggling to find consistency, and scoring crucial goals, some of them from the penalty-spot. He moved back north after the outbreak of hostilities and continued to make guest appearances for several clubs. Also a good cricketer and golfer.

BURLEY, Craig (1989-)   **Midfield**
Born: Ayr (Scotland), 24 September 1971.
6ft 1in; 11st 7lb.
Career: Chelsea (January 1989).
Honours: Scotland Youth international (10 caps).
Chelsea debut: 20 April 1991. Appearances: League 0(1).
Nephew of George Burley, the Scottish international and Ipswich Town defender, he first arrived at Stamford Bridge as a 16-year-old, graduating to first-team status via the Juniors and Reserves (for whom he was a regular in the 1990-91 Combination championship team).

BUSH, Robert James (1906-1907)   **Wing-half**
Born: West Ham 1884.
Career: West Ham United (1904), Chelsea (summer 1906).
Chelsea debut: 10 November 1906. Appearances: League 4; Goals: League 1.
Bush spent only one season at Stamford Bridge. Apart from four consecutive first-team games in November and December, he played entirely in the reserve team.

BUTLER, Dennis M. (1960-1963)   **Full-back**
Born: Fulham, 7 March 1943.
5ft 9in; 11st 10lb.
Career: Chelsea (May 1960), Hull City (June 1963, £10,000), Reading (December 1969), Retired (May 1974).
Honours: Third Division championship medal 1966.
Chelsea debut: 18 November 1961. Appearances: League 18.
Butler signed professional after two years as a Chelsea junior. A strong defender, who made a promising start but was unable to win a regular first-team place against the challenge of Ken Shellito and Eddie McCreadie, he subsequently made over 400 appearances in his League career.

BUTLER, Geoffrey (1967-1968)   **Full-back**
Born: Middlesbrough, 29 September 1946.
5ft 9in; 11st 2lb.
Career: Middlesbrough (May 1964), Chelsea (September 1967, £57,000), Sunderland (January 1968,

£65,000), Norwich City (October 1968), Baltimore Rockets (1974), Bournemouth & Boscombe Athletic (March 1976), Peterborough United (August 1981). *Chelsea debut: 23 September 1967. Appearances: League 8(1).*
Butler's stay at Stamford Bridge was limited to four months despite an obvious first-team vacancy at right-back. He made a promising start but never settled in London, although he subsequently made some 300 senior appearances for Norwich City and Bournemouth. He managed Salisbury City for a time after his playing career ended.

BYRNE, Michael T.G. (1905-1907)   **Goalkeeper**
Born: Bristol, 1881.
5ft 10in; 12st 7lb.
Career: Grenadier Guards, Bristol Rovers (1902), Southampton (cs 1903), Chelsea (August 1905), contract cancelled (April 1907), Glossop (May 1907). *Chelsea debut: 18 November 1905. Appearances: League 4, FA Cup 1.*
Byrne was a popular figure who was signed as deputy for Willie Foulke and who began the 1906-07 season as first-choice goalkeeper, following the big man's departure. He lost his place after dislocating his shoulder in the first game of that season and never played in the first team again.

CALDERHEAD, David (Junior) (1907-1914) Centre-half
Born: Dumfries.
5ft 8in; 11st.
Career: Lincoln City, Chelsea (September 1907), Leicester Fosse (1914), Motherwell (April 1914). *Chelsea debut: 21 January 1911. Appearances: League 34, FA Cup 9; Goals: League 1.*
The son of the Chelsea manager, David Calderhead snr, at one time he looked like becoming Chelsea's regular centre-half. But the signing of Andy Ormiston and Tom Logan in an endeavour to establish the club in the First Division, restricted his opportunities. He managed Lincoln City from 1921 to 1924.

CAMERON, David (1920-1926) Full-back/Wing-half
Born: Middleton (Borthwick), 12 September 1902.
5ft 11in; 12st.

Career: Queen's Park, Chelsea (June 1920), Helensburgh (loan), Heart of Midlothian (cs 1925), Dunfermline Athletic (1927), Nottingham Forest (June 1928), Colwyn Bay United (1930). *Chelsea debut: 28 August 1920. Appearances: League 73, FA Cup 8; Goals: League 2.*
Cameron was a tall, commanding defender whose promising career was marred by injury almost as soon as he arrived at Chelsea. During World War One he had served, appropriately, with the Cameron Highlanders and had played for two seasons with Queen's Park in the Scottish League after demobilization. 'There is no better defender in Scottish football today', wrote one commentator. After his initial set-back at Stamford Bridge, he found it difficult to hold his place in a side that was struggling to maintain its First Division status.

CAMERON, John ('Jock') (1907-1913)   **Full-back**
Born: Kirkwoodin (Lanarkshire).
Career: Kirkwood Thistle, St Mirren, Blackburn Rovers (April 1904), Chelsea (October 1907, £900), Burslem Port Vale (July 1913).
Honours: Scotland international (2 caps), Scottish League XI (3 appearances).
Chelsea debut: 12 October 1907. Appearances: League 179, FA Cup 15.
Jock Cameron was one of the outstanding full-backs in Chelsea's history. For six seasons he was an automatic choice in the first team, partnering Walter Bettridge in what was often considered to be the strongest full-back pairing in the country in those days. He captained Chelsea for much of his time with the club and was renowned for his sound defensive qualities, being a particularly fearsome tackler. He had won a Scottish international cap early in his career with St Mirren, and added to this when he played against England at the Crystal Palace in 1908-09.

CAMPBELL, Robert Inglis (1947-1954) Outside-right
Born: Glasgow, 28 June 1922.
5ft 9in; 11st 7lb.
Career: Falkirk (1941), Chelsea (May 1947), Reading (August 1954, free transfer), Retired (1960).
Honours: Scotland international (5 caps)
Chelsea debut: 4 November 1947. Appearances: League 188, FA Cup 25; Goals: League 36, FA Cup 4.
Signing for Falkirk in 1941, Campbell lost some of the best years of his career to wartime football but his talents were quickly realized when the game returned to normal and he was soon recognized by the national selectors. His arrival in London to take over the right-wing berth from long-serving Dick Spence was an immediate success as he scored twice on his debut and, for six seasons, he was first choice for his position. Fast and direct, he had spells on the left and also at inside-forward. His goal in a memorable Cup tie against Newcastle United in 1950 is often considered one of the best ever seen at Stamford Bridge. Running from the half-way line he outpaced all defenders on a treacherous surface, before drawing the goalkeeper to put the ball into the net. After retiring as a player, he was briefly coach at Reading before being appointed manager of Dumbarton in April 1961. The following year, in May, he moved to Bristol Rovers as chief coach, a position he held until he was appointed manager in November 1977. Finally, severing his

connection with the West Country club after 18 years, in September 1980, he was appointed manager of Gloucester City in November of that year.

CANOVILLE, Paul K. (1981-1986)   **Forward**
Born: Hillingdon, 4 March 1962.
5ft 10in; 11st 5lb.
Career: Hillingdon Borough, Chelsea (December 1981), Reading (August 1986, £50,000), Enfield, Burnham.
Chelsea debut: 12 April 1982. Appearances: League 53(26), FA Cup 2(3), League Cup 12(6), Full Members' Cup 0(1); Goals: League 11, FA Cup 1, League Cup 3.
Canoville was the first coloured player to play first-team football for Chelsea. A fast-running striker with a flair for scoring spectacular goals, he operated mainly down the flanks. Despite great ability, his inconsistency limited his chances and he was allowed to leave, moving to Reading after his provisional transfer to Brentford had been cancelled. Sadly his League career was curtailed by serious injury.

CARR, John James. (1928-1931)   **Full-back**
Born: Gateshead, 1909.
5ft 9in; 9st 11lb.
Career: Crewcrook Albion, Chelsea (June 1928), Crewcrook Albion (1931), Chester (June 1931), Gateshead (June 1933).
Chelsea debut: 17 April 1929. Appearances: League 1.
Signed early in the 1928-9 season, this lightweight full-back was a regular in the Combination side for three seasons, but was unable to break through to first-team football at a time when big-name stars were being signed for large fees.

CARTER, Robert (1929-1933)   **Centre-half**
Born: Bolton, 1911.
5ft 7½in; 11st 1lb.
Career: Army football, Chelsea (August 1929), Plymouth Argyle (May 1933), Watford.
Chelsea debut: 7 April 1931. Appearances: League 18; Goals: League 1.
Carter was discovered whilst playing football in the Army. Injury problems gave him an extended run in the first team early in the 1931-2 season, but the arrival of Peter O'Dowd and Allan Craig limited his opportunities and he moved on to Plymouth Argyle. A year later, after only three appearances, he was on the move again, this time to Watford.

CARTWRIGHT, William (1908-1913)   **Full-back**
Born: Burton upon Trent, 24 June 1884.
5ft 10in; 12st 9lb.
Career: Gainsborough Trinity (1906), Chelsea (May 1908), Tottenham Hotspur (May 1913), Swansea Town (cs 1919).
Chelsea debut: 12 September 1908. Appearances: League 44, FA Cup 2.
Cartwright was a full-back who played most of his football with Chelsea in the reserve side during a stay of five years. He then moved to Tottenham Hotspur, but is perhaps better remembered at Southend, where he gave the Essex club long and devoted service on their training staff before being granted a testimonial.

CASEY, Leonard J. (1954-1958)   **Wing-half**
Born: Hackney, 24 May 1931.
5ft 8in; 11st 7lb.
Career: Leyton, Chelsea (February 1954), Plymouth Argyle (December 1958, £12,000 combined fee with Wally Bellett), Retired (1963).
Honours: FA Amateur Cup winners' medal 1952.
Chelsea debut: 24 March 1956. Appearances: League 34, FA Cup 3.
Having won an FA Amateur Cup medal with Leyton at Wembley in 1952, Casey was one of several amateurs to be recruited to Chelsea by manager Ted Drake at that time. He found the transition to the professional game difficult to make, however, and failed to tie down a regular first-team place.

CASTLE, Sidney Rowland (1923-1926)   **Winger**
Born: Guildford, 12 March 1892; Died: 27 January 1978.
5ft 8in; 10st 8lb.
Career: Basingstoke Town, Thorneycroft Works, Tottenham Hotspur (March 1920), Charlton Athletic (May 1921), Chelsea (May 1923), Guildford United (cs 1926).
Chelsea debut: 27 August 1923. Appearances: League 32; Goals: League 2.
Castle was a fast and clever winger who looked as if he had established himself in the 1923-4 campaign. However, it was a traumatic time for the club, with relegation occurring at the end of the season, and soon Jackie Crawford had arrived to take over on the right wing. Castle remained a pillar of the reserve side for a time but was never given a further chance to develop his undoubted potential.

CHEYNE, Alexander George (1930-1931 & 1934-1936) Inside-forward
Born: Glasgow, 28 April 1907; Died: Arbroath, 5 August 1983.
5ft 8in; 10st 6lb.
Career: Shettleston Juniors, Aberdeen (December 1925), Chelsea (June 1930, £6,000), Nimes (May 1932), Chelsea (March 1934), Colchester United (1936), Retired (1939).
Honours: Scotland international (5 caps), Scottish League XI (1 appearance).
Chelsea debut: 30 August 1930. Appearances: League 62, FA Cup 7; Goals: League 12, FA Cup 1.
A versatile forward who played on the wing during the earlier part of his career, Cheyne was used entirely as an inside-forward for Chelsea. After five years with Aberdeen, where he won his five Scottish caps, he found it difficult to adjust to the greater speed of English football and rarely produced his best form south of the border. Along with others he became unsettled in London and went to France for two years where he had been enticed by a most attractive financial offer before coming back to Stamford Bridge where, again, he failed to do his great ability the justice it deserved. He drifted into the Southern League with Colchester United, and later managed Arbroath in the Scottish League from May 1949 to May 1955.

CHITTY, Wilfred Sidney (1930-1938) Winger/Full-back
Born: Walton-on-Thames, 10 July 1912.
5ft 10in; 10st 6lb.
Career: Wycombe Wanderers, Woking, Chelsea (March 1930), Plymouth Argyle (December 1938), Reading (August 1939), Retired (1947).
Chelsea debut: 6 April 1932. Appearances: League 45,

FA Cup 1; Goals: League 16.
Chitty was a loyal servant of Chelsea during most of the 1930s, spending the majority of his time at Stamford Bridge in reserve-team football. A speedy winger with a powerful shot, he perhaps lacked the necessary determination to win a permanent place in the senior side. For one season, too, he showed himself to be a competent full-back. After moving to Plymouth Argyle, he returned to play for Reading throughout the war and, indeed, in the first post-war season, after which he retired. He scouted for Chelsea and later Reading and West Ham United.

CHIVERS, Gary P.S. (1978-1983)   **Defender**
Born: Stockwell, 15 May 1960.
5ft 11in; 11st 7lb.
Career: Chelsea (July 1978), Swansea City (August 1983), Queen's Park Rangers (February 1984), Watford (September 1987), Brighton & Hove Albion (March 1988).
Chelsea debut: 21 April 1979. Appearances: League 128(5), FA Cup 7, League Cup 8; Goals: League 4.
Chivers joined Chelsea as a schoolboy and made his debut, against Middlesbrough, within nine months of becoming a professional. Almost his entire career at Stamford Bridge was played in the Second Division, often with the threat of further relegation looming and, partially as a result of this, he failed to do justice to his undoubted ability.

CLARE, James E. (1978-1981)   **Midfield**
Born: Islington, 6 November 1959.
5ft 8in; 9st 9lb.
Career: Chelsea (August 1978), Charlton Athletic (August 1981).
Chelsea debut: 4 October 1980. Appearances: League 0(1).
Clare graduated to the professional ranks via the Chelsea youth scheme as an apprentice, but failed to bridge the gap between reserve and first-team football. He did not appear in Charlton's first team.

CLARKE, Stephen, (1987-)   **Defender**
Born: Saltcoats, 29 August 1963.
5ft 9in; 11st 2lb.
Career: Beith Juniors, St Mirren, Chelsea (January 1987, £422,000).
Honours: Scotland international (5 caps), Scotland Under-21 (8 caps), Second Division championship medal 1989.
Chelsea debut: 24 January 1987. Appearances: League 134(2), FA Cup 7, League Cup 8, Full Members' Cup 9; Goals: League 5, FA Cup 1, League Cup 1, Full Members' Cup 1.
A talented defender, either at full-back or in the middle of the back-four. Clarke was signed in the face of stiff competition on both sides of the border and came from a family with a strong football tradition. A sound defensive player and good in the tackle, one of his greatest assets is his speed and acceleration which snuffs out many a dangerous situation and takes him away from opponents.

CLISS, David L. (1956-1962)   **Inside-forward**
Born: Enfield, 15 November 1939.
5ft 6in; 9st.
Career: Chelsea (November 1956), Guildford City (summer 1962).

Honours: England Youth international (4 caps).
Chelsea debut: 8 February 1958. Appearances: League 24; Goals: League 1.
A clever, intricate, ball-playing inside-forward whose skills delighted onlookers, his frail physique being something of a handicap. His Chelsea career was virtually ended when he broke his leg at the beginning of the 1960-61 season.

COADY, John (1986-1988)   **Full-back/Midfield**
Born: Dublin, 25 August 1960.
5ft 9in; 10st 10lb.
Career: Shamrock Rovers, Chelsea (Decmeber 1986, £35,000), Derry City (October 1988, £15,000).
Chelsea debut: 3 March 1987. Appearances: League 9(7), League Cup 0(1), Full Members' Cup 1(1); Goals: League 2, Full Members' Cup 1.
Coady had his first taste of full-time professional football at the age of 26 when he crossed the Irish Sea after several years experience with the Dublin club, Shamrock Rovers, with whom he had appeared in the European Cup. The former postman played in midfield as well as in his usual position of left-back.

COCK, John Gilbert MM (1919-1923) Centre-forward
Born: Hayle, Cornwall, 14 November 1893; Died: Kensington, 19 April 1966.
5ft 11in; 12st 5lb.

Career: Camborne Boys Brigade, West Kensington United, Forest Gate, Old Kingstonians (December 1912), Brentford (amateur March 1914), Huddersfield Town (April 1914), Chelsea (October 1919, £2,500), Everton (January 1923), Plymouth Argyle, Millwall (November 1927), Folkestone (July 1931), Walton & Hersham (March 1932).
Honours: England international (2 caps), Third Division South championship medal 1928.
Chelsea debut: 1 November 1919. Appearances: League 99, FA Cup 11; Goals: League 47, FA Cup 6.
Jack Cock is one of the many famous centre-forwards in Chelsea's history. A beautifully-built natural athlete,

he possessed a strong shot in either foot and was a particularly fine header of the ball. But for the outbreak of World War One he would have made an even bigger impact on the game and, undoubtedly, added to his scant reward of two international caps. His move from Chelsea to Everton came at a time when his powers seemed to be in decline but his form with the Merseysiders proved this to be a totally false assumption. His long League career extended into the 1930s and ended at Millwall, the club where he subsequently became manager, from November 1944 to August 1948. He won the Military Medal in 1917.

COLLINS, Ronald Michael (1951-1957)   Goalkeeper
Born: Redcar, 8 June 1933.
5ft 11in; 11st 6lb.
Career: Redcar Albion, Chelsea (November 1951), Watford (July 1957), Folkestone Town (August 1959).
Chelsea debut: 6 Mar 1954. Appearances: League 1.
Collins was a goalkeeper whose opportunities were restricted by the presence of Harry Medhurst, Bill Robertson and Charlie Thomson, who were all on the Chelsea staff at the time. After five years in the Combination team he moved to Watford where he played in the first team for two seasons.

COMPTON, John Frederick (1955-1960)   Wing-half
Born: Poplar, 27 August 1937.
5ft 9in; 10st.
Career: Chelsea (February 1955), Ipswich Town (July 1960), Bournemouth & Boscombe Athletic (July 1964).
Honours: Football League Championship medal 1962, Second Division championship medal 1961.
Chelsea debut: 28 April 1956. Appearances: League 12.
A member of the Chelsea youth scheme for two years before signing professional, Compton was offered few first team opportunities. At Ipswich, however, his career took off and he played more than a century of League games in their Championship years.

COOKE, Charles (1966-1972 & 1973-1978)
Winger/Midfield
Born: St Monace, Fife, 14 October 1942.
5ft 8in; 12st 2lb.
Career: Port Glasgow, Renfrew Juniors (1958), Aberdeen (October 1959), Dundee (December 1964), Chelsea (April 1966, £72,000), Crystal Palace (September 1972, £85,000), Chelsea (January 1974, £17,000), Los Angeles Aztecs (1976), Memphis Rogues (player-coach 1978), California Surf (1981).
Honours: Scotland international (16 caps), Scotland Under-23 (4 caps), Scottish League XI (4 appearances), FA Cup winners' medal 1970, runners-up medal 1967; European Cup-winners' Cup winners' medal 1971, Football League Cup runners-up medal 1972.
Chelsea debut: 11 May 1966. Appearances: League 289(10), FA Cup 32(2), League Cup 22(1), Fairs Cup 5, European Cup Winners' Cup; Goals: League 22, FA Cup 3, League Cup 4, Fairs Cup 1.
Charlie Cooke was one of the greatest entertainers of his time and one of the most highly-skilled players to appear for Chelsea — as well as one of the most popular. A true ball artist, he had begun his career in Scotland almost entirely as an 'old-fashioned' winger, but the changing tactics within the game dictated that he widened his scope to become a midfield player. He was a wonderful dribbler, often leaving a

series of bemused opponents in his wake. Perhaps his goal tally was disappointing for one of his type, but he was essentially a creator of chances for others. His Chelsea career was in two parts, punctuated by a 16-month spell at Crystal Palace. On his return he found the club fortunes in decline but, nevertheless, proceeded to play some of the most effective football of his Stamford Bridge career. After finally leaving the club he continued to play in the North American Soccer League.

COPELAND, David Campbell (1905-1907)
Inside/Centre-forward
Born: Ayr, 2 April 1875; Died: 16 November 1931.
Career: Ayr Parkhouse, Walsall (1897), Bedminster (1898), Tottenham Hotspur (1899), Chelsea (May 1905), Glossop (May 1907).
Honours: FA Cup winners' medal 1901.
Chelsea debut: 2 September 1905. Appearances: League 26; Goals: League 9.
Copeland was one of two players (Johnny Kirwan was the other) signed from Tottenham Hotspur in time for the first Chelsea season. A strong, aggressive forward, who could play either centre, or inside, forward, he was appointed club captain in September 1906 but was injured in the sixth match of the season.

COPELAND, James Leslie (1932-1937) Centre-forward
Born: Chorlton cum Hardy, 1 October 1909.
Career: Polygon Electric, Manchester United (amateur), Park Royal, West Ham United (amateur),

Chelsea (May 1932), Halifax Town (August 1937).
Chelsea debut: 9 September 1933. Appearances: League 2; Goals: League 1.
A prolific goalscorer in Combination football throughout most of his five seasons at Chelsea, Copeland found it impossible to break through into the first team ahead of three international centre-forwards, Hughie Gallacher, Joe Bambrick and George Mills.

CORTHINE, Peter A. (1957-1960)   **Winger**
Born: Highbury, 19 July 1937.
5ft 6in; 9st 12lb.
Career: Leytonstone, Chelsea (December 1957), Southend United (March 1960), Chelmsford City (July 1962).
Chelsea debut: 31 October 1959. Appearances: League 2.
Chelsea was Corthine's first professional club after he had been spotted playing in Army football. Reserve to Peter Brabrook in his two years on the Stamford Bridge staff, he subsequently played 73 League games (21 goals) for Southend United.

COURT, Colin Raymond (1954-1959)   **Winger**
Born: Ebbw Vale, 3 September 1937.
5ft 7½in; 10st 8lb.
Career: Chelsea (September 1954), Torquay United (May 1959), Weymouth (1961).
Honours: Welsh Schoolboy international.
Chelsea debut: 30 September 1958. Appearances: Fairs Cup 1.
Court graduated to professional status via Chelsea Juniors, but was unable to establish a place in the first team with Eric Parsons and Peter Brabrook on the staff at that time.

CRAIG, Allan (1933-1939)   **Centre-half**
Born: Paisley, 7 February 1904.
5ft 10½in; 11st 10lb.
Career: Celtic Victoria (Paisley Juniors), Motherwell,

Chelsea (January 1933, £4,000), not retained (May 1939).
Honours: Scotland international (3 caps), Scottish League XI (2 appearances), Scottish League Championship medal 1932, Scottish FA Cup runners-up medal 1931.
Chelsea debut: 7 January 1933. Appearances: League 196, FA Cup 15.
Craig was a tall, stylish centre-half who was a pillar of the Chelsea defence for seven seasons in the period leading up to the outbreak of World War Two and, indeed, captained the team for much of that time. Strangely, he played no football at school. He had spent nine years at Motherwell before coming south and his long and honourable career ended with the outbreak of war.

CRAIGIE, James (1905-1907)   **Half-back**
Born: Larkhall.
5ft 9in; 11st 3lb.
Career: Larkhall, Manchester City (May 1903), Chelsea (August 1905).
Chelsea debut: 7 October 1905. Appearances: FA Cup 2.
Craigie signed during the summer of 1905. He was one of a large pool of players who was on the staff at the beginning of Chelsea's first-ever season. In fact, his FA Cup debut was made when the recognized first team were fulfilling a Football League fixture, and he received only one further opportunity, also in an FA Cup tie.

CRAWFORD, John Forsyth (1923-1934)   **Winger**
Born: Jarrow, 26 September 1896; Died: Epsom, 27 July 1975.
5ft 2in; 10st.
Career: Jarrow Celtic, Palmer's Works (Jarrow), Jarrow Town, Naval Service (World War One), Hull City (December 1919), Chelsea (May 1923, £3,000), Queen's Park Rangers (May 1934), Retired (1937).
Honours: England international (1 cap).
Chelsea debut: 17 November 1923. Appearances: League 288, FA Cup 20; Goals: League 25, FA Cup 1.
Jackie Crawford was one of Chelsea's greatest-ever wingers, operating on either flank with equal facility. With intricate footwork, a good crosser of the ball, and a strong shot in either foot he was the complete player for his position, even if his goal tally was, perhaps, modest for one of such talent. In the dressing-room he was, also, a first-class influence, having the reputation of being a born optimist who expected to win every match. Altogether a most likeable personality, he coached at Queen's Park Rangers and, later, Malden Town after his playing career ended.

CROAL, James Anderson (1914-1922)   **Inside-forward**
Born: Glasgow, 27 July 1885; Died: St Petherton (Somerset), 16 September 1939.
5ft 8½in; 9st 1lb.
Career: Glasgow Rangers (1904), Ayr Parkhouse (loan), Alloa Athletic, Dunfermline Athletic, Falkirk (1910), Chelsea (April 1914, £2,000), Fulham (March 1922), Retired (cs 1924).
Honours: Scotland international (3 caps), Scottish League XI (3 appearances), Scottish FA Cup winners' medal (1913), FA Cup runners-up 1915.
Chelsea debut: 5 September 1914. Appearances: League 113, FA Cup 17; Goals: League 22, FA Cup 4.

Jimmy Croal, a schoolmaster by profession, had already won his three Scotland caps before his arrival at Stamford Bridge. He was renowned for his artistry, but lacked something in aggression, especially inside the opposition's penalty area. He was a most popular player and a great entertainer who, partnered by Bobby McNeil, played a major part in steering Chelsea to their first FA Cup Final, in 1915.

CROWTHER, Stanley (1958-1961)   **Wing-half**
Born: Bilston, 3 September 1935.
6ft 1½in; 13st 6lb.
Career: Bilston Town (1952), Aston Villa (August 1955), Manchester United (February 1958), Chelsea (December 1958, £10,000), Brighton & Hove Albion (March 1961), Rugby Town, Hednesford Town.
Honours: England Under-23 international (3 caps), FA Cup winners' medal 1957, runners-up medal 1958.
Chelsea debut: 20 December 1958. Appearances: League 51, FA Cup 4, League Cup 1, Fairs Cup 2.
A powerfully built, hard-tackling wing-half, Crowther appeared in consecutive FA Cup Finals before his arrival at Stamford Bridge, having been drafted in by Manchester United after the Munich air disaster. His time at Chelsea was during a transitional phase and he never fitted into Tommy Docherty's rebuilding plans.

CUNDY, Jason Victor (1988-)   **Centre-half**
Born: Wimbledon, 12 November 1969.
6ft 1in; 13st 10lb.
Career: Chelsea (August 1988).
Honours: England Under-21 international (2 caps).
Chelsea debut: 1 September 1990. Appearances: League 28(1), FA Cup 1, League Cup 6, Full Members' Cup 2; Goals: League 1.
Cundy progressed through the Chelsea ranks from trainee to junior and reserve-team captain. In 1987 he was the club's Young Player of the Year. A powerfully-built, rugged defender, within weeks of his debut, he had not only helped to shore up a suspect defence, but had also caught the eye of the England selectors, being capped at Under-21 level. Fearless and a strong tackler, his turn of speed is another priceless asset.

DALE, George Henry (1919-1922)   **Inside-forward**
Born: Nottingham, 2 May 1883.
5ft 6in; 10st 4lb.
Career: Stanley Works (Newark), Newark Town, Notts County (February 1914), Chelsea (May 1919).
Chelsea debut: 20 August 1919. Appearances: League 49, FA Cup 3; Goals: League 1.
Dale was a skilful dribbler who helped the club re-establish themselves in the First Division during the first season after normal football was resumed at the end of World War One. It was felt, however, that he did not have the necessary finishing power and never again commanded a regular place in the first team.

D'ARCY, Seamus Paul (1951-1952)   **Forward**
Born: Newry, 14 December 1921; Died: Sudbury (Suffolk), 22 February 1985.
6ft; 12st.
Career: Limerick City, Dundalk, Ballymena, Charlton Athletic (March 1948), Chelsea (October 1951, £6,000), Brentford (October 1952 — part-exchange Ron Greenwood).

Honours: Northern Ireland international (5 caps).
Chelsea debut: 27 October 1951. Appearances: League 23, FA Cup 8; Goals: League 13, FA Cup 1.
'Jimmy' D'Arcy proved a good investment in the short-term, being joint leading goalscorer with Roy Bentley in his first season season at Stamford Bridge. But he did not fit into manager Ted Drake's plans for building a Championship-winning team. A tall, somewhat awkwardly built man, on his day he was an accurate finisher.

DAVIDSON, Alexander M. (1946-1948)   **Inside-forward**
Born: Langholm, 6 June 1920.
5ft 7in; 11st.
Career: Hibernian, Chelsea (August 1946), Crystal Palace (August 1948), Clacton Town (1949).
Chelsea debut: 30 November 1946. Appearances: League 2.
The fair-haired Davidson's two years at Stamford Bridge were spent almost entirely in the Combination side. He played another ten League games after moving to Crystal Palace.

DAVIES, Gordon J. (1984-1985)   **Striker**
Born: Merthyr Tydfil, 8 August 1955.
5ft 7in; 10st 12lb.
Career: Merthyr Tydfil, Fulham (March 1978), Chelsea (November 1984, £90,000), Manchester City (October 1985, £100,000), Fulham (October 1986).
Honours: Wales international (18 caps). Wales Schoolboys.

Chelsea debut: 8 December 1984. Appearances: League 11(2), FA Cup 2; Goals: League 6.
Having scored over 100 League goals for Fulham, Davies moved to Stamford Bridge in an attempt to establish himself in First Division football. However, the consistency of Kerry Dixon and David Speedie limited his chances and, understandably impatient at

73

the age of 30, he moved to Manchester City after 11 months with Chelsea. Small and determined, with the eye for a half-chance, he will be remembered by Chelsea fans chiefly for his hat-trick in a League match at Goodison.

DEMPSEY, John Thomas (1969-1978)   **Centre-half**
Born: Hampstead, 15 March 1946.
6ft 1in; 11st 3lb.
Career: Fulham (March 1964), Chelsea (January 1969, £70,000), Philadelphia Fury (March 1978).
Honours: Republic of Ireland international (19 caps), FA Cup winners' medal 1970, European Cup-winners' Cup winners' medal 1971.
Chelsea debut: 1 February 1969. Appearances: League 161(14), FA Cup, 15(1), League Cup 15(2), European Cup-winners' Cup 9; Goals: League 4, FA Cup 2, European Cup-winners' Cup 1.
Dempsey was a dominant, uncompromising, centre-half who was a pillar of Chelsea's defence in the most successful period of the club's history. His height enabled him to control the majority of opponents in the air and he will also be remembered for scoring the vital goal in the European Cup-winners' Cup Final replay in Athens.

DICKENS, Alan William (1989-)   **Midfield**
Born: Plaistow, 3 September 1964.
5ft 11in; 12st.
Career: West Ham United (August 1982), Chelsea (August 1989, £650,000).
Honours: England Under-21 international (1 cap), England Youth (5 caps).
Chelsea debut: 19 August 1989. Appearances: League 33(5), League Cup 3, Full Members' Cup 3; Goals: League 1, Full Members' Cup 3.
After starting his career as an apprentice at West Ham United, Dickens went on to make more than 200 senior appearances for the Hammers as a creative and influential midfield player. At Chelsea he lost his first-team place after seven months, never quite doing justice to his considerable talents.

DICKIE, Murdoch M. (1945-1946)   **Outside-right**
Born: Dumbarton, 28 December 1919.
Career: Port Vale (1939), Guildford City, Chelsea (April 1945), Bournemouth & Boscombe Athletic (February 1947).
Chelsea debut: 7 September 1946. Appearances: League 1.
Although he played a handful of first-team games in the final season of regional wartime football, Dickie was unable to win a place in the senior side thereafter, but later played intermittently for Third Division Bournemouth for two seasons.

DICKIE, William Cunningham (1919-1921) Half-back
Born: Kilmarnock, 2 May 1893; Died: Sittingbourne (Kent), 1960.
5ft 7½in; 10st.
Career: Riccarton (1909), Kilbirnie Ladeside (1910), Kilmarnock (May 1912), Stoke (April 1921), Sittingbourne.
Chelsea debut: 20 August 1919. Appearances: League 35, FA Cup 5.
Although he was only a registered Chelsea player for

two seasons, Dickie's association with the club began in September 1917 when he made guest appearances in the unofficial regional wartime competitions. Further, he was a member of the Chelsea side which beat Fulham 3-0 in the London Victory Cup Final. Noted for his fitness and hard work, he was unable to hold a first-team place after his initial season in the League side.

DICKS, Alan V. (1951-1958)   **Half-back**
Born: Kennington, 29 August 1934.
5ft 10in; 11st 7lb.
Career: Dulwich Hamlet, Rainham Town, Millwall (amateur), Chelsea (August 1951), Southend United (November 1958, £12,000 — combined fee with Les Stubbs), Coventry City (February 1962).
Chelsea debut: 13 December 1952. Appearances: League 33, FA Cup 5; Goals: League 1.
Tall and athletically built, Dicks' only prolonged spell in the first team was in the latter part of the 1956-7 season. Otherwise, he remained a pillar of the Combination team for six seasons. After three years of first-team football at Southend, he moved to Coventry where he became assistant manager to Jimmy Hill before managing Bristol City for several years, then taking up similar posts in Greece, Qatar and USA before being appointed manager of Fulham in 1990. His brother, Ronnie, was a full-back with Middlesbrough from 1947 to 1958. Also, father of Julian Dicks.

DICKSON, William (1947-1953)   **Half-back**
Born: Lurgan, County Armagh, 15 April 1923.
5ft 10in; 12st 11lb.
Career: Glenavon, Notts County (1946), Chelsea (November 1947 — part exchange for Tommy Lawton), Arsenal (October 1953, £15,000), Mansfield Town (July 1956), Glenavon (January 1958).
Honours: Northern Ireland international (12 caps).
Chelsea debut: 1 January 1948. Appearances: League 101, FA Cup 18; Goals: League 4.
A powerfully built attacking wing-half (or useful centre-half), Dickson turned out to be much more than a 'make-weight' in the £20,000 (a then record) deal which took Tommy Lawton to Notts County. For three seasons he was outstanding in the first team, then in the process of being rebuilt, and it was surprising that he did not figure in manager Ted Drake's plans when he assembled the side that went on to win the Championship in 1954-5. Eagerly snapped up by Arsenal, his career at Highbury was affected by injuries.

DIGWEED, Perry (1988)   **Goalkeeper**
Born: London, 26 October 1959.
6ft; 11st 4lb.
Career: Fulham (September 1976), Brighton & Hove Albion (January 1981), West Bromwich Albion (loan), Charlton Athletic (loan), Newcastle United (loan), Chelsea (loan).
Chelsea debut: 3 March 1988. Appearances: League 3.
Following the serious injury which ended Eddie Niedzwiecki's career, Digweed was signed to provide cover for Roger Freestone, Chelsea's only other professional 'keeper at the time. Three weeks later, however, the club had signed Kevin Hitchcock from Mansfield Town, whereupon Digweed rejoined Brighton, where later he was restored to the first team.

74

DIXON, Kerry Michael (1983-)   **Striker**
Born: Luton, 24 July 1961.
6ft; 13st.
Career: Cheshunt, Tottenham Hotspur (apprentice), Dunstable Town (1979), Reading (July 1980), Chelsea (August 1983, £175,000).
Honours: England international (8 caps), England Under-21 (1 cap), Second Division championship medals 1984, 1989, Full Members' Cup winners' medal 1990.

Chelsea debut: 27 August 1983. Appearances: League 303(1), FA Cup 14(1), League Cup 38(1), Full Members' Cup 17; Goals: League 143, FA Cup 8, League Cup 25, Full Members' Cup 11.
Dixon had already made his reputation with 55 goals in 116 League games for Reading in the Fourth and Third Divisions before arriving at Stamford Bridge. As Chelsea surged to promotion, he then proceeded to head the Second Division's list and followed this up by topping the First Division's scorers to complete a unique quartet. A well-built natural athlete whose strength is his finishing ability, he was a member of England's 1986 World Cup squad.

DOCHERTY, James (1979)   **Striker**
Born: Broxburn, 8 November 1956.
5ft 10in; 10st 5lb.
Career: East Stirling, Chelsea (February 1979, £50,000), Dundee United (November 1979).
Chelsea debut: 3 March 1979. Appearances: League 2(1).
Failing to adjust to the demands of English football, Docherty was on the staff for ten months at a time when the club was going through a difficult period, both on the field and behind the scenes.

DOCHERTY, Thomas Henderson (1961-1962) Wing-half
Born: Glasgow, 24 August 1928.
5ft 9in; 11st 8lb.

Career: Shettleston Juniors, Glasgow Celtic (July 1948), Preston North End (November 1949), Arsenal (August 1958), Chelsea (September 1961).
Honours: Scotland international (25 caps), Scotland 'B' (2 caps), Second Division championship medal 1951, FA Cup runners-up medal 1954.
Chelsea debut: 9 September 1961. Appearances: League 4.
Tommy Docherty's move from Arsenal to Chelsea in the twilight of his playing days enabled him to launch forth on his career as a manager. It was, in fact, as player-coach that he was signed and he was promoted manager in January 1962, when he succeeded Ted Drake. He then went on to build a promotion team (1962-3), help win the Football League Cup (1965) and take Chelsea to their first Wembley FA Cup Final (1967) — after two unsuccessful semi-final appearances in the same competition — before leaving in controversial circumstances in October 1967. In turn he managed Rotherham United, Queen's Park Rangers, Aston Villa, Oporto, Hull City (assistant manager), Scotland, Manchester United, Derby County, Queen's Park Rangers (again), Sydney Olympic, Preston North End, South Melbourne, Sydney Olympic (again), Wolves and Altrincham.

DODD, George Frederick (1911-1913) Inside-forward
Born: Whitchurch (Salop), 7 February 1885.
5ft 9in; 11st 6lb.
Career: Wallasey Town, Stockport County (cs 1905), Workington, Notts County (December 1907), Chelsea (October 1911), Millwall (May 1913), Brighton & Hove Albion (December 1913), Darlington (cs 1914), West Ham United (1914), Treherbert (player-manager cs 1920), Charlton Athletic (May 1921), Retired (1924).
Chelsea debut: 14 October 1911. Appearances: League 29, FA Cup 2; Goals: League 8, FA Cup 1.
Dodd was a regular first-teamer for only his first year at Stamford Bridge, when he was succeeded by the legendary amateur Corinthian, V.J.Woodward. His main claim to a spot in Chelsea's history is the fact that he scored the first-ever goal recorded against the club in League football, when he notched the only goal of the game at Stockport on 2 September 1905. After his playing career ended he managed both Catford South End and Southend United. Brother-in-law of Bob Thomson.

DODDS, William (1986-1989)   **Striker**
Born: New Cumnock, 5 February 1969.
5ft 7in; 10st.
Career: Chelsea (May 1986), Partick Thistle (loan), Dundee (1989).
Chelsea debut: 3 March 1987. Appearances: League 0(1), Full Members' Cup 0(1).
Dodds joined Chelsea as a apprentice at the start of the 1985-6 season, during which he was top scorer for the Juniors (27 goals in 30 League and Cup games), as well as playing in several matches for the reserve team. A fast, nippy attacker with a keen eye for an opening and a strong finisher.

DOLBY, Hugh R. (1908-1912)   **Winger**
Born: Agra (India).
Career: Nunhead, Chelsea (cs 1908), Brentford (1912).
Chelsea debut: 11 December 1909. Appearances: League 2.

A dependable reserve player, in four years on the staff Dolby could not force his way into the first team ahead of Billy Brawn and Angus Douglas.

DOLDING, Desmond Leonard (1945-1948)   Winger
Born: Ooregaum, Kola Gold Field (India), 13 December 1922; Died: Wembley, 23 November 1954.
5ft 9in; 10st 7lb.
Career: Wealdstone, Chelsea (July 1945), Norwich City (July 1948), Margate (1951).
Chelsea debut: 12 February 1946. Appearances: League 26, FA Cup 1; Goals: League 2.
After a brief spell with amateurs Wealdstone, Dolding joined Chelsea at the end of World War Two in which he had served as a member of an RAF air-crew. He never fully established a first-team place and the arrival of 'expensive' signings such as Bobby Campbell, Johnny Paton and John McInnes limited the chances which came his way. A member of the MCC groundstaff, he played one game for Middlesex in 1951. He was almost 32 when he died in a car crash.

DONAGHY, Charles (1905-1907)   Winger
Born: India, 1883.
5ft 7½in; 11st 2lb.
Career: Glasgow Rangers, Chelsea (August 1905), contract cancelled (September 1906).
Chelsea debut: 18 November 1905. Appearances: League 2, FA Cup 1; Goals: League 1.
A member of the hastily assembled squad of players starting Chelsea's first-ever season in football, Donaghy played most of his career at Stamford Bridge in the reserve team.

DONALD, Alexander (1930-1932)   Full-back
Born: Kirkintilloch.
5ft 9in; 10st 11lb.
Career: Kirkintilloch Juniors, Partick Thistle, Heart of Midlothian, New York Nationals, Chelsea (July 1930), Bristol Rovers (May 1932), Dunfermline Athletic (July 1936).
Chelsea debut: 8 November 1930. Appearances: League 24.
Donald's arrival at Stamford Bridge from USA coincided with the club's promotion from the Second Division. Two spells in the first team, when he deputized for Scottish international Tommy Law, were insufficient to win him a more permanent place. Back where he started, he was coach to Kirkintilloch Boys Club in the early 1950s.

DORIGO, Anthony Robert (1988-1991)   Full-back
Born: Melbourne (Australia), 3 December 1965.
5ft 10in; 11st.
Career: Aston Villa (January 1982), Chelsea (July 1978, £475,000), Leeds United (May 1991, tribunal).
Honours: England international (5 caps), England 'B' (5 caps), England Under-21, (11 caps), Second Division championship medal 1989, Full Members' Cup winners' medal 1990.
Chelsea debut: 15 August 1987. Appearances: League 149, FA Cup 4, League Cup 14, Full Members' Cup 13; Goals: League 11, Full Members' Cup 1.
Dorigo quickly established a reputation as one of the most aggressive, attacking full-backs in the game. Great speed and acceleration enable him to go forward on the 'overlap' to become an extra attacker. Not the least of

his assets is the powerful shot which is frequently produced from long-range, either in open play or from dead-ball situations. His cleverly-flighted free-kick which produced the only goal of the 1990 Full Members' Cup Final is a typical example of his varied skills. The fee for his move to Leeds, set by a tribunal, would certainly be around £1 million, a record for an outgoing Chelsea player.

DOUGLAS, Angus (1908-1913)   Outside-right
Born: Lochmaben, Dumfries, 1 January 1889; Died: 14 December 1918.
5ft 8½in; 10st 10lb.
Career: Castlemilk, Lochmaben, Dumfries, Chelsea (May 1908), Newcastle United (October 1913, £1,100).
Honours: Scotland international (1 cap).
Chelsea debut: 1 September 1908. Appearances: League 96, FA Cup 7; Goals: League 12.
Chelsea had to compete with Everton for the signature of Douglas and he at once became a great favourite with the Stamford Bridge crowd. Fast and clever, with all the traditional Scottish ball skills, he shared the outside-right position with Billy Brawn in his early years on the staff, but had established himself when he was, surprisingly, transferred to Newcastle United — not a popular move with the Bridge regulars. He died of influenza shortly after serving in World War One.

DOWNING, Samuel (1909-1914)   Wing-half
Born: Willesden, 19 January 1883; Died: Cuckfield (Sussex), March 1974.
5ft 10in; 13st.
Career: West Hampstead, Willesden Town, Queen's

Park Rangers (cs 1900), Chelsea (April 1909), Croydon Common (cs 1914).
Chelsea debut: 9 April 1909. Appearances: League 134, FA Cup 10; Goals: League 9, FA Cup 1.
Although he was an artistic, constructive wing-half, Downing's lack of pace probably cost him more widespread recognition. A most popular player who was given a benefit match to mark his retirement, he skippered the side for a period. He was noted for his accurate and powerful long-range shooting and for his scrupulously fair play. He continued to live in North London until his death, at one time coaching cricket at a college in Maidenhead.

DRIVER, Philip A. (1980-1983)   **Winger**
Born: Huddersfield, 10 August 1959.
5ft 10in; 10st 12lb.
Career: Luton Town, Bedford Town, Wimbledon (December 1978), Chelsea (September 1980, £20,000), Wimbledon (July 1983), St Alban's City.
Chelsea debut: 8 October 1980. Appearances: League 25(19), FA Cup 0(1), League Cup 0(1); Goals: League 4.
Driver's speed on the wing combined with intricate footwork and the ability to cross the ball accurately made him, potentially, a fine player. Yet his comparatively short League career was hampered by injuries and he never did himself justice.

DROY, Michael R. (1970-1985)   **Central defender**
Born: Highbury, 7 May 1951.
6ft 4in; 15st 2lb.
Career: Hoddesdon Town, Wembley, Slough Town, Chelsea (October 1970), Luton Town (loan), Crystal Palace (free transfer) (March 1985), Brentford (November 1986), Kingstonian.

Chelsea debut: 13 February 1971. Appearances: League 263(9), FA Cup 21, League Cup 17(2), European Cup winners' Cup 1; Goals: League 13, FA Cup 4, League Cup 2.

It was Droy's misfortune that his career coincided with one of the most difficult phases in Chelsea's history. As a result, his lot was usually to shore up an inexperienced defence which lacked confidence, under a succession of different managers and with financial, and other, worries never far away. Nevertheless, he remained the pillar of the defence for a dozen or so seasons. Powerful in the air, he frequently displayed deft skills at ground level for such a big man, his 'telescopic' left foot dispossessing many a startled opponent with its immense range.

DUBLIN, Keith B.L. (1984-1987)   **Full-back**
Born: Wycombe, 29 January 1966.
5ft 11in; 11st 10lb.
Career: Chelsea (January 1984), Brighton & Hove Albion (August 1987, £3,500), Watford (cs 1990).
Chelsea debut: 7 May 1984. Appearances: League 50(1), FA Cup 5, League Cup 6, Full Members' Cup 5(1).

Well-built, full-back Keith Dublin came to Chelsea as an apprentice in July 1982 after Watford (where he had also signed apprentice forms), West Ham United and Crystal Palace had also shown interest. Speedy and a strong tackler, his debut came in the final home fixture of the 1983-4 season, when Chelsea were celebrating their return to Division One.

DUDLEY, Samuel Morton (1932-1934)   **Outside-left**
Born: Tipton, 1905.
5ft 7½in; 10st 2lb.
Career: Scottish Junior football, Preston North End (cs 1927), Bournemouth and Boscombe Athletic (June 1928), Coleraine (May 1929), Clapton Orient (July 1930), Chelsea (June 1932), Exeter City (June 1934).
Chelsea debut: 4 February 1933. Appearances: League 1.
Dudley's arrival at Stamford Bridge coincided with

a time when famous names were being signed in an endeavour to bring instant success for Chelsea and he was unable to displace such stars.

DUFFY, Bernard (1923-27)   **Wing-half**
Born: Uddington.
5ft 9in; 11st 8lb.
Career: Blantyre Caledonians, Burnbank, Bellshill Athletic (Glasgow), Chelsea (June 1923), Clapton Orient (March 1927), Shelbourne (Dublin) (June 1931).
Chelsea debut: 27 October 1923.Appearances: League 3.
Duffy came to Chelsea direct from junior football in the Glasgow area but failed to make his mark in English football, although he was a dependable member of Chelsea's reserve team for several seasons.

DUNN, John A. (1962-1966)   **Goalkeeper**
Born: Barking, 21 June 1944.
5ft 11in; 12st 6lb.
Career: Chelsea (February 1962), Torquay United (October 1966), Aston Villa (January 1968), Charlton Athletic (July 1971), Tooting & Mitcham (September 1974).
Chelsea debut: 27 March 1963. Appearances: League 13, FA Cup 3.
Honours: Football League Cup runners-up medal 1971.
Dunn was one of several talented 'keepers whose lot was to deputize for Peter Bonetti. Signed professional after joining Chelsea as an apprentice, he was a reliable and sound performer who went on to make more than a century of League appearances with both Aston Villa and Charlton.

DURIE, Gordon Scott (1986-)   **Striker**
Born: Paisley, 6 December 1965.
6ft; 11st 6lb.

Career: Hill O'Beath, East Fife, Hibernian, Chelsea (April 1986, £381,000).
Honours: Scotland international (12 caps), Scotland Under-21 (4 caps), Second Division championship medal 1989, Full Members' Cup winners' medal 1990.
Chelsea debut: 5 May 1986. Appearances: League 119(8), FA Cup 6, League Cup 11, Full Members' Cup 9; Goals: League 54, FA Cup 1, League Cup 7, Full Members' Cup 1.
A fast, well-built and brave striker, Durie moved from Scottish football where he had scored 41 goals (121 games) with his previous clubs. At Hibernian he had become something of a folk hero amongst the fans. Operating either in the middle or down the flanks, he won recognition from the Scotland selectors in his first season at Stamford Bridge, being called up for the Under-21 squad, and later graduated to the senior national team.

DYKE, Charles H. (1947-1951)   **Outside-right**
Born: Caerphilly, 23 September 1926.
5ft 6in; 10st 12lb.
Career: Troed-y-rhiw, Chelsea (November 1947), Barry Town (August 1951).
Chelsea debut: 21 February 1948. Appearances: League 24, FA Cup 1; Goals: League 2.
Cheerful and slightly-built, the ginger-haired Dyke was a great trier as a thrustful winger. But, having failed to oust Bobby Campbell from the League team, he returned to his native South Wales after four seasons at The Bridge.

EDWARDS, Robert Henry (1951-55) Inside-forward
Born: Guildford, 22 May 1931.
5ft 11in; 12st.
Career: Woking, Chelsea (November 1951), Swindon Town (July 1955), Norwich City (December 1959), Northampton Town (March 1961), King's Lynn (June 1962), Boston (1965).
Chelsea debut: 26 December 1952. Appearances: League 13; Goals: League 2.
Edwards signed professional forms immediately after demobilization from the RAF. He was an elegant player who understudied John McNichol for some four years and made one appearance in the League Championship season. Later, he played nearly 200 games in his four-year stay with Swindon Town. His elder brother, Leslie, played for Bristol Rovers.

ELLIOT, Sidney D. (1928-1930)   **Centre-forward**
Born: Sunderland, 1910.
Career: Arcade Mission, Margate, Durham City (June 1926), Fulham (May 1927), Chelsea (May 1928, £3,000), Bristol City (July 1930), Notts County (March 1932), Bradford City (June 1934), Rochdale (September 1935).
Chelsea debut: 25 August 1928. Appearances: League 30; Goals League 9.
Having scored more than 100 goals in a season for Arcade Mission in his native Sunderland, Elliot was snapped up by Third Division North club Durham City at the age of 16, and arrived at Stamford Bridge after one season at Craven Cottage. At the time, Chelsea were desperate to end their stay in the Second Division but did not consider his output of goals sufficient to give him extended opportunities.

ELMES, Timothy (1980-1982)   **Midfield**
Born: Thornton Heath, 28 September 1962.
5ft 10in; 12st.
Career: Chelsea (July 1980), Orient (1982).
Chelsea debut: 26 December 1980. Appearances: League 2(2).
Elmes, a sturdily-built, combative midfielder, signed professional forms after a year as an apprentice. Sadly, he failed to fulfill his undoubted potential and, after a brief spell with Orient, drifted out of League football altogether.

EVANS, Robert (1960-1961)   **Half-back**
Born: Glasgow, 16 July 1927.
5ft 8½in; 12st.
Career: Thornliebank Methodist FC, St Anthony's (Glasgow), Glasgow Celtic (1944), Chelsea (May 1960, £12,500), Newport County (player-manager May 1961), Morton (July 1962), Third Lanark (trainer-coach cs 1963), Third Lanark (player-manager June 1964), Raith Rovers (player cs 1965), Retired (1967).
Honours: Scotland international (48 caps), Scottish League XI (24 appearances), Scottish League Championship medal 1954, Scottish FA Cup winners' medals 1951, 1954, runners-up medals 1955, 1956, Scottish League Cup winners' medals 1957, 1958.
Chelsea debut: 20 August 1937. Appearances: League 32, FA Cup 1, League Cup 4; Goals: League Cup 1.
Evans' move to Chelsea, as his long and distinguished career was drawing to its close, was scarcely a success. At 33 he had lost his edge and being asked to operate at centre-half, having spent the majority of his career as a wing-half, also presented its problems. As a result, the young, emerging players around him never fully felt the benefit of his experience. Earlier he had had a magnificent and highly successful career with Celtic, having been virtually a permanent fixture in the Scotland side for ten years from 1949.

FAIRGRAY, Norman Murray (1907-1914)   **Outside-left**
Born: Dumfries, 28 October 1880.
5ft 5in; 9st 6lb.
Career: Maxwelltown Volunteers, Kilmarnock (November 1903), Maxwelltown Volunteers (July 1904), Lincoln City (December 1905), Chelsea (September 1907), Motherwell (May 1914), Queen of the South (August 1919).
Chelsea debut: 14 September 1907. Appearances: League 79, FA Cup 5; Goals: League 5.
In retrospect, it is surprising that 'Norrie' Fairgray did not play more frequently in the first team during his seven years on the staff. On his day he was a brilliant winger of the orthodox type, exhibiting tricky footwork and an extensive repertoire of ball skills. Certainly he was most popular with the Stamford Bridge regulars, but his slight physique was against him at a time when most full-backs were selected for their strength of tackle and ability to win the ball.

FALCO, Mark Peter (1982)   **Striker**
Born: Hackney, 22 October 1960.
6ft; 12st.
Career: Tottenham Hotspur (July 1978), Chelsea (November 1982, loan), Watford (October 1986), Glasgow Rangers (1987), Queen's Park Rangers (December 1987).
Honours: England Youth international.

Chelsea debut: 27 November 1982. Appearances: League 3.
Falco joined Chelsea on a month's loan in November 1982. A tall, well-built striker, he then returned to Tottenham where he had a long run in the first team before being transferred to Watford in October 1986.

FASCIONE, Joseph V. (1962-1969)   **Winger**
Born: Coatbridge, 5 February 1945.
5ft 4½in; 9st 12lb.
Career: Kirkintilloch Rob Roy, Chelsea (September 1962), Durham City (July 1969), Romford, Barking.
Chelsea debut: 23 September 1964. Appearances: League 22(7), League Cup 3, Fairs Cup 2; Goals: League 1.
A small, tricky winger, Fascoine's time at Chelsea was largely spent in the reserve team. However, he gave some excellent displays on the rare opportunities to show his true ability. After his playing career ended he coached at Whyteleafe, with Steve Kember.

FEELY, Peter J. (1970-1973)   **Striker**
Born: City of London, 3 January 1950.
5ft 11in; 12st 10lb.
Career: Enfield Town, Chelsea (April 1970), Bournemouth & Boscombe Athletic (February 1973, £1,000), Fulham (July 1974), Gillingham (January 1977), Sheffield Wednesday (February 1986), Stockport County (October 1974).
Honours: England Amateur international.
Chelsea debut: 24 April 1971. Appearances: League 4(1); Goals: League 2.
After scoring on his League debut, against Coventry City, Feely found it impossible to win a permanent place in the senior side in the era of Peter Osgood, Ian Hutchinson and Tommy Baldwin. One of soccer's nomads, his most successful spell was at Gillingham, where he averaged more than a goal in every two games.

FERGUSON, Christopher (1927-1930)   **Forward**
Born: Kirkonnel.
5ft 6in; 10st 2lb.
Career: Chelsea (October 1927), Queen's Park Rangers (May 1930), Wrexham (July 1931), Guildford City (cs 1932).
Chelsea debut: 28 April 1928. Appearance: League 1.
Younger brother of Willie Ferguson, his first professional club was Chelsea and he remained on the Stamford Bridge staff for three seasons, playing at inside, or centre-forward in the reserve team.

FERGUSON, Edward (1920-1923)   **Full-back**
Born: Seaton Burn, 2 August 1895.
5ft 7in; 11st.
Career: Ashington, Chelsea (March 1920), Ashington (June 1924), Nelson (August 1928), Annfield Plain (1930).
Chelsea debut: 7 May 1921. Appearances: League 2.
Ferguson's opportunities were strictly limited by the consistency of Jack Harrow, who was firmly installed at full-back in partnership with either Walter Bettridge or George Smith at this time.

FERGUSON, William (1921-1933)
Inside-forward/Wing-half
Born: Muirkirk, 13 February 1901; Died: 31 August 1960.

5ft 6in; 9st 13lb.
Career: Kellsbank Juveniles, Kelso Rovers, Queen of the South Wanderers, Chelsea (October 1921), Queen of the South (August 1933).
Chelsea debut: 30 March 1923. Appearances: League 272, FA Cup 22; Goals: League 11.
Willie Ferguson was one of the best-liked and most loyal players in Chelsea's history. He began his Stamford Bridge career in the forward line, but soon moved back to wing-half where he was undisputed first choice for nine seasons, in good times and bad. The disappointment of relegation in April 1924 was more than compensated for him by the return to Division One six years later. A terrier-like, consistent player, he overcame his lack of height and was noted both for his firm tackling and accurate distribution of the ball. After returning to his native land, he was appointed manager of Queen of the South in 1937 at the conclusion of his long and honourable playing career.

FERRIS, James (1920-1922)   **Inside-forward**
Born: Belfast; Died: Scotland, 10 October 1932.
5ft 7in; 9st 7lb.
Career: Distillery, Belfast Celtic, Chelsea (June 1920), Preston North End (March 1922), Belfast Celtic.
Honours: Northern Ireland international (5 caps), Irish League XI.
Chelsea debut: 6 September 1920. Appearances: League 33, FA Cup 6; Goals: League 8, FA Cup 1.
Ferris arrived at Chelsea with a big reputation but, although winning a further two international caps during his time at Stamford Bridge, he never settled in London. A forceful and clever schemer, but lacking pace and finishing power, after one season he unaccountably lost form, and moved to Preston North End, before finishing his playing career in his native land.

FILLERY, Michael C. (1978-1983)   **Midfield**
Born: Mitcham, 19 September 1960.
5ft 10in; 13st.
Career: Merton Schools, Chelsea (August 1978), Queen's Park Rangers (August 1983, £200,000), Portsmouth (July 1987), Oldham Athletic (October 1990), Millwall (March 1991, loan).
Honours: England Schoolboy and Youth international.
Chelsea debut: 4 April 1979. Appearances: League 156(5), FA Cup 11, League Cup 9; Goals: League 32, FA Cup 3, League Cup 6.
Signed after being an apprentice on the Stamford Bridge staff, Fillery was a highly talented and stylish midfield player who, at times, lacked the consistency and application to do his ability justice. His time in the first team was spent almost wholly in the Second Division and at a time of general instability both on and off the field which, perhaps, hindered his development and shaped an attitude which appeared casual and disinterested on occasions.

FINLAYSON, William (1920-1923)   **Centre-forward**
Born: Thornliebank (Renfrewshire).
5ft 7in; 9st 7lb.
Career: Ashfield (Glasgow), Thornliebank, Chelsea (June 1920), Clapton Orient (1923), Brentford.
Chelsea debut: 21 January 1922. Appearances: League 5; Goals: 1.

A junior player from Scotland, Finlayson spent most of his four years at Stamford Bridge in the reserve team at a time when Jack Cock and Andy Wilson were recognized centre-forwards on the staff.

FINNIESTON, Steven James (1971-1978)   **Striker**
Born: Edinburgh, 30 November 1954.
5ft 11in; 11st 3lb.
Career: Chelsea (December 1971), Cardiff City (loan), Sheffield United (June 1978, £90,000), Addlestone, Hartney Wintney.
Honours: Scotland Youth international
Chelsea debut: 1 February 1975. Appearance: League 78(2), FA Cup 4(2), League Cup 4; Goals: League 34, FA Cup 1, League Cup 2.
Finnieston joined Chelsea as an apprentice from school at Weybridge and became a prolific goalscorer in junior and reserve football who established himself in the senior side on the 1974 club tour of Australia. However, at a time of instability within the club, his career was adversely affected by a series of injuries and he was unable to do full justice to his undoubted ability. After a spell at Sheffield United he was forced to give up full-time football, as a result of another injury.

FLETCHER, James (1905-1906)   **Full-back**
Career: Chelsea (1905)
Chelsea debut: 28 April 1906. Appearances: League 1.
A somewhat mysterious character, Fletcher played one League game as an amateur in Chelsea's first ever season — without apparently being registered with the Football League.

FORD, Henry Thomas (1912-1924)   **Winger**
Born: Fulham, 1893.
5ft 7½in; 11st 4lb.
Career: Tunbridge Wells Rangers, Chelsea (April 1912), Retired (1924).
Honours: FA Cup runners-up medal 1915.
Chelsea debut: 7 September 1912. Appearances: League 222, FA Cup 26; Goals: League 41, FA Cup 5.

Harry Ford was spotted playing for Tunbridge Wells Rangers (for whom he scored 60 goals in the 1911-12 season) against Chelsea Reserves. He was a versatile performer who was prepared to turn out in any position, on one occasion even playing the role of deputy goalkeeper despite his lack of inches. It was, however, on the right wing where he most usually operated. One of the best in England at that time, he was very fast, could centre the ball with precision and also possessed impressive shooting power — two of his most crucial goals being instrumental in taking Chelsea to their first FA Cup Final in 1915. A most popular man, he would probably have established a club record for the number of games played if he had not lost four seasons in World War One.

FOSS, Sidney Richard (1936-1952)
Inside-forward/Wing-half
Born: Barking, 28 November 1912.
5ft 6in; 11st 7lb.
Career: Thames (FC) (May 1931) Tottenham Hotspur (amateur, May 1932), Southall, Chelsea (May 1936), Retired (1952).
Chelsea debut: 20 February 1937. Appearances: League 41, FA Cup 7; Goals: League 3.
Foss was one of the many professional footballers whose career was wrecked by World War Two. He played nearly 200 first-team wartime games yet, at the age of 33 when the war ended, he was unable to figure largely in manager Birrell's post-war rebuilding of his playing staff. Having started in the forward line, he became a sound wing-half. A shrewd reader of the game, it was no surprise when he became manager of the Chelsea youth scheme in 1952 after his career as a player ended. For 16 years he was largely instrumental in producing a regular and distinguished line of young stars who made their mark in international as well as club football. A most likeable man and a crucial figure in the history of Chelsea FC.

FOULKE, William Henry (1905-1906)   Goalkeeper
Born: Dawley, Salop, 12 April 1874; Died: 1 May 1916.
6ft 2in; 22st 3lb.
Career: Alfreton Blackwell Colliery, Sheffield United

(cs 1894), Chelsea (May 1905, £50), Bradford City (April 1906), Retired (November 1907).
Honours: England international (1 cap), FA Cup winners' medals 1899, 1902, runners-up medal 1901.
Chelsea debut: 2 September 1905. Appearances: League 34, FA Cup 1.
One of football's legendary characters, the stories surrounding Foulke are legion. 'Little Willie' was Chelsea's first goalkeeper and was a giant of a man in every sense of the word. Surprisingly agile for a person of such girth, he spent only one season in London before moving back to finish his playing career in Yorkshire. Possibly uniquely, his name at birth was registered as 'Foulk', and his death as 'Foulkes'. He played four matches as a professional cricketer for Derbyshire in 1900 and died from pneumonia, contracted on Blackpool Sands where he was earning his living by inviting members of the public to score goals against him.

FRANCIS, Stephen S. (1982-1987)   Goalkeeper
Born: Billericay, 29 May 1964.
5ft 11in; 11st 5lb.
Career: Chelsea (May 1982), Reading (February 1987, £15,000).
Honours: Full Members' Cup winners' medal 1986.
Chelsea debut: 6 October 1981. Appearances: League 71, FA Cup 10, League Cup 6, Full Members' Cup 1.

Francis signed apprentice forms in July 1980 and made an impressive debut at Southampton in the League Cup in October 1981, going on to establish himself as the regular first-team 'keeper in the next two seasons. Lost his place after the signing of Eddie Niedzwiecki, whose consistency limited further chances and, after an eventual recall, did not display his previous confidence.

FREEMAN, Charles Redfern (1907-1921) Inside-forward
Born: Overseal, (Derbyshire), 22 August 1887; Died: Fulham, 17 March 1956.
5ft 7in; 10st 13lb.
Career: Overseal Swifts, Burton United, Fulham (1906), Chelsea (1907), Gillingham (June 1921), Maidstone United (cs 1923).
Chelsea debut: 13 February 1909. Appearances: League 95, FA Cup 10; Goals: League 21, FA Cup 1.

Having impressed in a trial game, Freeman was signed as a professional and started an association with Chelsea FC which was to endure for 46 years. As a player his career at Stamford Bridge extended over eight seasons, not including the four lost in World War One. Yet, only in one did he win selection for more than half the games played. Always on hand to be recalled from the reserve team, he was a grafting and reliable inside-forward, if lacking in flair and originality. Noted for his dependability, it was entirely appropriate that on retiring as a player he became a member of the backroom staff. Performing a variety of tasks over the years he became trainer to the first team during World War Two, as well as groundsman. He finally retired in the summer of 1953.

FREESTONE, Roger (1987-)　　　　**Goalkeeper**
Born: Caerleon (Newport, Mon) 19 August 1968.
6ft 2ins; 13st 3lb.
Career: Newport County (April 1986), Chelsea (March 1987, £75,000). Swansea City (loan), Hereford United (loan).
Honours: Wales Under-21 international (1 cap), Second Division championship medal 1989.
Chelsea debut: 18 April 1987. Appearances: League 42, FA Cup 3, League Cup 2, Full Members' Cup 6.
Freestone, who joined Newport County as a YTS trainee, signed for Chelsea towards the end of the 1986-7 season, after only a handful of games for the Somerton Park club. He made his first-team debut within weeks of his arrival at Stamford Bridge. Magnificently built, with a safe pair of hands.

FREW, James (1922-1927)　　　　**Centre-half**
Born: Ballochmyle, 16 March 1900.
5ft 6in; 11st 2lb.
Career: Lanemark (May 1919), Hurlford (June 1920), Nithdale Wanderers (October 1920), Kilmarnock (December 1920), Nithdale Wanderers (loan 1920-21 and permanent transfer 1922), Chelsea (June 1922), Southend United (May 1927), Carlisle United (July 1929).
Chelsea debut: 14 February 1923. Appearances: League 42, FA Cup 1.
Most of Frew's five years at Stamford Bridge were spent in the reserve team but, despite his lack of inches, he proved a reliable and able deputy to Harold Wilding and George Rodger, the regular centre-halves of those days. A hard, but fair tackler.

FRIDGE, Leslie F. (1985-1987)　　　　**Goalkeeper**
Born: Inverness, 27 August 1968.
5ft 10in; 11st.
Career: Inverness Thistle, Chelsea (December 1985), St Mirren (January 1987, £50,000).
Honours: Scotland Under-21 international (2 caps), Scotland Youth.
Chelsea debut: 5 May 1986. Appearances: League 1.
Highly-rated north of the border, Fridge's chances at Stamford Bridge were limited by the form of Eddie Niedzwiecki and, later, Tony Godden on the staff. Strongly-built, he signed professional forms after a trial period and was the regular Juniors' 'keeper for his two full seasons at Chelsea.

FROST, James Lewis (1906-1908)　　　　**Outside-right**
Born: Wolverton, 1880.

Career: Wolverton (1896), Northampton Town (1901), Chelsea (December 1906, £350), West Ham United (cs 1908), Croydon Common (cs 1909), Clapton Orient (cs 1910).
Chelsea debut: 15 December 1906. Appearances: League 22; Goals: League 4.
A fast and direct winger, Frost came to Chelsea at a time when several other clubs were competing for his services. After seemingly establishing his first-team spot soon after his arrival, he then suffered injury and was unable to displace Billy Brawn, leaving Chelsea soon afterwards.

FROST, Lee A. (1976-1980)　　　　**Winger**
Born: Woking, 4 December 1957.
5ft 8½in; 10st 7lb.
Career: Chelsea (July 1976), Brentford (loan), Brentford (December 1980, £15,000).
Chelsea debut: 15 April 1978. Appearances: League 11(3); Goals: League 5.
Lee Frost joined Chelsea as a junior and progressed to the first team via reserve-team football. A speedy and potentially dangerous and direct forward, he nevertheless, failed to develop his early promise — this after scoring a hat-trick in a 7-3 win at Orient in November 1977.

GALLACHER, Hugh, Kilpatrick (1930-1934)
Centre-forward
Born: Bellshill (Lanarkshire), 2 February 1903; Died: Gateshead, 11 June 1957.
5ft 5in; 10st 10lb.
Career: Bellshill Academy, Bellshill Athletic, Queen of the South Wanderers (1921), Airdrieonians (May 21), Newcastle United (December 1925), Chelsea (May 1930, £10,000), Derby County (November 1934, £3,000), Notts County (September 1936), Grimsby Town (January 1938), Gateshead (June 1938), Retired (September 1939).
Honours: Scotland international (20 caps), Scottish League representative XI, Scottish FA Cup winners' medal 1924, Football League Championship medal 1927.
Chelsea debut: 30 August 1930. Appearances: League 132, FA Cup 12; Goals: League 72, FA Cup 9.
Hughie Gallacher is one of the legendary names of football history. Playing in the same school teams as Alex James, he had been a wartime munitions worker and coal-miner before starting his professional career

with Airdrieonians, for whom he scored 91 goals in 111 League games. Signing for Newcastle United in December 1925, for a £6,500 fee, Gallacher became idolized on Tyneside and, indeed, the largest crowd (68,386) ever seen at St James' Park was for the fixture

against Chelsea, less than four months after he moved to Stamford Bridge. He was the complete centre-forward. With superb ball-control, he loved to leave defenders trailing in his wake after his trickery and acceleration had bewildered them. Indeed, he was very fast, both mentally, in sizing up a situation and, physically, in speed over a short distance. And his heading for such a small man, brought him a good proportion of his goals. But for his fiery temperament, he would have achieved still more glory. Basically a kindly man, he easily lost his temper when provoked and was constantly in trouble with referees, on one occasion invoking a two-month suspension. Yet, at least one manager — Derby's George Jobey — found him easy to handle and a great club man. After two successful seasons at the Baseball Ground he moved into the lower divisions and ended his League career in 1938-9 with Gateshead, scoring 18 goals in 31 games. After a handful of matches at the beginning of the war he retired, with the formidable tally of 387 goals from 543 League matches. His private life was often as stormy as his football career and in 1957 he ended his life when he stepped in front of an express train near his Gateshead home.

GALLON, James (1919-1921)   **Wing-half**
Born: Burslem (Stoke-on-Trent), 1894.
5ft 9in; 11st 7lb.
Career: Hanley, Chelsea (August 1919), not retained (May 1921).
Chelsea debut: 4 February 1920. Appearances: League 2.
Signed after impressing as a trialist, Gallon played in the reserve team regularly for two seasons without being able to force his way into the senior side at a time of post-war rebuilding.

GALLOWAY, John A. (1946-1949)   **Inside-forward**
Born: Grangemouth, 29 October 1918.
5ft 10in; 11st 10lb.
Career: Glasgow Rangers, Chelsea (August 1946), Retired (1949).
Honours: Scotland Schoolboy international.
Chelsea debut: 31 August 1946. Appearances: League 4.
Galloway was a tall, well-built player who guested for Chelsea during the wartime 1940-41 season. A captain in the Royal Signals, he had served in the Middle East, being wounded in the Italy campaign, and was a member of the famous Army Wanderers (Middle East 'Select') soccer team. A school teacher by profession, he never adjusted to the pace and demands of English football and reverted to amateur status as a 'permit' player in October 1949, after which he played little football.

GARLAND, Christopher Stephen (1971-1975)   Striker
Born: Bristol, 24 April 1949.
5ft 9½in; 11st 8lb.
Career: Bristol City (May 1966), Chelsea (September 1971, £100,000), Leicester City (February 1975, £95,000), Bristol City (November 1976).
Honours: England Under-23 international (1 cap), Football League Cup runners-up medal 1972.
Chelsea debut: 4 September 1971. Appearances: League 89(3), FA Cup 7, League Cup 15; Goals: League 22, FA Cup 1, League Cup 8.
Signed as a cover for strikers Peter Osgood, Tommy Baldwin and Ian Hutchinson, Garland never did justice to his ability as a thrustful and dangerous attacker.

His period at Chelsea coincided with the gradual breakup of the Cup-winning sides of 1970 and 1971 and he was rarely certain of his first-team place.

GARNER, William D. (1972-1978)   **Striker**
Born: Leicester, 14 December 1947.
6ft ½in; 13st.
Career: Notts County (July 1966), Bedford Town, Southend United (November 1969), Chelsea (September 1972, £80,000), Cambridge United (November 1978, free transfer), Brentford (August 1983), Whyteleafe.
Chelsea debut: 9 September 1972. Appearances: League 94(11), FA Cup 9(1), League Cup 2(2); Goals: League 31, FA Cup 5.
A striker whose build made him a formidable opponent, Garner's height enabled him to win many balls in the air and he was difficult to dispossess. On his day his finishing could be an additional asset, but his game suffered from inconsistency and a temperament which constantly brought him into conflict with referees.

GIBBS, Derek William (1955-1960)   **Inside-forward**
Born: Fulham, 22 December 1934.
5ft 10in; 11st 7lb.
Career: Chelsea (April 1955), Leyton Orient (November 1960), Queen's Park Rangers (August 1963), Romford (February 1965).
Chelsea debut: 1 January 1957. Appearances: League 23, FA Cup 2; Goals: League 5, FA Cup 1.
Signed professional forms after originally joining Chelsea Juniors, Gibbs was a dependable reserve who never succeeded in establishing a first-team spot over such contemporaries as Jimmy Greaves, Tony Nicholas and Johnny Brooks.

GIBSON, George Bennett (1933-1938)   **Inside-left**
Born: Hamilton.
5ft 9½in; 12st 4lb.
Career: Hamilton Academical, Dundee, Bolton Wanderers (March 1927), Chelsea (February 1933), not retained (May 1938).
Honours: FA Cup winners' medal 1929.
Chelsea debut: 1 March 1933. Appearances: League 129, FA Cup 12; Goals: League 23, FA Cup 1.
One of Chelsea's many 'big-name' signings of the 1930s, Gibson possessed all the brilliant ball skills so often associated with Scottish players, so much so that he was at times likened to the great Alex James. A typical 'dribbler' of that period, gaining possession in midfield, he would set out for goal leaving defenders in his wake. A creator and scorer of goals, he was the complete inside-forward. His last game for Bolton before joining Chelsea saw him score the Trotters' goal in a 1-1 draw at Stamford Bridge.

GODDARD, Raymond (1946-1948)   **Half-back**
Born: Ecclesfield (Sheffield), 17 October 1920; Died: Gornal, 1 February 1974.
5ft 8in; 11st.
Career: Red Rovers, Wolverhampton Wanderers (September 1938), Chelsea (September 1946), Plymouth Argyle (July 1948), Exeter City (December 1949), Bideford Town (player-manager).
Chelsea debut: 7 September 1946. Appearances: League 14, FA Cup 1; Goals: League 1.

One of the famous pre-World War Two 'Buckley Babes', military service took Goddard to Burma as one of General Wingate's men. Subsequently he toured India, Burma and Ceylon with the Army soccer team. At home in any of the half-back positions, he was a tough, hard-tackling defender whose ability suggested he could have made a bigger reputation had he not lost seven of his best years to the war.

GODDEN, Anthony L. (1986-1987)   **Goalkeeper**
Born: Gillingham, 2 August 1955.
6ft ½in; 13st.
Career: Ashford Town, West Bromwich Albion (August 1975), Preston North End (loan), Luton Town (loan), Walsall (loan), Chelsea (August 1986, free-transfer), Birmingham City (July 1987, £35,000), Bury (loan), Sheffield Wednesday (loan), Wivenhoe (1990), Colchester United (March 1991, loan).
Chelsea debut: 5 April 1986. Appearances: League 34, FA Cup 1, League Cup 2, Full Members' Cup 1.
Hurriedly signed on loan to solve Chelsea's goalkeeping problem, following an injury to Eddie Niedzwiecki and Steve Francis' loss of form, Godden performed with distinction and bravery and was signed on a permanent basis before the start of the following season. He had previously played 267 League games for West Bromwich Albion.

GOODWIN, Joe (1905-1906)   **Outside-left**
Career: Chelsea (1905, amateur).
Chelsea debut:28 October 1905. Appearances: FA Cup 2.
Although playing twice in the FA Cup competition in Chelsea's first season, Goodwin never made a League appearance. Most of his career was spent in amateur football in the London area.

GOULDEN, Leonard Arthur (1945-1950)   **Inside-left**
Born: Plaistow, 16 July 1912.
5ft 8in; 10st 12lb.
Career: Holborn Road School, West Ham United (amateur 1931), Chelmsford City (loan), Leyton (loan), West Ham United (April 1933), Chelsea (August 1945, £4,500), Retired (cs 1950).
Honours: England international (14 caps), England Schoolboys (2 caps), Football League XI (2 appearances).
Chelsea debut: 5 January 1946. Appearances: League 99, FA Cup 12; Goals: League 17, FA Cup 2.
One of the outstanding inside-forwards of the immediate pre-World War Two period, Goulden came to Chelsea in the autumn of his career but was still a fine player and good influence on those around him in a team in the process of reconstruction. With his educated left foot he both scored regularly and carved out scoring opportunities for others. Late in his career he had a successful spell at wing-half before being appointed Chelsea coach at the end of the 1949-50 season. His professional career had begun at West Ham United in 1933 and, after he left Stamford Bridge, he was appointed manager of Watford in November 1952. He was later secretary-manager of Banbury United (1965-67) and trainer-coach at Oxford United (1969), having also spent two years coaching in Libya.

GRAHAM, George (1964-1966)   **Striker**
Born: Bargeddie, 30 November 1944.
5ft 10½in; 11st 10lb.

Career: Coatbridge Schools, Aston Villa (December 1961), Chelsea (June 1964, £5,000), Arsenal (September 1966, £50,000), Manchester United (December 1972), Portsmouth (November 1974), Crystal Palace (November 1976), Retired (cs 1980).
Honours: Scotland international (12 caps), Scotland Under-23 (2 caps), Scotland Schoolboys, FA Cup winners' medal 1971, runners-up medal 1972, Football League Championship medal 1971, Football League Cup runners-up medals 1963, 1968, 1969, Inter-Cities Cup winners' medal 1970.

Chelsea debut: 29 August 1964. Appearances: League 72, FA Cup 11, League Cup 8, Fairs Cup 11; Goals: League 35, FA Cup 3, League Cup 5, Fairs Cup 3.
During an all-too-short stay at Stamford Bridge, Graham immediately struck up a fruitful partnership with Barry Bridges — over 80 goals coming from their 'striker-duo' in the two seasons they were together. A stylish, elegant player of great intelligence, 'Stroller' was both a creator and strong finisher, being a particularly fine header of the ball. His playing career over, he was appointed to the Crystal Palace coaching staff in 1980, moving to Queen's Park Rangers in a similar capacity in the following year. In December 1982 he was appointed manager of Millwall, and manager of Arsenal in May 1986, steering the Gunners to the League Championship in 1989 and 1991.

GRAY, William Patrick (1949-1953) **Winger**
Born: Dinnington, Co Durham, 24 May 1927.
5ft 6in; 10st 1lb.

Career: Dinnington Colliery, Leyton Orient (May 1947), Chelsea (March 1949), Burnley (August 1953, £16,000), Nottingham Forest (June 1957), Millwall (player-manager November 1963).
Honours: England 'B' international (1 cap), FA Cup winners' medal 1959.
Chelsea debut: 30 April 1949. Appearances: League 146, FA Cup 26; Goals: League 12, FA Cup 3.
A fast and clever winger, Billy Gray was a first-team regular for four seasons, during which time Chelsea twice reached the FA Cup semi-finals. A most popular player, his move to Burnley was much regretted by supporters and he went on to give the Lancashire club, and later Nottingham Forest, years of excellent service, playing over 500 games in his distinguished League career. He later managed Millwall, Brentford and Notts County for brief periods and was groundsman at the City Ground, Nottingham, for several years.

GREAVES, James Peter (1957-1961) **Inside-forward**
Born: East Ham, 20 February 1940.
5ft 8in; 10st 4lb.
Career: Dagenham Schools, Lakeside Manor Boys' Club, Chelsea (May 1957), AC Milan (June 1961, £80,000), Tottenham Hotspur (November 1961), West Ham United (March 1970), Barnet.
Honours: England international (57 caps), England Under-23 (12 caps), England Youth, Football League XI, FA Cup winners' medals 1962, 1967, European Cup-winners' Cup winners' medal 1963, FA Youth Cup winners' medal 1958.
Chelsea debut: 24 August 1957. Appearances: League 157, FA Cup 7, League Cup 2, Fairs Cup 3; Goals: League 124, FA Cup 3, League Cup 2, Fairs Cup 3.
Jimmy Greaves was one of the most lethal goalscorers the game of football has ever known, and certainly

the most prolific scorer in Chelsea's history, as measured by goals-per-game. A former Chelsea Junior whose feats in finding the back of the net had already won him a reputation, he was soon skating through First Division defences with ridiculous ease. He possessed speed off the mark, the ability to go around opponents and an uncanny knack of stealing unnoticed into space, especially in the opponents' penalty area. Three times he scored five goals in a match for Chelsea, topping the list of scorers in each of his four seasons in the senior side. His transfer to Italy in the summer of 1961 aroused much publicity, and protests from Chelsea fans, and it was a further source of disappointment that, despite strenuous efforts on the part of the board, he did not return to Stamford Bridge when he came back to England in November 1961. He was Spurs' top scorer in each of his eight seasons with them and altogether in his career he netted 357 First Division goals, 35 in the FA Cup and 44 for England. Greaves, who had the remarkable record of scoring on every debut at every level, both in club and international football, later overcame alcoholism and carved out a new career as a TV soccer pundit.

GREENWOOD, Ronald (1940-1945 & 1952-1955) Centre-half
Born: Burnley, 11 November 1921.
5ft 10in; 10st.
Career: Burnley Schools, Chelsea and Belfast Celtic (1940-1945), Bradford (1946), Brentford (March 1949), Chelsea (October 1952, £5,000, part-exchange for Seamus D'Arcy), Fulham (February 1955, free transfer).
Honours: England 'B' international (1 cap), Football League Championship medal 1955.
Chelsea debut: 25 October 1952. Appearances: League 65, FA Cup 1.
Ron Greenwood first came to Chelsea as a boy and played for the club in wartime football. Then, with John Harris installed at centre-half in the first-team, he moved to Bradford where he was assured of regular League football. After nearly four seasons at Brentford, he arrived back at Stamford Bridge to play a vital role in bringing the League Championship to Chelsea, sharing the centre-half spot with Stan Wicks. One of the most knowledgeable and respected coaches of his time, he subsequently managed West Ham United and was the England manager from 1976 to 1982. In December 1983, he became a director of Brighton & Hove Albion.

GREGG, Robert Edmond (1933-1938) Inside-forward
Born: Ferryhill, 3 January 1904.
5ft 8in; 11st 7lb.
Career: Ferryhill Athletic, Cornford Juniors, Spennymoor United, Chilton Colliery, Darlington (September 1926), Sheffield Wednesday (May 1928), Birmingham (January 1931), Chelsea (September 1933), Boston United (June 1938).
Honours: Football League Championship medal 1929, FA Cup runners-up medal 1931.
Chelsea debut: 13 September 1933. Appearances: League 48, FA Cup 3; Goals: League 5, FA Cup 1.
Despite a distinguished career with his two previous clubs, Gregg failed to settle at Stamford Bridge and played the majority of his games in the Reserves. A clever ball player, his failing was an inability to play

the early ball and to spot an opening. He is often remembered as being the scorer of the best disallowed 'goal' in an FA Cup Final, at Wembley against West Bromwich Albion in 1931.

GRIFFITHS, Robert (1931-1941)   Half-back
Born: Chapleton (Scotland).
5ft 9in; 10st 8lb.
Career: Pollock Juniors, Chelsea (July 1931), Retired (1941).
Chelsea debut: 17 September 1932. Appearances: League 42, FA Cup 3.
Griffiths was a most loyal club servant during his ten years with the club and, although he lacked the necessary height to become a dominating centre-half, he nevertheless was a most skilled and resourceful performer. In turn he understudied Peter O'Dowd, Allan Craig and Bob Salmond and, for one season, he not only was the recognized first choice for his position, but also captained the side. He joined the Police War Reserve in 1939 and continued to make occasional appearances in wartime regional football until he retired.

HALES, Kevin P. (1979-1983)   Defender/Midfield
Born: Dartford, 13 January 1961.
5ft 7in; 10st 4lb.
Career: Chelsea (January 1979), Orient (August 1983).
Chelsea debut: 10 November 1979. Appearances: League 18(2), FA Cup 7; Goals: League 2.
Hales graduated to professional ranks after joining Chelsea after 18 months as an apprentice. A versatile player whose Stamford Bridge career was dogged by injuries which prevented him establishing a permanent first-team berth, but he became a pillar of the Orient team, either at full-back or in midfield.

HALL, Gareth David (1985-)   Full-back
Born: Croydon, 20 March 1969.
5ft 8in; 10st 7lb.
Career: Chelsea (August 1984).
Honours: Wales international (8 caps), Wales Under-21 (1 cap), England Schoolboys (9 caps), Second Division Championship medal 1989. Full Members' Cup Winners' medal 1990.
Chelsea debut: 5 May 1987. Appearances: League 64(12), FA Cup 2, League Cup 7, Full Members' Cup 6(2); Goals: League 1, Full Members' Cup 1.
Strongly-built defender who joined the club as an apprentice in August 1984, Hall graduated to the first team via the juniors and reserve teams. Chelsea Young Player of the Year in 1984-5, he also played cricket for Surrey Schools. Competing for the right-back position with Steve Clarke, and therefore never an automatic first-team choice, he still managed to attract the attention of the Welsh Selectors, winning his first 'full' international cap at the age of 19.

HALSE, Harold James (1913-1921)   Inside-forward
Born: Leytonstone, 1 January 1886; Died: Colchester, April 1951.
5ft 7in; 10st 10lb.
Career: Park Road School, Wanstead FC, Barking Town, Clapton Orient (1902), Southend United (June 1906), Manchester United (March 1908), Aston Villa (July 1912), Chelsea (May 1913), Charlton Athletic (July 1921), Retired (cs 1923).

Honours: England international (1 cap), Football League XI, FA Cup winners' medals 1909, 1913, runners-up medal 1915, Football League Championship medal 1911.
Chelsea debut: 6 September 1913. Appearances: League 96, FA Cup 15; Goals: League 23, FA Cup 2.
Halse was a slightly built inside-forward whose forte was his mastery of the ball. This, allied to deadly shooting power, made him one of the most respected forwards of his day. An infant prodigy, at the age of 13, in the West Ham District Schoolboys team, he went on to be the first man to play in FA Cup Finals for three different teams. It was surprising that he was only once recognized by the England selectors, although it must be remembered that he lost four of his potentially best seasons to World War One. After leaving Chelsea he captained Charlton Athletic in their first season in the Football League.

HAMILTON, Ian M. (1968) Forward/Midfield
Born: Streatham, 31 October 1950.
5ft 9½in; 10st 6lb.
Career: Chelsea (January 1968), Southend United (August 1968, £5,000), Aston Villa (June 1969), Sheffield United (July 1976), Minnesota Kicks (1978), San Jose Earthquakes (1982).
Honours: England Youth international.
Chelsea debut: 18 March 1967. Appearances: League 3(2); Goals: League 2.
Hamilton's somewhat curious Chelsea career began when he became the youngest player in the club's history to play in a senior competitive game. He was 16 years 4 months and 18 days when he played against Tottenham Hotspur in a League fixture at White Hart Lane and scored Chelsea's goal in a 1-1 draw. Yet, ultimately signing professional forms, he remained on the staff for only a further eight months before his transfer to Third Division Southend United. Later he played more than 200 senior games for Aston Villa.

HAMPTON, Colin Michael Kenneth (1914-1924) Goalkeeper
Born: Brechin.
5ft 11in; 11st 4lb.
Career: Brechin City, Motherwell, Chelsea (April 1914), Brechin City (cs 1924), Crystal Palace (December 1925).
Honours: Scottish League XI.
Chelsea debut: 25 April 1914. Appearances: League 79, FA Cup 3.
Most of Hampton's 11 years on the Chelsea staff was spent understudying such as Jim Molyneux and Benjamin Howard Baker, yet he was an extremely sound and reliable 'keeper. Perhaps more exciting were his exploits in World War One, when he served as a machine-gunner in Mesopotamia. After his car was shattered by shells he was taken prisoner, set out on foot to Constantinople, but never arrived as the Armistice was declared soon afterwards. He was awarded the Military Medal for gallantry in that campaign.

HANSON, Adolf Jonathan (1938-1946) Outside-left
Born: Bootle, 27 December 1912.
5ft 8½in; 10st 10lb.
Career: Bootle JOC, Everton (trialist to January 1931), Liverpool (November 1931), Chelsea (June 1938, £7,500), South Liverpool (player-manager 1945),

Shelbourne United (Dublin) (player-manager 1946), Ellesmere Port Town.
Chelsea debut: 27 August 1938. Appearances: League 37, FA Cup 6; Goals: League 8, FA Cup 1.
Hanson moved to London from Liverpool just before World War Two, having scored 50 goals in 166 games during five seasons at Anfield. A fast and direct left-winger, his career was virtually terminated by the outbreak of war, although he continued to play regional football as a guest player for various clubs in the north of England. He was a good cricketer and baseball player and his younger brother, Stan, kept goal for Bolton Wanderers for several years. Adolf Hanson was a plumber by trade.

HARMER, Thomas Charles (1962-1967) Inside-forward
Born: Hackney, 2 February 1928.
5ft 5in; 10st.
Career: Finchley, Tottenham Hotspur (August 1948), Watford (October 1960), Chelsea (September 1962, £3,500), Retired (1967).
Honours: England 'B' international (1 cap).
Chelsea debut: 20 October 1962. Appearances: League 8, League Cup 1; Goals: League 1.
Signed at the age of 34 with a view to mainly coaching the young players, Harmer nevertheless made a handful of appearances in the first team where he exhibited all his old mastery of the ball for which he was renowned. At Chelsea he will always be remembered for scoring the vital goal against Sunderland at Roker Park in the penultimate game of the 1962-3 season which virtually ensured promotion to the First Division. He stayed at Stamford Bridge as youth-team coach until June 1967, still making occasional appearances as a player in the Reserves.

HARDING, Augustus W. (1906-1913) Full-back
Born: Hereford.
5ft 9½in; 12st.
Career: Tottenham Hotspur (amateur), Chelsea (December 1906, amateur forms, professional June 1907), Exeter City (cs 1913).
Chelsea debut: 14 December 1907. Appearances: League 4, FA Cup 1.
For almost all of his seven years on the staff, Harding played reserve-team football, yet his loyalty was rewarded with a testimonial in February 1913. He was renowned as much for his fine sportsmanship as for his ability on the field.

HARRIS, Allan J. (1960-1964 & 1966-1967) Full-back
Born: Hackney, 28 December 1942.
5ft 8in; 10st 7lb.
Career: Chelsea (June 1960), Coventry City (November 1964, £35,000), Chelsea (May 1966, £45,000), Queen's Park Rangers (July 1967, £30,000), Plymouth Argyle (March 1971), Cambridge United (July 1973).
Honours: England Schoolboy and Youth international (3 caps), FA Cup runners-up medal 1967.
Chelsea debut: 24 October 1960. Appearances: League 82(2), FA Cup 7(1), League Cup 7(1), Fairs Cup 2; Goals: League Cup 1.
Originally signed from Chelsea Juniors and the elder brother of Ron, he was usually on the fringe of the first team, competing for the full-back spot with Eddie McCreadie, Ken Shellito or Marvin Hinton. Nevertheless, he chalked up some 300 games in his League

career. Later assistant manager at Queen's Park Rangers, FC Barcelona and Tottenham Hotspur before becoming manager of FC Barcelona.

HARRIS, Charles (1905-1909) Full-back/Centre-half
Born: Wanstead, 1 December 1885.
5ft 9in; 11st 4lb.
Career: Chelsea (1905).
Chelsea debut: 2 September 1905. Appearances: League 1, FA Cup 1.
Although Harris made only one appearance in League football, he was a stalwart of the reserve team for four seasons and was then appointed trainer of Swansea Town. He later returned to join the Stamford Bridge training staff to give more than 30 years' loyal service.

HARRIS, John (1945-1946) Centre-half/Full-back
Born: Glasgow, 30 June 1917.
5ft 10in; 12st.
Career: Swindon Town, Swansea Town (August 1934), Tottenham Hotspur (February 1939), Wolverhampton Wanderers (1939), Chelsea (August 1945, £5,000), Chester (player-manager April 1956).
Honours: Scotland wartime international, Football League Championship medal 1955.
Chelsea debut: 5 January 1946. Appearances: League 326, FA Cup 38; Goals: League 14.
After making 109 guest appearances in wartime football from 1943, John Harris was signed on a permanent basis and went on to give sterling service, first at centre-half and later at full-back, in the immediate post-war period. For most of his 14 seasons with the club he was a dominant figure on the field and an influential captain. He had led the team in their two wartime Wembley Cup Finals and was renowned for his hard tackling and shrewd positional sense. But for his comparative lack of inches he would have undoubtedly achieved more than his one wartime cap. He moved to Chester as player-manager in April 1956, subsequently joining Sheffield United in that capacity before beginning a long association with Sheffield Wednesday. His father was Neil Harris, who played for Swansea Town and Tottenham Hotspur.

HARRIS, Ronald E. (1961-1980) Defender
Born: Hackney, 13 November 1944.
5ft 8in; 11st 5lb.
Career: Hackney Schools, Chelsea (November 1961), Brentford (May 1980, free transfer).
Honours: England Schoolboy international (6 caps), England Youth, England Under-23 (4 caps), FA Cup winners' medal 1970, runners-up medal 1967, Football League Cup winners' medal 1965, runners-up medal 1972, European Cup-winners' Cup winners' medal 1971, FA Youth Cup winners' medal 1961. Also 1 FA Charity Shield appearance 1970.
Chelsea debut: 24 February 1962. Appearances: League 646(9), FA Cup 64, League Cup 46(2), Fairs Cup 14, European Cup-winners' Cup 13; Goals: League 13, European Cup-winners' Cup 1.
Nobody can equal Ron Harris' service over 19 seasons as a first-team player for Chelsea, during which he made more appearances than anyone else in the club's history. Throughout this time he was a pillar of the defence, whether at full-back or in the middle of the back line. A superbly fit and dedicated athlete, he joined the club as a junior in August 1960. He was a member

of the four Cup Final sides of his time, having already played in a winning FA Youth Cup team. And at Wembley, in 1967, he became the youngest man to captain an FA Cup Final side. A Chelsea legend, his strength in the tackle made 'Chopper' a respected and formidable opponent. He joined Brentford as player-coach after leaving Stamford Bridge and later managed Aldershot for six months in 1984.

HARRISON, Michael J. (1957-1962) Outside-left
Born: Ilford, 18 April 1940.
5ft 11½in; 11st 10lb.
Career: Chelsea (April 1957), Blackburn Rovers (September 1962, £18,000), Plymouth Argyle (September 1964), Luton Town (June 1968).
Honours: England Schoolboy international (1), England Under-23 (3 caps).
Chelsea debut: 15 April 1957. Appearances: League 61, Fairs Cup 3; Goals: League 8, Fairs Cup 1.
One of the many products of Chelsea's youth scheme, Harrison had the misfortune to be on the staff at a time when Frank Blunstone was the recognized first-team left-winger. Extremely quick and a direct attacker, he moved to Blackburn Rovers where, for five years, he was a regular first-team choice, making nearly 200 appearances.

HARROW, Jack Henry (1911-1926) Full-back
Born: Beddington, 8 October 1888; Died: 19 July 1958.
5ft 8½in; 11st 10lb.
Career: Mill Green Rovers, Croydon Common (1908), Chelsea (March 1911, £50), Retired (1926).
Honours: England international (2 caps), Football

League XI (1 appearance), FA Cup runners-up medal 1915.
Chelsea debut: 9 December 1911. Appearances: League 304, FA Cup 29; Goals: League 5.
One of Chelsea's most famous players, Harrow served the club for 27 years, first as a player and then on the training staff from which retired in 1938. His career was at its peak when it was interrupted by World War One, although he was demobilized from the Army in time to appear in the team which won the London Victory Cup in 1919. For eight years he was a pillar of the defence, playing mostly at left-back, and was acknowledged as one of the best players in this position

in the country. His strength lay in his defensive qualities. He was a strong tackler and had a sound positional sense. Originally he was signed as a wing-half but this, and his burning ambition to play at centre-forward, were soon forgotten. Almost certainly his total number of international caps would have been considerably increased but for the war. In December 1924, he received a hard facial blow from the ball which subsequently affected his eyesight, and his performance thereafter.

HARWOOD, Jack A. (1912-1913)   **Wing-half**
Born: Somerstown.
5ft 11in; 11st 10lb.

Career: Tooting Town, Southend United (1911), Chelsea (May 1912), Portsmouth (March 1913), Swansea Town (May 1922), Aberdare Athletic (August 1924), Barrow (October 1927).
Chelsea debut: 4 January 1913.Appearances: League 4.
Harwood's short spell at Stamford Bridge included four games as deputy for the injured Sam Downing. After his playing career ended he was trainer at Fulham for a time.

HATELEY, Anthony (1966-1967)   **Centre-forward**
Born: Derby, 13 June 1941.
6ft 1½in; 12st 7lb.
Career: Normanton Sports, Notts County (June 1958), Aston Villa (May 1963), Chelsea (October 1966, £100,000), Liverpool (July 1967, £100,000), Coventry City (September 1968), Birmingham City (August 1969), Notts County (November 1970), Oldham Athletic (July 1972), Bromsgrove Rovers, Prescot Town, Keyworth United.
Honours: FA Cup runners-up medal 1967, Fourth Division championship medal 1974.
Chelsea debut: 26 October 1966. Appearances: League 26(1), FA Cup 6; Goals: League 6, FA Cup 3.
Manager Tommy Docherty moved smartly to sign Hateley when Peter Osgood broke his right leg early in the 1966-7 season. Although he scored the goal in a semi-final tie against Leeds United which took Chelsea to their first Wembley Cup Final, he never justified his big fee at Stamford Bridge. One of the best headers of a ball in the game, he scored over 200 goals in a career which included seven different League clubs. He is the father of England international, Mark Hateley.

HAY, David (1974-1979)   **Midfield/Defender**
Born: Paisley, 29 January 1948.
5ft 11in; 11st 7lb.
Career: St Mirren's Boys Guild, Glasgow Celtic (1965), Chelsea (August 1974, £225,000), Retired (September 1979).
Honours: Scotland international (27 caps), Scotland Under-23 (3 caps), Scottish League XI (4 appearances), Scottish League Championship medals 1970, 1971, 1972, 1973, 1974, Scottish FA Cup winners' medals 1972, 1974, runners-up medals 1970, 1973, Scottish League Cup winners' medal 1970, runners-up medals 1971, 1972, 1973, 1974.
Chelsea debut: 17 August 1974. Appearances: League 107(1), FA Cup 6(1), League Cup 5; Goals: League 2, League Cup 1.
After a brilliant career in Scotland, during which he won every honour in the game, Hay's time at Chelsea was dogged by misfortune. Even before he arrived, he had experienced an eye injury (in an accident off the field), and later he had trouble with a knee which eventually brought about his premature retirement. At his best he was a dominating, aggressive midfield operator who could also play in any defensive position. He will be especially remembered for his outstanding performances for Scotland in the 1974 World Cup finals. After injury caused his retirement as a player in September 1979, he was appointed assistant manager of Motherwell two months later, and manager of the club in May 1982, before moving to Celtic as manager in July 1983. Appointed manager of St Mirren in March 1991.

89

HAYWOOD, Johnson William (1921-1924) Inside-forward
Born: Eckington.
5ft 8in; 10st 9lb.
Career: Eckington, Chelsea (March 1921), Halifax Town (May 1924), Yeovil & Petters, Portsmouth (May 1926), Barrow (November 1926), Scunthorpe United (October 1928).
Chelsea debut: 14 April 1922. Appearances: League 23; Goals: League 2.

After a promising start, Haywood failed to live up to his early promise. He began his first full season on the staff as a recognized first-team choice, but lost his place to Buchanan Sharp and never played regularly again.

HAZARD, Michael (1985-1990) Midfield
Born: Sunderland, 5 February 1960.
5ft 7in; 10st 5lb.
Career: Tottenham Hotspur (February 1978), Chelsea (September 1985, £310,000), Portsmouth (January 1990, £100,000), Swindon Town (September 1990).
Honours: FA Cup winners' medal 1982, UEFA Cup winners' medal 1984.
Chelsea debut: 21 September 1985. Appearances: League 78(3), FA Cup 4(2), League Cup 7(3), Full Members' Cup 5(1); Goals: League 9, FA Cup 1, League Cup 1, Full Members' Cup 1.
Hazard was a creative midfield player with great skill on the ball. A shrewd and accurate distributor, on his day, he could control the game from the middle of the park. Previously the whole of his professional career had been spent at Tottenham where, in his six years on the staff, he made less than 100 Legaue appearances.

HENDERSON, George Hunter (1905-1909) Half-back
Born: Ladhope (Selkirkshire), 2 May 1880.
Career: Queen's Park, Dundee, Glasgow Rangers, Middlesbrough, Chelsea (April 1905), Glossop (cs 1909).
Honours: Scotland international (1 cap), Scottish FA

Cup winners' medal 1903, runners-up medals 1904, 1905.
Chelsea debut: 16 April 1906. Appearances: League 60, FA Cup 4; Goals: League 1.
One of the first of many Scottish players who have found their way to Stamford Bridge, Henderson was an artistic, creative player, and also a strong player well known for his appetite for hard work. His Scotland cap came was against Ireland in 1904.

HEWITT, Thomas John (1911-1913) Full-back
Born: Connah's Quay, 26 April 1889; Died: Cardiff, 12 December 1980.
5ft 8in; 11st 10lb.
Career: Sandycroft (1906-07), Connah's Quay (1907-08), Saltney (July 1908), Wrexham (1910), Chelsea (March 1911, £350), South Liverpool (cs 1913), Swansea Town (cs 1914).
Honours: Wales international (8 caps).
Chelsea debut: 2 December 1911. Appearances: League 8.
Although winning three of his eight Welsh international caps whilst at Chelsea, Hewitt failed to break through into the senior side, partly as a result of the consistently good form of Walter Bettridge and Jock Cameron, but also through a series of injuries which kept him on the side-lines for much of his time at Stamford Bridge. He was appointed manager of Aberaman in June 1920.

HIGGS, Frank Jary (1928-30) Goalkeeper
Born: Willington (Northumberland), 1910.
6ft.
Career: Bedlington United, Seaton Delaval, Chelsea (October 1928), Linfield (Belfast) 1930, Barnsley (June 1931), Manchester City (June 1933), Aldershot (June 1933), Walsall (July 1934), Carlisle United (November 1935), Southend United (May 1937), Barrow (July 1938).
Honours: Irish FA Cup winners' medal.
Chelsea debut: 28 September 1929. Appearances: League 2.
Signed as cover for Sam Millington, Higgs made two first-team appearances but was unable to win a regular place and moved on after two years on the staff.

HILSDON, George Richard (1906-1912) Forward
Born: Bow (East London), 10 August 1885; Died: 7 September 1941.
Career: Boleyn Castle, South West Ham, British Empire, Clapton Orient, Luton Town, West Ham United, Chelsea (May 1906, free transfer), West Ham United (summer 1912, free transfer), Chatham Town (April 1919), Retired (May 1919).
Honours: England international (8 caps), Football League XI (2 appearances).
Chelsea debut: 1 September 1906. Appearances: League 150, FA Cup 14; Goals: League 98, FA Cup 9.
Signed at the age of 21 as an inside-forward, Hilsdon was soon converted into leading the attack, his powerful shooting winning him the nickname 'Gatling Gun' after he had scored five goals in his first League game for Chelsea, against Glossop, a feat which is still a club record. His 27 goals in his first season at Stamford Bridge was instrumental in the team winning promotion to the First Division for the first time. Then, after five successful years, his form deserted him. According to one writer he had been 'too sociable,

too careless with his strength and vitality'. Be that as it may, his return to West Ham revitalized the Upton Park team and his experience was of particular value to the youngsters on their staff. He played for them up to the outbreak of World War One in which he was badly affected by mustard-gas poisoning. The silhouette of a footballer which for many years adorned the old East Stand at Stamford Bridge was modelled on George Hilsdon, one of the most famous names in the club's history. A canary breeder, he also joined Fred Karno's Troop in 1924.

HINSHELWOOD, Walter Alexander (1951) Winger
Born: Lambeth, 27 October 1929.
Career: Sutton United (1945), Fulham (October 1946), Chelsea (January 1951, £20,000 part-exchange Jimmie Bowie), Fulham (May 1951), Reading (December 1952), Bristol City (February 1956), Millwall (June 1960), Canadian Football (cs 1961), Newport County (November 1961), Canterbury City, Deal Town.
Chelsea debut: 3 February 1951. Appearances: League 12, FA Cup 2; Goals: League 1.
Signed from Fulham, in part-exchange for Jimmy Bowie, Hinshelwood returned to the Craven Cottage club after only 15 weeks. Father of Paul and Martin Hinshelwood, the latter being appointed Chelsea reserve-team coach in 1985 after his playing career with Crystal Palace ended.

HINTON, Marvin (1963-1976)   **Defender**
Born: Norwood, 2 February 1940.
5ft 10¼in; 11st 11lb.
Career: Charlton Athletic (April 1952), Chelsea (August 1963, £30,000); Barnet (cs 1976), Crawley, Horsham, Peacehaven, Eastbourne United.
Honours: England Under-23 international (3 caps), FA Cup winners' medal 1970, runners-up medal 1967, Football League Cup winners' medal 1966. Also 1 FA Charity Shield appearance 1970.
Chelsea debut: 25 September 1963. Appearances: League 257(8), FA Cup 30(3), League Cup 22(3), Fairs Cup 13, European Cup-winners' Cup 5(2); Goals: League 3, European Cup-winners' Cup 1.
A cultured defender, Hinton was equally at home as a full-back or in the centre of defence. A member of Alf Ramsey's original 1966 World Cup squad, he possessed a fine positional sense. Indeed, 'Lou', as he was known, was also a most intelligent reader of the game. His long career at Chelsea was in the club's most successful era and he was a vital part of those days. He might have gone even further had he been rather more ambitious, for few contemporaries had more natural ability.

HITCHCOCK, Kevin Joseph (1988-)   **Goalkeeper**
Born: Custom House (London), 5 October 1962.
6ft 1in; 12st 10lb.
Career: Barking, Nottingham Forest (August 1983), Mansfield Town (loan), Mansfield Town (February 1984), Chelsea (March 1988, £250,000), Northampton Town (loan, December 1990).
Honours: Associate Members Cup winners' medal 1987.
Chelsea debut: 26 March 1988. Appearances: League 18, League Cup 1.
As manager Bobby Campbell's first signing, Hitchcock immediately took over the goalkeeping position which had been causing problems following Eddie Niedzwiecki's unfortunate retirement from the game. Then, just when he appeared to have established himself, Hitchcock, too, suffered injury which necessitated the signing of David Beasant and subsequently relegated Hitchcock to the role of deputy 'keeper.

HODDINOTT, Frank Thomas (1921-1923) Inside-forward
Born: Brecon, 29 November 1894; Died: 1980.
Career: Aberdare Athletic (1913), Watford (cs 1919), Chelsea (June 1921, £3,500), Crystal Palace (May 1923), Rhyl (cs 1926), New Brighton (May 1927), Newark Town (August 1928), Grantham Town (June 1931).
Honours: Wales international (2 caps).
Chelsea debut: 27 August 1921. Appearances: League 31, FA Cup 1; Goals: League 4.
Hoddinott had already won his two Welsh caps when he came to Chelsea. A direct inside-forward, he never fulfilled his reputation as a goalscorer during his short spell with the club, although it is fair to say that he was pitchforked into playing as an emergency centre-forward for most of his spell in the first team, due to an injury to Jack Cook.

HOLDEN, Arthur (1909-1910)   **Outside-left**
Born: Billingshurst, 23 September 1882.
5ft 7in; 11st.
Career: Portsmouth (cs 1903), Southend United (cs

1906), Plymouth Argyle (cs 1907), Chelsea (April 1909), Plymouth Argyle (1911).
Chelsea debut: 17 April 1909. Appearances: League 20; Goals: League 1.
Holden was a speedy winger who was first choice for his position during most of his short stay at Chelsea, but the signing of Marshall McEwan towards the end of the 1909-10 season ended his Football League career at Stamford Bridge.

HOLLINS, John William MBE (1963-1975 &
1983-1984) **Midfield/Defender**
Born: Guildford, 16 July 1946.
5ft 8in; 11st 7lb.
Career: Chelsea (July 1963), Queen's Park Rangers (June 1975, £80,000), Arsenal (July 1979), Chelsea (player-coach, June 1983).
Honours: England international (1 cap), England Under-23 (12 caps), Football League XI (3 appearances), FA Cup winners' medal 1970, runners-up medal 1967, Football League Cup winners' medal 1966, runners-up medal 1972, Second Division championship

medal 1984. European Cup-winners' Cup winners' medal 1971, runners-up medal 1980. Also 1 FA Charity Shield appearance 1970.
Chelsea debut: 25 September 1963. Appearances: League 465, FA Cup 51, League Cup 48, Fairs Cup 15, European Cup-winners' Cup 12; Goals: League 48, FA Cup 4, League Cup 7, Fairs Cup 1, European Cup-winners' Cup 4.
One of the great names in Chelsea's history, John Hollins quickly established himself as an outstanding, attacking midfield player whose energetic running, strong tackling and accurate distribution was a key factor in the most successful era of the club. It was a sad blow when he moved to Queen's Park Rangers in the summer of 1975, this following Chelsea's relegation to Division Two. Eight years later he returned as player-coach and his influence on and off the field made an immediate impact and was a major factor in the winning of the Second Division championship. Then, after two years in that role of John Neal's right-hand man, he was manager from June 1985 to March 1988. As a player he was one of the outstanding midfield men in the country, a fact never wholly recognized by the England selectors.

HOLTON, Patrick (1959-1960) **Full-back**
Born: Hamilton, 23 December 1935.
5ft 9in; 12st.
Career: Motherwell, Chelsea (March 1959, £6,000), Southend United (August 1960).
Chelsea debut: 28 March 1959. Appearances: League 1.
Holton never settled into the pattern of English League football and after his short stay with Chelsea he played a few games for Southend United.

HOPE, James P. (1930-1932) **Wing-half**
Born: East Wemyss.
5ft 7in; 10st 7lb.
Career: East Fife, South Shields (July 1928), Gateshead, Chelsea (June 1930), free transfer (May 1932).
Chelsea debut: 24 October 1931. Appearances: League 1.
Hope was a regular player in the reserve team for two seasons when he was unable to supplant Sam Irving, Willie Ferguson and Sid Bishop from the wing-half positions in the League side.

HORN, George (1909-1913) **Half-back**
Born: West Ham.
5ft 6½in; 10st 6lb.
Career: Tunbridge Wells Rangers, West Ham United, Chelsea (May 1909), Peterborough United (summer 1913, free transfer), Fletton United.
Chelsea debut: 2 April 1910. Appearances: League 2.
A sound wing-half, Horn was a regular member of the reserve team which twice won the South-East League Championship during his time at Chelsea.

HORTON, John William (1933-1937) **Outside-left**
Born: Castleford, 14 August 1905.
5ft 6½in; 11st.
Career: Castleford Town, Charlton Athletic (May 1926), Chelsea (March 1933), Crystal Palace (June 1937), Retired (cs 1939).
Honours: Third Division South championship medal 1929.

Chelsea debut: 18 March 1933. Appearances: League 59, FA Cup 7; Goals: League 15.
This stockily built winger had a reputation as a frequent scorer of goals, but he never quite justified this at Chelsea. He was the regular first-team choice for one season, but the signing of Willie Barraclough effectively ended his days in the League side at a time when no money or effort was spared in attempting to bring overdue success to Stamford Bridge.

HOUSEMAN, Peter M. (1962-1965)
Winger/Midfield/Full-back
Born: Battersea, 24 December 1945; Died: 19 March 1977.
5ft 8½in; 10st 8in.
Career: Battersea, Chelsea (December 1962), Oxford United (May 1975, £30,000).
Honours: FA Cup winners' medal 1970, European Cup-winners' Cup winners' medal 1971. Also 1 FA Charity Shield appearance 1970.
Chelsea debut: 21 December 1963. Appearances: League 252(17), FA Cup 25, League Cup 32(1), Fairs Cup 4, European Cup-winners' Cup 11; Goals: League 20, FA Cup 10, League Cup 4, Fairs Cup 1, European Cup-winners' Cup 4.

Houseman played an integral part in the Chelsea successes of the 1960s and early 1970s. Originally signing professional forms from the Juniors, he was primarily a left-winger whose accurate crosses produced many goals, but he could also operate effectively in midfield or at full-back. He was not a prolific goalscorer but he had a happy knack of finding the net in important FA Cup ties, his equalizer in the 1970 Wembley Final being a case in point. With his wife, Sally, he was tragically killed in a car crash hours after playing in a League game for Oxford United.

HOUSTON, Stewart Mackie (1967-1972)   Defender
Born: Dunoon, 20 August 1949.
5ft 11in; 12st 12lb.
Career: Port Glasgow Rangers, Chelsea (August 1967), Brentford (March 1972, £17,000), Manchester United (December 1973), Sheffield United (July 1980), Colchester United (player-coach August 1983).
Honours: Scotland international (1 cap), Scotland Under-23 (2 caps), Second Division championship medal 1975, Fourth Division championship medal 1982, FA Cup runners-up medal 1976.
Chelsea debut: 12 February 1968. Appearances: League 6(3), FA Cup 3, League Cup 1(1).
Houston's Chelsea career, which started so promisingly, was marred by a series of injuries. His fortunes improved after he left Stamford Bridge, first at Brentford and then Manchester United, where he made over 200 League appearances and won a Scotland cap. Later appointed coach at Plymouth Argyle, he moved to Colchester United, then Arsenal, where he became assistant manager.

HOWARD, Terry (1984-1987)   Defender
Born: Hornchurch, 26 February 1966.
6ft 1in; 11st 7lb.
Career: Chelsea (February 1984, £17,000), Crystal Palace (loan), Chester City (loan), Orient (March 1987).
Honours: England Youth international.
Chelsea debut: 16 April 1985. Appearances: League 6.
Howard was a tall defender who played either in the centre or on the flanks. A pillar of the reserve team for three seasons, where he was a regular goalscorer.

HUDSON, Alan Anthony (1968-1974 & 1983-1984)
Midfield
Born: Chelsea, 21 June 1951.
5ft 10½in; 12st 4lb.
Career: Chelsea (June 1968), Stoke City (January 1974, £240,000), Arsenal (December 1976), Seattle Sounders (October 1978), Chelsea (August 1983, £23,500), Stoke City (January 1984).
Honours: England international (2 caps), England Under-23 (10 caps), European Cup-winners' Cup winners' medal 1971, Football League Cup runners-up medal 1972. Also 1 FA Charity Shield appearance 1970.
Chelsea debut: 1 February 1969. Appearances: League 144(1), FA Cup 14, League Cup 16, European Cup-winners' Cup 13; Goals: League 10, League Cup 2, European Cup-winners' Cup 2.
Born and brought up in the King's Road, Chelsea, Hudson signed professional forms after being on the club's books as an apprentice. A most gifted player with an uncanny ability to pass the ball with pin-point accuracy, his two England caps were scant reward for

so much skill. One of the outstanding midfield players in the country in the early 1970s, he was a vital part of the Chelsea FA Cup side, although missing the Final through injury, and then went on to play some of the most effective football of his career at Stoke. Illness and injury prevented him playing his part in restoring Chelsea's fortunes when he returned to Stamford Bridge in 1983.

HUGHES, Harold James (1951-1952)   Centre-half
Born: Hinckley, 8 October 1929.
5ft 11½in; 13st.
Career: Symingtons, Southport (August 1950), Chelsea (February 1951), Bournemouth & Boscombe Athletic (June 1952), Gillingham (July 1958), Guildford City (1963).
Chelsea debut: 25 August 1951. Appearances: League 1.
A tall centre-half who came to Chelsea after his demobilization from the Army, as cover for John Harris, Hughes was unable to displace the Scot and moved on after 16 months.

HUGHES, Thomas A. (1965-1971)   Goalkeeper
Born: Dalmuir, 11 July 1947.
6ft 1in; 12st.
Career: Clydebank Juniors (1963), Chelsea (July 1965), Aston Villa (May 1971, £12,500), Brighton & Hove Albion (loan), Hereford United (August 1973).
Honours: Scotland Under-23 international (2 caps). Third Division championship medal 1972.
Chelsea debut: 19 November 1966. Appearances: League 11.
One of several goalkeepers who had the thankless task of understudying Peter Bonetti, Hughes ultimately moved on to seek regular League football. A capable 'keeper, he subsequently played more than 200 League games for Hereford United.

HUGHES, William Marshall (1948-1951)   Full-back
Born: Carmarthen, March 1918; Died: Birmingham, 16 June 1981.
5ft 10in; 12st 12lb.
Career: Archer Corinthians, Watchers Celtic, Birmingham (June 1935), Luton Town (July 1947), Chelsea (March 1948, £12,000), Hereford United (August 1951), Flint Town (January 1954), Retired (1955).
Honours: Wales international (10 caps).
Chelsea debut: 13 March 1948. Appearances: League 93, FA Cup 12.
Past his 30th birthday when he signed for Chelsea, this cultured full-back was an important addition to a side in the process of rehabilitation after World War Two. His total of international caps would have been much greater but for the war, during which he played for his country in many unofficial games. A good tackler and excellent distributor of the ball, especially with his educated left foot, he also played for the Great Britain team which beat the Rest of the World 6-1 at Hampden Park in 1947.

HUMPHREYS, Percy (1908-1909)   Inside-forward
Born: Cambridge, 3 December 1880; Died: Stepney, 13 April 1959.
Career: Cambridge St Mary's, Queen's Park Rangers (cs 1900), Leicester Fosse (June 1907), Chelsea (February 1908), Tottenham Hotspur (December 1909), Leicester Fosse (October 1911), Hartlepools United (player-manager cs 1912), Norwich City (November 1914).
Honours: England international (1 cap).
Chelsea debut: 29 February 1908. Appearances: League 45, FA Cup 1; Goals: League 13.
Humphreys was a strongly-built inside-forward who was noted for his dash and enthusiasm. As contemporary writers described him, he was 'a great trier'. Ironically, he is perhaps best remembered by Chelsea historians as the player who scored the vital goal for Spurs at White Hart Lane in the final match of the 1909-10 season, thus saving his own club from relegation but sending his previous employers back to Division Two.

HUNTER, George (1913-1914)   Wing-half
Born: Peshawar (India), August 1886; Died: February 1934.
5ft 7½in; 12st.
Career: Army football, Maidstone, Croydon Common (cs 1907), Aston Villa (February 1908), Oldham Athletic (January 1912), Chelsea (February 1913), Manchester United (March 1914), Portsmouth (August 1919).
Honours: Football League XI (2 appearances).
Chelsea debut: 1 March 1913. Appearances: League 30, FA Cup 2; Goals: League 2.
A stocky wing-half, Hunter was noted for his tough, vigorous tackling. As a result, although highly popular with his home supporters, he was not loved by opposing players and fans. One of the great characters of his day and noted comedian off the field, he burst into print with a light-hearted book about football. His somewhat fiery temperament made him a difficult customer to handle at times and it was this which led to his sudden and unexpected departure from Stamford Bridge. He was later banned *sine die* when with

Manchester United. He served with the Army in France and at Gallipoli.

HUTCHESON, John Hughes McGeavy (1934-1938) Wing-half
Born: Larbert, 31 March 1909.
5ft 10in; 11st 5lb.
Career: Falkirk, Chelsea (March 1934), Ipswich Town (June 1938) Crittall Athletic (June 1939).
Chelsea debut: 7 April 1934. Appearances: League 22; Goals: League 1.
A former miner who learned his football in Scottish junior circles, Hutcheson was a stalwart of the reserve side for some three seasons, deputizing competently for either Billy Mitchell or Harold Miller (both internationals). His career was effectively ended by cartilage trouble. Having been paid maximum compensation under the Football League's insurance scheme, he did, however, play for Ipswich Town in FA Cup ties and the Southern League in 1938.

HUTCHINGS, Christopher (1980-1983) Full-back/Midfield
Born: Winchester, 5 July 1957.
5ft 10in; 11st.
Career: Harrow Borough, Chelsea (July 1980, £5,000), Brighton & Hove Albion (November 1983, £50,000), Huddersfield Town (December 1987), Walsall (Aug 1990).

Chelsea debut: 31 October 1980. Appearances: League 83(4), FA Cup 7, League Cup 7; Goals: League 3.
A former bricklayer and part-time footballer, Hutchings was converted to full-back after beginning his professional career as an aggressive midfielder. Among his assets were boundless enthusiasm and a liking for moving forward to attack at every opportunity.

HUTCHINSON, Ian (1968-1976)   Striker
Born: Codnor (Derbyshire), 4 August 1948.
6ft 1in; 12st 12lb.
Career: Burton Albion, Cambridge United, Chelsea (July 1968, £5,000), Dartford (August 1976), Retired (1976).
Honours: England Under-23 international (2 caps), FA Cup winners' medal 1970. Also 1 FA Charity Shield appearance and 1 goal 1970.
Chelsea debut: 2 October 1968. Appearances: League 112(7), FA Cup 11, League Cup 10, European Cup-winners' Cup 3; Goals: League 44, FA Cup 6, League Cup 4, European Cup-winners' Cup 3.
A brave, thrustful striker, Hutchinson was always anxious to get into the centre of the action. A potentially great career was marred by a series of injuries which ultimately ended his football days, the latter part being played under severe physical handicap. Unpredictable, especially in the opposition's penalty area, he was a deadly marksman and a fine header of the ball. An immensely long throw (once measured at 112ft) was an added weapon in his armoury. It was his second equalizing goal in the 1970 Wembley Final which forced the replay against Leeds United.

HUXFORD Clifford G. (1955-1959)   Wing-half
Born: Stroud, 8 June 1937.
5ft 9in; 11st 12lb.
Career: Chelsea (February 1955), Southampton (May 1959, part-exchange Charlie Livesey), Exeter City (June 1967), Aldershot (1968).
Chelsea debut: 30 September 1958. Appearances: League 6, Fairs Cup 1.
Signing professional for Chelsea after two years as a junior, Huxford was a rugged, hard-tackling wing-half who was unable to win a first-team place, but moved on to Southampton where he played some 300 first-team games.

ILES, Robert J. (1978-1983)   Goalkeeper
Born: Leicester, 2 September 1955.
6ft 1in; 12st 7lb.
Career: AFC Bournemouth, Poole Town, Weymouth, Chelsea (June 1978, £10,000), Wealdstone (summer 1983). Yeovil Town, Bashley.
Chelsea debut: 7 October 1978. Appearances: League 14.
During his five years at Chelsea, he understudied such as Peter Bonetti, John Phillips, Petar Borota and Steve Francis. A tall 'keeper with a safe pair of hands he never received the extended trial in the first team which many felt that he deserved.

IRVING, Samuel Johnstone (1928-1932)   Wing-half
Born: Belfast, 28 August 1894; Died: 17 January 1969.
5ft 10in; 12st 1lb.
Career: Newcastle United (trialist), Galashiels United, Bristol City (cs 1913), Shildon (1919), Dundee (cs 1924), Cardiff City (August 1926), Chelsea (February 1928), Bristol Rovers (May 1932).
Honours: Northern Ireland international (18 caps), FA Cup winners' medal 1927.
Chelsea debut: 3 March 1928. Appearances: League 89, FA Cup 8; Goals: League 5.
Already past his 30th birthday when he came to Chelsea, Irving nevertheless played an important part in helping the club back to the First Division in the spring of 1930, his forceful and attacking flair proving

95

a great asset to a team which had previously lacked these qualities.

ISAAC, Robert C. (1983-1987) **Defender**
Born: Hackney, 30 November 1965.
Career: Chelsea (November 1983), Brighton & Hove Albion (February 1987, £35,000).
Honours: England Youth international.
Chelsea debut: 16 March 1985. Appearances: League 9, League Cup 2, Full Members' Cup 2.
Isaac was a central defender who could also play at full-back. He progressed through the Youth team and Reserves and performed impressively in the League side whenever called upon.

JACKSON, Alexander Skinner (1930-1932) **Winger**
Born: Renton, 12 May 1905; Died: Cairo, 15 November 1946.
5ft 10in; 10st 7lb.
Career: Renton School, Dumbarton Academy, Renton Victoria, Dumbarton (1922), Aberdeen (cs 1923), Bethlethem Star FC (USA) (1923-4), Aberdeen (1924), Huddersfield Town (May 1925), Chelsea (September 1930), Ashton Nationals (August 1932), Margate (February 1933), Le Touquet (France), Nice (France), Olympique (France).
Honours: Scotland international (17 caps), Football League Championship medal 1926, FA Cup runners-up medals 1928, 1930.
Chelsea debut: 15 September 1930. Appearances: League 65, FA Cup 12; Goals: League 26, FA Cup 4.
One of football's legendary figures, the 'Gay Cavalier' had already won a string of honours when he arrived at Chelsea, one of the first in a long line of big-money signings at that time. Primarily a winger, his speed, ball-control and directness of approach, allied to powerful shooting, made him a star box-office attraction (51,000 people watched his Stamford Bridge debut). Sadly, differences of opinion with the management abbreviated his career in London and he signed for the Lancashire non-League club, Ashton Nationals, never again to play League football after the age of 28. Jackson was killed in a road accident in Cairo, whilst serving as a major in the Army.

JACKSON, John (1933-1942) **Goalkeeper**
Born: Glasgow, 29 November 1906; Died: Nova Scotia, 12 June 1965.
5ft 9in; 10st 12lb.
Career: Boys Brigade Football, Kirkintilloch Rob Roy, Partick Thistle (cs 1926), Chelsea (June 1933), Guildford City (1945).
Honours: Scotland international (8 caps), Scottish League XI (4 appearances).
Chelsea debut: 26 August 1933. Appearances: League 49, FA Cup 2.
One of the best goalkeepers in Britain of his time, Jackson spent most of his days at Chelsea in the shadow of the great Vic Woodley, although he added a further four Scotland caps to a similar number won whilst with Partick Thistle. Along with Harry Hibbs he was one of the smallest goalkeepers to play international football, but he was, as his manager once said, 'brave as a lion, quick, safe, sure'. He played a further 74 games for Chelsea in wartime football, also guesting

for Brentford, before retiring. After the war he emigrated to Canada and became a golf professional, having played in the 1950 British Open Championship.

JACKSON, William (1928-1931) **Outside-left**
Born: Farnworth, 5 September 1902; Died: Blackpool, 1974.
5ft 9in; 10st 1lb.
Career: Leyland, Sunderland (May 1924), Leeds United (September 1925), West Ham United (May 1927), Chelsea (February 1928), Leicester City (May 1931), Bristol Rovers (May 1932), Cardiff City (May 1934), Watford (January 1935).
Chelsea debut: 31 March 1928. Appearances: League 26; Goals: League 6.
One of soccer's nomads, Jackson's three years at Chelsea were spent mostly in the reserve team understudying George Pearson. Given rare opportunities, he nevertheless performed creditably and was a strong winger with remarkable ball-control.

JASPER, Dale W. (1982-1986) **Midfield/Defender**
Born: Croydon, 14 January 1964.
Career: Chelsea (January 1982), Brighton & Hove Albion (May 1986, free transfer), Crewe Alexandra (July 1988).
Chelsea debut: 31 March 1984. Appearances: League

10, League Cup 3(1), Full Members' Cup 0(1).
Signed professional forms after joining Chelsea as a junior, Jasper was an elegant player in midfield and a versatile defender. His Chelsea days were marred by misfortune and injury, although he captained the Combination team to the Championship title in 1984-5.

JENKINS, Richard George Christopher (1924-1925) Outside-right
Born: London, 27 November 1903.
Career: Polytechnic, London University (1922-26), Oxford University (1927-28), Corinthians (1924-29), Chelsea (amateur) (1924-25).
Honours: England Amateur international (10 caps).
Chelsea debut: 30 August 1924. Appearances: League 4.
This famous Corinthian footballer, who signed amateur forms for Chelsea at the beginning of the 1924-5 season, assisted the club occasionally. He was a member of the Corinthians side which played Newcastle United in the famous FA Cup tie of 1927. He never played the game professionally.

JENKINS, Thomas Frederick (1949-1951) Inside-forward
Born: Stockton-on-Tees, 5 December 1925.
5ft 8in; 10st 8lb.
Career: Queen of the South, Chelsea (July 1949, £8,000), Barry Town (1951), Kettering Town, Leicester City (July 1954).
Chelsea debut: 25 February 1950. Appearances: League 5.
A slightly-built inside-forward, Jenkins moved into English football with a big reputation which he never justified. Most of his Chelsea days were spent in the reserve team. After leaving Stamford Bridge he returned to League football with Leicester City after a spell in the Southern League, but never played in their senior side.

JOHNSEN, Erland (1989-) Centre-half
Born: Fredrikstad (Norway), 5 April 1967.
6ft; 12st 10lb.
Career: Bayern Munich, Chelsea (December 1989, £306,000).
Honours: Norway international (18 caps), Full Members' Cup winners' medal 1990.
Chelsea debut: 9 December 1989. Appearances: League 24, FA Cup 4, Full Members' Cup 4.
As a Bayern Munich player, Johnsen was a member of the team which won the Bundesliga and reached the UEFA Cup semi-finals. At Chelsea, he soon established his place at centre-half in the first team, but injury early in his second season, allied to the establishment of the successful central defensive duo of Jason Cundy and Kenneth Monkou, made it difficult for him to become re-established.

JOHNSON, Gary J. (1978-1980) Striker/Midfield
Born: Peckham, 14 September 1959.
5ft 11in; 11st 7lb.
Career: South London Schools, Chelsea (August 1978), Crystal Palace (loan, 1978-9), Brentford (December 1980, £15,000), PG Rangers (SA), Aldershot (August 1985).
Chelsea debut: 15 January 1979. Appearances: League 16(3), FA Cup 1(1), League Cup 1; Goals: League 9.
Johnson joined Chelsea as a South London schools player, signing apprentice forms in May 1976. Primarily a striker, he promised more than he achieved

and at one time seemed on the verge of establishing a permanent first-team place.

JOHNSON, Geoffrey H. (1912-1913) Full-back
Born: Fulham.
5ft 10in; 12st.
Career: Clapton Orient (1910), Chelsea (March 1912), Portsmouth (cs 1913), Bournemouth & Boscombe Athletic (1914), Merthyr Town.
Chelsea debut: 16 March 1912. Appearances: League 4, FA Cup 1.
A full-back signed as cover for Walter Bettridge and Jock Cameron, Johnson was unable to displace either. The signing of Jimmy Sharp further restricted his opportunities in the senior side.

JOHNSTONE, Derek J. (1983-1985) Striker
Born: Dundee, 4 November 1953.
6ft; 13st 2lb.
Career: St Francis Boys' Club, St Columba's (Dundee), Glasgow Rangers (July 1970), Dundee United (loan), Chelsea (September 1983, £30,000), Glasgow Rangers (January 1985).
Honours: Scotland international (14 caps), Scotland Schoolboys, Youth & Amateur, Scotland Under-23 (6 caps), Scottish League XI (1 appearance), Scottish League Championship medals 1975, 1976, 1978, Scottish FA Cup winners' medals 1973, 1976, 1978, 1979, 1981, runners-up medal 1971, Scottish League Cup winners' medals 1971, 1978, 1979, 1982, runners-up medal 1983, European Cup-winners' Cup winners' medal 1972.
Chelsea debut: 24 February 1984. Appearances: League 1(3).
Johnstone was a famous Scottish international striker who was signed, at the age of 29, to provide cover for Kerry Dixon and David Speedie. In fact he had little opportunity to make his mark during 17 months in London. Appointed Patrick Thistle manager July 1986.

JONES, Evan (1909-1911) Inside-forward
Born: Trehaford (Pontypridd), 1889.
5ft 8in; 11st 10lb.
Career: Aberdare, Mardy, Chelsea (May 1909), Oldham Athletic (February 1911), Bolton Wanderers (May 1912), Newport County (Wartime guest), Swansea Town (August 1919), Aberdare (cs 1920), Llanbradach (cs 1921).
Honours: Wales international (7 caps)
Chelsea debut: 11 September 1909. Appearances: League 21; Goals: League 4.
An ebullient character, noted for his singing as well as his footballing ability, who, after an extended run in the first team when George Hilsdon was injured, was unable to stake a regular claim. He continued to score goals regularly in the reserve team before moving to Oldham Athletic.

JONES, Joseph Patrick (1982-1985) Defender
Born: Llandudno, 4 March 1955.
5ft 10in; 11st 7lb.
Career: Wrexham (January 1973), Liverpool (July 1975), Wrexham (October 1978), Chelsea (October 1982, £34,500), Huddersfield Town (August 1985, £35,000), Wrexham (August 1987).
Honours: Wales international (72 caps), Wales Under-23 (4 caps), Football League Championship medals

1976, 1977, Second Division championship medal 1984, European Cup winners' medal 1977, FA Cup runners-up medal 1977.
Chelsea debut: 30 October 1982. Appearances: League 76(2), FA Cup 5, League Cup 8; Goals: League 2.
Joey Jones had already had an eventful career with both his previous clubs before joining a Chelsea team where morale was low and success elusive. At once he helped to restore both these ingredients by his attitude in the dressing-room and his positive approach on the field. If lacking in the finer skills, his determination not to accept defeat lightly turned many a game and few players established such an immediate and obvious rapport with the supporters. A resourceful defender whether at full-back or in the centre of the defence.

JONES, Keith A. (1983-1987)   **Midfield**
Born: Dulwich, 14 October 1965.
5ft 9in; 10st 11lb.
Career: Chelsea (August 1983), Brentford, (September 1987, £40,000).
Honours: England Schoolboy international.
Chelsea debut: 26 March 1983. Appearances: League 43(9), FA Cup 1, League Cup 9(2), Full Members' Cup 4(1); Goals: League 7, League Cup 3.
A gifted and creative performer in midfield with a flair

for scoring spectacular goals, Jones progressed through the junior and reserve ranks to have several spells of first-team experience. Won a Robinson's Barley Water regional award for Young Player of the Month in December 1984.

JONES, Thomas Benjamin (1947-1953)   Outside-left
Born: Frodsham, 23 March 1920; Died: December 1972.
5ft 8½in; 12st 3lb.
Career: Ellesmere Port, Tranmere Rovers (1946), Chelsea (November 1947), Accrington Stanley (July 1953), Dartford (July 1954).
Chelsea debut: 29 November 1947. Appearances: League 55, FA Cup 7; Goals: League 11, FA Cup 2.
For most of his time at Chelsea, Benny Jones was on the fringe of the first team. A most popular player with the fans, he was noted for his wholehearted, bulldozing attacking play down the left-wing. Heavily-built, he possessed a strong shot, especially from his left foot, which made him a regular scorer of goals.

KELL, Leonard William (1952-1954)   Inside-forward
Born: Billingham, 27 May 1932.
5ft 8in; 10st 10lb.
Career: Chelsea (March 1952), Norwich City (June 1954, £2,000), Worcester City (1955), Poole Town (1957), Scarborough Town (1961), South Coast United (Wales) 1963, Lowestoft Town (1965).
Chelsea debut: 8 September 1953. Appearances: League 3.
Kell graduated to the ranks of full professional after four years as an apprentice on the Stamford Bridge staff. His time at Chelsea was spent almost entirely in the junior and reserve teams with Johnny McNichol and Les Stubbs the established first-team inside-forwards.

KEMBER, Stephen Dennis (1971-1975)   Midfield
Born: Croydon, 8 December 1948.
5ft 8in; 11st.

Career: Croydon School, Crystal Palace (December 1965), Chelsea (September 1971, £170,000), Leicester City (July 1975, £80,000), Crystal Palace (October 1978), Vancouver Whitecaps (1980), Whyteleafe.
Honours: England Under-23 international (3 caps), Second Division championship medal 1979.
Chelsea debut: 25 September 1971. Appearances: League 125(5), FA Cup 10(1), League Cup 9; Goals: League 13, League Cup 2.
A tireless runner in midfield and a strong tackler, Kember's time at Chelsea coincided with the fragmentation of the 1970 and 1971 Cup-winning squads and with a difficult financial period in the club. As a result he was rarely able to do justice to his considerable ability. After retiring from playing he was caretaker manager of Crystal Palace for a spell.

KENNEDY, George (1908-1910) Half-back
Born: Dumfries, c.1885.
5ft 6in; 11st 3lb.
Career: Maxwellstown Volunteers, Lincoln City (cs 1906), Chelsea (May 1908), Brentford (cs 1910).
Chelsea debut: 10 October 1908. Appearances: League 10, FA Cup 2.
Spending only two seasons at Stamford Bridge, Kennedy deputized for Bob McRoberts at centre-half in several matches and also appeared in both wing-half positions.

KEVAN, Derek Tennyson (1963) Centre/Inside-forward
Born: Ripon, 6 March 1935.
6ft 1in; 13st 8lb.
Career: Ripon County, Ripon YMCA, Bradford (October 1952), West Bromwich Albion (July 1953), Chelsea (March 1963, £45,000), Manchester City (August 1963, £40,000), Crystal Palace (July 1965), Peterborough United (March 1966), Luton Town (December 1966), Stockport County (March 1967), Macclesfield Town (August 1968), Boston United (October 1968), Stourbridge (1968-69) Ansells FC (1969).
Honours: England international (14 caps), England Under-23 (4 caps), Football League XI, Fourth Division championship medal 1967.
Chelsea debut: 23 March 1963. Appearances: League 7; Goals: League 1.
Kevan's five-month sojourn at Chelsea was punctuated by the winning of promotion from Division Two, as well as by differences of opinion with manager Tommy Docherty. A superbly built player, he scored nearly 250 goals in his League career, well over half of them for West Brom, the only club he served for more than two seasons.

KEY, George (1905-1909) Wing-half
Born: Dennistoun, 1882.
5ft 6in; 11st.
Career: Heart of Midlothian, Chelsea (August 1905), Retired (cs 1909).
Honours: Scotland Schoolboy international.
Chelsea debut: 2 September 1905. Appearances: League 54, FA Cup 2; Goals: League 2.
Chelsea's first right-half, 'Geordie' Key had the reputation of possessing an inexhaustible supply of energy. No cause was ever lost for him and he only vacated his first-team spot through injury early in the 1905-06 season. However, he was then unable to

displace George Henderson and was never an automatic choice afterwards.

KIRKUP, Joseph R. (1966-1968) Full-back
Born: Hexham, 17 December 1939.
5ft 11in; 12st 4lb.
Career: Hickley Juniors, West Ham United (May 1957), Chelsea (March 1966, £35,000) Southampton (February 1968, part-exchange David Webb), Durban City (player-coach, February 1974).
Chelsea debut: 12 March 1966. Appearances: League 48(5), FA Cup 6(2), League Cup 3, Fairs Cup 5; Goals: League 2.
A tall, stylish full-back, he became an important member of Chelsea's first-team squad during his two years with the club before manager Dave Sexton's exchange deal which brought the more aggressive Dave Webb to Stamford Bridge.

KIRWAN, John (1905-1908) Outside-left
Born: Wicklow, 1878; Died: 9 January 1959.
5ft 6½in; 10st 6lb.
Career: Southport, Everton (July 1898), Tottenham Hotspur (July 1899), Chelsea (May 1905), Clyde (May 1908).
Honours: Ireland international (17 caps), FA Cup winners' medal 1901.
Chelsea debut: 2 September 1905. Appearances: League 73, FA Cup 3; Goals: League 17, FA Cup 1.

Chelsea's famous outside-left for the club's first two seasons, 'Jock' Kirwan was fast, an accurate crosser of the ball and a regular goalscorer. A great character and favourite with the crowd, he won four of his Irish caps whilst at Stamford Bridge.

KITCHENER, Raymond Alan (1954-1956) Outside-left
Born: Letchworth, 31 October 1930.
5ft 9in; 11st.
Career: Letchworth Town (amateur), Hitchin Town (amateur), Chelsea (July 1954), Norwich City (September 1956), Biggleswade Town (July 1957), Amesbury Rovers, Retired (1965).
Chelsea debut: 11 February 1956.Appearances: League 1.
A regular reserve player for his two seasons at Chelsea, his first professional club, Kitchener understudied Frank Blunstone, and the further presence of amateur Jim Lewis meant that he had little prospect of ever gaining a regular first-team place.

KNOX, Thomas (1962-1965) Outside-left
Born: Glasgow, 5 September 1939.
5ft 7½in; 10st 4lb.
Career: East Stirling, Chelsea (June 1962, £5,000), Newcastle United (February 1965, £10,000), Mansfield Town (March 1967), Northampton Town (November 1967), St Mirren (June 1972), Tonbridge.
Chelsea debut: 22 September 1962. Appearances: League 20, League Cup 1.
Knox joined Chelsea from East Stirling two months after Eddie McCreadie had arrived from the same club. Having remained on the fringe of the first team for three years, he sought his fortune with Newcastle United, but again failed to establish himself as a regular and moved into Third Division football two years later.

LAKE, George (1913-1918) Wing-half
Born: Manchester; Died: France 1918.
5ft 8in; 10st.
Career: Chelsea (1913).
Chelsea debut: 14 April 1914. Appearances: League 1.
Lake signed professional early in the 1913-14 season after a period on trial. Any chance of establishing himself in the first team was ended by the outbreak of World War One and he was one of the last men to be killed in action before the signing of the Armistice.

LANGLEY, Thomas W. (1975-1980) Striker
Born: Lambeth, 8 February 1958.
5ft 11in; 11st 7lb.
Career: Chelsea (March 1975), Queen's Park Rangers (August 1980, £425,000), Crystal Palace (March 1981), AEK Athens, Coventry City (March 1984), Wolverhampton Wanderers (July 1984), Aldershot (loan), Aldershot (August 1986), Exeter City (cs 1988), Slough Town (1989).
Honours: England Under-21 international (1 cap), England Schoolboy & Youth.
Chelsea debut: 9 November 1974. Appearances: League 129(13), FA Cup 6, League Cup 4; Goals: League 40, FA Cup 2, League Cup 1.
Langley made his Football League debut, against Leicester City, when he was only 16 years 9 months old, four months before he signed professional forms. An enthusiastic, fast and totally committed player, for three difficult seasons he bore the brunt of leading the Chelsea attack, often in discouraging circumstances and in the light of much unfair criticism.

LANGTON, Joseph (1919-1922) Wing-half
Born: Crook, County Durham.
5ft 8in; 9st.
Career: Chelsea (October 1919, free transfer 1922).
Chelsea debut: 2 May 1921. Appearances: League 3.
During his three years on the staff, Langton was a regular member of the reserve team but could not displace such men as Tommy Meehan, Tom Wilding and David Cameron from the senior side.

LAVERICK, Robert M. (1955-1959) Outside-left
Born: Trimdon, Co Durham, 11 June 1938.
5ft 11in; 12st 6lb.
Career: Chelsea (June 1955), Everton (February 1959, free transfer), Brighton & Hove Albion (June 1960), Coventry City (July 1962).
Honours: England Youth international.
Chelsea debut: 2 February 1957.Appearances: League 7.
Laverick joined Chelsea as a 15-year-old groundstaff boy before signing professional. A powerful, sturdily built winger of direct approach, he was contemporary with Frank Blunstone, Jim Lewis and Mike Block and therefore found that few first-team opportunities came his way.

LAW, Thomas (1925-1939) Left-back
Born: Glasgow, 1 April 1908; Died: February 17 February 1976.
5ft 10in; 12st.

Career: Claremont FC, Bridgeton Waverley (Glasgow), Chelsea (June 1925, £10), free transfer (May 1939).
Honours: Scotland international (2 caps)
Chelsea debut: 18 September 1926. Appearances: League 293, FA Cup 26; Goals: League 15, FA Cup 4.
One of the most distinguished players in Chelsea's history, Law's entire professional career was spent at Stamford Bridge. Stockily built, he concealed his lack of pace with shrewd positional play. He was a fine passer of the ball and his constructive ideas launched many attacks from deep in his own half of the field. Strangely, he was selected only twice by the Scotland selectors, on each occasion to play against England at Wembley, one of these being in 1928 for the team which won 5-1 and were dubbed the 'Wembley Wizards'. For most of his time in the Chelsea side he was also the recognized penalty-taker, seldom failing from the spot. He continued to live in London until the time of his death and remained a regular and familiar figure at The Bridge.

LAWTON, Thomas (1945-1947)   Centre-forward
Born: Bolton, 6 October 1919.
6ft; 12st 8lb.
Career: Bolton Schools football, Hayes Athletic, Rossendale United, Bolton Wanderers (amateur), Sheffield Wednesday (amateur, 1935), Burnley (amateur, 1936), Burnley (October 1936), Everton (January 1937), Chelsea (November 1945, £11,500), Notts County (November 1947, £20,000), Brentford (March 1952), Brentford (player-manager, January 1953), Arsenal (September 1953), Kettering Town (player-manager, February 1956-April 1957).
Chelsea debut: 5 January 1946. Appearances: League 42, FA Cup 11; Goals: League 30, FA Cup 5.
One of football's most famous centre-forwards, Tommy Lawton was magnificently built, a brilliant header of the ball and an extremely skilful ball player with the most delicate footwork for such a big man. One of those players whose career was mutilated by World War Two, (15 wartime caps) he was one of Chelsea's big-money signings designed to bring the game's top honours to Stamford Bridge. Unhappily, he fell into dispute with the management after only one normal peacetime season and then became Britain's first £20,000 transfer when he moved, perhaps unwisely, into Third Division football with Notts County. At his peak, both before and after the war, he was recognized as the finest centre-forward in the game. He managed both Brentford, briefly, and Notts County from November 1963 to April 1964, when appointed a club director. He was then coach and chief scout to that club from October 1968 to April 1970.

LE SAUX, Graeme Pierre (1988-) Full-back/Midfield
Born: Harrow, 17 October 1968.
5ft 7in; 11st 2lb.
Career: St Paul's (Jersey), Chelsea (December 1988).
Honours: England Under-21 international (4 caps), England Youth.
Chelsea debut: 13 May 1989. Appearances: League 28(8), FA Cup 3(1), League Cup 4(3), Full Members' Cup 4; Goals: League 5, League Cup 1.
Chelsea discovered Le Saux in the comparative obscurity of Channel Islands football and in less than 18 months he had graduated to the first team. His immense promise was soon acknowledged at national

level, too, as his obvious talents blossomed. A competent defender at left-back, almost certainly his future lies as a midfield player whose speed and great acceleration have already caused alarm and embarrassment to some of the strongest defences in the country.

LEADBETTER, James Hunter (1949-1952) Inside-forward
Born: Edinburgh, 15 July 1928.
5ft 8½in; 9st 10lb.
Career: Edinburgh Thistle, Chelsea (July 1949), Brighton & Hove Albion (August 1952), Ipswich Town (June 1955).
Honours: Football League Championship medal 1962, Second Division championship medal 1961, Third Division South championship medal 1957.
Chelsea debut: 12 April 1952. Appearances: League 3.
Pencil-slim Scottish ball-playing inside-forward, Jimmy Leadbetter spent three seasons at Chelsea without his true potential being unearthed. After more than 100 games with Brighton he went on to win fame with Ipswich Town's team which won three League titles in six years, playing as a 'withdrawn' left-winger, a tactical role created for him by his manager Alf Ramsey.

LEE, Colin (1980-1987)   Centre-forward/Full-back
Born: Torquay, 12 June 1956.
6ft 1in; 11st 9lb.
Career: Bristol City (June 1974), Hereford United (November 1974), Torquay United (January 1977), Tottenham Hotspur (October 1977), Chelsea (January 1980, £200,000), Brentford (player-coach July 1987, £17,500).

Honours: Second Division championship medal 1984, Full Members' Cup winners' medal 1986.
Chelsea debut: 1 March 1980. Appearances: League 167(18), FA Cup 12, League Cup 20(4), Full Members' Cup 1(1); Goals: League 36, FA Cup 2, League Cup 1, Full Members' Cup 2.

For the first part of his career, Lee was recognized as a striker (32 goals from 99 League games before his arrival at Stamford Bridge), but the advent of David Speedie and Kerry Dixon limited his chances in the forward line and he developed into a sound, solid full-back, occupying that place during the latter part of the 1983-4 Second Division championship season with distinction. However, in the 1986 Full Members' Cup Final he was again pressed into service as a forward and responded by scoring twice. Manager of Watford 1990.

LEE, David John (1988-)   **Defender/Midfield**
Born: Bristol, 26 November 1969.
6ft 3in; 12st 7lb.
Career: Chelsea (June 1988).
Honours: England Under-21 international (6 caps), England Youth, Second Division championship medal 1989, Full Members' Cup winners' medal 1990.
Chelsea debut: 1 October 1988. Appearances: League 52(19), FA Cup 1(4), League Cup 6(2), Full Members' Cup 5(1); Goals: League 6, League Cup 1, Full Members' Cup 1.
Lee progressed from the junior ranks to first-team status in little over two years after his arrival at Stamford Bridge as a 17-year-old. Within months he had appeared in defence, midfield and attack. Indeed, it is this versatility which has largely prevented him from establishing a claim to a regular place in the senior side, although he remains an indispensable member of the squad.

LEE, John (1920-1924)   **Outside-left**
Born: Sheffield, 1890; Died: Hull, 10 August 1955.
5ft 10¼in; 11st 2lb.
Career: Bird-in-Hand (Sheffield), Hull City (cs 1913), Chelsea (February 1920, £1,500), Watford (cs 1924), Rotherham United (June 1925).
Chelsea debut: 13 March 1920. Appearances: League 7; Goals: League 1.
Signed for a relatively large fee, Lee won an immediate first-team place but failed to adjust to First Division football, playing mostly in the reserve team during his Stamford Bridge career.

LEWINGTON, Raymond (1974-1979)   **Midfield**
Born: Lambeth, 7 September 1956.
5ft 7in; 10st 13lb.
Career: Chelsea (February 1974), Vancouver Whitecaps (February 1979, £40,000), Wimbledon (September 1979), Fulham (March 1980), Sheffield United (July 1985), Fulham (player-manager July 1986).
Chelsea debut: 21 February 1976. Appearances: League 80(5), FA Cup 4, League Cup 3; Goals: League 4.
A ball-winning midfielder who first joined Chelsea as a schoolboy, Lewington was an ever-present in the 1976-7 Second Division promotion-winning team, but lacked the necessary pace to establish himself in the top class and was not part of manager Danny Blanchflower's plans for Chelsea's future. He spent a brief period in North American football before returning to this country to resume his Football League career. Player-manager of Fulham 1986-90.

LEWIS, Frederick Arthur (1946-1953)   **Left-back**
Born: Broughton Gifford (Wiltshire), 27 July 1923.
5ft 8in; 10st 12lb.
Career: Aylesbury Town, Chelsea (March 1946), Colchester United (June 1953).
Chelsea debut: 31 August 1946. Appearances: League 23, FA Cup 3.
A compact full-back with constructive ideas, Lewis came to Chelsea following demobilization from the Royal Navy. After a promising start he was unable to command a regular first-team place and spent most of his seven seasons on the staff in the Reserves.

LEWIS, James Leonard (1952-1958)
Winger/Centre-forward
Born: Hackney, 26 June 1927.
5ft 11in; 12st.
Career: Walthamstow Avenue (November 1950), Leyton Orient (amateur), Walthamstow Avenue, Chelsea (amateur, September 1952), Walthamstow Avenue (cs 1958), Eton Manor, Ilford, Leyton.
Honours: England Amateur international, Football League Championship medal 1955.
Chelsea debut: 4 October 1952. Appearances: League 90, FA Cup 5; Goals: League 38, FA Cup 2.
One of the famous amateur players who have assisted Chelsea down the years, Lewis was also one of the most prolific of goalscoring wingers. In the 1954-5 Championship season he shared the outside-left berth with Frank Blunstone. Of direct method he possessed both speed and clever footwork. The son of James William Lewis, also an England Amateur international player, he was presented with an illuminated address in November 1959 to commemorate his distinguished career at Stamford Bridge over six seasons.

LINFOOT, Frederick (1920-1924)   **Outside-right**
Born: Whitley Bay, 1901.
5ft 11in; 11st 1lb.
Career: Newcastle United Swifts, Smith's Dock, Leeds City (December 1918), Lincoln City (October 1919), Chelsea (July 1920), Fulham (March 1924).
Chelsea debut: 4 September 1920. Appearances: League 34, FA Cup 7; Goals: League 1.
Linfoot remained on the fringe of the first-team during his four seasons on the Chelsea staff at a time when a series of different players were competing for the right-wing spot.

LIVESEY, Charles Edward (1959-1961) Centre-forward
Born: West Ham, 6 February 1938.
5ft 11½in; 12st 8lb.

Career: Wolverhampton Wanderers (amateur), Southampton (March 1956), Chelsea (May 1959, £10,000, part-exchange for Cliff Huxford), Gillingham (August 1961, £5,500), Watford (October 1962), Northampton Town (August 1964), Brighton & Hove Albion (September 1965).
Chelsea debut: 22 August 1959. Appearances: League 39, FA Cup 2, League Cup 1; Goals: League 17.
Livesey was a robust centre-forward who was noted for his brisk and enthusiastic approach. Despite a most respectable scoring ratio, he never fully acclimatized to First Division football and moved on when losing his first-team place to Ron Tindall. He scored over 100 goals in his Football League career of some 360 games.

LIVINGSTONE, William Rennison (1955-1959) Centre-half
Born: Greenock, 8 February 1929.
6ft 1½in; 12st 8lb.
Career: Ardeer Recreation, Reading (April 1949), Chelsea (June 1955), Brentford (July 1959), Hastings United (July 1960).
Chelsea debut: 15 February 1956. Appearances: League 20, FA Cup 2.
A powerfully-built 'stopper' centre-half, Livingstone proved a reliable deputy following the retirement, through injury, of Stan Wicks and before the signing of John Mortimore. Most of his time at Chelsea, however, was spent in the reserve team.

LLOYD, Barry D. (1966-1969)   **Inside-forward**
Born: Hillingdon, 19 February 1949.
5ft 7½in; 10st 5lb.
Career: Hillingdon Borough, Chelsea (February 1966), Fulham (January 1969, £30,000), Hereford United (October 1976), Brentford (June 1977).
Honours: England Youth international.
Chelsea debut: 10 April 1967. Appearances: League 8(2).
Lloyd joined Chelsea as an apprentice from his local club. Unable to win a first-team place at a time when Chelsea had a surfeit of talent on the books, he moved on to Fulham when John Dempsey made the reverse move and went on to play over 250 games for the Cottagers. Appointed manager of Brighton and Hove Albion in January 1987.

LOCKE, Gary R. (1971-1983)   **Full-back**
Born: Kingsbury, 12 July 1954.
5ft 11in; 11st 5lb.
Career: Chelsea (July 1971), Crystal Palace (January 1983).
Chelsea debut: 30 September 1972. Appearances: League 270(2), FA Cup 24, League Cup 21; Goals: League 3, FA Cup 1.
A product of the Chelsea youth scheme, Locke was a pillar of the defence for 11 seasons at a time when the club was in severe financial difficulty, which was reflected by a marked lack of success on the field. As a result, he often failed to win the credit he deserved. Further, his career was disrupted by injuries. At his best he was a sound defensive player with an attacking flair, his speedy overlapping runs leading to goals on many occasions.

LOGAN, Thomas (1913-1920)   **Centre-half**
Born: Burnhead (Renfrewshire), 17 August 1888.

5ft 11in; 13st 4lb.
Career: Arthurlie, Falkirk, Chelsea (May 1913, £2,500), Retired (1921).
Honours: Scotland international (1 cap), Scottish FA Cup winners' medal 1913, FA Cup runners-up medal 1915.
Chelsea debut: 6 September 1913. Appearances: League 107, FA Cup 10; Goals: League 7, FA Cup 1.

Logan was a fine resourceful centre-half whose career was bisected by World War One, at a time when he was at his peak and well capable of adding to his undeserved tally of only one international cap. A powerful defender, he was never averse to moving forward to lend weight to attack, this in the days before the alteration of the offside law.

LUKE, George (1967-1968)   **Wing-half**
Born: Hetton-le-Hole (Co Durham), 9 November 1948; Died: December 1968.
Career: Newcastle United, Chelsea (March 1967), Durban City (August 1968).
Honours: England Schoolboy international (6 caps).
Chelsea debut: 9 May 1967. Appearances: League 1.
Contemporary with such as John Hollins, Ron Harris and John Boyle, Luke was unable to win a first-team place despite his undoubted ability and sought his fortune in South African football after little more than a year at Stamford Bridge.

LYON, Frank (1907-1908)   **Full-back**
Born: Crewe, 23 September 1879.
5ft 8in; 11st 3lb.
Career: Stockport County (cs 1905), Watford (amateur), Queen's Park Rangers, Chelsea (March 1907), Crewe Alexandra (cs 1908).
Chelsea debut: 14 September 1907. Appearances: League 6.
Lyon started the 1907-08 season as first choice at right-back but the arrival of Jock Cameron limited his chances to become established. Then injury forced his early retirement from the game. Noted for his powerful

kicking, he was also a sprinter who won many prizes at athletics meetings in this country. He subsequently opened a business in Crewe.

McALLISTER, Kevin (1985-)   **Winger**
Born: Falkirk, 8 November 1962.
5ft 5in; 11st.
Career: Falkirk, Chelsea (May 1985, £34,000), Falkirk (loan).
Honours: Full Members' Cup winners' medals 1986, 1990, Second Division championship medal 1989.
Chelsea debut: 14 September 1985. Appearances: League 78(31), FA Cup 3(2), League Cup 9(2), Full Members' Cup 11(4); Goals: League 7, FA Cup 1, League Cup 2, Full Members' Cup 3.

A lightweight winger with good ball-control and a wide range of skills, McAllister possessed a fine turn of speed but his chances at Stamford Bridge were limited by the consistent form of Pat Nevin with his greater scoring ability, until his fellow Scot moved to Everton in July 1988.

McANDREW, Anthony (1982-1984)   **Defender/Midfield**
Born: Lanark, 11 April 1956.
5ft 11½in; 13st 2lb.
Career: Middlesbrough (August 1973), Vancouver Whitecaps (1976), Chelsea (August 1982, £92,500), Middlesbrough (September 1984), Darlington (May 1986), Hartlepool United (March 1989). Assistant manager Darlington May 1991.
Honours: Second Division championship medal 1984.
Chelsea debut: 4 September 1982. Appearances: League 20, FA Cup 1, League Cup 2; Goals: League 4.
A solid player, McAndrew's Chelsea career was nevertheless dogged by a series of injuries. His signing was designed to add experience to the squad and he captained the side for a period during the 1983-4 championship season. After recovering full fitness he was unable to win back his place and soon returned

to Middlesbrough, where he made nearly 300 senior appearances for the Teesside club.

MACAULAY, James Austin Russell (1946-1951)
Wing-half
Born: Edinburgh, 19 October 1922.
5ft 9in; 11st 6lb.
Career: Edinburgh City, Chelsea (October 1946), Aldershot (August 1951).
Chelsea debut: 19 October 1946. Appearances: League 86, FA Cup 8; Goals: League 5.
Macaulay first came to Chelsea as a junior in 1940-41 and then signed professional forms on demobilization from the RAF in November 1946. A civil servant and part-time player, he was a strong, attacking wing-half in the immediate post-war period but lost his place to Frank Mitchell.

MACAULAY, Robert (1932-1936) **Full-back**
Born: Wishaw, 28 August 1904.
5ft 8in; 12st.
Career: Glasgow Rangers, Fall River (USA), Glasgow Rangers (cs 1930), Chelsea (May 1932), Cardiff City (December 1936), Workington (August 1938), Raith Rovers (cs 1939).
Honours: Scotland international (2 caps), Scottish FA Cup winners' medal 1932, Scottish League XI (1 appearance).
Chelsea debut: 3 September 1932. Appearances: League 66, FA Cup 8; Goals: League 1.
Scottish international full-back Macaulay arrived in London with a big reputation that he was never to fully justify. Stockily built, he lacked a little pace but was a good tackler and distributor of the ball. He was unable to hold a first-team place in competition with such as Tommy Law and George Barber. He was a scout for Glasgow Rangers and was appointed their Chief Scout in 1979.

McCALLIOG, James (1963-1965) **Inside-forward**
Born: Clydebank, 23 September 1946.
5ft 9in; 10st 5lb.
Career: Glasgow Schools, Leeds United (amateur), Chelsea (September 1963), Sheffield Wednesday (October 1965, £37,500), Wolverhampton Wanderers (August 1969), Manchester United (March 1974), Southampton (February 1975), Chicago Sting (1977), Norwegian soccer (1977-78), Lincoln City (September 1978), Runcorn (player-manager cs 1979).
Honours: Scotland international (5 caps), Scotland Under-23 (2 caps), Scotland Schoolboys, FA Cup winners' medal 1976, runners-up medal 1966, Second Division championship medal 1975, Fairs Cup runners-up medal 1972.
Chelsea debut: 23 September 1964. Appearances: League 7, League Cup 5; Goals: League 2, League Cup 1.
A slim Scotland Schoolboy international when he signed for Chelsea, McCalliog was unable to establish himself at a time when there was competition for first-team places and, unwisely many thought, was allowed to move on. He went on to play nearly 500 League games without ever quite fulfilling his great potential. Appointed manager of Halifax Town 1990.

McCARTNEY, David (1906-1907) **Centre-half**
Born: Ayrshire.
Career: Dalbeattie, Glossop (1901), Watford (1903),

Luton Town, Chelsea (May 1906), Northampton Town (cs 1907).
Chelsea debut: 12 January 1907. Appearances: League 1, FA Cup 2.
A strong, commanding centre-half, McCartney's first-team opportunities were limited by the consistent form of Bob McRoberts and after 12 months he moved on to seek a permanent spot in a senior team.

McCONNELL, English (1910-1912) **Centre-half**
Born: Larne.
5ft 9in; 11st 10lb.
Career: Cliftonville, Glentoran, Sunderland (October 1905), Sheffield Wednesday (May 1908), Chelsea (April 1910, £1,000), South Shields (cs 1912).
Honours: Ireland international (12 caps).
Chelsea debut: 16 April 1910. Appearances: League 21.
McConnell was signed, along with several other players, in an unavailing bid to avoid relegation in the closing weeks of the 1909-10 season after a long and distinguished career both in his native Ireland and in the north of England. He was a polished, stylish centre-half, very much in the attacking mould of those times, but his Stamford Bridge days came to an unfortunate end due to a cartilage operation 12 months after his arrival on the Chelsea scene.

McCREADIE, Edward Graham (1962-1974) **Full-back**
Born: Glasgow, 15 April 1940.
5ft 8½in; 10st 8lb.
Career: Drumchapel Amateurs, Clydebank Juniors, East Stirlingshire (1959), Chelsea (April 1962, £6,000), Retired (November 1974).
Honours: Scotland international (23 caps), FA Cup winners' medal 1970, runners-up medal 1967, Football League Cup winners' medal 1965.
Chelsea debut: 18 August 1962. Appearances: League 327(4), FA Cup 41, League Cup 21(1), Fairs Cup 13, European Cup-winners' Cup 3; Goals: League 4, League Cup 1.

McCreadie, one of Chelsea's best-ever bargain buys at £6,000, was an unknown from the Scottish Second Division. At once he struck up a formidable full-back duo with Ken Shellito which was an important part of the 1962-3 Second Division promotion-winning team. Aggressive and flamboyant in style, he went on to establish what was then a record number of international appearances for a Chelsea player. Latterly his career was plagued by injury and he was appointed coach in November 1974 before taking over from Ron Suart as manager, 12 months later. In management, too, his forceful style was much in evidence and he guided the team back to the First Division in May 1976. Then, with his future apparently assured, a dispute over contract ended his always eventful 14-year stay at Stamford Bridge and he continued his career with Memphis Rogues in the NASL.

McDERMOTT, Thomas (1905-1906) Inside-forward
Born: Glasgow, May 1882.
5ft 7½in; 11st 12lb.
Career: Cambuslang, Glasgow Celtic, Everton (cs 1903), Chelsea (October 1905), Dundee (1906), Bradford City (February 1908), Gainsborough Trinity (November 1908), Glasgow Celtic (1909), Vale of Leven (February 1912).
Chelsea debut: 21 October 1905. Appearances: League 31, FA Cup 1; Goals: League 10.
A scheming inside-forward, McDermott contested the inside-left position with Jimmy Windridge during Chelsea's first two seasons. Despite undoubted ability and an impressive scoring ratio, his play suffered from inconsistency and he moved on after two seasons.

McEWAN, Marshall (1909-1911)   Winger
Born: Rutherglen, 1885; Died: Belfast, 1966.
Career: Blackpool, Bolton Wanderers (1905), Chelsea (March 1909, £1,000), Linfield (cs 1911).
Chelsea debut: 2 April 1910. Appearances: League 33, FA Cup 2; Goals: League 3.
McEwan, a ball-playing Scottish winger, was one of a group of players signed towards the end of the 1909-10 season in a bid to stave off relegation. 'Slippery as an eel' was one description of this player who probably lacked the necessary physique to make a real impression in English football in those robust days.

McEWAN, Robert (1905-1906)   Full-back
Born: 1881.
5ft 10in; 12st 8lb.
Career: St Bernards, Bury, Glasgow Rangers, Heart of Midlothian, Chelsea (May 1905), Glossop North End (August 1906).
Chelsea debut: 2 September 1905. Appearances: League 19, FA Cup 1.
A Scottish full-back, McEwan was an 'ever-present' in Chelsea's first three months, but then lost his place to Tommy Miller through injury and was unable to displace him when he was fit again.

McFARLANE, Alexander (1913-1915)   Inside-forward
Born: Dundee, c.1878.
5ft 8½in; 12st.
Career: Baillieston, Airdrieonians, Newcastle United (October 1898), Dundee (November 1901), Chelsea (April 1913).
Honours: Scotland international (5 caps), Scottish

League XI (3 appearances), Scottish FA Cup winners' medal 1910.
Chelsea debut: 13 September 1913. Appearances: League 4.
Any chance of 'Sandy' McFarlane establishing himself in English football was ruined by the outbreak of World War One and, apart from one appearance in 1915-16, he never again played for Chelsea. He later managed both Dundee and Charlton Athletic (twice in each case), and Blackpool (1933-35).

MacFARLANE, Ian (1956-1958)   Full-back
Born: Lanark, 26 January 1933.
6ft 1in; 12st 7lb.
Career: Aberdeen, Chelsea (August 1956), Leicester City (May 1958), Bath City (July 1959).
Chelsea debut: 22 August 1956. Appearances: League 40, FA Cup 3.
MacFarlane, a powerfully-built full-back, was the regular first choice during his first season on the Chelsea staff, but loss of form led to his transfer to Leicester City after two seasons. He later became manager of Carlisle United (1970-72) for a spell and then coach at Leicester City, as well as assistant manager from 1977 to 1982.

MACHIN, Alexander Harold (1944-1948)
Inside-forward/Wing-half
Born: Shepherds Bush, 6 July 1920.
Career: Chelsea (1944), Plymouth Argyle (June 1948).
Chelsea debut: 5 January 1946. Appearances: League 53, FA Cup 2; Goals: League 8, FA Cup 1.
Machin was first spotted by Chelsea whilst serving with the Royal Hampshire Regiment during World War Two and became a full-time professional on demobilization. Then 25, he had already lost too much vital training and experience during his formative years and, doubtless as a result, never quite fulfilled his potential. A strong, forceful player, he lost his place to Ken Armstrong after one season in the first team and then moved to Plymouth Argyle, for whom he made a handful of League appearances.

McINNES, John Smith (1947-1951)   Outside-left
Born: Glasgow, 11 August 1927; Died: Bedford, October 1973.
5ft 8in; 10st.
Career: Morton, Chelsea (May 1947), Bedford Town (August 1951).
Chelsea debut: 3 May 1947. Appearances: League 37; Goals: League 5.
This willowy outside-left spent five years at Stamford Bridge, fighting injury and ill health for much of this time. Speedy and with clever ball-control, it was sad that such talent never had the chance to blossom. He died, prematurely, in Bedford where his abbreviated playing career ended.

MACINTOSH, Stanley Wilson (1930-1936)   Goalkeeper
Born: Brighton, 26 November 1905; Died: Brighton, 3 October 1976.
Career: London Caledonians, Chelsea (May 1930).
Chelsea debut: 6 December 1930.Appearances: League 1.
A capable goalkeeper, MacIntosh was content to remain at Stamford Bridge for six seasons without any real chance of displacing either Vic Woodley or Johnny Jackson, internationals both, and possibly the two best in their position in Britain.

106

McKENNA, Peter Joseph (1924-1931)   Goalkeeper
Born: Toxbeth Park, Liverpool, 8 December 1901;
Died: London, 27 July 1964.
5ft 10in; 12st.
Career: Bangor, Chelsea (May 1924).
*Chelsea debut: 8 November 1924. Appearances: League
62, FA Cup 4.*
McKenna's seven years of loyal service to Chelsea were
spent understudying first the legendary Howard Baker
and then Sam Millington. Reliable, he was just a little
lacking in height to make a dominant 'keeper.
Nevertheless, he was consistently sound whenever
called upon, which in his early seaons was frequently,
as Baker was often away on duty with either the
England Amateur side or the Corinthians.

McKENZIE, Duncan (1978-1979)   Striker/Midfield
Born: Grimsby, 10 June 1950.
5ft 9in; 11st.
Career: Nottingham Forest (July 1968), Mansfield
Town (loan), Leeds United (August 1974), Anderlecht,
Everton (December 1976), Chelsea (September 1978,
£165,000), Blackburn Rovers (March 1979, £80,000),
Tulsa Roughnecks (1981), Chicago Sting (1982), Hong
Kong football.

McKENZIE, Kenneth (1910-1911)   Winger
Career: Inverness Thistle, Chelsea (March 1910, £25),
Cardiff City (cs 1911).
Chelsea debut: 26 April 1911. Appearances: League 1.
Most of McKenzie's brief career at Chelsea was spent
in the reserve team at a time when the staff was well-
stocked with wingers.

McKENZIE, Kenneth W. (1920-1923)   Centre-half
Born: Montrose.
6ft; 12st 2lb.
Career: Queen's Park, Chelsea (August 1920), Cardiff
City (May 1923).
*Chelsea debut: 11 September 1920. Appearances:
League 21, FA Cup 1.*
Ideally built for a centre-half, McKenzie had an
extended run in the autumn of 1921, deputizing for
the injured Harold Wilding, yet was unable to displace
him on a permanent basis.

MACKIE, Robert (1905-1907)   Full-back
Born: Daltry (Ayr), August 1882.
5ft 10in; 12st.
Career: Stenhousemuir, Heart of Midlothian, Leicester
Fosse (May 1904), Chelsea (May 1905), Leicester Fosse
(November 1907), Airdrieonians (cs 1909).
*Chelsea debut: 2 September 1905. Appearances:
League 44, FA Cup 4; Goals: League 1.*

*Chelsea debut: 9 September 1978. Appearances:
League 15, FA Cup 1; Goals: League 4.*
McKenzie was a highly-talented performer who, in a
brief seven-month stay, never acclimatized himself to
a side of limited ability, often doubtful commitment,
and struggling to avoid inevitable relegation. He scored
some spectacular goals but too often failed to produce
his best form.

Mackie was Chelsea's first right-back. Extremely quick
and a great-hearted player who was popular with the
club's supporters, he lost his place through injury. The
signing of Joe Walton prevented him from regaining
it again on a regular basis.

McKNIGHT, Philip (1947-1954)   Wing-half
Born: Camlachie, 15 June 1924.

5ft 8in; 10st 7lb.
Career: Alloa Athletic, Chelsea (January 1947), Leyton Orient (July 1954).
Chelsea debut: 1 May 1948. Appearances: League 33; Goals: League 1.
McKnight was a loyal reserve wing-half who deputized capably whenever required. A hard-working player with a long throw-in, he went on to make almost 200 first-team appearances for Leyton Orient before retiring in 1960. He coached Orient's 'A' team and then Hendon for a spell from 1961.

McLAUGHLIN, Joseph (1983-1989)   **Centre-half**
Born: Greenock, 2 June 1960.
6ft 1in; 12st.
Career: Morton, Chelsea (May 1983, £95,000), Charlton Athletic (August 1989, £600,000), Watford (August 1990).
Honours: Scotland Under-23 international (10 caps), Second Division championship medals 1984, 1989, Full Members' Cup winners' medal 1986.
Chelsea debut: 27 August 1983. Appearances: League 224, FA Cup 9, League Cup 23, Full Members' Cup 12; Goals: League 5, League Cup 1, Full Members' Cup 1.

McLaughlin, a tall, commanding centre-half, had already made around 200 Scottish League appearances for Morton before his arrival at Stamford Bridge. Immediately establishing himself in the first team, he was the lynch-pin of the defence in the 1983-4 Second Division championship side and continued his impressive form in the First Division, coming under the close scrutiny of the Scotland international selectors.

McMILLAN, Eric (1958-1960)   **Wing-half**
Born: Beverley, 2 November 1936.
5ft 10½in; 11st 10lb.
Career: RAF football, Chelsea (April 1958), Hull City (July 1960, £2,000), Halifax Town (July 1965), Scarborough (July 1967), Port Elizabeth (SA), (January 1969).
Chelsea debut: 5 September 1959. Appearances: League 5.
McMillan first signed on amateur forms, after service with the RAF. Unable to break into the first team at Chelsea, he returned to his native Humberside to make 150 League appearances for Hull City.

McMILLAN, Paul A. (1967-1968)   **Wing-half**
Born: Lennox Castle, 13 July 1950.
5ft 10½in; 11st 9lb.
Career: Chelsea (August 1967), Retired on medical advice (February 1968), Clydebank.
Chelsea debut: 2 September 1967. Appearances: League 1.
A former Chelsea Junior, McMillan's career came to a most unfortunate end after eight months as a professional for medical reasons, although he did later play again, briefly, for Clydebank.

McNALLY, Errol A. (1961-1963)   **Goalkeeper**
Born: Lurgan, 27 August 1943.
5ft 10½in; 11st.
Career: Portadown, Chelsea (December 1961, £5,000), Glenavon (1963).
Chelsea debut: 17 March 1962. Appearances: League 9.
One of several goalkeepers saddled with the thankless task of playing second fiddle to Peter Bonetti, McNally's one extended run came in a dispirited side already doomed to relegation to Division Two.

McNAUGHT, John (1986-1987)   **Midfield**
Born: Glasgow, 19 June 1964.
5ft 11in; 11st 12lb.
Career: Auchengill Boys' Club, Hamilton Academical (1983), Chelsea (May 1986, £75,000), Partick Thistle (December 1987, free transfer).
Chelsea debut: 5 May 1986. Appearances: League 9(1), League Cup 3; Goals: League 2.
McNaught was a rugged midfielder, strong in the tackle and with a liking for moving on to the attack at every opportunity. He had played three seasons with Hamilton Academical in the Scottish League before his arrival at Stamford Bridge, scoring 19 goals in 109 outings.

McNEIL, Robert W. (1914-1929)   **Winger**
Born: Springburn (Glasgow), 1890.
5ft 7in; 10st 10lb.
Career: Hamilton Academical, Chelsea (summer 1914). Retired May 1929.
Honours: FA Cup runners-up medal 1915, Scottish League XI (5 appearances).
Chelsea debut: 5 September 1914. Appearances: League 279, FA Cup 28; Goals: League 27, FA Cup 5.
McNeil was one of Chelsea's best-loved players over his 14 seasons with the club, interrupted, of course, by World War One. But for this, his total number of games would have exceeded 400. Signed along with Jimmy Croal from Falkirk, he made up a left-wing partnership which took Chelsea to their first FA Cup Final at the end of his first season at Stamford Bridge.

Extremely fast, he possessed a clever football brain and was also a fine dribbler with the ball. Although not a prolific goalscorer, he could at times surprise friend and foe alike with the power and accuracy of his long-range shooting. After retiring, he returned to become trainer to his first love, Hamilton Academical.

McNICHOL, John (1952-1958)   **Inside-forward**
Born: Kilmarnock, 20 August 1925.
5ft 9in; 11st.
Career: Hurlford Juniors, Newcastle United (August 1946), Brighton & Hove Albion (August 1948), Chelsea (August 1952, £12,000), Crystal Palace (March 1958, £2,000)
Honours: Football League Championship medal 1955.
Chelsea debut: 23 August 1952. Appearances: League 181, FA Cup 21; Goals: League 59, FA Cup 7.
Manager Ted Drake's first signing for Chelsea, McNichol, then aged 27, had played all his League football in the Third Division but immediately made an impact in the higher sphere. A clever ball-playing and forceful inside-forward, he was a regular goalscorer as well as a creator of chances, especially for Roy Bentley. An integral part of the 1954-5 Championship winning side, he stayed in the game after retiring as a player, being employed at Crystal Palace in their commercial department.

McROBERTS, Robert (1905-1909)   **Centre-half/forward**
Born: Coatbridge, 1874; Died: Birkenhead, 27 February 1959.
5ft 8½in; 11st 9lb.
Career: Coatbridge, Airdrieonians, Albion Rovers, Gainsborough Trinity, Small Heath, Chelsea (April 1905, £100).
Chelsea debut: 2 September 1905. Appearances: League 104, FA Cup 2; Goals: League 10.
Chelsea's first signing, he was equally at home at either centre-half or centre-forward, McRoberts was in the team for Chelsea's inaugural League game, at Stockport, after a fine career with Small Heath.

Particularly noted for his sound positional play as a defender, he was a fine header of the ball and was appointed club captain at the start of the 1907-08 season. His 'joint' benefit match (with Jimmy Windridge) realized £666 in March 1911. He subsequently became manager of his old club, now renamed Birmingham FC, retiring from that position during World War One.

MAIR, Thomas (1909-1910)   **Outside-left**
Career: Galston, Ayr United, Leyton, (cs 1908), Chelsea (January 1909, £600)
Chelsea debut: 25 December 1908. Appearances: League 9; Goals: League 1.
Mair was at Chelsea for just over a year and was one of a number of players who occupied the outside-left position at a time when Chelsea were struggling, unsuccessfully as it turned out, to maintain their First Division status.

MALCOLM, Andrew (1961-1962)   **Wing-half**
Born: East Ham, 4 May 1933.
5ft 8in; 11st 10lb.
Career: Romford Schools, West Ham United (July 1950), Chelsea (November 1961, £12,000), Queen's Park Rangers (October 1962, £12,000), Port Elizabeth (SA) (June 1965).

Honours: England Schoolboy & Youth international, Football League XI.
Chelsea debut: 4 November 1961. Appearances: League 27, FA Cup1; Goals: League 1.
Malcolm was signed after a long and distinguished career with West Ham (over 300 games) to add stability and experience to a young Chelsea team, in a move which also took Ron Tindall to Upton Park. Perhaps he was already past his peak but, after one unhappy season during which Chelsea were relegated, manager Tommy Docherty placed his faith in 19-year-old Terry Venables. Malcolm moved to Queen's Park Rangers shortly afterwards.

MARSH, Wilson (1921-1924) **Goalkeeper**
Born: Woodhouse, (Nr Sheffield) 1894.
6ft 1½in; 13st.
Career: Eckington Works (Sheffield), Chelsea (May 1921), Dundee (August 1924).
Chelsea debut: 27 December 1921. Appearances: League 10, FA Cup 2.
For nearly three seasons, Marsh stood on the sidelines as as deputy goalkeeper to Jim Molyneux, Colin Hampton and the great Corinthian, Howard Baker. Not surprisingly, his opportunities were limited and when he was not retained at the end of the 1923-4 season, he moved to Dundee. He was also a notable golfer.

MARSHALL, Owen Thomas (1913-1920) **Full-back**
Born: Nottingham, 1892.
5ft 11in; 12st 8lb.
Career: Ilkeston United, Chelsea (January 1913, £120), Gillingham (November 1920), Maidstone United (cs 1923).
Chelsea debut: 8 September 1913. Appearances: League 34, FA Cup 2.
Marshall proved a reliable deputy for either Walter Bettridge or Jack Harrow and might have gone further in the game but for the interruption of his career by World War One.

MATTHEW, Damian (1989-) **Midfield**
Born: Islington, 23 September 1970.
5ft 11in; 10st 10lb.
Career: Chelsea (January 1989).
Honours: England Under-21 international (4 caps).
Chelsea debut: 20 January 1990. Appearances: League 8(2), League Cup 4, Full Members' Cup 1.
Matthew was one of a crop of highly promising young players who emerged together from the Chelsea Juniors, via the Reserves, and he immediately found his feet in the environment of the first team with a minimum of fuss. Recognized by the England selectors at Under-21 level, his creative play and good passing ability, allied to his pace, suggests a bright future in the game.

MATTHEWS, Reginald Derrick (1956-1961) Goalkeeper
Born: Coventry, 20 December 1933.
6ft; 11st 7lb.
Career: Coventry Schools, Coventry City, Chelsea (December 1956, £20,000), Derby County (October 1961, £10,000), Rugby Town (player-manager, August 1968).
Honours: England international (5 caps), England

Under-23 (4 caps), England 'B' (3 caps), Football League XI.
Chelsea debut: 17 November 1956. Appearances: League 135, FA Cup 9, League Cup 1, Fairs Cup 3.
Matthews was signed by Chelsea for what was then a record fee for a goalkeeper. He possessed lightning reflexes, was absolutely fearless and dominated his penalty area. By the time he came to Stamford Bridge he had already won his five England full international caps, being first capped as a Third Division player. At Chelsea he was not always seen at his best, being forced to play behind an unreliable and often square-lying defence. Ultimately he lost his place to Peter Bonetti and moved to Derby County, where he played more than 250 games, giving the Rams seven seasons of outstanding service and becoming a great favourite at the Baseball Ground.

MAYBANK, Edward G. (1974-1976) **Striker**
Born: Lambeth, 11 October 1956.
5ft 10in; 10st 12lb.
Career: South London Boys, Chelsea (February 1974), Fulham (November 1976, £65,000), Brighton & Hove Albion (November 1977), Fulham (December 1979), PSV Eindhoven (August 1980), Retired through injury (1981).
Chelsea debut: 19 April 1975. Appearances: League 28, FA Cup 4; Goals: League 6.
Maybank signed professional after two years as an apprentice at Stamford Bridge. A talented, if at times unpredictable, striker, he lost his place to Steve Finnieston and, with young Tommy Langley also in the wings, he was allowed to move on.

MAYES, Alan K. (1980-1983) **Striker**
Born: Edmonton, 11 December 1953.
5ft 7in; 10st 7lb.
Career: Queen's Park Rangers (July 1971), Watford (November 1974), Northampton Town (January 1976), Chelsea (December 1980, £200,000), Swindon Town (July 1983, free transfer), Carlisle United (July 1985), Blackpool (September 1986), Newport County (Loan).
Chelsea debut: 26 December 1980. Appearances: League 61(5), FA Cup 9, League 1; Goals: League 19, FA Cup 5.
Mayes was a free-scoring player throughout a career spent mostly in the lower divisions of the League. A neat ball-player with an accurate shot, he was especially adept at turning in a confined space to lose his marker. However, he became a victim of manager John Neal's 'sell-and-buy' policy in the close season of 1983, when the team was rebuilt. He managed Harrow Town for a spell after his playing career ended.

MAYES, Arnold John (1933-1942) **Wing-half**
Born: Wickford (Essex), 8 December 1913.
Career: Barking Town, Chelsea (March 1933), Retired (1942).
Chelsea debut: 28 December 1935. Appearances: League 12, FA Cup 1.
A strong tackling wing-half, Mayes was understudy to Irish international Billy Mitchell in the four seasons leading up to the outbreak of World War Two. He became a corporal in the Army during the hostilities and did not resume his football career afterwards.

MEDHURST, Harry Edward P. (1946-1952) Goalkeeper
Born: Byfleet, 5 February 1916; Died: April 1984.
5ft 9in; 10st 10lb.
Career: Woking, West Ham United (1936), Chelsea (December 1946, exchange Joe Payne), Brighton & Hove Albion (November 1952).
Chelsea debut: 25 December 1946. Appearances: League 143, FA Cup 14.
Already past his 30th birthday when he arrived at Chelsea to play in the First Division for the first time in his career, Medhurst immediately established himself in the senior side and gave sterling service for five seasons. On the small side for a goalkeeper, he compensated for this by his wonderful agility and his reliability. Originally an outside-left, he was pressed into service in goal in an emergency and remained there. After leaving Stamford Bridge he had six months at Brighton before returning as assistant trainer in the summer of 1953. He became head trainer in 1960 and physiotherapist in 1973, a post he held until his retirement in April 1975. A useful cricketer who played for Surrey Second XI.

MEEHAN, Thomas (1920-1924)   **Wing-half**
Born: Manchester, 1896; Died: 18 August 1924.
5ft 5in; 10st 7lb.
Career: Newtown, Walkden Central, Rochdale Town, Manchester United (cs 1917), Chelsea (December 1920, £3,300).
Honours: England international (1 cap), Football League XI (2 appearances).
Chelsea debut: 27 December 1920; Appearances: League 124, FA Cup 9; Goals: League 4.

One of the most popular, stylish and outstanding wing-halves of his time, Meehan was both a sound defensive player and a constructive user of the ball A non-smoker and teetotaller, his career was ended by his tragic death from sleeping sickness while still at the height of his powers. Some 2,000 attended his funeral at Wandsworth and a match between Chelsea and a Football League XI at Stamford Bridge in October 1924 raised

£1,500 for his dependants. His one international appearance for England was made only months before he died.

MEREDITH, John (1928-1930)   **Outside-right**
Born: Grimsby, 12 September 1899; Died: Grimsby, spring 1970.
5ft 6½in; 10st.
Career: Scunthorpe United, Blackpool (October 1923), Chelsea (May 1928), Reading (October 1930).
Chelsea debut: 27 October 1928. Appearances: League 23; Goals: League 6.
A lightweight right-winger, Meredith was on the staff for two seasons as deputy for Jackie Crawford. Most of his football was played in the reserve team, where was a regular scorer of goals.

MIDDELBOE, Nils (1913-1921)   **Half-back**
Born: Ardd, Denmark; Died: Copenhagen, September 1976.
6ft 3½in; 12st 6lb.
Career: Chelsea (1913).
Honours: Denmark international (13 caps).
Chelsea debut: 15 November 1913. Appearances: League 41, FA Cup 5.

A famous Danish amateur half-back, Middelboe appeared, all too irregularly, for Chelsea over a period of nine years, interrupted by World War One. With his long, raking stride and great skill he was a most popular personality at Stamford Bridge. Amateur in every sense of the word, he never claimed even his expenses. At the end of his playing career, his teammates presented him with a silver cigarette box, inscribed: 'To our captain and comrade — one of the best'. He played for Denmark against England in the 1908 Olympic Final.

MILLAR, John (1984-1987)   **Full-back**
Born: Coatbridge, 8 December 1966.
5ft 7in; 12st.
Career: Clyde Amateurs, Chelsea (August 1984),

Northampton Town (loan), Hamilton Academical (loan), Blackburn Rovers (July 1987, £25,000).
Honours: Scotland Youth international.
Chelsea debut: 8 February 1986.Appearances: League 11.
Scottish full-back Millar graduated to the first team via the Juniors (whom he captained) and Reserves. A sound left-back who made his debut as a 19-year-old, he has also played cricket for Scotland and was a student at London University. He had periods on loan to both Hamilton Academical and Northampton Town in the 1986-7 season.

MILLER, Harold Sydney (1923-1939)
Inside-forward/Wing-half
Born: St Albans, 20 May 1902.
5ft 8in; 9st 4lb.
Career: St Albans City, Charlton Athletic (January 1922), Chelsea (June 1923), Northampton Town (May 1939, free transfer).
Honours: England international (1 cap).
Chelsea debut: 25 August 1923. Appearances: League 337, FA Cup 26; Goals: League 41, FA Cup 3.
Miller was one of the longest-serving players in the history of Chelsea FC. Having won amateur honours, 'Dusty' turned professional with Charlton Athletic and came to Chelsea as an inside-forward with a reputation for scoring goals. Indeed, his ability had already been rewarded with an England cap. In the First Division he found life harder and was not always assured of his place in the team, especially when the big-money names began to arrive after the 1929-30 promotion season. Then, however, he converted to wing-half and his 'second' career began. Lightly built, he was a surprisingly hard tackler, but his forte was his constructive use of the ball. A good dribbler, he possessed dainty footwork and was also noted for his wonderful consistency.

MILLER, Thomas (1905-1909)   **Full-back**
Born: Falkirk.
5ft 6½in; 11st 10lb.

Career: Falkirk, Chelsea (May 1905), Falkirk (cs 1909).
Chelsea debut: 2 September 1905. Appearances: League 112, FA Cup 8.
Small and very fast, Miller was anything but the popular image of a full-back of those days in the early part of this century. Winning his first-team place as a result of an injury to Bob McEwan, he remained first choice for the next three seasons. A constructive user of the ball, if a little over-elaborate at times, after a couple of pints of beer he once claimed to be the 'best back in England'.

MILLINGTON, Simeon (1926-1932)   **Goalkeeper**
Born: Walsall, 1896.
5ft 10in; 11st 4lb.
Career: Wellington, Chelsea (January 1926), Retired through illness (1932).
Chelsea debut: 2 October 1926. Appearances: League 223, FA Cup 22.
A familiar figure in his cloth cap, Millington was a most reliable goalkeeper who spanned the period between Howard Baker, who retired at the end of the 1925-6 season, and Vic Woodley. He was never absent, other than through a rare injury, from his debut until illness forced his retirement from the game six seasons later. After missing out on promotion in the first four of these years, 'Sam' was very much an integral part of the side which eventually regained Chelsea's First Division place in 1930.

MILLS, George Robert (1929-1943)   Centre-forward
Born: Deptford, 29 December 1908; Died: Torquay, 15 July 1978.
6ft; 11st 12lb.

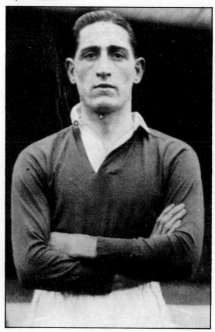

Career: Emerald Athletic, Bromley, Chelsea
(December 1929), Retired (1943).
Honours: England international (3 caps), Football
League XI (1 appearance).
*Chelsea debut: 21 December 1929. Appearances: League
220, FA Cup 19; Goals: League 117, FA Cup 7.*
Mills was plucked out of amateur football to be
pitchforked into the first team at Christmas 1929. It
was a happy debut, Chelsea won 5-0. Tall, well-built
and with an infectious enthusiasm for the game, he
went on to become Chelsea's first 'centurion'.
Strangely, he spent most of his Stamford Bridge career
contesting his place with a series of internationals, all
of whom had been signed at great expense, in contrast
to George's £10 signing-on fee. At times Hughie
Gallacher, Joe Bambrick and 'Ten-goal' Joe Payne all
ousted him from the side. Yet he ended the 1938-9
season as first choice for the centre-forward position.
But for such rivalry his figures would have been still
more impressive. He scored a hat-trick on his debut
for England, against Northern Ireland, and coached
Chelsea's 'A' team for a period after the war.

MITCHELL, David Stewart (1989-)   **Forward**
Born: Glasgow, 13 June 1962.
6ft 1in; 12st 7lb.
Career: Eintracht Frankfurt, Glasgow Rangers,
Feyenoord, Chelsea (January 1989, £200,000), NEC
Nijmegen (loan), Newcastle United (loan).
Honours: Australia international (27 caps).
*Chelsea debut: 10 January 1989. Appearances: League
7, Full Members' Cup 1.*
Mitchell was signed to provide cover for central
strikers, Dixon and Durie and was given his opportunity almost immediately. Adjusting to English
football for the first time, at the age of 26, posed
problems, later increased by injury, and his first-team
opportunities were further retarded by the arrival of
a crop of promising young players from the junior
team.

MITCHELL, Frank Rawlinson (1949-1952)   **Wing-half**
Born: Goulburn (Australia), 3 June 1922; Died: 2 April
1984.
5ft 11in; 12st 12lb.
Career: Coventry City (amateur), Birmingham City
(September 1943), Chelsea (January 1949), Watford
(August 1952, £7,000), Retired (1957).
*Chelsea debut: 5 February 1949. Appearances: League
75, FA Cup 10; Goals: League 1.*
Mitchell was a stylish, constructive wing-half whose
career was delayed by World War Two. He was
particularly adept in his use of the long cross-field pass
which he directed with pinpoint accuracy. His all-too-
brief Chelsea career ended when he lost his place to
Bill Dickson, but he went on to play some 200 games
for Watford. He was also a good cricketer who played
17 games for Warwickshire between 1946 and 1948.

MITCHELL, William (1933-1945)   **Wing-half**
Born: County Lurgan, 22 November 1910; Died: 1978.
5ft 5½in; 11st 4lb.
Career: Cliftonville, Distillery, Chelsea (June 1933),
Bath City (1945).
Honours: Northern Ireland international (15 caps).
*Chelsea debut: 24 February 1934. Appearances: League
108, FA Cup 9; Goals: League 2, FA Cup 1.*

Already capped by Northern Ireland when he arrived
at Stamford Bridge, Billy Mitchell was a terrier-type
wing-half, small of stature but immensely strong and
especially in the tackle. His somewhat fiery temperament sometimes got him into trouble with the
authorities but he was a magnificent team man and
it was sad that the outbreak of World War Two
prematurely ended his Chelsea career. Having played
as a guest player for Bristol City during hostilities,
he joined their coaching staff for a spell in 1946.

MOLYNEUX, James (1910-1922)   **Goalkeeper**
Born: Port Sunlight, 1887.
5ft 9in; 11st 9lb.
Career: Rock Ferry, Stockport County (cs 1906),
Chelsea (August 1910, £550), Stockport County
(January 1923). Retired 1925.
*Chelsea debut: 3 September 1910. Appearances:
League 210, FA Cup 29.*
Signed as understudy to Jack Whitley, Molyneux in
fact won a first-team place immediately and was then
almost an automatic choice for his 12 seasons
(including the war years) on the staff. Despite his lack
of inches, he was extremely agile with a good sense

113

Chelsea debut: 1 May 1989. Appearances: League 61(2), FA Cup 3, League Cup 10, Full Members' Cup 7; Goals: League 2.

Monkou had already had four seasons experience in the Dutch First Division before moving into English football with Chelsea, who obtained his services in keen competition with two West German sides and another Dutch club. Almost at once he established his place in the first team as a player of very considerable talent and resource. On his day, he can dominate in defence and his wide range of skills on the ball is an extra bonus for a defender who has already proved a bargain signing.

MOORE, Graham (1961-1963)   **Centre-/Inside-forward**
Born: Hengoed, 7 March 1941.
5ft 11½in; 13st 11lb.
Career: Cardiff City (May 1958), Chelsea (December 1961, £35,000), Manchester United (November 1963, £35,000), Northampton Town (December 1965), Charlton Athletic (June 1967), Doncaster Rovers (September 1971).
Honours: Wales international (21 caps), Wales Under-23 (9 caps), Football League XI.
Chelsea debut: 23 December 1961. Appearances: League 68, FA Cup 4; Goals: League 13, FA Cup 1.

Tommy Docherty paid a record club fee to obtain the services of the established Welsh international forward Graham Moore. But he failed to make the expected impact in the First Division, especially when it came to scoring goals, and soon Barry Bridges had forced his way into the first team. With other young players of promise in the pipeline, Moore was allowed to leave Stamford Bridge.

MORAN, Martin (1905-1908)   **Outside-right**
Born: Glasgow, 1878.

of anticipation and he became one of the most respected goalkeepers in the game. 'Moly', who was immensely popular with the Chelsea supporters, kept goal in the 1919 London Victory Cup Final against Fulham at Highbury.

MONKOU, Kenneth John (1989-)   **Defender**
Born: Necare (Surinam), 29 November 1964.
6ft 3in; 13st 8lb.
Career: Feyenoord, Chelsea (March 1989, £100,000).
Honours: Holland Under-21 international, Full Members' Cup winners' medal 1990.

5ft 5½in; 10st 7lb.
Career: Glasgow Celtic (April 1898), Sheffield United (August 1899), Millwall (August 1902), Heart of Midlothian (May 1904), Chelsea (May 1905), Glasgow Celtic (May 1908).
Chelsea debut: 2 September 1905. Appearances: League 63, FA Cup 4; Goals: League 7, FA Cup 1.
'The muscular midget', as Moran was affectionately known, was Chelsea's first right-winger and became renowned for his speedy dashes down the flank. Already a mature and experienced player, he was also described as the type of player 'to delight the heart of a manager'. 'Give it to Micky', was a familiar cry from the terraces in his playing days.

MORRISON, William (1924-1927)   Inside-forward
Born: Bo'ness, Scotland.
Career: Linlithgow Rovers, Chelsea (cs 1924).
Chelsea debut: 20 April 1945. Appearances: League 1.
A regular reserve-team player for his two seasons on the Stamford Bridge staff, Morrison was unable to displace such men as Andy Wilson, Albert Thain and Harold Miller from the inside-forward positions.

MORTIMORE, John H. (1957-1965)   Centre-half
Born: Farnborough, 23 September 1934.
6ft; 11st 9lb.
Career: Woking, Aldershot (amateur), Chelsea (August 1957), Queen's Park Rangers (September 1965, £8,000), Sunderland.
Honours: England Amateur international, England Youth, Football League Cup winners' medal 1965.
Chelsea debut: 28 April 1956. Appearances: League 249, FA Cup 16, League Cup 11, Fairs Cup 3; Goals: League 8, FA Cup 1, League Cup 1.
A commanding centre-half, especially powerful in the

air, Mortimore was still an amateur with Woking when he made his Chelsea debut. Strangely, for two seasons he was displaced, first by Bobby Evans (well past his best and not a centre-half in any event) and then by Mel Scott, both of whom were lesser performers in his position. But Mortimore was ever-present in the Second Division promotion team of 1962-3 and lent invaluable experience to manager Tommy Docherty's youthful protégés. Later he was assistant manager of Southampton after gaining coaching and managerial experience abroad. After The Dell he coached the Portuguese club Benfica and was then manager of Belenenses, before returning to Southampton, again as assistant manager.

MULHOLLAND, James (1962-1964)   Forward
Born: Knightswood, 10 April 1938.
5ft 8in; 10st 10lb.
Career: East Stirling, Chelsea (October 1962, £8,000), Morton (September 1964, part-exchange Billy Sinclair), Barrow (August 1965), Stockport County (October 1968), Crewe Alexandra (August 1970).
Chelsea debut: 3 November 1962. Appearances: League 11, FA Cup 1; Goals: League 2, FA Cup 1.
After a promising start, Mulholland failed to win a permanent place in the firstteam, either at centre-forward or on the wing, in the face of the stream of talent emerging from Chelsea Juniors.

MULLIGAN, Patrick Martin (1969-1972)
Full-back/Centre-half
Born: Dublin, 17 March 1945.
5ft 7in; 11st 9lb.
Career: Home Farm, Shamrock Rovers, Chelsea (October 1969, £17,500), Boston Beacons (loan), Crystal Palace (September 1972, £75,000), West Bromwich Albion (September 1975).
Honours: Republic of Ireland international (51 caps), Football League Cup runners-up medal 1972. Also 1 FA Charity Shield appearance 1971.
Chelsea debut: 20 December 1969. Appearances: League 55(3), FA Cup 3, League Cup 9, European Cup-winners' Cup 6(2); Goals: League 2.
Paddy Mulligan's move to Chelsea set up a record fee for any Republic of Ireland player up to that time. A rugged and powerful defender whose turn of speed made him a dangerous overlapping raider down the flanks, for a comparatively small man he was surprisingly good in the air and, although rarely certain of a permanent place in the team, it was a disappointment when he left the club.

MURPHY, Jerry Michael (1985-1988)   Midfield
Born: Stepney, 23 September 1959.
5ft 9in; 11st 10lb.
Career: Crystal Palace (October 1976), Chelsea (August 1985, free transfer), registration cancelled (May 1988), Basingstoke (March 1991).
Honours: Republic of Ireland international (3 caps), England Schoolboys.
Chelsea debut: 17 August 1985. Appearances: League 34, FA Cup 1, League Cup 3, Full Members' Cup 1; Goals: League 3.
After nine years as a professional with Crystal Palace (229 League games), Murphy was snapped up by Chelsea and immediately made an impact in the first team. A creative left-sided midfielder, as well as a

powerful tackler, he saw his early Stamford Bridge days punctuated by a series of injuries which hampered his progress in establishing himself as a regular member of the League side.

MURRAY, Albert G. (1961-1966)   Winger/Midfield
Born: Shoreditch, 22 September 1942.
5ft 7½in; 10st 8lb.
Career: Chelsea (May 1961), Birmingham City (August 1966, £25,000), Brighton & Hove Albion (February 1971), Peterborough United (September 1973).
Honours: England Under-23 international (6 caps), England Schoolboy & Youth, Football League Cup winners' medal 1965.
Chelsea debut: 21 October 1961. Appearances: League 156(4), FA Cup 14, League Cup 6, Fairs Cup 3; Goals: League 39, FA Cup 4, Fairs Cup 1.

Signed on professional forms after three years as a Chelsea junior, Murray was a most versatile player who began life as an orthodox right winger. He converted into a midfield operator before playing most of the latter part of his career at full-back and was also a capable 'emergency' goalkeeper. Lightly built, he possessed clever and intricate footwork and his total of 17 League goals in the 1964-5 season was the highest for a Chelsea winger since Dick Spence (19 in 1934-5).

MYERS, Andrew John (1990-)   Midfield
Born: Isleworth, 3 November 1973.
5ft 9in; 12st 6lb.

Career: FA National School (1988), Chelsea (July 1990).
Honours: England Under-16 international (12 caps), England Youth (2 caps).
Chelsea debut: 6 April 1991. Appearances: League 0(3).
At the age of 17, he was the youngest Chelsea player to make his first-team debut since Tommy Langley (9 November 1974). He originally signed for the club at the age of 13, having trials with both Arsenal and Watford, before winning a two-year scholarship with the GM Vauxhall FA National School at Lilleshall.

**NEVIN, Patrick Kevin Francis Michael
(1983-1988)   Winger**
Born: Glasgow, 6 September 1963.
5ft 6in; 10st.
Career: Gartcosh (1979), Clyde (1981), Chelsea (May 1983, £95,000), Everton (July 1988, £925,000).
Honours: Scotland international (10 caps), Scotland Under-21 (5 caps), Scotland Youth, Second Division championship medal 1984, Full Members' Cup winners' medal 1986, FA Cup runners-up medal 1989.
Chelsea debut: 13 September 1983. Appearances: League 194(3), FA Cup 8(1), League Cup 25(1), Full Members' Cup 10; Goals: League 37, FA Cup 1, League Cup 5, Full Members' Cup 2.

An artistic ball player in the true Scottish tradition, Nevin was a prolific creator of goalscoring chances for colleagues as well as being a strong and accurate finisher himself. A thoughtful person and severe self-critic, he was one of the outstanding entertainers in modern football and a most important ingredient in Chelsea's rise from the basement of Second Division football to the top bracket of clubs in the First Division.

116

NICHOLAS, Anthony Wallace (1955-1960) Inside-forward
Born: West Ham, 16 April 1938.
5ft 10in; 12st 3lb.
Career: Chelsea (May 1955), Brighton & Hove Albion (November 1960, £15,000), Chelmsford City, Leyton Orient (June 1965), Dartford (1966).
Honours: England Youth international.
Chelsea debut: 22 August 1956. Appearances: League 59, FA Cup 1, League Cup 1, Fairs Cup 2; Goals: League 18, League Cup 1, Fairs Cup 1.

Signing professional after service as a Chelsea junior, this strongly-built player never wholly fulfilled his potential as a free-scoring inside-forward. With thrust, as well as clever ball skills, it was his misfortune to be a contemporary of Jimmy Greaves, who restricted his opportunities. Yet it was surprising that he failed to make much of an impact with either of his two subsequent League clubs.

NICHOLAS, Charles Brian (1955-1958) Wing-half
Born: Aberdare, 20 April 1933.
5ft 9½in; 11st 7lb.
Career: Queen's Park Rangers (May 1950), Chelsea (July 1955, £5,000), Coventry City (February 1958, £3,000), Rugby Town (July 1962).
Honours: England Schoolboy international.
Chelsea debut: 5 September 1955. Appearances: League 26, FA Cup 3; Goals: League 1.
Signed after five years at Queen's Park Rangers, mostly as a first-team player, Nicholas understudied Ken Armstrong for two seasons and then, after the latter retired, was overlooked in favour of John Mortimore. As a result he moved on and played several seasons in Coventry City's League side. A tough tackler and sound defensive player.

NICHOLAS, Peter (1988-1991) Midfield
Born: Newport (Gwent), 10 November 1959.
5ft 8in; 11st 8lb.
Career: Crystal Palace (December 1976), Arsenal (March 1981), Crystal Palace (August 1984), Luton Town (January 1985), Aberdeen (cs 1987), Chelsea (August 1988, £350,000), Watford (March 1991, £175,000).
Honours: Wales international (71 caps), Wales Under-21 (3 caps), Second Division championship medals 1979, 1989, Full Members' Cup winners' medal 1990.
Chelsea debut: 27 August 1989. Appearances: League 79(1), FA Cup 2, League Cup 7, Full Members' Cup 4; Goals: League 2.

Peter Nicholas had already moved around the football scene at frequent intervals before arriving at Stamford Bridge at the age of 28 as an established international midfield player. His assets were his strength and tackling ability which, if they did not always endear himself to supporters, were, nevertheless, qualities which Chelsea needed at that time. He was always likely to be a short-term acquisition and declining pace, allied to injury, saw him struggling to hold his first-team place after two influential seasons in the side.

NIEDZWIECKI, A. Edward (1983-1988) Goalkeeper
Born: Bangor, 3 May 1959.
6ft; 11st.
Career: Wrexham (July 1976), Chelsea (May 1983, £45,000), Retired (May 1988).
Honours: Wales international (2 caps), Wales Schoolboys, Second Division championship medal 1984.
Chelsea debut: 27 August 1983. Appearances: League

136, FA Cup 8, Football League Cup 25, Full Members' Cup 6.

After seven years with Wrexham, he came to Stamford Bridge, immediately won his place in the first team and became a vital member of the Second Division championship team of 1983-4. An outstanding goalkeeper, respected and liked throughout the game, he proved to be an excellent handler of the ball with fine anticipation as well as being agile and courageous.

The recognized deputy to Neville Southall in the Welsh goal, his career suffered a major set-back in March 1986 when he severely injured a knee and was incapacitated for six months. He resumed, still some way short of full fitness, before being forced to retire in May 1988. Chelsea received £125,000 in insurance compensation. Appointed to the Chelsea coaching staff after his retirement, he then moved to Reading as coach and was assistant manager (1990-91).

NUTTON, Michael William (1977-1983) Central defender
Born: St John's Wood, 3 October 1959.
5ft 11in; 10st 12lb.
Career: Chelsea (October 1977), Reading (loan), Millwall (March 1983), Fisher Athletic (cs 1987).
Chelsea debut: 23 December 1978. Appearances: League 77(2), FA Cup 3, League Cup 1.
Nutton joined Chelsea as a schoolboy and graduated to the full-time professional ranks after 18 months as an apprentice. A competent defender in the middle of the back-four, he had several spells in the first team without ever establishing himself as an automatic choice. His misfortune was to come into a struggling team virtually doomed to relegation and in an era of many comings and goings. He lacked the height to dominate in defence but was a useful foil in partnership with Micky Droy.

OAKTON, Albert Eric (1932-1937) **Winger**
Born: Kiveton Park (Yorkshire), 28 December 1906; Died: 5 August 1981.
5ft 9in; 11st.
Career: Grimsby Town (amateur) (November 1927), Rotherham United (August 1930), Worksop Town, Sheffield United (November 1927), Scunthorpe United, Bristol Rovers, Chelsea (May 1932), Nottingham Forest (June 1937).
Chelsea debut: 27 August 1932. Appearances: League 107, FA Cup 5; Goals: League 27, FA Cup 1.
At home on either flank, Oakton was a fast, direct winger with a flair for scoring goals. For two seasons he was a regular choice in the first team but the arrival of Dick Spence and Willie Barraclough restricted his opportunities after that.

O'CONNELL, Seamus D. (1954-1956) Inside-forward
Born: Carlisle, 1 January 1930.
Career: Sligo Rovers, Queen's Park, Middlesbrough (amateur) (May 1953), Bishop Auckland, Chelsea (amateur, August 1954), Crook Town, Carlisle (amateur, February 1958).
Honours: England Amateur international, Football League Championship medal 1955, FA Amateur Cup winners' medal 1955, 1956, runners-up 1954.
Chelsea debut: 16 October 1954. Appearances: League 16, FA Cup 1; Goals: League 11, FA Cup 1.
O'Connell marked his debut with a hat-trick in the 6-5 home defeat by Manchester United and, when available, proved himself a prolific goalscorer at the top level. Well-built and a fine mover with the ball, his accurate shooting was his greatest asset. How much he might have achieved in the professional game will never be known, since he left soccer, to help his father in his cattle-dealing business, and made only spasmodic appearances thereafter for Crook Town and Carlisle United. He never relinquished his amateur status.

ODELL, Leslie Frank (1924-1937) **Full-back**
Born: Sandy (Bedfordshire).
6ft; 13st 4lb.
Career: Sandy, Biggleswade Town, Luton Town (amateur), Chelsea (amateur, August 1924; professional, September 1924), Bedford Town (player-manager, September 1937).
Chelsea debut: 20 December 1924. Appearances: League 101, FA Cup 2; Goals: League 7.
Curiously, this tall, commanding full-back could never claim a regular place throughout his 12 seasons at Stamford Bridge and this despite chalking up a century of appearances. He began in the Smith-Harrow era, partnered Scottish internationals Law and Macaulay, and finished as Barber and O'Hare were becoming established. A loyal servant whose strength was, not least, the length and power of his kicking, which was also put to good use from the penalty-spot.

O'DOWD, James Peter (1931-1934) **Centre-half**
Born: Halifax, 26 February 1908; Died: 8 May 1964.
5ft 11in; 10st 5lb.
Career: St Bees GS (Bradford), Apperley Bridge, Selby, Bradford (amateur 1926), Blackburn Rovers

(December 1926), Burnley (March 1930), Chelsea (November 1931, £5,250), Valenciennes (September 1934), Torquay United (March 1937).
Honours: England international (3 caps).
Chelsea debut: 14 November 1931. Appearances: League 80, FA Cup 7.
Those who were fortunate enough to see O'Dowd's all-too-brief Chelsea career mostly agree that he was the club's finest-ever centre-half. Quietly spoken, he was a stylist, an intelligent player with time in which to use the ball constructively, and always with an eye to move forward to lend weight to the attack. His performance for England against Scotland in 1932 was universally admired. Then, at the height of his powers, he fell out with the Stamford Bridge management, and went off to play in France for much greater financial reward.

OELOFSE, Roelf J. (1951-1953)   **Centre-half**
Born: Johannesburg, 12 November 1926.
5ft 11in; 12st 4lb.
Career: Berea Park (SA), Chelsea (October 1951) Watford (July 1953), South Africa football (1954).
Chelsea debut: 1 March 1952. Appearances: League 8.
One of several South African players who tried their hand in English football after World War Two, Oelofse was a dominating figure in defence. He played a few games as a deputy for John Harris before moving to Watford, then in the Third Division South.

O'HARA, Francis (1905-1906)   **Centre-forward**
Born: Coatbridge.
5ft 5½in; 9st 4lb.
Career: Albion Rovers, Chelsea (August 1905), not retained (May 1906).
Chelsea debut: 7 October 1905. Appearances: League 1, FA Cup 2; Goals: FA Cup 3.
One of the large squad assembled to launch Chelsea into the Football League. 'Pat' O'Hara was unable to force his way into the first team and was at Stamford Bridge for only one season.

O'HARE, John (1932-1941)   **Full-back**
Born: Armadale.
5ft 8in; 11st 4lb.
Career: Shawfield Juniors, Chelsea (June 1932), Retired (1941).
Chelsea debut: 24 February 1934. Appearances: League 102, FA Cup 6.
O'Hare was a fearless tackler who lacked the pace to become a top-class full-back. Nevertheless, he was a dependable player who was a peripheral first-teamer in the four seasons leading up to World War Two, despite competing for his place with the likes of George Barber, Ned Barkas, Tommy Law and Jack Smith. A centre-forward at school, he was converted to his defensive position by chance.

ORD, Thomas (1972-1973)   **Midfield**
Born: Woolwich, 15 October 1952.
5ft 9in; 11st 7lb.
Career: Erith and Belvedere, Chelsea (December 1972), Bristol City (loan), Montreal Olympic (May 1973), Rochester Lancers (May 1974), New York Cosmos (July 1975), Vancouver Whitecaps (April 1976), Seattle Sounders (July 1977), Tulsa Roughnecks (April 1980), Atlanta Chiefs (July 1980).

Chelsea debut: 7 April 1973. Appearances: League 3; Goals: League 1.
Despite scoring on his debut, Ord never succeeded in winning a first-team place at a time when the professional staff was being pruned for financial reasons. He played for a few seasons in the North American Soccer League.

ORMISTON, Andrew (1909-1918)   **Centre-half**
Born: Paisley, 1 March 1884; Died: 1952.
5ft 11½in; 12st 6lb.
Career: Hebburn Argyle, Lincoln City (1901), Chelsea (cs 1909), Lincoln City (1918).
Chelsea debut: 4 September 1909. Appearances: League 95, FA Cup 7; Goals: League 1.
'Alec' Ormiston was a commanding centre-half and a particularly fine header of the ball. One of several players who followed manager David Calderhead from Lincoln City to Chelsea at that time, he never quite succeeded in coming to terms with the demands of a higher class of football, although he played in the majority of the games in the promotion season of 1912-13.

O'ROURKE, John (1962-1963)   **Centre-forward**
Born: Northampton, 11 December 1945.
5ft 8½in; 10st 10lb.
Career: Arsenal (amateur), Chelsea (April 1962), Luton Town (December 1963), Middlesbrough (July 1966), Ipswich Town (February 1968), Coventry City (November 1969), Queen's Park Rangers (October 1971), Bournemouth and Boscombe Athletic (January 1974).
Honours: England Youth international.
Chelsea debut: 25 September 1963. Appearances: League Cup 1.
One of soccer's nomads, O'Rourke topped the Combination goalscorers list in 1962-3 but failed to win a first-team place at a time when Barry Bridges and Graham Moore were the recognized choices for the central attacking positions He went on to score some 150 League goals with six different clubs.

**OSGOOD, Peter Leslie (1964-1974 & 1978-1979)
Striker-Midfield**
Born: Windsor, 20 February 1947.
6ft 2in; 12st 9lb.
Career: Spital Old Boys, Windsor Corinthians, Windsor Eriths, Chelsea (September 1964), Southampton (March 1974, £275,000), Norwich City (loan), Philadelphia Fury (December 1977), Chelsea (December 1978, £25,000), Retired (September 1979).
Honours: England international (4 caps), England Under-23 (6 caps), England Youth, Football League XI (3 appearances), FA Cup winners' medal 1970, 1976, European Cup-winners' Cup winners' medal 1971, Football League Cup runners-up medal 1972. Also 1 FA Charity Shield appearance 1970.
Chelsea debut: 16 December 1964. Appearances: League 286(3), FA Cup 34, League Cup 30, Fairs Cup 14(1), European Cup-winners' Cup 11; Goals: League 105, FA Cup 19, League Cup 10, Fairs Cup 4, European Cup-winners' Cup 12.
An immensely talented player, whether as a striker or operating in midfield, Osgood arrived on the Stamford Bridge scene as an unknown amateur in March 1964. He scored two goals on his debut, nine

months later, and then became an automatic choice in the first-team for nine seasons until differences of opinion with manager Dave Sexton led to his departure. His flair and opportunism made him one of the most exciting players of his generation. High-spirited, and often unpredictable, off the field, he was not the easiest of players to handle and at times his irresponsible actions landed him in trouble with the authorities. But, equally, it must be said that he was not always sympathetically handled and it makes little

cartilage operation, developed into one of the outstanding players of the 1954-5 Championship team. An ever-present in that side, he scored many vital goals, as well as laying on others, especially for Roy Bentley. A firm favourite with the Chelsea crowd, who affectionately nicknamed him 'The Rabbit', he played nearly 500 senior games despite losing several seasons through World War Two at the start of his career.

sense that a player of such rare ability was recognized so infrequently at international level. In October 1966 he broke a leg and missed the rest of that season through injury. After an interval of more than four years he returned to Chelsea, at the age of 31, but some of the old magic, and pace, was missing and he was unable to retain a first-team place. After retirement, he coached at Butlin's holiday camps (from 1986), was Portsmouth Youth-team coach (1988) and, latterly, coached in the Far East and Gambia.

PARSONS, Eric George (1950-1956)   Outside-right
Born: Worthing, 9 November 1923.
5ft 7in; 10st 4lb.
Career: West Ham United, Chelsea (December 1950, £23,000), Brentford (November 1956, free transfer), Dover (July 1961).
Honours: England 'B' international (2 caps), Football League Championship medal 1955. Also 1 FA Charity Shield appearance 1955.
Chelsea debut: 2 December 1950. Appearances: League 158, FA Cup 18; Goals: League 37, FA Cup 5.
Parsons was a fast, clever outside-right who, after a

PATES, Colin George (1979-1988)   Defender/Midfield
Born: Carshalton, 10 August 1961.
5ft 11in; 11st.
Career: Chelsea (July 1979), Charlton Athletic (October 1988, £430,000), Arsenal (January 1990), Brighton & Hove Albion (loan).
Honours: England Youth international, Second Division championship medal 1984, Full Members' Cup winners' medal 1986.
Chelsea debut: 10 November 1979. Appearances: League 284(1), FA Cup 20, League Cup 32, Full Members' Cup 9; Goals: League 10.
Pates first came to Stamford Bridge as an apprentice in July 1977. A talented central defender who played in all 11 England Youth internationals in the 'Little World Cup' tournament of 1980-81. He quickly established himself as a member of Chelsea's first-team squad and was appointed captain in April 1984, for the last few matches of the Second Division championship season. He also played in midfield on occasions but was happiest in his defensive role, operating on the left-side.

PATON, John Aloysius (1946-1947)   Outside-left
Born: Glasgow, 2 April 1923.
5ft 8in; 11st.
Career: St Mungo's Academy, Dennistoun Waverley,
Glasgow Celtic, Chelsea (November 1946, £7,000),
Glasgow Celtic (cs 1947), Brentford (September 1949),
Watford (July 1952).
*Chelsea debut: 7 December 1946. Appearances: League
18, FA Cup 5; Goals: League 3.*
A Press photographer by profession, Paton was a
Chelsea player for less than one season but was the
recognized first-choice outside-left during his short
stay. With clever footwork and accurate crosses, his
play produced goals for others and, after returning
north of the border, he again came south to play a
further 200 games or so in English football. Watford
manager (1955-56).

PAYNE, Joseph (1938-1946)   Centre-forward
Born: Bolsover, 17 January 1914; Died: 22 April 1975.
6ft; 12st.
Career: Bolsover Colliery, Biggleswade Town, Luton
Town (cs 1934), Chelsea (March 1938, £5,000), West
Ham United (December 1946, part-exchange Harry
Medhurst), Millwall (September 1947), Worcester City
(October 1952).
Honours: England international (1 cap), Third Division
South championship medal 1937.
*Chelsea debut: 12 March 1938. Appearances: League
36, FA Cup 11; Goals: League 21, FA Cup 2.*

The statistic that Joe Payne scored 110 goals in his
118 League games is an impressive one. Even so, it
does not tell the full story of this remarkable player
who scored ten goals on his first appearance at centre-
forward, for Luton Town against Bristol Rovers in
April 1936. His Chelsea career was truncated by the
outbreak of World War Two and, later, by injury.
A fine header of the ball and blessed with powerful
and accurate shooting from either foot, he was a lethal
finisher. As Sergeant Payne (RAF), he scored 50 goals
(39 games) in the wartime 1943-4 season and 40 (29
games) in the following campaign. Sadly, he played
little football after the ending of hostilities despite
several brave attempts to overcome injury. He also
played Minor Counties cricket for Bedfordshire.

PEARCE, Ian (1990-)   Central Defender
Born: Bury St Edmunds, 7 May 1974.
Career: Chelsea (associated schoolboy, July 1990).
Chelsea debut: 11 May 1991. Appearances: League 0(1).
After a handful of games for the Chelsea Juniors
towards the end of the 1989-90 season, Pearce was
signed as an associated schoolboy at the start of the
following term. A tall, commanding defender, with the
ability to move forward, he first earned promotion
to the Reserves and then made a brief first-team
appearance in the final fixture of the season, at Villa
Park, a few days after his 17th birthday.

PEARSON, Frank (1905-1906)   Centre-forward
Born: Manchester, 18 May 1884.
5ft 9½in; 12st 7lb.
Career: Preston North End (1899), Manchester City
(June 1903), Chelsea (October 1905, £250), Hull City
(October 1906), Luton Town (May 1907), Rochdale
(September 1908), Eccles Borough (February 1909).
*Chelsea debut: 14 October 1905. Appearances: League
29, FA Cup 1; Goals: League 18.*
After an outstandingly successful first season for
Chelsea, when he frequently captained the side,
Pearson was, surprisingly, allowed to move on and
was subsequently never able to reproduce his best form.

PEARSON, George William M. (1926-1933)   Outside-left
Born: West Stanley, 1907.
5ft 2in; 10st 11lb.
Career: West Stanley, Bury (Trialist), Chelsea
(February 1926), Luton Town (June 1933), Walsall
(September 1934).
*Chelsea debut: 3 April 1926. Appearances: League 197,
FA Cup 18; Goals: League 33, FA Cup 2.*
Pearson came to Stamford Bridge from his native
North-East via Bury, where he had been a trialist.
Succeeding Bobby McNeil (the last survivor from the
1915 Cup Final team), he took over the left-wing
position and became an automatic choice for the next
six seasons. One of the smallest men ever to play for
Chelsea, he was extremely fast and direct with a
powerful shot and his most successful season with the
club was that of 1929-30, when Chelsea returned to
the First Division after an absence of six seasons.

PHILLIPS, John Thomas (1970-1980)   Goalkeeper
Born: Shrewsbury, 7 July 1951.
5ft 10½in; 10st 10lb.
Career: Shrewsbury Town (November 1968), Aston
Villa (October 1969), Chelsea (August 1970, £25,000),

Crewe Alexandra (August 1979, loan), Brighton & Hove Albion (March 1980), Charlton Athletic (July 1981), Crystal Palace (January 1983), Retired (1984).
Honours: Wales international (4 caps), Wales Under-23 (4 caps).
Chelsea debut: 24 October 1970. Appearances: League 125, FA Cup 11, League Cup 9, European Cup-winners' Cup 4.
Phillips spent the majority of his career at Chelsea understudying Peter Bonetti, although, as his total of first-team appearances suggests, he had several lengthy spells of duty in the senior side, notably when playing a crucial part in steering the club to the European Cup-winners' Cup Final in 1971. At his best he was a fine goalkeeper, but his game did suffer from inconsistency.

PICKERING, Peter Barlow (1948-1951)   Goalkeeper
Born: York, 24 March 1926.
5ft 11in; 12st 6lb.
Career: Earswick, York City (1946), Chelsea (May 1948), Kettering Town (summer 1951), Northampton Town (July 1955).
Chelsea debut: 9 October 1948. Appearances: League 27, FA Cup 8.
A magnificently-built and spectacular goalkeeper, Pickering shared the goalkeeping duties with Harry Medhurst for some three seasons. A lack of consistency prevented him going further in the game but he totalled 160 League games in a career delayed by World War Two. For York City he achieved the remarkable feat of saving 11 consecutive penalty-kicks. A good cricketer, he played one match for Northamptonshire and later became a first-class umpire in South Africa.

PINNER, Michael John (1961)   Goalkeeper
Born: Boston (Lincs), 16 February 1934.
Career: Boston GS, Boston, Cambridge University (1952-54), Pegasus, Corinthian Casuals, Aston Villa (amateur 1954), Sheffield Wednesday (amateur, December 1957), Queen's Park Rangers (amateur, July 1959), Manchester United (amateur February 1961), Chelsea (amateur October 1961), Swansea Town (amateur May 1962), Leyton Orient (October 1962, professional October 1963).
Honours: England Amateur international.
Chelsea debut: 20 April 1962. Appearances: League 1.
Pinner was a famous amateur goalkeeper who made occasional appearances for seven League clubs, Chelsea included, before signing professional forms for Leyton Orient. Over a period of almost 15 years he made 113 League appearances (77 with Orient).

PLUM, Seth Lewis (1924-1927)   Wing-half
Born: Edmonton, 15 July 1899; Died: 29 November 1969.
5ft 7½in; 10st 5lb.
Career: Mildmay Athletic (1912-13), Tottenham Park Avondale, Barnet, Charlton Athletic (August 1923), Chelsea (March 1924), Southend United (cs 1927).
Honours: England international (1 cap), England Amateur.
Chelsea debut: 30 August 1924. Appearances: League 26, FA Cup 1; Goals: League 1.
Plum was a wing-half who arrived, having won Amateur international honours, and began his Chelsea career in the first team. However, he was unable to

establish his place and played most of his football in the Reserves thereafter.

PORTER, William (1905-1907)   Outside-left
Career: London Caledonians, Chelsea (amateur, 1905-07), Luton Town.
Chelsea debut: 14 April 1906. Appearances: League 2.
Porter was one of several amateurs linked with Chelsea in their early days. His two first-team games, separated by 11 months, were both occasioned when he deputized for the injured Johnny Kirwan.

POTRAC, Anthony J. (1970-1973)   Inside-forward
Born: Victoria (London), 21 January 1953.
5ft 9½in; 11st.
Career: Chelsea (August 1970), Durban City (summer 1973).
Chelsea debut: 8 January 1972. Appearances: League 1.
Potrac was unable to break into the first team at a time when financial cuts were being forced on the club, and a large number of other junior players were also pressing for places.

PRIESTLEY, John (1920-1928)   Inside-forward
Born: Johnstone (Renfrew), 19 August 1900; Died: 9 January 1980.
5ft 8in; 10st 2lb.
Career: Johnstone FC, Chelsea (May 1920), Grimsby Town (May 1928), St Johnstone (August 1932), Cowdenbeath (1933).
Chelsea debut: 2 May 1921. Appearances: League 191, FA Cup 13; Goals: League 18, FA Cup 1.
Originally a wing-half, Priestley turned out to be a wonderful investment for Chelsea, remaining a pillar of the first team for six seasons. A strong tackler, he was an accurate passer of the ball and a consistent 'provider' of goals for others. Well liked and respected throughout the game.

PRIESTLEY, Thomas J.M. (1933-1934)   Inside-forward
Born: Belfast; Died: 1986.
5ft 9in; 11st.
Career: Coleraine, Linfield, Chelsea (June 1933, £2,000), Shelbourne, (September 1934).
Honours: Northern Ireland international (2 caps).
Chelsea debut: 26 August 1933. Appearances: League 23, FA Cup 4; Goals: League 1, FA Cup 1.
Chelsea secured his services in fierce competition with other English clubs. Easily identified by the fact that he wore a skull-cap to conceal his complete baldness, he was a gifted player on the field and quiet and withdrawn off it. After one season he returned home, without being in dispute with the club, and never returned. He remained on Chelsea's list of retained players for many years. A schoolmaster by profession and headmaster of a school in Londonderry.

PROUDFOOT, Peter (1906-1908)   Wing-half
Born: Wishaw; Died: 4 March 1941.
Career: St Mirren, Lincoln City, Millwall (October 1904), Clapton Orient (cs 1905), Chelsea (April 1906), Stockport County (cs 1908), Manchester United.
Chelsea debut: 13 April 1906. Appearances: League 12.
A terrier-type defender, Proudfoot's energetic and constructive play were the features of his game. Unable to win a regular first-team place at Chelsea, he was appointed manager of Clapton Orient in April 1922,

after his playing career had ended and after having held a commission in the Army during World War One.

PROUT, Stanley S. (1932-1934) **Outside-left**
Born: Fulham, 1911.
5ft 8in; 10st 5lb.
Career: Park Royal, Fulham (amateur), Chelsea (May 1932), Bristol Rovers (June 1934).
Chelsea debut: 12 November 1932. Appearances: League 16, FA Cup 1; Goals: League 3.
Having made the step-up from amateur to professional football with apparent ease, Prout lost his place to Jack Horton and, after a season in the Reserves, moved into the Third Division.

RANDALL, Ernest Albert Walter (1950-1953)
Centre-forward
Born: Bognor Regis, 13 January 1926.
6ft; 12st 11lb.
Career: Bognor Town, Chelsea (December 1950), Crystal Palace (June 1953), Bognor Town (August 1955).
Chelsea debut: 13 October 1951. Appearances: League 3; Goals: League 1.
A powerfully-built centre-forward and former policeman, Randall was unable to displace Roy Bentley from the first team, but was a regular goalscorer in the reserve and 'A' teams.

RANKIN, John Patterson (1930-1934) **Inside-forward**
Born: Coatbridge.
5ft 8½in; 10st 2lb.
Career: Dundee (1924), Charlton Athletic (September 1925), Chelsea (May 1930), Notts County (May 1934).
Chelsea debut: 25 March 1931. Appearances: League 62, FA Cup 4; Goals: League 9.
An engineer by profession, Rankin was an artistic, ball-playing inside-forward who had played over 200 first-team games with Charlton. At a period when Chelsea were spilling out large sums of money on new 'star' players, he never quite established himself as a regular first-teamer and the arrival of George Gibson virtually ended his opportunities in the senior side.

READ, William Henry (1911-1912) **Winger**
Born: Blackpool, 1885.
5ft 9in; 11st 8lb.
Career: Colne, Sunderland (cs 1910), Chelsea (May 1911), Dundee (March 1913).
Chelsea debut: 20 January 1912. Appearances: League 3, FA Cup 1.
Read spent almost two seasons in the Reserves as deputy to Billy Bridgeman on the left-wing.

REID, Ernest James (1937-1939)
Born: Pentrebach, 25 March 1914.
5ft 7in; 11st 9lb.
Career: Troed-y-rhiw, Swansea Town (1936), Chelsea (September 1937), Swansea Town (summer 1939), Norwich City (June 1945), Bedford Town (October 1947).
Chelsea debut: 5 November 1938.Appearances: League 1.
Reid was spotted in Welsh League football and spent two seasons in the Reserves, deputizing on one occasion for Sammy Weaver, but never quite fulfilled his promise. He made regular 'guest' appearances for Brighton and Hove Albion during the war, from 1942-45.

REILLY, Edward W. (1908-1909) Half-back/Inside-forward
Career: Chelsea (amateur, 1908-09), Fulham (1909).
Chelsea debut: 3 April 1909. Appearances: League 1.
Reilly was one of several amateurs associated with Chelsea in their early days. He was on the books for two seasons, but received only one opportunity in the first team. He did not appear in Fulham's first team after moving to Craven Cottage and drifted out of League circles.

RHOADES-BROWN, Peter (1979-1984) **Winger**
Born: Hampton, 2 January 1962.
5ft 11in; 10st 12lb.
Career: Chelsea (July 1979), Oxford United (January 1984, £85,000), Retired (March 1990).
Chelsea debut: 29 December 1979. Appearances: League 86(10), FA Cup 7(2), League Cup 4; Goals: League 4, FA Cup 1.

Rhoades-Brown first came to Chelsea as a schoolboy and was then an apprentice before signing as a full-time professional. A skilful and speedy left-side striker, his output of goals was disappointing and, partly as a result, the advent of Paul Canoville and Mickey Thomas rendered him superfluous to the needs of the first-team squad.

RICHARDSON, Frederick A. (1946-1947) Centre-forward
Born: Middlestone Moor, 18 August 1924.
5ft 9in; 11st 7lb.
Career: Spennymoor United, Bishop Auckland, Chelsea (September 1946), Hartlepools United

(October 1947), Barnsley (October 1948), West Bromwich Albion (June 1950), Chester (February 1952), Hartlepools United (November 1952), Retired 1955.
Honours: FA Amateur Cup runners-up medal 1946.
Chelsea debut: 12 April 1947. Appearances: League 2.
Kept in the Reserves by the presence of Tommy Lawton in the first season after World War Two, Richardson subsequently achieved success with his other clubs, chalking up nearly 250 League appearances (66 goals).

ROBERTS, Graham Paul (1988-1990)
Born: Southampton, 3 July 1959.
5ft 10in; 12st 12lb.
Career: Scholing School (Southampton), AFC Bournemouth, Dorchester Town, Weymouth, Totten-ham Hotspur (May 1980), Glasgow Rangers (December 1986), Chelsea (August 1988, £475,000), West Bromwich Albion (November 1990, £200,000).
Honours: England international (6 caps), England 'B' (1 cap), UEFA Cup winners' medal 1984, FA Cup winners' medals 1981, 1982. Scottish League Cup winners' medal 1988, Second Division championship medal 1989.
Chelsea debut: 27 August 1988. Appearances: League 70, FA Cup 4, League Cup 3, Full Members' Cup 6; Goals: League 18, League Cup 1, Full Members' Cup 3.
Graham Roberts was appointed captain soon after his arrival at Chelsea and immediately his powerful presence and aggression gave the team the quality of leadership which had been missing for some time. as Chelsea romped away with the Second Division

championship, his tally of 15 goals (mostly from the penalty-spot) was an additional bonus. Appointed coach upon the departure of Ian Porterfield to Reading, in November 1989, things began to go wrong almost immediately. Roberts lost form on the pitch, where his lack of pace was increasingly exposed by First Division strikers. Then problems over contractual obligations led to the termination of his appointment on the coaching staff and he never played for the first team again.

ROBERTSON, James (1905-1907)   **Inside-forward**
Born: Glasgow, 1883.
Career: Crewe Alexandra, Small Heath (cs 1903), Chelsea (April 1905, £150), Glossop (August 1907), Leyton (cs 1909), Partick Thistle, Ayr United, Barrow, Leeds City, Gateshead.
Chelsea debut: 30 September 1905. Appearances: League 29, FA Cup 2; Goals: League 21, FA Cup 1.
Robertson was a member of Chelsea's first-ever League side and a regular goalscorer when called upon during the first two seasons in the club's history. Strangely, in view of his impressive striking record, he was by no means assured of his first-team place, especially after the arrival of Billy Bridgeman in the autumn of 1906.

ROBERTSON, John Tait (1905-1906)   **Wing-half**
Born: Dumbarton, 25 February 1977; Died: 24 January 1935.
Career: Morton (1896), Southampton (May 1898), Glasgow Rangers (August 1899), Chelsea (player-manager, April 1905), Glossop (player-manager, October 1906).
Honours: Scotland international (16 caps), Scottish League XI (6 appearances), Scottish League Championship medals 1900, 1901, 1902, Scottish FA Cup winners' medals 1903, runners-up medals 1904, 1905.
Chelsea debut: 2 September 1905. Appearances: League 36, FA Cup 3; Goals: League 4.
'Jackie' Robertson is the only player-manager in Chelsea's history. He was appointed in the spring of 1905 and his experience of both Scottish and English football was crucial in assembling, at very short notice, a squad of players ready to do battle in the Football League. At the princely salary of £4 per week, his shrewd judgement of talent enabled him to build a team with a nice blend of experience and youth which took the club to third position in the Second Division at the very first attempt. He was also still a fine player and played regularly in the left-half position through-out that season. Subsequently he coached on the Continent.

ROBERTSON, William Gibb (1946-1960)   **Goalkeeper**
Born: Glasgow, 13 November 1928; Died: June 1973.
6ft; 13st.
Career: Arthurlie, Chelsea (July 1946), Leyton Orient (September 1960, £1,000), Dover Town (1963).
Honours: Football League Championship medal 1955.
Also 1 FA Charity Shield appearance 1955.
Chelsea debut: 21 April 1951. Appearances: League 199, FA Cup 14, Fairs Cup 1.
Robertson was a wonderfully solid, reliable goalkeeper who spent five years understudying Harry Medhurst before making his League debut against Liverpool on 21 April 1951. After 14 games without a win, Chelsea

were four points adrift at the bottom of the First Division and 'certainties' for relegation. But they won their last four games, avoided the drop by 0.44 of a goal, and Bill Robertson's career as first-choice 'keeper was well and truly launched. Later, after 51 League and Cup appearances for Leyton Orient he ended his career in the Southern League.

ROBERTSON, William Harold (1945-1948)   Goalkeeper
Born: Crowthorne (Berks), 25 March 1923.
6ft 1½in; 12st 9lb.
Career: RAF Lossiemouth, Chelsea (October 1945), Birmingham City (December 1948), Stoke City (June 1952).
Chelsea debut: 5 January 1946. Appearances: League 37, FA Cup 6.
Robertson had the unenviable task of succeeding Vic Woodley as Chelsea's first-choice goalkeeper. He played regularly in the 1945-6 transitional season but lost his place with the arrival of Harry Medhurst. He made over 200 first-team appearances for Stoke City.

ROBINSON, Arthur Charles (1908-1910) Goalkeeper
Born: Coventry, 28 February 1877; Died: 15 May 1929.
Career: Singer's FC, Small Heath (cs 1899), Chelsea (cs 1908), not retained (May 1910).
Honours: Irish League XI, Scottish League XI.
Chelsea debut: 7 September 1908. Appearances: League 3.
Robinson was signed in the 1908 close season as deputy for Jack Whitley. An experienced 'keeper, he was given few opportunities to prove himself in his two seasons at Chelsea, after nine seasons of distinguished service with Small Heath.

ROBSON, Bryan Stanley (1982-1983)   Striker
Born: Sunderland, 11 November 1945.
5ft 7in; 11st 8lb.
Career: Clare Vale Juniors, Newcastle United (November 1962), West Ham United (February 1971), Sunderland (July 1974), West Ham United (October 1976), Sunderland (July 1979), Carlisle United (March 1981), Chelsea (July 1982), Sunderland (August 1983), Carlisle United (July 1984).
Honours: England Under-23 international (2 caps), Football League XI, Second Division championship medal 1965, Fairs Cup winners' medal 1969.
Chelsea debut: 28 August 1982. Appearances: League 11(4), League Cup 1(1); Goals: League 3, League Cup 2.
After a long and distinguished career, 'Pop' Robson arrived at Stamford Bridge as senior professional just short of his 37th birthday. He was also involved in coaching duties with the Juniors but, unable to hold a first-team place, he returned to Sunderland for a third spell, after only one season at Stamford Bridge. In his prime he was a prolific goalscorer as his tally of some 250 League goals proves.

ROBSON, Thomas Henry (1965-1966)   Outside-left
Born: Gateshead, 31 July 1944.
5ft 7½in; 10st 3lb.
Career: Northampton Town (August 1961), Chelsea (November 1965, £30,000), Newcastle United (December 1966, £20,000), Peterborough United (October 1968), Nuneaton Borough (cs 1981).
Honours: England Youth international, Fourth

Division championship medal 1974.
Chelsea debut: 4 December 1965. Appearances: League 6(1).
A speedy left-winger, Robson's chances at Chelsea were stifled by the form and consistency of Bobby Tambling. On the staff for only 13 months, he later played some 500 first-team games for Peterborough United, scoring well over a century of goals.

RODGER, George B. (1924-1931)   Centre-half
Born: Cambuslang.
5ft 10in; 11st 2lb.
Career: Kilsyth Rangers, Chelsea (June 1924), Clachnacuddin (coach-manager, 1931).
Chelsea debut: 17 January 1925. Appearances: League 119, FA Cup 3; Goals: League 2.
Throughout his time at Stamford Bridge, Rodger faced keen competition for his place in the first team, both from Harry Wilding and, later, Jack Townrow. He did play a vital role in the 1929-30 promotion season but, before he had a real chance to establish himself in the First Division, a knee injury terminated his career.

ROFE, Dennis (1980-1982)   Full-back
Born: Fulham, 1 June 1950.
5ft 7½in; 11st 7lb.
Career: Orient (February 1968), Leicester City (April 1972), Chelsea (February 1980, £80,000), Southampton (July 1982).
Honours: England Under-23 international (1 cap).
Chelsea debut: 23 February 1980. Appearances: League 58(1), FA Cup 1(1), League Cup 2.

After a distinguished career with Orient and Leicester City, involving some 500 senior appearances, Rofe, a hard-tackling, aggressive full-back, was appointed captain in his first full season at Stamford Bridge and played 54 consecutive first-team games before, surprisingly, losing his place to Chris Hutchings. Soon he moved on to Southampton, where he subsequently became a member of the coaching staff, and was first-team coach from February 1987 to May 1991.

ROUGVIE, Douglas (1984-1987)   Defender
Born: Ballingry (Fifeshire), 24 May 1956.
6ft 1in; 12st.
Career: Dunfermline United, Aberdeen (1972), Chelsea (July 1984, £150,000), Brighton & Hove Albion (June 1987, £50,000), Shrewsbury Town (August 1988), Fulham (February 1989).
Honours: Scotland international (1 cap), Scottish League Championship medals 1980, 1984, Scottish FA Cup winners' medals 1982, 1983, 1984, Scottish League Cup runners-up medals 1979, 1980, European Cup-winners' Cup winners' medal 1983, Full Members' Cup winners' medal 1986.
Chelsea debut: 25 August 1984. Appearances: League 74, FA Cup 4, League Cup 16, Full Members' Cup 6; Goals: League 3.

Rougvie came to Chelsea at the age of 28 after 12 highly successful years with Aberdeen. A tall, strong defender, at home in any of the back-four positions, he was a hard tackler, good in the air and quick coming forward. Popular with the crowd, he played mainly in the left-back position at Chelsea competing for the number-three shirt with Keith Dublin.

ROUSE, Frederick William (1907-1909) Inside-forward
Born: Cranford (Middlesex), 18 November 1881; Died: Windsor, 1953.

Career: Southall, Wycombe Wanderers, Shepherd's Bush, Grimsby Town (1903), Stoke City (April 1904), Everton (November 1906), Chelsea (October 1907, £1,000), West Bromwich Albion (May 1909), Croydon Common (September 1910), Brentford (1911), Retired (1912).
Honours: Football League XI.
Chelsea debut: 19 October 1907. Appearances: League 38, FA Cup 4; Goals: League 11.
Chelsea's first-ever four-figure transfer signing, Rouse was a vigorous, bustling player who played in all three inside-forward positions for Chelsea and was a strong finisher.

RUSSELL, Robert Inglis (1944-1948)   Wing-half
Born: Aberdour, 27 December 1919.
5ft 7in; 10st 10lb.
Career: Airdrieonians, Chelsea (December 1944), Notts County (August 1948), Leyton Orient (October 1948).
Chelsea debut: 5 January 1946. Appearances: League 2, FA Cup 2.
Whilst the official record books show that Bobby Russell played only four 'official' first-team games for Chelsea, as a member of the renowned 'Russell-Harris-Foss' half-back line which formed the backbone of so many wartime games from 1943 to 1945, his total number of such appearances was 85 and included the

two Football League (South) Cup Finals at Wembley in 1944 and 1945. Unfortunately, injury limited his football once the war ended. He made only two appearances for Notts County and did not appear in League football for Leyton Orient.

RUSSELL, William (1927-1935)   **Wing-half**
Born: Hamilton.
5ft 7½in; 10st.
Career: Woodside (Hamilton), Larkhall (IOR), Blantyre Victoria, Chelsea (June 1927), Heart of Midlothian (December 1935), Rhyl (player-manager, August 1938).
Chelsea debut: 9 April 1928. Appearances: League 150, FA Cup 10; Goals: League 6.
Like his namesake Bobby, he was a flame-haired wing-half. An intelligent player, renowned for his strength in the tackle he was primarily a defensive player, but his clever use of the ball initiated many an attack — "The man who gets into the open space makes things easy," he once said. A welcome guest at the 1967 FA Cup Final banquet, he still followed the fortunes of his old club and was at the Liverpool-Chelsea game in November 1986.

SALES, Arthur Alfred (1924-1928)   **Centre-half**
Born: Lewes, 14 March 1900; Died: Lewes, 5 May 1977.
Career: Redhill, Chelsea (September 1924), not retained (May 1928).
Chelsea debut: 30 August 1924. Appearances: League 7.
Sales came to Stamford Bridge having established a high reputation for himself in amateur football. With George Rodger, Harry Wilding and Jack Townrow all on his books during his four seasons with the club, first-team opportunities were necessarily limited. He was also a fine athlete who once ran the 100 yards event in 10.5 seconds.

SALMOND, Robert C. (1938-1945)   **Centre-half**
Born: Kilmarnock.
5ft 11½in; 12st 7lb.
Career: Dundee North End, Portsmouth (May 1930), Chelsea (November 1938), Banbury Spencer (player-manager, 1945).
Chelsea debut: 12 November 1938. Appearances: League 24, FA Cup 5.
This tall and dominating centre-half was signed after eight years' service with Portsmouth to take over from Allan Craig who was nearing the end of his long career. The outbreak of World War Two, however, terminated his League career and at the end of hostilities he moved to Banbury Spencer as player-manager. It was a matter of surprise that he never received international recognition from the Scotland selectors.

SAUNDERS, Derek William (1953-1959)   **Wing-half**
Born: Ware, 6 January 1928.
5ft 10in; 11st 7lb.
Career: Walthamstow Avenue (amateur), Chelsea (July 1953), Retired (May 1959).
Honours: England Amateur international, Football League Championship medal 1955, FA Amateur Cup winners' medal 1952. Also 1 FA Charity Shield appearance 1955.
Chelsea debut: 5 September 1953. Appearances: League 203, FA Cup 17, Fairs Cup 2; Goals: League 9.

This red-haired, highly-skilled wing-half was an ever-present in the 1954-5 Championship team and his strong tackling and defensive play, as well as his constructive ideas, were crucial factors in that success. Appointed captain of Chelsea in August 1957, he joined the coaching staff on retirement as a player. Later, he was groundsman and chief football coach at Westminster School before joining Hampstead Cricket Club as groundsman.

SAUNDERS, Francis John (1948-1954)   **Centre-half**
Born: Middlesbrough, 24 August 1924.
6ft; 12st.
Career: Darlington, Chelsea (May 1948), Crystal Palace (August 1954), Chester (May 1957), Hyde United.
Chelsea debut: 10 December 1949. Appearances: League 52, FA Cup 8.
Saunders understudied John Harris in the centre-half position for five seasons until the arrival of Ron Greenwood and Stan Wicks. A tall, craggy defender, he made over 250 appearances in his League career, having first been spotted in Army football.

SAUNDERS, James E. (1909-1910)   **Goalkeeper**
Born: Birmingham.
5ft 9in; 11st 7lb.
Career: Glossop, Manchester United (October 1901), Lincoln City (1906), Chelsea (May 1909), Watford (cs 1910, £50).
Chelsea debut: 25 December 1909. Appearances: League 2.
Saunders deputized for Jack Whitley twice during his only season on the staff, one of the games being the home fixture against Newcastle United at Christmas,

when over 70,000 spectators were present. He had previously been with manager Dave Calderhead at Lincoln City.

SCOTT, Melvyn D. (1956-1963)   **Centre-half**
Born: Claygate, 26 September 1939.
6ft; 11st 9lb.
Career: Chelsea (November 1956), Brentford (March 1963, £10,000), Chicago Sting (1967), Oakland Clippers (February 1967).
Honours: England Under-23 international (4 caps).
Chelsea debut: 11 March 1958. Appearances: League 97, FA Cup 5, Fairs Cup 2.
One of the many products of the Chelsea youth scheme in its most prolific and successful period, Scott's early career as a professional was interrupted by National Service and thereafter he never quite fulfilled his true potential. Lack of domination in the air caused him to lose his place to John Mortimore, but he went on to become Brentford's regular pivot for five seasons. In 1967 and 1968 he appeared for Oakland Clippers in the North American Soccer League.

SHARP, Buchanan (1919-1923)   **Inside-forward**
Born: Alexandria, 2 November 1894; Died: Bolton, 1956.
5ft 11in; 12st 2lb.
Career: Vale of Leven, Chelsea (November 1919), Tottenham Hotspur (March 1923), Leicester City (January 1925), Nelson (June 1926), Southport (October 1928).
Chelsea debut: 28 February 1920. Appearances: League 65, FA Cup 7; Goals: League 20, FA Cup 3.
Renowned for his close, Scottish-style, dribbling and ball-control, as well as for his strong shooting powers, Sharp played for Chelsea in the 1920 FA Cup semi-final against Aston Villa at Bramall Lane, yet took some time to find his bearings in the Football League. Even so, it was a surprise when he was allowed to move towards the end of his most successful season at Stamford Bridge.

SHARP, James (1912-1915)   **Full-back**
Born: Jordanstone, 11 October 1880; Died: Ayrshire, 18 November 1949.
5ft 9½in; 13st 7lb.
Career: East Craigie (Dundee), Dundee (1899), Fulham (cs 1904), Woolwich Arsenal (cs 1905), Glasgow Rangers (April 1908), Chelsea (November 1912, £1,750).
Honours: Scotland international (5 caps), Scottish League XI (2 appearances).
Chelsea debut: 23 November 1912. Appearances: League 61, FA Cup 3.
The experienced Sharp was signed to take over from Jock Cameron at full-back. A fine defender, with a good tactical sense, he was a little lacking in pace and the emergence of Jack Harrow limited his first-team opportunities, which were ended altogether by the outbreak of World War One. Subsequently he became trainer-coach with Fulham (1919-26) and was later associated both with Walsall (1926-28) and Cliftonville (1928-29).

SHAW, Colin M. (1960-1963)   **Centre-forward**
Born: St Albans, 19 June 1943.
5ft 6½in; 10st 6lb.

Career: Chelsea (May 1960), Norwich City (August 1963, £3,500), Leyton Orient (March 1965), Natal (SA) (1966).
Chelsea debut: 3 February 1962. Appearances: League 1.
A prodigous goalscorer in junior and reserve football (including seven goals against Fulham in an FA Youth Cup tie), Shaw never established himself at senior level and with his three professional clubs (11 appearances in all) he failed to find the net in a League fixture.

SHEARER, Duncan N. (1983-1986)   **Striker**
Born: Fort William, 28 August 1962.
5ft 10in; 10st 9lb.
Career: Clachnacuddin, Chelsea (November 1983), Huddersfield Town (March 1986, £10,000), Swindon Town (June 1988).
Chelsea debut: 1 February 1986. Appearances: League 2; Goals: League 1.

A tall centre-forward who scored goals regularly in the reserve team, Shearer's opportunities were restricted by the consistent form of Kerry Dixon and David Speedie. He was an instant success at Huddersfield Town, however, scoring five goals in his first two full games.

SHELLITO, Kenneth J. (1957-1969)   **Full-back**
Born: East Ham, 18 April 1940.
5ft 10in; 12st 6lb.
Career: Chelsea (April 1957), Retired January 1969.
Honours: England international (1 cap), England Under-23 (1 cap), FA Youth Cup winners' medal 1958.
Chelsea debut: 15 April 1959. Appearances: League

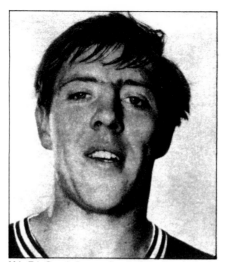

114, FA Cup 4, League Cup 1, Fairs Cup 4; Goals: League 2.
Shellito, who first joined Chelsea as a junior in 1955, was an outstanding, aggressive full-back whose career was dogged, and prematurely ended, by injury. After four operations on his left knee he was forced to retire. Yet months earlier he might well have been part of England's triumphant 1966 World Cup campaign. As it was, he had only one full season in Chelsea's first team, partnering Eddie McCreadie in one of the best young full-back duos in the League in the 1962-3 Second Division promotion season. After coaching the Juniors, he succeeded Frank Blunstone as manager of the youth section and was appointed manager of Chelsea FC before the start of the 1977-8 season, resigning after 15 months. After leaving Chelsea in December 1978, he was, in turn, assistant manager with Queen's Park Rangers (May 1979 to 1980), on the Crystal Palace coaching staff (1980-81) and assistant manager with that club (cs 1982 to November 1983), first-team coach at Wolverhampton Wanderers (January 1985) and manager of Cambridge United from March to December 1985.

SHERBORNE, John L. (1936-1945)   **Forward**
Born: Bolton, 1 May 1916.
Career: Chorley, Chelsea (February 1937), Retired 1945.
Chelsea debut: 18 December 1937. Appearances: League 5.
Apart from a brief spell in the League side in February and March 1937, Sherborne had to be content with reserve-team football, although he played a handful of games in the first season of wartime soccer before joining the Army. After suffering wounds on active service in France, he never played again.

SHERWOOD, Stephen (1971-1976)   **Goalkeeper**
Born: Selby, 10 December 1953.
6ft 3in; 14st.
Career: Chelsea (July 1971), Brighton & Hove Albion (loan), Millwall (loan), Brentford (loan), Watford

(November 1976, £5,000), Grimsby Town (July 1987).
Honours: FA Cup runners-up medal 1984.
Chelsea debut: 1 January 1972. Appearances: League 16, League Cup 1.
Recommended to Chelsea whilst playing football in the West Riding, Sherwood was an apprentice for a year before signing professional forms. The son of a former Huddersfield Town goalkeeper and brother of Olympic hurdler John Sherwood, Steve began the 1975-6 season as first-choice goalkeeper before the re-signing of Peter Bonetti effectively ended his opportunities.

SILLETT, John Charles (1954-1962)   **Full-back**
Born: Southampton, 20 July 1936.
6ft; 12st 12lb.
Career: Southampton (amateur), Chelsea (April 1954), Coventry City (April 1962, £3,000), Plymouth Argyle (July 1966).
Honours: Football League XI (1 appearance).
Chelsea debut: 1 January 1957. Appearances: League 93, FA Cup 5, League Cup 2, Fairs Cup 2; Goals: League Cup 1.
Son of a former Southampton player Charles Sillett, John came to Stamford Bridge as an amateur with brother Peter in May 1953 and signed professional 12 months later. A strong, hard-tackling full-back, he was in partnership with Peter, on the flanks of the defence for some three seasons before losing his place to Ken Shellito. After retiring as a player, he was a coach with Bristol City, managed Hereford United (1974-78) before being appointed chief coach and then manager with Coventry City. He steered Coventry to victory in the 1987 FA Cup Final and announced his retirement three years later.

SILLETT, Richard Peter (1953-1962)   **Full-back**
Born: Southampton, 1 February 1933.
6ft 1in; 14st 9lb.
Career: Normansland, Southampton (June 1950), Chelsea (May 1953, £12,000), Guildford City (June 1962, free transfer), Folkestone Town, Ashford Town (player-manager, July 1965).
Honours: England international (3 caps), England Under-23 (3 caps), England 'B' (1 cap), Football League XI (1 appearance), Football League Championship medal 1955. Also 1 FA Charity Shield appearance 1955.
Chelsea debut: 19 August 1953. Appearances: League 260, FA Cup 20, League Cup 3, Fairs Cup 4; Goals: League 29, FA Cup 2, League Cup 2, Fairs Cup 1.
A sound and respected full-back who was a particularly fine kicker of the ball, Peter Sillett obtained most of his goals either from the penalty-spot or from free-kicks. A member of the 1954-5 Football League Championship side, he shared the right-back position with John Harris and is well remembered for his goal against Wolverhampton Wanderers in front of 75,000 spectators, an effort which virtually clinched the title when he hit a penalty-kick with stunning power past England goalkeeper Bert Williams. Lacking the pace to make a permanent impact on the international scene, he was manager of Ashford Town, Folkestone and Poole Town for spells, and a Coventry City scout (1987-1990).

SIMNER, Joseph (1947-1949)   **Centre-forward**
Born: Sedgley, 13 March 1923.
Career: Folkestone Town, Chelsea (October 1947), Swindon Town (July 1949).

Chelsea debut: 6 March 1948. Appearances: League 1.
Simner spent two years in the reserve team at a time
when Roy Bentley and Hugh Billington were vying
for the centre-forward berth in the first team. He
remained at Swindon Town for three years.

SINCLAIR, Frank (1990-) **Full-back**
Born: Lambeth, 3 December 1971.
5ft 9in; 12st.
Career: Chelsea (May 1990).
Chelsea debut: 6 April 1991. Appearances: League 4.
A product of Pimlico School, in signing for Chelsea
he followed in the footsteps of Alan Hudson. He earned
his first-team chance after some impressive displays
in the 1990-91 Football Combination championship
team.

SINCLAIR, William I. (1964-1966) **Midfield**
Born: Glasgow, 21 March 1947.
5ft 6in; 11st 2lb.
Career: Greenock Morton, Chelsea (September 1964,
part-exchange Jim Mulholland), Released (March
1966), Glentoran.
Chelsea debut: 24 April 1965. Appearances: League 1.
After playing in the junior and reserve sides, Sinclair
made one League appearance, then went on the club
tour of Australia the following summer but did not
receive any further first-team opportunities.

SISSONS, John Leslie (1974-1975) **Outside-left**
Born: Hayes, 30 September 1945.
5ft 7in; 10st 12lb.
Career: Hayes School, West Ham United (October
1962), Sheffield Wednesday (August 1970), Norwich
City (December 1973), Chelsea (August 1974, £70,000),
contract cancelled (May 1975), Tampa Bay Rowdies
(May 1975), Cape Town City.
Honours: England Under-23 international (10 caps),
England Youth, England Schoolboys, FA Cup winners'
medal 1964, European Cup-winners' Cup winners'
medal 1965, Football League Cup runners-up medal
1966.
*Chelsea debut: 17 August 1974. Appearances: League
10(1), FA Cup 1, League Cup 1.*
A left-winger who had played over 400 senior games,
most of them for West Ham United, when he arrived
at Stamford Bridge, Sissons was already past his best
and failed to establish himself in a team struggling
to maintain its First Division status.

SITTON, John Edmund (1977-1980) **Central defender**
Born: Hackney, 21 October 1959.
6ft; 12st 2lb.
Career: Chelsea (October 1977), Millwall (February
1980 £10,000), Gillingham (September 1981), Orient
(July 1985).
*Chelsea debut: 21 February 1979. Appearances: League
11(2), League Cup 1.*
A strongly-built centre-half, Sitton first came to
Chelsea as an apprentice in May 1976. He had a run
of games in the first team towards the end of the
1978-9 season, in a side already doomed to relegation
from the First Division, but did not figure in manager
Geoff Hurst's plans and played mostly reserve-team
football thereafter. He skippered Orient to promotion
to Division Three in 1989.

SMALE, Douglas M. (1937-1945) **Outside-left**
Born: Victoria (London), 27 March 1916.
5ft 7in; 11st.
Career: Kingstonian, Chelsea (March 1937), Retired
(1945).
Chelsea debut: 29 March 1937. Appearances: League 9.
One of many players whose career was terminated by
World War Two, Smale was was on the fringe of the
first team at the outbreak of hostilities, as deputy for
regular left-winger Alf Hanson. During the war he
served with the RAF in India and had retired from
football by the time normal soccer was resumed in
1946.

SMART, James (1965-1966) **Inside-forward**
Born: Dundee, 9 January 1947.
5ft 7½in; 10st 8lb.
Career: Greenock Morton, Chelsea (February 1965),
contract cancelled (March 1966), Highlands Park (SA).
Chelsea debut: 24 April 1965. Appearances: League 1.
Spending only just over 12 months at Stamford Bridge,
in the Reserves, Smart was unable to make an impact
in English football and, with a stream of young talent
emerging from the Juniors at that time, was allowed
to move on.

SMETHURST, Derek (1968-1971) **Striker**
Born: Durban, South Africa, 24 October 1947.
6ft 1in; 11st 7lb.
Career: Durban University, Durban City, Chelsea
('permit player' December 1968, professional January
1971), Millwall (September 1971, £35,000), Tampa Bay
Rowdies (April 1975), San Diego Sockers (May 1978),
Seattle Sounders (April 1979).
Honours: European Cup-winners' Cup winners' medal
1971.
*Chelsea debut: 1 September 1970. Appearances: League
14, League Cup 1, European Cup-winners' Cup 3(1);
Goals: League 4, European Cup-winners' Cup 1.*
Smethurst proved himself an extremely able deputy
for such as Peter Osgood and Ian Hutchinson during
his time at The Bridge and he played an important
role in the semi-final and final of the successful
European Cup-winners' Cup campaign in 1970-71.
Surprisingly, he was allowed to move on but made
little impact with his only other English club, Millwall.
One of the original Tampa Bay Rowdies, he helped
them win the North American Soccer League title in
1975, scoring 18 goals in 22 regular season games, and
73 in his career on that side of the Atlantic.

SMITH, Arthur John (1938-1945) **Full-back**
Born: Merthyr, 1912; Died: 1975.
5ft 10in; 11st 7lb.
Career: West Bromwich Albion (trialist), Wolverhampton Wanderers (May 1930), Swindon Town (cs 1934),
Chelsea (March 1938), Retired (1945).
*Chelsea debut: 12 March 1938. Appearances: League
45, FA Cup 4.*
An excellent acquisition from Third Division football,
Jack Smith went straight into the first team at left-
back and a very promising career was then truncated
by the outbreak of World War Two, during which
he served as a Flight-Sergeant in the RAF. Unfortunately, any chance of resuming his career afterwards
was ruined by injuries received in a road accident. He
won an unofficial wartime cap for Wales and was later

130

trainer to Wolverhampton Wanderers and manager of West Bromwich Albion (1948-52), guiding them back to the First Division during his first season at the helm. He also managed Reading (1952-55).

SMITH, George W. (1921-1932) **Full-back**
Born: Parkhead.
5ft 9½in; 11st 12lb.
Career: Wishaw, YMCA, Vale of Clyde Juniors, Parkhead, Chelsea (May 1921), East Fife (1932).
Chelsea debut: 27 August 1921. Appearances: League 351, FA Cup 19.
One of the best bargains for a £10 signing-on fee Chelsea have ever made. For almost ten full seasons the dependable and resourceful George Smith was a permanent fixture in the first team, having made his debut within weeks of his arrival from Scottish junior football. During the 1920s, few English club teams were better served at full-back than Chelsea were by Smith and his two distinguished partners, Jack Harrow and, later, Tommy Law. Further, few men were more noted for their sportsmanship and fair play — and few were more respected and liked by supporters. Smith's final full season saw Chelsea return to the First Division after a six-year interval and soon afterwards a serious injury effectively ended his career.

SMITH, James Harold (1951-1955) **Winger**
Born: Sheffield, 6 December 1930.
Career: Shildon, Chelsea (April 1951), Leyton Orient (July 1955), Retired (1958).
Chelsea debut: 8 September 1951. Appearances: League 19, FA Cup 4; Goals: League 3.
This nippy, clever winger never quite fulfilled his early promise and the consistency of Eric Parsons and Frank Blunstone condemned him to reserve-team football for his last three years on the staff. He did not make much of an impact with Leyton Orient before being forced to retire through injury in 1958.

SMITH, Phillip (1910) **Centre-forward**
Career: Crewe Alexandra, Chelsea (April 1910, £250), Burnley (September 1910).
Chelsea debut: 16 April 1910. Appearances: League 1.
Smith was one of several players signed in the final weeks of the 1909-10 season in an unavailing bid to stave off relegation. After one game he was dropped and played only a handful of reserve games at the start of the following season.

SMITH, Robert Alfred (1950-1955) **Centre-forward**
Born: Lingdale, Yorkshire, 22 February 1923.
5ft 9in; 12st.
Career: Redcar Boys Club, Redcar United, Tudor Rose, Chelsea (May 1950), Tottenham Hotspur (December 1955, £16,000), Brighton & Hove Albion (May 1964), Hastings United (October 1965), Banbury United (cs 1968), Retired (1968).
Honours: England international (15 caps), Football League Championship medal 1961, FA Cup winners' medals 1961, 1962. Fourth Division championship medal 1965.
Chelsea debut: 4 September 1950. Appearances: League 74, FA Cup 12; Goals: League 23, FA Cup 7.
Bobby Smith was one of the outstanding products of the Chelsea youth scheme, coming to Stamford Bridge as a schoolboy from Redcar in 1948. Making his debut

as a 17-year-old, this strongly-built and aggressive centre-forward made an immediate impact with his enthusiasm and bustling methods. Yet he lost his place to Roy Bentley and never quite fitted into the scheme of things, although it was a matter of regret when he moved to Tottenham just at a time when further chances were coming his way. Once at White Hart Lane, Smith proved the folly of his release from Stamford Bridge, by winning a string of international caps and being a member of the famous Spurs 'double' side.

SMITH, Stephen (1921-1923) **Wing-half**
Born: Byker.
5ft 7in; 10st 1lb.
Career: Newcastle Junior football, Chelsea (January 1921), Merthyr Tydfil (cs 1923).
Chelsea debut: 29 August 1921. Appearances: League 22, FA Cup 1; Goals: League 1.
Although Smith had an extended run in the first team in 1921-2, he never succeeded in establishing a permanent place in the League side and the switching of Harry Wilding from centre to wing-half in September 1922 effectively ended his Chelsea career.

SORRELL, Dennis J. (1962-1964) **Wing-half**
Born: Lambeth, 7 October 1940.
5ft 5½in; 10st 10lb.
Career: Woodford Town, Leyton Orient (October 1957), Chelsea (March 1962, £10,000), Leyton Orient (September 1964, £3,000), Romford (December 1966).
Chelsea debut: 9 March 1962. Appearances: League 3, FA Cup 1; Goals: FA Cup 1.
A strong-tackling wing-half, Sorrell was on the staff at a time when Terry Venables and Ron Harris were establishing themselves in his position. He played over 100 games for Leyton Orient in two spells with that club.

SPACKMAN, Nigel J. (1983-1987) **Midfield**
Born: Romsey, 2 December 1960.
6ft 1in; 12st 4lb.

Career: Andover Town, AFC Bournemouth (May 1980), Chelsea (June 1983, £40,000), Liverpool (February 1987, £400,000), Queen's Park Rangers (February 1989), Glasgow Rangers (November 1989). Honours: Football League Championship medal 1988, Second Division championship medal 1984, Full Members' Cup winners' medal 1986. Football League Cup runners-up medal 1987, Scottish League Championship medals 1990, 1991.
Chelsea debut: 27 August 1983. Appearances: League 139(2), FA Cup 8, League Cup 22(1), Full Members' Cup 7; Goals: League 12, FA Cup 1, Full Members' Cup 1.
A powerful midfield player, strong in the tackle with boundless energy, Spackman proved ever-ready to move up in support of his forwards and had a good shot, especially from long range. The practical joker of the side, he was a highly popular player with colleagues and fans alike and was an ever-present member of the 1984 Second Division championship team.

SPARROW, John P. (1974-1981) Full-back
Born: Bethnal Green, 3 June 1957.
5ft 10in; 12st.
Career: Chelsea (August 1974), Millwall (loan), Exeter City (January 1981, £5,000).
Honours: England Youth international, England Schoolboys.
Chelsea debut: 13 March 1974. Appearances: League 63(6), FA Cup 2, League Cup 3; Goals: League 2.
Sparrow made his debut as a 16-year-old in March 1974, three months before signing professional forms and after two years as an apprentice. He promised rather more than he achieved and was never able to hold down a regular place at a time of instability within the club. Brother of Brian Sparrow, who played for a number of London clubs, notably Crystal Palace, John retired from League football in 1983.

SPECTOR, Miles D. (1952-1953) Outside-left
Born: Hendon, 4 August 1934.
Career: Hendon, Chelsea (1952-53, amateur), Millwall, Hendon.
Honours: England Youth international, England Amateur, FA Amateur Cup winners' medal 1960.
Chelsea debut: 7 February 1953. Appearances: League 3, FA Cup 3.
As an 18-year-old Hendon Grammar Schoolboy, Spector made an immediate impact in both the League and FA Cup competitions, with his speedy, direct raids down the left flank. Unable to be assured of a regular place, with Frank Blunstone and Jim Lewis (another amateur player) available, little more was seen of him and he remained in amateur football throughout his career thereafter.

SPEEDIE, David Robert (1982-1987) Striker
Born: Glenrothes, 20 February 1960.
5ft 7in; 11st.
Career: Barnsley (October 1978), Darlington (June 1980), Chelsea (May 1982, £65,000), Coventry City (July 1987, £750,000), Liverpool (February 1991).
Honours: Scotland international (10 caps), Scotland Under-21 (1 cap), Second Division championship medal 1984, Full Members' Cup winners' medal 1986.
Chelsea debut: 18 September 1982. Appearances:

League 155(7), FA Cup 12, League Cup 23(1), Full Members' Cup 7; Goals: League 47, FA Cup 5, League Cup 7, Full Members' Cup 5.
A highly-talented striker, or occasional midfield player, Speedie's lightning quick reactions and skill on the ball were a menace to opponents. A man with an excitable temperament, for a comparatively small player he was a powerful header of the ball and had the ability to outjump taller opponents. His relentless determination and aggression were vital components in Chelsea's surge from the Second Division to the upper reaches of the First.

SPENCE, Richard (1934-1950) Outside-right
Born: Platt's Common near Barnsley, 18 July 1908; Died: Ealing, March 1983.
5ft 7in; 9st.
Career: Thorpe Colliery, Platt's Common YMCA, Barnsley (February 1933), Chelsea (October 1934, £5,000), Retired (1950).
Honours: England international (2 caps), Third Division North championship medal 1934.
Chelsea debut: 6 October 1934. Appearances: League 221, FA Cup 25; Goals: League 62, FA Cup 3.
A loyal and well-loved servant of Chelsea FC for more than 40 years, Dick Spence was a bargain signing from his home-town club, Barnsley. He was an automatic choice for the right-wing position in the five seasons leading to the outbreak of World War Two, during which he served in the police force and, later, in the Army. A wiry lightweight man to whom fitness came easily, he resumed his career in 1945 and when he made his final first-team appearance on 13 September 1947, at 40 years and 57 days, he was the oldest player to appear for Chelsea in a League fixture. Before the war he was unfortunate enough to have been a contemporary of international wingers Sammy Crooks and Stanley Matthews, but still played twice for England.

132

Extremely fast, he was very much a winger of the old school and loved to make direct tracks on goal. He possessed a surprisingly powerful shot for such a small man and his tally of 19 goals in his first season on the staff remains a record for any Chelsea winger — this after he arrived with eight games of that season already played. During wartime football he made 170 appearances (50 goals) to show what further records could have come his way but for the hostilities. He joined the training staff on his retirement as a player and continued to be a frequent visitor to Stamford Bridge almost to the time of his death.

SPOTTISWOODE, Joseph (1919-1920) Outside-left
Born: Carlisle.
5ft 9in; 12st.
Career: Chelsea (1919), Swansea Town (January 1920), Queen's Park Rangers (June 1925).
Chelsea debut: 3 January 1920. Appearances: League 1.
Spottiswoode signed for Chelsea soon after the resumption of normal football in August 1919, but was unable to make an impression, although subsequently enjoying considerably more success with his other clubs.

STANLEY, Gary E. (1971-1979) Midfield
Born: Burton upon Trent, 4 March 1954.
5ft 9½in; 11st 7lb.
Career: Chelsea (March 1971), Fort Lauderdale Strikers (1979), Everton (August 1979, £300,000), Swansea City (October 1981), Portsmouth (January 1984), Bristol City (November 1988), Waterlooville.
Chelsea debut: 16 August 1975. Appearances: League 105(4), FA Cup 4(1), League Cup 6; Goals: League 15.
An attacking midfield player, Stanley was recommended to Chelsea by former player Frank Upton, who had spotted him in Derbyshire Schools football. His forceful play was an important ingredient in the 1976-7 promotion team and, in many ways, he reflected manager Eddie McCreadie's attitude towards the game. He was allowed to move in order to ease the financial situation at Stamford Bridge but never quite fulfilled his true potential.

STARK, James (1907-1908) Centre-half
Born: Ruchzie (Glasgow), 1880.
Career: Mansewood, Pollokshaws Eastwood, Glasgow Perthshire, Glasgow Rangers (May 1900), Chelsea

(May 1907), Glasgow Rangers (October 1908), Greenock Morton (cs 1910).
Honours: Scotland international (2 caps), Scottish League XI (2 appearances), Scottish League Championship medal 1901, Scottish FA Cup winners' medal 1903, runners-up medals 1904, 1905, 1909.
Chelsea debut: 5 October 1907. Appearances: League 30, FA Cup 2; Goals: League 2.
Scotland international centre-half Jimmy Stark was signed early in the 1907-08 season in order to establish Chelsea in their first experience of First Division football, for the largest fee paid by the club up to that time. Disappointingly, however, he decided to return to his native land after one season in London. He was a dominating defender, but one who enjoyed moving upfield to lend weight to his fellow attackers, as was the centre-half's style of those days.

STEER, William H.O. (1911-1918)   **Centre-forward**
Born: Kingston upon Thames.
5ft 8in; 11st 6lb.
Career: Queen's Park Rangers, Old Kingstonians, Chelsea (cs 1911), Newry County, Retired (1918).
Honours: England Amateur international (4 caps).
Chelsea debut: 21 December 1912. Appearances: League 4; Goals: League 1.
Former amateur international Steer signed professional forms for Chelsea but never succeeded in winning a regular first-team place. He played irregularly in wartime football, after which he retired.

STEFFEN, Willi (1946-1947)   **Full-back**
Born: Switzerland, 17 March 1925.
Career: Swiss football, Chelsea (1946-7), amateur.
Honours: Switzerland international (7 caps).
Chelsea debut: 30 November 1946. Appearances: League 15, FA Cup 5.
A former pilot in the Swiss Air Force, this outstanding defender played for Chelsea, as an amateur, whilst in London in the first season after World War Two. Superbly built and standing over 6ft tall, he made an immediate impression. A strong tackler and dominating in the air, he was universally popular with his fellow players and with supporters, and it was a matter of great regret when he returned home after his five-month stay in England.

STEPNEY, Alex Cyril (1966)   **Goalkeeper**
Born: Mitcham, 18 September 1942.
6ft; 12st 8lb.
Career: Achilles FC, Fulham (trial), Tooting and Mitcham (1958), Millwall (May 1963), Chelsea (May 1966, £50,000), Manchester United (September 1966, £50,000), Goole Town, Dallas Tornado (January 1979), Goole Town, Altrincham (player-coach, September 1979).
Honours: England international (1 cap), England Under-23 (3 caps), Football League XI, Football League Championship medal 1967, European Cup winners' medal 1968, Second Division championship medal 1975, FA Cup winners' medal 1977, runners-up medal 1976.
Chelsea debut: 3 September 1966. Appearances: League 1.
Signed at a time when Peter Bonetti's future with Chelsea was uncertain, Stepney remained at Stamford Bridge for only four months before moving to Manchester United where he played some 500 first-team games.

STONE, George (1924-1928)   **Outside-left**
Born: Hemel Hempstead, 27 July 1902; Died: Hemel Hempstead, February 1940.
5ft 5in; 9st.
Career: Hemel Hempstead, Apsley, Chelsea (September 1924), not retained (May 1928), Watford (September 1929).
Chelsea debut: 29 August 1925. Appearances: League 25; Goals: League 2.
After playing regularly in the first team during the first half of the 1925-6 season, Stone lost his place to the veteran Bobby McNeil and was never again recognized as a first choice.

STRIDE, David Roy (1976-1979)   **Full-back**
Born: Lymington, 14 March 1958.
5ft 9in; 11st 5lb.
Career: Chelsea (January 1976), Memphis Rogues (November 1979, £90,000), Minnesota Kicks (April 1981), Jacksonville Tea Men (April 1982), Millwall (February 1983), Orient (July 1984), USA soccer.
Chelsea debut: 23 September 1978. Appearances: League 35, FA Cup 1, League Cup 1.
Stride joined Chelsea as an apprentice and was converted to full-back from his previous position as a left winger. He developed into a speedy, overlapping defender before his career was interrupted by a hairline fracture of the skull, after having apparently established himself in the first team. He played in the North American Soccer League before joining Orient and after leaving the Football League scene he returned to the USA to play indoor soccer.

STUART, Graham Charles (1989-)   **Midfield/Striker**
Born: Tooting, 24 October 1970.
5ft 8in; 11st 6lb.
Career: Chelsea (June 1989).
Honours: England Under-21 international (5 caps).
Chelsea debut: 16 April 1990. Appearances: League19(2), FA Cup 1, League Cup 5, Full Members' Cup 1(1); Goals: League 5, League Cup 1, Full Members' Cup 1.
One of a promising bunch of young players who burst on to the scene during 1990, Graham Stuart graduated to Chelsea via the FA/GM National School of Excellence at Lilleshall. A most versatile performer, his pace and strength equip him for either a midfield role or, more dangerously, a wide attacking player. Scoring on his debut, he was a member of the England Under-21 squad in Toulon during the 1990 close-season.

STUBBS, Leslie L. (1952-1958)   **Inside-forward**
Born: Great Wakering, 18 February 1929.
5ft 10in; 12st.
Career: Great Wakering, Southend United (May 1948), Chelsea (November 1952, £10,000), Southend United (November 1958, £12,000 combined fee with Alan Dicks), Bedford Town (July 1960).
Honours: Football League Championship medal 1955. Also 1 FA Charity Shield appearance 1955.
Chelsea debut: 15 November 1952. Appearances: League 112, FA Cup 10; Goals: League 34, FA Cup 1.
A forceful inside-forward who was a regular goalscorer,

Stubbs played an important role in the 1954-5 Championship team. Strongly-built, he possessed a powerful shot, if somewhat lacking pace and mobility.

SWAIN, Kenneth (1973-1978)   **Striker/Full-back**
Born: Birkenhead, 28 January 1952.
5ft 9in; 11st 7lb.
Career: Liverpool and Merseyside District Schools, Kirkby Boys, Shoreditch College (Surrey), SE Counties Colleges. Wycombe Wanderers, Chelsea (August 1973), Aston Villa (December 1978, £100,000), Nottingham Forest (October 1982), Portsmouth (July 1985), West Bromwich Albion (loan), Crewe Alexandra (player-coach, August 1988).
Honours: First Division Championship medal 1981, European Cup winners' medal 1982.
Chelsea debut: 16 March 1974. Appearances: League 114(5), FA Cup 7, League Cup 6; Goals: League 26, FA Cup 2, League Cup 1.
Although Swain played almost exclusively as a full-back after leaving Chelsea, at Stamford Bridge he was primarily a left winger. With clever footwork and the ability to cross the ball accurately, he was an effective attacker, if lacking a little pace. It was a matter of regret when financial economies, as much as anything else, dictated his move to Aston Villa.

TAMBLING, Robert Victor (1958-1970)   **Forward**
Born: Storrington (Sussex), 18 September 1941.
5ft 8½in; 12st 6lb.

Career: Chelsea (September 1958), Crystal Palace (January 1970 £40,000), Cork Celtic (October 1973), Waterford (1977), Shamrock Rovers (1978).
Honours: England international (3 caps), England Under-23 (13 caps), England Schoolboys, Football League XI (1 appearance), FA Cup runners-up medal 1967, Football League Cup winners' medal 1965, FA Youth Cup winners' medal 1960.
Chelsea debut: 7 February 1959. Appearances: League 298(4), FA Cup 36, League Cup 18, Fairs Cup 14; Goals: League 164, FA Cup 25, League Cup 10, Fairs Cup 3.
The most prolific scorer in Chelsea's history, and only Jimmy Greaves (41) has bettered his 35 League goals in a season, Tambling's coming in the Second Division promotion campaign of 1962-3. He first came to Chelsea as a 15-year-old junior in July 1957 and made his senior debut, aged 17, scoring a goal against West Ham United in front of a crowd of over 52,000. He possessed great speed and acceleration, qualities which, allied to his accurate shooting — especially with his left foot — brought him a regular harvest of goals. He scored five times in the away fixture against Aston Villa in September 1966 and four goals on four separate occasions. After his move to Crystal Palace he returned to Chelsea to be presented with an illuminated address to commemorate his outstanding feats of scoring goals throughout his remarkable Chelsea career.

TAYLOR, Frederick (1909-1919)   **Wing-half**
Born: Rotherham.
5ft 8½in; 12st 5lb.
Career: Gainsborough Trinity, Chelsea (December 1909), Brentford (July 1919), Maidstone United (cs 1920).
Honours: Football League XI (1 appearance), FA Cup runners-up medal 1915.
Chelsea debut: 25 December 1909. Appearances: League 155, FA Cup 16; Goals: League 4.
A strong wing-half, Taylor was especially noted for his speed. He became a cornerstone of the Chelsea defence in the seasons leading up to World War One, which ended his first-team career, apart from isolated games made in the regional football played during the hostilities. In recognition of his loyal service to the club he was granted a benefit in 1920 which realized £120.

TENNANT, Albert E. (1934-1953)
Inside-forward/Wing-half/Full-back
Born: Ilkeston (Derbyshire), 29 October 1917; Died: 1986.
5ft 9in; 12st.
Career: Stanton Ironworks, Chelsea (November 1934), Retired (May 1953).
Chelsea debut: 5 January 1946. Appearances: League 2, FA Cup 6.
It was only during World War Two that Tennant blossomed into a valuable first-team player, albeit in the less demanding climate of regional football. He had been unable to break through previously, appearing in the Reserves and 'A' team as an inside-forward in the five seasons leading up to the war. But he played no fewer than 148 wartime games, first at wing-half and latterly as a most dependable full-back. Injury struck him down early in the 1946-7 season and he played little football thereafter, becoming coach in

1953 before, finally leaving Stamford Bridge to take over as manager of Guildford City in the summer of 1959.

THAIN, Albert Edward (1922-1931)   Inside-forward
Born: Southall, 20 April 1900; Died: Beverley, 1979.
5ft 9in; 10st 3lb.
Career: Metropolitan Railway, Southall, Chelsea (April 1922), Bournemouth & Boscombe Athletic (June 1931).
Chelsea debut: 30 September 1933. Appearances: League 144, FA Cup 9; Goals: League 44, FA Cup 6.
Thain was a clever ball player with a long-striding run which frequently took him clear of all opposition to score a regular supply of goals. Having learnt his football with a local railway works team, he jokingly said he chose Chelsea as his professional club because he could listen to the underground trains passing during games at Stamford Bridge, which made him feel at home. Injury abbreviated a fine career, after which this loyal clubman would often pay his fare to support his team at away matches.

THOMAS, Michael Reginald (1984-1985)   Midfield
Born: Mochdre, 7 July 1954.
5ft 6in; 10st 7lb.
Career: Wrexham (May 1972), Manchester United (November 1978), Everton (August 1981), Stoke City (August 1982), Chelsea January 1984, £75,000), West Bromwich Albion (September 1985, £100,000), Derby County (loan), Shrewsbury Town (August 1988), Leeds United (June 1989), Stoke City (loan), Stoke City (August 1990).
Honours: Wales international (51 caps), Wales Under-23 (2 caps), FA Cup runners-up medal 1979, Third Division championship medal 1978, Second Division championship medal 1984.
Chelsea debut: 14 January 1984. Appearances: League 43(1), FA Cup 3, League Cup 7; Goals: League 9, League Cup 2.
Thomas proved a vital signing midway through the 1983-4 Second Division championship season. An ebullient left-sided midfield player or winger, he was very fast, extremely tenacious and determined both as defender and attacker. After a somewhat chequered career he quickly settled at Stamford Bridge and became one of the most popular players the club has had. It was a matter of some concern amongst supporters when he was allowed to leave.

THOMPSON, James William (1927-1929)   Forward
Born: West Ham, 19 April 1898; Died: August 1984.
5ft 11in; 12st 1lb.
Career: West Ham Schoolboys, Custom House, Charlton Athletic (Amateur), Wimbledon, Millwall (December 1921), Coventry City (May 1923), Clapton Orient (August 1924), Luton Town (August 1925), Chelsea (May 1927), Norwich City (May 1929), Sunderland (May 1930), Fulham (October 1930), Hull City (October 1931), Tunbridge Wells Rangers (December 1931), Sittingbourne (1932), Peterborough United (August 1934), Belfast Linfield, Aldershot, Lucerne (Switzerland 1935).
Chelsea debut: 27 August 1927. Appearances: League 37, FA Cup 5; Goals: League 33, FA Cup 1.
Thompson came to Chelsea having played mainly as a left winger, but once at Stamford Bridge he was

converted into a highly successful centre-forward. Indeed, no other player in the club's history can match his goal average over a comparable number of games. Most surprisingly, he was dropped at the start of his second season, returned briefly to score a few more goals, and was then allowed to leave the following summer. Despite such outstanding feats of goalscoring he is perhaps even better remembered as the scout who unearthed so much youthful talent for Chelsea, particularly from the East End of London, during the years after World War Two. Jimmy Greaves, Terry Venables and Bobby Tambling were among those he 'discovered'. After finishing as a player, he was also trainer of Enfield (1937-39) and was then appointed manager of Dartford. After the war he also had spells scouting in South Africa and the USA. Not for nothing was he known as the 'champion rolling stone'.

THOMSON, Charles Richard (1952-1957)   Goalkeeper
Born: Perth, 2 March 1930.
5ft 11in; 12st.
Career: Clyde, Chelsea (October 1952, £5,000), Nottingham Forest (August 1957).
Honours: FA Cup winners' medal 1959, Football League Championship medal 1955.
Chelsea debut: 26 December 1952. Appearances: League 46, FA Cup 13.
'Chick' Thomson was a sound and reliable 'keeper who shared the duties of guarding Chelsea's net with Bill Robertson for four seasons, playing an especially valuable role in the 1954-5 Championship season. His father had also been a professional goalkeeper in the Scottish League.

THOMSON, James S. (1965-1968)   Defender
Born: Provinside, Glasgow, 1 October 1946.
5ft 10½in; 11st 3lb.
Career: Provinside Hibernian, Chelsea (January 1965), Burnley (September 1968, £40,000).
Chelsea debut: 4 May 1966. Appearances: League 33(6), FA Cup 5(1), Fairs Cup 2; Goals: League 1.
A reliable defender, Thomson was in, or on the verge of, the first team during his three and a half years on the staff, playing in any of the defensive positions. Unable to claim a regular spot, he moved to Burnley where he went on to play over 300 senior games.

THOMSON, Robert John (1911-1922)   Centre-forward
Born: Croydon, 29 December 1890; Died: South Norwood, 9 January 1971.
5ft 6in; 11st.
Career: Dartford, Croydon Common (cs 1910), Chelsea (September 1911), Charlton Athletic (March 1922).
Honours: FA Cup runners-up medal 1915.
Chelsea debut: 21 October 1911. Appearances: League 83, FA Cup 12; Goals: League 23, FA Cup 6.
Thomson succeeded George Hilsdon as first-team centre-forward, yet was rarely assured of a permanent place during more than seven 'normal' seasons with the club, interrupted by World War One. He is perhaps best remembered for two reasons not directly connected with his performances on the field. First, he was renowned for having only one eye ("I just shut the other one and play from memory," he once said), and secondly he played in the FA Cup Final, even though the famous amateur, Vivian Woodward (normally first choice) was unexpectedly available, having been given

leave from his duties in the Army. Having played in every Cup tie up to the Final, Woodward sportingly insisted that Bob Thomson should play.

TICKRIDGE, Sidney (1951-1955)   **Full-back**
Born: Stepney, 10 April 1923.
5ft 10in; 11st 11lb.
Career: Royal Navy, Tottenham Hotspur (1946), Chelsea (March 1951, £10,000), Brentford (July 1955, free transfer).
Honours: England Schoolboy international.
Chelsea debut: 23 March 1951. Appearances: League 61, FA Cup 12.
Tickridge came to Chelsea after 15 years on the Tottenham staff, which he had joined as an amateur in 1936. Although he played only one full season in the first team, he proved an excellent signing, lending stability to a suspect defence and also doing the same job in the reserve team where his experience helped the younger players. He was also assistant trainer at Millwall from 1957-59.

TINDALL, Ronald Albert Ernest (1953-1961)
Centre-forward/Full-back
Born: Streatham, 23 September 1935.
5ft 10in; 10st 9lb.
Career: Camberley Wanderers, Chelsea (April 1953), West Ham United (November 1961, part-exchange Andy Malcolm), Reading (October 1962), Portsmouth (September 1964).
Honours: Football League XI (1 appearance).
Chelsea debut: 12 November 1955. Appearances: League 160, FA Cup 9, League Cup 3, Fairs Cup 2; Goals: League 67, FA Cup 2.
A tall, speedy centre-forward, Tindall turned professional after working in the Chelsea FC offices. Spotted by Ted Drake, he was an industrious player, strong in the air, who in the latter part of his time, played almost exclusively at full-back. In an emergency he could also perform creditably in goal. He made over 400 senior appearances in his career, scoring almost a century of goals. A good cricket all-rounder, from 1956 to 1966 he played 172 first-class games for Surrey. Emigrated to Australia and was appointed director of coaching for Western Australia.

TOOMER, James (1905-1906)   **Forward**
Born: Southampton, February 1883. Died: December 1962.
Career: Fulham (amateur) Chelsea (amateur, summer 1905), Southampton (amateur, summer 1906).
Chelsea debut: 18 November 1905. Appearances: FA Cup 1.
One of the large squad of players signed for Chelsea's inaugural season of 1905-06, Toomer played regularly in the reserve team but made only one first-team appearance, in an FA Cup tie when the recognized first-choice players were fulfilling a League fixture. After World War One he became a teacher and then opened a sports outfitters business in Southampton that bears his name today. In 1949 he became a director of Southampton FC.

TOWNROW, John Ernest (1927-1932)   **Centre-half**
Born: Stratford (East London), 28 March 1901; Died: Knaresborough, 11 April 1969.
5ft 11½in; 13st 7lb.

Career: Fairbairn House, Clapton Orient (August 1919), Chelsea (February 1927, £5,000), Bristol Rovers (May 1932).
Honours: England international (2 caps), England Schoolboys.
Chelsea debut: 26 February 1927. Appearances: League 130, FA Cup 10; Goals: League 3.
Already an international player when he signed for Chelsea, Jack Townrow was one of the most capable and respected centre-halves of his time. Very much an 'attacking' pivot by nature, he was forced to change his game once the new offside law was introduced in 1925, although he always enjoyed moving upfield when given the opportunity. He was a fine tackler, very strong in the air and with the ability to use the ball constructively. His Chelsea career was hampered by injuries but he was an important member of the 1929-30 promotion team and he also helped to establish the side in the First Division the following season. Elder brother of Frank Townrow (Bristol Rovers).

TOWNSEND, Andrew David (1990-)   **Midfield**
Born: London, 23 July 1963.
5ft 10in; 12st 7lb.

137

Career: Weymouth, Southampton (January 1985), Norwich City (August 1988), Chelsea (July 1990, £1,200,000).
Honours: Republic of Ireland international (23 caps).
Chelsea debut: 25 August 1990. Appearances: League 34, FA Cup 1, League Cup 9, Full Members' Cup 1; Goals: League 2, League Cup 3.
A late starter in professional football, Townsend's career blossomed as he became an integral member of the highly successful Norwich City team in 1988-9. A creative midfield player, whose astute and long-range passing ability make him one of the outstanding performers in this area of the game at the present time. At Chelsea he took over the captaincy of the team from Peter Nicholas in November 1990, as he increasingly justified the outlay of his transfer fee.

TUCK, Peter G. (1951-1954)   **Inside-forward**
Born: Plaistow, 14 May 1932.
5ft 8in; 10st 6lb.
Career: Chelsea (May 1951), Retired (1954).
Chelsea debut: 20 October 1951. Appearances: League 3; Goals: League 1.
Signing professional after graduating from the Chelsea Juniors, any hopes Tuck had of a successful career were dashed when he broke his leg and never played serious football again.

TURNBULL, James McLachlan (1912-1914)
Inside/Centre-forward
Born: Bannockburn, 23 May 1884.
5ft 10in; 12st 11lb.
Career: Falkirk, East Stirlingshire, Falkirk, Dundee, Glasgow Rangers, Preston North End (1905), Leyton (cs 1906), Manchester United (cs 1907), Bradford, Chelsea (cs 1912), Manchester United (August 1914).
Honours: Football League Championship medal 1908.
Chelsea debut: 2 September 1912. Appearances: League 20, FA Cup 2; Goals: League 8.
One of the best-known centre-forwards of his day, 'Trunky' Turnbull was considered most unlucky never to have won international honours. A contemporary writing of him said that in 1907-08, when he led Manchester United's Championship-winning forward line, he gave 'one of the finest expositions of centre-forward play we have seen in the present decade'. His season at Chelsea came towards the end of his long career, but was instrumental in helping the club to avoid relegation. Rejoined Manchester United after leaving Chelsea but did not make a first team appearance. After he retired, Turnbull became a prosperous money-lender.

TURNBULL, Robert Hamilton (1925-1928)
Centre-forward
Born: Dumbarton, 22 June 1894; Died: 1946.
5ft 8in; 11st 7lb.
Career: Royal Engineers, Arsenal (January 1921), Charlton Athletic (November 1924), Chelsea (February 1925), Clapton Orient (March 1928), Southend United, Chatham (August 1930), Crystal Palace (July 1931).
Chelsea debut: 7 February 1925. Appearances: League 80, FA Cup 7; Goals: League 51, FA Cup 7.
Turnbull was originally a full-back who was converted to centre-forward during an Arsenal goalscoring crisis and responded by becoming the Gunners' leading scorer in 1922-3. He was signed in order to solve Chelsea's scoring 'famine' during their first season after relegation from Division One and this he did with great success, achieving one of the best scoring ratios of any player in the club's history. He lost his place to Jimmy Thompson early in the 1927-8 season but was a wholehearted, enthusiastic player, skilful with a strong shot from either foot. He was Crystal Palace trainer for a spell before World War Two.

TYE, Edward (1914-1915)   **Full-back**
Born: Stamford.
5ft 6in; 9st 5lb.
Career: Stamford, Chelsea (1914-15).
Chelsea debut: 28 December 1914. Appearances: League 1.
A diminutive full-back, Tye's speed unfortunately did not compensate for his slight physique. He played consistently well for the Reserves in the last season before the outbreak of World War One but was never able to displace either Bettridge or Harrow.

UPTON, Frank (1961-1965)   **Wing-half**
Born: Ainsley Hill, 18 October 1934.
6ft; 13st 4lb.
Career: Nuneaton Borough, Northampton Town (March 1953), Derby County (June 1954), Chelsea (August 1961, £15,000), Derby County (August 1965), Notts County (September 1966), Worcester City (July

1967), Workington (player-manager, January 1968-July 1968).
Honours: Third Division North championship medal 1957.
Chelsea debut: 19 August 1961. Appearances: League 74, FA Cup 8, League Cup 4; Goals: League 3.
Upton was a strongly-built, hard-tackling wing-half who played a crucial part in the 1962-3 promotion team. In his long career he played nearly 400 League games and was player-manager of Workington for a brief period. He had always been interested in the coaching side of the game. While at Derby County he was helping at Repton School and after leaving Workington he was in turn involved with Northampton Town (1969), Aston Villa (1970-77), Chelsea (1977-78), Randers Freja (1979-80), Dundee (1980), Al-Arabi (1981), Wolverhampton Wanderers (1982-84), before briefly trying his hand as manager of Bedworth United (1984), then moving to Coventry City as coach-assistant manager (1985-87) and going abroad to coach IBK Keflavik in May 1987. His latest venture took him to Malaysia as coach to Borneo's national team, returning to England in December 1990.

VENABLES, Terence Frederick (1960-1966) Midfield
Born: Bethnal Green, 6 January 1943.
5ft 8½in; 11st 6lb.
Career: Dagenham Schools, Chelsea (August 1960), Tottenham Hotspur (May 1966, £80,000), Queen's Park Rangers (June 1969), Crystal Palace (September 1974).

Honours: England international (2 caps), England Under-23 (4 caps), England Schoolboys, England Youth, England Amateur, Football League XI (1 appearance), Football League Cup winners' medal 1966, FA Cup winners' medal 1967, FA Youth Cup winners' medals 1960, 1961.
Chelsea debut: 6 February 1960. Appearances: League 202, FA Cup 19, League Cup 8, Fairs Cup 8; Goals: League 26, FA Cup 1, League Cup 1, Fairs Cup 3.
Terry Venables is the only player to have represented England at five different international levels. He arrived at The Bridge as a 15-year-old in 1958-9 and developed into an outstanding midfield player, strong in the tackle and a brilliant passer of the ball. He was in the 1962-3 Second Division promotion side and in the teams which then went on to finish fifth, third and fifth again, in the first three seasons back in the top flight. After his playing career ended he managed Crystal Palace, Queen's Park Rangers, Barcelona and Tottenham Hotspur, proving just as successful a manager as player. He steered Palace from the Third Division to the First and took Barcelona to the Spanish League title and into a European Cup Final. Then, in 1991, his Spurs team won the FA Cup Final at Wembley. A man of many talents, Venables also co-authored the TV series *Hazell*.

VILJOEN, Colin (1980-1982)   Midfield
Born: Johannesburg (South Africa), 20 June 1948.
5ft 9in; 11st 8lb.
Career: South Transvaal FC, Ipswich Town (August

139

1967), Manchester City (August 1978), Chelsea (March
1980, £45,000), contract cancelled (May 1982).
Honours: England international (2 caps), Second
Division championship medal 1968.
*Chelsea debut: 15 March 1980. Appearances: League
19(1), League Cup 3.*
Viljoen adopted British nationality in 1971. After a
distinguished career he arrived at Chelsea, aged 31,
but never fitted into the scheme of things and seemed
not to possess the necessary motivation. As a result
his appearances were isolated and his place never
assured.

WALDRON, Colin (1967)   **Centre-half**
Born: Bristol, 22 June 1948.
6ft; 12st 8lb.
Career: Bury (May 1966), Chelsea (June 1967, £25,000),
Burnley (October 1967, £30,000), Manchester United
(May 1976), Sunderland (February 1977), Tulsa
Rougnecks (1978), Atlanta Chiefs (1979), Rochdale
(October 1979), Philadelphia Fury, Atlanta Chiefs.
*Chelsea debut: 19 August 1967. Appearances: League
9, League Cup 1.*
This tall fair-haired centre-half spent an unhappy four
months at Stamford Bridge, failing to find his form
and not settling in London. However, after moving
to Burnley he went on to play more than 300 League
games for the Lancastrians in a nine-year stay at Turf
Moor. His brother, Alan, played for Bolton Wanderers
and Blackpool.

WALKER, Andrew M. (1913-1920)   **Half-back**
Born: Dalkeith.
5ft 10½in; 12st 7lb.
Career: Dundee, Chelsea (May 1913), Newport County
(cs 1920), Accrington Stanley (June 1922).
Honours: FA Cup runners-up medal 1915.
*Chelsea debut: 13 September 1913. Appearances:
League 18, FA Cup 5; Goals: League 2.*
Something of a utility player, Walker played in a variety
of positions from centre-forward, where he made his
debut after the team had been stricken with a mystery
illness *en route* to their away fixture at Oldham, to
full-back. Never a regular first teamer, his career was
interrupted by World War One when he might have
had a chance of establishing himself. His main claim
to fame was playing at left-half for Chelsea in the 1915
FA Cup Final.

WALKER, Clive (1975-1984)   **Winger**
Born: Oxford, 26 June 1957.
5ft 8½in; 11st 4lb.
Career: Chelsea (April 1975), Fort Lauderdale Strikers
(1979), Sunderland (July 1984, £75,000), Queen's Park
Rangers (December 1985), Fulham (October 1987,
Brighton & Hove Albion (August 1990).
Honours: England Schoolboy international.
*Chelsea debut: 19 April 1977. Appearances: League
168(30), FA Cup 14(2), League Cup 9(1); Goals: League
60, FA Cup 3, League Cup 2.*
A speedy striker down either flank, or in the centre
of the attack, Walker's flair for scoring spectacular
goals made him an exciting player. Particularly
remembered was his long-range effort at Bolton which
staved off relegation to the Third Division at the end
of the 1982-3 season. At times an unpredictable and
erratic performer, he was playing the most consistently

good football of his career when injury caused him
to drop out of the first team and, unable to regain
his place, he was soon transferred, whilst still in his
prime.

WALKER, Thomas, OBE (1946-1948)   **Inside-forward**
Born: Livingstone Station, 26 May 1915.
5ft 9in; 11st 7lb.
Career: Berryburn Rangers, Livingstone Violet,
Broxburn Rangers, Heart of Midlothian (May 1932),
Chelsea (September 1946, £6,000), Heart of Midlothian
(player-assistant manager, December 1948).
Honours: Scotland international (20 caps), Scotland
Schoolboys, Scottish League XI (5 appearances).
*Chelsea debut: 9 September 1946. Appearances: League
97, FA Cup 7; Goals: League 23, FA Cup 1.*
One of the most famous players ever to wear the
Chelsea shirt, Tommy Walker was known as one of
soccer's gentlemen. He had 'guested' for the club during
World War Two and his permanent signing, albeit in
the autumn of his career, was a great coup. During
his two and a half seasons at Stamford Bridge he
delighted crowds with his marvellous skills and ball-
control, his dribbling being one of his greatest assets.

At one time destined for a career in the church, he attached himself to a London boys' club and won great respect and affection during his time in the capital. He later became manager of Hearts (1951-66), Dunfermline Athletic (1966) and Raith Rovers (1967-69) before joining the board of directors of his first professional club, Heart of Midlothian. He was awarded the OBE in 1960.

WALTON, Joseph (1906-1911) **Full-back**
Born: North Shields, 1884.
5ft 9in; 12st 4lb.
Career: Wallsend Park Villa, New Brompton (cs 1904), Chelsea (August 1906), not retained (May 1911), Swansea Town.
Chelsea debut: 1 September 19u6. Appearances: League 53.

Playing only one season as undisputed first choice, Walton was a calm, unruffled defender, respected as a strong tackler and a most reliable player. After suffering an injury in the opening fixture of 1907-08, he lost his place to Jock Cameron and was subsequently unable to regain it on a regular basis.

WARD, Joseph (1920-1922) **Half-back**
Born: Sion Mills, County Tyrone.
5ft 8in; 10st 10lb.

Career: St Johnstone, Chelsea (May 1920), Swansea Town (summer 1922).
Chelsea debut: 16 October 1920. Appearances: League 14, FA Cup 2.
Having been signed as a centre-half, Ward played most of his football at Stamford Bridge in the wing-half positions. Not the most fortunate of players, injury robbed him of an Irish international cap, he was selected to play against Wales in April 1921, and was never picked again.

WARREN, Benjamin (1908-1912) **Wing-half**
Born: Newhall (Derbyshire), 1879; Died: Mickleover (Derbyshire), 15 January 1917.
5ft 8½in; 12st 8lb.
Career: Newhall Town, Newhall Swifts, Derby County (May 1899), Chelsea (August 1908, £1,250), Retired (February 1912).
Honours: England international (22 caps), Football League XI (5 appearances), FA Cup runners-up medal 1903.
Chelsea debut: 1 September 1908. Appearances: League 92, FA Cup 9; Goals: League 4, FA Cup 1.

An outstanding right-half, Warren's total of 22 international caps is testimony to his ability, at a time when far fewer games were played at this level. He was renowned for his fitness and enthusiasm for the

141

game, as well as for his scrupulously fair play. One of the most famous players of his day, he moved from Derby County after they were relegated in 1907, then resumed his First Division career with Chelsea. Illness forced him to retire when he was still at the height of his career and in April 1914, Chelsea staged a benefit match for his dependents at Stamford Bridge, between sides representing North and South. Certified insane, poor Warren spent a period in Derbyshire Lunatic Asylum before dying in tragic circumstances. His son, Harry, played for Blackpool, and was manager of Southend United from 1946 to 1956.

WARREN, Robert E. (1948-1951) Centre-half
Born: Devonport (Plymouth), 8 January 1927.
6ft 11st 10lb.
Career: Plymouth United, Plymouth Argyle (1946), Chelsea (July 1948), Torquay United (August 1951).
Chelsea debut: 9 April 1949. Appearances: League 1.
Warren spent three seasons at Stamford Bridge, playing almost entirely in the Reserves and 'A' team, as understudy to John Harris.

WATSON, Ian L. (1962-1965) Full-back
Born: Hammersmith, 7 January 1944.
5ft 11in; 11st 11lb.
Career: Chelsea (February 1962), Queen's Park Rangers (July 1965, £10,000).
Chelsea debut: 30 January 1963. Appearances: League 5, FA Cup 1, League Cup 3; Goals: League 1.
Watson signed professional forms after two years as a Chelsea junior. A well-built full-back who was discovered by Wilf Chitty, the former Chelsea player, he never achieved a permanent place in the first team but played some 200 senior games after moving to Queen's Park Rangers.

WATSON, James (1905-1906) Inside-forward
Born: Inverness, 1883.
5ft 10in; 12st 2lb.
Career: Inverness Thistle, Clyde, Sunderland (cs 1903), Chelsea (September 1905), Brentford (summer 1906).
Chelsea debut: 9 September 1905. Appearances: League 13, FA Cup 1.
Signed before the start of Chelsea's first season, 'Dougal' Watson provided cover for player-manager Jackie Robertson and, in fact, was called upon to play in almost half the games.

WEAVER, Reginald William (1929-1932) Centre-forward
Born: Radstock (Somerset), 14 September 1905; Died: Gloucester, 16 July 1970.
Career: Newport County (1925), Wolverhampton Wanderers (November 1927), Chelsea (March 1929), Bradford City (June 1932), Chesterfield (March 1933), Newport County (1934).
Chelsea debut: 13 March 1929. Appearances: League 20; Goals: League 8.
Noted for his speed, he was a Powderhall sprinter, Weaver was Wolves' leading goalscorer in 1928-9 and, in his restricted opportunities, found the net with regularity at Stamford Bridge. But with George Mills already on the staff, and the signing of Hughie Gallacher shortly after his arrival, he was allowed to move on after two full seasons. Brother of Walter Weaver (Wolves).

WEAVER, Samuel (1936-1945) Wing-half
Born: Pilsley (Derbyshire), 8 February 1909; Died: 15 April 1985.
5ft 9in; 11st 7lb.
Career: Pilsley Red Rose, Sutton Junction, Sutton Town (1926), Hull City (March 1928), Newcastle United (November 1929), Chelsea (August 1936, £4,166), Stockport County (December 1945), Retired (1947).
Honours: England international (3 caps), FA Cup winners' medal 1932.
Chelsea debut: 29 August 1936. Appearances: League 116, FA Cup 9; Goals: League 4.
Weaver was the automatic choice for the left-half position in the three seasons immediately before World War Two and was first-team captain in 1938-9. He was a stylish player and the first to develop the tactical use of the long throw (once measured to be 35 yards), now fairly commonplace in the game. After his playing career had virtually ended his playing career, he was a coach at Leeds United and Millwall before being associated with Mansfield Town as coach, manager, trainer and scout. In addition he was masseur to Derbyshire CCC for many years, having played two matches for Somerset in 1939 as a left-handed batsman.

WEBB, David James (1968-1974) Defender
Born: Stratford (East London), 9 April 1946.
6ft; 12st 13lb.
Career: West Ham United (amateur), Leyton Orient (May 1963), Southampton (March 1966), Chelsea (February 1968, £40,000, part-exchange Joe Kirkup), Queen's Park Rangers (May 1974, £100,000), Leicester City (September 1977), Derby County (December 1978), AFC Bournemouth (player-manager, May 1980), Torquay United (player-manager, February 1984).
Honours: FA Cup winners' medal 1970, European Cup-winners' Cup winners' medal 1971, Football

League Cup runners-up medal 1972. Also 1 FA Charity Shield appearance 1970.

Chelsea debut: 2 March 1968. Appearances: League 230, FA Cup 23, League Cup 27, Fairs Cup 4, European Cup-winners' Cup 14; Goals: League 21, FA Cup 6, League Cup 3, European Cup-winners' Cup 3.

David Webb wrote his name indelibly into the Chelsea history book by scoring the winning goal against Leeds United in the 1970 FA Cup Final replay. A strong, defensive player whose enthusiasm for the game was a morale-booster to those playing around him, his versatility saw him wearing every shirt on the field, with the exception of number 11. His emergency appearance as goalkeeper, against Ipswich Town on Boxing Day 1971, when he kept a clean sheet, typified his value to the club. After his playing career ended he managed AFC Bournemouth, Torquay United and Southend United, on two occasions.

WEGERLE, Roy Connon (1986-1988)   **Striker**
Born: Johannesburg (South Africa), 19 March 1964.
5ft 8in; 10st 2lb.
Career: Tampa Bay Rowdies, Chelsea (June 1986, £75,000), Swindon Town (loan), Luton Town (July 1988, £75,000), Queen's Park Rangers (December 1989).
Chelsea debut: 8 November 1986. Appearances: League 15(8), FA Cup 1(1), Full Members' Cup 2(1); Goals: League 3, FA Cup 1.

Brought up in South Africa in a rugby football environment, Wegerle joined a local soccer club where he was coached by Roy Bailey, the former Ipswich Town goalkeeper. After a brief flirtation with Manchester United, he went to the USA to begin a university career and became a professional soccer player in the death throes of the North American Soccer League. He came to Stamford Bridge for two months early

in the 1985-6 season, returning to sign professional forms the following summer. A fine natural athlete of great potential as an attacker, both down the flanks or through the middle, he possessed considerable skill and pace, as well as being a strong finisher.

WELLER, Keith (1970-1971)   **Forward**
Born: Islington, 11 June 1946.
5ft 10in; 12st 1lb.
Career: Arlington Boys' Club, Tottenham Hotspur (January 1964), Millwall (June 1967), Chelsea (May 1970, £100,000), Leicester City (September 1971, £100,000), New England Tea Men (February 1979), Fort Lauderdale Strikers (July 1980).
Honours: England international (4 caps), Football League XI, European Cup-winners' Cup winners' medal. Also 1 FA Charity Shield appearance 1971.
Chelsea debut: 15 August 1970. Appearances: League 34(4), FA Cup 3, League Cup 3, European Cup-winners' Cup 8(1); Goals: League 14, League Cup 1.

Having played mainly as a central striker before his arrival at Chelsea, Weller was utilized as an attacker down the right flank, where his speed and strong shooting power were considerable assets. After eight seasons with Leicester City he played in the North American Soccer League and continued to coach in the USA (Dallas Sidekicks) after his playing career ended.

WEST, Colin William (1985-1990)   **Striker**
Born: Middlesbrough, 19 September 1967.
5ft 7in; 11st.
Career: Chelsea (September 1985), Partick Thistle (loan), Swansea City (loan), Dundee (July 1990, £105,000)

County (cs 1908).
Chelsea debut: 12 January 1907. Appearances: League 10, FA Cup 3; Goals: League 1, FA Cup 1.
Whitehouse began and ended his football career in the Birmingham League, his chief claim to fame in his time at Chelsea was to score the fastest-ever recorded goal by the club, in 13 seconds against Blackburn Rovers on 2 December 1907.

WHITING, Robert (1906-1908)   **Goalkeeper**
Born: West Ham, 6 January 1884.
5ft 11in; 13st 12lb.
Career: South West Ham, Tunbridge Wells Rangers, Chelsea (summer 1906), Brighton & Hove Albion (summer 1908).
Chelsea debut: 28 April 1906. Appearances: League 52, FA Cup 2.

Honours: England Youth international.
Chelsea debut: 7 March 1987. Appearances: League 8(8); Goals: League 4.
A speedy front-runner and regular goalscorer, West made a dramatic entry when, after seven months on loan to Partick Thistle in the Scottish First Division, he scored within five minutes of his first-team debut against Arsenal at Stamford Bridge. He first arrived at Chelsea as an apprentice in August 1983.

WHIFFEN, Kingsley (1966-1967)   **Goalkeeper**
Born: Welshpool, 3 December 1950.
Career: Chelsea (August 1966, apprentice), Plymouth Argyle (1967, trialist).
Chelsea debut: 9 May 1967. Appearances: League 1.
Whiffen never signed professional forms and spent only one season at Stamford Bridge, playing almost entirely for the Juniors. He made no further appearances in the Football League after leaving Chelsea.

WHITE, Alexander (1937-1948)   **Full-back**
Born: Armadale (West Lothian), 28 January 1916.
5ft 7in; 11st 10lb.
Career: Bonnyrigg Rose, Chelsea (February 1937), Swindon Town (July 1948), Southport (player-coach, July 1950).
Chelsea debut: 14 September 1946. Appearances: League 17, FA Cup 1.
One of the many players whose career was disrupted by World War Two, White was a solid defender who made two appearances for Scotland v England in Army internationals during the war, during which he served as a sergeant-instructor.

WHITEHOUSE, Ben (1906-1908)   **Inside-forward**
Born: Coseley (Staffs).
5ft 7in; 10st 7lb.
Career: Bilston, Chelsea (November 1906), Stockport

Whiting was saddled with the unenviable task of taking over from Willie Foulke. Yet Bob (or 'Pom-Pom' as he was affectionately known) played a sterling part in the club's first promotion season of 1906-07. Noted

144

for the enormous length of his kicking, he lost his place to Jack Whitley at Christmas 1907 and never played for the first team again. He then played regularly for Brighton & Hove Albion in the Southern League, for the seven seasons leading up to the outbreak of World War One.

WHITLEY, Jack (1907-1914)   **Goalkeeper**
Born: Cornwall, 1880; Died: London, c.1955.
6ft ½in; 14st 2lb.

Career: Liskeard YMCA (1897), Darwen (1899), Aston Villa (May 1900), Everton (1902), Stoke (August 1905), Leeds City (April 1906), Lincoln City (1906), Chelsea (cs 1907), Retired (1914).
Chelsea debut: 23 September 1907. Appearances: League 127, FA Cup 11.
As player and trainer, Whitley was a part of the Chelsea scene for 32 years. He was a sound and competent goalkeeper who shared the custodian's duties with Jim

Molyneux for most of that time, his best season being the promotion campaign of 1911-12. However, it is perhaps as head trainer that he is best remembered. A father figure to generations of Chelsea players, he retained that post from 1914 to May 1939 and his energetic dashes on to the field, bald-headed and coat-tails flapping, were very much part of the Chelsea scene during the inter-war years.

WHITTAKER, Richard (1952-1960)   **Full-back**
Born: Dublin, 10 October 1934.
5ft 9in; 11st.
Career: St Mary's Boys' Club (Dublin), Chelsea (May 1952), Peterborough United (July 1960), Queen's Park Rangers (July 1963), Stamford (player-coach, May 1967).
Honours: Republic of Ireland international (1 cap), Republic of Ireland Under-23 (1 cap), Irish Schoolboys.
Chelsea debut: 28 April 1956. Appearances: League 48, FA Cup 1, Fairs Cup 2.
Signed professional after joining the Chelsea ground-staff, this compact full-back remained on the fringe of a regular first-team place for five seasons, usually coming in as deputy for one of the Sillett brothers, before seeking regular League football in the lower divisions.

WHITTINGHAM, Robert (1909-1919)
Inside/Centre-forward
Born: Goldenhill· (Stoke); Died: Goldenhill (Stoke), 1919.
5ft 8in; 12st 1lb.
Career: Blackpool, Bradford City (January 1909), Chelsea (April 1909, £1,300), Stoke (September 1919).
Chelsea debut: 16 April 1910. Appearances: League 119, FA Cup 10; Goals: League 71, FA Cup 9.
This bustling, vigorous, well-built forward was renowned for his powerful shooting and he became a scourge of goalkeepers: 'I'd rather face his Satanic Majesty than Whittingham', one was said to have remarked. Many of his goals came from long-range efforts and he delighted in picking up loose balls in midfield and setting off on lightning dashes towards goal. He played in one Victory international for England against Scotland in 1919 and died soon after his transfer to Stoke, later that year.

WHITTON, William A. (1923-1926)   **Centre-forward**
Born: Aldershot.
5ft 8½in; 10st 10lb.
Career: Tottenham Hotspur (1920), Chelsea (March 1923), contract cancelled (April 1926).
Chelsea debut: 17 March 1923. Appearances: League 38, FA Cup 1; Goals: League 19.
One of several players brought to Stamford Bridge in an attempt to solve the goalscoring 'famine' and keep the club in the First Division, Whitton failed to do either. But he scored regularly in Division Two in the first part of the 1924-5 season before losing his form and deciding to give up the game and take up a business career.

WICKS, Stanley Maurice (1954-1956)   **Centre-half**
Born: Reading, 11 July 1928; Died: Henley-on-Thames, 20 February 1983.
6ft 2½in; 13st 3lb.
Career: Reading, Chelsea (January 1954, £10,500),

Retired through injury (1956).
Honours: England 'B' international (1 cap), Football League XI (1 appearance), Football League Championship medal 1955. Also 1 FA Charity Shield appearance 1955.
Chelsea debut: 6 November 1954. Appearances: League 71, FA Cup 9; Goals: League 1.

This tall, dominating centre-half followed manager Ted Drake to Stamford Bridge from Reading, having already played nearly 200 first-team games for the Berkshire club in Division Three South. Making the transition to the higher class of football with ease, he took over the centre-half spot from Ron Greenwood in the second half of the League Championship season, won representative honours and, just when, even at the age of 28, a full England cap seemed within his reach, he was cruelly struck down by a knee injury and never played football again.

WICKS, Stephen John (1974-1979 & 1986-1988)
Centre-half
Born: Reading, 3 October 1956.
6ft 2in; 13st 2lb.
Career: Chelsea (June 1974), Derby County (January 1979, £275,000), Queen's Park Rangers (September 1979), Crystal Palace (January 1981), Queen's Park Rangers (March 1982), Chelsea (July 1986, £450,000), Retired (July 1988, £262,000 compensation).
Honours: England Under-23 international (1 cap), England Youth, Second Division championship medal 1983, Football League Cup runners-up medal 1986.
Chelsea debut: 31 March 1975. Appearances: League 151(1), FA Cup 8, League Cup 4; Goals: League 6, FA Cup 2.

Like his namesake, Stan, Steve Wicks was a powerful giant of a centre-half and from the same place of birth. He graduated to the professional ranks from the Juniors and was a first-team regular at the age of 19. Dominant in the air and firm in the tackle, with a strong left foot, he was a member of the 1976-7 Second Division promotion team before moving to Derby County the following year. He was at the Baseball Ground only briefly, but it was more than seven years later that he returned to Stamford Bridge, at a new record fee for a player signed by Chelsea FC. He retired through injury and was then a coach with Tampa Bay Rowdies before being appointed assistant manager of Portsmouth.

WILDING, Harry Thomas MM (1914-1928)
Centre-forward/Centre-half
Born: Wolverhampton, 27 June 1894; Died: Earlsfield, 12 December 1958.
6ft 1in; 12st 12lb.
Career: Chelsea (April 1914), Tottenham Hotspur (November 1928), Bristol Rovers (November 1930).
Chelsea debut: 20 August 1919. Appearances: League 241, FA Cup 24; Goals: League 22, FA Cup 3.
Wilding's career was interrupted by the outbreak of World War One before he had played in the first team. But, having won the Military Medal whilst serving with the Coldstream Guards, he returned to become a pillar of the side in the immediate post-war period. First

WILKINS, Raymond Colin (1973-1979)   **Midfield**
Born: Hillingdon, 14 September 1956.
5ft 7in; 10st 10lb.
Career: Chelsea (October 1973), Manchester United (August 1979, £875,000), AC Milan (June 1984), Paris St-Germain (July 1987), Glasgow Rangers (November 1987), Queen's Park Rangers (November 1989).
Honours: England international (84 caps), England Under-23 (2 caps), England Under-21 (1 cap), Football League XI (1 appearance), England Youth, FA Cup winners' medal 1983.
Chelsea debut: 26 October 1973. Appearances: League 176(3), FA Cup 11(1), League Cup 6(1); Goals: League 30, FA Cup 2, League Cup 2.
Younger brother of Graham, Ray Wilkins graduated to full professional status after beginning his Stamford Bridge career as an apprentice in October 1973. He made his senior debut the same month. An immensely gifted central midfield player whose accuracy and range of passing the ball was his trademark, he was Chelsea's youngest-ever captain when appointed in April 1975, aged 18. Financial problems dictated his transfer to

at centre or inside-forward, but more permanently at centre-half, he was a dominating figure, possessing clever ball skills as well as being a fine header of the ball. Greatly respected by his fellow professionals, he was noted for his consistency and strength in the tackle.

WILEMAN, Arthur Harold MM (1909-1911)
Inside-forward
Born: Newhall (Derbyshire), 1889. Killed in action at Ypres, 28 April 1918.
5ft 7in; 10st 9lb.
Career: Burton Albion, Chelsea (cs 1909), Millwall (cs 1911), Luton Town (cs 1912), Southend United (cs 1913).
Chelsea debut: 25 September 1909. Appearances: League 14; Goals: League 5.
Wileman was signed together with his brother and was soon making an impression in the League side with his clever footwork and ball skills. However, apart from two spells in a season ending with relegation from Division One, he never fulfilled his early promise and the signing of Bob Whittingham finally ended his Chelsea first-team career. He served in the Royal Sussex Regiment as a Sergeant during World War One and was awarded the Military Medal.

WILKINS, Graham C. (1972-1982)   **Full-back**
Born: Hillington, 28 June 1955.
5ft 6½in; 10st 2lb.
Career: Chelsea (July 1972), Brentford (July 1982, free transfer), Southend United (loan).
Chelsea debut: 26 December 1972. Appearances: League 136(1), FA Cup 5, League Cup 7; Goals: League 1.
Son of former Brentford player, George Wilkins, he signed professional from the apprentice ranks. A stylish, lightweight, full-back, he was rarely assured of his place in the first team at a time of many comings and goings in the club, and he lacked the consistency and physique to become a top-class defender.

Manchester United for a, then, Chelsea record fee, just when he was establishing himself as one of the country's leading midfield players.

WILLEMSE, Stanley B. (1949-1956)   **Full-back**
Born: Brighton, 23 August 1924.
5ft 10½in; 11st 9lb.
Career: Brighton & Hove Albion (June 1946), Chelsea (July 1949, £6,500), Leyton Orient (June 1956, £4,500), Retired (1958).
Honours: England 'B' international (1 cap), England Schoolboys, Football League XI (1 appearance), Football League Championship medal 1955. Also 1 FA Charity Shield appearance 1955.
Chelsea debut: 31 August 1949. Appearances: League 198, FA Cup 22; Goals: League 2.
A rugged, fearless, hard-tackling full-back (and useful emergency striker) this one-time Royal Marine was signed to take over from Welsh international Billy Hughes. For seven seasons his wholehearted enthusiasm endeared him to supporters and he was a vital member of the 1954-5 League Championship side.

WILLIAMS, Ernest W. (1909-1910)   **Outside-left**
Born: Ryde (Isle of Wight).
Career: Chelsea (December 1909, amateur), Portsmouth (amateur).
Chelsea debut: 18 December 1909. Appearances: League 6, FA Cup 2; Goals: FA Cup 1.
This amateur winger signed forms at the same time as Vivian Woodward, then went straight into the first team. He held his place until the middle of February, after which he never played for Chelsea again. He was noted for his speed and direct approach to goal.

WILLIAMS, Paul J. (1980-1983)   **Centre-half**
Born: Lambeth, 16 November 1962.
6ft; 11st 7lb.
Career: Chelsea (July 1980), free transfer (May 1983), Leatherhead.
Chelsea debut: 9 April 1983. Appearances: League 1.
He signed apprentice forms in July 1979 and then spent three years on the staff as a full professional, playing in the junior and reserve teams.

WILLIAMS, Reginald F. (1945-1951)
Wing-half/Inside-forward
Born: Watford, 28 January 1922.
5ft 11in; 12st 3lb.
Career: Watford (amateur), Chelsea (October 1945), Retired (October 1951).
Chelsea debut: 5 January 1945. Appearances: League 58, FA Cup 16; Goals: League 13, FA Cup 4.
Williams was a most talented player whose career was later to be mirrored by Ken Shellito. For much of his six years on the staff he was in hospital, or on the treatment table, fighting a series of injuries which ultimately caused his premature retirement from the game. Well-built and of graceful movement, he was a skilful, yet forceful, player either in defence or attack. Called up for the England international squad for the matches against France and Switzerland in 1946, he was destined never to play a full season and his promising career, already retarded by the outbreak of World War Two, petered out sadly.

WILLIAMS, William Dennis (1927-1928)   **Inside-forward**
Born: Leytonstone, 1904.
5ft 8in; 11st 6lb.
Career: Fairbairn House Boys, West Ham United (1922), Chelsea (June 1927), not retained (May 1928), Dagenham.
Honours: England Schoolboy international.
Chelsea debut: 26 December 1927. Appearances: League 2.
Apart from deputizing for Albert Thain in two games, Williams' Chelsea career, limited to one season, consisted of playing in the reserve team. He toured Australia with an FA party in 1925, and became trainer to Leyton after his playing career ended.

WILSON, Andrew Nesbitt (1923-1931)
Centre/Inside-forward
Born: Newmains (Lanarkshire), 14 February 1896; Died: October 1973.
5ft 6½in; 12st 5lb.

Career: Cambuslang Rangers, Middlesbrough (February 1914), Chelsea (November 1923, £6,500), Queen's Park Rangers (October 1931), Nimes FC (France, May 1932), Retired (1934).
Honours: Scotland international (12 caps).
Chelsea debut: 1 December 1923. Appearances: League 238, FA Cup 15; Goals: League 59, FA Cup 3.
One of the most loyal and popular players to have worn the Chelsea shirt, Andy Wilson had already won his 12 Scotland caps before moving to London and it was, indeed, strange that the selectors never recognized him again. At Stamford Bridge he was converted to inside-forward (having previously played almost entirely as leader of the attack), in a 'W' formation evolved largely as a result of the change of the offside law. A fine dribbler and passer of the ball, he was a true artist and overcame the handicap of having a hand shattered by a shell fragment at Arras whilst serving in the 16th Royal Scots early in 1918. Despite this disability he was a fine golfer, billiards and bowls player. After the war, Middlesbrough held his registration but allowed him to play in the Scottish League and the 'rebel' Scottish Central League before he rejoined them in August 1921. The First Division's leading scorer in 1921-2, he signed for Chelsea for a record £6,500 early in the 1923-4 season. When both Chelsea and Middlesbrough were relegated at the end of that season, Wilson was leading scorer for both clubs. After ending his English career with QPR, he moved briefly into French football before returning to become trainer-manager with Clacton Town, then manager at Walsall (1934-37) and, later Gravesend & Northfleet. Then he retired to live in London where he was a familiar figure at Stamford Bridge almost up until his death. His son, Jimmy, was on the Chelsea professional staff in the 1950s.

WILSON, Clive (1987-1990) **Midfield**
Born: Aylesbury, 13 November 1961.
5ft 7in; 10st.
Career: Manchester City (December 1979), Chester City (loan), Manchester City (loan), Chelsea (March 1987, £250,000), Queen's Park Rangers (July 1990, £4,000).
Honours: Second Division championship medal 1989, Full Members' Cup winners' medal 1990.
Chelsea debut: 15 August 1987. Appearances: League 71(13), FA Cup 4, League Cup 3(3), Full Members' Cup 7(2); Goals: League 5.
Somehow, Clive Wilson's talents were never fully appreciated, or put to the best use at Stamford Bridge. This highly talented left-side midfield player possessed both speed and excellent passing ability and ball-control, yet was rarely automatically assured of his first-team place, although extremely popular with the fans.

WILSON, Kevin James (1987-) **Striker**
Born: Banbury, 18 April 1961.
5ft 7in; 10st 10lb.
Career: Ruscote Sports, Banbury United (1978), Derby County (December 1979), Ipswich Town (January 1985), Chelsea (June 1987, £335,000).
Honours: Northern Ireland international (21 caps), Second Division championship medal 1989, Full Members' Cup winners' medal 1990.
Chelsea debut: 15 August 1987. Appearances: League 111(22), FA Cup 6, League Cup 8(2), Full Members'

Cup 10(3); Goals: League 41, FA Cup 1, League Cup 4, Full Members' Cup 6.
Kevin Wilson is a tireless worker and a striker with a natural flair for scoring goals. At Chelsea he has had to compete with Gordon Durie for the right to partner Kerry Dixon in the club's main strike-force. Too often, and not always with regard to justice, he has found himself relegated to the substitutes' bench. A great trier, his infectious enthusiasm for the game is not the least of his assets, and no cause is ever lost, as he chivvies opposing defenders into enforced errors.

WINDRIDGE, James Edwin (1905-1911) Inside-forward
Born: Sparkbrook (Birmingham), 21 October 1882;
Died: 23 September 1939.
5ft 7½in; 11st 3lb.
Career: Small Heath (1902), Chelsea (April 1905, £190), Middlesbrough (November 1911, £1,000), Birmingham (April 1914).
Honours: England international (8 caps).
Chelsea debut: 2 September 1905. Appearances: League 143, FA Cup 9; Goals: League 54, FA Cup 4.
The 'Wizard' played at inside-left in Chelsea first-ever League fixture and, indeed, outlasted all his colleagues in the team that day by remaining at Stamford Bridge for more than six seasons. Renowned as a 'scientific close dribbler', the ball was seemingly glued to his boot and he was also a good distributor of it, and a powerful

signing, becoming a fixture as a skilful and reliable right-back in the first four post-war seasons. He was one whose League career was disrupted by the war and it is most likely this prevented him having a fruitful international career. He played for Chelsea in the 1944-5 Football League (South) Cup Final at Wembley.

WISE, Dennis Frank (1990-)   **Forward**
Born: Kensington, 15 December 1966.
5ft 6in; 9st 5lb.
Career: Southampton (amateur), Wimbledon (March 1985), Chelsea (July 1990, £1,600,000).
Honours: England international (1 cap), England Under-21 (1 cap), FA Cup winners' medal 1988.
Chelsea debut: 25 August 1990. Appearances: League 33, FA Cup 1, League Cup 7, Full Members' Cup 1; Goals: League 10, League Cup 2, Full Members' Cup 1.

marksman. He was also a county cricketer with Warwickshire CCC, playing seven matches as an all-rounder between 1909 and 1913.

WINTER, Daniel Thomas (1945-1951)   **Full-back**
Born: Tonypandy, 14 June 1918.
5ft 8½in; 11st 1½lb.
Career: Tonypandy Juniors, Bolton Wanderers, Chelsea (December 1945, £5,000), Worcester City (cs 1951).
Chelsea debut: 5 January 1946. Appearances: League 131, FA Cup 24.
A Welsh wartime international, Winter had made his League debut for Bolton Wanderers in the 1937-8 season. He first made his mark at Chelsea, whilst guesting for the club when serving as a bombardier in the Army in 1944. He went on to play 57 games in wartime football and then proved himself a bargain

Chelsea paid a record fee (£1,600,000) to obtain the services of this lively, diminutive wide attacker. Not a prolific goalscorer, at Wimbledon, Wise immediately assumed the responsibility of taking penalty-kicks and solved a problem which, apart from Graham Roberts during the 1988-89 season, had sorely afflicted the club for several years. A clever ball-player, his aggressive temperament sometimes gets him into trouble (he was sent off in his second game for Chelsea) and, possibly

150

in view of his place on the edge of the England squad, for a time he seemed less willing to commit himself in physical contact, reducing his effectiveness and causing him to be omitted from the team for several games.

WOLFF, Frank (1905-1906)　　　　　**Centre-half**
5ft 9½in; 12st 7lb.
Career: Hull City (1904), Chelsea (August 1905), not retained (May 1906).
Chelsea debut: 18 November 1905. Appearances: FA Cup 1.
A member of the Chelsea professional staff during the club's first season, Wolff was a regular in the reserve team and made only one senior appearance, in an FA Cup tie on a day when the first team were fulfilling a League fixture.

WOOD, Darren Terence (1984-1989)　　　**Full-back**
Born: Scarborough, 9 June 1964.
5ft 10in; 11st.
Career: Middlesbrough (July 1981), Chelsea (September 1984, £50,000), Sheffield Wednesday (January 1989, £350,000).
Honours: England Schoolboy international, Full Members' Cup winners' medal 1986.
Chelsea debut: 27 October 1984. Appearances: League 134(10), FA Cup 9, League Cup 11, Full Members' Cup 13(1); Goals: League 3.
After making more than 200 appearances for Middlesbrough by the age of 20, Wood rejoined his former manager, John Neal, at Chelsea. Immediately winning his place in the first team, he showed himself to be a competent full-back or occasional midfield player. Speedy and strong in the tackle, he was a long kicker of the ball and good auxiliary attacker.

WOODLEY, Victor Robert (1931-1945)　**Goalkeeper**
Born: Cippenham (Bucks), 26 February 1910; Died: Trowbridge, October 1978.
6ft; 12st 4lb.
Career: Windsor & Eton (cs 1930), Chelsea (May 1931), Bath City (December 1945), Derby County (March 1946), Bath City (player-manager, March 1947). Retired (1949).
Honours: England international (19 caps), Football League XI (4 appearances), FA Cup winners' medal 1946.
Chelsea debut: 29 August 1931. Appearances: League 252, FA Cup 20.
One of Chelsea's greatest goalkeepers, Woodley's sequence of 19 England caps in succession was only terminated by the outbreak of World War Two. Pitchforked into the First Division from amateur football within weeks of his arrival at Stamford Bridge, he became a permanent fixture between the posts for the next 15 years, despite strong competition from Johnny Jackson, Scotland's international 'keeper. Indeed, it was Woodley's wonderful consistency and sure handling which kept Chelsea in the First Division in some difficult seasons for most of the 1930s. He played a further 109 wartime games before apparently moving out to grass with Bath City. In the early months of 1946, however, Derby County found themselves without an experienced 'keeper and Woodley filled the breach. Within weeks he had crowned his long career by keeping goal for the Rams in their FA Cup Final

victory over Charlton Athletic, a fairy-tale ending to his football days. The glory of Wembley over, Woodley returned to the backwaters of the Southern League.

WOODWARD, Vivian John (1919-1915) Centre-forward
Born: Kennington, 3 June 1879; Died: Earling, 31 January 1954.
5ft 11in; 11st.
Career: Aschum College, Clacton, Harwich & Parkestone, Corinthians, Tottenham Hotspur (amateur, 1901), Chelsea (amateur 1909)
Honours: England international (23 caps), England Amateur (38 caps), Football League XI (3 appearances), Olympic football gold winners' medals 1908, 1912.
Chelsea debut: 27 November 1909. Appearances: League 106, FA Cup 10; Goals: League 30, FA Cup 4.
Woodward was the greatest amateur centre-forward of his time and one of the famous Corinthians. An architect by profession, often described as the 'perfect attacker', he was noted for his solo dribbling, besides being a fine distributor of the ball. Equally impressive was his heading and powers of shooting. 'A human chain of lightning; the footballer with magic in his boots', wrote one commentator. He captained the Great Britain team which won the Olympic soccer title in 1908 and 1912. Having obtained special leave from the Army to play for Chelsea in the 1915 FA Cup Final, he sportingly stood down at the last minute to

possessed high skills and artistry. He won four 'blues' at Cambridge, played Davis Cup tennis for Great Britain and won the 1921 Wimbledon doubles (with Lycett) and the 1920 Olympic Games doubles (with Turnbull). A broken leg, sustained in a collision with a wooden paled fence at Manchester City's old Hyde Road ground, eventually ended his football career, shortly after playing his only full international for England, against Wales in 1922. He was president of the Corinthian Casuals FC for a time.

allow Bob Thomson (who had appeared in the earlier rounds) to take his place. In fact, Woodward never played for Chelsea again as the war ended his brilliant career. He was a director of Chelsea FC from 1922 to 1930 and had been a member of the Spurs' board in his playing days with that club (1908-09). He scored Spurs' first goal in the Football League and was leading scorer in their promotion-winning side of 1908-09 before shocking them by resigning on the eve of their first season in Division One. It was an even bigger shock for the White Hart Lane club when he returned to League football with Chelsea. In fact, in an interview, he said he had been persuaded to move to Stamford Bridge by Claude Kirby, the club's chairman, but, also, that the ground was much nearer than White Hart Lane for his friends and relatives to come to see him play!

WOOSNAM, Maxwell (1914) Centre-half
Born: Liverpool, 6 September 1892; Died: 14 July 1965.
Career: Winchester College (1908-11), Cambridge University (1912-14), Corinthians (1913-21), Chelsea (amateur, 1913-14), Manchester United (amateur, October 1919), Northwich Victoria (amateur cs 1925), Brentford (amateur, May 1929).
Honours: England international (1 cap), England Amateur (2 caps).
Chelsea debut: 21 March 1914. Appearances: League 3.
Woosnam, son of a former Canon of Chester, played three games for Chelsea in the latter part of the 1913-14 season. A centre-half very much in the old-style amateur tradition, he was a six-footer renowned for his ferocious shoulder-charging, but he also

WOSAHLO, Roger Frank (1964-1967) Winger
Born: Cambridge, 11 September 1947.
5ft 7½in; 10st 4lb.
Career: Chelsea (December 1964), Ipswich Town (April 1967), Peterborough United (June 1968), Ipswich Town (July 1969).
Honours: England Schoolboy international.
Chelsea debut: 22 April 1967. Appearances: League 0(1).
Wosahlo, a former apprentice, signed professional forms after being leading goalscorer for Chelsea Juniors. He was a regular member of the reserve team in 1966-7 but was never able to break through into the senior side, being restricted to one appearance as a substitute. Emigrated to South Africa in 1970.

YOUNG, Allan Robert (1961-1969) Centre-half
Born: Hornsey, 20 January 1941.
6ft; 12st 10lb.
Career: Barnet Juniors, Arsenal (April 1959), Chelsea (November 1961, £6,000), Torquay United (January 1969, £8,000).
Chelsea debut: 23 December 1961. Appearances: League 20, FA Cup 2, League Cup 1, Fairs Cup 3; Goals: FA Cup 1.
Young gave loyal service to Chelsea for more than seven years. He was usually in the reserve team but proved a dependable deputy whenever called up to play in the senior side.

Cover of the programme for the 1922 FA Cup Final held at Stamford Bridge.

Chelsea line-up in 1905. Back row (left to right): J.T.Robertson (manager), H.A.Mears (chairman), Byrne, F.W.Parker (director), McRoberts, Foulke (captain), Copeland, Mackie, James Miller, McEwan, Harry Ransom (trainer), Craigie, William Lewis (secretary), Jack White (assistant trainer). Seated: Moran, Donaghy, T.Miller, J.Robertson, O'Hara, Windridge, Key, Kirwan. On ground: Dowland, Slater, Wolff, Watson.

Match to Remember 1   2 September 1905

Stockport County 1   Chelsea 0
Dodd

AS IT turned out, there was little memorable about Chelsea's first competitive match, a Football League Second Division fixture away to Stockport. Walking from the railway station to the ground, Willie Foulke, the 22st goalkeeper, was accosted by a young home-team supporter. "You'll get licked t'day," he warned the giant. Unworried and unmoved, Foulke calmly retorted, "Then it'll be the first time this season, me lad."

A record Edgeley Park crowd had gathered to welcome the League newcomers, intrigued by the publicity which had accompanied their entry into football, but Chelsea were totally unable to live up to their star-billing.

Making a nervous, hesitant start, the nimble Stockport forwards made rings around the more static Pensioners' defence. At least it gave the fans plenty of opportunity to watch Foulke in action as he coped capably with several shots, only one of which, a hard hit low drive, caused him any difficulty.

After a goalless first half, during which Stockport's wing-half, Cresser, grazed the bar, the home team soon took the lead. Winger Schofield was unceremoniously upended in the penalty box, and, although Foulke saved that player's spot-kick, Bardsley, following up, picked on the rebound and crossed for George Dodd, later to become a Chelsea player, to score easily.

As the game moved towards its conclusion, Chelsea began to find some semblance of rhythm, especially down the right flank where Martin Moran and the veteran Dave Copeland combined threateningly. Once, Moran's weak finishing let him down when he should have scored. But, despite some striking individual play, Chelsea were handicapped by indifferent teamwork in what was generally agreed to have been 'a terribly hard game'.

Stockport County: Pemble; Haywood, Waters, Stuart, Hall, Cresser, Schofield, Crump, Manson, Dodd, Bardsley.

Chelsea: Foulke; Mackie, McEwan, Key, McRoberts, Miller, Moran, Robertson, Copeland, Windridge, Kirwan.

Referee: D.Hammond (Heywood)   *Attendance: 7,000*

Match to Remember 2   11 January 1908

Chelsea 9   Worksop Town 1
Hilsdon 6, Bridgeman, Windridge 2   *Richardson*

RECORDS are made to be broken, but no Chelsea player has yet equalled George Hilsdon's half-dozen goals in an FA Cup tie more than 80 years ago, let alone bettered it.

The circumstances leading up to the match were in themselves somewhat unusual. Second out of the green baize bag, the Chelsea directors persuaded their Worksop counterparts to transfer the game to Stamford Bridge on the dubious grounds that 'we have only one First League match at home between Boxing Day and the third week in February'. Without doubt, financial considerations played a part, certainly so far as the Dukeries club were concerned.

In any event, some 19,000 turned up to watch a game so one-sided that a contemporary writer observed 'the emotions of the crowd were never stirred'. Yet, Worksop should have scored in the first minute, but, having been shaken, Chelsea promptly took the game over.

Jimmy Windridge scores one of his two goals as the Worksop goalkeeper looks on.

155

George Hilsdon, Jimmy Windridge (twice) and Billy Bridgeman all scored before half-time to give Chelsea an unassailable lead before the visitors' captain, inside-forward Richardson, replied, But, that was merely a foretaste of what was to come.

Hilsdon proceeded to add a further three goals in the opening five minutes after the resumption, helped no doubt by the absence of the Worksop left-half who was injured and off the field. But his long-range drives simply flashed into the net, justifying his 'Gatling Gun' nickname. And, although he added another two before the end, in truth, only the heroic goalkeeping of Fern kept the score within reasonable limits. Bravely, Worksop plugged away and their centre-forward, Padley, hit the bar on one occasion, whilst inside-left Walker scorned an easy scoring chance.

Consolation for the men from Nottinghamshire came in the form of their share of the 'gate', a cheque for £381, no doubt a vastly bigger sum than they could have expected had the tie taken place at their Central Avenue headquarters.

Chelsea were not entirely happy, despite the outcome. Having claimed that it was absurd to suggest that the choice of ground affected the result, one club official went on to add that, but for a disinclination to take too many risks on the frozen ground, Chelsea's score might easily have been 20 or more! He then criticized Worksop's 'none too clean methods in stopping', drawing attention to a particularly ugly foul on Hilsdon.

'Instant ordering off is the only proper treatment for the football hooligan', he concluded.

Chelsea: Whitley; Cameron, Harding, Henderson, Stark, Birnie, Brawn, Whitehouse, Hilsdon, Windridge, Bridgeman.

Worksop Town: Fern; Coupe, Gregory, Parramore, Walters, Westwood, Cooke, Richardson, Padley, Walker, Bale.

Referee: J.W.Bailey (Leicester)   *Attendance: 18,995*

Match to Remember 3   24 April 1915

Sheffield United 3   Chelsea 0
Simmons, Fazackerley, Kitchen

CHELSEA'S first FA Cup Final should have been the climax to their first ten seasons as a football club. Yet, for a variety of reasons, fate conspired to make it a day they would rather not recall.

World War One had already been in progress for eight months and, increasingly, the feeling was gaining ground that normal football in such circumstances should be abandoned. Inevitably, games were being staged in front of dwindling crowds and in an air of unreality.

The venue of the Final was switched from the Crystal Palace to Old Trafford, Manchester, and, to make matters worse, the game was played on a grey, sunless day. Indeed, at one point, it seemed quite possible that fog would halt the proceedings.

Sheffield United had arrived at the Final through victories over northern teams, beating in turn, Blackpool, Liverpool, Bradford, Oldham Athletic (after a replay) and Bolton Wanderers in a semi-final at Blackburn. Chelsea had had a somewhat rougher ride against opposition which included Woolwich Arsenal, Manchester City, Newcastle United, and Everton in the semi-final.

But, on the day, there was only ever going to be one winner. Sheffield simply brushed Chelsea aside, as one writer said 'as if they were novices'. Their strength lay in their half-back line, with George Utley outstanding. Poor Harry Ford scarcely got a kick at the ball and centre-half Brelsford, despite his lack of inches, was

156

Chelsea's FA Cup Final line-up in 1915. Back row (left to right): Taylor, Whitley, Bettridge, Molyneux, Logan, Walker, Harrow. Front row: Ford, Halse, Thomson, Croal, McNeil.

too strong for brave little Bob Thomson, who had only recently recovered from a dislocated elbow.

For virtually the whole of the game the Chelsea defence was subjected to constant pressure and became increasingly ragged — even Walter Bettridge uncharacteristically losing his composure at times. After 36 minutes, Simmons opened the scoring by beating two men to the ball and rocketing the ball past Jim Molyneux. And although afterwards Chelsea managed to keep the Blades' attack at bay until near the end, goals from Utley and Kitchen in the last six minutes gave a more realistic look to the score-sheet.

J.A.H.Catton, one of the leading football writers of the day, summed it up by saying: "Chelsea were as helpless as a reed shaken in the wind. They would not have scored had they played for a week."

Sheffield United: Gough; Cook, English, Sturgess, Brelsford, Utley, Simmons, Fazackerley, Kitchen, Masterman, Evans.
Chelsea: Molyneux; Bettridge, Harrow, Taylor, Logan, Walker, Ford, Halse, Thomson, Croal, McNeil.
Referee: H.H.Taylor (Altrincham)   *Attendance: 49,557*

Match to Remember 4   4 September 1922

Chelsea 3   Stoke 2
Wilding, Cock, Sharp   *J.Broad 2 (1 pen)*

FOR 17 years Chelsea had been striving to reach the top of the tree. At ease in the Second Division of the Football League, they had found the greater challenge

Chelsea, 1922-3. Back row (left to right): Bell, Smith, Sharp, Howard Baker, Hoddinott. Front row: Harrow, Wilding, Ford, Cock, Meehan, McNeil.

of the upper branches a good deal harder to come to terms with. Cup-tie football, with its lesser demand for consistency, was more to their liking.

Then, in the autumn of 1922, they got away to a rapid start. After a 1-1 draw at home to Birmingham, Stoke were beaten 2-1 in the Potteries, and Birmingham by a single goal in the return at St Andrew's. So it was, when Stoke made their first-ever visit to Stamford Bridge on the first Monday in September.

On a warm evening, the game opened uneventfully. Gradually, Chelsea's greater aggression saw them gaining control in midfield and Harry Wilding, an old-style attacking half-back, who could also play in the forward line, scored shortly before half-time. Earlier, Jack Cock had missed a good chance.

The goal, however, stung Stoke into action and, almost immediately, Jim Broad equalized. And after the interval they continued to dictate the run of play until Cock restored Chelsea's advantage following a defensive mix-up after a corner.

Straightaway, Cock hit a post when it seemed easier to score and, after the same player had retired for treatment to an injury, Buchanan Sharp then made it 3-1. Jim Broad's second goal, from the penalty-spot, came in the final minute of the game and was too late to cause alarm. At last, Chelsea could look down on all rivals from the top of the Championship table.

With only four games played, reactions were understandably guarded. 'It would be unwise to chortle prematurely', said the programme editor, while admitting that Chelsea's display: 'gave substantial grounds for a certain amount of optimism'.

As things turned out, Chelsea enjoyed their position for another 12 days, before defeat at Middlesbrough, the Teessiders themselves occupying second place in the table at the time, knocked them off their perch. And, in fact, any euphoria quickly evaporated still further as Chelsea tumbled down the ladder to end the season in 19th position and six points ahead of Stoke, who were relegated. Fame and success can, indeed, be fleeting.

Chelsea: Howard Baker; Smith, Harrow, Wilding, Cameron, Meehan, Haywood, Ford, Cock, Sharp, McNeil.

Stoke: Scott; McGrory, Milne, Clarke, Beswick, Rouse, T.Broad, Groves, J.Broad, Watkin, Tempest.

Referee: A.E.Caseley (Wolverhampton)   *Attendance: 20,000*

Cardiff City 3   Chelsea 2
Irving, Davies, H.Ferguson (pen)   *Priestley, Turnbull*

NOWADAYS, cup ties fall thick and fast throughout the football season, as new competitions continually burst on the scene. Before 1960, when the Football League introduced their own Cup, there was only one recognized national knock-out competition for senior teams and, as a result, there was a unique flavour and atmosphere about each FA Cup tie, not always experienced today.

One such occasion paired Chelsea and Cardiff City, to produce two games still discussed by those survivors of the more than 100,000 spectators who were able to force their way through the turnstiles before they were closed. First, at Stamford Bridge in difficult conditions, the teams fought out a goalless draw, with each claiming that they had been baulked by ill-fortune. If that match contained high drama, it was nothing compared with what followed in Wales four days later.

Despite the 3pm midweek kick-off, Ninian Park was full to overflowing well before

A Cardiff forward heads for the Chelsea goal with full-back George Smith in pursuit.

the start and, within 20 minutes, the home team were two goals ahead. First, Sam Irving (to join Chelsea 12 months later) put the Welshmen into the lead, and then Len Davies added a second.

But the incident, still discussed, and to have far-reaching effect, occurred ten minutes before the interval. Cardiff centre-half Tommy Sloan fouled Bob Turnbull in the 18-yard area and Chelsea were awarded a penalty. City goalkeeper, Tom Farquharson was then seen to retire into the back of his net and, as Andy Wilson shaped to take the kick, proceeded to charge forward and smother the shot on the edge of the six-yard area. As a result of such sharp tactics, the law was later changed to prevent a goalkeeper from moving until after the ball is kicked.

Small consolation for Chelsea that day, however. And, although John Priestley scored with almost the last kick before half-time, and Turnbull equalized soon after the interval, it was another penalty, this time to Cardiff, which settled this day.

Priestley's goal, too, had sparked off controversy. His angled shot appeared to have passed out of play beyond the far post when the referee was seen to signal a Chelsea goal, much to the consternation of the Cardiff players. In fact, the force of the shot had ripped up the pegs holding down the side-netting under which the ball had passed. After the Cardiff players had made clear their dissatisfaction, the official then consulted a policeman standing behind the goal before allowing the goal to stand.

But, not only had it been Cardiff's day, they then went on to beat Arsenal in the FA Cup Final at Wembley, to take the Cup out of England for the only time, and to complete the most memorable season in their history.

Cardiff City: Farquharson; Nelson, Watson, Keenor, Sloan, Hardy, H.Ferguson, Irving, Davies, Curtis, McLachlan.
Chelsea: Millington; Smith, Law, Priestley, Wilding, W.Ferguson, Crawford, Thain, Turnbull, Wilson, Pearson.

Referee: J.V.Pennington (Reading)   *Attendance: 47,353*

Match to Remember 6   3 September 1930

Newcastle United 1   Chelsea 0
Cape

EVERY now and then football produces a star personality who catches the imagination of its public by his extraordinary skills and spectacular deeds. One such, between the two world wars, was Hughie Gallacher, still considered by some as the greatest centre-forward of all time.

Standing a mere 65 inches tall, he was a fine header of the ball, often out-jumping defenders who should have towered above him. On the ground his close ball-control and swift changes of direction regularly produced panic amongst the opposition. Throughout almost 20 years his magnetic appeal, and prolific goalscoring, attracted extra thousands through the turnstiles wherever he played.

For five years he was the idol of Tyneside, a part of England where the game is more a religion than a mere pastime. His transfer from Newcastle to Chelsea in May 1930 was therefore a mortal blow to his army of black and white fans in the North-East and his return there, albeit in the blue Chelsea shirt, in the first week of the following season is an occasion still recalled by those present.

Had St James' Park been able to accommodate 90,000 it would still have been filled to capacity. As it was, the 68,386, who crammed in before the gates were

Hughie Gallacher in action in Chelsea colours. For a small man he was effective in the air.

closed will forever remain the largest crowd to watch a game in the famous stadium. Many saw very little of the action. Extra police were called to come to the assistance of the hard-worked ambulance men. As one 'Geordie' put it, 'I paid eighteen pence to get in; I wish I could have paid eighteen pence to get out'.

Chelsea, back in the First Division for the first time for five seasons, had brandished the chequebook to ensure they remained in the top class. And it was obvious from the start that they were the superior craftsmen. They were ultra-clever. But intricate patterns and over-elaboration became worn-out by repetition. Newcastle, for their part, fought determinedly for every inch of the way and were rewarded by scoring the only goal of a tense encounter in the 76th minute.

Down to ten men, following an injury to Jimmy Nelson, winger Wilkinson broke away down the right flank and his centre was met on the far side of the penalty area by Cape who headed firmly past Sam Millington. For the remaining minutes, Chelsea counter-attacked strongly but found McInroy in brilliant form, two of his saves from Alex Cheyne and Gallacher being especially fine.

Too late they had begun to play with a directness which had been lacking earlier. 'Chelsea must remember that the object of the game is to put the ball in the net', summed up one reporter.

Newcastle United: McInroy; Nelson, Fairhurst, Mathieson, Hill, Naylor, Cape, Starling, Lindsay, McDonald, Wilkinson.
Chelsea: Millington; Smith, Law, Russell, Townrow, Bishop, Crawford, Cheyne, Gallacher, Miller, Pearson.

Referee: J.E.Williams (Bolton)   *Attendance: 68,386*

Match to Remember 7   29 October 1932

Blackpool 4   Chelsea 0
Wilkinson, Hampson 3

THE English professional footballer is a hardy soul, as needs he must be. His playing season opens before the heat of summer has finally retreated. It proceeds unconcernedly on its way through autumn rains into the snow and ice of winter until the warmth of spring eases his physical burden. Spectators, of course, are subjected to the same extremes, but for them attendance is at least not obligatory.

On this final Saturday of October 1932, the local Lancastrian reporter, covering Chelsea's visit to Blackpool, described the seaside afternoon as 'the worst day climatically for many seasons'. Seven days later writing in the following week's programme, the editor of the *Chelsea Chronicle* was more specific.

'Drenched to the skin again and again by the incessant downpour and frequent immersion in the icy lake which covered the pitch, chilled to the marrow by the piercing wind . . .Blackpool is all right in summer time, but simply pitiless when a wintry north-westerly gale is driving sheets of rain or snow across it'.

Perhaps the home team were better prepared? By half-time, with the hurricane at their backs, they were already three goals ahead, and, shortly afterwards, Jimmy Hampson added another to complete his hat-trick, and the scoring. Certainly Blackpool played more intelligently, using long passes to open up the play with sweeping movements, whilst Chelsea played into their hands by trying to progress with persistent, intricate, close-passing patterns, which inevitably became bogged down in the standing water.

But, more memorable by far than such details is the fact that Chelsea finished the game with only six players on the field. One had already given up the struggle by half-time. Three more called it a day with a quarter of an hour still to play, and another opted for his early bath before the referee mercifully blew for time. The voluntary withdrawal of nearly half a team in a Football League fixture is surely a statistical freak that will never be repeated.

Yet, the loyal Chelsea programme writer would hear no criticism. 'Those ready to disparage the 'quitters' should know that in each instance the player had barely enough strength left to reach the dressing-room before collapsing. Common humanity suggests that the game should have been abandoned.'

Blackpool: McDonagh; Wassell, Everest, A.Watson, P.R.Watson, Crawford, Wilkinson, McClelland, Hampson, Douglas, Rattray.

Chelsea: Woodley; Odell, Law, Allum, O'Dowd, Ferguson, Oakton, Rankin, Mills, Miller, Pearson.

Referee: G.W.Jones (Nottingham) *Attendance: 7,311*

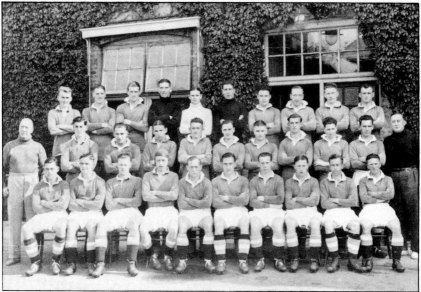

Chelsea in 1933. Back row (left to right): Allum, Craig, Barber, Macintosh, Jackson, Woodley, Macaulay, Law, Griffiths, Mitchell. Middle row: J.Whitley (trainer), O'Dowd, Dudley, Buchanan, O'Hare, Pollock, Brown, Sime, Russell, Rankin, C.Harris (assistant trainer). Front row: Oakton, Copeland, Chitty, Priestley, Gallacher, Gibson, Horton, Prout, Miller, Crawford.

Match to Remember 8   12 October 1935

Chelsea 1   Arsenal 1
Bambrick   Crayston

THE huge crowds which were increasingly attracted to big football games in the first half of this century have vanished for ever. The fact that they could be accommodated in such numbers says much for their tolerance of appalling conditions which saw them herded together, often in grossly overcrowded conditions, and on cinder steps open to the elements. Many, indeed, never had more than the occasional glimpse of what was going on below them.

Conditions at Stamford Bridge were better than most. The steeper terracing allowed an uninterrupted view for the majority. Boys at the back would be handed down over the heads of people already in position and allowed to spill on to the greyhound-racing track at the front, on which tarpaulins were spread for the purpose.

In October 1935, the largest crowd ever to attend a Football League fixture up to that time watched the Chelsea and Arsenal game at The Bridge. Lying fifth in the table, and striving to add to their three consecutive Championship titles, Arsenal held the upper hand for most of the match.

Early on, it was obvious that they were the masters in the finer points of the game, and in their teamwork. But Chelsea made up for any such deficiencies with their dash and determination.

Both goals came in the second half. First, Billy Mitchell and Jimmy Argue, opening up the left flank of the Arsenal defence, made an easy opportunity for Joe Bambrick to score. Soon afterwards, with the Chelsea defence in disarray, Jack Crayston equalized after a corner kick had failed to be cleared.

Often local 'derbies' fail to live up to their promise. But, against a perpetual tumult of noise, the vast throng was well entertained. Tommy Law and Eddie Hapgood, on opposing sides, each gave a superb demonstration of classic full-back play. George Gibson's artistry at inside-forward overshadowed even that of Alex James, for once subdued by the constant attentions of Mitchell, who at times incurred the displeasure of the referee. The pace of the game generated excitement for its customers throughout the 90 minutes.

Chelsea won their point in a fascinating struggle deservedly, even if their spoiling

Arsenal skipper Eddie Hapgood clears as George Gibson and George Male look on.

164

tactics prevented Arsenal from playing their normal game. And had Willie Barraclough accepted an easy chance late in the game they could well have snatched victory.

Chelsea: Jackson; O'Hare, Law, Mitchell, Craig, Miller, Spence, Argue, Bambrick, Gibson, Barraclough.
Arsenal: Wilson; Male, Hapgood, Crayston, Roberts, Hill, Milne, Bowden, Drake, James, Bastin.

Referee: A.E.Fogg (Bolton) *Attendance: 82,905*

Match to Remember 9   13 November 1945

. **Chelsea 3**   **Dinamo Moscow 3**
Goulden, Williams, Lawton   *Kartsev, Archangelski, Bobrov*

STAMFORD Bridge had never experienced anything like it. Well before midday, Fulham Road was packed with football fans who had arrived from all over London, and far beyond, to see the much heralded and mysterious men from Russia. For days the newspapers had built up Dinamo Moscow as a team of superstars, the equal of whom had not before been seen in England.

The turnstiles were opened at one o'clock and closed again, little more than an hour later, with the ground already full. But still the crowds arrived — and many somehow managed to gain entry. Gates were torn from their hinges; people clambered over garden walls; ladders appeared from nowhere enabling hundreds to climb in; even more found their way in via the railway embankment.

The official 'gate' figure of 74,496 is a meaningless statistic. Estimates of the real size of the crowd varied from 90-100,000. The crowd poured on to the greyhound track, and then up to the touch-lines. Hundreds occupied vantage points on the roof of East Stand. Police and stewards were powerless. Ambulance men coped as best they could and it was miraculous that no one was seriously hurt.

Reg Williams gets the ball past Dinamo goalkeeper Khomich to score Chelsea's second goal.

165

And the drama off the field was more than matched by the game itself. Superbly trained, the Russians moved the ball with bewildering speed and accuracy. Their stamina was remarkable and they seemed to be going faster at the end of the game than at the beginning. Only their finishing let them down. Several clear-cut openings were ruined by wild shooting.

Chelsea, too, emerged with enormous credit. Drawing on their considerable experience, they were never overawed and made the most of the few opportunities which came their way. Len Goulden opened the scoring after a bad defensive blunder. Ten minutes later, Reg Williams added another goal. And when Leonid Soloviev saw Vic Woodley save his penalty-kick, it seemed as if Chelsea would win a famous victory.

But, first Vasili Kartsev scored from long range and then right-winger Archangelski equalized. Suddenly Chelsea were being overrun and outplayed. Yet, with nine minutes remaining, Tommy Lawton climbed above Dinamo captain, Mikhail Semichastny, to make the score 3-2. But it was the Russians who had the final say. Four minutes later, their lanky inside-forward, Bobrov, made it 3-3 from a seemingly offside position. Eyebrows were raised as the linesman's flag remained down. But there were no protests. It was that sort of occasion.

At least diplomacy had been served, and the Russian radio commentator rightly claimed 'we have passed our first exam with honour'. Going on to beat Cardiff City (10-1) and Arsenal (4-3) before drawing with Glasgow Rangers (2-2), they were certainly one of the greatest club sides in the world at that time.

Chelsea: Woodley; Tennant, Bacuzzi (Fulham), Russell, Harris, Taylor (Fulham), Buchanan, Williams, Lawton, Goulden, Bain.
Dinamo Moscow: Khomich; Radikovsky, Stankevich, Blinkov, Semichastny, L.Soloviev, Archangelski, Kartsev, Beksov, Bobrov, S.Soloviev.

Referee: Lt-Commander G.Clark   *Attendance: 74,496*

Match to Remember 10   18 March 1950

Chelsea 2   Arsenal 2
Bentley 2   Cox, L.Compton

NEATLY dressed in his grey suit and invariably courteous and polite, Billy Birrell had perhaps the roughest ride of any Chelsea manager. With only two first-team players reporting back for duty after the seven years of World War Two, he successfully achieved the monumental task of keeping Chelsea in the First Division during his time in charge.

Inevitably he was forced to 'buy experience'. Tommy Walker (aged 31), Len Goulden (33), Harry Medhurst (30), Billy Hughes (30) and Hugh Billington (32) were examples of his shrewd and successful, if essentially short-term, purchases in the transfer market which kept his ship afloat. And, just once, the immediate post-war Chelsea team came agonizingly close to winning a major trophy.

The 1950 FA Cup campaign produced two outstanding victories over clubs then at the height of their fame. In the fourth round, Newcastle United were comprehensively beaten by three clear goals on a treacherous, frozen Stamford Bridge

Arsenal's Joe Mercer watches as the ball rolls between George Swindin and Hugh Billington.

pitch. Five weeks later, also at The Bridge, Manchester United were dispatched from the competition, 2-0, in another equally compelling performance. Accordingly, the pairing of Chelsea with Arsenal in the semi-final was rightly given 'five-star' billing.

And after 25 minutes of the game it seemed as if Chelsea were on course for their first peacetime Wembley Final. Roy Bentley, probably the outstanding centre-forward in the land at that time, first ran on to a John Harris pass deep out of defence, and, bisecting two Arsenal defenders, beautifully lobbed the ball over George Swindin as he advanced off his line.

Ten minutes later he was again on hand, this time to head Billy Hughes' long cross-ball inches inside the right-hand post, apparently bringing Arsenal to their knees. But, seconds before half-time their famous, or infamous, luck came to the rescue. Freddie Cox hit the second of two corners with the outside of his right foot and the ball, head-high, swung wickedly into the net at the near post as Medhurst, possibly unsighted by Hughes, made his late and unavailing effort to punch the ball to safety. At a stroke, the whole balance of the match had changed.

Never again did Chelsea command their early authority. And when Leslie Compton, ignoring his captain Joe Mercer's instructions, went upfield to head in brother Denis' corner for the equalizer, the despair of every man in a blue shirt was all too evident. Indeed, Arsenal had two golden chances to clinch the tie before the final whistle.

Four days later, with batteries recharged but morale inevitably dented, Chelsea took the Gunners to extra-time, only for Freddie Cox, again, to make his mark, this time scoring the only goal of the game with a low shot from the edge of the penalty area. Chelsea's dream of glory had vanished. For Birrell and several members of this ageing team, for ever.

Chelsea: Medhurst; Winter, Hughes, Armstrong, Harris, Mitchell, Gray, Goulden, Bentley, Billington, Williams.
Arsenal: Swindin; Scott, Barnes, Forbes, L.Compton, Mercer, Cox, Logie, Goring, Lewis, D.Compton.

Referee: R.J.Leafe (Nottingham)   *Attendance: 67,752*

167

Chelsea 4   Bolton Wanderers 0
Bentley 2, Smith 2

FOOTBALL history contains many remarkable acts of escape at the death, when all was apparently lost. But surely there can be few, if any, to compare with Chelsea's last-ditch efforts in 1950-51, when they retained their First Division place by 0.044 of a goal.

On 18 April, when Huddersfield Town won 2-1 in their League fixture against the Pensioners, it seemed merely to confirm what had appeared increasingly likely from Chelsea's last victory, way back in mid-January. Since then their result sequence read: D D L L D L L D L L L D L L. Optimists could point to the fact that three of their remaining games were at home, but a glance at the bottom of the table quickly dispelled any real hopes of salvation.

Pos		P	W	D	L	F	A	Pts
20	Everton	39	11	8	20	46	78	30
21	Sheffield W	39	10	8	21	55	81	28
22	Chelsea	38	8	8	22	44	63	24

'Chelsea Sunk', announced one headline. And, even with only two teams being relegated in those days, few could disagree.

When Liverpool, not then the power in the game they were later to become, were defeated by a single goal, little interest was aroused. Four days after, and profiting from some eccentric refereeing, Chelsea came from a goal behind to beat Wolverhampton Wanderers, 2-1. Next, an identical situation and scoreline, saw Chelsea win at Fulham to bring them, incredibly, within striking range of both

Bob Campbell (7) raises his arms in delight as Roy Bentley scores his second goal in three minutes.

Everton and Sheffield Wednesday. Everton still had a two-point advantage, but Wednesday were level on 30 points with Chelsea. The final scene was set as the table now read:

Pos		P	W	D	L	F	A	Pts
20	Everton	41	12	8	21	48	80	32
21	Chelsea	41	11	8	22	49	65	30
22	Sheffield W	41	11	8	22	58	83	30

To increase the drama, the fixture-planners had paired the other two companions in distress, at Hillsborough, on the final day, whilst Chelsea's visitors were Bolton Wanderers, enjoying a 'safe' position in the upper half of the table.

Within a minute at Stamford Bridge, Bobby Smith had put the ball into the net, only for the referee to rule his effort offside. And Bolton soon showed they had come to win by launching dangerous attacks on a Chelsea defence, not surprisingly beset by nervousness. After 17 minutes, however, Roy Bentley scored the type of goal which had become his hallmark. Soaring above everyone else in a packed goalmouth, he headed Billy Gray's corner past Stan Hanson. Two minutes later he repeated his act, this time outjumping Bryan Edwards to flick the ball inside the post. Before half-time Smith had made it 3-0, with the same player adding his second soon after half-time.

The game was decided, but not yet the relegation issue. On the old half-time score-board at the railway end of the ground, many eyes had been focussed on the letter 'A' which was charting the progress of the game in Sheffield. At the half-way stage, and much to Chelsea's advantage, Wednesday were three goals ahead. Fifteen minutes from the end, the board showed that the Owls had won 6-0 (the Hillsborough match having kicked-off a quarter of an hour earlier than Chelsea's).

So it was the statisticians who had the final say (and there were no electronic calculators then). When the final sums had been completed, with the three clubs all on 32 points, it was declared that Chelsea (goal-average 0.815) had wriggled clear of Wednesday (0.771) and Everton (0.558). The scenes of jubilation, on and off the field, could scarcely have been excelled had the Championship itself been won.

Chelsea: Robertson; Bathgate, Tickridge, Dickson, J.Saunders, Mitchell, Campbell, Bentley, R.Smith, Armstrong, Gray.
Bolton Wanderers: Hanson; Ball, Howe, Wheeler, Barrass, Edwards, Codd, Corfield, Lofthouse, Moir, Langton.

Referee: G.L.Iliffe (Leicester)   *Attendance: 38,926*

Match to Remember 12   16 October 1954

Chelsea 5   Manchester United 6
S.O'Connell 3, J.L.Lewis, Armstrong   *Viollet 3, Taylor 2, Blanchflower*

ELEVEN goals for 'two bob' (10p) represents good value by any yardstick. And when the teams concerned are Chelsea and Manchester United, obviously the game in question is one to recall fondly, regardless of its outcome. At the time, United were lagging one point behind Sunderland, leading the table, whilst Chelsea were comfortably tucked away in ninth position, quite unconsciously *en route* to their first Championship title.

The teams provided an interesting contrast. Chelsea could well be described as a collection of mature and seasoned professionals plus two amateurs, one of whom,

Jim Lewis gives Chelsea the lead for the only time in the 6-5 thriller against Manchester United.

Seamus O'Connell, was making his debut for the club. United, on the other hand, were already reaping the reward of their enlightened youth policy with the 'Busby Babes' constantly attracting the attention of the headline writers.

Although the large crowd were forced to wait a quarter of an hour before the scoring started, it was soon obvious that both attacks had the measure of their opposing defenders. Dennis Viollet began it all by taking advantage of a lucky deflection. Then, two elementary errors allowed amateurs O'Connell and Jim Lewis to nose Chelsea in front. But by half-time, Tommy Taylor and Viollet had restored United's lead before Chelsea forced several corners in their desperate efforts to level the score.

Eight minutes after the interval it looked all over. Little Johnny Berry, enjoying a field day down his right-hand touch-line, laid on chances from which first Taylor and, then, Viollet again, scored easily. Ken Armstrong's header from Eric Parsons' corner temporarily closed the gap to 3-5, but only for Jackie Blanchflower to reply in kind almost immediately. Being three goals in arrears seemed to inspire Chelsea, however, and none more so than O'Connell, one of the more enigmatical figures in the Chelsea story. Totally unaffected by the occasion, having scored with a powerful drive from 20 yards, he was then on hand to tap in Chelsea's fourth goal and to go on to complete his hat-trick as Parsons' header obligingly rebounded off the crossbar to his feet.

Still there were 14 minutes remaining and the crowd, some of whom were uncertain

Seamus O'Connell completes his hat-trick to mark an unforgettable League debut for Chelsea.

170

of the score, were in a fever of excitement. Storming through, Chelsea's forwards laid siege to United's goal and, at the end, it was goalkeeper Ray Wood whose magnificent save from Derek Saunders' free-kick saved the day for United and ensured his name on the roll of honour in this extraordinary contest.

The catalogue of the 11 goals is worthy of record: 0-1 (15 minutes); 1-1 (20), 2-1 (35), 2-2 (38), 2-3 (41), 2-4 (47), 2-5 (57), 3-5 (61), 3-6 (63), 4-6 (67), 5-6 (76).

Chelsea: Robertson; Harris, Willemse, Armstrong, Greenwood, Saunders, Parsons, McNichol, Bentley, S.O'Connell, J.L.Lewis.

Manchester United: Wood; Foulkes, Byrne, Gibson, Chilton, Edwards, Berry, Blanchflower, Taylor, Viollet, Rowley.

Referee: C.W.Kingston (Newport)   *Attendance: 55,966*

Match to Remember 13   4 December 1954

Wolverhampton Wanderers 3 Chelsea 4
Broadbent, Swinbourne, Hancocks (pen)   McNichol, Bentley 2, Stubbs

CHELSEA'S Championship season of 1954-5 stands out above every other in the club's story. Historians usually acknowledge that it was the victory over challengers Wolverhampton Wanderers at Stamford Bridge on Easter Saturday which virtually clinched the title, with more than 70,000 crammed into the stadium. Much less well remembered is the contest which took place between the same teams at Molineux four months earlier.

That morning, Wolves were at the top of the table, three points clear of their nearest rival. Chelsea found themselves languishing in the anonymity of 11th place, a comfortable enough situation at that stage but not one indicating the glamour and distinction which was to follow.

The scoreline itself suggests an exciting game, yet conveys nothing of the final drama that accompanied it. Johnny McNichol had given Chelsea the lead after 16 minutes as he hooked Roy Bentley's pass over Bert Williams' head and into the net. Inside a minute, Wolves were level, Peter Broadbent squirming Johnny Hancocks' centre over the line.

That set the scene for a thrilling match. Bill Robertson distinguished himself with a series of fine saves in the Chelsea goal and, when he was beaten, Stan Willemse headed Roy Swinbourne's shot off the line. At the opposite end, Williams, was also in frequent action.

Soon after half-time, Bentley scored for Chelsea when Eric Parsons' shot obligingly rebounded from the post to his feet. There matters stayed until, with a quarter of an hour remaining, goals by Swinbourne and Hancocks (from a hotly-disputed penalty) appeared to have settled the issue. But then came a climax, more at home in schoolboy fiction than reality.

John Harris, Chelsea's leading protester in the penalty incident moments earlier, took the ball out of defence to set Parsons free down the right-hand touch-line. Away went 'The Rabbit', outpacing defenders, and his measured cross was easily turned into the net from close range by Les Stubbs. Three-all with six minutes remaining. Incredibly, within 60 seconds Bentley found himself alone in the middle of the field, deep inside the Wolves' half with the ball at his feet. As Billy Wright trailed yards behind, and Williams desperately came off his line, the Chelsea centre-forward decisively whiplashed the ball inside the far post from some 15 yards to win a famous victory.

Bert Williams' dive is enough to thwart John McNichol, whose shot goes wide of the Wolves goal. Billy Wright covers.

Excited fans waited to accompany the players back to the nearby railway station, cheering and dancing with a fervour which could never have grasped the full significance of the victory. Only Chelsea's single-goal win over the same opponents the following April was to put this remarkable game into perspective.

Wolverhampton Wanderers: Williams; Stuart, Shorthouse, Slater, Wright, Flowers, Hancocks, Broadbent, Swinbourne, Wilshaw, Smith.
Chelsea: Robertson; Harris, Willemse, Armstrong, Greenwood, Saunders, Parsons, McNichol, Bentley, Stubbs, Blunstone.

Referee: J.W.Malcolm (Leicester)   *Attendance: 32,095*

Match to Remember 14   21 May 1963

Chelsea 7   Portsmouth 0
Kevan, Tambling 4, Blunstone,
Venables (pen)

IT WAS a night of carnival. A new era in the Chelsea story was dawning. Chelsea had returned to the First Division after 12 months in the wilderness, their team restyled by the ebullient Tommy Docherty, whose 'ducklings' had swept all before them. The future was once more alive with possibility.

The 1962-3 season had been a strange, almost unreal one, certainly for Chelsea. After victory at Luton on Boxing Day, a six-point gap had opened at the top of the table with Chelsea, ten wins and a draw from the previous 11 games, leading the field. Promotion seemed a formality, such was the confidence in the side and the high quality, non-stop football they were producing.

172

Derek Kevan heads Chelsea's first goal against Portsmouth and puts them on the road back to Division One.

Then came the snow and the ice. Chelsea played no League fixtures in January and managed only two, both lost, in February. March produced one victory in five games. Sunderland took over at the top and Chelsea were now 'just' the club immediately behind them, marginally ahead of several other challengers. April was a 'see-saw' month and only a desperate and fortuitous 1-0 win at Roker Park had restored a situation almost beyond control.

Unlike earlier end-of-season situations, there were no complicated mathematics this time. Chelsea 'merely' had to win their final fixture to go up. Opponents Portsmouth, although in the lower reaches of the table, were clear of relegation, with, supposedly, nothing to win — or lose. It seemed straightforward enough. Inevitably, though, the nerve-ends were twanging and tension was in the air.

A few weeks earlier, Docherty had paid £45,000 for West Bromwich Albion's England international forward, Derek Kevan. His time at Stamford Bridge was to be brief and not notably successful. But his goal after 90 seconds on this evening not only settled those nerves but also effectively decided the outcome of the match. Thereafter, goals simply arrived at regular intervals as Chelsea's greater skill and enthusiasm overpowered Pompey.

Only once did danger threaten, and then towards the end and from an unexpected source. With four minutes of the game left, many of the large crowd mistook the referee's signal for a free-kick as the full-time whistle. Almost every young football supporter in West London, and some more elderly citizens besides, swarmed over the perimeter wall. For a brief moment there were visions of the match necessarily having to be abandoned. But sanity prevailed, as roars of 'off, off' from the stands and packed terraces cleared the playing area. Minutes later, when the game had ended, the ground was once more awash with spectators.

Details of Chelsea's performance seemed almost insignificant. Bobby Tambling's pace and ball-skills stood out. Frank Blunstone's 'head-down' dribbling created numerous openings. Venables' midfield leadership was crucial. But, for many, the

Tommy Docherty joins the celebrations as Chelsea go back to Division One.

mastery of Tommy Harmer, the elder statesman, was not the least important factor. On a dusty, worn pitch, his control of the lively ball was superb.

Chelsea: Bonetti; Shellito, McCreadie, Venables, Mortimore, R.Harris, Blunstone, Kevan, Upton, Harmer, Tambling.
Portsmouth: Armstrong; Gunter, Wilson, Brown, Dickinson, Campbell, Barton, Gordon, Saunders, McCann, Lill.

Referee: R.Aldous (Ipswich) *Attendance: 54,558*

Match to Remember 15 16 December 1964

Chelsea 2   Workington 0
Osgood 2

THE night was cold and frosty, the stands and terraces sparsely populated. The Football League Cup competition was still in its infancy and shunned by several of the major clubs. And to compound matters, Workington, albeit at the time riding high in Division Three, could scarcely be described as a star attraction by any standards, and certainly not the sort of opposition to lure the casual supporter away from his Christmas shopping.

Yet, this was the occasion when manager Tommy Docherty chose to put on display

Workington goalkeeper Ian Ower stops this shot from Peter Osgood, but Osgood went on to beat him twice for a memorable senior debut.

a genuine diamond of a discovery, unearthed from the unlikely soil of amateur football in Windsor. Already, Peter Osgood had been scoring goals with regularity for both Juniors and Reserves (where he averaged more than one goal a game). But his name meant little to the majority of fans. His first-team debut was carefully planned, and another youngster, Jim McCalliog, later to play for Scotland, was also given a place in an otherwise virtual full-strength team.

For more than 80 minutes, Workington held their own in this replay (the teams had fought out a 2-2 draw in Cumberland some three weeks before). Showing a poise and range of skills well above their station, they extended Chelsea to the full, and that with winger Geoff Martin a limping passenger for the final half-hour.

Indeed, had Kit Napier not swung wildly and missed the ball altogether six yards from goal, Workington could well have fought the closing stages of the game clinging to a slender lead. With six minutes left, however, and extra-time looming, Terry Venables slipped a through-pass down the middle of the visitor's defence, and young Osgood raced through to place his left-foot shot past the advancing goalkeeper, Ian Ower, with the nonchalance of a seasoned veteran.

Scarcely had the congratulations from his excited teammates abated when, after an untidy scramble in the Workington goalmouth, it was again Osgood who finally put the ball into the net for his second goal. A new star had arrived, or was about to emerge. Docherty, unpredictable as ever, promptly returned the youngster to the reserve team for the rest of the season, as Chelsea went on to lift the League Cup, winning a two-legged Final against Leicester City.

Meanwhile, one writer suggested that the Chelsea manager should offer a prayer of gratitude to the Post Office. It was Osgood, missed by the talent scouts, who had himself written to the club the previous April requesting a trial. Immediately accepted, he had signed professional forms only three months before the Workington game.

Chelsea: Bonetti; Hinton, McCreadie, Venables, Mortimore, Upton, Murray, Graham, Osgood, McCalliog, Knox.
Workington: Ower; Ogilvie, Lumsden, Hale, Brown, Burkinshaw, Watson, Carr, Napier, Moran, Martin.

Referee: H.G.New (Havant)   *Attendance: 7,936*

Match to Remember 16   16 February 1966

Chelsea 2   AC Milan 1
Graham, Osgood   *Sormani*

AS ANYONE with experience of European football well knows, these games have their own sense of occasion, and more especially is this so in the later rounds of the competitions when the giants of the major footballing nations are paired. One such meeting brought Chelsea and AC Milan together and the 110,000 or so spectators who watched the three instalments of this tie, in the third round of the Inter-Cities Fairs Cup, will doubtless ever remember the skill, drama and almost unbearable tension generated by those matches.

First, in Italy, a last-minute goal by George Graham restricted Milan to a one-goal advantage in the first leg, after Rivera had put the home side 2-0 ahead three minutes earlier. This all-important strike was enough to set up what promised to be an epic second encounter. Certainly the fans thought this to be the case. Seats were all sold well in advance and before the kick-off the terrace turnstiles were closed, with many unable to gain admission, and record receipts for Stamford Bridge announced.

The game duly lived up to its potential, and in ten minutes Chelsea were level on aggregate. Graham, loitering with intent on the edge of the Milan penalty area, as Bobby Tambling took a corner on the right, timed his run to perfection to soar above everyone else and firmly plant his header past Balzarini.

If that goal was memorable, the one which followed was even more so. Nine further minutes had elapsed when Peter Osgood, receiving an awkward pass from Graham and, seemingly walled in by a black and red border of Milan players, swayed to his right, then moved left, and finally and arrogantly hit the ball into the top right-hand corner of the net from 18 yards.

If Chelsea seemed rampant and likely to add to their lead, the menace of Milan remained an obvious threat, and before half-time they had indeed struck back. An untypically careless throw-out from Peter Bonetti was immediately returned into the Chelsea goalmouth where Sormani, surprisingly alone and unmarked, drove the ball past the unhappy goalkeeper. If that ended the evening's scoring, the battle, too severe at times, continued unabated. Chelsea attacked ferociously. Milan might well have been awarded a penalty when Eddie McCreadie upended Lodetti. John Hollins, receiving treatment on the touch-line, rushed back on to the field to plug a glaring gap in defence, uninvited, and unpunished, by the referee. It was that sort of game.

And when it was all over, with the sides still locked together on a 3-3 aggregate, Chelsea lost the toss for choice of ground for the third game. So, it was to be

176

George Graham almost scores a third goal for Chelsea in the closing stages but AC Milan goalkeeper Balzarini makes a brilliant save from close range.

back to San Siro once more, when again the teams finished all-square, this time at 1-1. But Ron Harris, never one to make the same error twice, now called correctly as the coin fell to earth to decide the outcome of a wonderful tie, albeit in a manner unworthy of what had gone before.

Chelsea: Bonetti; Harris, McCreadie, Hollins, Hinton, Boyle, Bridges, Graham, Osgood, Venables, Tambling.
AC Milan: Balzarini; Schnellinger, Trebbi, Santin, Maldini, Maddé, Sormani, Lodetti, Angelillo, Rivera, Amarildo.

Referee: E.Bostrom (Sweden)   *Attendance: 59,541*

Match to Remember 17   26 April 1970

Chelsea 2   Leeds United 1
(after extra-time)
Osgood, Webb   Jones

AT LAST, at their 55th attempt, Chelsea won the FA Cup on an early spring evening, not at Wembley, but on the same ground in Manchester where their first appearance in the Final of this competition had ended so ignominiously more than half a century earlier.

Three semi-final appearances, only one of which had taken the club into the Final, had already marked the five previous Cup campaigns, inevitably giving rise to scepticism and predictions of impending doom, which had been further fuelled by the desperate 2-2 draw at Wembley 18 days earlier. Now, however, it all came right on the night and the victory was achieved with typical Chelsea style and panache.

177

Dave Sexton (left) and Don Revie lead out their teams for the 1970 FA Cup Final at Wembley.

For three-quarters of 'normal' time the outcome appeared utterly predictable. In the first half, Allan Clarke had weaved his way past a mass of flailing tackles to send Mick Jones through to beat Peter Bonetti with a minimum of fuss. Earlier, the Chelsea goalkeeper had received treatment to a knee injury, for what seemed an age, before pluckily carrying on. Ominously, Billy Bremner and Johnny Giles were in total control of midfield and dictating the flow and pattern of the match. Leeds, in fact, were looking what many considered them to be. Simply, the best team in the land.

Then, as the game went into its final quarter, a change became noticeable. John Hollins and Charlie Cooke began to exert their influence. And it was the latter's delicate chip which sent Peter Osgood sprinting through to nod the ball past David Harvey. Poor Leeds, who earlier in the month had seen their hopes of both European Cup and Football League Championship melt away, wilted visibly as Chelsea surged forward with growing conviction.

Inevitably, the game moved into extra-time and towards its climax. Terry Cooper's surging runs down the left flank still caused particular concern. But in the 14th

Peter Osgood dives to head Chelsea's equalizer in the Cup Final replay.

178

David Webb climbs high above the Leeds defence to give the Chelsea the FA Cup.

Goalscorers David Webb and Peter Osgood kiss the Cup after Chelsea's dramatic victory.

minute of this additional period came the goal (and probably the most talked-of in Chelsea's long history) which settled the contest. Yards short of the left-hand corner-flag, Ian Hutchinson's 35-yard throw into the goalmouth was challenged by the ruck of players. The ball grazed the head of Jackie Charlton, as he leapt despairingly to head away to safety, only for David Webb, stationed at the far post, to head firmly, and decisively, into the net.

Even so, all was not over. The final 15 minutes seemed endless to Chelsea supporters. Leeds threw everything into attack and shots rained in on Bonetti's goal. But, with Marvin Hinton coming on as an additional defender, somehow the final onslaught was survived, and the celebrations simultaneously began in Manchester and London. Just over 12 hours later the FA Cup was on its way from Euston to Stamford Bridge and all the years of frustration and disappointment were over.

Chelsea: Bonetti; Harris, McCreadie, Hollins, Dempsey, Webb, Baldwin, Cooke, Osgood(Hinton), Hutchinson, Houseman.
Leeds United: Harvey; Madeley, Cooper, Bremner, Charlton, Hunter, Lorimer, Clarke, Jones, Giles, E.Gray.

Referee: E.T.Jennings (Stourbridge)   *Attendance: 62,078*

Match to Remember 18   22 May 1971

Chelsea 2   Real Madrid 1
Dempsey, Osgood   *Fleitas*

IN SOME respects history repeated itself when, just over 12 months after the FA Cup victory, Chelsea became the fourth English team to win the European Cup-winners' trophy. Again a second chapter was required. Again a late enemy counter-

Real Madrid's defenders are crestfallen after a shot from John Dempsey (not in picture) gives Chelsea the lead in the 1971 European Cup-winners' Cup Final replay.

attack was successfully warded off. And, again also, the Fulham Road was packed tight as the open-topped double-decker bus inched its way through the crowds for the civic reception at Fulham Town Hall, a hard-earned prize brandished triumphantly.

But the Karaiskaki Stadium was a far cry from Old Trafford. Two days earlier a furious 1-1 draw had taken place in the same arena. Peter Osgood had given Chelsea a second-half lead, only for Real to equalize with the last kick of normal time, and then to go on to dominate the proceedings in extra-time.

For the second instalment, Chelsea changed tactics, with a '4-2-4' formation bringing in Tommy Baldwin to add support to Osgood in the middle of the attack. Further, John Hollins was an absentee through injury. Certainly, the carefully planned change seemed to upset the Spaniards by helping Chelsea to establish mastery, as they scored twice within seven minutes.

After Borja had punched away Peter Houseman's corner-kick, John Dempsey was on hand to score one of his rare goals by volleying home a strong right-foot shot into the roof of the net from some 15 yards range. Soon, Baldwin, picking up a pass from Harris, had slipped the ball through to Osgood, who dummied nicely before shooting low past the 'keeper. Chelsea, adopting a positive and direct style which contrasted with the more subtle elaborations of Real, seemed home and dry.

But before long things had changed and, as at Old Trafford the year before, the game ended with Chelsea desperately struggling to cling on to their hard-won,

181

advantage. With 15 minutes remaining, Fleitas, showing brilliant individualism, turned past David Webb and John Boyle before pushing the ball into the corner of the net. At once, Peter Bonetti was plunging to his left to keep out a shot from Zoco. And the final crisis was reserved for the very last moments. A strong drive from Amancio was fumbled by Bonetti. But as the Real forwards surged in for the kill, Dempsey somehow bravely scrambled the ball away for a corner, and a famous victory was secure.

Chelsea, as the banner headlines proclaimed, were the 'Kings of Europe'. And if only a handful of the original blue army of fans had been able to stay on for the extra 48 hours to witness it all, it was another glorious night for Chelsea — and for English football.

Chelsea: Bonetti; Boyle, Harris, Cooke, Dempsey, Webb, Weller, Baldwin, Osgood(Smethurst), Hudson, Houseman.
Real Madrid: Borja; Jose Luis, Zunzunegui, Pirri, Benito, Zoco, Fleitas, Amancio, Grosso, Velazquez(Gento), Bueno(Grande).

Referee: A.Bucheli (Switzerland)   *Attendance: 41,000*

Match to Remember 19   5 January 1972

Tottenham Hotspur 2   Chelsea 2
(Chelsea won 5-4 on aggregate)
Chivers, Peters (pen)   *Garland, Hudson*

IN RECENT years, confrontations between Chelsea and North London rivals, Tottenham Hotspur, have assumed a special significance to the supporters of both clubs, and not always for altogether healthy reasons. Victory, therefore, has a particularly satisfying flavour, not least where Cup-tie football is concerned.

The two Football League Cup semi-final duels of 1971-2, interrupted by the Christmas festivities, were a case in point. First, a pulsating match in the first leg at Stamford Bridge which saw Spurs score twice in two minutes to inch ahead, 2-1, only for Chris Garland to head an equalizer and John Hollins to smash home a penalty just before full-time, set the scene nicely for the chapter at White Hart Lane.

With the high quality of both sides much in evidence, a match of great distinction and excitement unfurled, three of the four goals coming almost at the death. A keenly-contested first half had almost run its course when Ralph Coates' centre was gracefully headed back for Martin Chivers to volley powerfully past Bonetti to level the scores on aggregate.

When Peter Osgood, uncharacteristically, squandered a good chance after the restart, it seemed likely to be costly. But, soon, Chris Garland had put Chelsea ahead once more when, following clever approach work from Osgood and Charlie Cooke, he unleashed a rocket of a shot from the edge of the penalty area to leave Pat Jennings helpless. And it seemed as if that goal had settled matters until Spurs were given an unexpected gift, too generous to refuse.

A long throw into the penalty area from Chivers, bouncing awkwardly, appeared to hit Alan Hudson on the hand — and surely without intent? The referee, however, was of a different opinion and Martin Peters gladly scored from the spot with little fuss and effort. Lying 4-4 on aggregate, with seven minutes of normal time remaining. And that is how matters remained with seconds left to play, and extra-

Chris Garland scores with a cracking left-foot shot in the second-leg at White Hart Lane.

time seeming inevitable. Hudson, however, then proceeded to settle the argument with a goal which must rate as one of the most macabre in Chelsea's annals.

From a free-kick just outside the penalty area, and from the acutest of angles, as defenders and attackers jostled for position anticipating the chip into the danger area, the 'midfield generalissimo' steered the ball through a forest of legs and into the net just inside the far post. Spurs defender, Cyril Knowles, had swung wildly at the ball, making no contact whatsoever. Jennings, maybe bemused, was wrong-footed and stood passively watching the disaster. Players and spectators were dumbfounded for a second or two before the celebrations, and accusations and inquests, broke loose.

For Chelsea it meant a third major Cup Final in three years. Yet, within two months, hopes of a 'hat-trick' of successes had been shattered and soon the finest team in their history was falling apart at the seams. Where once there had been unity and achievement, now there was to be disharmony and failure.

Tottenham Hotspur: Jennings; Evans, Knowles, Pratt(Pearce), England, Beal, Coates, Perryman, Chivers, Peters, Gilzean.
Chelsea: Bonetti; Mulligan, Harris, Hollins, Dempsey, Webb, Cooke, Garland, Osgood, Hudson, Houseman.

Referee: E.W.Smith (Stonehouse)   *Attendance: 52,775*

183

Bolton Wanderers 0   Chelsea 1
Walker

FOOTBALL historians, and of course supporters of the game all over the world, are frequently in disagreement. And opinions, usually unasked for, are invariably in ready supply. Yet few would argue that the lowest point in the story of Chelsea Football Club arrived at the beginning of May 1983. Not for the first time was the cloud of relegation hovering over Stamford Bridge. But now there was a difference. This time it was Division Three that was lurking just round the corner.

Burnden Park, Bolton, has long since been shorn of the glamour it once enjoyed. And when two of the most famous teams in the land confronted each other on a damp spring afternoon, both were desperately fighting for their lives. The portents for an enjoyable day out were not promising, and a heavy 'dead' pitch did nothing to improve matters.

Determination and aggression, with violence never far away, were the order of the day. The towering figure of Micky Droy dominated the Chelsea end of the field as he constantly kicked clear or headed away Bolton's best efforts. At the other end, half an hour passed before Chelsea managed a shot on target and then John Bumstead's effort through a ruck of players was magnificently saved by Jim McDonagh. Twice in the other goalmouth, Steve Francis equally distinguished himself.

The relief brought by the interval was heightened by a band of kilted pipers, shortly followed, less acceptably, by a torrential downpour of rain, serving only to increase the gloom of the occasion. Slowly, Chelsea gaining a measure of control

Clive Walker scores his spectacular winner at Burnden Park.

in midfield, began to push forward. At last a clear-cut opportunity was carved out as Colin Lee ran loose down the middle to the edge of the penalty area where he was felled by McDonagh (already booked for an earlier offence).

Almost immediately followed the goal, which must be rated among the most important ever scored by a Chelsea player, and coming as a result of a rare flash of skill allied to a measure of good fortune. Paul Canoville, cleverly keeping possession, threaded his way past Steve Whitworth to set up a chance for Clive Walker, easily the game's outstanding player. From some 25 yards out, his fiercely struck shot swerved viciously as it beat McDonagh's despairing leap to fly into the far corner of the net. A goal as unforgettable as it was vital.

Surprisingly, the final 20 minutes passed without real crisis. Chelsea, indeed, twice threatened to increase their advantage, as Bolton seemed prepared to accept their fate. At the end blue shirts were torn from tired, wet, bodies and thrown into the sea of Chelsea supporters on the railway embankment as a measure of gratitude for their undying support on such a crucial day and throughout such a depressing season. As it turned out, the most vital corner of all had been turned.

Seven days later, Chelsea scrambled to safety, by two points, to leave Bolton, in last place in the table, to face a much less rosy future.

Bolton Wanderers: McDonagh; Whitworth, Deakin, Gray, McElhinney, Doyle, Joyce, Rudge, Moores, Hoggan, Borrows(Chandler).

Chelsea: Francis; Jones, Hutchings, Chivers, Droy, Pates, Fillery, Bumstead, Lee, Canoville, Walker.

Referee: T.Holbrook (Wolverhampton)   *Attendance: 8,687*

Match to Remember 21   12 May 1984

Grimsby Town 0   Chelsea 1
Dixon

AS IN the political world, so in football a week can be a long time. A year can completely transform even the most unpromising situation. Who would have believed that 12 months after the desperate Bolton 'rescue act', Chelsea would be on the threshold of a championship title? But, where there had been despair, now there was hope and anticipation.

For five months, since before Christmas, Chelsea and Sheffield Wednesday had been locked together in a see-saw battle at the top of the division. Both clubs were almost assured of promotion, with Wednesday favourites, most of the time, to end up as champions. But, at the last, it was Chelsea who had inched in front on goal-difference, and a win in the last fixture at Grimsby was required to clinch the top prize.

The M180 is not Britain's best known, or most frequented, motorway. But on that bright May morning in 1984 it was congested by a column of vehicles of varying vintage and reliability, heading eastward towards the traditional 'fish capital' of England. The mood was already one of noisy celebration. Promotion had been assured four matches before. Ticketed or not, the fans were not going to miss out on this one.

So often tension can spoil such occasions. But not this time. A cracking good match evolved, highlighted by Grimsby's battling qualities and Chelsea's obviously higher skills. Only a brief, unscheduled, interruption, as crushed visiting supporters behind a goal were shepherded by police to a safer area of the ground (an operation totally misinterpreted by sections of the media), was not part of the script.

185

Kerry Dixon gets up high to head home Pat Nevin's cross and Chelsea can begin to celebrate.

At one end, Joe McLaughlin's defensive qualities were needed to ward off persistent Grimsby attacks, and, several times he and his colleagues were fully extended. At the other, Nigel Batch twice dashed off his line bravely to throw himself down at the feet of Kerry Dixon. But he was powerless to prevent the blond striker's header from a measured centre from Pat Nevin, following a lovely run down the wing, bulging the net for what was to prove the only goal of the game.

Nevin, himself, should have scored in the second half. David Speedie, dashing clear of defenders, was unceremoniously felled by Andy Moore inside the penalty area, only for Batch to dive spectacularly to turn the little Scot's kick round the post, Chelsea's fifth penalty miss of the season. But, hard though Grimsby pressed towards the end, they were held at bay and, immediately after the final whistle, the celebrations began.

And, if police horses and dog handlers did not provide the perfect ending for such an occasion, there were few distasteful incidents as an estimated 8,000 Chelsea fans joyously gave vent to their feelings.

Grimsby Town: Batch; A.Moore, Crombie, Speight, Nicholl, K.Moore, Ford, Wilkinson, Drinkell, Bonnyman, Henshaw(Lund).
Chelsea: Niedzwiecki; Hollins, Jasper, Pates, McLaughlin, Bumstead, Nevin, Spackman, Dixon, Speedie, Thomas.

Referee: D.Shaw (Sandbach)   *Attendance: 13,995*

Match to Remember 22   30 January 1985

Sheffield Wednesday 4   Chelsea 4
Lyons, Chapman, Marwood, Sterland (pen)   *Canoville 2, Dixon, Thomas*

TALES of the unexpected abound in Football history. And, mathematically at any rate, there have been few more spectacular fight-backs from 'certain' defeat than

Kerry Dixon (9) has just scored Chelsea's second goal at Hillsborough.

Chelsea's remarkable recovery in a Football League Cup replay on a chilly winter's night at Hillsborough. The transformation was astonishing by any standards.

Two days earlier, the first game at Stamford Bridge had ended 1-1, with no suggestion of the excitement and drama which was to follow. And with Sheffield Wednesday now scoring in the 8th, 21st and 44th minutes, the second half seemed little more than formality. Although David Speedie had rattled a shot against a post on one occasion, Chelsea's petulance and lack of discipline never for one moment suggested what they had in store for the second period.

The recovery began with the substitution of Paul Canoville in place of Colin Lee (the fourth Chelsea player to be booked by the referee before half-time). Like a greyhound springing from his trap, the replacement had reduced the three-goal deficit within 11 seconds of the restart, darting forward in time to turn Speedie's inviting pass into the net. Twenty minutes later, a shrewd through ball from Mickey Thomas sent Kerry Dixon racing clear of defenders to draw Martin Hodge from his line and score comfortably to further reduce the deficit, and to bring the contest bubbling to life.

And it was Thomas, whose tireless energy and skill had been instrumental in demonstrating to his colleagues that no cause is ever lost, who notched the equalizer. After another ten minutes of furious attack, he drove Pat Nevin's cross, gleefully and unstoppably, past Hodge. Unable to grasp the changed situation, Wednesday were reeling and it seemed all part of the script when Canoville scored his second goal after being set up by clever approach work from Dixon and Nevin. A 0-3 scoreline had become 4-3 and, with four minutes remaining, disconsolate and unbelieving home supporters began their trudge towards the exit gates. But, all is never lost in this type of extravaganza, and the final twist was still to come.

With a handful of seconds left, Mel Sterland ran through down the right, going forward menacingly and despairingly into the penalty area, only to be brought down on the turf by Doug Rougvie's desperate ill-judged, and illegal, tackle. And it was Sterland, himself, who scored from the resultant penalty. Extra-time brought chances to both teams, but legs were now tiring and this epic Cup tie simply found itself unable to sustain the thrills and action of the first hour and a half.

It then remained only for Chelsea to win the toss for the right to stage the third instalment of this trial, which they went on to win 2-1 in another tense and dramatic game at Stamford Bridge.

Sheffield Wednesday: Hodge; Sterland, Shirtliff, Madden, Lyons, Worthington, Marwood, Blair, Varadi, Chapman(Oliver), Shelton.

Chelsea: Niedzwiecki; J.Jones, Rougvie, Lee(Canoville), McLaughlin, Jasper, Nevin, Spackman, Dixon, Speedie, Thomas.

Referee: G.M.Tyson (Sunderland)   *Attendance: 36,508*

Match to Remember 23   28 May 1988

Chelsea 1   Middlesbrough 0
(after extra-time – Middlesbrough won 2-1 on aggregate)
Durie

WHOEVER thought up the idea of subjecting football clubs to the torture of League 'play-offs' at the end of the marathon, almost nine-month long, season must have been concerned only with financial considerations. The Englishman's traditional sense of fair play clearly flew out of the window. That said, the situation in which Chelsea found themselves, a few days after England's cricketers had incredibly beaten the West Indies in the Texaco Trophy by three matches to nil, was entirely of their own making. Standing second in the First Division table at the end of September, their season had deteriorated alarmingly from that point onwards. Mismanagement, dressing-room rancour and delayed remedial treatment brought its just reward, even though 'normally' Chelsea would have escaped the indignity of relegation by seven clear points.

Three days earlier on Teesside, Middlesbrough, themselves denied 'automatic' promotion by the new scheme of things, had won the first leg of the contest by two clear goals, Trevor Senior and Bernie Slaven erecting what was to prove an insurmountable barrier.

Glaring misses at both ends of the park soon underlined the anxiety and tension under which the players were operating. Pat Nevin should have scored for Chelsea; Slaven should have put away an even easier chance for 'Boro. However, after some 18 minutes of feverish activity, Gordon Durie volleyed Nevin's cross past Steve Pears to reduce the deficit and set the game alight. Relentlessly, Chelsea now pushed forward, yet, apart from one header from Kerry Dixon, a goal seldom seemed likely.

For Middlesbrough, half-time came both as a sanctuary and a watershed. Visibly, Chelsea's confidence and self-belief drained away. If their opponents rarely seemed likely to breach Kevin Hitchcock's defences, only twice did Chelsea seriously threaten at the other end, to be thwarted by interceptions from Pears and Tony Mowbray. Even the strange sight of Eddie Niedzwiecki and Mickey Hazard, side-lined through injury, urging the inhabitants of the 'Shed' to even greater vocal efforts from behind

Nevin, Durie and Clarke are happy, for Durie has just scored against Middlesbrough. But it was not enough and Chelsea went down again.

the goal failed to inspire, and may even have proved counter-productive. In the end, it was difficult to escape the conclusion that justice had been done, at least as far as these two games were concerned.

So, it was back to Division Two once more. But not, sadly, before a minority loutish element of the fans had made their own mark. As the final whistle sounded, hundreds of Chelsea 'supporters' swarmed across the pitch to hurl bottles and bricks at the terrified Middlesbrough contingent, caged in at the other end of the ground. Only belatedly could police reinforcements restore some semblance of order.

As a result, the Football Association subsequently imposed a £75,000 fine on the club and ordered that all standing areas at Stamford Bridge must remain closed for the first six League and League Cup games in the following season. A depressing night had had even more dire repercussions.

Chelsea: Hitchcock; Clarke, Dorigo, Wicks, McLaughlin, Pates(Hall), Nevin, Bumstead, Dixon, Durie, K.Wilson(McAllister).
Middlesbrough: Pears; Parkinson, Cooper, Mowbray, Hamilton, Pallister, Slaven, Ripley, Senior, Kerr, Glover.

Referee: B.Hill (Kettering) *Attendance: 40,550*

Tottenham Hotspur 0   Chelsea 3

Townsend, Dixon, Wise(pen)

ALMOST 20 years had sped by since Chelsea's last confrontation with Spurs in the Football League Cup. In the interim, Tottenham had distinguished themselves by winning that trophy on one occasion to add to their two FA Cup and two UEFA Cup victories. Chelsea, on the other hand, had totally failed to reach such heights, rather being remembered for 'banner headline' defeats at such places as Crewe Alexandra, Scarborough, Wigan Athletic, Cardiff City (twice) and Reading.

Such ignominious events, however, counted for nothing as the team and its faithful supporting legions made their way to White Hart Lane once more, on a mission which should never have been necessary. Seven days earlier, in the first chapter at Stamford Bridge, Chelsea had dominated the proceedings almost throughout, yet failed to translate this superiority into goal advantage.

Again, the traditional 'sense of occasion', accompanied by the usual unoriginal taunting chants of the rival fans, was as much a test for nerve as for skill, with a trio of Chelsea's latest batch of emergent juniors facing the biggest test of their footballing lives up to that time.

As it turned out, they, and indeed the entire team, were to pass their examination with flying colours. A day which had begun with Tottenham Hotspur being taken to court over a £800 redundancy claim ended even more embarrassingly for the North Londoners.

For 15 minutes the traffic moved in one direction — menacingly towards Dave Beasant's goal. Now it was Spurs who were failing to put away their opportunities. Once, Jason Cundy scythed down Paul Gascoigne, only for the referee, happily for Chelsea, to be satisfied with the legality of the challenge.

Dixon latches on to the rebound to put Chelsea two-up at White Hart Lane.

And it was Beasant's long downfield clearance which, at last, produced the counterflow. Gordon Durie, fastening on to the loose ball, managed a crucial touch-on for Kerry Dixon's resultant short pass to reach Andy Townsend through the gap between Gary Mabbutt and Dave Howells, and for the Chelsea captain to deceive Erik Thorstvedt with a bobbling shot inside his right-hand post.

Beasant, too, made an important save from a Gary Lineker header, at close range. But that, and another valid penalty claim, this time against Kenny Monkou for hand-ball in the second half, were as near as Tottenham came to scoring. When another Townsend shot beat the goalkeeper and Dixon was on hand to meet the rebound and tuck it into the net, it was virtually over. Dennis Wise scoring, ironically, from the penalty-spot after Durie had been bowled over by Justin Edinburgh, merely added extra icing to the Chelsea cake.

Celebrations for players and supporters were justifiable, for it was a compelling performance. Discussion tended to centre on Gascoigne's elbowing Townsend in the face, leaving the Irish international clutching his head and losing a contact lens. But nothing could mar Chelsea's night.

With Second Division opposition to be faced in the forthcoming semi-final, it seemed as if Chelsea might, at long last, once more be on their way to a major Wembley Final. But, with their unfailing panache for inconsistency, such hopes were shortly to be dashed and dreams to become another mirage. The 1990s were starting as the 1930s had done. The Chelsea 'riddle' which had defied Leslie Knighton in his time as manager was now tormenting and perplexing Bobby Campbell.

Tottenham Hotspur: Thorstvedt; Fenwick(Sedgley), Edinburgh, Samways(Nayim), Howells, Mabbutt, Stewart, Gascoigne, Walsh, Lineker, Allen.
Chelsea: Beasant; Hall, Dorigo, Townsend, Cundy, Monkou, Stuart(Bumstead), Matthew, Dixon, Durie, Wise.

Referee: B.Hill (Kettering) *Attendance: 33,861*

Dennis Wise scores from the penalty-spot to put the game beyond Spurs' reach.

Chelsea's League Record & Top Scorer
1905-06 - 1990-91

	P	W	D	L	F	A	W	D	L	F	A	Pts	Pos	Top League Scorer	Goals
			Home						*Away*						

Division Two

	P	W	D	L	F	A	W	D	L	F	A	Pts	Pos	Top League Scorer	Goals
1905-06	38	13	4	2	58	16	9	5	5	32	21	53	3rd	Frank Pearson	18
1906-07	38	18	0	1	55	10	8	5	6	25	24	57	2nd	George Hilsdon	27

Division One

1907-08	38	8	3	8	30	35	6	5	8	23	27	36	13th	George Hilsdon	24
1908-09	38	8	7	4	33	22	6	2	11	23	39	37	11th	George Hilsdon	25
1909-10	38	10	4	5	32	24	1	3	15	15	46	29	19th	Jimmy Windridge	6

Division Two

1910-11	38	17	2	0	48	7	3	7	9	23	28	49	3rd	Bob Whittingham	30
1911-12	38	15	2	2	36	13	9	4	6	28	21	54	2nd	Bob Whittingham	26

Division One

1912-13	38	7	2	10	29	40	4	4	11	22	33	28	18th	Vivian Woodward	10
1913-14	38	12	3	4	28	18	4	4	11	18	37	39	8th	Harold Halse	10
1914-15	38	8	6	5	32	25	0	7	12	19	40	29	19th	Bob Thomson	12
1919-20	42	15	3	3	33	10	7	2	12	23	41	49	3rd	Jack Cock	21
1920-21	42	9	7	5	35	24	4	6	11	13	34	39	18th	Jack Cock	12
1921-22	42	9	6	6	17	16	8	6	7	23	27	46	9th	Jack Cock	13
1922-23	42	5	13	3	29	20	4	5	12	16	33	36	19th	Harry Ford & Buchanan Sharp	10
1923-24	42	7	9	5	23	21	2	5	14	8	32	32	21st	Andy Wilson	5

Division Two

1924-25	42	11	8	2	31	12	5	7	9	20	25	47	5th	William Whitton	16
1925-26	42	10	7	4	42	22	9	7	5	34	27	52	3rd	Bob Turnbull	29
1926-27	42	13	7	1	40	17	7	5	9	22	35	52	4th	Bob Turnbull	17
1927-28	42	15	2	4	46	15	8	6	7	29	30	54	3rd	Jimmy Thompson	25
1928-29	42	10	6	5	40	30	7	4	10	24	35	44	9th	George Biswell & Andy Wilson	9
1929-30	42	17	3	1	49	14	5	8	8	25	32	55	2nd	George Mills	14

Division One

1930-31	42	13	4	4	42	19	2	6	13	22	48	40	12th	Hughie Gallacher	14
1931-32	42	12	4	5	43	27	4	4	13	26	46	40	12th	Hughie Gallacher	24
1932-33	42	9	4	8	38	29	5	3	13	25	44	35	18th	Hughie Gallacher	19
1933-34	42	12	3	6	44	24	2	5	14	23	45	36	19th	George Mills	14
1934-35	42	11	5	5	49	32	5	4	12	24	50	41	12th	Dick Spence	19
1935-36	42	11	7	3	39	27	4	6	11	26	45	43	8th	Joe Bambrick	15
1936-37	42	11	6	4	36	21	3	7	11	16	34	41	13th	George Mills	22
1937-38	42	11	6	4	40	22	3	7	11	25	43	41	10th	George Mills	13
1938-39	42	10	5	6	43	29	2	4	15	21	51	33	20th	Joe Payne	17
1946-47	42	9	3	9	33	39	7	4	10	36	45	39	15th	Tommy Lawton	26
1947-48	42	11	6	4	38	27	3	3	15	15	44	37	18th	Ken Armstrong & Bobby Campbell	11
1948-49	42	10	6	5	43	27	2	8	11	26	41	38	13th	Roy Bentley	21
1949-50	42	7	7	7	31	30	5	9	7	27	35	40	13th	Roy Bentley & Hugh Billington	17
1950-51	42	9	4	8	31	25	3	4	14	22	40	32	20th	Roy Bentley	8
1951-52	42	10	3	8	31	29	4	5	12	21	43	36	19th	Roy Bentley & Jimmy D'Arcy	12
1952-53	42	10	4	7	35	24	2	7	12	21	42	35	19th	Roy Bentley	12
1953-54	42	12	3	6	45	26	4	9	8	29	42	44	8th	Roy Bentley	21
1954-55	42	11	5	5	43	29	9	7	5	38	28	52	1st	Roy Bentley	21
1955-56	42	10	4	7	32	26	4	7	10	32	51	39	16th	Roy Bentley	14
1956-57	42	7	8	6	43	36	6	5	10	30	37	39	13th	John McNichol & Ron Tindall	10
1957-58	42	10	5	6	47	34	5	7	9	36	45	42	11th	Jimmy Greaves	22
1958-59	42	13	2	6	52	37	5	2	14	25	61	40	14th	Jimmy Greaves	32
1959-60	42	7	5	9	44	50	7	4	10	32	41	37	18th	Jimmy Greaves	29
1960-61	42	10	5	6	61	48	5	2	14	37	52	37	12th	Jimmy Greaves	41
1961-62	42	7	7	7	34	29	2	3	16	29	65	28	22nd	Bobby Tambling	20

192

		Home					Away								
	P	W	D	L	F	A	W	D	L	F	A	Pts	Pos	Top League Scorer	Goals
Division Two															
1962-63	42	15	3	3	54	16	9	1	11	27	26	52	2nd	Bobby Tambling	35
Division One															
1963-64	42	12	3	6	36	24	8	7	6	36	32	50	5th	Bobby Tambling	17
1964-65	42	15	2	4	48	19	9	6	6	41	35	56	3rd	Barry Bridges	20
1965-66	42	11	4	6	30	21	11	3	7	35	32	51	5th	George Graham	17
1966-67	42	7	9	5	33	29	8	5	8	34	33	44	9th	Bobby Tambling	21
1967-68	42	11	7	3	34	25	7	5	9	28	43	48	6th	Peter Osgood	16
1968-69	42	11	7	3	40	24	9	3	9	33	29	50	5th	Bobby Tambling	17
1969-70	42	13	7	1	36	18	8	6	7	34	32	55	3rd	Peter Osgood	23
1970-71	42	12	6	3	34	21	6	9	6	18	21	51	6th	Keith Weller	13
1971-72	42	12	7	2	41	20	6	5	10	17	29	48	7th	Peter Osgood	18
1972-73	42	9	6	6	30	22	4	8	9	19	29	40	12th	Chris Garland & Peter Osgood	11
1973-74	42	9	4	8	36	29	3	9	9	20	31	37	17th	Tommy Baldwin	9
1974-75	42	4	9	8	22	31	5	6	10	20	41	33	21st	Ian Hutchinson	7
Division Two															
1975-76	42	7	9	5	25	20	5	7	9	28	34	40	11th	Ray Wilkins	11
1976-77	42	15	6	0	51	22	6	7	8	22	31	55	2nd	Steve Finnieston	24
Division One															
1977-78	42	7	11	3	28	20	4	3	14	18	49	36	16th	Tommy Langley	11
1978-79	42	3	5	13	23	42	2	5	14	21	50	20	22nd	Tommy Langley	15
Division Two															
1979-80	42	14	3	4	34	16	9	4	8	32	36	53	4th	Clive Walker	13
1980-81	42	8	6	7	27	15	6	6	9	19	26	40	12th	Colin Lee	15
1981-82	42	10	5	6	37	30	5	7	9	23	30	57	12th	Clive Walker	16
1982-83	42	8	8	5	31	22	3	6	12	20	39	47	18th	Mike Fillery	9
1983-84	42	15	4	2	55	17	10	9	2	35	23	88	1st	Kerry Dixon	28
Division One															
1984-85	42	13	3	5	38	20	5	9	7	25	28	66	6th	Kerry Dixon	24
1985-86	42	12	4	5	32	27	8	7	6	25	29	71	6th	Kerry Dixon & David Speedie	14
1986-87	42	8	6	7	30	30	5	7	9	23	34	52	14th	Kerry Dixon	10
1987-88	40	7	11	2	24	17	2	4	14	26	51	42	18th	Gordon Durie	12
Division Two															
1988-89	46	15	6	2	50	25	14	6	3	46	25	99	1st	Kerry Dixon	25
Division One															
1989-90	38	8	7	4	31	24	8	5	6	27	26	60	5th	Kerry Dixon	20
1990-91	38	10	6	3	33	25	3	4	12	25	44	49	10th	Gordon Durie	12

Chelsea Against Other League Clubs

Since 1905, Chelsea have met 80 different clubs in Football League games. Here is a summary of their results against each opponent including play-off matches. All games against clubs under previous names (ie Leicester Fosse, Clapton Orient) are covered here.

| | P | | Home | | | | | Away | | | |
		W	D	L	F	A	W	D	L	F	A
Arsenal	108	18	18	18	67	71	16	14	24	69	85
Aston Villa	88	22	8	14	69	57	8	12	24	63	97
Barnsley	28	10	0	4	33	19	4	5	5	19	23
Birmingham City	68	18	10	6	63	39	12	9	13	57	62
Blackburn Rovers	68	21	6	7	67	40	8	12	14	36	48
Blackpool	76	19	10	9	78	45	15	4	19	52	63
Bolton Wanderers	82	20	10	11	67	49	9	12	20	56	85
Bournemouth & BA	2	1	0	0	2	0	0	0	1	0	1
Bradford	14	5	0	2	16	5	3	1	3	9	9
Bradford City	30	12	1	2	35	17	3	6	6	18	30
Brentford	10	4	0	1	10	8	1	1	3	4	5
Brighton & HA	4	2	0	0	3	0	2	0	0	3	1
Bristol City	24	7	5	0	25	9	0	6	6	7	16
Bristol Rovers	8	3	1	0	5	0	1	0	3	3	7
Burnley	78	19	5	15	61	50	7	11	21	35	79
Burton United	4	2	0	0	4	0	1	0	1	5	4
Bury	10	4	0	1	16	8	0	1	4	4	10
Cambridge United	10	4	1	0	16	3	4	0	1	4	1
Cardiff City	34	10	2	5	30	15	5	6	6	22	29
Carlisle United	10	3	1	1	9	6	2	1	2	5	5
Charlton Athletic	50	11	6	8	49	36	7	9	9	34	44
Chesterfield	4	1	0	1	7	2	1	1	0	2	0
Coventry City	34	11	4	2	29	17	6	4	7	27	27
Crystal Palace	22	4	6	1	15	10	4	4	3	14	11
Darlington	4	1	1	0	7	4	0	2	0	3	3
Derby County	80	14	15	11	54	49	10	8	22	45	76
Everton	104	26	15	11	96	51	8	15	29	66	125
Fulham	44	12	8	2	32	13	14	4	4	43	28
Gainsborough Trinity	8	3	0	1	9	4	2	1	1	6	4
Glossop	8	3	1	0	12	2	3	0	1	8	5
Grimsby Town	40	15	2	3	52	19	5	5	10	21	28
Hereford United	2	1	0	0	5	1	0	1	0	2	2
Huddersfield Town	56	13	7	8	47	30	10	1	17	35	55
Hull City	26	11	2	0	28	2	6	3	4	17	15
Ipswich Town	28	9	3	2	31	14	6	2	6	19	23
Leeds City	8	4	0	0	14	3	1	3	0	4	3
Leeds United	64	15	9	8	61	36	3	8	21	24	68
Leicester City	74	26	8	3	83	34	6	14	17	42	59
Leyton Orient	28	7	4	3	23	15	8	2	4	23	14
Lincoln City	6	3	0	0	13	2	2	1	0	9	1
Liverpool	96	25	9	14	89	57	4	11	33	48	108
Luton Town	36	9	5	4	33	21	5	6	7	23	27
Manchester City	102	24	16	11	82	60	11	14	26	57	85

		Home					Away				
	P	W	D	L	F	A	W	D	L	F	A
Manchester United	98	14	11	24	73	93	13	15	21	46	80
Middlesbrough	78	24	10	5	73	33	7	13	19	45	72
Millwall	8	2	1	1	8	4	1	1	2	4	6
Newcastle United	98	26	13	10	96	62	10	12	27	52	79
Northampton Town	2	1	0	0	1	0	1	0	0	3	2
Norwich City	22	5	5	1	17	9	1	4	6	8	19
Nottingham Forest	72	19	11	6	55	40	9	11	16	42	70
Notts County	30	9	3	3	32	20	3	4	8	15	28
Oldham Athletic	42	13	6	2	42	21	5	6	10	28	27
Oxford United	10	3	1	1	11	7	1	3	1	10	10
Plymouth Argyle	8	1	3	0	10	5	3	0	1	8	4
Portsmouth	60	12	12	6	61	47	8	9	13	42	55
Port Vale	14	6	1	0	19	5	1	3	3	10	8
Preston North End	70	18	10	7	62	31	10	6	19	41	62
Queen's Park Rangers	30	6	5	4	21	21	3	6	6	18	24
Reading	8	2	2	0	3	1	1	1	2	7	9
Rotherham United	6	1	1	1	5	5	1	0	2	1	7
Scunthorpe United	2	1	0	0	3	0	0	0	1	0	3
Sheffield United	66	18	10	5	65	35	11	5	17	44	57
Sheffield Wednesday	82	19	12	10	57	40	4	15	22	49	90
Shrewsbury Town	12	4	0	2	14	7	1	2	3	7	11
South Shields	8	2	2	0	11	2	0	2	2	3	8
Southampton	48	10	6	8	40	32	8	9	7	35	40
Stockport County	12	4	2	0	12	5	2	2	2	5	8
Stoke City	68	17	10	7	58	45	13	6	15	37	51
Sunderland	88	27	11	6	87	44	11	8	25	53	89
Swansea City	18	5	3	1	23	8	2	3	4	6	12
Swindon Town	2	1	0	0	3	2	0	1	0	1	1
Tottenham Hotspur	86	17	7	19	52	64	12	10	21	58	85
Walsall	4	1	0	1	2	1	2	0	0	12	1
Watford	16	1	3	4	9	15	5	0	3	16	13
West Bromwich Albion	100	22	14	14	98	72	16	13	21	56	89
West Ham United	52	11	7	8	44	44	5	4	17	30	60
Wimbledon	8	0	2	2	3	10	1	1	2	5	6
Wolverhampton Wanderers	92	17	14	15	87	73	13	12	21	61	95
Wrexham	6	2	1	0	7	3	1	0	2	4	3
York City	2	0	1	0	0	0	0	1	0	2	2

There were 2 points for a win until 1981-2, since when 3 points for win have been awarded.

56 seasons were spent in Division One, 19 in Division Two, totalling 75 League seasons.

Overall Total 1905-06 to 1990-91

	P	W	D	L	F	A
Home	1554	793	399	362	2811	1829
Away	1554	408	408	738	1908	2755
Total	3108	1201	807	1100	4719	4584

1905-06

Manager: John Tait Robertson

1	Sep	2	(a)	Stockport C	L 0-1		7,000
2		9	(a)	Blackpool	W 1-0	J.T.Robertson	4,000
3		11	(h)	Hull C	W 5-1	Windridge 3, Copeland 2	6,000
4		16	(a)	Bradford C	D 1-1	McRoberts	17,000
5		23	(h)	West Brom A	W 1-0	McRoberts	20,000
6		30	(a)	Leicester F	W 1-0	James Robertson	7,000
7	Oct	14	(a)	Lincoln C	W 4-1	McRoberts, Pearson 2, Windridge	3,000
8		21	(h)	Chesterfield	L 0-1		10,000
9		30	(a)	Burslem Port Vale	L 2-3	Moran, Windridge	5,000
10	Nov	4	(h)	Barnsley	W 6-0	Pearson 2, McDermott 2, Copeland, McRoberts (pen)	8,000
11		11	(a)	Clapton O	W 3-0	Pearson 2, Copeland	8,000
12		18	(h)	Burnley	W 1-0	McRoberts	8,000
13		25	(a)	Leeds C	D 0-0		20,000
14	Dec	2	(h)	Burton U	W 3-0	Moran, McDermott, James Robertson	7,000
15		9	(h)	Grimsby T	W 2-0	Kirwan, McDermott	7,000
16		16	(a)	Gainsborough T	W 2-0	James Robertson, Hall (og)	8,000
17		23	(h)	Bristol C	D 0-0		25,000
18		25	(a)	Manchester U	D 0-0		35,000
19		26	(a)	Glossop	W 4-2	McRoberts, J.T.Robertson, Kirwan 2	6,000
20		30	(h)	Stockport C	W 4-2	Pearson, James Robertson 3	12,000
21	Jan	6	(h)	Blackpool	W 6-0	Kirwan, J.T.Robertson, Pearson 2, Moran, James Robertson	6,000
22		20	(h)	Bradford C	W 4-2	Kirwan, McDermott, Copeland, James Robertson	14,000
23		27	(a)	West Brom A	D 1-1	Pearson	25,000
24	Feb	5	(h)	Leicester F	D 3-3	Pearson, Windridge, James Robertson	6,000
25		10	(a)	Hull C	L 3-4	J.T.Robertson, Windridge, James Robertson	7,000
26		17	(h)	Lincoln C	W 4-2	Pearson, McDermott, Key, McRoberts (pen)	3,000
27		24	(a)	Chesterfield	W 2-0	Kirwan, Pearson	7,000
28	Mar	3	(h)	Burslem Port Vale	W 7-0	McRoberts (pen), Moran, James Robertson, Pearson, Kirwan 2, J.T.Robertson	10,000
29		10	(a)	Barnsley	W 2-1	Windridge, Pearson	7,900
30		17	(h)	Clapton O	W 6-1	Windridge 2, Donaghy, James Robertson, J.T.Robertson (pen), Pearson	15,000
31		24	(a)	Burnley	L 0-2		8,000
32		31	(h)	Leeds C	W 4-0	McRoberts (pen), Pearson, Windridge, McDermott	9,000
33	Apr	7	(a)	Burton U	W 4-2	Windridge 3, James Robertson	10,000
34		13	(h)	Manchester U	D 1-1	McDermott	67,000
35		14	(a)	Grimsby T	D 1-1	J.T.Robertson	6,000
36		16	(h)	Glossop	D 0-0		30,000
37		21	(h)	Gainsborough T	L 1-3	Mackie	10,000
38		28	(a)	Bristol C	L 1-2	Pearson	14,000

FINAL LEAGUE POSITION: 3rd in Division Two

Appearances
Goals

FA Cup

P1	Oct	7	(h)	1st Btn Grenadiers	W 6-1	Moran, James Robertson, O'Hara 2, Windridge 2	5,000
P2		28	(a)	Southend U	W 1-0	McDermott	7,000
P3	Nov	18	(a)	Crystal P	L 1-7	O'Hara	3,000

Aggregate League attendances:
Home: 273,000 (average 14,368)
Away: 204,900 (average 10,784)

Appearances
Goals

Appearance / shirt-number grid (numbers indicate the shirt worn by each player in each match; blank = did not play).

Foulke W	Mackie R	McEwan R	Miller T	Key G	McRoberts R	Robertson JT	Moran M	Copeland D	Windridge J	Kirwan J	Watson D	Robertson, James	Pearson F	McDermott T	Byrne M	Porter W	Donaghy C	Proudfoot P	Harris C	Henderson G	O'Hara F	Whiting R	Fletcher J	Craigie J	Goodwin J	Wolff F	Toomer J	
1	2	3	6	4	5	8	7	9	10	11																		1
1	2	3		4	9	6	7	8	10	11	5																	2
1	2	3		4	9	6	7	8	10	11	5																	3
1	2	3		4	9	6	7	8	10	11	5																	4
1	2	3		4	9	6	7	8	10	11	5																	5
1	2	3		4		6	7	9	10	11	5	8																6
1	2	3		4	5	6	7		10	11		8	9															7
1	2	3		4	5	6	7		10	11			9	8														8
1	2	3		4	5	6	7		10	11		8		9														9
1	2	3		4	5		7		10	11		6	9	8														10
1	2	3		4	5		7		10	11		6	9	8														11
1	2	3		4	5		7		10	11		6	9	8														12
1	2	3		4	5	8	7		10	11		6	9															13
1	2	3		4	5	6	7			11		8	9	10														14
1	2		3	4	5	6	7			11		8	9	10														15
1	2		3	4	5	6	7		10	11		8	9															16
1	2		3	4	9	6	7	8		11	5			10														17
1	2		3	4	5	6	7		10	11			9	8														18
1	2		3	4	9	6	7	8		11	5			10														19
1	2		3	4	5	6	7		10	11		8	9															20
1	2		3	4	5	6	7			11		8	9	10														21
1	2		3	4	5	6		8		11		7	9	10														22
1		2	3	4	5	6		8		11		7	9	10														23
1		2	3	4	5	6	7		10	11		8	9															24
	2	3		4	5		8	10	11		6	7	9		1													25
1	2		3	4	5	6	7		10				9	8			11											26
1	2		3	4	5	6	7		10	11			9	8														27
1	2		3	4	5	6	7		10	11		8	9															28
1	2		3	4		6	7	5	10	11			9	8														29
	2	3		4	5	6	7		10	11		8	9			1												30
1	2	3	5	4		6	7		10	11			9	8														31
1	2	3		4	5	6	7		10	11			9	8														32
1	2		3	4	5	6	7		10	11		8	9															33
1	2	3			5	6	7		10	11			9	8				4										34
1	2	3			5	6	7			11		8	9	10				4										35
1	2	3				6	7	8		11	5		9	10					4									36
	2		8		5		7			11			10		1			4		3	6	9						37
	2		8		5		7			11			9	10	1			4		6			3					38
34	35	19	24	33	34	33	34	20	20	36	13	16	29	22	3	1	1	4	1	3	1	1	1					
	1			1	9	7	4	5	14	8		13	18	8			1											

I own-goal

Foulke W	Mackie R	McEwan R	Miller T	Key G	McRoberts R	Robertson JT	Moran M	Copeland D	Windridge J	Kirwan J	Watson D	Robertson, James	Pearson F	McDermott T	Byrne M	Porter W	Donaghy C	Proudfoot P	Harris C	Henderson G	O'Hara F	Whiting R	Fletcher J	Craigie J	Goodwin J	Wolff F	Toomer J	
1	2		3	4		6	7		10	11		8									9		5					P1
1		3		4	5	6	7		10		2		9	8								11						P2
			3		6			8							1		10	2			9	4	11	5	7			P3
1	2	1	2	2	1	3	2	2	1	1	2	1	1	1	1	1	2	2	2	1	1							
			1					2			1		1									3						

1906-07

Manager: John Tait Robertson

1	Sep	1	(h)	Glossop	W	9-2	McDermott, Hilsdon 5, Copeland, Kirwan, Key	12,000
2		8	(a)	Blackpool	D	0-0		6,000
3		15	(h)	Bradford C	W	5-1	Moran, McDermott, Hilsdon, Copeland 2	10,000
4		22	(a)	West Brom A	W	2-1	McDermott, Copeland	25,000
5		29	(h)	Leicester F	W	1-0	Hilsdon	20,000
6	Oct	6	(a)	Nottingham F	L	1-3	Hilsdon	24,000
7		13	(h)	Lincoln C	W	2-0	Kirwan 2	10,000
8		20	(a)	Burton U	L	1-2	McRoberts	4,000
9		27	(h)	Grimsby T	W	2-0	Hilsdon 2 (1 pen)	18,000
10	Nov	3	(a)	Burslem Port Vale	L	0-2		5,000
11		10	(h)	Burnley	W	2-0	Hilsdon 2	10,000
12		17	(a)	Leeds C	W	1-0	James Robertson	8,000
13		24	(h)	Barnsley	W	2-1	Windridge, Hilsdon	14,000
14	Dec	1	(a)	Chesterfield	D	0-0		6,000
15		8	(a)	Wolves	W	2-1	Hilsdon, Windridge	8,000
16		15	(h)	Clapton O	W	2-1	Windridge, Frost	15,000
17		22	(a)	Gainsborough T	D	1-1	Hilsdon	3,000
18		25	(a)	Hull C	W	1-0	Windridge	16,000
19		29	(a)	Glossop	W	1-0	Hilsdon	4,000
20	Jan	1	(a)	Stockport C	W	2-1	Hilsdon, Bridgeman	7,000
21		5	(h)	Blackpool	W	3-0	Hilsdon, Windridge, Frost	15,000
22		26	(h)	West Brom A	W	2-0	Windridge, Bridgeman	38,000
23	Feb	2	(a)	Leicester F	D	1-1	Birnie	17,000
24		9	(h)	Nottingham F	L	0-2		15,000
25		16	(a)	Lincoln C	W	5-0	James Robertson 3, Windridge, Bridgeman	3,000
26		23	(h)	Burton U	W	1-0	Windridge	11,000
27	Mar	2	(a)	Grimsby T	L	1-2	James Robertson	6,000
28		4	(h)	Stockport C	W	2-0	Hilsdon (pen), Frost	8,000
29		9	(h)	Burslem Port Vale	W	2-1	Hilsdon (pen), Frost	8,000
30		16	(a)	Burnley	D	1-1	James Robertson	7,000
31		19	(a)	Bradford C	L	3-6	Kirwan 2, Windridge	6,000
32		23	(h)	Leeds C	W	2-0	Hilsdon 2 (1 pen)	25,000
33		29	(h)	Hull C	W	3-0	Hilsdon 2, Windridge	48,000
34		30	(a)	Barnsley	L	1-3	Bridgeman	5,000
35	Apr	6	(h)	Chesterfield	W	7-1	Hilsdon 2, James Robertson 2, Windridge 3	12,000
36		13	(h)	Wolves	W	4-0	Kirwan 2, Windridge 2	30,000
37		20	(h)	Clapton O	W	1-0	Moran	18,000
38		27	(h)	Gainsborough T	W	4-1	Hilsdon (pen), Windridge 3	15,000

FINAL LEAGUE POSITION: 2nd in Division Two

Appearances
Goals

FA Cup

1	Jan	12	(a)	Lincoln C	D	2-2	Kirwan, Whitehouse	5,000
R		16	(h)	Lincoln C	L	0-1*		11,883

*After extra-time

Appearances
Goals

Aggregate League attendances:
Home: 334,000 (average 17,578)
Away: 178,000 (average 9,368)

Whiting R	Walton J	Miller T	Henderson G	McRoberts R	Birnie E	Moran M	McDermott T	Hilsdon G	Copeland D	Kirwan J	Byrne M	Key G	Robertson, James	Robertson JT	Windridge J	Donaghy C	Brebner RG	Proudfoot P	Bush R	Bridgeman W	Frost J	Mackie R	McCartney D	Whitehouse B	Porter W	
	2	3	6	5		7	8	9	10	11	1	4														1
1	2	3	4	5	6	7		9	10	11			8													2
1	2	3	4	5	6	7	8	9	10	11																3
1	2	3	4	5	6	7	8	9	10						11											4
1	2	3	4	5	6	7	8	9	10						11											5
1	2	3	4	5	6	7	8	9		11					10											6
1	2	3	4	9	5	7	10			11		8	6													7
1	2	3	6	5		7	10	9		11			4		8											8
	2	3	4	5		7	8	9		11					10	1	6									9
1	2	3	6	5		7	8	9	10	11		4														10
1	2	3	4	5		7		9		11			8		10			6								11
1	2	3	4	5		7		9		11			8		10			6								12
1	2	3	4	5		7		9		11			8		10			6								13
1	2	3	4	5		7		9		11					10			6	8							14
1	2	3	4	5	6	7		9		11					10					8						15
1	2	3	4	5	6			9		11					10					8	7					16
1	2	3	4	5	6			9		11					10					8	7					17
1	2	3	4	5	6			9		11					10					8	7					18
1		3	4	5	6			9		11					10					8	7	2				19
1		3	4	5	6			9		11					10					8	7	2				20
1		3	4	5	6			9		11					10					8	7	2				21
1	2	3	4	5	6			9		11					10					8	7					22
1	2	3	4	5	6			9		11					10					8	7					23
1	2	3	4	5	6	7		9		11					10					8						24
1	2	3	4	5	6					11			8		10					9	7					25
1	2	3	4	5	6								8		10					9	7			11		26
1	2	3	4	5	6					11			8		10					9	7					27
1	2	3	4	5	6			9		11					10					8	7					28
1	2	3	4	5	6			9		11					10					8	7					29
1	2	3	4	5	6					11			9		10					8	7					30
1	2	3	4	5						11			9		10					8	7		6			31
1	2	3	4	5	6			9		11					10					8	7					32
1	2	3		5	4			9		11			8		10			6			7					33
1	2	3	4	5				9		11					10			6		8	7					34
1	2	3	4	5				9		11			8		10			6			7					35
1	2	3	4					5		11			8		10			6		9	7					36
1	2	3	4			7		9		11	5				10			6		8						37
1	2	3	4			7		9		11	5				10			6		8						38
36	35	38	37	35	24	18	9	32	6	35	1	4	13	3	31	1	1	7	4	23	20	3	1		1	
			1	1	2	3	27	4	7		1	8			18					4	4					

Whiting R	Walton J	Miller T	Henderson G	McRoberts R	Birnie E	Moran M	McDermott T	Hilsdon G	Copeland D	Kirwan J	Byrne M	Key G	Robertson, James	Robertson JT	Windridge J	Donaghy C	Brebner RG	Proudfoot P	Bush R	Bridgeman W	Frost J	Mackie R	McCartney D	Whitehouse B	Porter W	
1		3	4			6	7		9		11									10		2	5	8		1
1		3	4			6	7		9		11									10		2	5	8		R
2		2	2			2	2		2		2									2		2	2	2		
																								1		

1907-08

Manager: David Calderhead

1	Sep	7	(h)	Sheffield U	L	2-4	Hilsdon, Windridge	25,000
2		14	(a)	Newcastle U	L	0-1		30,000
3		21	(a)	Nottingham F	L	0-6		20,000
4		23	(h)	Newcastle U	W	2-0	Bridgeman, Windridge	20,000
5		28	(h)	Manchester U	L	1-4	Hilsdon	30,000
6	Oct	5	(a)	Blackburn R	L	0-2		10,000
7		12	(h)	Bolton W	L	1-3	Hilsdon	35,000
8		19	(a)	Birmingham	D	1-1	Hilsdon	20,000
9		26	(h)	Everton	W	2-1	Windridge 2	50,000
10	Nov	2	(a)	Sunderland	L	0-3		13,000
11		9	(h)	W Arsenal	W	2-1	Hilsdon 2	55,000
12		16	(a)	Sheffield W	L	1-3	Hilsdon	22,000
13		23	(h)	Bristol C	W	4-1	Hilsdon 4	20,000
14		30	(a)	Notts C	L	0-2		12,000
15	Dec	2	(h)	Blackburn R	W	1-0	Whitehouse	18,000
16		7	(h)	Manchester C	D	2-2	Brawn, Hilsdon	50,000
17		14	(a)	Preston NE	W	4-2	Stark, Rouse 2, Brawn	8,000
18		21	(h)	Bury	L	3-4	Hilsdon 2, Lindsay (og)	35,000
19		25	(a)	Liverpool	W	4-1	Henderson, Hilsdon 2, Windridge	30,000
20		26	(h)	Middlesbrough	W	1-0	Rouse	40,000
21		28	(a)	Aston Villa	D	0-0		30,000
22	Jan	1	(a)	Middlesbrough	L	1-3	Brawn	30,000
23		4	(a)	Sheffield U	W	3-0	Hilsdon, Windridge 2	5,000
24		18	(h)	Nottingham F	L	0-4		35,000
25		25	(a)	Manchester U	L	0-1		30,000
26	Feb	8	(a)	Bolton W	W	2-1	Hilsdon, Windridge	18,000
27		15	(h)	Birmingham	D	2-2	Fairgray, Brawn	30,000
28		29	(h)	Sunderland	W	2-1	Rouse 2	32,000
29	Mar	7	(a)	W Arsenal	D	0-0		30,000
30		14	(h)	Sheffield W	W	3-1	Hilsdon, Windridge, Stark	30,000
31		21	(a)	Bristol C	D	0-0		15,000
32	Apr	1	(a)	Everton	W	3-0	Hilsdon 3	10,000
33		4	(a)	Manchester C	W	3-0	Rouse, Humphreys, Jackson (og)	15,000
34		11	(h)	Preston NE	D	0-0		40,000
35		18	(a)	Bury	D	1-1	Hilsdon	11,000
36		20	(h)	Liverpool	L	0-2		40,000
37		25	(h)	Aston Villa	L	1-3	Birnie	30,000
38		29	(h)	Notts C	L	1-2	Hilsdon	10,000

FINAL LEAGUE POSITION: 13th in Division One

Appearances
Goals

FA Cup

1	Jan	11	(h)	Worksop T	W	9-1	Bridgeman, Hilsdon 6, Windridge 2	18,995
2	Feb	1	(a)	Manchester U	L	0-1		25,000

Appearances
Goals

Aggregate League attendances:
Home: 625,000 (average 32,894)
Away: 359,000 (average 18,894)

Appearance and goalscoring grid (numbers denote the shirt number worn in each match; right-hand column is the match number).

Whiting R	Walton J	Miller T	Henderson G	McRoberts R	Birnie E	Frost J	Bridgeman W	Hilsdon G	Windridge J	Kirwan J	Fairgray N	Lyon F	Mackie R	Key G	Moran M	Proudfoot P	Whitley J	Stark J	Whitehouse B	Rouse F	Cameron J	Brawn W	Harding A	Humphreys P	
1	2	3	4	5	6	7	8	9	10	11															1
1			4	5	6	7	9	8	10		11	3	2												2
1			4	5	6	7	8	9	10		11	2	3												3
				5	6		8	9	10		11	2	3	4	7		1								4
				5			8	9	10		11	2	3	4	7	6	1								5
		3			6		8	9	10		11		2	4	7		1	5							6
1					6		8	9		11				4	7			5	10	3	2				7
1		3	4	5				9	10		11			6	7					8	2				8
1		3			6			9	10		11			4	7			5		8	2				9
1		3			6			9	10		11			4	7			5		8	2				10
1		3			6			9	10		11			4	7			5		8	2				11
1		3	4		6			9	10		11				7			5		8	2				12
1		3	4		6			9	10		11							5		8	2	7			13
1		3			6		10	9			11			4				5	8		2	7			14
1		3			6			9			11			4				5	10	8	2	7			15
1		3			6			9			11			4				5	10	8	2	7			16
1			4		6		11	9										5	10	8	2	7	3		17
1		3	4		6		11	9										5	10	8	2	7			18
		3	4		6		11	9	10								1	5		8	2	7			19
		3	4		6		11	9	10								1	5		8	2	7			20
		3	4		6		11	9	10								1	5		8	2	7			21
		3	4	6			11	9	10								1	5		8	2	7			22
		3	4		6		11	9	10								1	5	8		2	7			23
		3	4		6		11	9	10								1	5	8		2	7			24
		3		5	6			9			11		4				1	8	10		2	7			25
		3	4		6			9	10		11						1	5		8	2	7			26
		3	4		6		9				11				7		1	5	10		2	8			27
		3	4		6				10		11						1	5		8	2	7		9	28
		3	4		6			9	10		11						1	5			2	7		8	29
			4		6			9	10		11	2					1	5			3	7		8	30
		3	4		6			9	10		11						1	5			2	7		8	31
		3	4		6			9	10		11						1	5			2	7		8	32
		3		5	6		8				11			4			1		10		2	7		9	33
		3	4		6			9	10		11						1	5			2	7		8	34
		3	4		6			9	10		11						1	5			2	7		8	35
		3	4		6			9	10		11						1	5			2	7		8	36
		3	4		6				10		11						1	5		8	2	7		9	37
			4		6			9	10		11	3					1	5			2	7		8	38
15	1	30	14	20	36	3	18	33	29	2	28	6	6	13	10	1	23	30	10	20	32	26	1	11	
		1		1			1	24	9		1							2	1	6		4		1	

2 own-goals

Whiting R	Walton J	Miller T	Henderson G	McRoberts R	Birnie E	Frost J	Bridgeman W	Hilsdon G	Windridge J	Kirwan J	Fairgray N	Lyon F	Mackie R	Key G	Moran M	Proudfoot P	Whitley J	Stark J	Whitehouse B	Rouse F	Cameron J	Brawn W	Harding A	Humphreys P	
			4		6		11	9	10								1	5	8		2	7	3		1
		3	4		6		11	9	10								1	5		8	2	7			2
		1	1	1	2		2	2	2								2	2	1	1	2	2	1		
							1	6	2																

1908-09

Manager: David Calderhead

1	Sep	1	(h)	Preston NE	D	0-0	25,000
2		5	(a)	Liverpool	L	1-2	Hilsdon	25,000
3		7	(a)	Preston NE	L	0-6	6,000
4		12	(h)	Bury	W	4-1	Warren, Humphreys, Hilsdon, Bridgeman	50,000
5		19	(a)	Sheffield U	W	3-1	Brawn, Humphreys, Hilsdon	15,000
6		21	(h)	Nottingham F	W	2-1	Hilsdon, Windridge	20,000
7		26	(h)	Aston Villa	L	0-2	40,000
8	Oct	3	(a)	Nottingham F	L	1-2	Humphreys	18,000
9		10	(h)	Sunderland	W	2-0	Windridge, Rouse	35,000
10		17	(h)	Sheffield W	D	2-2	Rouse 2	25,000
11		24	(a)	Blackburn R	L	0-2	15,000
12		31	(h)	Bradford C	D	1-1	Hilsdon	30,000
13	Nov	7	(a)	Manchester U	W	1-0	Hilsdon (pen)	20,000
14		14	(h)	Everton	D	3-3	Hilsdon 3 (1 pen)	40,000
15		21	(a)	Leicester F	L	2-5	Warren, Hilsdon	15,000
16		28	(h)	W Arsenal	L	1-2	Hilsdon	55,000
17	Dec	5	(a)	Notts C	L	0-3	12,000
18		12	(h)	Newcastle U	L	1-2	Humphreys	25,000
19		19	(a)	Bristol C	L	0-1	10,000
20		25	(a)	Manchester C	W	2-1	Brawn, Rouse	35,000
21		26	(h)	Manchester C	L	1-2	Humphreys	40,000
22	Jan	1	(a)	Middlesbrough	W	4-1	Hilsdon 3, Windridge	25,000
23		2	(h)	Liverpool	W	3-0	Hilsdon (pen), Windridge, Rouse	30,000
24		23	(h)	Sheffield U	D	1-1	Brawn	25,000
25		30	(a)	Aston Villa	D	0-0	18,000
26	Feb	13	(a)	Sunderland	W	2-1	Birnie, Douglas	16,000
27		27	(h)	Blackburn R	D	1-1	Hilsdon (pen)	10,000
28	Mar	13	(h)	Manchester U	D	1-1	Bridgeman	25,000
29		20	(a)	Everton	L	2-3	Hilsdon (pen), Windridge	25,000
30		22	(a)	Sheffield W	L	1-5	Windridge	12,000
31		31	(a)	Bury	L	1-2	Hilsdon	3,000
32	Apr	3	(a)	W Arsenal	D	0-0	20,000
33		9	(h)	Middlesbrough	W	3-0	Humphreys, Hilsdon 2	50,000
34		10	(h)	Notts C	W	3-2	Warren, Humphreys, Hilsdon (pen)	30,000
35		17	(a)	Newcastle U	W	3-1	Humphreys, Hilsdon 2 (1 pen)	30,000
36		20	(a)	Bradford C	L	0-3	14,000
37		26	(h)	Bristol C	W	3-1	Humphreys, Hilsden 2	12,000
38		29	(h)	Leicester F	W	1-0	Bridgeman	10,000

FINAL LEAGUE POSITION: 11th in Division One

Appearances
Goals

FA Cup

1	Jan	16	(a)	Hull C	D	1-1	Hilsdon	18,100
R		20	(h)	Hull C	W	1-0	Warren	25,792
2	Feb	6	(a)	Blackburn R	L	1-2	Hilsdon	31,897

Aggregate League attendances:
Home: 577,000 (average 30,368)
Away: 334,000 (average 17,578)

Appearances
Goals

Appearance/line-up grid (jersey numbers by player and match). Columns are players; rows 1–38 are matches.

#	Whitley J	Cameron J	Miller B	Warren B	McRoberts R	Kennedy G	Birnie E	Brawn W	Humphreys P	Hilsdon G	Windridge J	Fairgray N	Rouse F	Bridgeman W	Cartwright W	Walton J	Douglas A	Downing S	Henderson G	Freeman C	Holden A	Key G	Mair T	Robinson A C	Reilly E
1	1	2	3	4	5		6		8	9	10	11					7								
2	1	2	3	4	5		6			9	10	11	8				7								
3		2	3	4	5					9	10		8	11			7					6		1	
4		2		4	5		7	8	9			10	11	3								6		1	
5	1	2		4	5		7	8	9	10		11		3								6			
6	1	2		4	5		7	8	9	10		11		3								6			
7	1	2		4	5		6	7	8	9	10	11		3											
8	1	2		4	5		6	7	8	9	10	11		3											
9	1	2				4	6	7	5	9	10	11	8	3											
10	1	2	3	4		5	6	7	8	9		11	10												
11	1	2	3	4	5		6	7	8		11	9	10												
12	1	2		4	5		6			9	10	11	8		3		7								
13	1	2	3	4	5		6	7		9	10	11	8												
14	1	2	3	4			5	7	6	9	10	11	8												
15	1	2	3	4			5	7	6	9	10	11	8												
16	1	2	3	4	5		6	7		9	10	11	8												
17	1	2	3	4	5	6		7		9	10		8	11											
18	1	2		4	5	6		7	8	9	10		11	3											
19	1	2		4		5	6	7	8	9	10		11	3											
20	1	2	3	4		5	6	7	8		10		9										11		
21	1	2	3	4		5	6	7	8		10		9										11		
22	1	2	3	4		5	6	7		9	10		8										11		
23	1	2	3	4		5	6	7		9	10	11	8												
24	1	2	3	4	5		6	7		9	10	11	8												
25	1	2	3		5	4	6	7		9	10	11	8												
26	1	2	3				6		8			11		10		5	7	4	9						
27	1	2	3				6	7	8	9	10	11			5			4							
28	1	2	3	5				7		9	10	11		8	6			4							
29	1	2		5			6	7		9	10	11		8	3			4							
30	1		3	5			6	7		9	10			8	2			4					11		
31	1	2		5			6	7		9	10	11		8	3			4							
32	1						5	7	4	9	10				2	3	11		6						8
33	1	2		4			5	7	8	9	10			3					11		6				
34	1	2		4			6	7	8	9	10		3						11		5				
35	1	2		4			6	7	8	9	10			3					11	5					
36	1	2		4			6	7	8	9	10			3					11	5					
37	1	2		4			6	7	8	9	10			3					11	5					
38	1			4			6			9	10		8	2	3	7	5		11						
Total	36	35	20	34	15	10	31	32	23	34	34	18	18	16	12	12	7	6	6	4	4	4	4	2	1
			3		1	3	9	25	6			5	3			1									

#	Whitley J	Cameron J	Miller B	Warren B	McRoberts R	Kennedy G	Birnie E	Brawn W	Humphreys P	Hilsdon G	Windridge J	Fairgray N	Rouse F	Bridgeman W	Cartwright W	Walton J	Douglas A	Downing S	Henderson G	Freeman C	Holden A	Key G	Mair T	Robinson A C	Reilly E
1	1	2	3	5		4	6	7		9	10		8	11											
R	1	2	3	5		4	6	7		9	10	11	8												
2	1	2	3	5			6		8	9	10	11	7					4							
Total	3	3	3	3		2	3	2	1	3	3	2	3	1				1							
									2				1												

203

1909-10

Manager: David Calderhead

1	Sep	1	(h)	Notts C	D	2-2	Humphreys, Hilsdon	12,000
2		4	(h)	Liverpool	W	2-1	Hilsdon (pen), Windridge	27,000
3		11	(a)	Aston Villa	L	1-4	Humphreys	30,000
4		18	(h)	Sheffield U	D	2-2	Downing, Windridge	36,000
5		25	(a)	W Arsenal	L	2-3	Wileman, Fairgray	20,000
6	Oct	2	(h)	Bolton W	W	3-2	Downing, Windridge, Jones	35,000
7		9	(a)	Middlesbrough	W	1-0	Jones	12,000
8		16	(a)	Blackburn R	L	0-1		10,000
9		23	(h)	Nottingham F	L	0-1		30,000
10		27	(h)	Preston NE	W	2-0	Humphreys, Fairgray	25,000
11		30	(a)	Sunderland	L	0-4		10,000
12	Nov	6	(h)	Everton	L	0-1		35,000
13		13	(a)	Manchester U	L	0-2		10,000
14		20	(h)	Bradford C	L	0-3		24,000
15		27	(a)	Sheffield W	L	1-4	Downing	15,000
16	Dec	4	(h)	Bristol C	W	4-1	Jones, Woodward 2, Bradshaw	20,000
17		11	(a)	Bury	L	2-4	Bradshaw, Mair	5,000
18		18	(h)	Tottenham H	W	2-1	Windridge, Bradshaw	40,000
19		25	(a)	Notts C	L	1-2	Windridge	20,000
20		27	(h)	Newcastle U	W	2-1	Brawn, Woodward	70,000
21	Jan	1	(a)	Newcastle U	L	0-1		25,000
22		8	(a)	Liverpool	L	1-5	Woodward	15,000
23		10	(a)	Preston NE	L	0-2		9,000
24		22	(h)	Aston Villa	D	0-0		30,000
25	Feb	12	(a)	Bolton W	L	2-5	Freeman 2	8,000
26		19	(h)	Middlesbrough	W	2-1	Downing, Hilsdon	20,000
27		26	(h)	Blackburn R	W	3-1	Holden, Douglas, Woodward	30,000
28	Mar	5	(a)	Nottingham F	D	0-0		7,000
29		7	(a)	Sheffield U	D	0-0		8,000
30		12	(h)	Sunderland	L	1-4	Downing	15,000
31		19	(a)	Everton	D	2-2	Wileman 2	10,000
32		26	(h)	Manchester U	D	1-1	Wileman	25,000
33		28	(h)	W Arsenal	L	0-1		40,000
34	Apr	2	(a)	Bradford C	L	1-4	Horn	16,000
35		9	(h)	Sheffield W	W	4-1	Brawn 2, Wileman, McEwan	25,000
36		16	(a)	Bristol C	L	0-1		16,000
37		23	(h)	Bury	W	2-0	Douglas, Whittingham	35,000
38		30	(a)	Tottenham H	L	1-2	Windridge	35,000

FINAL LEAGUE POSITION: 19th in Division One

Appearances
Goals

FA Cup

1	Jan	15	(h)	Hull C	W	2-1	Brawn, Williams	34,700
2	Feb	5	(h)	Tottenham H	L	0-1		31,776

Appearances
Goals

Aggregate League attendances:
Home: 574,000 (average 30,210)
Away: 281,000 (average 14,789)

	Whitley J	Walton J	Cameron J	Warren B	Birnie E	Downing S	Brawn W	Humphreys P	Hilsdon G	Windridge J	Holden A	Ormiston A	Jones E	Wileman A	Fairgray N	Harding A	Freeman C	Bettridge W	Cartwright W	Douglas A	Woodward VJ	Bridgeman W	Bradshaw J	Mair T	Dolby H	Williams EW	Saunders J	Taylor F	Horn G	McEwan M	Robinson A	McConnell E	Whittingham R	Smith P	
1	1	2	3	4	5	6	7	8	9	10	11																								1
2	1	2	3	4		6	7	8	9	10	11		5																						2
3	1	2	3	4	5	6	7	8		10	11		9																						3
4	1	2	3	4	5	6	7	8		10	11		9																						4
5	1	2	3	4		6		7		10			5	9	8	11																			5
6	1		3	4		6	7			10			5	9	8	11	2																		6
7	1		3	4		6	7						5	9	8	11	2	10																	7
8	1			4		6	7		10	11			5	9	8				2	3															8
9	1			4	5	6	7	8	10	11				9					2	3															9
10	1			4		6		8	10				5	9		11			2	3	7														10
11	1			4		6		8					5	9		11	10		2	3	7														11
12	1		3	4		6	7	8	9				5			11	10		2																12
13	1		3	4		6		8			11		5		9		10		2		7														13
14	1		3	4		6		8			11		5		9		10		2		7														14
15	1		3	4		6	7	8			11		5						2			9	10												15
16	1		3	4	5	6	7							9					2		8			10	11										16
17	1		3		4	6			10			5	9						2		8			11	7										17
18	1			4	6	7			10			5	9						2	3	8				11										18
19				5	6	7			10				9						2	3	8			11	1	4									19
20				5	6	7			10				9						2	3	8			11	1	4									20
21	1				6	7	9						10						2	3	8		5		11	4									21
22	1				6	7	9						10						2	3	8		5		11	4									22
23	1				6	7	9						5	10					2	3	8			11		4									23
24	1				6	7	9	10					5						2	3	8			11		4									24
25	1				6								5	8	9		10	2	3	7				11		4									25
26	1	3			6	7		9	10				5		8				2					11		4									26
27	1	3			6		9	10	11	5									2	7	8					4									27
28	1	3			6		9	10	11	5									2	7	8					4									28
29	1	3	4		6		9	10	11										2	7	8					5									29
30	1	3			6		9	10	11	5									2	7	8					4									30
31	1	3			6		9		11	5			8				10		2	7						4									31
32	1	3			6		9		11	5			8				10		2	7						4									32
33	1	3			6				11	5	9	8					10	2		7						4									33
34	1	3			6	7			5			8	2						9							4	10	11							34
35		3			6	7	9	10		8					2											5	4	11	1						35
36	1	3			6	7			10										2							4	11			5	8	9			36
37	1	3			6				10										2	7	9					4	11			5	8				37
38	1	3			6				10										2	7	9					4	11			5	8				38
	35	5	26	17	10	37	23	11	15	23	16	24	18	14	6	3	9	18	24	14	13	2	6	5	1	6	2	20	2	5	1	3	3	1	
			5	3	3	3	6	1		3	5	2					2			2	5					3	1			1	1		1		

	Whitley J	Walton J	Cameron J	Warren B	Birnie E	Downing S	Brawn W	Humphreys P	Hilsdon G	Windridge J	Holden A	Ormiston A	Jones E	Wileman A	Fairgray N	Harding A	Freeman C	Bettridge W	Cartwright W	Douglas A	Woodward VJ	Bridgeman W	Bradshaw J	Mair T	Dolby H	Williams EW	Saunders J	Taylor F	Horn G	McEwan M	Robinson A	McConnell E	Whittingham R	Smith P	
1	1				6	7			9	10			5						2	3	8					11	4								1
2	1				6	7			9	10			5						2	3	8					11	4								2
	2				2	2			2	2			2						2	2	2					2	2								
						1																					1								

205

1910-11

Manager: David Calderhead

1	Sep	3	(a)	Derby C	W	4-1	Hilsdon 3, Windridge	12,000
2		10	(h)	Barnsley	W	3-1	Whittingham, Hilsdon, McEwan	21,000
3		17	(a)	Leicester F	L	0-1		16,000
4		24	(h)	Wolves	W	2-0	Whittingham 2	29,000
5	Oct	1	(h)	Bolton W	W	3-0	Whittingham 2, Hilsdon	25,000
6		8	(a)	Clapton O	D	0-0		25,000
7		15	(h)	Blackpool	D	0-0		30,000
8		22	(a)	Glossop	L	1-2	McEwan	7,000
9		29	(h)	Lincoln C	W	7-0	Downing, Woodward 2, Whittingham 2, Hilsdon 2	25,000
10	Nov	12	(h)	Birmingham	D	2-2	Whittingham 2	17,000
11		19	(a)	West Brom A	W	3-1	Woodward, Whittingham, Jones	25,000
12		26	(h)	Hull C	W	2-0	Whittingham 2	17,000
13	Dec	3	(a)	Fulham	L	0-1		35,000
14		10	(h)	Bradford	W	3-0	Whittingham 2, Hilsdon	14,000
15		17	(a)	Burnley	D	1-1	Hilsdon	7,000
16		24	(h)	Gainsborough T	W	3-0	Downing, Douglas, Whittingham	16,000
17		26	(a)	Leeds C	D	3-3	Hilsdon 3	18,000
18		27	(h)	Stockport C	W	2-0	Whittingham 2	30,000
19		31	(h)	Derby C	W	3-2	Douglas, Whittingham 2	32,000
20	Jan	2	(a)	Stockport C	D	2-2	Whittingham, Hilsdon	5,000
21		7	(a)	Barnsley	L	2-3	Whittingham, Hilsdon	7,000
22		21	(h)	Leicester F	W	2-0	Whittingham, Hilsdon	18,000
23		28	(a)	Wolves	D	0-0		16,000
24	Feb	8	(a)	Clapton O	W	1-0	Hilsdon	41,000
25		18	(a)	Blackpool	W	2-0	Douglas, Freeman	6,000
26	Mar	4	(a)	Lincoln C	D	0-0		4,000
27		6	(h)	Glossop	W	2-0	Hilsdon, Bridgeman	12,000
28		18	(a)	Birmingham	L	1-2	Warren	25,000
29		20	(h)	Huddersfield T	W	2-0	Whittingham, Hilsdon	12,000
30		29	(h)	West Brom A	W	2-1	Douglas, Whittingham	25,000
31	Apr	1	(a)	Hull C	D	1-1	Whittingham	12,000
32		8	(h)	Fulham	W	2-0	Douglas, Whittingham	45,000
33		14	(h)	Leeds C	W	4-1	Douglas, Woodward, Whittingham, Bridgeman	35,000
34		15	(a)	Bradford	L	1-2	Whittingham	15,000
35		18	(a)	Huddersfield T	L	1-3	Freeman	9,000
36		22	(h)	Burnley	W	3-0	Woodward, Whittingham 2	36,000
37		26	(a)	Bolton W	L	0-2		35,000
38		29	(a)	Gainsborough T	L	1-3	Woodward	7,000

FINAL LEAGUE POSITION: 3rd in Division Two

Appearances
Goals

FA Cup

1	Jan	14	(h)	Leyton	D	0-0		19,167
R		19	(a)	Leyton	W	2-0	Downing, Hilsdon	14,000
2	Feb	4	(a)	Chesterfield T	W	4-1	Woodward 2, Whittingham 2 (1 pen)	28,400
3		25	(a)	Wolves	W	2-0	Woodward, Freeman	33,000
4	Mar	13	(h)	Swindon T	W	3-1	Whittingham 2, Bridgeman	77,952
SF		25	(a*)	Newcastle U	L	0-3		34,000

*Played at St Andrew's, Birmingham.

Appearances
Goals

Aggregate League attendances:
Home: 480,000 (average 22,263)
Away: 268,000 (average 15,052)

Molyneux J	Whitley J	Bettridge W	Cameron J	Cartwright W	Warren B	Taylor F	Calderhead D	Ormiston A	Downing S	Douglas A	Brawn W	Woodward VJ	Whittingham R	Hilsdon G	Freeman C	McConnell E	Windridge J	McEwan M	Bridgeman W	Jones E	Fairgray N	McKenzie K	Dolby HR	No.
1		2	3		4				6	7			8	9		5	10	11						1
1		2	3		4				6	7			8	9		5	10	11						2
1		2	3		4				6	7			8	9		5	10	11						3
1		2	3		4	6						10	8	9		5		11			7			4
1		2	3		4				6	7		10	8	9		5		11						5
1		2	3		4				6	7		10	8	9		5		11						6
1		2	3		4				6	7		10	8	9		5		11						7
1		2	3		4				6	7		10	8	9		5		11						8
1		2	3		4				6	7		10	8	9		5		11						9
1		2	3		4				6	7		10	8	9		5		11						10
1		2	3	6	4					7		10	8			5		11	9					11
1		2	3	6	4					7		10	8			5		11	9					12
1		2	3	6	4					7		10	8			5		11	9					13
1		2	3		4				6	7		10	8	9		5		11						14
1		2	3		4				6	7		10	8	9		5		11						15
1		2	3		4				6	7		10	8	9		5		11						16
1		2	3		4				6	7			8	9		5	10	11						17
1		2	3		4				6	7		10	8	9		5		11						18
1		2	3	5	4				6	7		10	8	9				11						19
1		2	3	5	4				6	7			8	9	10			11						20
1		2	3	5	4				6	7			8	9	10			11						21
	1	2	3		4		5		6	7			8	9	10			11						22
1		2	3		4		5		6	7			8	9	10			11						23
1		2	3			4	5		6	7			8	9	10			11						24
1		2	3		4		5		6	7			8	9	10			11						25
1		2	3		4		5		6	7			8	9	10			11						26
1		2	3		4		5		6	7			8	9	10			11						27
1		2	3		4		5		6				8	9	10	7		11						28
1		2	3		4		5		6	7			8	9	10			11						29
1		2	3		4		5		6	7			8		10				11		9			30
1		2	3			4	5		6	7			8		10				11		9			31
1		2	3		4		5		6	7			8		10				11		9			32
1		2	3			4	5		6	7	10		8						11		9			33
1		2	3		4	5			6	7			8		10				11		9			34
1		2	3		4	5			6	7			8		10			9		11				35
1		2	3		4		5		6	7			8	9	10				11			4		36
1		3	2				5		6				8	9	10				11		4			37
1		2	3	5	4				6				8	9	10				11					38
37	1	37	34	5	31	14	10	6	34	24	12	19	38	26	18	18	4	28	15	3	2	1	1	
			1		2	6			6	30	18	2			1	2	2	1						

Molyneux J	Whitley J	Bettridge W	Cameron J	Cartwright W	Warren B	Taylor F	Calderhead D	Ormiston A	Downing S	Douglas A	Brawn W	Woodward VJ	Whittingham R	Hilsdon G	Freeman C	McConnell E	Windridge J	McEwan M	Bridgeman W	Jones E	Fairgray N	McKenzie K	Dolby HR	No.
1		2	3		4		5		6	7			8	9	10			11						1
1		2	3		4		5		6	7			8	9	10			11						R
1		2	3		4		5		6	7			10	8	9			11						2
1		2	3		4		5		6	7			8	9	10			11						3
1		2	3		4		5		6	7			8	9	10			11						4
1		2	3		4		5		6	7			9	8	10			11						SF
4	2	6	6		6				6	6			6	6	3	5	5	5	2	4				
			1						3	4	1	1				1								

1911-12

Manager: David Calderhead

1	Sep	2	(h)	Stockport C	D 0-0		28,000
2		9	(a)	Leeds C	D 0-0		15,000
3		11	(h)	Derby C	W 1-0	Freeman	20,000
4		16	(h)	Wolves	W 4-0	Brown, Woodward, Freeman 2	32,000
5		23	(a)	Leicester F	L 0-2		15,000
6		30	(h)	Gainsborough T	W 1-0	Whittingham (pen)	30,000
7	Oct	7	(a)	Grimsby T	L 1-2	Douglas	8,000
8		14	(h)	Nottingham F	W 2-0	Whittingham, Dodd	24,000
9		21	(a)	Burnley	D 2-2	Bridgeman 2	12,000
10		28	(a)	Clapton O	W 4-1	Douglas, Whittingham 2 (1 pen), Dodd	25,000
11	Nov	4	(h)	Bristol C	D 2-2	Whittingham 2	25,000
12		11	(a)	Birmingham	W 4-1	Dodd 3, Thomson	25,000
13		18	(h)	Huddersfield T	W 3-1	Whittingham (pen), Thomson 2	5,000
14		25	(a)	Blackpool	L 0-1		12,000
15	Dec	2	(h)	Glossop	W 1-0	Thomson	25,000
16		9	(a)	Hull C	L 0-1		14,000
17		16	(h)	Barnsley	W 2-1	Whittingham, Bridgeman	20,000
18		23	(a)	Bradford	D 1-1	Dodd	20,000
19		25	(a)	Fulham	W 1-0	Whittingham	40,000
20		26	(h)	Fulham	W 1-0	Dodd	41,761
21		30	(a)	Stockport C	W 1-0	Whittingham	7,000
22	Jan	6	(h)	Leeds C	W 4-2	Downing, Bridgeman, Dodd, Thomson	10,000
23		20	(a)	Wolves	L 1-3	Whittingham	9,000
24		27	(h)	Leicester F	W 2-1	Ormiston, Whittingham	27,000
25	Feb	10	(h)	Grimsby T	W 4-1	Whittingham 2 (1 pen), Freeman, Thomson	25,000
26		17	(a)	Nottingham F	W 3-2	Whittingham 3	9,000
27		24	(h)	Burnley	L 0-2		30,000
28	Mar	2	(h)	Clapton O	W 3-0	Whittingham 3	45,000
29		9	(a)	Bristol C	D 1-1	Whittingham	15,000
30		16	(h)	Birmingham	L 0-2		27,000
31		20	(a)	Gainsborough T	W 2-0	Whittingham, Hilsdon	3,000
32		23	(a)	Huddersfield T	W 3-1	Whittingham 2, Woodward	13,000
33	Apr	6	(a)	Glossop	W 2-1	Whittingham (pen), Taylor	4,000
34		8	(a)	Derby C	L 0-2		17,000
35		13	(h)	Hull C	W 1-0	Freeman	35,000
36		22	(h)	Blackpool	W 4-1	Bridgeman 2, Thomson, Taylor	27,000
37		25	(a)	Barnsley	W 2-0	Whittingham, Freeman	7,000
38		27	(h)	Bradford	W 1-0	Freeman	40,000

FINAL LEAGUE POSITION: 2nd in Division Two

Appearances
Goals

FA Cup

1	Jan	13	(h)	Sheffield U	W 1-0	Dodd	34,400
2	Feb	3	(a)	Bradford C	L 0-2		21,070

Aggregate League attendances:
Home: 516,761 (average 27,191)
Away: 270,000 (average 14,210)

Appearances
Goals

Appearances and goals grid (players as columns, matches 1–38 as rows; figures are position numbers):

	Molyneux J	Bettridge W	Cameron J	Warren B	Ormiston A	Downing S	Douglas A	Whittingham R	Hilsdon G	Windridge J	Fairgray N	Brown WY	Whitley J	Woodward VJ	Freeman C	Bridgeman W	Dodd G	Buchanan R	Thomson R	Taylor F	Calderhead D	Hewitt T	Harrow J	Read W	Johnson G	Cartwright W	
1	1	2	3	4	5	6	7	8	9	10	11																1
2	1	2	3	4	5	6	7		9	10	11	8															2
3		2	3	4	5	6	7	8	9		11		1			10											3
4		2	3	4	5	6	7		9		11		1	8		10											4
5		2	3	4	5	6	7		9		11		1	8		10											5
6		2	3	4	5	6	7	8			11		1	9		10											6
7		2	3	4	5	6	7		9				1	8	11	10											7
8		2	3	4	5	6	7	8					1	9	11	10											8
9			3	4	5	6	7	8					1		11	10	2	9									9
10			3	4	5	6	7	8					1		11	10	2	9									10
11			3		5	6	7	8					1		11	10	2	9	4								11
12		2	3		5		7	8					1		11	10			9	4	6						12
13		2	3		5	6	7	8					1		11	10			9	4							13
14		2	3		5	6	7	8			11		1			10			9	4							14
15			3		5	6	7	8					1	10			11		9	4	2						15
16			3		5		7	8					1	10			11		9	4	2	6					16
17			3		5		7	8					1		11	10			9	4	2	6					17
18			3		5	6	7	8					1		11	10			9	4	2						18
19			3		5	6	7	8					1		11	10			9	4	2						19
20			3		5	6	7						1	8	11	10			9	4	2						20
21			3		5	6	7	8					1		11	10			9	4	2						21
22			3		5	6	7	8					1		11	10			9	4	2						22
23		2	3		5	6		8					1		11	10			9	4			7				23
24		2	3		5	6		8					1		11	10			9	4			7				24
25		2	3		5	6		8			11		1			10			9	4			7				25
26		2	3		5	6	7	8			11		1			10			9	4							26
27		2	3		5	6	7	8			11		1			10			9	4							27
28	1	2	3		5		7	8	9						10	11				6			4				28
29	1	2	3		5		7	8	9						10	11				6			4				29
30			3		5	6	7	8					1		10	11			2	4					9		30
31	1	2	3		5		7	8	9						10	11				6			4				31
32	1	2	3			6	7	8	9						10	11				5			4				32
33	1	2	3		5		7	8	9							10				6			4				33
34	1	2	3		5	6	7	8	9							11	10						4				34
35	1	2	3		5		7	8								10	11		9	6			4				35
36	1	2	3		5		7									8	10	11	9	6			4				36
37	1	2			5	6	7	8								9	10	11		4				3			37
38	1	2			5		7	8								9	10	11		6			4		3		38
Apps	12	26	36	10	37	28	35	32	10	2	10	3	26	14	15	26	18	3	21	27	1	8	12	3	2	1	
Goals				1	1	2	26	1					1		2	7	6	8		7	2						

	Molyneux J	Bettridge W	Cameron J	Warren B	Ormiston A	Downing S	Douglas A	Whittingham R	Hilsdon G	Windridge J	Fairgray N	Brown WY	Whitley J	Woodward VJ	Freeman C	Bridgeman W	Dodd G	Buchanan R	Thomson R	Taylor F	Calderhead D	Hewitt T	Harrow J	Read W	Johnson G	Cartwright W	
1		2	3			6	7	8					1			11	10		9	5			4				1
2		2	3		5	6		8					1			11	10		9	4			7				2
		2	2		1	2	1	2					2			2	2		2	2			1	1			
																		1									

209

1912-13

Manager: David Calderhead

1	Sep	2	(a)	Aston Villa	L 0-1		28,000
2		7	(a)	Bolton W	L 0-1		21,666
3		9	(h)	Liverpool	L 1-2	Ford	25,000
4		14	(h)	Sheffield U	W 4-2	Turnbull, Woodward 3	40,000
5		21	(a)	Newcastle U	L 2-3	Fairgray 2	25,000
6		28	(h)	Oldham A	D 1-1	Turnbull	30,000
7	Oct	5	(h)	Sunderland	W 2-0	Turnbull, Whittingham	25,000
8		12	(a)	W Arsenal	W 1-0	Bridgeman	22,000
9		19	(h)	Bradford C	L 0-3		40,000
10		26	(a)	Manchester C	L 0-2		40,000
11	Nov	2	(h)	West Brom A	L 0-2		40,000
12		9	(a)	Everton	L 0-1		20,000
13		16	(h)	Sheffield W	L 0-4		27,000
14		23	(a)	Blackburn R	D 1-1	Woodward	15,000
15		30	(h)	Derby C	W 3-1	Woodward, Bridgeman, Whittingham	30,000
16	Dec	7	(a)	Tottenham H	L 0-1		36,771
17		14	(h)	Middlesbrough	L 2-3	Thomson, Whittingham	35,000
18		21	(a)	Notts C	D 0-0		10,000
19		25	(h)	Manchester U	L 1-4	Douglas	30,000
20		26	(a)	Manchester U	L 2-4	Ford, J.A.Brown	25,000
21		28	(h)	Bolton W	L 2-3	Woodward, W.Y.Brown	35,000
22	Jan	4	(a)	Sheffield U	D 3-3	Woodward, Whittingham 2	7,000
23		18	(h)	Newcastle U	W 1-0	Turnbull	50,000
24		25	(a)	Oldham A	L 2-3	Turnbull 2	18,000
25	Feb	8	(a)	Sunderland	L 0-4		12,000
26		15	(h)	W Arsenal	D 1-1	Ford	20,000
27		22	(a)	Bradford C	D 2-2	Woodward, Whittingham (pen)	10,000
28	Mar	1	(h)	Manchester C	W 2-1	Turnbull, Hunter	35,000
29		8	(a)	West Brom A	W 1-0	J.A.Brown	15,000
30		15	(h)	Everton	L 1-3	Steer	45,000
31		21	(h)	Aston Villa	L 1-2	Downing	65,000
32		22	(a)	Sheffield W	L 2-3	Whittingham, J.A.Brown	8,000
33		24	(a)	Liverpool	W 2-1	J.A.Brown, Freeman	15,000
34		29	(h)	Blackburn R	L 1-6	Woodward	30,000
35	Apr	5	(a)	Derby C	L 1-3	Freeman	10,000
36		12	(h)	Tottenham H	W 1-0	Ford	50,000
37		19	(a)	Middlesbrough	W 3-0	Woodward, Ford 2	8,000
38		26	(h)	Notts C	W 5-2	Turnbull, Ford 3, Freeman	20,000

FINAL LEAGUE POSITION: 18th in Division One

Appearances
Goals

FA Cup

1	Jan	11	(h)	Southend U	W 5-2	Woodward, Whittingham 4 (2 pens)	14,569
2	Feb	1	(h)	Sheffield W	D 1-1	Whittingham	33,606
R		5	(a)	Sheffield W	L 0-6		35,860

Aggregate League attendances:
Home: 672,000 (average 35,368)
Away: 346,437 (average 18,233)

Appearances
Goals

Brebner RG	Bettridge W	Cameron J	Harrow J	Ormiston A	Downing S	Douglas A	Turnbull J	Thomson R	Woodward VJ	Bridgeman W	Ford H	Dodd G	Fairgray N	Taylor F	Molyneux R	Whittingham R	Brown WY	Johnson G	Calderhead D	Sharp J	Steer W	Cartwright W	Brown JA	Harwood J	Freeman C	Hunter G	Whitley J	#
1	2	3	4	5	6	7	8	9	10	11																		1
1	2	3	4	5	6	7		9			8	10	11															2
1	2	3	4	5	6	7		9			8	10	11															3
1	2	3		5	6	7		9	8			10	11	4														4
1	2	3		5	6	7		9	8				11	4														5
1	2	3		5	6	7		9	10		8		11	4														6
	2	3		5	6	7	9			11		10		4	1	8												7
1	2	3		5	6	7		9	11			10		4		8												8
1	2	3		5	6	7			11			10		4		8	9											9
1	2	3		5	6	7		9	11			10		4		8												10
1	2	3		5	6	7		9	11			10		4		8												11
1	2				6	7		9		11	8	10		4					3	5								12
1	2				6	7		9	10	11	8			4					3	5								13
	2				6			9	10	11	7			4	1	8			5	3								14
	2		4					9	10	11	7			6	1	8			5	3								15
	2		4					9	10	11	7			6	1	8			5	3								16
	2		4	6				9	10	11	7				1	8			5	3								17
1	2				6		10	9	11	7				4					5	3	8							18
1	2			5	6	7		10	11	9				4						3	8							19
1				5	6			9		7	10			4		8				3		2	11					20
1	2			5	6				9		7		11	4		8	10			3								21
1		3						9	11	7				4		8	10		5	2				6				22
		3			6			9	10	11	7			4	1	8			5	2								23
		3			6			9	10		7		11	4	1	8			5	2								24
	2	3				7	9			11				4	1	8	10		5					6				25
	2							9	10	11	7			4	1	8			5	3				6				26
	2							9	10		7		11	4	1	8			5	3				6				27
	2	3							9		7			4	1	8	11		5						10	6		28
	2								10		7			4	1				5	3	9		11		8	6		29
	2								10		7			4	1				5	3	9		11		8	6		30
	2				6				9		7			4	1	8				3			11		10	5		31
	2				6				9		7			4	1	8				3			11		10	5		32
	2				6				9		7			4		8				3			11		10	5	1	33
	2				6		9		8		7			4						3			11		10	5	1	34
	2				6		9		8		7			4						3			11		10	5	1	35
	2	5					9		8		7			4	1					3			11		10	6		36
	2			5	6		9		8		7				1					3			11		10	4		37
				5	6		9		8		7				1					3		2	11		10	4		38
17	**33**	**16**	**6**	**20**	**25**	**16**	**19**	**10**	**27**	**17**	**29**	**11**	**9**	**32**	**18**	**20**	**6**	**2**	**16**	**23**	**4**	**2**	**11**	**4**	**11**	**11**	**3**	
				1	1		8	1	10	2	9		2	7	1	1							4		3	1		

Brebner RG	Bettridge W	Cameron J	Harrow J	Ormiston A	Downing S	Douglas A	Turnbull J	Thomson R	Woodward VJ	Bridgeman W	Ford H	Dodd G	Fairgray N	Taylor F	Molyneux R	Whittingham R	Brown WY	Johnson G	Calderhead D	Sharp J	Steer W	Cartwright W	Brown JA	Harwood J	Freeman C	Hunter G	Whitley J	#
1	2			5				9	11	7				4		8	10		6	3								1
	2			5				9	10		7		11	4	1	8			6	3								2
	2			5				9	10		7		11	4	1	8		3	6									R
1	1	2		3			2		3	1	3		2	3	2	3	1	1	3	2								
					1														5									

1913-14

Manager: David Calderhead

1	Sep	6	(h)	Tottenham H	L 1-3	Halse	61,500
2		8	(h)	West Brom A	D 1-1	Halse	5,000
3		13	(a)	Oldham A	L 2-3	Whittingham, Walker	20,000
4		20	(h)	Manchester U	L 0-2		40,000
5		27	(a)	Burnley	L 1-6	Whittingham (pen)	30,000
6	Oct	4	(h)	Preston NE	W 2-0	Halse 2	30,000
7		11	(a)	Newcastle U	L 0-1		18,000
8		18	(h)	Liverpool	W 3-0	Ford, Halse, Bridgeman	40,000
9		25	(a)	Aston Villa	W 2-1	Ford, Halse	36,000
10	Nov	1	(h)	Middlesbrough	W 3-2	Calderhead, Whittingham, Bridgeman	40,000
11		8	(a)	Sheffield U	L 2-3	Hunter, Ford	14,000
12		15	(h)	Derby C	W 2-1	Whittingham, Freeman	28,000
13		22	(a)	Manchester C	L 1-2	Whittingham	20,000
14		29	(h)	Bradford C	W 2-1	Woodward 2	45,000
15	Dec	6	(a)	Blackburn R	L 1-3	Whittingham (pen)	10,000
16		13	(h)	Sunderland	D 1-1	Halse	30,000
17		20	(a)	Everton	D 0-0		20,000
18		25	(h)	Sheffield W	W 2-1	Woodward, Walker	40,000
19		26	(a)	Sheffield W	L 0-3		30,000
20		27	(a)	Tottenham H	W 2-1	Ford, Woodward	29,305
21	Jan	3	(h)	Oldham A	W 2-1	Ford, Halse	30,000
22		17	(a)	Manchester U	W 1-0	Freeman	20,000
23		24	(h)	Burnley	D 0-0		35,000
24	Feb	7	(a)	Preston NE	D 3-3	Logan (pen), Ford, Thomson	25,000
25		10	(a)	Bolton W	D 1-1	Halse	10,000
26		14	(h)	Newcastle U	L 0-1		40,000
27		28	(h)	Aston Villa	L 0-3		58,000
28	Mar	7	(a)	Middlesbrough	L 0-2		14,000
29		14	(h)	Sheffield U	W 2-0	Logan, Freeman	19,000
30		18	(a)	Liverpool	L 0-3		20,000
31		21	(h)	Derby C	W 1-0	Ford	10,000
32		28	(h)	Manchester C	W 1-0	Ford	25,000
33	Apr	4	(a)	Bradford C	D 0-0		10,000
34		11	(h)	Blackburn R	W 2-0	Ford, Freeman	50,000
35		13	(h)	Bolton W	W 2-1	Halse, Freeman	40,000
36		14	(a)	West Brom A	L 1-3	Taylor	20,000
37		18	(a)	Sunderland	L 0-2		15,000
38		25	(h)	Everton	W 2-0	Brittan 2	30,000

FINAL LEAGUE POSITION: 8th in Division One

Appearances
Goals

FA Cup

1	Jan	10	(a)	Millwall	D 0-0		24,500
R		14	(h)	Millwall	L 0-1		35,800

Appearances
Goals

Aggregate League attendances:
Home: 686,500 (average 36,131)
Away: 371,305 (average 19,542)

Football appearance/lineup grid (positions by player and match).

	Molyneux J	Whitley J	Bettridge W	Marshall O	Sharp J	Harrow J	Taylor F	Logan T	Ormiston A	Calderhead D	Hunter G	Ford H	Halse HJ	Whittingham R	Thomson R	Turnbull J	Woodward VJ	Freeman C	Bridgeman W	Downing S	Fairgray N	Middelboe N	Walker A	Brown JA	Woosnam M	Brittan H	Hampton C	Lake G	McFarlane A	
	1		2		3		4	5				7	8	9			10		6			11								1
	1			2	3		4	5			6	7	8	9			10					11								2
	1			2	3		4					6	7	8	5		9		11							10				3
	1		2		3		4	5				6	7	8			9		11							10				4
	1				3		4	5	6			7	2		9	8			11							10				5
	1		2		3		4	5			6	7	8	9			10	11												6
	1		2		3		4	5			6	7	8	9			10	11												7
	1		2		3		4	5				7	8	9			10	11	6											8
	1			2	3		4	6		5		7	8	9			10	11												9
	1			2	3		4	6		5		7	8	9			10	11												10
	1			2	3		4	5			6	7	8	9			10		11											11
	1			2	3		4				6	7	8	9			10		11	5										12
	1			2	3		4	5				7	8	9			10	11	6											13
	1			2	3			5				6	7	8	9		10	11	4											14
	1		2		3		4	5			6	7	8	9			10	11												15
	1		2		3			5			6	7	8	9			10	11	4											16
	1			3	2		4	5				6	7		8		10	11					9							17
	1			3	2		4	5				6	7		9		10	11					8							18
	1			3	2		4	6		5	8	7		9			10	11												19
	1		2		3			5			6	7		9			8	10			11	4								20
	1		2		3		4		5	6	7	8					9	10	11											21
	1		2			3	4	5		6	7	8					9	10				11								22
	1		2			3	4	5		6	7	8					9	10	11											23
	1		2		3		4	5	6		7	8	9				10	11												24
	1		2		3		4	5	7		6	8	9				10	11												25
	1		2			3	4	5	6		7	8	10	9				11												26
	1		2		3			5		6	7		8	9	4	10	11													27
	1		2			3	4	5	6		7	8		9	10	11														28
	1			2	3		4	5	6		7	8		9	10	11														29
	1			2	3		4	5		6	7			8	9	10	11													30
		1		2	3		4	5			7			9	8	10	11							6						31
		1		2	3		4	5				7	8		9	10	11							6						32
		1		2	3		4		5				7	8	9	10	11	6												33
	1			2	3		4	5				7	8		9	10	11							6						34
	1			2	3		4	5				7	8		9	10	11	6												35
	1		2				3	4	5			7	8	9			10	11									6			36
	1		2				3	4	5	6		7	8	9				11							10					37
			2				3	4	5			7	8		9			11				6			10	1				38
	34	3	16	18	21	20	31	35	8	7	19	37	30	20	9	1	27	21	29	4	6	6	3	3	3	2	1	1	3	
									1	2			1	1	9	10	6	1			4	5	2			2			2	

	Molyneux J	Whitley J	Bettridge W	Marshall O	Sharp J	Harrow J	Taylor F	Logan T	Ormiston A	Calderhead D	Hunter G	Ford H	Halse HJ	Whittingham R	Thomson R	Turnbull J	Woodward VJ	Freeman C	Bridgeman W	Downing S	Fairgray N	Middelboe N	Walker A	Brown JA	Woosnam M	Brittan H	Hampton C	Lake G	McFarlane A	
	1		2	3		4		5			6	7	8				9	10	11											1
	1			2	3	4		5	6		7	8					9	10		11										R
	2		1	2		2	1	1	1		2	2	2				2	2	1			1								

213

1914-15

Manager: David Calderhead

1	Sep	5	(a)	Tottenham H	D	1-1	McNeil	26,000
2		9	(a)	Bradford C	D	2-2	Halse, Croal	14,000
3		12	(h)	Newcastle U	L	0-3		14,000
4		19	(a)	Middlesbrough	L	0-3		12,000
5		26	(h)	Sheffield U	D	1-1	McNeil	25,000
6	Oct	3	(a)	Aston Villa	L	1-2	Abrams	20,000
7		10	(h)	Liverpool	W	3-1	Ford, Thomson, McNeil	20,000
8		17	(a)	Bradford	L	0-3		20,000
9		24	(h)	Oldham A	D	2-2	Abrams 2	20,000
10		31	(a)	Manchester U	D	2-2	Halse 2	15,000
11	Nov	7	(h)	Bolton W	W	2-1	Halse, Thomson	24,000
12		14	(a)	Blackburn R	L	2-3	Halse, Thomson	21,000
13		21	(h)	Notts C	W	4-1	Logan, Abrams (pen), Thomson 2	16,000
14		28	(a)	Sunderland	L	1-2	Abrams	6,000
15	Dec	5	(h)	Sheffield W	D	0-0		15,000
16		12	(a)	West Brom A	L	0-2		7,000
17		19	(a)	Everton	W	2-0	Logan, Freeman	18,000
18		25	(h)	Manchester C	D	0-0		20,000
19		26	(a)	Manchester C	L	1-2	Thomson	26,000
20		28	(h)	Burnley	L	1-4	Ford	20,000
21	Jan	2	(h)	Tottenham H	D	1-1	Freeman	30,000
22		23	(h)	Middlesbrough	D	2-2	Halse, Croal	7,500
23	Feb	6	(h)	Aston Villa	W	3-1	Thomson, Croal, Brown	15,000
24		13	(a)	Liverpool	D	3-3	Halse, Thomson, Croal	20,000
25		27	(a)	Oldham A	D	0-0		6,000
26	Mar	1	(h)	Bradford	L	0-1		19,000
27		8	(a)	Sheffield U	D	1-1	Thomson	14,000
28		17	(a)	Newcastle U	L	0-2		20,000
29		20	(h)	Blackburn R	L	1-3	Thomson	22,000
30	Apr	2	(h)	Bradford C	W	2-0	Logan (pen), Halse	24,000
31		3	(h)	Sunderland	W	3-0	Thomson 2, Woodward	20,000
32		5	(a)	Burnley	L	0-2		10,000
33		10	(a)	Sheffield W	L	2-3	Thomson, Croal	18,000
34		14	(h)	Bolton W	L	1-3	Brittan	10,000
35		17	(h)	West Brom A	W	4-1	Ford, Halse 2, Woodward	25,000
36		19	(h)	Manchester U	L	1-3	Woodward	30,000
37		26	(a)	Everton	D	2-2	Logan (pen), Brittan	30,000
38		28	(a)	Notts C	L	0-2		10,000

FINAL LEAGUE POSITION: 19th in Division One

Appearances
Goals

FA Cup

1	Jan	9	(h)	Swindon T	D	1-1	Thomson	28,000
R		16	(a*)	Swindon T	W	5-2	Ford, Thomson 3, McNeil	18,610
2		30	(h)	W Arsenal	W	1-0	Halse	40,372
3	Feb	20	(a)	Manchester C	W	1-0	Thomson	39,000
4	Mar	6	(h)	Newcastle U	D	1-1†	Thomson	58,760
R		13	(a)	Newcastle U	W	1-0†	Ford	49,827
SF		27	(a‡)	Everton C	W	2-0	Halse, Croal	22,000
F	Apr	24	(a§)	Sheffield U	L	0-3		49,557

*Played at Stamford Bridge by arrangement.   †After extra-time.
‡Played at Villa Park, Birmingham.   §Played at Old Trafford, Manchester.

Appearances
Goals

Aggregate League attendances:
Home: 384,500 (average 20,236)
Away: 305,000 (average 16,052)

Molyneux J	Bettridge W	Sharp J	Marshall O	Taylor F	Logan T	Walker A	Abrams L	Ford H	Halse HJ	Thomson R	Croal J	Woodward VJ	Freeman C	McNeil R	Bridgeman W	Brittan H	Middelboe N	Brown JA	Hampton J	McFarlane A	Tye E	Harrow J	
1	2	3	4	5		6	7	8		10		9		11									1
1	2	3		5	6		8	9	10				7	11								4	2
1	2		4	5		6	7	8	10			9		11								3	3
1	2		5	4	6			9						11	10	8	7					3	4
1		3	4		6	7	8	9						11		10	5					2	5
1		3	4	9	6	7	8							11		10	5					2	6
1	2	3	4	5		7	8	9	10		6			11									7
		3	4	5	6	7	8	9	10					11					1			2	8
1		3	4	5	6	7	8	9	10					11								2	9
1		3	4	5	6	7	8	9	10					11								2	10
1		3	4	5	6	7	8	9	10					11								2	11
1		3	4	5	6	7	8	9	10					11								2	12
1		3		5	6	7	8	9	10					11		2						4	13
1	2	3	5	4	6	7	8	9	10					11									14
1	2	3	4	5	6		8	9	10					11		7							15
1	2	3	4	5	6			9	10				7	11		8							16
1	2	3	4	5	6	7		9	10				8	11									17
1	2	3	4	5	6	7		9	10				8	11									18
1	2	3	5	4	6	7		9	10				8	11									19
1	2		4	5	6	7			10				8	11			9					3	20
1	2		4	5	6	7	8	9	10					11								3	21
1	2	3	4	5	6	7	8	9	10					11									22
1	2		4	5	6	7	8	9	10								11					3	23
1	2		4	5	6	7	8	9	10					11								3	24
1	2		4	5	6	7	8	9	10					11								3	25
1	2		4	5	6	7	8	9	10					11								3	26
1	2		4	5		7	8	9	10					11			6					3	27
1	2		4	5	6	7		9					8	11			10					3	28
1	2	3	4	5	6	7	8	9	10					11									29
1	2		4	5	6	7	8	9	10					11								3	30
1	2		4	5	6	7	8	9	10					11								3	31
1	2		4	5	6			9	10				8	11		7						3	32
1	2	3	4	5	6	7	8	9	10					11									33
1	2	3	4	5	6	7		9					8	11			10						34
1	2	3	4	5	6	7	8	9	10					11									35
1	2	3	4	5	6	7	8	9	10					11									36
1	2		5	4	6	7	8		10					11			9					3	37
1	2			5	6	7	8	9	10					11						4		3	38
37	25	17	11	31	35	12	31	33	27	30	27	6	15	37	1	9	7	2	1	1	1	22	
			4		5	3	10	12	6	3	2	3		2		1							

Molyneux J	Bettridge W	Sharp J	Marshall O	Taylor F	Logan T	Walker A	Abrams L	Ford H	Halse HJ	Thomson R	Croal J	Woodward VJ	Freeman C	McNeil R	Bridgeman W	Brittan H	Middelboe N	Brown JA	Hampton J	McFarlane A	Tye E	Harrow J	
1	2		4	5	6	7	8	9	10					11								3	1
1	2	3	4	5	6	7	8	9	10					11									R
1	2		4	5	6	7	8	9	10					11								3	2
1	2		4	5	6	7	8	9	10					11								3	3
1	2		4	5	6	7	8	9	10					11								3	4
1	2		4	5	6	7	8	9	10					11								3	R
1	2		4	5	6	7	8	9	10					11								3	SF
1	2		4	5	6	7	8	9	10					11								3	F
8	8	1	8	6	5	5	8	8	8	6				2		8						7	
						2	2	6	1					1									

1919-20

Manager: David Calderhead

1	Aug	20	(a)	Everton	W 3-2	Wilding, Halse, Whittingham (pen)	35,000
2	Sep	1	(h)	Sunderland	W 2-0	Wilding, Croal	50,000
3		6	(h)	Everton	L 0-1		60,000
4		10	(a)	Sunderland	L 2-3	Croal, Brittan	35,000
5		13	(h)	Newcastle U	D 0-0		12,000
6		20	(a)	Newcastle U	L 0-3		45,000
7		27	(h)	Burnley	L 0-1		38,000
8	Oct	4	(a)	Burnley	W 3-2	Abrams 2, Croal	25,000
9		11	(h)	Liverpool	W 1-0	Brittan	35,000
10		18	(a)	Liverpool	W 1-0	Brittan	25,000
11		25	(a)	Bradford	L 0-1		18,000
12	Nov	1	(h)	Bradford	W 4-0	Ford, Cock 2, Croal	36,000
13		8	(a)	Preston NE	L 1-3	Cock	20,000
14		15	(h)	Preston NE	W 4-0	Cock 3, McNeil	34,000
15		22	(a)	Middlesbrough	D 0-0		20,000
16		29	(h)	Middlesbrough	W 3-1	Cock 2, Croal	50,000
17	Dec	6	(a)	Arsenal	D 1-1	Cock	50,000
18		13	(h)	Arsenal	W 3-1	Ford, Cock, McNeil	60,000
19		20	(a)	Sheffield U	L 1-3	Halse	25,000
20		25	(a)	Aston Villa	L 2-5	Dale, McNeil	30,000
21		26	(h)	Oldham A	W 1-0	Harrow	40,000
22		27	(h)	Sheffield U	W 1-0	Cock	40,000
23	Jan	1	(a)	Oldham A	L 0-1		12,000
24		3	(a)	Manchester U	W 2-0	Cock 2	25,000
25		17	(h)	Manchester U	W 1-0	Cock	40,000
26		24	(a)	Bradford C	L 1-3	Browning	18,000
27	Feb	4	(h)	Bradford C	W 1-0	Logan	25,000
28		7	(a)	Bolton W	W 2-1	Cock, Croal	20,000
29		14	(h)	Bolton W	L 2-3	Cock 2	45,000
30		28	(h)	Blackburn R	W 2-1	Sharp 2	52,000
31	Mar	11	(a)	Blackburn R	L 1-3	Logan	12,000
32		13	(a)	Notts C	W 1-0	Sharp	15,000
33		17	(h)	Notts C	W 2-0	Wilding, Cock	25,000
34		20	(h)	Sheffield W	D 1-1	Lee	47,000
35	Apr	2	(a)	Aston Villa	W 2-1	Cock, Hardy (og)	70,000
36		3	(h)	Manchester C	W 1-0	Cock	40,000
37		6	(a)	Sheffield W	W 2-0	Halse, Cock	15,000
38		10	(a)	Manchester C	L 0-1		25,000
39		17	(h)	Derby C	D 0-0		40,000
40		24	(a)	Derby C	L 0-5		20,000
41		26	(h)	West Brom A	W 2-0	Harrow (pen), Ford	25,000
42	May	1	(a)	West Brom A	L 0-4		35,000

FINAL LEAGUE POSITION: 3rd in Division One

Appearances
Goals

FA Cup

1	Jan	10	(a)	Bolton W	W 1-0	Cock	35,398
2		31	(h)	Swindon T	W 4-0	Ford, Cock, McNeil 2	67,054
3	Feb	21	(h)	Leicester C	W 3-0	Ford, Cock, Browning	40,000
4	Mar	6	(h)	Bradford	W 4-1	Wilding, Logan, Sharp 2	61,223
SF		27	(n*)	Aston Villa	L 1-3	Croal	37,771

*Played at Bramall Lane, Sheffield.

Appearances
Goals

Aggregate League attendances:
Home: 864,000 (average 41,142)
Away: 525,000 (average 25,000)

Player appearance and goalscoring grid (shirt numbers by match).

Molyneux J	Hampton C	Bettridge W	Harrow J	Dickie W	Wilding H	Logan T	Hale H	Abrams L	Middelboe N	Ford H	Dale G	Whittingham R	Cock J	Croal J	Sharp B	McNeil R	Freeman C	Browning J	Brittan H	Lee J	Gallon J	Marshall O	Walker A	Spottiswood R	Baxter T	#
1		2	3	5	9			4	6			7	8		10	11										1
1		2	3	5	9			4	6			7	8		10	11										2
1			3		9			4	6			7	8		10	11						2	5			3
1		2	3		9		6			4			8		10	11		7	5							4
1		2	3		9		6			4			8		10	11		7	5							5
1		2	3	5	9			4	6			7	8		10	11										6
1		2	3	6	5							7	8		10	11			9				4			7
	1	2	3	6	5			4	11			7	8		10				9							8
	1	2	3	6	5			4	11			7	8		10				9							9
	1	2	3	6	5			4	11			7	8		10				9							10
	1	2	3	6	5			4	11			7	8		10				9							11
	1	2	3	6	5			4	11			7	8	9	10											12
	1	2	3	6	5			4	11			7	8	9	10											13
1		2	3	5	6		8			4	7			9	10	11										14
1		2	3	5	6		4				7		8	9	10	11										15
1		2	3	5	6		8			4	7			9	10	11										16
1		2	3	6	5		8			4	7			9	10	11										17
1		2	3	5	6		8			4	7			9	10	11										18
1		2	3	5	6		4				7		8	9	10	11										19
1		2	3	5	6		4				7		8	9	10	11										20
1		2	3	5			6			4	7		8	9	10	11										21
1		2	3	5			6			4	7		8	9	10	11										22
1		2	3	4	5						7		8	9	10	11			6							23
1		2	3	4	5						7		8	9	10	11			6							24
1		2	3	4	5		6				7			9	10	11			8							25
1		2	3	4	5	9					7				10	11	8		6							26
1		2	3	4	5						7		8	9	10	11			6							27
1			3	4	5						7		8	9	10	11			6			2				28
1			3	4	5		6				7		8	9	10	11						2				29
1			3	4	5		6			11	7		8		10				9			2				30
1		2	3	4	9	5	6				7		8		10	11										31
1		2	3	4	5		6				7		8	9	10	11										32
	1	2	3	4	5		6				7			9	10	11			8							33
1		2	3	4	5		6				7		8	9	10	11										34
1		2	3	4	6	5					7		8	9	10	11										35
1		2	3	4	6	5					7		8	9	10	11										36
1		2	3	4	6	5					7		8	9	10	11										37
1		2	3	4	6	5					7		8	9	10	11										38
	1	2	3	4	5		6				7		8	9	10	11										39
1		2	3	4	9	5	6				7		8		10	11										40
1		2	3	4	5		6				7		8	9	10	11										41
1		2	3	4	6	5					7		8		10	11										42
27	15	41	39	28	35	22	31	13	9	30	36	6	25	32	11	26	2	5	13	4	2	5	3	1	1	
			2	4	1	3	2			3	1	1	21	6	3	3		1	3	1						

1 own-goal

Molyneux J	Hampton C	Bettridge W	Harrow J	Dickie W	Wilding H	Logan T	Hale H	Abrams L	Middelboe N	Ford H	Dale G	Whittingham R	Cock J	Croal J	Sharp B	McNeil R	Freeman C	Browning J	Brittan H	Lee J	Gallon J	Marshall O	Walker A	Spottiswood R	Baxter T	#
1		2	3	5			4				6	7		9	10	11			8							1
1		2	3	5	6		4				7		8	9	10	11										2
1		2	3	4	5		6				7		8	9	10	11										3
1		2	3	4	5	6	8			11		7		9	10											4
1		2	3	4	5		6				7		8	9	10	11										SF
5		5	5	2	4	3	5			2	5	3	5	4	2	3			1						1	
				1	1		2						3	1	2	2			1							

1920-21

Manager: David Calderhead

1	Aug	28	(a)	Derby C	D	0-0		25,000
2	Sep	1	(h)	Bolton W	W	1-0	McNeil	35,000
3		4	(h)	Derby C	D	1-1	Cock	42,000
4		6	(a)	Bolton W	L	1-3	Ferris	40,000
5		11	(a)	Manchester U	L	1-3	Bell	40,000
6		18	(h)	Manchester U	L	1-2	Bell	35,000
7		25	(a)	Burnley	L	0-4		27,000
8	Oct	2	(h)	Burnley	D	1-1	Cock	45,000
9		9	(a)	Tottenham H	L	0-5		50,000
10		16	(h)	Tottenham H	L	0-4		76,000
11		23	(h)	Oldham A	D	1-1	McNeil	38,000
12		30	(a)	Oldham A	W	2-1	Cock, McNeil	20,000
13	Nov	6	(h)	Preston NE	D	1-1	Croal	35,000
14		13	(a)	Preston NE	W	1-0	Ferris	20,000
15		20	(h)	Sheffield U	W	2-1	Wilding, Ford	25,000
16		27	(a)	Sheffield U	W	1-0	Ferris	15,000
17	Dec	4	(h)	Arsenal	L	1-2	Cock	60,000
18		11	(a)	Arsenal	D	1-1	Ferris	50,000
19		18	(h)	Bradford	W	4-1	Ferris 2, Cock, McNeil	40,000
20		25	(h)	Liverpool	D	1-1	Cock	50,000
21		27	(a)	Liverpool	L	1-2	Croal	40,000
22	Jan	1	(a)	Bradford	W	2-0	Ferris, Croal	23,000
23		15	(h)	Manchester C	W	2-1	Cock, McNeil	36,000
24		22	(a)	Manchester C	L	0-1		30,000
25	Feb	5	(h)	Newcastle U	W	2-0	Wilding, Ferris	56,000
26		9	(a)	Newcastle U	L	0-1		50,000
27		12	(h)	West Brom A	W	3-0	Cameron, Thomson, Croal	42,000
28		26	(h)	Everton	L	0-1		44,000
29	Mar	12	(h)	Sunderland	W	3-1	Logan, Cock, Croal	35,000
30		14	(a)	West Brom A	D	1-1	Ford	15,000
31		19	(a)	Sunderland	L	0-1		20,000
32		26	(a)	Bradford C	D	1-1	Ford	28,000
33		28	(a)	Aston Villa	L	0-3		30,000
34		29	(h)	Aston Villa	W	5-1	Harrow (pen), Ford, Cock 2, Croal	25,000
35	Apr	2	(h)	Bradford C	W	3-1	Harrow (pen), Cameron, Thomson	38,500
36		6	(a)	Everton	L	1-5	Cock	25,000
37		9	(a)	Huddersfield T	L	0-2		14,000
38		16	(h)	Huddersfield T	D	1-1	McNeil	37,500
39		23	(a)	Middlesbrough	D	0-0		20,000
40		30	(h)	Middlesbrough	D	1-1	Cock	30,000
41	May	2	(a)	Blackburn R	D	0-0		8,000
42		7	(h)	Blackburn R	L	1-2	Croal	20,000

FINAL LEAGUE POSITION: 18th in Division One

Appearances
Goals

FA Cup

1	Jan	8	(a)	Reading	D	0-0		15,836
R		12	(h)	Reading	D	2-2*	Cock, Croal	34,582
2R		16	(h)	Reading	W	3-1	Wilding, Ferris, Sharp	29,450
2		29	(a)	Swindon T	W	2-0	Cock 2	20,651
3	Feb	19	(a)	Plymouth A	D	0-0		37,749
R		24	(h)	Plymouth A	D	0-0*		59,871
2R		28	(n†)	Plymouth A	W	2-1	Croal, McNeil	26,007
4	Mar	5	(a)	Cardiff C	L	0-1		45,000

*After extra-time.   † Played at Ashton Gate, Bristol.

Appearances
Goals

Aggregate League attendances:
Home: 845,000 (average 40,238)
Away: 625,000 (average 29,761)

Player appearance / shirt-number grid (season match-by-match).

Molyneux J	Hampton C	Bettridge W	Barrett F	Harrow J	Meehan T	Dickie W	Wilding H	Logan T	McKenzie KW	Middelboe N	Cameron D	Ward J	Ford H	Linfoot F	Bell Dr JB	Ferris J	Halse HJ	Cock J	Thomson R	Croal J	Sharp B	Priestley J	McNeil R	Ashford J	Dale G	Ferguson E	Lee J	Langton J	#
1		2	3		5	4			6			7				9		10	8		11								1
1		2	3		5	4		6				7				9		10	8		11								2
1		2	3		5	4					7				6	9		10			11	8							3
1		2	3	4	5	6						7		8				10			11	9							4
1		2	3		9	5	4				8		7	6				10			11								5
1			2	3	4	5		6				8	7			9		10			11								6
1			2	3	9	5	4				8		7	6				10			11								7
	1	2	3		5		4				7				6	9		10			11	8							8
1		2	3		5	4					7				6	9		10			11	8							9
1		2	3	4	8	5			6			7				9		10			11								10
1			2	3	4	5		7				6	9				10			11	8								11
1		2	3	4	5			6				7			9		10			11	8								12
1		2	3	4	5			6				8				9		10			11	7							13
1		2	3	4	5			6	7				8		9		10			11									14
1		2	3	4	5		6					7				8	9		10			11							15
	1	2	3		5		4		6	7				8			9	10					11						16
	1	2	3		5		4		6	7				8	9		10			11								17
	1	2	3		5		4		6	7				8	9		10			11								18
1		2	3	4	5						6		7		8	9		10			11								19
1		2			3	2	5		4			6	7			8	9		10			11							20
1			2	3	4	5					6	7			8		9	10		11									21
1			2	3	4	5				6	7				8	9		10			11								22
1		2	3	4	5			6				7			8	9		10			11								23
1		2	3	4	6	5					7				8	9		10			11								24
1		2	3		5		4	6				7			8	9		10			11								25
1		2	3	10	4	5			6			7			8	9					11								26
1		2	3		5		4	6				7			8	9	10			11									27
1		2	3		5		4			7				6		9	10		8			11							28
1			2	3	4	5		6				7		8	9		10			11									29
	1	2	3	4			5				7				8	6	9	10			11								30
1		2	3	4		5			6	7				8	9		10			11									31
1		2	3	4	5			6	7				8	9	11	10													32
1	2	3		4	5		6				7				8	9		10			11								33
1		2	3	4	5		6				7				9	8	10			11									34
1		2	3	4	5		6	7				8	9	10				11											35
1		2	3	4	5		6	7		8	9	10				11													36
	1	2	3	4	6	5			7	8	9		10				11												37
1		2	3	4	5		6	7		8	9	10				11													38
1			3	4	5		6	7			9	8	10			11	2												39
1			3	4	5		6	7		8	9	10				11	2												40
1			3	4	5		7		8	9	10	11	2				6												41
1				4	5		6	7		9	8	10				11	2	3											42
36	6	28	10	40	19	7	40	15	3	14	13	12	23	13	6	27	8	32	13	33	8	1	39	4	8	1	2	1	
		2			3					2			4			2	8			12	2		7			6				

Molyneux J	Hampton C	Bettridge W	Barrett F	Harrow J	Meehan T	Dickie W	Wilding H	Logan T	McKenzie KW	Middelboe N	Cameron D	Ward J	Ford H	Linfoot F	Bell Dr JB	Ferris J	Halse HJ	Cock J	Thomson R	Croal J	Sharp B	Priestley J	McNeil R	Ashford J	Dale G	Ferguson E	Lee J	Langton J	#
1	.	2	3	4		5						6	7			8		9		10			11						1
1		2	3	4		5						6	7			8		9		10			11						R
1		2		3	6	4	5						7			8		9			10		11						2R
1		2	3		5			4	6			7				8		9		10			11						2
1		2	3		5			4	6			7				8		9	10				11						3
1		2	3	4	5			6				7				8		9	10			11							R
1		2	3	4	5			6	7						9	10	8		11										2R
1		2	3	8	5			4	6	7					9	10			11										4
8		6	2	8	4	3	8			3	5	2	4	4		6		6	2	6			3		8				
		1								1	3		2	1		1													

1921-22

Manager: David Calderhead

1	Aug	27	(a)	Blackburn R	D	1-1	Cock	30,000
2		29	(h)	Birmingham	L	1-2	Cock	30,000
3	Sep	3	(h)	Blackburn R	W	1-0	Cock	48,000
4		5	(a)	Birmingham	L	1-5	Cock	30,000
5		10	(h)	Manchester U	D	0-0		30,000
6		17	(a)	Manchester U	D	0-0		28,000
7		24	(h)	Liverpool	L	0-1		38,000
8	Oct	1	(a)	Liverpool	D	1-1	Hoddinott	40,000
9		8	(h)	Newcastle U	D	1-1	Hoddinott	40,000
10		15	(a)	Newcastle U	L	0-1		40,000
11		22	(a)	Burnley	L	0-5		15,000
12		29	(h)	Burnley	W	4-1	Hoddinott, Croal 2, McNeil	35,000
13	Nov	5	(h)	Sheffield U	L	0-2		30,000
14		12	(a)	Sheffield U	W	2-1	Cock, Croal	20,000
15		19	(h)	Bradford C	W	1-0	Howard Baker (pen)	35,000
16		26	(a)	Bradford C	W	1-0	Bell	15,000
17	Dec	3	(h)	Preston NE	D	0-0		30,000
18		10	(a)	Preston NE	L	0-2		25,000
19		17	(a)	Tottenham H	D	0-0		50,000
20		24	(h)	Tottenham H	L	1-2	Ford	60,000
21		26	(a)	Middlesbrough	W	1-0	Bell	30,000
22		27	(h)	Middlesbrough	D	1-1	Bell	67,000
23		31	(h)	Arsenal	L	0-2		50,000
24	Jan	14	(a)	Arsenal	L	0-1		40,000
25		18	(h)	Bolton W	L	0-3		15,000
26		21	(a)	Bolton W	W	2-0	Cock 2	20,000
27	Feb	4	(a)	Oldham A	W	3-0	S.Smith, Bell, Ford	10,000
28		8	(a)	Cardiff C	L	0-2		25,000
29		11	(h)	Oldham A	W	1-0	Sharp	30,000
30		25	(h)	Cardiff C	W	1-0	Sharp	65,000
31	Mar	4	(a)	West Brom A	D	2-2	Sharp, McNeil	20,000
32		11	(h)	West Brom A	D	1-1	Sharp	30,000
33		18	(h)	Manchester C	D	0-0		40,000
34		25	(a)	Manchester C	D	0-0		25,000
35	Apr	1	(h)	Everton	W	1-0	Ford	30,000
36		8	(a)	Everton	W	3-2	Cock 2, Sharp	30,000
37		10	(h)	Huddersfield T	W	1-0	Cock	18,000
38		14	(h)	Aston Villa	W	1-0	Haywood	60,000
39		15	(h)	Sunderland	W	1-0	Sharp	40,000
40		17	(a)	Aston Villa	W	4-1	Bell, Cock 2, Sharp	20,000
41		22	(a)	Sunderland	W	2-1	Harrow (pen), Cock	10,000
42	May	6	(a)	Huddersfield T	L	0-2		15,000

FINAL LEAGUE POSITION: 9th in Division One

Appearances
Goals

FA Cup

1	Jan	7	(a)	West Brom A	L	2-4	Bell, Ford	32,800

Appearances
Goals

Aggregate League attendances:
Home: 821,000 (average 39,095)
Away: 548,000 (average 26,095)

Player appearance / shirt-number grid (28 players × 42 matches).

Howard Baker B	Hampton C	Molyneux J	Marsh W	Smith GW	Harrow J	Barrett F	Meehan T	Smith S	Wilding H	McKenzie KW	Cameron D	Middelboe N	Bell Dr JB	Linfoot F	Ferris J	Dale G	Ford H	Cock J	Hoddinott F	Croal J	Sharp B	McNeil R	Haywood J	Ashford J	Langton J	Ward J	Finlayson W	
		1		3	2		4		5		6						7		9	8	10	11						1
		1		3	2		4	6	5								7		9	8	10	11						2
		1		3	2		4		5		6						7		9	8	10	11						3
		1		3	2		4		5		6						7		9	8	10	11						4
		1		3	2				5		6						7		9	8	10	11		4				5
		1		3	2		4		5		6						7		9	8	10	11						6
		1		3	2		4		5			6	8				7		9		10	11						7
		1		3	2		4		5			6	8				7		9		10	11						8
		1		3	2		4		5			6	8				7		9		10	11						9
1				3	2		4		5		6		8				7		9		10	11						10
1				3	2		4		5				8				7		9		10	11			6			11
1				3	2		4		5			6					7		9	8	10	11						12
1				3	2		4		5			6					7		9	8	10	11						13
1				3	2		4	6	5								7		9	8	10	11						14
1				3	2		4	6	5								7		9	8	10	11						15
1				3	2		4	6	5								7	8	9		10	11						16
	1			3	2		4	6	5								7	8	9		10	11						17
1				3	2		4		5							8	7		9		10	11			6			18
1					2	3	4	6	5				8				7		9		10	11						19
1					2	3	4	6	5				8				7		9		10	11						20
1					2	3	4		5	6							7	8	9		10	11						21
			1		2	3	4		5	6							7	8	9		10	11						22
1					2	3	4		5	6							7	8	9		10	11						23
1				3	2		4		5						6		7	8	9		10	11						24
1				3	2		4		5		6						7		9		10	11						25
1				3	2		4		5								7		9		10	11		8	6			26
	1			3	2		4	6	5								7	8	9		10	11						27
	1			3	2		4	6	5								7	8	9		10	11						28
1				3	2		4	6	5								7	8	9		10	11						29
1				3	2		4	6	5								7	8	9		10	11						30
1				3	2		4		5							6	7	8	9		10	11						31
1				3	2		4	6	5								7	8	9		10	11						32
1				3	2		4	6	5								7	8	9		10	11						33
1				3	2		4	6	5								7	8	9		10	11						34
1				3	2		4	6	5								7	8	9		10	11						35
1				3	2		4	6	5								7		9	8	10	11						36
	1			3	2		4	6	5								7		9	8	10	11						37
	1			3	2		4		5						6		7		9		10	11	8					38
	1				2		4		5						6		7		9		10	11	8			3		39
	1				2		4		5						6		7		9		10	11	8			3		40
	1			3	2		4		5						6		7		9		10	11	8					41
	1			3	2		4		5						6		7		9		10	11	8					42
23	9	9	1	35	38	9	37	20	29	18	13	5	24	2	6	5	29	31	23	21	21	42	5	2	2	2	1	
1		1					1						5					3	13	3	3	7	2	1				

Howard Baker B	Hampton C	Molyneux J	Marsh W	Smith GW	Harrow J	Barrett F	Meehan T	Smith S	Wilding H	McKenzie KW	Cameron D	Middelboe N	Bell Dr JB	Linfoot F	Ferris J	Dale G	Ford H	Cock J	Hoddinott F	Croal J	Sharp B	McNeil R	Haywood J	Ashford J	Langton J	Ward J	Finlayson W	
1				2	3		4	5	6								7		8		9	10		11				1
1				1	1		1	1	1								1		1		1	1		1				
																	1		1									

1922-23

Manager: David Calderhead

1	Aug	26	(h)	Birmingham	D	1-1	Bell	40,000
2		28	(a)	Stoke	W	2-1	Sharp 2	20,000
3	Sep	2	(a)	Birmingham	W	1-0	Sharp	35,000
4		4	(h)	Stoke	W	3-2	Wilding, Cock, Sharp	20,000
5		9	(h)	Middlesbrough	D	1-1	McNeil	40,000
6		16	(a)	Middlesbrough	L	1-2	Sharp	20,000
7		23	(h)	Oldham A	W	4-0	Ford, Hoddinott, McNeil, Haywood	30,000
8		30	(a)	Oldham A	L	0-2		20,000
9	Oct	7	(h)	Sheffield U	D	0-0		35,000
10		14	(a)	Sheffield U	W	2-0	Ford 2	25,000
11		21	(h)	Sunderland	L	1-3	Meehan (pen)	38,000
12		28	(a)	Sunderland	D	1-1	Sharp	25,000
13	Nov	4	(a)	Preston NE	L	0-2		15,000
14		11	(h)	Preston NE	L	0-1		25,000
15		18	(a)	Burnley	L	0-1		15,000
16		25	(h)	Burnley	L	0-1		25,000
17	Dec	2	(h)	Huddersfield T	D	2-2	Meehan (pen), Sharp	25,000
18		9	(a)	Huddersfield T	L	0-3		15,000
19		16	(h)	Tottenham H	D	0-0		50,000
20		23	(a)	Tottenham H	L	1-3	Armstrong	40,000
21		25	(h)	Nottingham F	D	2-2	Ford, McNeil	35,000
22		26	(a)	Nottingham F	W	4-0	Ford, Armstrong 2, Sharp	20,000
23		30	(h)	Liverpool	D	0-0		40,000
24	Jan	6	(a)	Liverpool	L	0-1		30,000
25		20	(h)	Newcastle U	W	3-0	Ford, Armstrong 2	27,000
26		27	(a)	Newcastle U	D	0-0		20,000
27	Feb	10	(a)	Everton	L	1-3	Sharp	30,000
28		14	(h)	Everton	W	3-1	Ford, Armstrong, Sharp	20,000
29		17	(h)	Arsenal	D	0-0		45,000
30		24	(a)	Arsenal	L	1-3	Ford	40,000
31	Mar	3	(h)	Cardiff C	D	1-1	Bell	32,000
32		10	(a)	Cardiff C	L	1-6	Ford	26,000
33		17	(a)	West Brom A	D	0-0		18,000
34		30	(a)	Aston Villa	L	0-1		30,000
35		31	(a)	Manchester C	L	0-3		30,000
36	Apr	2	(h)	Aston Villa	D	1-1	McNeil	30,000
37		7	(h)	Manchester C	D	1-1	Armstrong	30,000
38		14	(a)	Bolton W	D	1-1	Whitton	15,000
39		21	(h)	Bolton W	W	3-0	Priestley, Wilding, Whitton	20,000
40		25	(h)	West Brom A	D	2-2	Meehan (pen), Wilding	25,000
41		28	(a)	Blackburn R	D	0-0		10,000
42	May	5	(h)	Blackburn R	D	1-1	Ford	12,000

FINAL LEAGUE POSITION: 19th in Division One

Appearances
Goals

FA Cup

1	Jan	13	(h)	Rotherham C	W	1-0	Armstrong	30,500
2	Feb	3	(h)	Southampton	D	0-0		67,105
R		7	(a)	Southampton	L	0-1		15,781

Aggregate League attendances:
Home: 644,000 (average 30,666)
Away: 499,000 (average 23,761)

Appearances
Goals

Hampton C	Howard Baker B	Smith GW	Harrow J	Meehan T	Priestley J	Smith S	Wilding H	Cameron D	Linfoot F	Bell Dr JB	Ford H	Armstrong J	Cock J	Hoddinott F	Sharp B	McNeil R	Haywood J	Frew J	Ferguson E	Thain A	Whitton W	Ashford J	Bennett W	Lee J	
	1	2	3	6		4	5			7			9		10	11	8								1
	1	2	3	6			4	5			8		9		10	11	7								2
	1	2	3	6			4	5			8		9		10	11	7								3
	1	2	3	6			4	5			8		9		10	11	7								4
	1	2	3	6			4	5			8		9		10	11	7								5
	1	2		6			4	5			8			9	10	11	7		3						6
	1	2	3	6			4	5			8			9	10	11	7								7
	1	2	3	6			4	5			8			9		11	7			10					8
	1	2	3	6			4	5		7	8			9		11	10								9
	1	2	3	6			4	5		7	8			9		11	10								10
	1	2		6		4	5			7	8			9		11	10					3			11
	1	2	3	6			4	5		7	8			9	10	11									12
	1	2	3	6			4	5		7	8			9	10	11									13
1		2	3	6			4	5		7	8		9		10	11									14
	1	2	3	6			4		7				9		10	11				8			5		15
	1	2	3	6			4	5	7				9		10	11				8					16
	1	2	3	6			4	5	7				9		10	11				8					17
	1	2	3	6			4	5	7				9		10	11	8								18
1		2	3	6			4	5		7	8		9				10							11	19
1		2	3	6			4	5		7	8	9				11	10								20
1		2	3	6			4	5		7	8	9			10	11									21
1		2	3	6	4			5	7		8	9			10	11									22
1		2	3	6	4			5	7		8	9			10	11									23
1		2	3	6	4			5	7		8	9			10	11									24
1		2	3	6	4			5	7		8	9			10	11									25
1		2	3	6	10		4	5	7		8	9				11									26
1		2	3	6	4		9	5		7	8				10	11									27
1		2	3	6	4				7		8	9			10	11		5							28
1		2	3	6	4				7		8	9			10	11		5							29
1		2	3	6	4				7		8	9			10	11		5							30
1		2	3	6	4				7	8					10	11		5		9					31
1		2	3	6			4	5			8				10	11	7			9					32
1		2	3	6	4						7					11	10	5		8	9				33
1		2	3	6	4				7		8	9				11		5	10						34
1		2	3	6	4						8	9				11		5	7	10					35
1		2	3	6	4						8	9				11		5	7	10					36
1		2	3	6	4					7	8	9				11		5	10						37
1		2	3	6	4		8				7					11		5	10		9				38
1		2	3	6	4		10				8					11		5	7		9				39
1		2	3	6	4		10				8					11		5	7		9				40
1		2	3	6	4		10				8					11		5	7		9				41
1		2	3	6	4		10				8					11		5	7		9				42
25	17	42	40	42	20	2	29	25	14	13	36	14	11	8	25	41	16	14	10	9	6	1	1	1	
				3	1		3			2	10	7	1	1	10	4	1				2				

1		2	3	6	4			5	7		8	9			10	11	1
1		2	3	6	10		4	5	7		8	9				11	2
1		2	3	6	4		9	5		7	8				10	11	R
3		3	3	3	3		2	3	2	1	3	2			2	3	
												1					

1923-24

Manager: David Calderhead

1	Aug	25	(a)	Blackburn R	L	0-3	15,000
2		27	(h)	Tottenham H	L	0-1	35,000
3	Sep	1	(h)	Blackburn R	W	2-0 Castle, Thain	31,000
4		3	(a)	Tottenham H	W	1-0 Linfoot	40,000
5		8	(h)	Aston Villa	D	0-0	46,000
6		15	(a)	Aston Villa	D	0-0	20,000
7		22	(h)	Sheffield U	D	1-1 Whitton	26,000
8		29	(a)	Sheffield U	L	0-1	20,000
9	Oct	6	(h)	Cardiff C	L	1-2 Castle	47,000
10		13	(a)	Cardiff C	D	1-1 Finlayson	37,000
11		17	(a)	Sunderland	L	0-2	20,000
12		20	(h)	West Ham U	D	0-0	50,000
13		27	(a)	West Ham U	L	0-2	26,000
14	Nov	3	(h)	Bolton W	D	0-0	26,500
15		10	(a)	Bolton W	L	0-4	20,000
16		17	(a)	Middlesbrough	L	0-2	10,000
17		24	(h)	Middlesbrough	W	2-0 Priestley, Meehan	18,000
18	Dec	1	(a)	Preston NE	D	1-1 Wilson	16,000
19		8	(h)	Preston NE	L	1-2 Miller	36,000
20		15	(a)	Burnley	L	0-2	15,000
21		22	(h)	Burnley	W	3-2 Crawford 2, Miller	17,500
22		25	(a)	Nottingham F	L	0-2	20,000
23		26	(h)	Nottingham F	D	1-1 Wilson	30,000
24		29	(a)	Arsenal	L	0-1	38,000
25	Jan	1	(a)	Liverpool	L	1-3 Wilson	30,000
26		5	(h)	Arsenal	D	0-0	38,000
27		19	(a)	Huddersfield T	W	1-0 Ferguson	25,000
28		26	(h)	Huddersfield T	L	0-1	36,000
29	Feb	9	(h)	Notts C	L	0-6	15,000
30		16	(a)	Everton	L	0-2	25,000
31		23	(h)	Everton	D	1-1 Wilson	30,000
32	Mar	1	(a)	West Brom A	D	2-2 Miller, Brown	18,000
33		5	(a)	Notts C	D	0-0	20,000
34		12	(h)	West Brom A	D	0-0	28,000
35		15	(h)	Birmingham	D	1-1 Wilson (pen)	34,000
36		22	(a)	Birmingham	L	0-1	25,000
37	Apr	5	(a)	Manchester C	L	0-1	20,000
38		12	(a)	Newcastle U	L	1-2 Wilding	15,000
39		18	(h)	Liverpool	W	2-1 Armstrong, Brown	35,000
40		19	(h)	Newcastle U	W	1-0 Armstrong	30,000
41		26	(h)	Sunderland	W	4-1 Wilding, Crawford, Brown 2	24,000
42		30	(h)	Manchester C	W	3-1 Priestley, Wilding 2	40,000

FINAL LEAGUE POSITION: 21st in Division One

Appearances
Goals

FA Cup

1	Jan	12	(h)	Southampton	D	1-1 Wilson	34,586
R		16	(a)	Southampton	L	0-2	18,415

Appearances
Goals

Aggregate League attendances:
Home: 673,000 (average 32,047)
Away: 475,000 (average 22,619)

Football player appearance grid (shirt numbers by match). Player columns left→right; match number at far right.

Hampton C	Marsh W	Smith GW	Harrow J	Priestley J	Wilding H	Meehan T	Cameron D	Castle S	Linfoot F	Ford H	Crawford J	Thain A	Whitton W	Wilson A	Armstrong J	Miller H	Ferguson W	McNeil R	Barrett F	Frew J	Bennett W	Finlayson W	Duffy B	Haywood J	Brown W	Howard Baker B	Bower AG	#
1		2		4		6	7				8		9			10		11	3	5								1
1		2		4	5	6		7			8		9			10		11	3									2
1		2		4	5	6		7			8		9			10		11	3									3
1		2		4	5	6			7		8		9			10		11	3									4
1		2	3	4	5	6		7					9			10	8	11										5
1		2	3	4	5	6		7			8		9			10		11										6
1		2	3	4	5	6		7			8		9			10		11										7
1		2	3		5			7					9			8	10	11			4		6					8
1		2	3	4	5	6		7			8						10	11				9						9
1		2	3	4	5	6	7									8	11	10				9						10
1		2	3	4	5	6	7									8	11	10				9						11
1		2	3	4				7							9	8	11	10	5	6								12
1		2	3	4	5			7							9	8	10	11					6					13
1		2	3	4	6	5	7	8								10		11				9						14
1		2	3	5	4	6	9	7	8							10		11										15
1		2	3	4	5	6		7			8				9	10		11										16
1		2	3	4	5	6		7			8				9	10		11										17
1		2	3	4	5	6			7		8			9		10		11										18
1		2	3	4	5	6		7			8			9		10		11										19
1		2	3	4	5	6		7			8			9		10	11											20
1		2	3	4	5	6		7			8			9		10	11											21
	1	2	3	4	5	6		7			8			9		10	11											22
	1	2	3	4	5	6		7			8			9		10	11											23
	1	2	3	4	5	6		7			8			9			11							10				24
	1	2	3	4	5	6			7					9			10	11				8						25
	1	2	3	4	5	6			7					9			10	11				8						26
	1	2	3	4	5	6		7						9	8	10	11											27
	1	2	3	4	5	6		7						9	8	10	11											28
	1	2	3	4	5	6		7					9			8	10	11										29
1		2	3	4	5								7	9	8	10	6	11										30
	1	2	3	4	5	6			7					9	8	10	11											31
			3	4	5				7					9		10	6	11							8	1	2	32
			3	4	5				7					9		10	6	11							8	1	2	33
			3	4	5				7					9		10	6	11							8	1	2	34
		2	3	4	5	6			7					9		10	11								8	1		35
		2	3	4	5				7					9		10	6	11							8	1		36
		2	3	4	10		6	7						9				11				5			8	1		37
		2	3	4	10		6	7					9					11				5			8	1		38
		2	3	4	10		6	7							9			11				5			8	1		39
		2	3	4	10		6	7						8				11				5			9	1		40
		2	3	4	10		6	7						8				11				5			9	1		41
		2	3	4	10		6	7						8				11				5			9	1		42
22	9	39	38	40	39	26	11	24	5	4	21	6	10	19	13	32	27	29	4	8	4	4	1	2	11	11	3	
		2	4	1		2	1				3	1	1	5	2	3	1					1			4			

Hampton C	Marsh W	Smith GW	Harrow J	Priestley J	Wilding H	Meehan T	Cameron D	Castle S	Linfoot F	Ford H	Crawford J	Thain A	Whitton W	Wilson A	Armstrong J	Miller H	Ferguson W	McNeil R	Barrett F	Frew J	Bennett W	Finlayson W	Duffy B	Haywood J	Brown W	Howard Baker B	Bower AG	#
1		2	3	4	5	6		7						9		8	10	11										1
1		2	3	4	5	6			7					9		8	11	10										R
2	2	2	2	2	2			1	1					2		2	2	2										
														1														

1924-25

Manager: David Calderhead

1	Aug	30	(h)	Coventry C	W 1-0	Brown	35,000
2	Sep	1	(a)	Leicester C	L 0-4		25,000
3		6	(a)	Oldham A	W 5-0	Brown 2, Whitton 3	30,000
4		8	(h)	Leicester C	W 4-0	Whitton 4	32,000
5		13	(h)	Sheffield W	D 0-0		35,000
6		20	(a)	Clapton O	D 0-0		35,000
7		22	(a)	Stoke	L 0-1		8,000
8		27	(h)	Crystal P	D 2-2	Brown 2	42,000
9	Oct	4	(a)	Southampton	D 0-0		15,000
10		11	(h)	Fulham	D 0-0		40,000
11		18	(h)	Stockport C	D 1-1	Priestley	35,000
12		25	(a)	Portsmouth	D 0-0		24,000
13	Nov	1	(h)	Hull C	W 1-0	Crawford	8,500
14		8	(a)	Blackpool	W 2-1	Ferguson, Wilson	12,000
15		15	(h)	Derby C	D 1-1	Wilson	33,000
16		22	(a)	South Shields	D 1-1	Whitton	27,000
17		29	(h)	Bradford C	W 3-0	Whitton, Wilson, McNeil	28,000
18	Dec	6	(a)	Port Vale	D 1-1	Whitton	12,000
19		13	(h)	Middlesbrough	W 2-0	Whitton, Wilson	22,000
20		20	(a)	Barnsley	D 3-3	Whitton, Wilson 2 (1 pen)	11,000
21		25	(h)	Wolves	W 1-0	Miller	30,000
22		26	(a)	Wolves	W 1-0	Plum	33,264
23		27	(a)	Coventry C	W 3-0	Brown, Whitton 2	6,000
24	Jan	1	(a)	Manchester U	L 0-1		28,000
25		3	(h)	Oldham A	W 4-1	Wilson, Miller 3	30,000
26		17	(a)	Sheffield W	L 1-2	Whitton	20,000
27		24	(h)	Clapton O	D 1-1	Wilson	35,000
28	Feb	7	(h)	Southampton	W 1-0	Turnbull	37,000
29		14	(a)	Fulham	W 2-1	Miller, Turnbull	30,000
30		21	(a)	Stockport C	L 0-4		12,000
31		28	(h)	Portsmouth	L 2-3	Brown, McNeil	37,000
32	Mar	7	(a)	Hull C	L 0-1		10,000
33		14	(h)	Blackpool	W 3-0	Ferguson, Wilson, Miller	27,000
34		21	(a)	Derby C	L 0-1		18,000
35	Apr	1	(a)	Crystal P	L 0-1		20,000
36		4	(a)	Bradford C	L 0-2		15,000
37		11	(h)	Port Vale	W 1-0	Whitton	30,000
38		13	(h)	Manchester U	D 0-0		40,000
39		18	(a)	Middlesbrough	D 1-1	Wilding	14,000
40		20	(h)	South Shields	D 1-1	Wilson	24,000
41		25	(h)	Barnsley	L 0-1		20,000
42		27	(h)	Stoke	W 2-1	Turnbull, McNeil	25,000

FINAL LEAGUE POSITION: 5th in Division Two

Appearances
Goals

FA Cup

1	Jan	10	(a)	Birmingham	L 0-2		32,000

Appearances
Goals

Aggregate League attendances:
Home: 645,500 (average 30,714)
Away: 405,264 (average 19,298)

Howard Baker B	McKenna P	Smith GW	Harrow J	Barrett F	Priestley J	Frew J	Wilding H	Plum S	Ferguson W	Cameron D	Crawford J	Brown W	Whitton W	Wilson A	Miller H	Turnbull R	Armstrong J	McNeil R	Sales A	Jenkins R	Thain A	Castle S	Odell L	Ashford J	Rodger G	Duffy B	Morrison W	#
1		2	3	4		10	6	11				9						5	7	8								1
1		3		4	5		6		7	8								11	9	10		2						2
1		2	3	4	5		6	8	7	11		9		10				11										3
1		2	3	4	5		6		7	8		9		10				11										4
1		2	3	4	5		6		7	8		9		10				11										5
1		2	3	4	5		6		7	8		9	10					11										6
1		2	3	4	5		6		7	8		9	10					11										7
1		2	3	4		5	6	11	7	8			9	10														8
1		2	3	4		5	6	11		8			9	10									7					9
1		2	3	4		5	6	11		8			9	10									7					10
1		2	3	4			6						9	10				11	5	7	8							11
1		2	3	8	5	4	6		7				9	10				11										12
1		2	3	4	5		6		7			9	8	10				11										13
	1	2	3	4	5		6		7			9	8	10				11										14
	1	2	3	4	5		6		7			9	8	10				11										15
	1	2	3	4	5		6		7			9	8	10				11										16
1		2	3	4	5	10	6		7				9	8				11										17
1		2	3	4	5		6	10	7				9	8				11										18
1		2	3	4	5		6	10	7				9	8				11										19
1		2		4	5		6		7				9	8	10			11						3				20
	1	2	3	4	5		6		7				9	10	8			11										21
	1	2	3		5	4	6		7				9	8	10			11										22
1		2	3		5	4	6		7			11	9	8	10			11										23
	1	2	3		5	4	6		7				9	10	8			11										24
1		2	3		5	4	6		7				9	8	10			11										25
1		2	3				6			4		8	9	10				11		7					5			26
1		2	3		5		6			4		8	9	10				11				7						27
	1	2	3	4	5		6					8		10		9		11				7						28
1		2	3	4	5		6					8		10		9		11				7						29
1		2	3	4	5		6					8		10		9		11				7						30
	1	2	3	4	5		6					8		10		9		11				7						31
1		2	3	4	5		6	11				8		10		9						7						32
1		2	3	4					7		6	8		10		9		11							5			33
	1	2	3	4					7		6	8		10		9		11							5			34
1		2	3	4					7		6	8		10			9	11							5			35
1			3						7		6	8		10		9		11	4			2			5			36
	1	2	3	4			6		7				9	8	10			11							5			37
	1	2	3	4			6		7				9	8	10			11							5			38
	1	2	3	4			9		6		7	8		10				11							5			39
	1	2	3	4			6		7			8		10				11							5	9		40
1		2	3	4			6		7	8			9	10				11							5			41
1		2	3			5			7		10	8		9				11	6						4			42
28	14	40	34	7	35	18	17	17	30	11	26	18	22	36	30	9	1	35	5	4	2	8	2	1	10	1	1	
			1		1	1	2	1	1			7	16	10	6	3		3										

Howard Baker B	McKenna P	Smith GW	Harrow J	Barrett F	Priestley J	Frew J	Wilding H	Plum S	Ferguson W	Cameron D	Crawford J	Brown W	Whitton W	Wilson A	Miller H	Turnbull R	Armstrong J	McNeil R	Sales A	Jenkins R	Thain A	Castle S	Odell L	Ashford J	Rodger G	Duffy B	Morrison W	#
1		2	3		5	4	6		7				9	8	10			11										1
1		1	1		1	1	1		1				1	1	1			1										1

227

1925-26

Manager: David Calderhead

1	Aug	29	(h)	Bradford C	W	2-0	Thain, Turnbull	31,443
2		31	(a)	Nottingham F	W	5-1	Turnbull 2, Wilson 2, Stone	9,981
3	Sep	5	(a)	Port Vale	W	6-0	Crawford, Thain, Turnbull 2, Wilson, Stone	12,801
4		7	(h)	Nottingham F	D	0-0		22,352
5		12	(h)	Barnsley	W	3-2	Turnbull 3	35,161
6		19	(a)	Clapton O	W	2-1	Turnbull 2	15,538
7		26	(h)	Fulham	W	4-0	Crawford, Thain, Wilson, Bagge (og)	49,379
8	Oct	3	(h)	Hull C	W	4-0	Priestley, Thain, Turnbull, Wilson (pen)	47,428
9		10	(a)	Darlington	D	1-1	Turnbull	16,897
10		17	(a)	South Shields	D	0-0		11,805
11		24	(h)	Preston NE	W	5-0	Thain 2, Turnbull 2, Wilson	40,539
12		31	(a)	Oldham A	D	1-1	Thain	15,531
13	Nov	7	(h)	Stockport C	W	3-2	Turnbull 3	29,139
14		14	(a)	Wolves	D	0-0		17,185
15		21	(h)	Swansea T	L	1-3	Wilding	43,827
16		28	(a)	Sheffield W	L	1-4	Miller	23,827
17	Dec	5	(h)	Stoke C	D	1-1	Thain	23,382
18		12	(a)	Middlesbrough	W	2-1	Barrett, Turnbull	14,395
19		19	(h)	Portsmouth	D	0-0		29,010
20		25	(a)	Blackpool	D	0-0		13,690
21		26	(h)	Blackpool	L	2-3	Thain, Turnbull	49,707
22		28	(h)	Derby C	L	2-4	Barrett, Thain	25,108
23	Jan	2	(a)	Bradford C	L	2-4	Priestley, Turnbull	14,702
24		16	(h)	Port Vale	W	3-1	Thain, Turnbull, McNeil	15,568
25		23	(a)	Barnsley	W	3-2	Crawford, Thain, McNeil	7,031
26	Feb	6	(a)	Fulham	W	3-0	Barrett (pen), Priestley, Thain	42,611
27		10	(h)	Clapton O	L	1-3	McNeil	14,000
28		13	(a)	Hull C	W	1-0	Thain	9,464
29		20	(h)	Darlington	W	5-2	Barrett 2, Priestley, Wilson, Wilding	34,442
30		27	(h)	South Shields	D	0-0		38,242
31	May	6	(a)	Preston NE	L	1-3	Miller	16,463
32		13	(h)	Oldham A	W	3-0	Turnbull 2, McNeil	28,889
33		20	(a)	Stockport C	D	0-0		7,828
34		27	(h)	Wolves	D	3-3	Brown, Turnbull 2	26,889
35	Apr	2	(h)	Southampton	D	0-0		43,391
36		3	(a)	Swansea T	D	0-0		20,993
37		5	(a)	Southampton	W	1-0	Turnbull	14,408
38		10	(h)	Sheffield W	D	0-0		41,817
39		17	(a)	Stoke C	W	3-1	Turnbull 2, McNeil	10,268
40		24	(h)	Middlesbrough	L	0-1		25,552
41		26	(h)	Derby C	W	2-1	Thain, Turnbull	9,335
42	May	1	(a)	Portsmouth	L	0-4		17,235

FINAL LEAGUE POSITION: 3rd in Division Two

Appearances
Goals

FA Cup

3	Jan	9	(a)	Plymouth A	W	2-1	Turnbull, McNeil	31,025
4		30	(a)	Crystal P	L	1-2	Thain	‡41,000

‡Record attendance for Selhurst Park.

Appearances
Goals

Aggregate League attendances:
Home: 679,492 (average 32,356)
Away: 337,761 (average 16,083)

This page is a player appearances/line-up grid. The columns are players (listed as vertical headings) and each numbered row (1–42 at the right) is a match, with the figures showing the shirt number worn by each player. The two rows at the foot of the main grid are total appearances and total goals; a separate block of rows below gives two further matches (3 and 4).

McKenna P	Howard Baker B	Smith GW	Barrett F	Harrow J	Priestley J	Plum S	Rodger G	Frew J	Ferguson W	Crawford J	Thain A	Miller H	Brown W	Turnbull R	Wilson A	Armstrong J	Wilding H	McNeil R	Stone G	Bower AG	Duffy B	Odell L	Pearson G	#
	1	2		4	5		6		7	8				9	10			11		3				1
	1	2	3	4	5		6		7	8				9	10			11						2
	1	2		4	5		6		7	8				9	10			11		3				3
	1	2	3	4	5		6		7	8				9	10			11						4
	1	2		4	5		6		7	8				9	10			11		3				5
	1	2		4	5		6		7	8				9	10			11		3				6
	1	2	3	4	5		6		7	8				9	10			11						7
	1	2	3	4	5		6		7	8				9	10			11						8
	1	2		4	5		6		7	8				9	10			11		3				9
	1		3	4	5		6		7	8				9	10			11		2				10
1		2	3	4	5		6		7	8				9	10			11						11
1		2	3	4			6		7	8	10			9			5	11						12
1		2	3	4			6		7	8				9	10		5	11						13
1		2	3	4			6		7	8				9	10		5	11						14
1		2	3	4			6		7	8				9	10		5	11						15
1		2	3	4			6		7		10	9	8				5	11						16
1		2	3	4	5		6		7	8				9	10			11						17
1		2	3	4	5		6		7	8				9	10				11					18
1		2	3	4	5		6		7	8				9	10				11					19
1		2	3	4	5		6		7	8				9	10				11					20
1		2	3	4	5		6			8				9	10	7			11					21
1			3		5		6			8	4				10		7	11	9	2				22
1		2	3	4	5		6			8				9			7	10	11					23
1		2	3	4	5		6		7	8				9				10	11					24
1		2	3	4	5		6		7	8				9				10	11					25
1		2	3	4	5				7	8		10	9					6	11					26
1		2	3	4	5				7	8	6			9				10	11					27
1		2	3	4					7	8	6			9			5	10	11					28
1		2	3	4	5				7	8	6				10			9	11					29
1		2	3	4	5				7	8		10		9			5		11					30
1		2	3	4	5				7	8		10		9				6	11					31
1		2	3	4		6			7		10	8		9			5		11					32
1		2	3	4	5	6			7		10	8		9					11					33
1		2	3	4		6			7		10	8		9			5		11					34
1		2	3	4		6			7		10	8		9			5		11					35
1		2	3	4	5	6				8		10		9					11			7		36
1		2	3	4	5	6					10	8		9					11	7				37
1		2	3	4	5	6			7		10	8		9					11					38
1		2	3	4		6			7		10	8		9			5		11					39
1		2	3	4	5	6					10	8		9					11				7	40
1		2	3	4	5		6		7	8		10		9					11					41
1		2	3	4	5		6		7	8		10		9					11					42
29	13	34	28	15	39	9	32	2	27	36	32	20	12	36	23	1	19	24	22	6	1	1	1	
		5		4						3	15	2	1	29	7			2	5	2				

1 own-goal

McKenna P	Howard Baker B	Smith GW	Barrett F	Harrow J	Priestley J	Plum S	Rodger G	Frew J	Ferguson W	Crawford J	Thain A	Miller H	Brown W	Turnbull R	Wilson A	Armstrong J	Wilding H	McNeil R	Stone G	Bower AG	Duffy B	Odell L	Pearson G	#
1		2	3	4	5		6		7					8	9			10	11					3
1		2	3	4	5		6		7	8				9				10	11					4
2		2	2	2	2		2		2	1		1		2				2	2					
											1			1					1					

1926-27

Manager: David Calderhead

1	Aug	28	(h)	Middlesbrough	W	3-0	Thain, Miller, McNeil	29,849
2		30	(a)	Wolves	W	3-0	Miller, Turnbull, Brown	16,874
3	Sep	4	(a)	Port Vale	D	0-0		14,720
4		6	(h)	Notts C	W	2-0	Turnbull 2	15,572
5		11	(h)	Southampton	L	2-3	Barrett (pen), Turnbull	30,298
6		13	(a)	Notts C	L	0-5		9,094
7		18	(a)	Bradford C	W	1-0	Thain	16,350
8		25	(h)	Fulham	D	2-2	Turnbull, Pearson	46,084
9	Oct	2	(h)	Preston NE	W	2-1	Thain 2	32,398
10		9	(a)	South Shields	L	1-5	Priestley	3,705
11		16	(a)	Portsmouth	W	3-2	Miller, Turnbull 2	17,689
12		23	(h)	Oldham A	W	1-0	Turnbull	25,232
13		30	(a)	Grimsby T	D	0-0		12,423
14	Nov	6	(h)	Blackpool	D	1-1	Wilson	25,366
15		13	(a)	Reading	L	1-2	Thain	11,589
16		20	(h)	Swansea T	D	2-2	Brown 2	18,140
17		27	(a)	Nottingham F	L	1-4	Pearson	12,841
18	Dec	4	(h)	Barnsley	W	4-2	Thain, Brown 3	21,904
19		11	(a)	Manchester C	L	0-1		26,868
20		18	(h)	Darlington	D	2-2	Priestley, Crawford	19,953
21		25	(h)	Hull C	W	1-0	Thain	34,306
22		27	(a)	Hull C	W	1-0	Brown	23,440
23	Jan	1	(h)	Clapton O	W	2-1	Priestley 2 (2 pens)	28,279
24		15	(a)	Middlesbrough	D	0-0		23,964
25	Feb	5	(h)	Bradford C	W	5-2	Priestley 2, Thain 2, Pearson	25,835
26		12	(a)	Fulham	W	2-1	Turnbull, Wilson	31,501
27		26	(h)	South Shields	W	4-1	Thain 2, Turnbull 2	31,191
28	Mar	12	(a)	Oldham A	W	2-1	Turnbull, Wilson (pen)	12,298
29		16	(h)	Port Vale	W	2-0	Thain 2	18,169
30		19	(h)	Grimsby T	W	2-0	Turnbull 2	35,239
31		21	(a)	Preston NE	W	2-0	Wilding, Ferguson	14,995
32		26	(h)	Blackpool	L	1-3	Thain	8,251
33	Apr	2	(h)	Reading	D	0-0		35,424
34		4	(a)	Southampton	D	1-1	Turnbull	5,638
35		9	(a)	Swansea T	L	1-2	Crawford	10,435
36		16	(h)	Nottingham F	W	2-0	Turnbull 2	44,855
37		18	(h)	Wolves	W	1-0	Ferguson	28,945
38		23	(a)	Barnsley	L	0-3		9,641
39		28	(a)	Clapton O	L	0-3		25,329
40		30	(h)	Manchester C	D	0-0		39,995
41	May	4	(h)	Portsmouth	D	0-0		40,037
42		7	(a)	Darlington	D	2-2	Ferguson, Crawford	12,937

FINAL LEAGUE POSITION: 4th in Division Two

Appearances
Goals

FA Cup

3	Jan	8	(h)	Luton T	W	4-0	Thain 2, Turnbull 2	41,441
4		29	(h)	Accrington S	W	7-2	Thain 2, Turnbull 3, Wilson 2	30,142
5	Feb	19	(h)	Burnley	W	2-1	Wilding, Thain	63,238
6	Mar	5	(h)	Cardiff C	D	0-0		70,184
R		9	(a)	Cardiff C	L	2-3	Priestley, Turnbull	47,353

Appearances
Goals

Aggregate League attendances:
Home: 627,071 (average 29,860)
Away: 320,582 (average 15,265)

Millington S	McKenna P	Smith GW	Law T	Barrett F	Priestley J	Rodger G	Townrow J	Wilding H	Ferguson W	Crawford J	Thain A	Miller H	Turnbull R	Wilson A	McNeil R	Brown W	Pearson G	Stone G	Sales A	
	1	2	3	4	5			6	7	8	10	9		11						1
	1	2	3	4	5			6	7		10	9			8	11				2
	1	2	3	4	5			6	7	8	10	9		11						3
	1	2	3	4	5			6	7	8	10	9		11						4
	1	2	3	4	5			6	8		10	9				11	7			5
	1	2	3	4	5			6	8		10	9				11	7			6
	1	2	3	4			5	6	8		10	9				11	7			7
	1	2	3	4	5			6	7	8	10	9				11				8
1		2	3		4	5		6	7	8	10	9				11				9
	1	2	3		4	5		6	7	8	10	9				11				10
1		2	3		4	5		6	7	8	10	9				11				11
1		2	3		4	5		6	7	8	10	9				11				12
1		2	3		4	5		6	7	8	10	9				11				13
1		2	3		4	5		6	7	8	10			9		11				14
1		2	3			5		6	7	8	4		10	9	11					15
	1	2	3			5		6	7	8		10	9	11			4			16
1		2	3		4	5		6	7	8				9	10	11				17
1		2	3		4	5		6	7	8				9	10	11				18
1		2	3		4	5		6	7	8				9	11	10				19
1		2	3		4	5		6	7		8			9	10	11				20
1		2	3		4	5		6	7	8				9	10	11				21
1		2	3		4		5	6	7	8				9	10	11				22
1		2	3		4		5	6	7	8				9	10	11				23
1		2	3		4		5	6	7	8				9	10		11			24
1		2	3		4		5	6	7	8				9	10		11			25
1		2	3		4		5	6	7	8				9	10		11			26
1		2	3		4	5		6	7	8				9	10		11			27
1		2	3		4		5	6	7	8				9	10		11			28
1		2	3		4		5	6	7	8				9	10		11			29
1		2	3		4		5	10	6	7	8			9			11			30
1		2	3		4		5	6	7	8				9	10		11			31
1		2	3		4		5	6	7	8				9	10		11			32
1		2	3		4		5	6	7	8				9	10	11				33
1		2	3			4	5	6	7					9	10	11	8			34
1		2	3		4	10	5	6	7	8				9	11					35
1		2	3		4		5	6	7	8	10	9					11			36
1		2	3		4		5	6	7	8	10	9					11			37
1		2	3		4		5	6	7	8	10	9					11			38
1		2	3		4	5		6	7	8	10	9					11			39
1		2	3		4	5		6	7	8	9	10					11			40
1		2	3		4	5		6	7	8	9	10					11			41
1		2	3		4		5	6	7	8	9	10					11			42
32	10	42	36	6	39	20	9	16	42	39	39	20	32	24	6	11	35	3	1	
			1	6		1	3	3	14	3	17	3	1	7	3					

Millington S	McKenna P	Smith GW	Law T	Barrett F	Priestley J	Rodger G	Townrow J	Wilding H	Ferguson W	Crawford J	Thain A	Miller H	Turnbull R	Wilson A	McNeil R	Brown W	Pearson G	Stone G	Sales A	
1		2	3		4		5	6	7	8				9	10		11			3
1		2	3		4		5	6	7	8				9	10		11			4
1		2	3		4		5	6	7	8				9	10		11			5
1		2	3		4		5	6	7	8				9	10		11			6
1		2	3		4		5	6	7	8				9	10		11			R
5		5	5		5		5	5	5	5				5	5		5			
			1				1			5		6	2							

1927-28

Manager: David Calderhead

1	Aug	27	(a)	Reading	W 2-1	Crawford, Thompson	24,529
2	Sep	3	(h)	Blackpool	W 3-0	Wilding, Thompson, Pearson	36,529
3		7	(h)	Notts C	W 5-0	Wilding, Thain, Thompson 2, Wilson	18,416
4		10	(a)	Fulham	D 1-1	Thain	39,860
5		17	(a)	Clapton O	L 1-2	Wilson	34,838
6		24	(h)	West Brom A	D 1-1	Thompson	44,724
7	Oct	1	(a)	Bristol C	D 1-1	Wilson	24,005
8		4	(a)	Notts C	W 1-0	Wilson	9,127
9		8	(h)	Stoke C	W 1-0	Crawford (pen)	41,472
10		15	(a)	Southampton	W 4-2	Thain, Thompson, Pearson 2	14,724
11		22	(h)	Hull C	W 2-0	Thompson, Wilson	15,153
12		29	(a)	Preston NE	W 3-0	Thompson 2, Pearson	23,107
13	Nov	5	(h)	Swansea T	W 4-0	Crawford 2, Thain, Thompson	41,220
14		12	(a)	Manchester C	W 1-0	Thompson	52,830
15		19	(h)	Nottingham F	W 2-1	Thain, Thompson	28,743
16		26	(a)	Port Vale	D 1-1	Crawford	14,115
17	Dec	3	(h)	South Shields	W 6-0	Priestley, Miller, Thompson 4	28,719
18		10	(a)	Leeds U	L 0-5		22,059
19		17	(h)	Wolves	W 2-0	Turnbull, Wilson	24,340
20		24	(a)	Barnsley	L 1-3	Priestley	5,634
21		26	(a)	Grimsby T	D 1-1	Turnbull	18,630
22		31	(h)	Reading	D 0-0		26,525
23	Jan	7	(a)	Blackpool	W 4-2	Wilding, Brown, Thompson, Wilson	8,704
24		21	(h)	Fulham	W 2-1	Thompson, Wilson	42,297
25		28	(h)	Clapton O	W 1-0	Wilding	17,875
26	Feb	4	(a)	West Brom A	L 0-3		23,718
27		11	(h)	Bristol C	W 5-2	Priestley 2, Ferguson, Thain, Wilson	31,949
28		20	(a)	Stoke C	L 0-1		15,770
29		25	(h)	Southampton	L 0-2		46,567
30	Mar	3	(a)	Hull C	W 2-0	Thompson 2	12,679
31		10	(h)	Preston NE	W 2-1	Law (pen), Thompson	47,780
32		14	(h)	Grimsby T	W 4-0	Thain, Thompson 3	14,278
33		17	(a)	Swansea T	D 0-0		15,563
34		24	(h)	Manchester C	L 0-1		51,813
35		31	(a)	Nottingham F	D 2-2	Thompson, Jackson	10,989
36	Apr	6	(h)	Oldham A	W 2-1	Thain 2	53,309
37		7	(h)	Port Vale	W 1-0	Crawford	39,278
38		9	(a)	Oldham A	L 1-2	Thain	18,992
39		14	(a)	South Shields	L 1-2	Irving	3,395
40		21	(h)	Leeds U	L 2-3	Rodgers, Wilson	47,562
41		28	(a)	Wolves	W 2-1	Wilson, Jackson	16,727
42	May	5	(h)	Barnsley	L 1-2	Biswell	13,707

FINAL LEAGUE POSITION: 3rd in Division Two

Appearances

Goals

FA Cup

3	Jan	14	(a)	Wolves	L 1-2	Brown	32,134

Aggregate League attendances:
Home: 712,256 (average 33,916)
Away: 409,965 (average 19,522)

Appearances

Goals

Football appearances and goals grid (season of 42 matches).

Millington S	McKenna P	Smith GW	Law T	Priestley J	Irving S	Russell W	Townrow J	Wilding H	Rodger G	Ferguson W	Crawford J	Thain A	Miller H	Brown W	Thompson J	Turnbull R	Wilson A	Pearson G	Jackson W	Odell L	Anderson G	Biswell G	Williams W	Ferguson C	Sales A	#
1		2	3				5	4	6	7	8	9					10	11								1
1		2	3				5	4	6	7	8	9					10	11								2
1		2	3				5	4	6	7	8	9					10	11								3
1		2	3				5	4	6	7	8	9					10	11								4
1		2	3				5	4	6	7	8	9					10	11								5
	1	2	3				5	4	6	7	8	9					10	11								6
	1	2	3				5	4	6	7	8	9					10	11								7
1		2	3				5	4	6	7	8	9					10	11								8
1		2	3				5	4	6	7	8	9					10	11								9
1		2	3	4			5		6	7	8	9					10	11								10
1		2	3	4			5		6	7	8	9					10	11								11
1		2	3	4			5		6	7	8	9					10	11								12
1		2	3	4			5		6	7	8	9					10	11								13
1		2	3	4			5		6	7	8	9					10	11								14
1		2	3	4			5		6	7	8	9					10	11								15
1		2	3	4				5	6	7	8	9					10	11								16
1		2	3	4				5	6	7		9		8			10	11								17
1		2	3	4				5		7		9		8			10	11						6		18
1		2	3	4				5	6	7	8				9		10	11								19
1		2	3	4				5	6	7	8				9		10	11								20
1		2	3	4				5	6	7							10	11					8			21
1		2	3	4				5	6	7		9					10	11					8			22
1		2	3				5	4	6	7	8	9					10	11								23
1		2	3				5	4	6	7	8	9					10	11								24
1			3				5	4	6		8	9					10	11			2	7				25
1			3	4			5	8	6								10	11		7	2	9				26
1		2	3	4			5		6	7	8						10	11				9				27
1		2	3	4			5		6	7	8						10	11			9					28
1		2	3	4			5		6	7	8						10	11				9				29
1		2	3		4			5	6	7	8	9					10	11								30
1		2	3		4			5	6	7	8	9					10	11								31
1		2	3		4			5	6	7	8	9					10	11								32
1		2	3		4			5	6	7	8						10	11		9						33
1		2	3		4			5	6	7	8	9					10	11								34
1		2		4			5		6	7	8	9	10						11	3						35
1		2	3	4			5		6	7	8	9	10						11							36
1		2	3	4			5		6	7	8	9					10		11							37
1		2	3		4			5	6	7	8	10						11	9							38
1		2	3	4			5		6	7	8	10						11	9							39
1		2		4			5		6	7	8	9					10	11		3						40
1		2		4			5		6	7		9					10	8	11	3						41
1		2			8		5		6	9							10	11	7	3	4					42
40	**2**	**40**	**38**	**17**	**11**	**2**	**25**	**17**	**13**	**41**	**39**	**31**	**11**	**2**	**29**	**3**	**38**	**35**	**8**	**6**	**5**	**5**	**2**	**1**	**1**	Apps
		1	4	1	4	1	1	6	10	1	1	25	2		11		4	2	1							Goals

Millington S	McKenna P	Smith GW	Law T	Priestley J	Irving S	Russell W	Townrow J	Wilding H	Rodger G	Ferguson W	Crawford J	Thain A	Miller H	Brown W	Thompson J	Turnbull R	Wilson A	Pearson G	Jackson W	Odell L	Anderson G	Biswell G	Williams W	Ferguson C	Sales A	#
1		2	3	4			5		6	7	8	9					10	11								3
1		1	1	1			1		1	1	1	1					1	1								
											1															

1928-29

Manager: David Calderhead

						Result	Scorers	Attendance
1	Aug	25	(h)	Swansea T	W	4-0	Crawford, Biswell, Pearson, Elliot	47,264
2		27	(a)	Bradford	W	2-1	Biswell, Wilson	20,801
3	Sep	1	(a)	Blackpool	W	1-0	Wilson	17,653
4		5	(h)	Bradford	W	3-1	Bishop, Wilson, Pearson	21,556
5		8	(h)	Middlesbrough	W	2-0	Thain, Wilson	48,775
6		15	(h)	Barnsley	W	1-0	Wilson	34,793
7		22	(a)	Bristol C	D	0-0		24,748
8		29	(h)	Nottingham F	W	3-0	Jackson, Biswell 2	38,139
9	Oct	6	(a)	West Brom A	L	0-3		28,969
10		13	(h)	Clapton O	D	2-2	Wilson 2 (1 pen)	39,890
11		20	(a)	Oldham A	L	0-1		13,385
12		27	(h)	Southampton	D	1-1	Meredith	33,197
13	Nov	3	(a)	Wolves	D	1-1	Meredith	22,178
14		10	(h)	Preston NE	W	2-1	Wilson, Meredith	33,285
15		17	(a)	Millwall	L	1-2	Meredith	37,774
16		24	(h)	Port Vale	D	3-3	Thain, Biswell 2	23,305
17	Dec	1	(a)	Hull C	D	2-2	Biswell 2	16,925
18		8	(h)	Tottenham H	D	1-1	Townrow	45,840
19		15	(a)	Reading	D	3-3	Crawford, Pearson, Meredith	13,338
20		22	(h)	Notts C	D	1-1	Thain	19,560
21		25	(a)	Stoke C	W	1-0	Miller	21,862
22		26	(h)	Stoke C	W	3-1	Thompson 3	15,251
23		29	(a)	Swansea T	W	1-0	Thompson	12,659
24	Jan	5	(h)	Blackpool	L	2-3	Irving, Pearson	20,069
25		19	(a)	Middlesbrough	W	5-4	Law (pen), Thain, Thompson 2, Miller	24,768
26		30	(a)	Barnsley	W	1-0	Miller	7,886
27	Feb	2	(h)	Bristol C	W	3-0	Thompson 2, Pearson	19,768
28		9	(a)	Nottingham F	L	0-3		10,829
29		23	(a)	Clapton O	L	0-1		18,844
30	Mar	2	(h)	Oldham A	L	2-3	Miller, Odell (pen)	29,538
31		9	(a)	Southampton	W	2-1	Biswell, Pearson	23,829
32		13	(a)	Notts C	L	3-4	Bishop, Weaver 2	11,235
33		16	(h)	Wolves	L	0-2		30,383
34		23	(a)	Preston NE	L	0-3		14,415
35		29	(a)	Grimsby T	L	0-1		23,644
36		30	(h)	Millwall	L	0-3		42,637
37	Apr	1	(h)	Grimsby T	W	3-2	Townrow, Jackson, Weaver	25,079
38		6	(a)	Port Vale	L	0-1		11,701
39		13	(h)	Hull C	D	0-0		9,654
40		17	(h)	West Brom A	L	2-5	Elliot, Odell	7,086
41		20	(a)	Tottenham H	L	1-4	Elliot	24,356
42		27	(h)	Reading	W	2-1	Wilson, Weaver	12,898

FINAL LEAGUE POSITION: 9th in Division Two

Appearances
Goals

FA Cup

						Result	Scorers	Attendance
3	Jan	12	(h)	Everton	W	2-0	Thompson, Miller	61,316
4		27	(h)	Birmingham	W	1-0	Miller	56,953
5	Feb	16	(h)	Portsmouth	D	1-1	Law	38,474
R		20	(a)	Portsmouth	L	0-1		31,966

Appearances
Goals

Aggregate League attendances:
Home: 595,967 (average 28,379)
Away: 401,799 (average 19,133)

Millington S	McKenna P	Smith GW	Law T	Irving S	Russell W	Townrow J	Rodger G	Ferguson W	Bishop S	Crawford J	Jackson W	Thain A	Biswell G	Wilson A	Thompson J	Miller H	Pearson G	Meredith J	Elliot S	Weaver R	Odell L	Anderson G	Carr J	
1		2	3	4		5			6	7			8	10			11		9					1
1		2	3	4		5			6	7			8	10			11		9					2
1		2	3	4		5			6	7	8			10			11		9					3
1		2	3	4		5			6	7	8			10			11		9					4
1		2	3	4		5			6	7	8			10			11		9					5
1		2	3	4		5			6	7	8			10			11		9					6
1		2	3	4		5			6	7	8			10			11		9					7
1		2	3	4		5			6	7	11	8	9	10										8
1		2	3	4		5			6	7		8	9	10			11							9
1		2	3	4		5			6	7		8	9	10			11							10
1		2	3	4		5			6	7		8	9	10			11							11
1		2	3		5	6		4		11		8		10		7	9							12
1		2	3	4	5	6						8		10			11	7	9					13
1		2	3	4	5	6						8		10			11	7	9					14
1		2	3	4		5			6			8		10			11	7	9					15
1		2	3	4		5		6				8			9	10	11	7						16
1		2	3	4		5		6				8			9	10	11	7						17
1		2	3	4		5		6				8				10	11	7				9		18
1		2	3	4		5		6		7						10	11	8				9		19
1		2	3	4		5		6				8				10	11	7				9		20
1			3	8	4	5		6		7						10	11			2	9			21
1			3	8	4	5		6		7					9	10	11			2				22
1		2	3		4	5		6		7			8		9	10	11							23
1		2	3	8	4	5		6		7					9	10	11							24
1		2	3	4		5		6		7			8		9	10	11							25
1		2	3	4		5		6		7			8		9	10	11							26
1		2	3	4		5		6		7			8		9	10	11							27
1		2	3	4		5		6		7			8		9	10	11							28
	1	2	3	4	5	6					11	8	9			10		7						29
1		2		4	5	6					11	8			9	10		7		3				30
1		2	3	4		5			6	7		8			9	10	11							31
1		2	3	4		5			6	7			8			10	11		9					32
1		2	3	4		5			6			8				10	11	7	9					33
1		2	3	4		5			6	7		8				10	11		9					34
1		2	3		4	5			6	7		8	9				11		10					35
1		2	3		4	5			6	11	7		8	10					9					36
1			3	4	8	5			6	11						10		7	9	2				37
	1		3		6	5		4		11			8			10		7	9	2				38
	1	2	3		4	5			6	8						10	11	7	9					39
	1			4	5				6	11		8					7	10	9	2		3		40
1		2	3		4	5			6	7	11	10						9	8					41
1		2			4	5			6	7	11			10				9	8	3				42
38	4	37	39	32	13	41	2	22	21	27	9	23	18	21	8	22	32	16	14	11	7	4	1	
	1	1		2						2	2	2	4	9	9	8	4	6	5	3	4	2		

Millington S	McKenna P	Smith GW	Law T	Irving S	Russell W	Townrow J	Rodger G	Ferguson W	Bishop S	Crawford J	Jackson W	Thain A	Biswell G	Wilson A	Thompson J	Miller H	Pearson G	Meredith J	Elliot S	Weaver R	Odell L	Anderson G	Carr J	
1		2	3	4		5			6	7		8			9	10	11							3
1		2	3	4		5			6	7		8			9	10	11							4
1		2	3	4		5			6	7	8				9	10	11							5
1		2	3		4	5			6	7		8			9	10	11							R
3	1	4	4	3	1	4		4		4		3	1		4	4	4							
		1														1	2							

235

1929-30

Manager: David Calderhead

1	Aug	31	(h)	Nottingham F	W	2-0	Elliot, Weaver	26,832
2	Sep	7	(a)	Oldham A	L	2-4	Miller, Pearson	20,299
3		11	(h)	Barnsley	W	2-0	Jackson, Wilson	11,353
4		14	(h)	Millwall	W	3-0	Crawford, Miller, Pearson	35,858
5		21	(a)	Southampton	L	2-4	Miller 2	15,569
6		23	(h)	Bury	W	5-3	Crawford, Wilson, Pearson 2, Elliot	12,640
7		28	(h)	Tottenham H	W	3-0	Bishop, Pearson 2	46,770
8	Oct	5	(a)	West Brom A	L	0-2		19,274
9		12	(h)	Bradford	L	1-2	Miller	27,171
10		19	(a)	Notts C	D	2-2	Weaver, Jackman (og)	13,878
11		26	(h)	Reading	W	1-0	Weaver	29,238
12	Nov	2	(a)	Charlton A	D	1-1	Weaver	27,642
13		9	(h)	Hull C	W	3-0	Ferguson, Elliot 2	23,416
14		16	(a)	Stoke C	D	1-1	Ferguson	10,298
15		23	(h)	Wolves	D	1-1	Miller	16,144
16		30	(a)	Bradford C	W	1-0	Elliot	11,333
17	Dec	7	(h)	Swansea T	W	1-0	Elliot	16,548
18		14	(a)	Cardiff C	L	0-1		10,526
19		21	(h)	Preston NE	W	5-0	Rodger, Bishop, Crawford, Miller 2	12,769
20		25	(a)	Blackpool	D	1-1	Wilson	14,882
21		26	(h)	Blackpool	W	4-0	Wilson 2 (1 pen), Mills, Pearson	53,819
22		28	(a)	Nottingham F	D	0-0		14,772
23	Jan	1	(a)	Barnsley	D	1-1	Bishop	8,773
24		4	(h)	Oldham A	D	1-1	Pearson	33,345
25		18	(a)	Millwall	D	0-0		31,355
26		25	(h)	Southampton	W	2-0	Wilson (pen), Pearson	25,268
27	Feb	1	(a)	Tottenham H	D	3-3	Crawford, Mills, Pearson	33,623
28		8	(h)	West Brom A	W	2-0	Mills 2	23,146
29		22	(h)	Notts C	W	3-1	Wilson, Mills, Miller	27,103
30	Mar	1	(a)	Reading	L	1-3	Miller	14,672
31		8	(h)	Charlton A	D	1-1	Mills	39,523
32		12	(a)	Bradford	W	3-1	Mills 2, Miller	11,087
33		15	(a)	Hull C	W	3-1	Jackson, Mills 2	4,813
34		22	(h)	Stoke C	W	3-2	Mills, Pearson, Meredith	35,621
35		29	(a)	Wolves	W	1-0	Mills	16,967
36	Apr	5	(h)	Bradford C	W	3-2	Wilson 2 (1 pen), Pearson	26,068
37		12	(a)	Swansea T	L	0-3		14,944
38		18	(h)	Bristol C	W	2-1	Wilson, Mills	36,038
39		19	(h)	Cardiff C	W	1-0	Miller	23,100
40		21	(a)	Bristol C	L	1-2	Irving	17,488
41		26	(a)	Preston NE	W	2-1	Mills, Miller	13,475
42	May	3	(a)	Bury	L	0-1		15,689

FINAL LEAGUE POSITION: 2nd in Division Two

Appearances
Goals

FA Cup

3	Jan	11	(a)	Arsenal	L	0-2		55,579

Appearances
Goals

Aggregate League attendances:
Home: 584,770 (average 27,846)
Away: 341,359 (average 16,255)

Appearance and goalscoring grid (League). Player shirt numbers are shown for each match (rows 1–42); blank = did not play.

Match	Millington S	McKenna P	Smith GW	Law T	Russell W	Irving S	Rodger G	Townrow J	Bishop S	Ferguson W	Crawford J	Jackson W	Wilson A	Thain A	Biswell G	Mills G	Miller H	Pearson G	Elliot S	Odell L	Weaver R	Meredith J	Higgs F
1	1	2	3	4		5	6	7									10	11	9		8		
2	1	2	3	4	5		6	7									10	11	9		8		
3	1	2	3		4	5	6			7	8						10	11		9			
4		1	2	3		4	5	6		7			8				10	11		9			
5	1	2	3		4	5	6		7				8				10	11	9				
6	1	2	3		4	5	6		7				8				10	11	9				
7		2	3		4	5	6		7				8				10	11	9			1	
8		2	3	4		5	6		7				8				10	11	9			1	
9	1	2	3		4	5	6		7				8				10	11		9			
10	1	2	3	4	5	6			7				8				10	11		9			
11	1	2	3	4	5	6			7				8				10	11		9			
12	1	2	3	4	5		6		7				8				10	11		9			
13	1	2	3	4	5		6	7					8				10	11	9				
14	1	2	3	4	5		6	7			10		8					11	9				
15	1	2	3	4	5		6	7					8				10	11	9				
16	1	2	3		5	4	6	7					8				10	11	9				
17	1	2	3	4	5		6	7					8				10	11	9				
18	1	2	3	4	5		6	7			10		8					11	9				
19	1	2	3	4	5		6	7					8				10	11					
20	1	2	3	4	5		6	7					8				10	11	9				
21	1	2	3	4	5		6	7		9			8				10	11					
22	1	2	3	4	5		6	7		9			8				10	11					
23	1	2	3	4	5		6				7		8				10	11	9				
24	1	2	3	4	5		6						8				10	11	9			7	
25	1		3	4	5		6				7		8				10	11	9	2			
26	1	2	3	4	5		6	7					8				10	11	9				
27	1		3	4	5		6	7		9			8				10	11		2			
28	1		3	4	5		6	7		9			8				10	11		2			
29	1	2	3	4	5		6	7		9			8				10	11					
30	1	2	3	4	5		6	7		9			8				10	11					
31	1		3		5	6	4	7		9			8				10	11		2			
32	1		3	4	5	6		7		9			8				10			2			11
33	1		3	4	5	6		7		9			8				10			2			11
34	1		3	4	5	6				9			8				10	11		2		7	
35	1	2	3	4	5	6				9			8				10	11				7	
36	1	2		4	5	6				9			8				10	11		3		7	
37	1		3	4	5	6		7		9			8				10	11		2			
38	1		3	4	5	6		7		9	11		8				10			2			
39	1		3	4	5		6	7		9	11		8				10			2			
40	1		3	4	5		6	7		9		8					10	11		2			
41	1		3	4	5		6	7		9		8					10	11		2			
42	1	2	3		5	6	4			9			8				10	11				7	
Apps	38	2	30	41	20	17	28	14	36	11	32	7	39	2	1	20	40	38	16	13	8	7	2
Goals						1	1		3	2	4		2			10	14	13	12	6		4	1

1 own-goal

Match	1	2	3	4	5	6	7	8	9	10	11
3	1	2	3	4	5	6	7	8	9	10	11
Apps	1	1	1	1	1	1	1	1	1	1	1

1930-31

Manager: David Calderhead

1	Aug	30	(a)	Grimsby T	W	1-0	Law (pen)	20,294
2	Sep	3	(a)	Newcastle U	L	0-1		68,386
3		6	(h)	Manchester U	W	6-2	Townrow, Cheyne 3, Gallacher 2	48,648
4		8	(a)	Sheffield W	D	1-1	Wilson	21,182
5		13	(a)	West Ham U	L	1-4	Law (pen)	31,334
6		15	(h)	Sheffield W	D	0-0		51,960
7		20	(h)	Bolton W	L	0-1		48,347
8		27	(a)	Liverpool	L	1-3	Cheyne	41,386
9	Oct	4	(h)	Middlesbrough	W	4-0	Jackson, Wilson 2, Pearson	48,395
10		11	(a)	Huddersfield T	D	1-1	Russell	25,853
11		18	(h)	Sheffield U	W	1-0	Law (pen)	59,700
12		25	(a)	Birmingham	L	2-6	Law (pen), Gallacher	17,277
13	Nov	1	(h)	Blackpool	W	3-0	Jackson, Cheyne, Gallacher	32,755
14		8	(a)	Blackburn R	L	0-2		21,008
15		15	(h)	Manchester C	W	2-0	Cheyne, Gallacher	25,671
16		22	(a)	Leeds U	W	3-2	Jackson 2, Pearson	13,602
17		29	(h)	Arsenal	L	1-5	Law (pen)	74,667
18	Dec	6	(a)	Derby C	L	2-6	Jackson, Miller	12,731
19		13	(h)	Sunderland	W	5-0	Law (pen), Cheyne, Gallacher 2, Crawford	31,295
20		20	(a)	Portsmouth	D	1-1	Jackson	22,687
21		25	(h)	Aston Villa	L	0-2		40,990
22		26	(a)	Aston Villa	D	3-3	Gallacher, Odell 2	53,580
23		27	(h)	Grimsby T	W	5-0	Jackson 2, Cheyne, Gallacher, Odell (pen)	23,467
24	Jan	3	(a)	Manchester U	L	0-1		8,966
25		17	(h)	West Ham U	W	2-1	Jackson, Cheyne	40,011
26		31	(h)	Liverpool	D	2-2	Mills, Crawford	35,936
27	Feb	4	(a)	Bolton W	D	1-1	Mills	9,678
28		7	(a)	Middlesbrough	D	2-2	Jackson, Pearson	16,443
29		18	(h)	Huddersfield T	L	1-2	Wilson	17,546
30		21	(a)	Sheffield U	L	0-4		26,694
31	Mar	7	(a)	Blackpool	L	1-2	Irving	12,271
32		14	(h)	Blackburn R	W	3-2	Gallacher, Crawford, Odell (pen)	32,623
33		21	(a)	Manchester C	L	0-2		27,866
34		25	(h)	Birmingham	W	1-0	Gallacher	12,968
35		28	(h)	Leeds U	W	1-0	Gallacher	25,446
36	Apr	4	(a)	Arsenal	L	1-2	Gallacher	53,867
37		6	(h)	Leicester C	W	1-0	Pearson	26,157
38		7	(a)	Leicester C	L	1-2	Rankin	19,848
39		11	(h)	Derby C	D	1-1	Irving	28,224
40		18	(a)	Sunderland	L	0-2		8,854
41		25	(h)	Portsmouth	W	2-0	Gallacher, Odell (pen)	19,521
42	May	2	(h)	Newcastle U	D	1-1	Jackson	22,860

FINAL LEAGUE POSITION: 12th in Division One

Appearances
Goals

FA Cup

3	Jan	10	(a)	West Ham U	W	3-1	Jackson 2, Wade (og)	21,000
4		24	(h)	Arsenal	W	2-1	Bishop, Mills	62,475
5	Feb	14	(h)	Blackburn R	W	3-0	Law (pen), Cheyne, Mills	61,170
6		28	(h)	Birmingham	D	2-2	Jackson, Crawford	55,298
R	Mar	4	(h)	Birmingham	L	0-3		74,365

Appearances
Goals

Aggregate League attendances:
Home: 747,317 (average 31,138)
Away: 533,807 (average 25,419)

Player appearance and goalscoring grid (shirt numbers by match). Columns left-to-right:

Millington S · McKenna P · Barber G · Smith GW · Law T · Irving S · Russell W · Rodger G · Townrow J · Ferguson W · Bishop S · Jackson A · Cheyne A · Gallacher H · Mills G · Wilson A · Miller H · Crawford J · Pearson G · Jackson W · Odell L · Donald A · Rankin J · Carter R · Macintosh S

Mil	McK	Bar	Smi	Law	Irv	Rus	Rod	Tow	Fer	Bis	JaA	Che	Gal	Mls	Wil	Mir	Cra	Pea	JaW	Ode	Don	Ran	Car	Mac	#
1		2	3		4	5		6			8	9				10	7	11							1
1		2	3		4	5		6			8	9				10	7	11							2
1		2	3		4	5	6				8	9			10		7	11							3
1		2	3		4	5	6				8	9			10		7	11							4
	1	2	3		4	5		6			8	9				10	7	11							5
1		2	3		4	5		6		7	8	9			10			11							6
1		2	3		4	5		6		7	8	9			10			11							7
1		2	3		4	5		6		7	8	9			10			11							8
1			3		4	5		6		7	8				10		11	9		2					9
1			3		4	5		6		7	8				10		11	9		2					10
1			3		4	5		6		7	8	9			10		11			2					11
1			3	4	5			6		7	8	9			10		11			2					12
1			3	4	5			6		7	8	9			10		11			2					13
1				4	5			6		7	8	9			10		11			2	3				14
1					5		4	6		7	8	9			10		11			2	3				15
1					5		4	6		7	8		9		10		11			2	3				16
1		3			5		4	6		7	8		9		10		11			2					17
		2	3		4	5		6		7	8		9		10		11						1		18
1		2	3	4	5			6		7	8	9			10		11								19
1		2	3	4	5			6		7	8	9			10		11								20
1			3	4	5			6		7	8				10		11			2					21
1		2		4	5			6		7	8				10		11				3				22
1		2		4	5		6			7	8	9			10		11				3				23
1		2		4	5		6			7	8		9		10		11				3				24
1		2	3	4	5			6		7	8	9			10		11								25
1		2	3	4	5			6		7	8	9			10		11								26
1		2	3	4	5		6			7	8	9			10		11								27
1		2	3	4	5		6			7	8	9			10			11							28
1		2	3	4	5			6		7	8	9			10		11								29
1		2	3		4	5		6		7	8	9				10	11								30
1		2	3	4	5			6		7	8		9		10		11								31
1				4	5			6			8	9			10		11	7		2	3				32
1				4	5			6			8	9			10		11	7		2	3				33
1				4	5			6		7		9			10		11			2	3	8			34
1				4	5			6			8	9			10	11		7		2	3				35
1			3	4	5			6				9			10		11	7		2		8			36
1			3	4	5	6						9			10		11	7		2		8			37
1		2		4				6				9			10		11	7			3	8	5		38
1				4	5	6						9			10		11	7		2	3	8			39
1				4	5	6						9			10		11	7		2	3	8			40
1				4	5			6		7	8	9			10		11			2	3				41
1					5		4	6		7	8	9			10		11			2	3				42
40	1	11	11	27	20	17	14	27	25	22	29	34	30	7	34	10	32	26	2	23	12	6	1	1	
				6	2	1		1				11	9	14	2	4	1	3	4		5		1		

Mil	McK	Bar	Smi	Law	Irv	Rus	Rod	Tow	Fer	Bis	JaA	Che	Gal	Mls	Wil	Mir	Cra	Pea	JaW	Ode	Don	Ran	Car	Mac	#
1		2		3	4			5			6	7	8	9			10			11					3
1		2		3	4			5			6	7	8		9		10			11					4
1		2		3	4			5			6	7	8		9		10			11					5
1		2		3	4			5			6	7	8		9		10			11					6
1		2		3	4			5			6	7	8		9		10			11					R
5		5		5	5			5			5	5	5	1	4		5			5					
				1							1	3	1		2					1					

I own-goal

1931-32

Manager: David Calderhead

#					Result	Scorers	Attendance
1	Aug	29	(a)	Middlesbrough	W 2-0	Jackson, Gallacher	24,510
2		31	(a)	West Ham U	L 1-3	Gallacher	28,338
3	Sep	5	(h)	Huddersfield T	L 0-1		42,961
4		9	(h)	Sheffield W	L 2-3	Jackson, Gallacher	31,426
5		12	(a)	Newcastle U	L 1-4	Mills	28,562
6		19	(h)	Aston Villa	L 3-6	Jackson 2, Miller	56,698
7		21	(a)	Sheffield W	D 2-2	Jackson, Gallacher	11,809
8		26	(a)	Leicester C	L 0-1		19,189
9	Oct	3	(h)	Liverpool	W 2-0	Jackson 2	40,597
10		10	(a)	Grimsby T	W 2-1	Rankin, Cheyne	16,050
11		17	(a)	Sunderland	L 1-2	Pearson	17,294
12		24	(h)	Blackburn R	L 1-2	Carter	35,688
13		31	(a)	Portsmouth	L 0-1		19,813
14	Nov	7	(h)	Derby C	W 2-1	Jackson, Gallacher	31,991
15		14	(a)	Everton	L 2-7	Jackson, Mills	32,758
16		21	(h)	Arsenal	W 2-1	Rankin, Gallacher	64,427
17		28	(a)	Sheffield U	L 2-4	Rankin, Mills	16,264
18	Dec	5	(h)	Manchester C	W 3-2	Gallacher, Mills, Felton (og)	27,509
19		12	(a)	West Brom A	L 0-4		24,196
20		19	(h)	Birmingham	W 2-1	Jackson, Gallacher	17,551
21		25	(a)	Blackpool	W 4-2	Russell, Gallacher 2, Pearson	20,378
22		26	(h)	Blackpool	W 4-1	Law (pen), Gallacher, Mills 2	38,569
23	Jan	1	(a)	Bolton W	L 0-1		28,232
24		2	(h)	Middlesbrough	W 4-0	Rankin, Gallacher 2, Pearson	25,259
25		16	(a)	Huddersfield T	L 1-2	Goodall (og)	16,645
26		30	(a)	Aston Villa	W 3-1	Jackson, Mills 2	35,993
27	Feb	6	(h)	Leicester C	W 1-0	Miller	34,077
28		20	(h)	Grimsby T	W 4-1	Russell, Ferguson, Gallacher, Miller	24,422
29	Mar	2	(h)	Sunderland	D 2-2	Gallacher 2	20,087
30		5	(a)	Blackburn R	D 2-2	Gallacher 2	13,691
31		16	(h)	Portsmouth	D 0-0		13,050
32		19	(a)	Derby C	L 0-1		14,791
33		25	(h)	Bolton W	W 3-0	Jackson 2, Gallacher	38,515
34		26	(h)	Everton	D 0-0		56,298
35	Apr	2	(a)	Arsenal	D 1-1	Gallacher	56,124
36		6	(a)	Liverpool	L 1-2	Chitty	7,873
37		9	(h)	Sheffield U	D 1-1	Gallacher	16,840
38		14	(h)	Newcastle U	W 4-1	Jackson, Gallacher 3	12,605
39		16	(a)	Manchester C	D 1-1	Jackson	20,124
40		23	(a)	West Brom A	L 0-2		23,873
41		30	(a)	Birmingham	L 0-4		14,861
42	May	7	(h)	West Ham U	W 3-2	Russell, Ferguson, Pearson	24,386

FINAL LEAGUE POSITION: 12th in Division One

Appearances

Goals

FA Cup

#					Result	Scorers	Attendance
3	Jan	9	(a)	Tranmere R	D 2-2	Gallacher 2	13,300
R		13	(h)	Tranmere R	W 5-3	Law, Jackson, Gallacher, Mills, Pearson	35,402
4		23	(h)	West Ham U	W 3-1	Gallacher, Mills 2	36,657
5	Feb	13	(a)	Sheffield W	D 1-1	Law	39,000
R		17	(h)	Sheffield W	W 2-0	Mills, Miller	60,004
6		27	(a)	Liverpool	W 2-0	Gallacher, Pearson	57,000
SF	Mar	12	(a*)	Newcastle U	L 1-2	Gallacher	36,709

*Played at Leeds Road, Huddersfield.

Appearances

Goals

Aggregate League attendances:
Home: 635,322 (average 30,253)
Away: 467,595 (average 22,266)

Football appearances and goals grid (page 241).

Millington S	Woodley V	Barber G	Odell L	Law T	Smith GW	Russell W	Irving S	O'Dowd P	Townrow J	Ferguson W	Bishop S	Jackson A	Crawford J	Rankin J	Cheyne A	Gallacher H	Wilson A	Mills G	Miller H	Pearson G	Carter R	Donald A	Chitty W	Hope J	Weaver R	
	1	2				4		5		6	7	11			8	9	10					3				1
	1	2				4		5		6	7	11			8	9	10					3				2
	1	2				4		5		6	7	11			8	9	10					3				3
	1	2				4		5		6	7	11			8	9	10					3				4
	1	2				4		5	6		7				8			9	10	11		3				5
	1	2				4		5	6		7				8	9			10	11		3				6
1			2			4		5		6	7	8				9		10	11			3				7
1		2				4		5		6	7	8				9		10	11			3				8
1		2				4		5		6	7	8				9		10	11			3				9
1		2						5	6		7	8		10	9				11	4		3				10
1		2						5	6		7	8		10	9				11	4		3				11
1		2	3					5			7	8		10	9				11	4				6		12
1		2	6	3				5			7	11	10		8	9		4								13
1		2	3	4				5			7	11			8	9		10		6						14
1		2	3	4			5				7	11			8	9		10		6						15
1		2		3			5			6	7	11			8	9		10		4						16
1		2		3			5			6	7	11			8	9		10		4						17
1		2		3			5			6	7	11			8	9		10		4						18
1		2						5		6	7				8	9		10	11	4	3					19
1		2	3	4				5		6	7	10			8	9				11						20
1		2	3	4		5			6		7				8	9		10		11						21
1		2	3	4		5			6		7				8	9		10		11						22
1		2	3	4		5			6		7				8	9		10		11						23
1		2	3	4		5			6		7				8	9		10		11						24
1		2	3			5			6		7				8	9		10		11	4					25
1		2	3	4		5			6		7				8			10	9	11						26
1		2	3	4		5			6		7				8	9				11					10	27
1		2	3	4		5			6				7		8	9		10		11						28
1		2		4		5			6		7					9		10	8	11		3				29
1		2	3	4		5			6		7				8	9		10		11						30
1			2	3	4				6		7	8				9		10		11		5				31
1		2	3	4		5			6		7				8	9		10		11						32
1		2	3	4		5			6		7				8	9		10		11						33
1		2	3	4		5			6		7				8	9		10		11						34
1		2	3	4		5			6		7				8	9		10		11						35
1		2	3	4					6		7				8	9		10			5		11			36
1		2	3	4					6				7		8	9		10			5		11			37
1		2	3	4					6		7				8	9		10			5		11			38
1		2	3	4		5			6		7				8	9		10					11			39
1		2	3	4		5			6		7				8	9		10					11			40
	1	2	3	4		5			6		7				8	9				11				10		41
1		2	3	4		5			6				7		8	9		10		11						42
35	7	33	11	27	1	24	9	24	14	21	17	36	21	24	19	36	4	14	22	27	16	12	6	1	1	
			1	3								2	15		4	1		24		8	3	4		1	1	

2 own-goals

Millington S	Woodley V	Barber G	Odell L	Law T	Smith GW	Russell W	Irving S	O'Dowd P	Townrow J	Ferguson W	Bishop S	Jackson A	Crawford J	Rankin J	Cheyne A	Gallacher H	Wilson A	Mills G	Miller H	Pearson G	Carter R	Donald A	Chitty W	Hope J	Weaver R	
1		2	3	4		5			6		7				8	9		10		11						3
1		2	3	4		5			6		7				8	9		10		11						R
1		2	3	4		5			6		7				8	9		10		11						4
1		2	3	4		5			6		7					9		10	8	11						5
1		2	3	4		5			6		7					9		10	8	11						R
1		2	3	4		5			6		7				9	8		10		11						6
1		2	3	4		5			6		7				9	8		10		11						SF
7		6	1	7		7			7		7		7		3	2		5	7	4	7					
													2			1		6	4	1	2					

241

1932-33

Manager: David Calderhead

1	Aug	27	(h)	Blackburn R	D	2-2 Gallacher, Miller	32,657
2		31	(a)	Portsmouth	L	0-2	20,856
3	Sep	3	(a)	Huddersfield T	L	0-2	13,032
4		7	(h)	Portsmouth	D	4-4 Rankin, Gallacher 2, Miller	20,984
5		10	(h)	Sheffield U	W	3-0 Rankin, Gallacher 2	32,775
6		17	(a)	Wolves	W	2-1 Gallacher 2	31,922
7		24	(h)	Newcastle U	L	0-1	51,857
8	Oct	1	(a)	Aston Villa	L	1-3 Miller	32,684
9		8	(h)	Middlesbrough	W	2-1 Mills, Chitty	18,181
10		15	(a)	Bolton W	W	3-2 Mills 2, Chitty	15,021
11		22	(h)	Derby C	L	1-3 Oakton	37,834
12		29	(a)	Blackpool	L	0-4	7,311
13	Nov	5	(h)	Birmingham	W	4-2 Law (pen), Oakton, Mills 2	25,619
14		12	(a)	West Brom A	L	2-3 Law (pen), Oakton	21,577
15		19	(h)	Sheffield W	L	0-2	20,677
16		26	(a)	Leeds U	L	0-2	19,739
17	Dec	3	(h)	Everton	W	1-0 Rankin	33,962
18		10	(a)	Arsenal	L	1-4 Russell	53,206
19		17	(h)	Manchester C	W	3-1 Mills 2, Prout	26,240
20		24	(a)	Sunderland	L	1-2 Mills	21,494
21		26	(a)	Liverpool	L	0-3	34,777
22		27	(h)	Liverpool	L	0-2	36,784
23		31	(a)	Blackburn R	W	3-1 Gallacher 2, Prout	10,583
24	Jan	7	(h)	Huddersfield T	L	0-1	23,844
25		21	(a)	Sheffield U	L	1-4 Mills (pen)	13,622
26		28	(h)	Wolves	W	3-1 Rankin, Oakton, Gallacher	16,919
27	Feb	4	(a)	Newcastle U	L	0-2	29,405
28		11	(h)	Aston Villa	L	0-1	34,378
29		25	(h)	Bolton W	D	1-1 Mills	12,590
30	Mar	1	(a)	Middlesbrough	L	1-2 Mills (pen)	8,219
31		11	(h)	Blackpool	W	1-0 Mills	31,222
32		18	(a)	Birmingham	D	0-0	19,620
33		25	(h)	West Brom A	L	1-2 Gallacher	33,371
34		29	(a)	Derby C	W	1-0 Gallacher	7,141
35	Apr	1	(a)	Sheffield W	D	2-2 Oakton, Gibson	10,121
36		8	(h)	Leeds U	W	6-0 Oakton, Mills, Gallacher, Gibson 2, Prout	31,095
37		14	(h)	Leicester C	W	4-1 Oakton, Gallacher, Horton 2	45,608
38		15	(a)	Everton	L	2-3 Gibson, Thomson (og)	27,635
39		18	(a)	Leicester C	D	1-1 Gallacher	22,647
40		22	(h)	Arsenal	L	1-3 Gallacher	72,260
41	May	3	(a)	Manchester C	W	4-1 Oakton, Gallacher 3	14,827
42		6	(h)	Sunderland	D	1-1 Gibson	22,322

FINAL LEAGUE POSITION: 18th in Division One

Appearances
Goals

FA Cup

3	Jan	14	(a)	Brighton & HA	L	1-2 Barber	23,580

Appearances
Goals

Aggregate League attendances:
Home: 661,179 (average 31,484)
Away: 435,509 (average 20,738)

Appearance and goal grid (player position numbers by match).

Match	Woodley V	Odell L	Law T	Barber G	Macaulay R	Russell W	Allum L	O'Dowd P	Craig A	Griffiths R	Rankin J	Ferguson W	Bishop S	Oakton E	Crawford J	Mills G	Gallacher H	Miller H	Gibson G	Prout S	Horton J	Pearson G	Chitty W	Carter R	Dudley S
1	1		3	2		4					6		8	7	11		9	10					5		
2	1		3	2		4		5			6		8	7	11		9	10							
3	1		3		2	4		5			6		8	7	11		9	10							
4	1		3		2	4		5			6		8	7	11		9	10							
5	1		3	2		4		5			6		8	7	11		9	10							
6	1		3	2		4		5	10		6			7	11	8	9								
7	1	2	3			4		5			6		10	7	11	8	9								
8	1	2	3			4		5			6		9	7		8		10					11		
9	1	2	3			4		5			6		9	7		8		10					11		
10	1	2	3			4		5			6	9		7		8		10					11		
11	1	2	3			4		5			6			7		8	9	10					11		
12	1	2	3				4	5			6	9		7		8		10			11				
13	1	2	3				4	5			6	9		7		8		10			11				
14	1	2	3			4	8	5			6			7			9		11						
15	1	2	3			4	10	5			6			7		8	9		11						
16	1	2	3			4	8	5			6			7			9	10	11						
17	1		3	2		4		5			6		8	7			9	10	11						
18	1		3	2		4		5			6		8	7			9	10	11						
19	1		3	2		4		5			6		10	7		8	9		11						
20	1		3	2		4	10	5			6			7		8	9		11						
21	1	2	3			4	10	5			6			7		8	9		11						
22	1	2		3		4		5					6	7		8	9	10	11						
23	1	2		3		4	6	5					8	7			9	10	11						
24	1	2		3		4			5	10	6		8	7			9		11						
25	1		3	2		4		5			6		10	7		8	9		11						
26	1	2		3	4			5			6		10	7		8	9		11						
27	1	2		3	4			5			6		10	7		8	9								11
28	1	2		3	4			5					6	8		10	9					11	7		
29	1		3	2				5	4		6	10		7		8	9		11						
30	1		3	2		4		5	6					7		8	9			10	11				
31	1		3	2		4		5			6	11		7		8	9			10					
32	1		3	2		4		5			6		7			8	9			10	11				
33	1		3	2		4		5			6		7			8	9			10	11				
34	1		3	2		6		5	4					7		8	9			10	11				
35	1		3	2		6		5	4					7		8	9			10			11		
36	1		3	2		4		5	6					7		8	9			10	11				
37	1		3	2		4		5	6					7		8	9			10	11				
38	1		3	2		4		5	6					7		8	9			10	11				
39	1		3	2		4		5	6					7		8	9			10	11				
40	1			2	3	4		5	6					7		8	9			10	11				
41	1			2	3	4		5		8	6			7			9			10	11				
42	1			2	3	4		5	6					7		8	9			10	11				
Apps	42	17	33	24	10	31	13	36	19	2	29	17	7	34	15	31	36	17	13	16	9	3	6	1	1
Goals		2		1							4			8		13	19	3	5	3	2		2		

1 own-goal

Match	Woodley V	Odell L	Law T	Barber G	Macaulay R	Russell W	Allum L	O'Dowd P	Craig A	Griffiths R	Rankin J	Ferguson W	Bishop S	Oakton E	Crawford J	Mills G	Gallacher H	Miller H	Gibson G	Prout S	Horton J	Pearson G	Chitty W	Carter R	Dudley S
3	1	2	3		4			5	6					7		8	9			10	11				
	1	1	1		1			1	1					1		1	1			1	1				
			1																						

1933-34

Manager: Leslie Knighton

					Result	Scorers	Attendance
1	Aug	26	(a)	Stoke C	L 0-1		32,725
2	Sep	2	(h)	Wolves	W 5-2	Oakton, Gallacher 2, Mills 2	31,792
3		4	(a)	Huddersfield T	L 1-6	Oakton	7,508
4		9	(a)	Sheffield U	L 1-4	Copeland	13,598
5		13	(h)	Huddersfield T	L 2-3	Oakton 2	20,006
6		16	(h)	Aston Villa	W 1-0	Mills	44,679
7		23	(a)	Leicester C	D 1-1	Gibson	21,164
8		30	(h)	Tottenham H	L 0-4		67,454
9	Oct	7	(a)	Liverpool	L 0-3		31,039
10		14	(h)	Middlesbrough	L 2-3	Gallacher, Mills	16,078
11		21	(a)	Blackburn R	L 2-4	Gallacher, Gibson	12,570
12		28	(h)	Newcastle U	W 2-1	Oakton, Gallacher	26,657
13	Nov	4	(a)	Sheffield W	L 1-2	Law	10,248
14		11	(h)	Derby C	L 0-2		24,422
15		18	(a)	West Brom A	L 1-3	Chitty	12,340
16		25	(h)	Birmingham	D 1-1	Barkas (og)	17,843
17	Dec	2	(a)	Everton	L 1-2	Priestley	15,584
18		9	(h)	Manchester C	L 1-2	Mills	18,048
19		16	(a)	Arsenal	L 1-2	Miller	43,897
20		23	(h)	Leeds U	D 1-1	Law (pen)	18,157
21		26	(h)	Sunderland	W 4-0	Law (pen), Gallacher, Horton, Gregg	12,800
22		30	(h)	Stoke C	W 2-0	Law, Oakton	24,487
23	Jan	1	(a)	Sunderland	D 0-0		12,820
24		6	(a)	Wolves	D 1-1	Oakton	21,459
25		20	(h)	Sheffield U	W 5-0	Oakton, Gallacher 2, Horton 2	31,287
26	Feb	8	(a)	Aston Villa	L 0-2		15,688
27		12	(a)	Tottenham H	L 1-2	Gregg	39,652
28		21	(h)	Liverpool	W 2-0	Oakton, Gallacher	14,152
29		24	(a)	Middlesbrough	D 2-2	Gallacher 2 (1 pen)	12,962
30	Mar	3	(h)	Blackburn R	W 3-0	Oakton, Gallacher 2 (1 pen)	26,409
31		10	(a)	Newcastle U	D 2-2	Gibson 2	14,108
32		17	(h)	Sheffield W	L 0-1		31,606
33		24	(a)	Derby C	L 0-1		13,644
34		30	(a)	Portsmouth	W 2-0	Horton 2	29,100
35		31	(h)	West Brom A	W 3-2	Gibson, Mills 2	36,593
36	Apr	2	(h)	Portsmouth	W 4-0	Oakton, Gibson, Horton, Mills	47,114
37		7	(a)	Birmingham	W 3-0	Oakton, Gibson 2	29,104
38		14	(h)	Everton	W 2-0	Horton, Mills	34,029
39		21	(a)	Manchester C	L 2-4	Horton, Mills	25,861
40		23	(h)	Leicester C	W 2-0	Mills 2	16,304
41		28	(h)	Arsenal	D 2-2	Horton, Mills	65,344
42	May	5	(a)	Leeds U	L 1-3	Mills	6,092

FINAL LEAGUE POSITION: 19th in Division One

Appearances
Goals

FA Cup

					Result	Scorers	Attendance
3	Jan	13	(h)	West Brom A	D 1-1	Gregg	51,451
R		17	(a)	West Brom A	W 1-0	Gallacher	20,061
4		27	(h)	Nottingham F	D 1-1	Priestley	53,269
R		31	(a)	Nottingham F	W 3-0	Gallacher 2, Gibson	37,187
5	Feb	17	(a)	Stoke C	L 1-3	Oakton (pen)	42,219

Appearances
Goals

Aggregate League attendances:
Home: 625,261 (average 29,774)
Away: 475,163 (average 22,626)

Woodley V	Barber G	Law T	Russell W	Craig A	O'Dowd P	Oakton E	Priestley T	Gallacher H	Gibson G	Horton J	Mills G	Jackson J	Odell L	Gregg R	Rankin J	Chitty W	Allum L	Macaulay R	Copeland J	Griffiths R	Miller H	Mitchell W	Hutcheson J	Argue J	O'Hare J	
	2	3	4	5	6	7	8	9	10	11		1														1
	3	4	5	6	7			9	10	11	8	1	2													2
	3	4	5	6	7			9	10	11	8	1	2													3
	3	4	5	6	7				10	11		1	2	8					9							4
	2	3	4	5	6	7	11	9	10			1		8												5
1	2	3	4	5	6	7	11	9	10					8												6
1	2	3	4	5	6	7	11	9	10					8												7
1	2	3	4	5	6	7	11	9	10					8												8
1		3	4	6	5	7	11	9	10					8				2								9
1		3	4	5		7		9	10	11	8			6				2								10
1	2	3		5		7	11	9	10		8					6	4									11
1	2	3		5		7	11	9	10		8						4				6					12
1	2	3		5		7	11	9	10		8						4				6					13
1	2	3		5		7	8	9	10	11							4				6					14
1	2	3		5			8	9	10	11							4	7			6					15
1	2	3	4	5		11	8	9	10									7			6					16
1	2	3	4	5		11	8	9	10									7			6					17
1		3	4	5		11		9	10				2					7			6		8			18
1		3		5		7	8	9	10	11			2				4				6					19
1		3		5		7	8	9	10	11			2				4				6					20
1		3		5		7	8	9	10	11			2				4				6					21
1		3		5		7	8	9	10	11			2				4				6					22
1	2	3		5		7	8	9	10	11							4				6					23
1	2	3		5		7	8	9	10	11							4				6					24
1	2	3		5		7	8	9	10	11							4				6					25
1	2			5		7	8	9	10	11				3			4				6					26
1	2		4	5		7		9	10	11	8			3							6					27
1	2		4	5		7		9	10	11	8			3							6					28
1			4	5		7		9	10	11	8			3			5					6			2	29
1	2		4	5		7	8	9	10	11				3								6				30
1	2		4	5		7		9	10	11	8			3							6					31
1	2		4	5		7		9	10	11	8			3							6					32
1	2		4	5		7		9	10	11	8			3							6					33
1	2		4	5		7		9	10	11	8			3							6					34
1	2		4	5		7		9	10	11	8			3							6					35
1	2		4	5		7		9	10	11	8			3							6					36
1	2		4	5		7		9	10	11	8			3									6			37
1	2		4	5		7		9	10	11	8			3									6			38
1	2		4	5		7		9	10	11	8			3									6			39
1	2		4	5		7		9	10	11	8			3									6			40
1	2		4	5		7		9	10	11	8			3									6			41
	2		4	5		7		9	10	11	8	1		3							6					42
36	31	25	29	30	20	41	23	23	32	30	24	6	14	28	3	5	14	13	1	1	23	2	6	1	1	
			4			12	1	13	9	8	14			2			1	1			1					

1 own-goal

Woodley V	Barber G	Law T	Russell W	Craig A	O'Dowd P	Oakton E	Priestley T	Gallacher H	Gibson G	Horton J	Mills G	Jackson J	Odell L	Gregg R	Rankin J	Chitty W	Allum L	Macaulay R	Copeland J	Griffiths R	Miller H	Mitchell W	Hutcheson J	Argue J	O'Hare J	
1	2	3		5		7	8	9		11							4				6					3
1	2	3		5		7	8	9	10	11							4				6					R
1	2			5		7	8	9	10	11				3			4				6					4
1	2			5		7	8	9	10	11				3			4				6					R
1	2			5		7		9	10	11	8			3			4	6								5
5	5	2		5		5	4	5	4	5	2			4			3				1	5				
				1		1		3	1					1												

245

1934-35

Manager: Leslie Knighton

1	Aug	25	(a)	Derby C	L	0-3		20,265
2		29	(h)	Sheffield W	L	1-2	Oakton	19,756
3	Sep	1	(h)	Leicester C	W	3-1	Mills 2, Cheyne	20,084
4		3	(a)	Sheffield W	L	1-3	Mills	13,029
5		8	(a)	Sunderland	L	0-4		33,592
6		15	(h)	Tottenham H	L	1-3	Russell (pen)	46,715
7		22	(a)	Preston NE	L	0-2		18,332
8		29	(h)	Grimsby T	W	2-0	Horton 2	25,373
9	Oct	6	(a)	Everton	L	2-3	Mills, Horton	17,827
10		13	(h)	Huddersfield T	W	2-1	Mills, Spence	32,151
11		20	(a)	Birmingham	W	1-0	Gallacher	22,572
12		27	(h)	Stoke C	L	0-2		39,160
13	Nov	3	(a)	Leeds U	L	2-5	Mills, Gallacher	13,295
14		10	(h)	West Brom A	L	2-3	Gregg, Spence	18,362
15		17	(a)	Blackburn R	W	2-1	Mills 2	10,781
16		24	(h)	Arsenal	L	2-5	Macaulay, Gregg	43,419
17	Dec	1	(a)	Portsmouth	D	1-1	W.Smith (og)	18,076
18		8	(h)	Liverpool	W	4-1	Spence 4	29,005
19		15	(a)	Manchester C	L	0-2		28,797
20		22	(h)	Middlesbrough	W	2-1	Spence, Argue	23,724
21		25	(h)	Aston Villa	W	2-0	Spence 2	46,746
22		26	(a)	Aston Villa	W	3-0	Gibson, Barraclough, Argue	52,886
23		29	(h)	Derby C	D	1-1	Argue	50,687
24	Jan	5	(a)	Leicester C	L	0-1		14,593
25		19	(h)	Sunderland	D	2-2	Horton, Spence	37,096
26		29	(a)	Tottenham H	W	3-1	Barraclough, Spence, Bambrick	28,121
27	Feb	2	(h)	Preston NE	D	0-0		31,994
28		9	(a)	Grimsby T	L	1-3	Bambrick	12,442
29		20	(h)	Everton	W	3-0	Barraclough, Mercer (og), Bambrick	11,701
30		23	(a)	Huddersfield T	L	0-3		13,593
31	Mar	6	(h)	Birmingham	D	2-2	Spence, Bambrick	13,016
32		9	(a)	Stoke C	W	1-0	Bambrick	13,186
33		16	(h)	Leeds U	W	7-1	Spence 2, Bambrick 4, Burgess	35,698
34		23	(a)	West Brom A	D	2-2	Bambrick, Argue	13,831
35		30	(h)	Blackburn R	W	4-2	Spence 3, Burgess	34,470
36	Apr	6	(a)	Arsenal	D	2-2	Barraclough, Spence	54,020
37		13	(h)	Portsmouth	D	1-1	Bambrick	44,787
38		19	(h)	Wolves	W	4-2	Hutcheson, Barrowclough, Argue, Burgess	44,636
39		20	(a)	Liverpool	L	0-6		14,297
40		22	(a)	Wolves	L	1-6	Spence	32,703
41		27	(h)	Manchester C	W	4-2	Bambrick 4	22,593
42	May	4	(a)	Middlesbrough	D	2-2	Gregg, Barrowclough	17,505

FINAL LEAGUE POSITION: 12th in Division One

Appearances
Goals

FA Cup

3	Jan	12	(h)	Luton T	D	1-1	Argue	46,492
R		16	(a)	Luton T	L	0-2		23,041

Appearances
Goals

Aggregate League attendances:
Home: 671,173 (average 31,960)
Away: 453,843 (average 21,611)

Player appearance and goalscoring grid (shirt numbers shown per match).

Woodley V	Barber G	Macaulay R	Russell W	Craig A	Miller H	Oakton E	Gregg R	Mills G	Gibson G	Horton J	Hutcheson J	Cheyne A	Gallacher H	Odell L	Jackson J	Allum L	Barraclough W	Spence R	Copeland J	Bambrick J	O'Hare J	Argue J	Mitchell W	Burgess H	#
1	2	3	4	5	6	7	8	9	10	11															1
1	2	3	4	5		7	8	9	10	11	6														2
1	2	3	4	5		7		9	10	11	6	8													3
1		3	4	5	6	7		9	10	11		8		2											4
1		3	4	5		7		9	10	11	6	8		2											5
1	2	3	4	5	6	7		9	10	11			8												6
	2	3	4	5	6	7		9	10	11			8		1										7
1	2	3		5	6	7	8	9	10	11						4									8
1	2	3		5	10		8	9		11	6					4		7							9
1	2	3	4	5			8	10		11	6		9					7							10
1	2	3	4	5			8	10		11	6		9					7							11
1	2	3	4	5			8	10		11	6		9					7							12
1	2	3	4	5			8	10			6		9				11	7							13
1	2	3		5	6		10	9								4	11	7				8			14
	2	3		5	6			9			10				1	4	11	7				8			15
	2	3		5	6		10	9							1	4	11	7				8			16
	2	3		5	6			9	10						1	4	11	7				8			17
	2	3		5	6			9	10						1	4	11	7				8			18
	2	3		5	6				10						1	4	11	7	9			8			19
	2	3		5	6			9	10						1	4	11	7				8			20
1		3		5	6				10					2		4	11	7		9		8			21
		3		5	6				10					2	1	4	11	7		9		8			22
		3		5	6				10					2	1	4	11	7		9		8			23
	2	3		5	6				10						1	4	11	7		9		8			24
	2	3		5	6				10	11					1			7		9		8	4		25
	2	3		5	6				10						1		11	7		9		8	4		26
	2	3		5	6				10						1		11	7		9		8	4		27
	2	3		5					10						1	4	11	7		9		8	6		28
	2	3		5	6				10						1	4	11	7		9		8			29
	2	3		5	6				10						1	4	11	7		9		8			30
	2	3		5	6				10						1	4	11	7		9		8			31
	2	3		5	6		10								1	4	11	7		9		8			32
	2	3		5	6										1	4	11	7		9		8		10	33
	2	3		5	6										1	4	11	7		9		8		10	34
	2	3		5	6										1	4	11	7		9		8		10	35
1	2	3		5	6											4	11	7		9		8		10	36
	2	3		5	6										1	4	11	7		9		8		10	37
	2	3		5	6										1	4	11	7		9		8		10	38
	2	3		5	6										1	4	11	7		9		8		10	39
	2	3	4	5	6			9							1		11	7				8		10	40
		3	4	5	6		8								1		11	7		9	2			10	41
		3	4	5	6		8								1		11	7		9	2			10	42
15	39	38	14	42	34	8	13	20	23	13	11	3	7	5	27	22	29	34	1	21	2	27	4	10	
	1	1		1	3	8	1	4	1	1	2					6	19			15		5	3		

2 own-goals

Cup appearances:

Woodley V	Barber G	Macaulay R	Russell W	Craig A	Miller H	Oakton E	Gregg R	Mills G	Gibson G	Horton J	Hutcheson J	Cheyne A	Gallacher H	Odell L	Jackson J	Allum L	Barraclough W	Spence R	Copeland J	Bambrick J	O'Hare J	Argue J	Mitchell W	Burgess H	
	2	3		5	6				10						1	4	11	7		9		8			3
	2	3	4	5	6				10	11					1			7		9		8			R
	2	2	1	2	2				2	1					2	1	1	2		2		2			
																		1							

247

1935-36

Manager: Leslie Knighton

1	Aug	31	(h)	Liverpool	D	2-2	Bambrick 2	41,224
2	Sep	4	(h)	Stoke C	L	3-5	Bambrick 3	23,687
3		7	(a)	Grimsby T	W	3-1	Spence, Bambrick, Burgess	14,917
4		9	(a)	Stoke C	L	0-3		21,310
5		14	(h)	Leeds U	W	1-0	Burgess	35,720
6		16	(a)	Blackburn R	L	0-1		14,610
7		21	(a)	West Brom A	W	2-1	Argue, Mills	17,308
8		28	(h)	Sunderland	W	3-1	Gibson, Mills 2	61,051
9	Oct	5	(a)	Birmingham	L	1-2	Burgess	22,625
10		12	(h)	Arsenal	D	1-1	Bambrick	82,905
11		19	(a)	Everton	L	1-5	Mills	18,934
12		26	(h)	Bolton W	W	2-1	Miller, Horton	36,080
13	Nov	2	(a)	Huddersfield T	L	0-2		16,684
14		9	(h)	Middlesbrough	W	2-1	Bambrick 2	33,408
15		16	(a)	Aston Villa	D	2-2	Spence 2	58,717
16		23	(h)	Brentford	W	2-1	Spence, Cheyne	56,624
17		30	(a)	Sheffield W	L	1-4	Gibson	16,014
18	Dec	14	(a)	Preston NE	L	0-2		16,178
19		21	(h)	Wolves	D	2-2	Spence, Barraclough	20,063
20		25	(a)	Manchester C	D	0-0		36,074
21		26	(h)	Manchester C	W	2-1	Gibson, Bambrick	41,732
22		28	(a)	Liverpool	W	3-2	Burgess, Oakton 2	26,523
23	Jan	4	(h)	Grimsby T	L	0-2		30,381
24		18	(a)	Leeds U	L	0-2		18,999
25	Feb	1	(a)	Sunderland	D	3-3	Gibson, Bambrick 2	23,755
26		8	(h)	Birmingham	D	0-0		30,268
27		22	(h)	Everton	D	2-2	Bambrick 2	17,136
28	Mar	4	(a)	Middlesbrough	L	1-4	Barraclough	7,968
29		7	(h)	Sheffield W	L	1-2	Burgess	27,221
30		11	(h)	West Brom A	D	2-2	Allum, Burgess	13,225
31		14	(a)	Bolton W	W	3-2	Spence, Bambrick, Mills	18,925
32		21	(h)	Aston Villa	W	1-0	Mills	48,761
33		28	(a)	Brentford	L	1-2	Argue	33,486
34	Apr	4	(h)	Huddersfield T	W	1-0	Burgess (pen)	22,369
35		10	(h)	Derby C	D	1-1	Spence	54,336
36		11	(a)	Portsmouth	L	0-2		18,605
37		13	(a)	Derby C	D	1-1	Spence	21,407
38		18	(h)	Preston NE	W	5-2	Spence 3, Burgess, Oakton	26,274
39		22	(h)	Portsmouth *	W	1-0	Mills	13,982
40		25	(a)	Wolves	D	3-3	Burgess, Mills 2	12,683
41		27	(a)	Arsenal	D	1-1	Mills	40,402
42	May	2	(h)	Blackburn R	W	5-1	Spence 2, Burgess 2, Mills	18,078

FINAL LEAGUE POSITION: 8th in Division One
*Original match on 7 December was abandoned after 78 minutes, with Portsmouth leading 2-1.

Appearances
Goals

FA Cup

3	Jan	11	(a)	Norwich C	D	1-1	Mitchell	32,398
R		15	(h)	Norwich C	W	3-1	Bambrick 3	31,734
4		25	(h)	Plymouth A	W	4-1	Bambrick, Burgess, Barraclough, McNeil (og)	53,703
5	Feb	19	(h)	Fulham	D	0-0		52,096
R		24	(a)	Fulham	L	2-3	Barraclough 2	30,696

Appearances
Goals

Aggregate League attendances:
Home: 734,525 (average 34,977)
Away: 476,124 (average 22,672)

Jackson J	Barber G	Macaulay R	Allum L	Craig A	Miller H	Spence R	Gibson G	Bambrick J	Burgess H	Barraclough W	Mitchell W	O'Hare J	Argue J	Law T	Odell L	Mills G	Gregg R	Woodley V	Cheyne A	Griffiths R	Horton J	Hutcheson J	Oakton E	Chitty W	Mayes A	
1	2	3	4	5	6	7	8	9	10	11																1
1	2	3	4	5	6	7	8	9	10	11																2
1		3	4	5		7	8	9	10	11		6	2													3
1		3	4	5		7	8	9	10	11		6	2													4
1	2			5	6	7		9	10	11	4		8	3												5
1				5	6	7			10	11	4	2	8	3		9										6
1				5	6	7	10			11	4	2	8	3		9										7
1				5	6	7	10			11	4	2		3		9			8							8
				5	6	7	10		8	11	4	2		3		9		1								9
1				5	6	7	10	9		11	4	2	8	3												10
1				5	6	7	10			11			2	8	3		9					4				11
				5	6	7	10	9	8		4	2		3				1				11				12
				5	6	7	10	9			4	2		3		8		1				11				13
					6	7	10	9			4	2		3				1	8	5	11					14
				5	6	7	10	9		11	4	2		3				1	8							15
				5	6	7	10	9			4	2		3				1	8			11				16
				5	6	7	10	9			4	2		3				1	8			11				17
				5	6	7	10	9		11	4	2		3				1	8							18
				5	6	7	10			11	4	2		3		9		1	8							19
				5	6	7			9	10	11	4	2		3			1	8							20
	3			5	6	7	10	9	8	11	4	2						1								21
	2			5				10		11	4			3		9		1	8				7		6	22
	2			5				10	9	11	4			3				1	8				7		6	23
	2	3		5	6	7	10	9	8	11	4							1								24
	2	3		5	6	7	10	9	8	11	4							1								25
	2	3		5		7	10	9	8	11	4							1				6				26
	2		4	5	6	7	10	9	8	11				3				1								27
	2		4	5	6	7		9	10	11			8	3				1								28
	3		4	5	6	7		9	10	11		2	8					1								29
	3		4	5	6	7		9	10	11		2	8					1								30
	3		4	5		7	8		10	11		2				9		1				6				31
	3		4	5		7			10	11		2	8			9		1				6				32
	3		4	5		7			10	11		2	8			9		1				6				33
	3		4	5	6	7	10		8	11		2				9		1								34
	3			5	6	7	10	9	8	11	4	2						1								35
	3			5	6	7	10		8		4	2				9		1					11			36
	3			5	6	7	10		8		4	2				9		1					11			37
	2			5	6	7	10		8		4		3			9		1					11			38
	2			5	6	7	10		8		4		3			9		1					11			39
	2			5	6	7	10		8		4		3			9		1					11			40
	2			5	6	7	10		8		4		3			9		1					11			41
	3			5	6	7	10		8		4	2				9		1					11			42
10	27	5	12	41	34	40	33	25	31	30	31	27	9	23	2	19	3	32	6	1	5	5	8	1	2	—
		1			1	13	4	15	11	2				2		11			1				1		3	

Jackson J	Barber G	Macaulay R	Allum L	Craig A	Miller H	Spence R	Gibson G	Bambrick J	Burgess H	Barraclough W	Mitchell W	O'Hare J	Argue J	Law T	Odell L	Mills G	Gregg R	Woodley V	Cheyne A	Griffiths R	Horton J	Hutcheson J	Oakton E	Chitty W	Mayes A	
	3			5		7	10	9	8	11	4	2						1					6			3
	2	3		5	6	7	10	9	8	11	4							1								R
	2	3		5	6	7	10	9	8	11	4							1								4
	2	3	4	5	6	7	10	9	8	11								1								5
	2		4	5	6	7	10	9	8	11				3				1								R
	5	3	2	5	4	5	5	5	5	5	3	1		1				5					1			
							4	1	3	1																

1 own-goal

249

1936-37

Manager: Leslie Knighton

#					Result	Scorers	Att.
1	Aug	29	(a)	Leeds U	W 3-2	Spence 2, Mills	19,379
2	Sep	2	(h)	Grimsby T	W 3-2	Weaver 2, Mills	25,671
3		5	(h)	Birmingham	L 1-3	Mills	32,803
4		8	(a)	Grimsby T	L 0-3		12,667
5		12	(a)	Middlesbrough	L 0-2		21,278
6		16	(h)	Liverpool	W 2-0	Bambrick 2	18,123
7		19	(h)	West Brom A	W 3-0	Gibson, Oakton 2	41,112
8		26	(a)	Manchester C	D 0-0		30,004
9	Oct	3	(h)	Portsmouth	D 1-1	Burgess	45,735
10		10	(a)	Preston NE	L 0-1		20,040
11		17	(h)	Sheffield W	D 1-1	Burgess	34,488
12		24	(a)	Manchester U	D 0-0		29,854
13		31	(h)	Derby C	D 1-1	Argue	15,529
14	Nov	7	(a)	Wolves	W 2-1	Mills 2	16,510
15		14	(h)	Sunderland	L 1-3	Mills	48,901
16		21	(a)	Huddersfield T	L 2-4	Spence 2	12,382
17		28	(h)	Everton	W 4-0	Weaver, Mills 3	31,623
18	Dec	5	(a)	Bolton W	L 1-2	Burgess	13,439
19		12	(h)	Brentford	W 2-1	Spence, Mills	51,079
20		19	(a)	Arsenal	L 1-4	Oakton	49,917
21		25	(a)	Stoke C	L 0-2		24,897
22		26	(h)	Leeds U	W 2-1	Spence, Chitty (pen)	27,761
23		28	(h)	Stoke C	W 1-0	Mills	16,675
24	Jan	2	(a)	Birmingham	D 0-0		17,673
25		9	(h)	Middlesbrough	W 1-0	Mills	30,201
26		23	(a)	West Brom A	L 0-2		9,722
27	Feb	3	(h)	Manchester C	D 4-4	Mills 3, Gibson	11,620
28		6	(a)	Portsmouth	L 1-4	Gibson	16,447
29		13	(h)	Preston NE	D 0-0		27,465
30		20	(a)	Sheffield W	D 1-1	Mills	16,052
31		27	(h)	Manchester U	W 4-2	Mills 2, Argue 2	16,382
32	Mar	6	(a)	Derby C	D 1-1	Argue	15,010
33		13	(h)	Wolves	L 0-1		34,078
34		20	(a)	Sunderland	W 3-2	Spence, Mills, Argue	21,825
35		26	(h)	Charlton A	W 3-0	Burgess, Mills, Argue	64,463
36		27	(h)	Huddersfield T	D 0-0		31,384
37		29	(a)	Charlton A	L 0-1		45,860
38	Apr	3	(a)	Everton	D 0-0		20,648
39		10	(h)	Bolton W	L 0-1		23,271
40		17	(a)	Brentford	L 0-1		22,042
41		24	(h)	Arsenal	W 2-0	Mills 2	53,325
42	May	1	(a)	Liverpool	D 1-1	Spence	8,278

FINAL LEAGUE POSITION: 13th in Division One

Appearances
Goals

FA Cup

					Result	Scorers	Att.
3	Jan	16	(h)	Leeds U	W 4-0	Spence 2, Mills, Argue	34,859
4		30	(a)	Millwall	L 0-3		42,000

Appearances
Goals

250

Woodley V	O'Hare J	Barber G	Mitchell W	Craig A	Weaver S	Spence R	Burgess H	Mills G	Gibson G	Barraclough W	Argue J	Miller H	Oakton A	Gregg R	Chitty W	Griffiths R	Horton J	Buchanan P	Allum L	Jackson J	Smale D	Bambrick J	Foss SR	#
1	2	3	4	5	6	7	8	9	10	11														1
1	2	3	4	5	6	7		9	10	11	8													2
1	2	3	4	5	6	7	8	9	10	11														3
1	2	3	4	5	6	7	8	9	10	11														4
1	2	3	4	5	6	7	8	9	10	11														5
1	2	3	4	5		7	8		10			6	11									9		6
1	2	3	4	5		7	8	10				6	11									9		7
1	2	3	4	5	10	7	8					6	11									9		8
1	2	3	4	5		7	10				8	6	11									9		9
1	2	3		5	6	7	10				8	4	11									9		10
1	2	3	4	5	6	7	10				8		11									9		11
1	2	3	4	5	6		10				11	8			7							9		12
1	2	3		5	6		10				11	8	4		7							9		13
1	2	3		5	6	7	10	9			8	4	11											14
1	2	3		5	6	7	10	9			8	4	11											15
1	2	3		5	6	7	10	9			8	4	11											16
1	2	3	4	5	6	7	10	9			11	8												17
1	2	3	4	5	6	7	10	9			11	8												18
1	2	3	4	5	6	7	10	9			11	8												19
1	2	3	4	5	6		10	9			11	8			7									20
1		3		5	6	7		9			8	4	11	10	2									21
1		3		5	6	7		9			8	4	11	10	2									22
1		3		5	6	7		9			8	4	11	10	2									23
1		3	4			7	8	9	10	11	6			2	5									24
1	2	3	4	5	6	7	8	9	10	11														25
1	2	3		5	6	7	10	9			8	4	11											26
1	2	3		5	6	7		9	10		8	4					11							27
1	2	3		5	6	7		9	10		8	4					11							28
1	2	3	4	5	6	11		9	10		8							7						29
1	2	3	4	5	6	7		9			11	8										10		30
1	2	3	4	5	6	7		9			11	8										10		31
1	2	3	4	5	6	7		9			8				11							10		32
1	2	3	4	5	6	7	11	9			8											10		33
1	2	3		5	6	7	11	9	10		8								4					34
1	2	3		5	6	7	11	9	10		8								4					35
1	2		4	5	6	7	11	9	10		8			3										36
1	2	3	4	5	6	7		9	10		8										11			37
1	2	3	4	5	6	7	8		10												11	9		38
1	2	3	4	5	6	7			10		8										11	9		39
	2	3		5	6	7	10	9			8								4	1	11			40
1		3		5	6	7	10	9			8					2			4		11			41
1		3	4	5	6	7		9	10		8					2					11			42
41	36	41	27	41	38	39	29	32	19	15	32	16	16	3	8	1	2	1	4	1	6	10	4	
				3	8	4	22	3			6	3			1						2			

Woodley V	O'Hare J	Barber G	Mitchell W	Craig A	Weaver S	Spence R	Burgess H	Mills G	Gibson G	Barraclough W	Argue J	Miller H	Oakton A	Gregg R	Chitty W	Griffiths R	Horton J	Buchanan P	Allum L	Jackson J	Smale D	Bambrick J	Foss SR	#
1	2	3		5	6	7	10	9			11	8	4											3
1	2	3		5	6	7		9	10		8	4					11							4
2	2	2		2	2	2	1	2	1	1	2	2					1							
				2		1						1												

1937-38

Manager: Leslie Knighton

1	Aug	28	(h)	Liverpool	W	6-1	Mitchell, Argue, Mills 3, Burgess	41,553
2	Sep	1	(a)	Leeds U	L	0-2		18,858
3		4	(a)	West Brom A	L	0-4		23,100
4		8	(h)	Leeds U	W	4-1	Argue, Mills 2, Buchanan	17,300
5		11	(h)	Birmingham	W	2-0	Burgess (pen), Gibson	34,072
6		15	(h)	Grimsby T	W	1-0	Chitty	15,617
7		18	(a)	Middlesbrough	L	3-4	Burgess (pen), Buchanan, Chitty	19,631
8		25	(h)	Stoke C	W	2-1	Argue, Chitty	38,504
9	Oct	2	(a)	Portsmouth	W	4-2	Mitchell, Mills, Buchanan, Chitty	25,233
10		9	(h)	Arsenal	D	2-2	Argue, Mills	75,952
11		16	(a)	Blackpool	W	2-0	Argue, Buchanan	23,974
12		23	(h)	Brentford	W	2-1	Argue, Bambrick	56,810
13		30	(a)	Bolton W	D	5-5	Argue 3, Mills, Chitty	22,293
14	Nov	6	(h)	Sunderland	D	0-0		50,554
15		13	(a)	Everton	L	1-4	Mills	29,930
16		20	(h)	Manchester C	D	2-2	Mills, Burgess	40,197
17		27	(a)	Leicester C	L	0-1		18,883
18	Dec	4	(h)	Huddersfield T	W	3-1	Spence, Bidewell 2	31,475
19		11	(a)	Derby C	L	0-4		12,886
20		18	(h)	Wolves	L	0-2		31,314
21		27	(a)	Charlton A	L	1-3	Chitty	51,125
22	Jan	1	(a)	Liverpool	D	2-2	Burgess, Chitty	39,062
23		15	(h)	West Brom A	D	2-2	Mills, Burgess	20,378
24		22	(a)	Birmingham	D	1-1	Buchanan	18,480
25		29	(h)	Middlesbrough	L	0-1		27,081
26	Feb	5	(a)	Stoke C	L	1-2	Spence	22,693
27		12	(h)	Portsmouth	W	3-1	Mills, Buchanan, Chitty	18,323
28		19	(a)	Arsenal	L	0-2		49,513
29		26	(h)	Blackpool	L	1-3	Mills	27,301
30	Mar	9	(a)	Brentford	D	1-1	Foss	20,401
31		12	(h)	Bolton W	D	0-0		38,171
32		19	(a)	Sunderland	D	1-1	Chitty	19,327
33		26	(h)	Everton	W	2-0	Payne, Chitty	27,043
34	Apr	2	(a)	Manchester C	L	0-1		31,033
35		9	(h)	Leicester C	W	4-1	Weaver, Spence, Chitty, Sharman (og)	20,211
36		15	(h)	Preston NE	L	0-2		54,735
37		16	(a)	Huddersfield T	W	2-1	Spence, Payne	18,356
38		18	(a)	Preston NE	D	0-0		32,096
39		23	(h)	Derby C	W	3-0	Foss 2, Payne	25,032
40		27	(h)	Charlton A	D	1-1	Payne	21,843
41		30	(a)	Wolves	D	1-1	Burgess	27,718
42	May	7	(a)	Grimsby T	L	0-2		14,601

FINAL LEAGUE POSITION: 10th in Division One

Appearances
Goals

FA Cup

3	Jan	8	(h)	Everton	L	0-1		41,946

Appearances
Goals

Aggregate League attendances:
Home: 713,466 (average 33,974)
Away: 539,193 (average 25,675)

Woodley V	O'Hare J	Barber G	Mitchell W	Griffiths R	Weaver S	Spence R	Argue J	Mills G	Burgess H	Smale D	Gibson G	Buchanan P	Allum L	Bambrick J	Jackson J	Miller H	Barkas E	Bidewell S	Gregg R	Law T	Mayes A	Foss SR	Payne J	Smith AJ	Craig A	Sherborne J	Chitty W	No.
1	2	3	4	5	6	7	8	9	10	11																		1
1	2	3	4	5	6	7	8	9	11		10																	2
1	2	3	4	5	6	7	8	9	11		10																	3
1	2	3	4	5	6	11	8	9	10			7																4
1	2	3	4	5	6	11		9	8		10	7																5
1	2	3	4	5	6		8	9	10			7															11	6
1	2	3	4	5	6		8	9	10			7															11	7
1	2	3	4	5	6		8	9	10			7															11	8
1	2	3	4	5	6		8	9	10			7															11	9
1	2	3	4	5	6		8	9	10			7															11	10
1	2	3	4	5	6		8	9	10			7															11	11
	2	3		5			8		10			7	4	9	1	6											11	12
1	2	3	4	5			8	9	10			7				6											11	13
1	2	3	4	5	6		8	9	10			7															11	14
1	2	3	6	5	10		8	9				7	4														11	15
1	2	3	4	5	6	11	8	9	10			7																16
1	2	3	4	5	6	11	8	9	10			7																17
1	2	3	4	5	6	11	8		10			7					9											18
1	2	3	4	5	6	11		9	10			7					8											19
1	2	3	4	5	6				10			7					8									9	11	20
1	2	3	4	5	6			9	10			7					8										11	21
1		3	4	5	6			9	10			7					2				8						11	22
1		3		5	6	11	8	9	10			7				4	2											23
1		3		5	6	11	8	9	10			7				4	2											24
1		3		5	6	11	8	9	10			7				4	2											25
1				5	6	7	8	9									2					3	4			10	11	26
1				5	6		8	9				7					2					3	4			10		27
1				5	6		8	9	11			7					2					3	4			10		28
1				5	6		8	9	11			7					2					3	4			10		29
1	2	3		5	6	11	8					7	4	9								10						30
1	2			5	6	11			10			7	4	9								8		3				31
1				5	6	7			8				4				2					10	9	3			11	32
1				5		7			8				4			6	2					10	9	3			11	33
1				5	6	7			8				4				2					10	9	3			11	34
				5	6	7		9	8				4		1		2					10		3			11	35
1					6	11			8			7	4				2					10	9	3	5			36
1					6	11			8			7	4				2					10	9	3	5			37
1	2				6	11			8			7	4									10	9	3	5			38
1					6	7			8	11			4				2					10	9	3	5			39
1					6	7			8	11			4				2					10	9	3	5			40
1					6	7			8	11	10		4				2						9	3	5			41
1		3			6	7			8		10	11	4				2						9	3	5			42
40	22	29	21	35	39	28	21	27	36	2	9	33	15	3	2	6	18	4	1	4	4	11	10	11	7	5	19	
		2		1	4	9	13	7		1	6		1				2					3	4				11	

1 own-goal

Woodley V	O'Hare J	Barber G	Mitchell W	Griffiths R	Weaver S	Spence R	Argue J	Mills G	Burgess H	Smale D	Gibson G	Buchanan P	Allum L	Bambrick J	Jackson J	Miller H	Barkas E	Bidewell S	Gregg R	Law T	Mayes A	Foss SR	Payne J	Smith AJ	Craig A	Sherborne J	Chitty W	No.
1		3		5	6			9	10			7	4				2	8										3
1		1		1	1			1	1			1	1				1	1										

1938-39

Manager: Leslie Knighton

1	Aug	27	(a)	Liverpool	L	1-2	Allum	33,868
2		31	(h)	Preston NE	W	3-1	Spence 2, Hanson	24,821
3	Sep	3	(h)	Leicester C	W	3-0	Mills 2, Hanson	37,323
4		5	(a)	Bolton W	W	2-0	Hanson 2	19,616
5		10	(a)	Middlesbrough	D	1-1	Mills	28,359
6		17	(h)	Birmingham	D	2-2	Spence, Mills	39,505
7		24	(a)	Manchester U	L	1-5	Burgess (pen)	34,557
8	Oct	1	(h)	Stoke C	D	1-1	Burgess	35,320
9		8	(a)	Blackpool	L	1-5	Payne	24,878
10		15	(h)	Arsenal	W	4-2	Burgess, Mills, Hanson 2	64,443
11		22	(a)	Brentford	L	0-1		31,425
12		29	(h)	Derby C	L	0-2		37,919
13	Nov	5	(a)	Grimsby T	L	1-2	Mills	11,461
14		12	(h)	Sunderland	W	4-0	Spence, Burgess, Hanson, Argue	37,103
15		19	(a)	Aston Villa	L	2-6	Mills, Argue	41,678
16		26	(h)	Wolves	L	1-3	Mills	32,456
17	Dec	3	(a)	Everton	L	1-4	Mills	27,959
18		10	(h)	Huddersfield T	W	3-0	Burgess, Payne 2	23,257
19		17	(a)	Portsmouth	L	1-2	Mills	21,536
20		24	(h)	Liverpool	W	4-1	Spence, Burgess (pen), Payne 2	6,801
21		26	(a)	Leeds U	D	1-1	Mills	27,586
22		27	(h)	Leeds U	D	2-2	Spence, Mills	32,692
23		31	(a)	Leicester C	L	2-3	Argue 2	13,180
24	Jan	14	(h)	Middlesbrough	W	4-2	Argue, Payne 3	26,750
25		28	(h)	Manchester U	L	0-1		31,265
26	Feb	4	(a)	Stoke C	L	1-6	Spence	25,205
27		18	(a)	Arsenal	L	0-1		54,510
28		25	(h)	Brentford	L	1-3	Payne	33,511
29	Mar	8	(a)	Derby C	W	1-0	Spence	6,697
30		11	(h)	Grimsby T	W	5-1	Spence 2, Burgess, Hanson, Payne	17,102
31		15	(h)	Blackpool	D	1-1	Payne	12,971
32		18	(a)	Sunderland	L	2-3	Burgess (pen), Argue	10,954
33		25	(h)	Aston Villa	W	2-1	Spence, Argue	31,225
34	Apr	1	(a)	Wolves	L	0-2		28,744
35		7	(a)	Charlton A	L	0-2		29,014
36		8	(h)	Everton	L	0-2		51,481
37		10	(h)	Charlton A	L	1-3	Payne	27,070
38		15	(a)	Huddersfield T	L	1-3	Payne	11,731
39		22	(h)	Portsmouth	W	1-0	Payne	28,744
40		26	(a)	Birmingham	D	1-1	Payne	28,637
41		29	(a)	Preston NE	D	1-1	Payne	13,333
42	May	6	(h)	Bolton W	D	1-1	Payne	18,232

FINAL LEAGUE POSITION: 20th in Division One

Appearances
Goals

FA Cup

3	Jan	7	(h)	Arsenal	W	2-1	Argue 2	58,095
4		21	(h)	Fulham	W	3-0	Hanson, Argue, Payne	69,987
5	Feb	11	(h)	Sheffield W	D	1-1	Burgess (pen)	60,920
R		13	(a)	Sheffield W	D	0-0*		47,549
2R		20	(n†)	Sheffield W	W	3-1	Burgess 2, Payne	51,879
6	Mar	4	(h)	Grimsby T	L	0-1		45,409

*After extra-time.   †Played at Arsenal Stadium, Highbury, London.

Appearances
Goals

Aggregate League attendances:
Home: 629,991 (average 29,999)
Away: 524,928 (average 24,996)

Woodley V	Barkas E	Smith AJ	Allum L	Craig A	Weaver S	Spence R	Burgess H	Mills G	Foss SR	Hanson A	Argue J	Griffiths R	Mitchell W	Barber G	Payne J	Reid E	Salmond R	O'Hare J	Mayes A	Buchanan P	Alexander D	Gibson G	Jackson J	Smale D	No.
1	2	3	4		6	7	10	9		11	8	5													1
1	2	3	4		6	7	8	9	10	11		5													2
1	2	3		5	6	7	8	9	10	11			4												3
1	2	3		5	6	7	8	9	10	11			4												4
1	2	3	4	5	6	7	8	9	10	11															5
1	2	3	4	5	6	7	8	9	10	11															6
1	2	3	4	5	6	7	8	9	10	11															7
1		3	4	5	6	7	8	9	10	11				2											8
1		3	4	5	6	7			10	11	8			2	9										9
1		3	4	5	6	7	10	9		11	8			2											10
	2	3	4	5	6	7	10	9		11	8										1				11
1		3	4	5	6	7	10			11	8			2	9										12
1		3	4	5		7	10	9		11	8			2		6									13
1		3	4		6	7	10	9		11	8			2			5								14
1		3	4		6	7	10			11	8			2			5								15
1		3			6	7	10	9		11	8			2			5		4						16
1		3			6	7		9	10	11			4	2	8		5								17
1		3			6	7	10	9		11			4	2	8		5								18
1					6	7	10	9		11			4	3	8		5	2							19
1					6	7	10	9		11			4	3	8		5	2							20
1					6	7		9		11			4	3	8		5	2					10		21
1					6	7	10	9		11	8		4	3			5	2							22
1		3			6	7	10				8		4		9		5	2					11		23
1					6	7	10			11	8		4	3	9		5	2							24
1					6	7	10			11	8		4	3	9		5	2							25
1					6	7	10			11	8		4	3	9		5	2							26
1		3			6	7		9	10	11			4	2	8		5								27
1		3		5	6	7	10	9		11			4		8			2							28
1		3			6	7			10	11	8		4	2	9		5								29
		3			6	7	10			11	8		4	2	9		5					1			30
1		3			6	7	10			11	8		4	2	9		5								31
1		3			6	7	10			11	8		4	2	9		5								32
1		3			6	11	10				8		4	2	9		5			7					33
1		3			6	11	10	9			8		4	2			5			7					34
1		3			6	11	10				8			2	9		5			7			4		35
1		3			6		10			11	8			2	9		5		4	7					36
1		3			6	7	10			11	8			2	9		5		4						37
		3			6	11	10				8				9		5	2	4	7				1	38
1		3		5	6	7		9		11	8				10			2	4						39
1		3		5	6	7	10	9		11			4		8			2							40
1		3		5		7	10	9		11			6		8			2	4						41
1		3		5	6	7	10			11	8		4		9			2							42
39	9	34	13	16	39	41	36	26	11	37	27	2	23	27	26	1	24	14	6	5	1	1	3	1	
			1		11	8	12			8	7						17								

Woodley V	Barkas E	Smith AJ	Allum L	Craig A	Weaver S	Spence R	Burgess H	Mills G	Foss SR	Hanson A	Argue J	Griffiths R	Mitchell W	Barber G	Payne J	Reid E	Salmond R	O'Hare J	Mayes A	Buchanan P	Alexander D	Gibson G	Jackson J	Smale D	No.
1					6	7	10			11	8		4	3	9		5	2							3
1					6	7	10			11	8		4	3	9		5	2							4
1		3			6	7	10			11	8		4		9		5	2							5
1		3			6	7	10	9		11			4	2	8		5								R
1		3			6	7	10	9		11			4	2	8		5								2R
1		3		5	6	7	10	9		11			4	2	8										6
6	4	1		6	6	6	3			6	3		6	5	6		5	3							
							3			1	3						2								

1946-47

Manager: William Birrell

1	Aug	31	(h)	Bolton W	W	4-3	Spence 2, Lawton 2	62,850
2	Sep	4	(h)	Manchester U	L	0-3		27,750
3		7	(a)	Liverpool	L	4-7	Goulden, Argue, Machin 2	49,995
4		9	(a)	Sheffield U	D	2-2	Lawton, Dolding	41,545
5		14	(h)	Leeds U	W	3-0	Lawton, Walker 2	56,484
6		18	(a)	Manchester U	D	1-1	Machin	30,275
7		21	(a)	Grimsby T	L	1-2	Lawton	21,932
8		28	(h)	Charlton A	D	2-2	Goulden, Walker	63,859
9	Oct	5	(a)	Middlesbrough	L	2-3	Goulden 2 (1 pen)	44,082
10		12	(h)	Stoke C	L	2-5	Lawton 2	67,935
11		19	(a)	Portsmouth	W	2-0	Spence, Lawton	36,474
12		26	(h)	Arsenal	W	2-1	Lawton 2	56,432
13	Nov	2	(a)	Blackpool	L	0-1		23,365
14		9	(h)	Brentford	W	3-2	Lawton, Bain, Walker	50,242
15		16	(a)	Sunderland	W	2-1	Spence, Lawton	41,227
16		23	(h)	Aston Villa	L	1-3	Spence	63,896
17		30	(a)	Derby C	L	1-3	Walker	27,946
18	Dec	7	(h)	Everton	D	1-1	Macaulay	41,255
19		14	(a)	Huddersfield T	W	4-1	Spence, Lawton 3	9,011
20		21	(h)	Wolves	L	1-2	Lawton	43,006
21		25	(h)	Preston NE	L	1-2	Lawton	37,126
22		26	(a)	Preston NE	D	1-1	Paton	40,167
23		28	(a)	Bolton W	D	1-1	Paton	36,048
24	Jan	4	(h)	Liverpool	W	3-1	Lawton 2, Goulden	59,226
25		18	(a)	Leeds U	L	1-2	Lawton	37,884
26	Feb	1	(a)	Charlton A	W	3-2	Lawton, Goulden (pen), Walker	32,959
27		8	(h)	Grimsby T	D	0-0		17,896
28		15	(a)	Stoke C	L	1-6	Machin	30,408
29	Mar	1	(a)	Arsenal	W	2-1	Williams, Goulden (pen)	52,606
30		8	(h)	Blackpool	L	1-4	Williams	30,365
31		15	(a)	Brentford	W	2-0	Machin, Paton	33,498
32		22	(h)	Sunderland	W	2-1	Lawton, Goulden (pen)	45,415
33		29	(a)	Aston Villa	L	0-2		37,627
34	Apr	4	(h)	Blackburn R	L	0-2		37,840
35		5	(h)	Derby C	W	3-0	Lawton 2, Goulden	52,886
36		7	(a)	Blackburn R	W	2-1	Lawton, Walker	35,646
37		12	(a)	Everton	L	0-2		30,970
38		19	(h)	Huddersfield T	W	1-0	Walker	39,753
39		26	(a)	Wolves	L	4-6	Spence, Lawton, Goulden, Machin	44,260
40	May	3	(h)	Sheffield U	L	1-4	McInnes	32,110
41		10	(h)	Middlesbrough	W	2-0	Machin, Walker	22,482
42		26	(h)	Portsmouth	L	0-3		26,048

FINAL LEAGUE POSITION: 15th in Division One

Appearances
Goals

FA Cup

3	Jan	11	(h)	Arsenal	D	1-1	Walker	70,257
R		15	(a)	Arsenal	D	1-1*	Lawton	53,350
2R		20	(a†)	Arsenal	W	2-0	Lawton 2	59,590
4		25	(h)	Derby C	D	2-2	Williams, Lawton	49,484
R		29	(a)	Derby C	L	0-1		19,079

*After extra-time. †Played at White Hart Lane, London.

Appearances
Goals

Aggregate League attendances:
Home: 934,856 (average 44,516)
Away: 737,925 (average 35,139)

Robertson WH	Winter D	Lewis F	Williams R	Harris J	Foss SR	Spence R	Galloway J	Lawton T	Goulden L	Bain J	Dolding L	Argue J	Dickie M	Goddard R	Machin A	Walker T	White A	Davidson A	Macaulay J	McInnes J	Medhurst H	Paton J	Richardson F	Steffen W	Tennant A	Bathgate S	Russell R	#
1	2	3	4	5	6	7	8	9	10	11																		1
1	2	3	4	5	6	7	8	9	10	11																		2
1	2	3		5				9	10		11	6	7	4	8													3
1	2	3	4	5				9	10		11				6	7	8											4
1	2		4	5	6	7		9	10		11						8	3										5
1	2		4	5	6	7			10		11				9		8	3										6
1	2		4	5	6	7		9	10		11						8	3										7
1	2		4	5	6	7			10		11				9		8	3										8
1	2			5	6	7		9	10		11					4	8	3										9
1	2			5	6	7		9			11				10	4	8	3										10
1	2	3		5		7		9	10		11					4	8			6								11
1	2	3		5		7		9	10		11					4	8			6								12
1	2			5		7		9	10	11						4	8	3		6								13
1	2			5		7		9	10	11						4	8	3		6								14
1	2			5		7		9	10	11						4	8	3		6								15
1	2			5		7		9	10	11						4	8	3		6								16
1	2			5		7		9	10							4	8		11	6					3			17
1	2			5		7		9	10							4	8			6			11		3			18
1	2			5		7		9	10							4	8			6			11		3			19
1	2			5		7		9	10							4	8			6			11		3			20
	2			5		7		9	10							4	8			6		1	11		3			21
	2			5				9			7						8	10		6		1	11		3		4	22
	2			5				9			7						8	10		6		1	11		3		4	23
	2			5		7		9							10		8			6		1	11		3		4	24
		3		5		7	10	9			11					4	8	2		6		1						25
	2			5		7		9	10							4	8			6		1	11		3			26
	2			5		7		9	10							4	8			6		1	11		3			27
	2			5		7		9	10							4	8			6		1	11		3			28
	2			5	9	7			10							4	8			6		1	11		3			29
	2			5	9	7			10							4	8			6		1	11		3			30
	2			5		7		9	10							4	8			6		1	11		3			31
	2			5		7		9	10							4	8			6		1	11		3			32
	2			5		7		9	10							4	8			6		1	11		3			33
	2			5		7		9	10							4	8			6		1	11		3			34
	2			5		7		9	10		11					4	8			6		1			3			35
	2			5		7		9	10		11					4	8			6		1			3			36
	2			5	9				10		11					4	8			6	7	1			3			37
	2			5	6	7		9	10							4	8					1	11		3			38
	2			5		7		9	10							4	8			6		1	11		3			39
	2			5	9	7			10							4	8			6		1	11	3				40
1	2			5	6	7		9	10							4	8	3					11					41
1	2			5	6	7		9	10							4	8	3					11					42
22	41	7	9	41	12	33	3	34	38	9	17	1	1	1	5	37	39	13	2	30	3	20	18	2	15	1	7	
	2					7		26	10	1	1	1				7	9			1		1			3			

Robertson WH	Winter D	Lewis F	Williams R	Harris J	Foss SR	Spence R	Galloway J	Lawton T	Goulden L	Bain J	Dolding L	Argue J	Dickie M	Goddard R	Machin A	Walker T	White A	Davidson A	Macaulay J	McInnes J	Medhurst H	Paton J	Richardson F	Steffen W	Tennant A	Bathgate S	Russell R	#
	2					7		9	10							4	8			6		1	11	5	3			3
			5		7			9	10							4	8	2		6		1	11		3			R
	2			5		7		9	10							4	8			6		1	11		3			2R
	2		7	5				9	10							4	8			6		1	11		3			4
	2			5		7		9	10						6	4	8					1	11		3			R
	4	1	4	4		5		5	5							5	5	1		5		5	5	1	5			
		1						4									1											

257

1947-48

Manager: William Birrell

1	Aug	23	(a)	Blackpool	L 0-3	27,389
2		27	(h)	Blackburn R	W 1-0 Armstrong	36,375
3		30	(h)	Derby C	W 1-0 Lawton	59,919
4	Sep	6	(a)	Huddersfield T	L 1-3 Walker	24,837
5		10	(h)	Sunderland	D 1-1 Dolding	30,085
6		13	(h)	Bolton W	D 1-1 Armstrong	41,242
7		17	(a)	Sunderland	W 3-2 Lawton, Bowie 2	31,444
8		20	(h)	Everton	W 3-1 Armstrong 2, Goulden	42,955
9		27	(a)	Wolves	L 0-1	51,365
10	Oct	4	(h)	Aston Villa	W 4-2 Lawton 2, Campbell 2	67,789
11		11	(a)	Liverpool	L 0-3	51,359
12		18	(h)	Middlesbrough	W 4-2 Armstrong 2, Goulden, Bowie	49,398
13		25	(a)	Charlton A	L 1-3 Armstrong	58,866
14	Nov	1	(h)	Arsenal	D 0-0	67,277
15		8	(a)	Preston NE	L 0-2	31,986
16		15	(h)	Stoke C	W 4-1 Armstrong 3, Campbell	41,835
17		22	(a)	Sheffield U	L 1-3 Machin	28,103
18		29	(h)	Manchester U	L 0-4	43,617
19	Dec	6	(a)	Burnley	L 0-1	30,865
20		13	(h)	Portsmouth	W 1-0 Goulden (pen)	41,096
21		20	(h)	Blackpool	D 2-2 Harris, Walker	48,421
22		25	(a)	Grimsby T	D 0-0	19,666
23		27	(h)	Grimsby T	L 2-3 Campbell 2	34,068
24	Jan	1	(a)	Blackburn R	D 1-1 Campbell	18,365
25		3	(a)	Derby C	L 1-5 Goulden	27,929
26		17	(h)	Huddersfield T	L 2-4 Harris, Campbell	41,908
27		31	(a)	Bolton W	L 1-2 Armstrong	24,232
28	Feb	14	(h)	Wolves	D 1-1 Goddard	56,416
29		21	(a)	Aston Villa	L 0-3	19,082
30		28	(h)	Liverpool	W 3-1 Walker (pen), Campbell, Bowie	39,078
31	Mar	6	(a)	Middlesbrough	D 0-0	28,174
32		13	(h)	Charlton A	W 3-0 Walker, Campbell, Bowie	61,566
33		20	(a)	Arsenal	W 2-0 Campbell, Bentley	56,596
34		26	(h)	Manchester C	D 2-2 Bentley, Billington	64,396
35		27	(h)	Preston NE	W 2-0 Walker, Billington	55,561
36		29	(a)	Manchester C	L 0-1	31,643
37	Apr	3	(a)	Stoke C	L 0-2	26,408
38		10	(h)	Sheffield U	W 1-0 Dyke	43,949
39		14	(a)	Everton	W 3-2 Walker, Campbell, Bentley	28,366
40		17	(a)	Manchester U	L 0-5	44,366
41		24	(h)	Burnley	L 0-2	33,390
42	May	1	(a)	Portsmouth	L 1-2 Walker	24,055

FINAL LEAGUE POSITION: 18th in Division One

Appearances
Goals

FA Cup

3	Jan	10	(h)	Barrow	W 5-0 Armstrong 2, Goulden, Campbell, Bowie	44,336
4		24	(a)	Manchester C	L 0-2*	45,059

*After extra-time

Appearances
Goals

Aggregate League attendances:
Home: 1,000,381 (average 47,637)
Away: 684,996 (average 32,618)

Appearances and goalscorers grid (shirt numbers by match). Players listed across the top; match numbers 1–42 down the right‑hand side.

Match	Robertson WH	Medhurst H	Bathgate S	Goddard R	Harris J	Armstrong K	Spence R	Macaulay J	Walker T	Goulden L	Dolding L	Machin A	Lawton T	Campbell R	Bowie J	McInnes J	Foss SR	Winter D	Jones B	Bentley R	Lewis F	Dyke C	Hughes W	Billington H	Dickson W	Galloway J	McKnight P	Simmer J	White A
1	1		3	4	5	6	7		9	10	11	8						2											
2	1		3	4	5	6	7	8	9	10	11							2											
3	1		3		5	6	7	8		10	11	4	9					2											
4	1		3		5	6	7	8		10	11	4	9					2											
5	1		3		5	6	7	8		10	11	4	9					2											
6	1		3	4	5	6	7	8			11	10	9					2											
7	1		3		5	4				10			7	9	8	11	6	2											
8	1		3		5	9		4		10			7		8	11	6	2											
9	1		3		5	6		4	9	10			7		8	11		2											
10	1		3		5	6		4	9	10				7	8	11		2											
11	1		3		5	6		4	9	10				7	8	11		2											
12	1		3		5	6			9	10		4		7	8	11		2											
13	1		3		5	6			9	10		4		7	8	11		2											
14	1		3		5	6			9	10		4		7	8	11		2											
15		1	3		5	6			9	10		4		7	8	11		2											
16		1	3	4	5	6			9	10				7	8	11		2											
17		1	3		5	6			9	10		4		7	8	11		2											
18		1	3	4	5	6			9	10		8		7				2	11										
19		1	3	4	5	6			9	10				7	8			2	11										
20		1	3	4	5	6			9	10				7	8			2	11										
21		1	3		5	6			9	10		4		7	8	11													2
22		1	3		5	6			9	10		4		7	8	11													2
23		1	3		5	6			9	10		4		7	8	11													2
24		1	3		5	6			9			10		7	8	11								4					2
25		1	3		5	4			9	10		8		7		11				2						6			
26		1	3		5	6			9			4		7	8			2	11	10									
27		1	3		5	9				10		4		7	8	11	6	2											
28		1	3		5	6			9	10		4		7		11		2		8									
29		1			5	6			9	10		4		7		11				8	3								
30		1			5	6			9	10		4				11		2		8	3	7							
31		1			5	6				10		4				11		2		8	3	7					9		
32		1			5	6				10		4				11		2			3	7	8	9					
33		1			5	6				10		4				11		2			3	7	8	9					
34		1			5	6				10		4				11		2			3	7	8	9					
35		1			5	6				10		4				11				2	3	7	8	9					
36	1				5	6			10			4				11				2	3	7	8	9					
37		1			5	6				10		4				11				2	3	7	8	9					
38		1			5	6				10		4				11				2	3	7	8	9					
39		1			5	6				10		4				11				2	3	7	8	9					
40		1	3		5	6				10		4				11				7	8	2		9					
41		1	3		5	6				10		4				11				8	2	7		9					
42		1	3		5	4				10						11			8	2	7	6		9					
Apps	15	27	32	9	41	42	6	15	38	27	9	16	8	32	22	15	3	28	11	14	12	13	8	11	1	1	1	1	4
Goals			1	2	11				7	4	1	1	1	4	11	5			3		1		2						

Cup / additional matches:

Match	Robertson WH	Medhurst H	Bathgate S	Goddard R	Harris J	Armstrong K	Spence R	Macaulay J	Walker T	Goulden L	Dolding L	Machin A	Lawton T	Campbell R	Bowie J	McInnes J	Foss SR	Winter D	Jones B	Bentley R
3		1	3		5	9				10		4		7	8			6	2	11
4		1	3	5		9				10		4		7				6	2	11	8
Apps	2	2	1	1	2				2	2		2	1		2	2	2	1		
Goals					2									1	1					

1948-49

Manager: William Birrell

1	Aug	21	(h)	Middlesbrough	W	1-0	Bentley	60,981
2		25	(a)	Newcastle U	D	2-2	Bentley, Billington	58,020
3		28	(a)	Birmingham C	L	0-1		48,264
4	Sep	1	(h)	Newcastle U	L	2-3	Walker (pen), Jones	50,207
5		4	(h)	Bolton W	D	2-2	Campbell 2	42,971
6		8	(a)	Charlton A	D	1-1	Williams	38,492
7		11	(h)	Everton	W	6-0	Macaulay, Campbell, Bowie, Walker (pen), Bentley 2	42,736
8		16	(h)	Charlton A	D	2-2	Macaulay, Bowie	45,357
9		18	(a)	Preston NE	L	2-3	Walker 2 (2 pens)	32,164
10		25	(h)	Burnley	W	1-0	Walker (pen)	53,193
11	Oct	2	(a)	Stoke C	L	3-4	Walker, Bentley 2	31,004
12		9	(a)	Liverpool	D	1-1	Bowie	42,709
13		16	(h)	Blackpool	D	3-3	Bowie 2, McInnes	77,696
14		23	(a)	Derby C	L	1-2	McInnes	29,369
15		30	(h)	Arsenal	L	0-1		56,476
16	Nov	6	(a)	Huddersfield T	W	4-3	Bentley 2, Williams, McInnes	18,693
17		13	(h)	Manchester U	D	1-1	Bentley	62,542
18		20	(a)	Sheffield U	L	1-2	McInnes	29,646
19		27	(h)	Aston Villa	W	2-1	Macaulay, Bentley	32,920
20	Dec	4	(a)	Sunderland	L	0-3		38,934
21		11	(h)	Wolves	W	4-1	Bowie 2, Bentley 2	43,971
22		18	(a)	Middlesbrough	D	1-1	Walker	23,464
23		25	(h)	Portsmouth	L	1-2	Jones	43,422
24		27	(a)	Portsmouth	L	2-5	Bentley 2	43,624
25	Jan	1	(h)	Birmingham C	W	2-0	Harris (pen), Campbell	28,850
26		22	(a)	Everton	L	1-2	Jones	52,700
27	Feb	5	(a)	Preston NE	W	5-3	Macaulay, Bentley 2, Williams, Jones	41,483
28		19	(a)	Burnley	L	0-3		28,754
29		26	(h)	Stoke C	D	2-2	Campbell, Bentley	39,259
30	Mar	5	(h)	Liverpool	W	2-1	Armstrong, Bentley	42,746
31		12	(a)	Blackpool	L	1-2	Bentley	20,292
32		19	(h)	Sheffield U	W	1-0	Billington	42,394
33		26	(a)	Aston Villa	D	1-1	Mitchell	40,954
34	Apr	2	(h)	Huddersfield T	W	5-0	Campbell, Bentley, Jones 2, Stewart (og)	48,136
35		9	(a)	Manchester U	D	1-1	McInnes	30,123
36		15	(a)	Manchester C	L	0-1		36,554
37		16	(h)	Derby C	L	0-3		60,299
38		18	(h)	Manchester C	D	1-1	Campbell	25,864
39		23	(a)	Arsenal	W	2-1	Goulden, Billington	54,604
40		30	(h)	Sunderland	L	0-1		32,003
41	May	4	(a)	Bolton W	D	1-1	McInnes	19,084
42		7	(a)	Wolves	D	1-1	Bentley	36,720

FINAL LEAGUE POSITION: 13th in Division One

Appearances
Goals

FA Cup

3	Jan	8	(a)	Bristol C	W	3-1	Bentley 2, Jones	36,454
4		29	(h)	Everton	W	2-0	Bowie, Williams	56,671
5	Feb	12	(a)	West Brom A	L	0-3		57,843

Aggregate League attendances:
Home: 973,586 (average 46,361)
Away: 754,168 (average 35,912)

Appearances
Goals

Football appearances grid.

Medhurst H	Pickering P	Winter D	Bathgate S	Hughes W	Lewis F	Armstrong K	McKnight P	Harris J	Macaulay J	Dickson W	Warren R	Campbell R	Dyke C	Bowie J	Walker T	Bentley R	Goulden L	Billington H	Williams R	McInnes J	Jones B	Mitchell F	Gray W	Tennant A	
1		2	3	4				5	6			7			10	8		9		11					1
1		2	3	4				5	6			7			10	8		9		11					2
1		2	3			4		5	6			7			10	8		9		11					3
1		2	3			4		5	6			7			10	8		9		11					4
1		2	3				5	4	6			7			10	8		9		11					5
	1	2	3	5					6			7			10	9	4			8	11				6
	1	2	3	5					6			7		8	10	9	4				11				7
	1	2	3	5					6			7		8	10	9	4				11				8
	1	2	3	5					6			7		8	10	9		4			11				9
	1	2	3	5					6			7		8	10	9		4			11				10
	1	2	3	5					6			7		8	10	9		4			11				11
	1	2	3	5					6			7		8	10	9	4				11				12
	1	2	3	5					6			7		8	10	9	4				11				13
	1	2	3	5					6					8	10	9	4		7	11					14
1		2	3	5					6			7			10	9	4			8	11				15
1		2	3	5					6			7			10	9	4			8	11				16
1		2	3	5					6			7			10	9	4			8	11				17
1		2	3	5					6			7			10	9	4			8	11				18
1		2	3	4				5	6			7		8	10	9					11				19
1		2	3	4				5	6			7		8	10	9					11				20
1		2	3	4				5	6			7		8	10	9					11				21
1		2	3	4				5	6			7		8	10	9					11				22
1		2	3	4				5	6					8	10	9				11	7				23
	1	2	3	4				5	6			7		8	10	9					11				24
	1	2	3	4				5	6			7		8		9	10				11				25
	1	2	3	4				5	6			7		8		9	10				11				26
	1	2	3	4				5	8			7				9	10				11	6			27
	1	2	3	4				5	8			7				9	10				11	6			28
	1	2	3	10				5	4			7		8		9					11	6			29
	1	2	3	10				5	4			7		8		9					11	6			30
1		2	3	4				5	6			7				9	10	8			11				31
1		2	3	4				5				7				9	10	8			11	6			32
1		2	3	4				5				7				9	10	8			11	6			33
1		2	3	4				5				7				9	10	8			11	6			34
1		2	3	4				5				7			10	9		8			11	6			35
1		2	3	4				5				7				9	10			8	11	6			36
1		2	3	4				5				7				9	10	8			11	6			37
1		2	3	4				5	6			7				9	10	8			11				38
1		2	3	4				5	6			7				9	10	8			11				39
1		2	3	4				5	6							9	10	8			11		7		40
1		2	3	4				5	6					8		9	10			11			7		41
1			3	4				5	8			7				9	10				11	6		2	42
26	16	25	17	38	3	25	2	41	36	2	1	36	2	22	21	40	20	16	13	18	28	11	2	1	
				1				1	4			7		7	7	21	1	3	3	6	6	1			

1 own-goal

Medhurst H	Pickering P	Winter D	Bathgate S	Hughes W	Lewis F	Armstrong K	McKnight P	Harris J	Macaulay J	Dickson W	Warren R	Campbell R	Dyke C	Bowie J	Walker T	Bentley R	Goulden L	Billington H	Williams R	McInnes J	Jones B	Mitchell F	Gray W	Tennant A	
	1	2	3	4				5	6			7		8		9	10				11				3
	1	2	3	4				5	6			7		8		9	10				11				4
	1	2	3	4				5	6			7		8		9	10				11				5
	3	3	3	3				3	3			3		3		3	3				3				
														1		2	1				1				

1949-50

Manager: William Birrell

1	Aug	20	(a)	Birmingham C	W	3-0	Bentley, Williams 2	45,068
2		24	(h)	Arsenal	L	1-2	Harris (pen)	63,196
3		27	(h)	Derby C	L	1-2	Bentley	59,038
4		31	(a)	Arsenal	W	3-2	Billington 2, Bentley	52,901
5	Sep	3	(a)	West Brom A	D	1-1	Bentley	45,111
6		7	(h)	Sunderland	W	3-1	Campbell, Billington, Williams	40,061
7		10	(h)	Manchester U	D	1-1	Gray	61,357
8		17	(a)	Fulham	D	1-1	Gray	45,924
9		24	(a)	Stoke C	W	3-2	Billington, Bentley 2	28,674
10	Oct	1	(h)	Burnley	L	0-1		54,574
11		8	(h)	Manchester C	W	3-0	Bentley 2, Goulden	45,153
12		15	(a)	Charlton A	L	0-1		48,181
13		22	(h)	Aston Villa	L	1-3	Goulden	44,705
14		29	(a)	Wolves	D	2-2	Campbell, Bentley	42,008
15	Nov	5	(h)	Portsmouth	L	1-4	Billington	31,650
16		12	(a)	Huddersfield T	W	2-1	Jones, Bowie	12,565
17		19	(h)	Everton	W	3-2	Billington 2, Jones	34,190
18		26	(a)	Middlesbrough	L	1-2	Bowie	24,815
19	Dec	3	(h)	Blackpool	D	1-1	Bowie	47,636
20		10	(a)	Newcastle U	D	2-2	Billington 2	43,329
21		17	(h)	Birmingham C	W	3-0	Harris (pen), Campbell, Billington	28,672
22		24	(a)	Derby C	D	2-2	Billington 2	28,899
23		26	(h)	Liverpool	D	1-1	Harris (pen)	55,920
24		27	(a)	Liverpool	D	2-2	Billington, Bentley	58,757
25		31	(h)	West Brom A	W	2-1	Billington, Bentley	41,610
26	Jan	14	(a)	Manchester U	L	0-1		48,466
27		21	(h)	Fulham	D	0-0		52,254
28	Feb	4	(h)	Stoke C	D	2-2	Williams, Bowie	45,097
29		18	(a)	Burnley	W	2-1	Bentley, Attwell (og)	23,446
30		25	(a)	Manchester C	D	1-1	Trautmann (og)	29,950
31	Mar	8	(h)	Charlton A	L	1-3	Bentley	26,407
32		11	(a)	Everton	D	1-1	Billington	50,328
33		25	(a)	Portsmouth	L	0-4		29,100
34		29	(h)	Middlesbrough	W	2-1	Campbell, Billington	15,513
35	Apr	1	(h)	Huddersfield T	W	3-1	Billington, Bentley 2	32,064
36		7	(h)	Bolton W	D	1-1	Williams	52,985
37		8	(a)	Aston Villa	L	0-4		37,730
38		10	(a)	Bolton W	L	0-1		23,658
39		15	(h)	Wolves	D	0-0		30,254
40		22	(a)	Blackpool	D	0-0		26,066
41		29	(h)	Newcastle U	L	1-3	Billington	24,677
42	May	6	(a)	Sunderland	L	1-4	Bentley	21,567

FINAL LEAGUE POSITION: 13th in Division One

Appearances
Goals

FA Cup

3	Jan	7	(a)	Brentford	W	1-0	Bowie	38,000
4		28	(h)	Newcastle U	W	3-0	Campbell, Billington 2	64,664
5	Feb	11	(a)	Chesterfield	D	1-1	Bowie	27,500
R		15	(h)	Chesterfield	W	3-0	Billington, Bentley 2	59,660
6	Mar	4	(h)	Manchester U	W	2-0	Campbell, Bentley	70,362
SF		18	(n*)	Arsenal	D	2-2	Bentley 2	67,752
R		22	(n*)	Arsenal	L	0-1†		65,482

*Played at White Hart Lane, London.   †After extra-time.

Appearances
Goals

Aggregate League attendances:
Home: 887,013 (average 42,238)
Away: 766,543 (average 36,502)

Medhurst H	Winter D	Willemse S	Armstrong K	Harris J	Mitchell F	Campbell P	Billington H	Bentley R	Williams R	Gray W	Jones B	Hughes W	Goulden L	Bathgate S	Macaulay J	McInnes J	Bowie J	Saunders FJ	Jenkins TF	Dickson W	McKnight P	Pickering P	
1	2		4	5	6	7		9	10			3	8			11							1
1	2		4	5	6	7		9	10		11	3	8										2
1	2		4	5	6	7		9	10		11	3	8										3
1	2	3	4	5	6	7	10	9		11			8										4
	2	3	4	5	6	7	10	9		11			8					1					5
1	2	3	4	5	6	7	8	9	10	11													6
1	2	3	4	5	6	7	8	9	10	11													7
1	2		4	5	6	7	10	9		11		3	8										8
1	2		4	5	6	7	10	9		11		3	8										9
1	2		4	5	6	7	8	9		11		3	10										10
1	2		4	5	6	7	8	9		11		3	10										11
1	2		4	5	6	7	8	9		11		3	10										12
1			4	5	6	7	8	9		11		3	10	2									13
1			4	5		7	10	9	8	11		3		2	6								14
1			4	5			8	9	11	7		3	10	2	6								15
1			4	5			10	9		7	11	3		2	6		8						16
1			4	5			10	9		7	11	3		2	6		8						17
1			4	5		11	10	9		7		3		2	6		8						18
1	2		4	5	6	11	10	9		7		3					8						19
1	2		4		6	11	10	9		7		3					8	5					20
1	2		4	5	6	11	10	9		7		3					8						21
1	2		4	5	6	11	10	9		7		3					8						22
1	2		4	5	6	11	10	9		7		3					8						23
1	2			5	6	11	10	9	4	7		3					8						24
1	2		4	5	6	11	10	9		7		3					8						25
1	2	3	4	5	6	11	10	9		7							8						26
1	2	3	4	5	6	11	10	9		7							8						27
1	2		4	5	6	11		9	10	7		3					8						28
1	2	3	4	5	6		10	9	11	7							8						29
1	2	3	4	5	6		10		11	7							8		9				30
1	2	3	4		6		9	10	7	11							8		5				31
1	2		4	5	6		10	9	8	7	11	3											32
1	2		4	5	6	7		9	8	11		3							10				33
1	2	3	4	5	6	11	10	9		7							8						34
1	2	3	4	5	6	11	10	9	8	7													35
1	2	3	4	5	6	11	10	9	8	7													36
1	2	3	4	5	6	11		9	8	7									10				37
1	2	3	4			11	10			7					5	6			9				38
1		3	4	5	6	11	9		10	7		8	2										39
1		3	4	5		11	10	9	8	7			2							6			40
1		3	4	5		11	10	9	8	7			2							6			41
1		3	4	5		11	10	9	8	7			2							6			42
41	32	18	41	39	33	35	35	39	21	39	6	24	14	10	5	1	16	3	5	3	1	1	
				3		4	17	17	5	2	2		2				4						

2 own-goals

Medhurst H	Winter D	Willemse S	Armstrong K	Harris J	Mitchell F	Campbell P	Billington H	Bentley R	Williams R	Gray W	Jones B	Hughes W	Goulden L	Bathgate S	Macaulay J	McInnes J	Bowie J	Saunders FJ	Jenkins TF	Dickson W	McKnight P	Pickering P	
1	2		4	5	6	11	9		10	7		3					8						3
1	2		4		6	11	10	9		7		3					8	5					4
1	2		4	5	6	11	10	9		7		3					8						5
1	2		4	5	6	11	10	9		7		3					8						R
1	2		4	5	6		10	9	8	7		3											6
1	2		4	5	6		10	9	11	7		3	8										SF
1	2		4	5	6	7		9	10	11		3	8										R
7	7		7	6	7	6	6	6	4	7		7	2				4	1					
							2	3	5				2										

1950-51

Manager: William Birrell

#	Month	Date	Venue	Opponent	Result	Scorers	Attendance
1	Aug	19	(h)	Sheffield W	W 4-0	Gray, Bentley 2, Billington	48,468
2		25	(a)	Arsenal	D 0-0		61,166
3		26	(a)	Middlesbrough	L 0-3		41,573
4		30	(h)	Arsenal	L 0-1		48,792
5	Sep	2	(h)	Huddersfield T	L 1-2	Harris (pen)	41,112
6		4	(a)	Bolton W	L 0-1		25,457
7		9	(a)	Newcastle U	L 1-3	Armstrong	56,903
8		16	(h)	West Brom A	D 1-1	Harris (pen)	39,570
9		23	(a)	Stoke C	L 1-2	Gray	25,521
10		30	(h)	Everton	W 2-1	Gray, Campbell	34,970
11	Oct	7	(a)	Blackpool	L 2-3	Bowie, Bentley	29,240
12		14	(h)	Tottenham H	L 0-2		65,992
13		21	(a)	Wolves	L 1-2	Billington	40,014
14		28	(h)	Sunderland	W 3-0	Billington, Campbell 2	51,315
15	Nov	4	(a)	Charlton A	W 2-1	Campbell, Dyke	29,913
16		11	(h)	Manchester U	W 1-0	Billington	51,882
17		18	(a)	Aston Villa	L 2-4	Gray, Billington	27,609
18		25	(h)	Derby C	L 1-2	Campbell	26,908
19	Dec	2	(a)	Liverpool	L 0-1		28,717
20		9	(h)	Fulham	W 2-0	Jones, Smith	43,835
21		23	(h)	Middlesbrough	D 1-1	Billington	35,313
22		25	(a)	Portsmouth	W 3-1	Bowie, Bentley, Smith	23,645
23		26	(h)	Portsmouth	L 1-4	Harris (pen)	41,909
24	Jan	13	(h)	Newcastle U	W 3-1	Williams, Smith 2	43,840
25		20	(a)	West Brom A	D 1-1	Gray	30,985
26	Feb	3	(h)	Stoke C	D 1-1	Gray	27,061
27		17	(a)	Everton	L 0-3		33,005
28		24	(a)	Sheffield W	D 2-2	Harris (pen), Dickson	40,964
29		28	(h)	Blackpool	L 0-2		36,074
30	Mar	3	(a)	Tottenham H	L 1-2	Campbell	59,449
31		17	(a)	Sunderland	D 1-1	Hinshelwood	24,270
32		23	(a)	Burnley	L 1-2	Harris (pen)	22,266
33		24	(h)	Charlton A	L 2-3	Bentley, Williams	38,196
34		26	(h)	Burnley	L 0-2		23,723
35		31	(a)	Manchester U	L 1-4	Willemse	25,779
36	Apr	7	(h)	Aston Villa	D 1-1	Williams	28,569
37		14	(a)	Derby C	L 0-1		16,364
38		18	(h)	Huddersfield T	L 1-2	Gallogly (og)	23,999
39		21	(h)	Liverpool	W 1-0	Smith	30,134
40		25	(h)	Wolves	W 2-1	Armstrong, Bentley (pen)	36,410
41		28	(a)	Fulham	W 2-1	Armstrong 2	24,897
42	May	5	(h)	Bolton W	W 4-0	Bentley 2, Smith 2	38,928

FINAL LEAGUE POSITION: 20th in Division One

Appearances
Goals

FA Cup

#	Month	Date	Venue	Opponent	Result	Scorers	Attendance
3	Jan	9	(a)	Rochdale	W 3-2	Bentley 2, Billington	17,249
4		27	(a)	Exeter C	D 1-1	Williams	20,000
R		31	(h)	Exeter C	W 2-0	Smith 2	46,134
5	Feb	10	(h)	Fulham	D 1-1	Bentley	69,434
R		14	(a)	Fulham	L 0-3		29,346

Aggregate League attendances:
Home: 831,001 (average 39,571)
Away: 697,736 (average 33,225)

Appearances
Goals

Medhurst H	Bathgate S	Willemse S	Armstrong K	Harris J	Mitchell F	Gray W	Bowie J	Bentley R	Billington H	Jones B	Williams R	Campbell B	McKnight P	Dyke C	Smith R	Dickson W	Saunders J	Pickering P	Hughes W	Parsons E	Hinshelwood W	Winter D	Tickridge S	Robertson WG	#
1	2	3	4	5	6	7	8	9	10	11															1
1	2	3	4	5	6	7	8	9	10		11														2
1	2	3	4	5	6	7	8	9	10			11													3
1	2	3	4	5	6	7	8	9	10			11													4
1	2	3	9	5	6	7	8		10			11	4												5
1	2	3	6	5		11	8					10	4	7	9										6
1	2	3	4	5		11	8					9	6	7		10									7
1	2	3	4	5		7	8	9				11	6			10									8
1	2	3	4	5		7	8	9				11	6			10									9
1	2	3	4		6	7	8	9				11				10	5								10
1	2	3	4		6	11	8	9	10			7					5								11
1	2	3	4	5	6		11	8	9	10		7													12
	2		4	5	6	11		10	9			8		7			1	3							13
	2		4	5	6	11		10	9			8		7			1	3							14
	2		4	5	6	11		10	9			8		7			1	3							15
	2		4	5	6	11		10	9			8		7			1	3							16
	2		4	5	6	11		10	9			8		7			1	3							17
	2		4	5	6	11		10	9			8		7			1	3							18
1	2		4	5	6		8	10	9	11								3	7						19
1	2		4	5	6		8	10		11						9		3	7						20
1	2		4	5	6			10	8	11						9		3	7						21
1	2	3	4	5	6		8	10		11						9			7						22
1	2	3	4	5	6		8	10		11						9			7						23
	2		4	5	6			10	8	11					7	9		1	3						24
	2		4	5	6	7		10		11	8					9		1	3						25
	2		4	5		11		10				8				9	6	1	3	7					26
			4	5				10	9	8				11		6		1	3	7	2				27
1			4	5	6			9	10					11		8		3	7	2					28
1			4	5	6			9	10					11		8		3	7	2					29
1			8	5	6			9		4	11					10		3	7	2					30
1				5			11		10			4	8			9	6	3	7	2					31
1				5			11		10			4	8			9	6	3	7			2			32
1			4	5			11		10			9	8				6	3	7			2			33
1	2		4	5			11		10	9						8	6	3	7						34
1	2	11	4	5					10						9	8	6	3	7						35
1	2		4	5			11		10						9	8	6	3	7						36
1			4	5			11		10				8			9	6	3	7	2					37
1	2		10	4		11		8				6	7			9	5		3						38
	2		10			11		8				4	7			9	6	5					3	1	39
	2		10		6	7		8		11			9	4	5								3	1	40
	2		10		6			8					11	7		9	4	5					3	1	41
	2		10		6				11			8		7		9	4	5					3	1	42
28	34	15	40	36	27	31	16	38	20	7	13	33	5	9	16	20	7	10	23	5	12	5	8	4	
	1		4	5		6	2	8	6	1	3	6		1	7	1			1						

1 own-goal

Medhurst H	Bathgate S	Willemse S	Armstrong K	Harris J	Mitchell F	Gray W	Bowie J	Bentley R	Billington H	Jones B	Williams R	Campbell B	McKnight P	Dyke C	Smith R	Dickson W	Saunders J	Pickering P	Hughes W	Parsons E	Hinshelwood W	Winter D	Tickridge S	Robertson WG	#
	2		4	5	6	11		10	8					7	9		1	3							3
	2		4	5	7			10		11	8					9	6	1	3						4
	2		4	5	7			10					11	8		9	6	1	3						R
			4	5		11		10						8		9	6	1	3	7	2				5
			4	5		11		10						8		9	6	1	3	7	2				R
3		5	5	1	5		5	1		2	4		1	5	4		5	5		2	2				
					3	1		1				2													

265

1951-52

Manager: William Birrell

1	Aug	18	(a)	Blackpool	W 2-1	Campbell, R.Smith	31,172
2		22	(h)	Arsenal	L 1-3	Campbell	59,143
3		25	(h)	Liverpool	L 1-3	Armstrong	44,055
4		29	(a)	Arsenal	L 1-2	R.Smith	45,768
5	Sep	1	(a)	Portsmouth	L 0-1		23,901
6		5	(h)	Derby C	L 0-1		25,191
7		8	(h)	Fulham	W 2-1	R.Smith, Bentley	47,582
8		15	(h)	Huddersfield T	W 2-1	Bentley, J.Smith	25,165
9		22	(a)	Wolves	L 3-5	Campbell, Bentley, J.Smith	35,184
10		29	(h)	Sunderland	W 2-1	Bentley, R.Smith	49,762
11	Oct	6	(a)	Middlesbrough	D 0-0		30,010
12		13	(h)	West Brom A	L 1-3	Bentley	34,917
13		20	(a)	Newcastle U	L 1-3	Bentley	52,168
14		27	(h)	Bolton W	L 1-3	Armstrong (pen)	45,287
15	Nov	3	(a)	Stoke C	W 2-1	Bentley, Tuck	26,121
16		10	(h)	Manchester U	W 4-2	R.Smith, Bentley, D'Arcy 2	48,960
17		17	(a)	Tottenham H	L 2-3	Campbell, Bentley	48,985
18		24	(h)	Preston NE	D 0-0		43,873
19	Dec	1	(a)	Burnley	D 1-1	R.Smith	21,773
20		8	(h)	Charlton A	W 1-0	D'Arcy	38,343
21		15	(h)	Blackpool	W 2-1	D'Arcy 2	38,912
22		22	(a)	Liverpool	D 1-1	D'Arcy	26,459
23		25	(h)	Manchester C	L 0-3		34,850
24		26	(a)	Manchester C	L 1-3	R.Smith	49,791
25		29	(h)	Portsmouth	D 1-1	R.Smith	43,389
26	Jan	5	(a)	Fulham	W 2-1	Parsons, Campbell	43,880
27		19	(a)	Huddersfield T	L 0-1		19,315
28		26	(h)	Wolves	L 0-1		40,586
29	Feb	9	(a)	Sunderland	L 1-4	Jones	37,298
30		16	(h)	Middlesbrough	W 5-0	Bentley 2, D'Arcy 3	37,805
31	Mar	1	(a)	West Brom A	W 1-0	Gray	24,291
32		12	(h)	Newcastle U	W 1-0	Allister	42,948
33		15	(a)	Bolton W	L 0-3		31,448
34		22	(h)	Stoke C	W 1-0	D'Arcy	36,880
35	Apr	12	(a)	Preston NE	L 0-1		28,081
36		14	(h)	Aston Villa	D 2-2	Randall, Jones	28,005
37		15	(a)	Aston Villa	L 1-7	J.Smith	29,649
38		19	(h)	Burnley	W 4-1	R.Smith 2, D'Arcy 2	26,349
39		21	(a)	Manchester U	L 0-3		39,272
40		26	(a)	Charlton A	D 1-1	Bentley	20,851
41		30	(h)	Tottenham H	L 0-2		46,574
42	May	3	(a)	Derby C	D 1-1	R.Smith	8,582

FINAL LEAGUE POSITION: 19th in Division One

Appearances
Goals

FA Cup

3	Jan	12	(h)	Chester	D 2-2	Armstrong (pen), Gray	42,954
R		16	(a)	Chester	W 3-2‡	R.Smith, Bentley, Lee (og)	20,500
4	Feb	2	(h)	Tranmere R	W 4-0	Armstrong, Bentley 2, Jones	59,101
5		23	(a)	Leeds U	D 1-1	R.Smith	52,328
R		27	(h)	Leeds U	D 1-1‡	D'Arcy	60,851
2R	Mar	3	(n*)	Leeds U	W 5-1	R.Smith 3, Gray, Bentley	30,504
6		8	(a)	Sheffield U	W 1-0	Bentley	43,677
SF	Apr	5	(n†)	Arsenal	D 1-1	Gray	68,084
R		7	(n†)	Arsenal	L 0-3		57,450

*Played at Villa Park, Birmingham.   †Played at White Hart Lane, London.   ‡After extra-time.

Appearances
Goals

Aggregate League attendances:
Home: 838,576 (average 39,932)
Away: 673,999 (average 32,095)

Appearance and scoring grid (player columns left-to-right; match number/round at right).

Robertson W/G	Bathgate S	Tickridge S	McKnight P	Saunders FJ	Dickson W	Parsons E	Campbell R	Smith R	Armstrong K	Gray W	Williams R	Hughes H	Bentley R	Smith J	Harris J	Randall E	Tuck P	D'Arcy S	Willemse S	Jones B	Mitchell F	Medhurst H	Oelofse R	Allister J	Leadbetter J	No.
1	2	3	4	5	6	7	8	9	10	11																1
1	2	3	4	5	6	7	8	9	10	11																2
1	2	3			6	7	8	9	10	11	4	5														3
1	2	3		5	6	7	8	9	10	11	4															4
1	2	3	4	5	6	7	8	9	10	11																5
1	2	3	4	5	6	7	8	9	10	11																6
1	2	3	4	5	6		8	9		7			10	11												7
1	2	3	4	5	6		8	9		7			10	11												8
1	2	3	4	5	6		8	9		7			10	11												9
1	2	3		5	6		8	9	4	7			10	11												10
1	2	3		5			8	9	4	7			10	11	6											11
1	2	3		5	6		8		4	7			10	11		9										12
1	2	3			6		11	9	4	7			10		5			8								13
1	2	3		5	6		11		4	7			10				8	9								14
1	2	3		5	6		11		4	7			10				8	9								15
1	2	3			6		11	9	4	7			10		5			8								16
1	2	3			6		11	9	4	7			10		5			8								17
1	2	3			6		11	9	4	7			10		5			8								18
1	2	3			6		11	9	4	7			10		5			8								19
1	2	3			6		11	9	4	7			10		5			8								20
1	2	3			6		11	9	4	7			10		5			8								21
1	2	3			6		11	9	4	7			10		5			8								22
1	2	3			6		11	9	4	7			10		5			8								23
1	2	3			6		11	9	4	7		8	10		5											24
1	2	3			6		11	9	4	7			10		5			8								25
1	2	3			6		11		4	7			10		5	9		8								26
1	2	3			6		11	9	4	7			8		5			10								27
1	2	3			6		11	9	4	7			8		5			10	3							28
1	2	3			6		11		4	7			10		8	9										29
1	2	3			6			9	4	7			10		5			8			11					30
	2	3					8	9	4	7			11	6	10						6	1	5			31
1	2	3			6				4	7			10					8			11			5	9	32
1	2	3			6				4	7			10					8			11			5	9	33
1	2	3			6			9	4	7			10		5			8			11					34
1	2	3	6					9	4	7					5						11			8	10	35
1	2								4	7			8		5			9		3	11	6			10	36
1	2								4	7			8		11	5		9		3		6			10	37
1	2	4			6			9		7			10		11			5	8	3						38
1	2	4			6			8		7			10		11			5	9	3						39
1	2				6			9	4	7			10					8	5	3	11					40
1	2				6			9	4	7			10					8	5	3	11					41
1	2				6			9	4	7			10		11			5	8	3						42
41	32	41	12	13	37	11	32	32	37	42	2	1	32	16	26	3	3	21	11	3	4	1	3	3	3	
							1	5	11	2	1				12	3		1	1	12		2		1		

Cup matches:

Robertson W/G	Bathgate S	Tickridge S	McKnight P	Saunders FJ	Dickson W	Parsons E	Campbell R	Smith R	Armstrong K	Gray W	Williams R	Hughes H	Bentley R	Smith J	Harris J	Randall E	Tuck P	D'Arcy S	Willemse S	Jones B	Mitchell F	Medhurst H	Oelofse R	Allister J	Leadbetter J	Rd
1	2	3			6		11		4	7			10		5	9		8								3
1	2				6		11	9	4	7			10		5			8	3							R
1	2				6		8		4	7			10		5			9		3	11					4
1	2				6			9	4	7			10		5			8	3		11	6				5
1	2				6			9	4	7			10		5			8	3		11	6				R
1	2	3			6			9	4	7			10		5			8			11					2R
1	2	3			6			9	4	11			10		7	5		8								6
1	2	3			6			9	4	11			10		7	5		8								SF
1	2	3			6			9	4	11			10		7	5		8								R
9	6	8			7	2	4	7	9	9			9	4	9			8	4	2	2					
								5	2	3				5						1	1					

1 own-goal

1952-53

Manager: Ted Drake

1	Aug	23	(a)	Manchester U	L	0-2		43,629
2		27	(h)	Derby C	D	1-1	Harris (pen)	34,467
3		30	(h)	Portsmouth	W	2-0	Parsons, Gray	53,470
4	Sep	3	(a)	Derby C	L	2-3	Dickson, McNichol	15,227
5		6	(a)	Bolton W	D	1-1	McNichol	29,877
6		10	(h)	Blackpool	W	4-0	D'Arcy 2, Bentley, Gray	47,632
7		13	(h)	Aston Villa	W	4-0	McNichol, Bentley 2, Campbell	56,653
8		15	(a)	Blackpool	L	1-3	Bentley	28,892
9		20	(a)	Sunderland	L	1-2	Bentley	40,388
10		27	(h)	Wolves	L	1-2	Bentley	63,781
11	Oct	4	(a)	Charlton A	D	2-2	Bentley (pen), Lewis	36,653
12		11	(h)	Preston NE	W	5-3	Parsons 2, McNichol, Bentley, Campbell	51,426
13		18	(a)	Burnley	D	1-1	Bentley	27,692
14		25	(h)	Tottenham H	W	2-1	McNichol, Willis (og)	62,688
15	Nov	1	(a)	Sheffield W	L	0-1		48,027
16		8	(h)	Cardiff C	L	0-2		52,139
17		15	(a)	Newcastle U	L	1-2	Parsons	37,178
18		22	(h)	West Brom A	L	0-2		33,304
19		29	(a)	Middlesbrough	L	0-4		19,683
20	Dec	13	(a)	Manchester C	L	0-4		20,733
21		20	(h)	Manchester U	L	2-3	Dickson, R.Smith	23,261
22		26	(a)	Stoke C	D	1-1	Campbell	31,011
23		27	(h)	Stoke C	D	0-0		17,173
24	Jan	3	(a)	Portsmouth	L	0-2		31,571
25		17	(h)	Bolton W	W	1-0	Parsons	36,572
26		24	(a)	Aston Villa	D	1-1	Armstrong	30,376
27	Feb	7	(h)	Sunderland	W	3-2	Parsons, Bentley 2	40,720
28		18	(a)	Wolves	D	2-2	Bentley, Gray	13,957
29		21	(h)	Charlton A	L	0-1		53,176
30		28	(a)	Preston NE	L	1-2	Parsons	30,501
31	Mar	7	(h)	Burnley	L	0-2		39,214
32		14	(a)	Tottenham H	W	3-2	Lewis, Edwards, Blunstone	47,903
33		21	(h)	Sheffield W	W	1-0	McNichol	36,191
34		23	(h)	Liverpool	W	3-0	Lewis, Edwards, Blunstone	17,337
35		28	(a)	Cardiff C	D	3-3	Dickson, McKnight, Montgomery (og)	19,830
36	Apr	3	(h)	Arsenal	D	1-1	Parsons	72,614
37		4	(h)	Newcastle U	L	1-2	Harris (pen)	40,218
38		6	(a)	Arsenal	L	0-2		40,536
39		11	(a)	West Brom A	W	1-0	McNichol	26,194
40		18	(h)	Middlesbrough	D	1-1	McNichol	40,042
41		25	(a)	Liverpool	L	0-2		47,699
42		29	(h)	Manchester C	W	3-1	Harris (pen), McNichol, Lewis	48,594

FINAL LEAGUE POSITION: 19th in Division One

Appearances
Goals

FA Cup

3	Jan	10	(a)	Derby C	D	4-4	Armstrong, Parsons, D'Arcy, Bentley	24,867
R		14	(h)	Derby C	W	1-0‡	Parsons	38,115
4		31	(h)	West Brom A	D	1-1	Bentley	58,912
R	Feb	4	(a)	West Brom A	D	0-0‡		37,974
2R		9	(n*)	West Brom A	D	1-1‡	Bentley	33,534
3R		11	(n†)	West Brom A	W	4-0	Parsons, Bentley 2, Campbell	27,997
5		14	(h)	Birmingham C	L	0-4		45,872

*Played at Villa Park, Birmingham.   †Played at Arsenal Stadium, Highbury, London.   ‡After extra-time.

Appearances
Goals

Aggregate League attendances:
Home: 920,675 (average 43,842)
Away: 667,557 (average 31,788)

Player appearance and goalscoring grid (shirt numbers worn in each match; row numbers at right).

Robertson WG	Tickridge S	Willemse S	Armstrong K	Harris J	Dickson W	Parsons E	McNichol J	D'Arcy S	Bentley R	Gray W	Bathgate S	Lewis F	Smith R	Saunders FJ	Campbell R	Oelofse R	Allister J	Lewis JL	Greenwood R	Stubbs L	Dicks A	Thomson C	Edwards R	Smith J	Spector M	Blunstone F	McKnight P	
1	2	3	4	5	6	7	8	9	10	11																		1
1		3	4	5	6	7	8	9	10	11	2																	2
1		3	4	5	6	7	8		10	11	2		9															3
1		3	4	5	6	7	8		10	11	2		9															4
1		3	4	2	6	7	10		9	11				5	8													5
1		3	4	2	6	7	10		9	11					8	5												6
1		3	4	2	6	7	10		9	11					8	5												7
1		3	4	2	6	7	10		9	11					8	5												8
1		3	4	2	6	7	10		9	11					8	5												9
1		3	4	2	6	7	10		9	11					8	5												10
1		3	4				10		9	11		2		5	8	6	7											11
1		3	4	2	6	7	10		9	11				5	8													12
1		3	4	2	6	7	10		9	11				5	8													13
1		3	4	2	6	7	10		9	11				5	8													14
1		3	4	2	6	7	10		8	11			9	5														15
1		3	4	2	6	7	8		10	11			9	5														16
1		3	4	2	6	7	10		8	11				5						9								17
1		3	4	2	6	7	8		9	11				5						10								18
1	2	3	4	5	6		10		8	11								7	9									19
1	2	3	5	4		7	10		9	11					8				6									20
1	2	3	4		6		10		8	7				9					5							11		21
	2	3	4		6	7	10			11				9	5							1	8					22
	2	3	4		6	7	10			11				9	5							1	8					23
	2	3	4		6				8					9	7				5			1	10	11				24
		3	4	2	6	7	10		9	11				5	8							1						25
		3	4	2	6	7			9	11				5	8							1	10					26
		3	4	2	6	7	10		9						8				5			1				11		27
1		3	4	2	6	7	10		8					5					9						11			28
1	2	3	4		6	7	10		8					5					9						11			29
		3	4	2	6	7	10		8	11				5								1	9					30
		3	4	2	6	7	10		8	11				5								1	9					31
		3	4	2	6				8					5	7				9			1	10			11		32
		3	4	2			8		7					5	9							1	10			11	6	33
		3	4	2			7		8					5	9							1	10			11	6	34
		3	4	2			9		7					5	8							1	10			11	6	35
		3	4	2	6	7			8					5						9		1	10			11		36
		3	4	2		7	10		8					5						9		1				11	6	37
	2	3	4		6	7	10		8					5						9		1				11		38
1		3	4	2	6	7	8		9										5				10			11		39
1		3	4	2	6	7	8		9										5				10			11		40
1		3	4	2	6	7	8		9										5				10			11		41
1		3	4	2	6	7	8		10					9					5							11		42
27	12	39	41	36	38	33	39	2	37	32	3	1	7	20	18	5	1	9	11	5	1	15	12	1	2	11	4	
			1	3	3	8	11		12	3			1		3				4				2			2	1	

2 own-goals

Robertson WG	Tickridge S	Willemse S	Armstrong K	Harris J	Dickson W	Parsons E	McNichol J	D'Arcy S	Bentley R	Gray W	Bathgate S	Lewis F	Smith R	Saunders FJ	Campbell R	Oelofse R	Allister J	Lewis JL	Greenwood R	Stubbs L	Dicks A	Thomson C	Edwards R	Smith J	Spector M	Blunstone F	McKnight P	
	2	3	4		6	7	10		9	11				5	8							1						3
	2	3	4		6	7	10		9	11				5	8							1						R
		3	4	2	6	7	10		9	11				5	8							1						4
		3	4	2	6	7	10		9	11				5	8							1						R
		3	4	2	6	7	10		9					5	8							1				11		2R
	2	3	4		6	7	10		9					5	8							1				11		3R
	2	3	4		6	7	10		9	8				5								1				11		5
	4	7	7	3	7	7	7		7	5				7	6							7				3		
				1			3		1						5											1		

1953-54

Manager: Ted Drake

#	Month	Date		Opponent	Result	Scorers	Attendance
1	Aug	19	(a)	Manchester U	D 1-1	McNichol	30,759
2		22	(a)	Blackpool	L 1-2	Lewis	28,440
3		25	(h)	Portsmouth	W 4-3	Lewis 3, McNichol	40,090
4		29	(h)	Charlton A	W 3-1	Bentley, McNichol 2	49,245
5	Sep	2	(a)	Portsmouth	L 2-3	Armstrong, Hall (og)	29,571
6		5	(h)	Sheffield U	L 1-2	McNichol	49,824
7		8	(a)	Arsenal	W 2-1	Bentley, Lewis	54,946
8		12	(a)	Huddersfield T	L 1-3	Stubbs	29,613
9		15	(h)	Arsenal	L 0-2		60,652
10		19	(h)	Aston Villa	L 1-2	Moss (og)	47,487
11		26	(a)	Wolves	L 1-8	Bentley	36,134
12	Oct	3	(h)	Sunderland	D 2-2	Bentley, Lewis	56,685
13		10	(a)	Sheffield W	L 0-2		32,214
14		17	(h)	Middlesbrough	D 1-1	Lewis	23,513
15		25	(a)	West Brom A	L 2-5	Bentley 2	32,254
16		31	(h)	Liverpool	W 5-2	Armstrong, Bentley 2, Blunstone, Stubbs	32,867
17	Nov	7	(a)	Tottenham H	L 1-2	Stubbs	44,795
18		14	(h)	Burnley	W 2-1	Bentley, McNichol	39,731
19		21	(a)	Bolton W	D 2-2	McNichol 2	30,635
20		28	(h)	Preston NE	W 1-0	Bentley	40,922
21	Dec	5	(a)	Newcastle U	D 1-1	Stubbs	41,728
22		12	(h)	Manchester U	W 3-1	McNichol 2, Parsons	37,153
23		19	(h)	Blackpool	W 5-1	Bentley, McNichol 3, Stubbs	34,865
24		26	(h)	Cardiff C	W 2-0	Blunstone, Stubbs	61,336
25		28	(a)	Cardiff C	D 0-0		36,958
26	Jan	2	(a)	Charlton A	D 1-1	McNichol	29,017
27		16	(a)	Sheffield U	W 3-1	Blunstone, Stubbs, Parsons	22,569
28		23	(h)	Huddersfield T	D 2-2	Bentley, McNichol	45,041
29	Feb	6	(a)	Aston Villa	D 2-2	Bentley, McNichol	20,625
30		13	(h)	Wolves	W 4-2	Bentley 2, Stubbs, Parsons	60,289
31		20	(a)	Sunderland	W 2-1	Bentley, Parsons	45,755
32		27	(h)	Sheffield W	L 0-1		54,498
33	Mar	6	(a)	Middlesbrough	D 3-3	Bentley, Parsons 2	27,920
34		17	(h)	West Brom A	W 5-0	Bentley, Lewis, McNichol, D.Saunders, Stubbs	46,089
35		20	(a)	Liverpool	D 1-1	Parsons	35,947
36		27	(h)	Tottenham H	W 1-0	McNichol	49,315
37	Apr	3	(a)	Burnley	W 2-1	Bentley, Lewis	20,312
38		10	(h)	Bolton W	W 2-0	Bentley, Parsons	49,433
39		16	(h)	Manchester C	L 0-1		59,794
40		17	(a)	Preston NE	L 0-1		27,172
41		19	(a)	Manchester C	D 1-1	Bentley	30,620
42		24	(h)	Newcastle U	L 1-2	Parsons	46,991

FINAL LEAGUE POSITION: 8th in Division One

Appearances
Goals

FA Cup

3	Jan	9	(a)	West Brom A	L 0-1		35,294

Appearances
Goals

Aggregate League attendances:
Home: 985,822 (average 46,943)
Away: 687,984 (average 32,761)

Robertson WG	Sillett P	Willemse S	Armstrong K	Greenwood R	McKnight P	Bentley R	Smith R	Lewis JL	McNichol J	Blunstone F	Campbell R	Saunders FJ	Saunders D	Spector M	Kell L	Stubbs L	Parsons E	Harris J	Smith J	Bowman A	Dicks A	Thomson C	Collins M	
1	2	3	4	5	6	7	8	9	10	11														1
1	2	3	4	5	6	7	8	9	10	11														2
1	2	3	4	5	6	7	8	9	10	11														3
1	2	3	4	5	6	7	8	9	10	11														4
1	2	3	4	5	6	7	8	9	10	11														5
1	2	3	4			7		9	10		8	5	6	11										6
1		3	4			7		9	8	11		5	6		10			2						7
1		3	4			7			8	11		5	6		10	9		2						8
1		3	4	5		7	8	9	10	11			6					2						9
1		3	4	5		9			8	11			6		10		7	2						10
1	2	3	4	5		7	8	9	10	11			6											11
1		3	4		6		8	9	10	11		5					7	2						12
1		3	4		6		8	9		11		5				10	7	2						13
1		3				8	9	7	10	11		5	6					2		4				14
1		3	4			9			8	11		5	6			10	7	2						15
1		3	4			9			8	11		5	6			10	7	2						16
1		3	4			9			8	11		5	6			10	7	2						17
1		3	4	5		9			8	11						10	7	2			6			18
1		3	4	5		9			8	11						10	7	2			6			19
1		3	4	5		9		11	8				6			10	7	2						20
1		3	4	5		9			8	11			6			10	7	2						21
1		3	4	5		9			8	11			6			10	7	2						22
1		3	4	5		9			8	11			6			10	7	2						23
1		3	4	5		9			8	11			6			10	7	2						24
1	3		4	5		9			8	11			6			10	7	2						25
		3	4	5		9			8	11			6			10	7	2				1		26
		3	4	5		9			8	11			6			10	7	2				1		27
		3	4	5		9			8	11			6			10	7	2				1		28
		3	4	5		9			8	11			6			10	7	2				1		29
		3	4	5		9			8	11			6			10	7	2				1		30
		3	4	5		9			8	11			6			10	7	2				1		31
		3	4	5		9			8	11			6			10	7	2				1		32
	3	11	4	5		9			8				6			10	7	2					1	33
1		3	4	5		9		11	8				6			10	7	2						34
1		3	4	5		9		11	8				6			10	7	2						35
1		3	4	5		9			8	11			6			10	7	2						36
1		3		5	4	9		11	8				6			10	7	2						37
1		3	4	5		9		11	8				6			10	7	2						38
1		3	4	5				9	8	11			6			10	7	2						39
1	2	3	4	5		9		11	8				6			10	7							40
1	2	3	4	5		9		11	8				6			10	7							41
1	2	3	4	5		9			8	11			6			10	7							42
34	12	41	40	33	8	41	8	20	41	32	2	9	33	1	3	30	29	32	2	1	2	7	1	
		2				21		9	18	3			1			9	9							

2 own-goals

Robertson WG	Sillett P	Willemse S	Armstrong K	Greenwood R	McKnight P	Bentley R	Smith R	Lewis JL	McNichol J	Blunstone F	Campbell R	Saunders FJ	Saunders D	Spector M	Kell L	Stubbs L	Parsons E	Harris J	Smith J	Bowman A	Dicks A	Thomson C	Collins M	
		3	4	5		9			8	11			6			10	7	2				1		3
		1	1	1		1			1	1			1			1	1	1				1		

1954-55

Manager: Ted Drake

1	Aug	21	(a)	Leicester C	D	1-1	Bentley	38,941
2		23	(h)	Burnley	W	1-0	Parsons	30,239
3		28	(h)	Bolton W	W	3-2	Bentley, Lewis, Ball (og)	52,756
4		31	(a)	Burnley	D	1-1	Bentley	28,472
5	Sep	4	(h)	Cardiff C	D	1-1	Lewis	42,688
6		6	(h)	Preston NE	L	0-1		36,947
7		11	(a)	Manchester C	D	1-1	Bentley	36,230
8		15	(a)	Preston NE	W	2-1	Parsons, McNichol	27,549
9		18	(h)	Everton	L	0-2		59,199
10		20	(a)	Sheffield U	W	2-1	Stubbs, Lewis	14,137
11		25	(a)	Newcastle U	W	3-1	McNichol, Bentley 2	45,659
12	Oct	2	(h)	West Brom A	D	3-3	Parsons, Bentley, Lewis	67,440
13		9	(a)	Huddersfield T	L	0-1		29,556
14		16	(h)	Manchester U	L	5-6	Lewis, Armstrong, O'Connell 3	55,966
15		23	(a)	Blackpool	L	0-1		19,694
16		30	(h)	Charlton A	L	1-2	Parsons	54,113
17	Nov	6	(a)	Sunderland	D	3-3	McNichol 2, Stubbs	42,416
18		13	(h)	Tottenham H	W	2-1	Bentley, Lewis	52,961
19		20	(a)	Sheffield W	D	1-1	McNichol	25,913
20		27	(h)	Portsmouth	W	4-1	McNichol, Bentley, Stubbs, Blunstone	40,358
21	Dec	4	(a)	Wolves	W	4-3	McNichol, Bentley 2, Stubbs	32,095
22		11	(h)	Aston Villa	W	4-0	Parsons, McNichol 2, Bentley	36,162
23		18	(h)	Leicester C	W	3-1	Parsons, McNichol, Milburn-Froggatt (og)	33,215
24		25	(a)	Arsenal	L	0-1		47,178
25		27	(h)	Arsenal	D	1-1	O'Connell	65,922
26	Jan	1	(a)	Bolton W	W	5-2	Sillett (pen), Bentley 2, O'Connell, Higgins (og)	30,988
27		22	(h)	Manchester C	L	0-2		34,160
28	Feb	5	(a)	Everton	D	1-1	Bentley	50,658
29		12	(h)	Newcastle U	W	4-3	McNichol, Bentley 3	50,667
30		26	(h)	Huddersfield T	W	4-1	Parsons, Bentley, Stubbs, Blunstone	35,786
31	Mar	5	(a)	Aston Villa	L	2-3	Parsons, McNichol	24,467
32		9	(a)	West Brom A	W	4-2	Sillett 2, Saunders, Bentley	7,651
33		12	(h)	Blackpool	D	0-0		55,227
34		19	(a)	Charlton A	W	2-0	Blunstone, O'Connell	41,415
35		23	(a)	Cardiff C	W	1-0	O'Connell	16,649
36		29	(h)	Sunderland	W	2-1	Willemse, McDonald (og)	33,203
37	Apr	2	(a)	Tottenham H	W	4-2	Sillett (pen), McNichol 2, Wicks	53,159
38		8	(h)	Sheffield U	D	1-1	Parsons	50,978
39		9	(h)	Wolves	W	1-0	Sillett (pen)	75,043
40		16	(a)	Portsmouth	D	0-0		40,230
41		23	(h)	Sheffield W	W	3-0	Sillett, Parsons 2	51,421
42		30	(a)	Manchester U	L	1-2	Bentley	34,933

FINAL LEAGUE POSITION: 1st in Division One

Appearances
Goals

FA Cup

3	Jan	8	(h)	Walsall	W	2-0	Stubbs, O'Connell	40,020
4		29	(a)	Bristol R	W	3-1	Parsons, McNichol, Blunstone	35,972
5	Feb	19	(a)	Notts C	L	0-1		41,930

Appearances
Goals

Aggregate League attendances:
Home: 1,017,451 (average 48,450)
Away: 696,008 (average 33,143)

Robertson WG	Sillett P	Willemse S	Harris J	Greenwood R	Saunders D	Parsons E	McNichol J	Bentley R	Stubbs L	Blunstone F	Smith R	Lewis JL	Armstrong K	O'Connell S	Wicks S	Thomson C	Brabrook P	Dicks A	Edwards R	
1	2	3	4	5	6	7	8	9	10	11										1
1	2	3	4	5	6	7	8		10		9	11								2
1		3	2	5	6	7	8	9	10	11		4								3
1		3	2	5	6	7	8	9	10	11		4								4
1		3	2	5	6	7	8	9	10	11		4								5
1		3	2	5	6	7	8	9		11		4					10			6
1		3	2	5	6	7	8	9	10	11		4								7
1		3	2	5	6	7	8	9	10	11		4								8
1		3	2	5	6	7	8	9	10	11		4								9
1		3	2	5	6	7	8	9	10	11		4								10
1		3	2	5	6	7	8	9		11	10	4								11
1		3	2	5	6	7	8	9		11	10	4								12
1		3	2	5	6	7	8	9	10	11		4								13
1		3	2	5	6	7	8	9		11		4	10							14
1		3	2	5	6	7	8	9		11		4	10							15
1		3	2	5	6	7		9		8	11	4	10							16
1		3	2		6	7	8	9	10	11		4		5						17
1		3	2		6	7	8	9	10	11		4		5						18
1		3	2		6	7	8	9	10	11		4		5						19
1		3	2	5	6	7	8	9	10	11		4								20
1		3	2	5	6	7	8	9	10	11		4								21
1		3	2	5	6	7	8	9	10	11		4								22
1	3		2	5	6	7	8	9	10	11		4								23
1		3	2	5	6	7	8	9	10	11		4								24
1	2	3			6	7	8	9		11		4	10	5						25
1	2	3			6	7		9	10	11		4	8	5						26
	2	3			6	7	8	9	10	11		4		5	1					27
	2	3			6	7	8	9	10	11		4		5	1					28
	2	3			6	7	8	9	10	11		4		5	1					29
	2	3			6	7	8	9	10	11		4		5	1					30
	2	3			6	7	8	9	10			11	4	5	1					31
	3		2		6	7	8	9	10	11		4		5	1					32
	3		2		6	7	8	9	10	11		4		5	1					33
	3		2		6	7	8	9		11		4	10	5	1					34
	3		2		6	7	8	9		11		4	10	5	1					35
	3	11	2		6	7	8	9				4		5	1	10				36
	3	11	2		6	7	8	9				5	1	10	4					37
	3		2		6	7	8	9		11		4		5	1	10				38
	2	3			6	7	8	9		11		4	10	5	1					39
	2	3			6	7	8	9	10	11		4		5	1					40
	2	3			6	7	8	9		11		4	10	5	1					41
	2	3			6	7	8	9	10	11		4		5	1					42
26	21	36	31	21	42	40	41	27	23	4	17	39	10	21	16	3	1	1		
	6	1			1	11	14	21	5	3		6	1		7	1				

4 own-goals

Robertson WG	Sillett P	Willemse S	Harris J	Greenwood R	Saunders D	Parsons E	McNichol J	Bentley R	Stubbs L	Blunstone F	Smith R	Lewis JL	Armstrong K	O'Connell S	Wicks S	Thomson C	Brabrook P	Dicks A	Edwards R	
1	2	3			6	7		9	10	11		4	8	5						3
	2	3			6	7	8	9	10	11		4		5	1					4
	2	3			6	7	8	9	10	11		4		5	1					5
1	3	3			3	3	2	3	3	3		3	1	3	2					
					1	1			1	1			1							

1955-56

Manager: Ted Drake

1	Aug	20	(h)	Bolton W	L 0-2		44,454
2		24	(a)	Huddersfield T	W 3-1	Parsons, O'Connell, Blunstone	20,308
3		27	(a)	Arsenal	D 1-1	O'Connell	56,034
4		29	(h)	Huddersfield T	D 0-0		25,983
5	Sep	3	(h)	Portsmouth	L 1-5	O'Connell	48,273
6		5	(a)	Blackpool	L 1-2	Brabrook	30,563
7		10	(a)	Sunderland	L 3-4	Bentley, Stubbs 2	45,240
8		17	(h)	Aston Villa	D 0-0		35,221
9		24	(a)	Wolves	L 1-2	Parsons	43,017
10	Oct	1	(h)	Manchester C	W 2-1	McNichol, Smith	44,583
11		8	(a)	Charlton A	W 2-1	Smith 2	40,980
12		15	(h)	Tottenham H	W 2-0	Bentley, Smith	48,195
13		22	(a)	Preston NE	W 3-2	Parsons, Bentley, Docherty (og)	17,799
14		29	(h)	Burnley	D 0-0		39,069
15	Nov	5	(a)	Birmingham C	L 0-3		30,499
16		12	(h)	West Brom A	W 2-0	Sillett, Tindall	41,898
17		19	(a)	Manchester U	L 0-3		22,365
18		26	(h)	Sheffield U	W 1-0	Bentley	30,032
19	Dec	3	(a)	Everton	D 3-3	Parsons 2, Brabrook	33,473
20		10	(h)	Newcastle U	W 2-1	Brabrook, Tindall	37,327
21		17	(a)	Bolton W	L 0-4		24,129
22		24	(h)	Arsenal	W 2-0	Bentley, Blunstone	43,022
23		26	(a)	Cardiff C	D 1-1	Bentley	26,794
24		27	(h)	Cardiff C	W 2-1	McNichol, Stubbs	36,740
25		31	(a)	Portsmouth	D 4-4	Blunstone 3, Stubbs	28,955
26	Jan	14	(h)	Sunderland	L 2-3	Bentley, Bone (og)	43,999
27		21	(a)	Aston Villa	W 4-1	Parsons, Blunstone, Stubbs 2	22,059
28	Feb	4	(h)	Wolves	L 2-3	Tindall 2	37,740
29		11	(a)	Manchester C	D 2-2	O'Connell, Lewis	26,642
30		22	(h)	Charlton A	W 3-1	Bentley, Tindall	8,473
31		25	(a)	Tottenham H	L 0-4		46,767
32	Mar	3	(h)	Manchester U	L 2-4	Parsons, Bentley	32,050
33		10	(a)	Burnley	L 0-5		18,670
34		21	(h)	Birmingham C	L 1-2	Stubbs	12,637
35		24	(a)	West Brom A	L 0-3		20,091
36		30	(a)	Luton T	D 2-2	Dicks, Sillett (pen)	24,276
37		31	(h)	Preston NE	L 0-1		31,450
38	Apr	2	(h)	Luton T	D 0-0		26,364
39		7	(a)	Sheffield U	L 1-2	Tindall	23,398
40		14	(h)	Everton	W 6-1	Bentley 3, Lewis, Stubbs 2	13,825
41		21	(a)	Newcastle U	D 1-1	Stubbs	24,322
42		28	(h)	Blackpool	W 2-1	Bentley 2	35,427

FINAL LEAGUE POSITION: 16th in Division One

Appearances
Goals

FA Cup

3	Jan	7	(a)	Hartlepools U	W 1-0	Moore (og)	16,700
4		28	(a)	Burnley	D 1-1	Parsons	44,897
R	Feb	1	(h)	Burnley	D 1-1§	Blunstone	26,661
2R		6	(n*)	Burnley	D 2-2§	Sillett (pen), Bentley	21,921
3R		13	(n†)	Burnley	D 0-0§		42,757
4R		15	(n‡)	Burnley	W 2-0	Lewis, Tindall	27,210
5		18	(a)	Everton	L 0-1		61,572

*Played at St Andrew's, Birmingham. †Played at Arsenal Stadium, Highbury, London.
‡Played at White Hart Lane, London. §After extra-time.

Appearances
Goals

Aggregate League attendances:
Home: 716,762 (average 34,131)
Away: 626,381 (average 29,827)

Thomson C	Sillett P	Willemse S	Armstrong K	Wicks S	Saudners D	Parsons E	McNichol J	Bentley R	O'Connell S	Blunstone F	Robertson WG	Nicholas B	Lewis JL	Brabrook P	Stubbs L	Smith R	Tindall R	Dicks A	Bellett W	Kitchener R	Casey L	Whittaker R	Mortimore J	Compton J	Harris J	Livingstone W	
1	2	3	4	5	6	7	8	9	10	11																	1
1	2	3	4	5	6	7	8	9	10	11																	2
1	2	3	4	5	6	7	8	9	10	11																	3
1	2	3	4	5	6	7	8	9	10	11																	4
1	2	3	4	5	6	7	8	9	10	11																	5
	2	3		5	6			9		11	1	4	7	8	10												6
	2	3		5	6	7		9		11	1	4		8	10												7
	2	3	4	5	6	7		9		11	1			8	10												8
	2	3	4	5	6	7	8	9		11	1					10											9
	2	3	4	5	6	7	8	9		11	1					10											10
	2	3	4	5	6	7	8	9		11	1					10											11
	2	3	4	5	6	7	8	9		11	1					10											12
	2	3	4	5	6	7	8	9		11	1					10											13
	2	3	4	5	6	7	8	9		11	1					10											14
	2	3	4	5	6	7	8	9		11	1					10											15
	2	3	4	5	6	7		10		11	1			8			9										16
	2	3	4	5	6	7		10		11	1			8			9										17
	2	3	4	5	6	7		10		11	1			8			9										18
	2	3	4	5	6	7		10		11	1			8			9										19
	2	3	4	5	6	7		10		11	1			8			9										20
	2	3	4	5	6	7		10		11	1			8			9										21
	2	3	4	5	6	7	8	9		11	1				10												22
	2	3	4	5	6	7	8	9		11	1				10												23
	2	3	4	5	6	7	8	9		11	1				10												24
	2	3	4	5	6	7	8	9		11	1				10												25
	2	3	4	5	6	7	8	9		11	1				10												26
	2	3		5	6	7	8			11	1				10		9	4									27
	2	3		5	6	7				11	1			8	10		9	4									28
1				5	6				10			4	7	8			9		3	11					2		29
1	2	3		5	6		8	9		11		4	7				10										30
1	2	3		5	6		8	9		11		4	7				10										31
	2	3		5	6	7		9		11	1	4		8			10										32
	2	11		5	6	7				10	1	4		8			9		3								33
	2	3		5	6	7	8	9		11	1	4			10												34
	2	3		5	4	7	8	9		11	1				10						6						35
	2	3		5		7	8	9		11	1				10			4			6						36
	2	3		5		7	8	9		11	1				10			4			6						37
	3			5				10		11	1	4	7	8			9				6				2		38
	3			5				10		11	1	4	7	8			9				6				2		39
	2	3		5	4			9		11	1		7	8	10						6						40
	2	3		5	4			9		11	1		7	8	10						6						41
	3			5				9		11	1		7	8	10							2	4	6			42
8	41	38	24	42	37	33	24	38	6	41	34	10	9	18	17	7	15	4	2	1	7	1	1	1	3		
	2					7	2	14	4	6			2	3	10	4	7	1									

2 own-goals

	2	3		5	6	7	8	9		11	1				10			4									3
	2	3		5	6	7	8	9		11	1				10			4									4
	2	3		5	6	7	8	9		11	1				10			4									R
	2	3		5	6	7		10		11	1			8			9	4									2R
1	2	3		5	6	7	8	9		11		4			10												3R
1	2	3			6		8	9		11		4	7				10									5	4R
1	2	3		5	6		8	9		11		4	7				10										5
3	7	7		6	7	5	6	7		7	4	3	2	1	4		3	4								1	
	1					1		1		1			1				1										

1 own-goal

1956-57

Manager: Ted Drake

1	Aug	18	(a)	Burnley	L	0-2		21,960
2		22	(a)	Sheffield W	L	0-4		35,338
3		25	(h)	Preston NE	W	1-0	Tindall	21,832
4	Sep	1	(a)	Leeds U	D	0-0		38,679
5		5	(h)	Manchester U	L	1-2	Blunstone	29,082
6		8	(a)	Cardiff C	D	1-1	McNichol	22,362
7		15	(h)	Birmingham C	W	1-0	Parsons	40,530
8		19	(h)	Sheffield W	D	0-0		21,971
9		22	(a)	West Brom A	L	1-2	Stubbs	24,525
10		29	(h)	Portsmouth	D	3-3	Lewis 3	31,620
11	Oct	6	(h)	Tottenham H	L	2-4	Armstrong (pen), Lewis	55,788
12		13	(a)	Everton	W	3-0	Stubbs 2, Tindall	34,897
13		20	(h)	Wolves	D	3-3	Stubbs, Blunstone, Brabrook	43,558
14		27	(a)	Bolton W	D	2-2	Saunders, Blunstone	21,299
15	Nov	3	(h)	Charlton A	L	1-3	Lewis	28,727
16		10	(a)	Sunderland	W	3-1	A.Nicholas, Tindall 2	27,182
17		17	(h)	Luton T	W	4-1	McNichol, A.Nicholas 2, Tindall	30,823
18		24	(a)	Aston Villa	D	1-1	Armstrong	26,949
19	Dec	1	(h)	Blackpool	D	2-2	P.Brabrook, Tindall	45,327
20		8	(a)	Manchester C	L	4-5	Armstrong, McNichol, A.Nicholas 2	24,412
21		15	(h)	Burnley	W	2-0	Blunstone 2	18,371
22		25	(h)	Arsenal	D	1-1	McNichol	34,094
23		26	(a)	Arsenal	L	0-2		22,126
24		29	(h)	Leeds U	D	1-1	McNichol	43,860
25	Jan	1	(a)	Manchester U	L	0-3		42,282
26		12	(h)	Cardiff C	L	1-2	Saunders	28,828
27		19	(a)	Birmingham C	W	1-0	McNichol	30,157
28	Feb	2	(h)	West Brom A	L	2-4	McNichol, Allen	29,362
29		9	(a)	Portsmouth	D	2-2	McNichol 2	22,964
30		20	(a)	Tottenham H	W	4-3	Saunders, McNichol, Allen 2	20,849
31		23	(h)	Bolton W	D	2-2	Nicholas, Edwards (og)	13,647
32	Mar	2	(a)	Wolves	L	1-3	Stubbs	30,437
33		9	(h)	Manchester C	W	4-2	Allen, P.Sillett, Gibbs, Paul (og)	35,664
34		16	(a)	Charlton A	L	1-3	P.Sillett	20,701
35		23	(h)	Sunderland	L	0-2		36,160
36		30	(a)	Luton T	W	4-0	Lewis 2, Tindall 2	15,831
37	Apr	6	(h)	Aston Villa	D	1-1	Brabrook	28,025
38		13	(a)	Blackpool	L	0-1		17,176
39		19	(a)	Newcastle U	W	2-1	Saunders, Stubbs	30,708
40		20	(h)	Everton	W	5-1	Saunders 2, Brabrook, B.Nicholas, Dunlop (og)	28,317
41		22	(h)	Newcastle U	W	6-2	Stubbs, Lewis 2, Brabrook 2, Tindall	20,795
42		27	(a)	Preston NE	L	0-1		13,592

FINAL LEAGUE POSITION: 13th in Division One

Appearances
Goals

FA Cup

3	Jan	5	(a)	Leyton O	W	2-0	McNichol, Brabrook	27,756
4		26	(a)	Tottenham H	L	0-4		66,398

Aggregate League attendances:
Home: 666,051 (average 31,716)
Away: 544,426 (average 25,925)

Appearances
Goals

276

Football club season appearance-and-goals grid (shirt numbers by player and match).

Robertson WG	Whittaker R	Bellett W	Armstrong K	Wicks S	Saunders D	Parsons E	McNichol J	Bentley R	Stubbs L	Blunstone F	MacFarlane I	Lewis JL	Brabrook P	Nicholas A	Tindall R	Allen L	Livingstone W	Dicks A	Casey L	Sillett P	Matthews R	Mortimore J	Sillett J	Gibbs D	Laverick R	Nicholas B	Berry P	Harrison M	#
1	2	3	4	5	6	7	8	9	10	11																			1
1		3	4	5	6			9		11	2	7	8	10															2
1		3	4	5	6					11	2	7	8	10	9														3
1		3	4	5	6					11	2		8	10	9	7													4
1	3		4	5	6					11	2	7	8	10	9														5
1		3	4	5	6		8			11	2	7		10	9														6
1		3	4	5	6	7	8		10	11	2							9											7
1		3	4	5	6	7	8		10	11	2							9											8
1			4			7	8			11	2			10	9			3	5	6									9
1		3	4	5				9		11	2	7	8		10				6										10
1		3	4	5				9		11	2	7	8		10				6										11
1			4		6				10	11	2		8	7	9		5			3									12
1			4		6				10	11	2	7	8		9		5			3									13
1		3	4		6	7				11	2		8	10	9					5									14
1			4		6					11	2	7	8	10	9		5			3									15
1			4		6		8			11	2	7		10	9		5			3									16
			4		6		8			11	2	7		10	9		5			3	1								17
			4		6		8			11	2	7		10	9		5			3	1								18
			4		6		8			11	2	7		10	9		5			3	1								19
			4		6		8			11	2	7		10	9		5			3	1								20
			4		6		8			11	2	7		10	9		5			3	1								21
					6		8			11	2	7		10	9		5			3	1	4							22
			4		6		8		10	11	2		9	7			5			3	1								23
			4		6		8			11	2	7		10	9		5			3	1								24
					6					11		7		10	9		5			3	1	4	2	8					25
			4		6		8			11		7		10	9		5			3	1		2						26
	2		4		6		8		10	11		7			9		5			3	1								27
			4		6		8		10		2	7			9		5			3	1				11				28
1			4		6		8		10		2	7			9		5			3					†11				29
1					6		8		10		2	11	7		9		5			3						4			30
					6		8				2	11	7	10	9		5			3	1					4			31
					6				10		2	7	8		9		5			3	1				11	4			32
1			4		6		8				2	7			9					3				10	11		5		33
			4		6		8				2	7			9					3	1			10	11		5		34
	2		4		6		8					7			9		5			3	1			10	11				35
1	2		4		6				10	11		7	8		9		5			3									36
	2		4		6				10	11		7	8		9		5			3	1								37
	2		4		6				10			7	8		9		5			3	1							11	38
	2				6				10	11		7	8		9		5			3	1					4			39
	2				6		8			11		7		10	9		5			3	1					4			40
	2				6				10	11		7	8		9		5			3	1					4			41
	2				6				10	11		7	8		9		5			3	1					4			42
20	11	10	33	8	41	5	24	4	18	27	30	18	38	20	26	19	12	19	3	30	22	2	2	4	6	7	2	1	
	3		6	1	10		7		5	9	6	6	9	4						2					1	1			

3 own-goals

Robertson WG	Whittaker R	Bellett W	Armstrong K	Wicks S	Saunders D	Parsons E	McNichol J	Bentley R	Stubbs L	Blunstone F	MacFarlane I	Lewis JL	Brabrook P	Nicholas A	Tindall R	Allen L	Livingstone W	Dicks A	Casey L	Sillett P	Matthews R	Mortimore J	Sillett J	Gibbs D	Laverick R	Nicholas B	Berry P	Harrison M	#
			4		6		8			11			7	10	9			5		3	1	2							3
	2		4		6		8		10	11		7			9			5		3	1								4
	1		2		2		2		1	2		1	1	1	2			2		2	2	1							
												1			1														

1957-58

Manager: Ted Drake

1	Aug	24	(a)	Tottenham H	D 1-1	Greaves	52,580
2		28	(h)	Manchester C	L 2-3	Greaves, Lewis	43,722
3		31	(h)	Birmingham C	W 5-1	Brabrook, Allen, Greaves 2, Lewis	43,806
4	Sep	4	(a)	Manchester C	L 2-5	Brabrook, Lewis	27,943
5		7	(a)	Everton	L 0-3		45,066
6		11	(h)	West Brom A	D 2-2	Tindall 2	29,824
7		14	(a)	Newcastle U	W 3-1	Tindall 2, Block	44,560
8		18	(a)	West Brom A	D 1-1	Greaves	36,680
9		21	(h)	Burnley	W 6-1	Brabrook, Tindall, Greaves, A.Nicholas 2, Block	42,449
10		28	(a)	Preston NE	L 2-5	Tindall, A.Nicholas	17,944
11	Oct	5	(h)	Sheffield W	W 1-0	Tindall	38,722
12		12	(h)	Aston Villa	W 4-2	Tindall 2, A.Nicholas 2	40,769
13		19	(a)	Wolves	L 1-2	A.Nicholas	37,524
14		26	(h)	Arsenal	D 0-0		66,007
15	Nov	2	(a)	Blackpool	L 1-2	Greaves	17,817
16		9	(h)	Luton T	L 1-3	Block	34,102
17		16	(a)	Sunderland	D 2-2	Lewis, Stubbs	32,678
18		23	(h)	Leicester C	W 4-0	Tindall, Lewis 2, McNichol	27,757
19		30	(a)	Bolton W	D 3-3	Brabrook, Lewis, Stubbs	18,815
20	Dec	7	(h)	Leeds U	W 2-1	McNichol, Stubbs	17,038
21		14	(a)	Manchester U	W 1-0	Tindall	37,073
22		21	(h)	Tottenham H	L 2-4	McNichol, Bellett	39,747
23		25	(h)	Portsmouth	W 7-4	P.Sillett, Tindall, Greaves 4, Rutter (og)	27,036
24		26	(a)	Portsmouth	L 0-3		32,236
25		28	(h)	Birmingham C	D 3-3	P.Sillett, Brabrook, Greaves	37,436
26	Jan	11	(h)	Everton	W 3-1	Greaves 2, McNichol	29,490
27		18	(h)	Newcastle U	W 2-1	Greaves, Lewis	37,327
28	Feb	1	(a)	Burnley	L 1-2	Allen	20,599
29		8	(h)	Preston NE	L 0-2		42,704
30		15	(a)	Sheffield W	W 3-2	Greaves 3	16,876
31		22	(a)	Aston Villa	W 3-1	Mortimore, Brabrook, Tindall	20,538
32	Mar	8	(a)	Arsenal	L 4-5	Tindall, Greaves 2, Block	41,570
33		11	(h)	Wolves	L 1-2	Greaves	46,835
34		15	(h)	Blackpool	L 1-4	Greaves	49,471
35		22	(a)	Leicester C	L 2-3	P.Sillett, Tindall	27,849
36		29	(h)	Sunderland	D 0-0		32,929
37	Apr	4	(h)	Nottingham F	D 0-0		44,288
38		5	(a)	Luton T	W 2-0	Brabrook, Tindall	15,285
39		7	(a)	Nottingham F	D 1-1	Gibbs	25,130
40		12	(h)	Bolton W	D 2-2	P.Sillett (pen), Brabrook	27,994
41		19	(a)	Leeds U	D 0-0		20,515
42		26	(h)	Manchester U	W 2-1	Allen, Cliss	45,011

FINAL LEAGUE POSITION: 11th in Division One

Appearances
Goals

FA Cup

3	Jan	4	(a)	Doncaster R	W 2-0	McNichol 2	19,888
4		25	(h)	Darlington	D 3-3	Tindall, Lewis, McNichol	40,759
R		29	(a)	Darlington	L 1-4*	McNichol	15,150

*After extra-time

Appearances
Goals

Aggregate League attendances:
Home: 806,755 (average 38,416)
Away: 626,714 (average 29,843)

Matthews R	Whittaker R	Sillett P	Mortimore J	Dicks A	Saunders D	Brabrook P	Tindall R	Allen L	Greaves J	Lewis JL	MacFarlane I	McNichol J	Bellett W	Stubbs L	Nicholas A	Block M	Livingstone W	Nicholas B	Berry P	Laverick R	Casey L	Cliss D	Scott M	Gibbs D	Compton J	Sillett J	Harrison M	
1	2	3	4	5	6	7	8	9	10	11																		1
1	2	3	4	5	6	7	8	9	10	11																		2
1		3	4	5	6	7		9	10	11	2	8																3
1			4	5	6	7		9		11	2	8	3	10														4
1		2	4	5	6	7		9	10	11		8	3															5
1	2	3	4	5	6	7	9		8						10	11												6
1	2	3	4		6	7	9		8						10	11	5											7
1	2	3			6	7	9		8						10	11		4	5									8
1	2	3	5		6	7	9		8						10	11		4										9
1	2	3	5		6	7	9		8						10	11		4										10
1	2		5		6	7	9		8				3		10			4		11								11
1	2	3	5		6	7	9		8						10	11		4										12
1	2	3	5		6		9		8					10	7	11		4										13
1	2	3	5		6	7	9		8						10	11		4										14
1	2	3	5		6	7	9		8					10		11		4										15
1		2	5		6	7	10	9	8				3			11					4							16
1		2				7	9			11		8	3	10			5	4			6							17
1		2			6	7	9			11		8	3	10			5				4							18
1		2	5		6	7	9			11		8	3	10							4							19
1		2	5		6	7	9			11		8	3	10							4							20
1		2	5		6	7	9			11		8	3	10							4							21
1		2	5		6	7	9			11		8	3	10							4							22
1		2	5		6	7	9		10	11		8	3								4							23
1		3	5		6	7	9		10	11		8					2				4							24
1		3	5		6	7	9		10	11	2				8						4							25
1		2	5		6	7	9		10	11		8	3								4							26
1		2	5		6	7	9		10	11		8	3								4							27
1		2	5		6	7		9	8		3				10	11					4							28
1		2	5		6	7		9	10		3					11					4	8						29
1		2	4			7	9		10		3					11	5				6	8						30
1		2	4			7	9		10		3					11	5				6	8						31
1		2	4			7	9		10		3					11	5				6	8						32
1		2	4			7	9		10		3					11					6	8	5					33
1		2	4			7	9		10		3					11					6	8	5					34
1		2	4			7	9		10				3			11					6	8	5					35
1		2	4		6	8	9		10	7			3			11							5					36
1		2	4		6	7	9		10				3			11						8	5					37
1		2	4		6	7	9		11				3	10									5	8				38
1		2	4			7	9		11				3	10									5	8	6			39
1		2	4			7	9		11				3	10									5	8	6			40
1		2	4			7	9		11				3	10			5							8	6			41
1		2	4			7		9	10												6	8	5			3	11	42
42	12	40	39	6	31	41	36	9	35	17	10	13	20	13	11	20	8	9	1	1	21	9	9	4	3	1	1	
		4	1			8	16	3	22	8		4	1	3	6	4						1		1				

1 own-goal

1		2	5		6	7		9	10	11	3	8									4							3
1		2	5		6	7	9		10	11	3	8									4							4
1		2	5		6	7	9			11	3	8		10							4							R
3		3	3		3	3	2	1	2	3	3	3		1							3							
							1			1		4																

1958-59

Manager: Ted Drake

1	Aug	23	(a)	Manchester U	L	2-5	Greaves 2	52,382
2		27	(h)	Tottenham H	W	4-2	Greaves, Nicholas, Tindall 2	59,203
3		30	(h)	Wolves	W	6-2	Greaves 5, Block	62,118
4	Sep	3	(a)	Tottenham H	L	0-4		50,299
5		6	(a)	Portsmouth	D	2-2	Nicholas, Tindall	31,795
6		10	(h)	Newcastle U	W	6-5	Brabrook, Greaves 2, Nicholas, Tindall 2	46,601
7		13	(h)	Aston Villa	W	2-1	P.Sillett, Greaves	44,023
8		17	(a)	Newcastle U	W	2-1	Mortimore, Harrison	50,283
9		20	(a)	West Ham U	L	2-4	Greaves 2	31,127
10		27	(h)	Nottingham F	W	4-1	Greaves 3, Nicholas	48,093
11	Oct	4	(a)	Burnley	L	0-4		22,902
12		11	(h)	Bolton W	L	0-1		49,229
13		18	(a)	Luton T	L	1-2	Tindall	24,864
14		25	(h)	Leicester C	W	5-2	Sillett, Saunders, Brabrook, Tindall 2	40,369
15	Nov	1	(a)	Preston NE	L	0-2		21,513
16		8	(h)	Leeds U	W	2-0	Greaves 2	31,757
17		15	(a)	Manchester C	L	1-5	Greaves	19,778
18		22	(h)	Arsenal	L	0-3		57,910
19		29	(a)	Everton	L	1-3	Tindall	30,638
20	Dec	6	(h)	Birmingham C	W	1-0	Greaves	27,773
21		13	(a)	West Brom A	L	0-4		19,557
22		20	(h)	Manchester U	L	2-3	P.Sillett (pen), Brabrook	48,550
23		25	(a)	Blackburn R	W	3-0	P.Sillett 2 (1 pen), Greaves	32,149
24		27	(h)	Blackburn R	L	0-2		46,312
25	Jan	3	(a)	Wolves	W	2-1	Tindall, Gibbs	36,093
26		17	(h)	Portsmouth	D	2-2	Greaves, Tindall	24,356
27		31	(a)	Aston Villa	L	1-3	Greaves	33,575
28	Feb	7	(h)	West Ham U	W	3-2	Greaves, Bridges, Tambling	52,968
29		21	(h)	Burnley	L	1-3	Greaves	27,564
30	Mar	4	(a)	Bolton W	L	0-6		24,258
31		7	(h)	Luton T	D	3-3	Brabrook, Nicholas, Blunstone	29,175
32		14	(a)	Leicester C	W	3-0	P.Sillett, Brabrook, Greaves	20,110
33		21	(h)	Preston NE	W	3-1	Greaves 2, Tindall	31,270
34		27	(a)	Blackpool	L	0-5		19,887
35		28	(a)	Leeds U	L	0-4		16,676
36		30	(h)	Blackpool	W	3-1	P.Sillett (pen), Brabrook, Harrison	40,537
37	Apr	4	(h)	Manchester C	W	2-0	Greaves, Blunstone	32,554
38		11	(a)	Arsenal	D	1-1	Greaves	40,722
39		15	(a)	Nottingham F	W	3-1	Brabrook, Greaves, Allen	18,339
40		18	(h)	Everton	W	3-1	Greaves (pen), Allen 2	24,366
41		22	(h)	West Brom A	L	0-2		31,948
42		25	(a)	Birmingham C	L	1-4	Tindall	19,580

FINAL LEAGUE POSITION: 14th in Division One

Appearances
Goals

FA Cup

3	Jan	19	(a)	Newcastle U	W	4-1	Mortimore, Brabrook, Greaves, Gibbs	57,038
4		24	(h)	Aston Villa	L	1-2	Greaves	55,994

Aggregate League attendances:
Home: 836,676 (average 39,841)
Away: 616,527 (average 29,538)

Appearances
Goals

Appearance and goalscoring grid (shirt numbers worn by each player, per match).

Matthews R	Sillett P	Sillett J	Mortimore J	Scott M	Saunders D	Brabrook P	Greaves J	Allen L	Nicholas A	Block M	Robertson WG	Tindall R	Whittaker R	Harrison M	Huxford C	Stubbs L	Bellett W	Casey L	Blunstone F	Cliss D	Gibbs D	Crowther S	Bridges B	Tambling R	Holton P	Anderton S	Shellito K	#
1	2	3	4	5	6	7	8	9	10	11																		1
1	2	3	4	5	6	7	8		10	11		9																2
	2	3	4	5	6	7	8		10	11	1	9																3
	2	3	4	5	6	7	8		10	11	1	9																4
		3	4	5	6	7	8		10	11	1	9	2															5
	2	3	4	5	6	7	8		10	11	1	9																6
	2	3	4	5	6	7	8		10	11	1	9																7
	2	3	4	5	6	7	8		10		1	9		11														8
	2	3	4	5	6	7	8		10		1	9		11														9
1	2	3	4	5	6	7	8		10			9		11														10
1	2	3	4	5	6		8		7			9		11	10													11
1		3	4	5		7	8		10			9	2	11	6													12
1	2	3	4	5	6	7	8			11		9			10													13
1	2	3	4	5	6	7	8		10	11		9																14
1	2	3	4	5	6	7	8		10	11		9																15
1	2	3	4	5	6	7	8	9		11		10																16
1	2	3	4	5	6	7	8	9		11		10																17
1	2	3		5	6	7	8		10			9	11	4														18
1			5				8		10			7	2	4		3	6		11			9						19
1		4	5			7	8		10				2	3			6		11			9						20
1			5			7	8		10			9	2	4		3	6		11									21
1	3	2	4	5		7	8		10			9							11			6						22
1	3	2	4	5	10	7	8												11		9	6						23
1	3	2	5		10	7	8							4					11		9	6						24
1	3	2	4	5		7	8					9							11		10	6						25
1	3	2	4	5		7	8					9							11		10	6						26
1	3	2	5			7	8					11	9	4							10	6						27
1	2	3	4	5		7	8					10										6	9	11				28
1	2	3	4	5		7	8					10									11	6	9					29
1	2	3	4	5		7	8		9			10							11			6						30
1	2		4	5		7	8		10			9		3					11			6						31
1	2		4	5		7	8		10			9		3					11			6						32
1	2		4	5			8		10			9		3					11			6	7					33
1	2		4	5		7	8		10			9		3					11			6						34
1	2		5			7	8					10							9		11	6	3			4		35
1	2		5			7	8					9		3					11		10	6				4		36
1	2		5			7	8					9		3					11		10	6				4		37
1	2		5			7	8					9		3					11		10	6				4		38
			5			7	8		1			9		3					11		10	6				4	2	39
			5			7	8		1			9		3					11		10	6				4	2	40
1	2		5			7	8					9		3					11		10	6				4		41
1	2		5			7	8					9		3					11		10	6				4		42
32	35	27	37	34	19	39	42	11	21	13	10	29	16	16	6	2	3	3	21	3	8	21	2	1	1	8	2	
7		1			1	7	32	3	5	1		13		2					2		1			1	1			

Matthews R	Sillett P	Sillett J	Mortimore J	Scott M	Saunders D	Brabrook P	Greaves J	Allen L	Nicholas A	Block M	Robertson WG	Tindall R	Whittaker R	Harrison M	Huxford C	Stubbs L	Bellett W	Casey L	Blunstone F	Cliss D	Gibbs D	Crowther S	Bridges B	Tambling R	Holton P	Anderton S	Shellito K	#
1	3	2	4	5		7	8					11	9									10	6					3
1	3	2	5	4		7	8					11	9									10	6					4
2	2	2	1	2	1	2	2					2	2									2	2					
		1			1	2																1						

1959-60

Manager: Ted Drake

1	Aug	22	(h)	Preston NE	D	4-4 Brabrook, Greaves 3	42,891
2		26	(a)	Manchester U	W	1-0 Greaves	57,903
3		29	(a)	Leicester C	L	1-3 Brabrook	29,341
4	Sep	2	(h)	Manchester U	L	3-6 P.Sillett 2 (1 pen), Greaves	66,579
5		5	(h)	Burnley	W	4-1 Brabrook, Greaves, Livesey 2	36,023
6		9	(a)	Birmingham C	D	1-1 Tambling	28,132
7		12	(a)	Leeds U	L	1-2 Greaves	17,011
8		16	(h)	Birmingham C	W	4-2 Greaves 3, Blunstone	31,651
9		19	(h)	West Ham U	L	2-4 Livesey, Blunstone	54,349
10		26	(a)	Fulham	W	3-1 P.Sillett (pen), Greaves, Livesey	40,814
11	Oct	3	(a)	West Brom A	W	3-1 Livesey 2, Allen	27,784
12		10	(h)	Bolton W	L	0-2	28,702
13		17	(a)	Luton T	W	2-1 Livesey, Pacey (og)	18,831
14		24	(h)	Everton	W	1-0 Greaves	37,114
15		31	(a)	Nottingham F	L	1-3 Harrison	30,268
16	Nov	7	(h)	Blackburn R	W	3-1 Anderton, Livesey, Harrison	27,677
17		14	(a)	Manchester C	D	1-1 Greaves	24,364
18		21	(h)	Arsenal	L	1-3 Gibbs	52,748
19		28	(a)	Wolves	L	1-3 Tindall	32,894
20	Dec	5	(h)	Sheffield W	L	0-4	33,177
21		12	(a)	Blackpool	L	1-3 Brooks	12,410
22		19	(a)	Preston NE	W	5-4 Greaves 5	15,775
23		26	(h)	Newcastle U	D	2-2 Greaves	48,462
24		28	(a)	Newcastle U	D	1-1 P.Sillett (pen)	43,295
25	Jan	2	(h)	Leicester C	D	2-2 Livesey, Brooks	23,719
26		16	(a)	Burnley	L	1-2 Brooks	21,916
27		23	(h)	Leeds U	L	1-3 Ashall (og)	18,963
28	Feb	6	(a)	West Ham U	L	2-4 Brabrook, Tindall	29,655
29		13	(h)	Fulham	W	4-2 Greaves 2, Tindall 2	38,687
30		24	(h)	West Brom A	D	2-2 Greaves 2	26,225
31		27	(a)	Sheffield W	D	1-1 Blunstone	41,403
32	Mar	5	(h)	Luton T	W	3-0 Greaves 2, Tindall	33,679
33		12	(a)	Everton	L	1-6 P.Sillett	50,963
34		19	(h)	Blackpool	L	2-3 Nicholas, Blunstone	40,262
35		30	(a)	Blackburn R	L	0-1	15,832
36	Apr	2	(h)	Manchester C	W	3-0 Greaves, Blunstone, Brooks	34,044
37		9	(a)	Arsenal	W	4-1 P.Sillett (pen), Brabrook 2, Brooks	40,525
38		15	(h)	Tottenham H	L	1-3 Brabrook	67,819
39		16	(h)	Nottingham F	D	1-1 Greaves	24,542
40		18	(a)	Tottenham H	W	1-0 Greaves	37,205
41		23	(a)	Bolton W	L	0-2	19,432
42		30	(h)	Wolves	L	1-5 Tindall	61,567

FINAL LEAGUE POSITION: 18th in Division One

Appearances
Goals

FA Cup

3	Jan	9	(h)	Bradford	W	5-1 Brabrook 2, Greaves, Livesey, Blunstone	32,212
4		30	(h)	Aston Villa	L	1-2 P.Sillett (pen)	66,671

Aggregate League attendances:
Home: 828,610 (average 39,457)
Away: 619,978 (average 29,522)

Appearances
Goals

Matthews R	Sillett P	Whittaker R	Anderton S	Mortimore J	Compton J	Brabrook P	Greaves J	Livesey C	Nicholas A	Blunstone F	Scott M	McMillan E	Tambling R	Allen L	Crowther S	Sillett J	Cliss D	Corthine P	Harrison M	Shellito K	Gibbs D	Block M	Brooks J	Venables T	Tindall R	Robertson WG	Bonetti P	Bridges B	No.
1	2	3	4	5	6	7	8	9	10	11																			1
1	2	3	4	5	6	7	8	9	10	11																			2
1	2	3	4	5	6	7	8	9	10	11																			3
1	2	3	4		6	7	8	9	10	11	5																		4
1	2				6	7	8	9		11	5	4	10												3				5
1	2				6	7	8	9		11	5	4	10												3				6
1	2				6	7	8	9		11	5	4	10												3				7
1	2	3			6	7	8	9	10		5	4							11										8
1	2	3			6	7	8	9		11	5	4	10																9
1	2		4	5		7	8	9		11				10	6										3				10
1	2		4	5		7	8	9		11				10	6										3				11
1	2		4	5		7	8			11				10	6										3			9	12
1	3		4	5		7		9		11				10	6	2	8												13
1	2		4	5		7	8	9		11					6		10								3				14
1	3		4	5		9	8								6	2	10	7	11										15
1	3		4	5		7	8	9						10	6				11	2									16
1	3		4	5	6	7	8			11						2					10				9				17
1	3		4	5			8	9		11						2		7			10								18
1	3		4	5		7	8	10							6	2			11						9				19
1	3		4	5		7		10							6	2			11						9				20
1	3		4	5	6	7	10	9		11						2							8						21
1	3		4	5		7	10	9		11					6	2							8						22
1	3		4	5		7	10	9		11					6	2							8						23
1	3		4	5		7	10	9		11					6	2							8						24
1	3	2	4	5		7	10	9		11					6								8						25
1	3		4			7	10	9		11				5	6	2							8						26
1	3		4			7	10	9		11				5	6	2							8						27
1	3	6	5			7	10			11						2							8	4	9				28
	3		4	5		7	10			11					6	2							8		9	1			29
	3		4	5		7	10			11					6	2							8		9	1			30
1	3		4	5		7				11					6	2					10		8		9				31
1	3		4	5		7	10			11					6	2							8		9				32
1	3	2	4	5		7	10								6				11				8		9				33
1			4			7	8	9	10	11				5	6	2									3				34
	2		4	5		7	8	9		11					6								10		3	1			35
	3		4	5		7	8			11					6	2							10		9		1		36
	3		4	5		7	8			11					6	2							10		9		1		37
	3		4	5		7	8			11					6	2							10		9		1		38
	3		4	5		7	8	9	10						6	2			11								1		39
	3		4	5		8				11					6	2					10		7		9		1		40
	3		4	5		7	8			11					6	2							10		9		1		41
1	3		4	5		7	8			11					6	2							10		9				42
33	41	8	40	33	8	39	40	25	7	37	9	5	4	5	30	21	4	2	5	5	4	2	20	1	24	3	6	1	
	6			1		7	29	9	1	5				1	1	2			1				5		6				

2 own-goals

Matthews R	Sillett P	Whittaker R	Anderton S	Mortimore J	Compton J	Brabrook P	Greaves J	Livesey C	Nicholas A	Blunstone F	Scott M	McMillan E	Tambling R	Allen L	Crowther S	Sillett J	Cliss D	Corthine P	Harrison M	Shellito K	Gibbs D	Block M	Brooks J	Venables T	Tindall R	Robertson WG	Bonetti P	Bridges B	No.
1	3		4			7	10	9		11				5	6	2							8						3
1	3		4			7	10	9		11				5	6	2							8						4
2	2		2			2	2	2		2				2	2	2							2						
	1					2	1	1		1																			

1960-61

Manager: Ted Drake

1	Aug	20	(a)	Aston Villa	L	2-3	Brabrook, Gibbs	42,247
2		24	(h)	Leicester C	L	1-3	Bradbury	24,691
3		27	(h)	Wolves	D	3-3	Greaves 3	41,681
4		31	(a)	Leicester C	W	3-1	P.Sillett, Greaves, Brooks	21,087
5	Sep	3	(a)	Bolton W	L	1-4	Greaves	21,609
6		7	(h)	Blackburn R	W	5-2	Greaves 3, Livesey 2	23,224
7		10	(h)	West Ham U	W	3-2	Greaves, Blunstone, Livesey	37,873
8		17	(a)	Fulham	L	2-3	Blunstone, Livesey	37,423
9		19	(a)	Blackburn R	L	1-3	Brabrook	21,508
10		24	(a)	Blackpool	W	4-1	Greaves 2, Livesey 2	26,546
11	Oct	1	(h)	Everton	D	3-3	Greaves, Blunstone, Livesey	31,457
12		15	(a)	Birmingham C	L	0-1		23,334
13		22	(h)	Burnley	L	2-6	Brabrook, Greaves	29,080
14		29	(a)	Preston NE	W	2-0	Tambling, Tindall	14,174
15	Nov	5	(h)	Newcastle U	W	4-2	Brabrook, Tindall 3	30,489
16		12	(a)	Arsenal	W	4-1	Greaves, Tambling, Mortimore, Tindall	38,666
17		19	(h)	Manchester C	W	6-3	Greaves 3, Tambling, Tindall 2	37,346
18		26	(a)	Nottingham F	L	1-2	Brabrook	22,121
19	Dec	3	(h)	West Brom A	W	7-1	Brabrook, Greaves 5, Tindall	19,568
20		10	(a)	Cardiff C	L	1-2	Greaves	21,840
21		17	(a)	Aston Villa	L	2-4	Greaves 2	23,805
22		24	(h)	Manchester U	L	1-2	Brabrook	37,601
23		26	(a)	Manchester U	L	0-6		50,164
24		31	(a)	Wolves	L	1-6	Anderton	28,503
25	Jan	14	(h)	Bolton W	D	1-1	Livesey	20,461
26		21	(a)	West Ham U	L	1-3	Blunstone	21,829
27	Feb	4	(h)	Fulham	W	2-1	Greaves, Bridges	39,185
28		11	(h)	Blackpool	D	2-2	P.Sillett (pen), Greaves	21,993
29		18	(a)	Everton	D	1-1	Greaves	34,449
30		25	(a)	Sheffield W	L	0-1		21,936
31	Mar	4	(h)	Birmingham C	W	3-2	Greaves, Tambling, Tindall	27,727
32		11	(a)	Burnley	D	4-4	Greaves 2, Tambling	19,435
33		18	(h)	Preston NE	D	1-1	Tindall	22,031
34		25	(a)	Newcastle U	W	6-1	Greaves 4, Tindall 2	28,975
35		31	(a)	Tottenham H	L	2-4	Brabrook, Tindall	65,032
36	Apr	1	(h)	Cardiff C	W	6-1	Greaves, Tambling, Tindall 2, Bridges, Harrington (og)	22,697
37		3	(h)	Tottenham H	L	2-3	Greaves, Blunstone	57,103
38		8	(a)	Manchester C	L	1-2	Tambling	27,720
39		15	(h)	Arsenal	W	3-1	Tambling, Tindall, Neill (og)	38,233
40		22	(a)	West Brom A	L	0-3		17,691
41		26	(h)	Sheffield W	L	0-2		24,258
42		29	(h)	Nottingham F	W	4-3	Greaves 4 (1 pen)	22,775

FINAL LEAGUE POSITION: 12th in Division One

Appearances
Goals

FA Cup

3	Jan	7	(h)	Crewe A	L	1-2	Blunstone	32,574

Appearances
Goals

League Cup

1	Oct	10	(a)	Millwall	W	7-1	P.Sillett 2, Evans, Brabrook, Greaves 2, Brooks	15,007
2		24	(h)	Workington	W	4-2	Brabrook, Tambling, Mortimore, Nicholas	5,630
3	Nov	16	(a)	Doncaster R	W	7-0	J.Sillett, Brabrook 2, Blunstone 2, Tambling 2	9,951
4	Dec	14	(a)	Portsmouth	L	0-1		13,054

Aggregate League attendances:
Home: 633,258 (average 30,155)
Away: 606,289 (average 28,870)

Appearances
Goals

Appearance and goalscoring grid (shirt numbers per match).

Bonetti P	Sillett J	Sillett P	Venables T	Evans R	Bradbury T	Brabrook P	Greaves J	Gibbs D	Brooks J	Blunstone F	Livesey C	Matthews R	Anderton S	Tambling R	Harris A	Mortimore J	Crowther S	Tindall R	Nicholas A	Block M	Bridges B	Harrison M	Scott M	Match
1	2	3	4	5	6	7	8	9	10	11														1
1	2	3	4	5	6	7	8		10	11	9													2
1	2	3	4	5	6	7	8		10	11	9													3
1	2	3	4	5	6	7	8		10	11	9													4
1	2	3	4	5	6	7	8		10	11	9													5
1	2	3	4	5	6	7	8		10	11	9													6
1	2	3	4	5	6	7	8		10	11	9													7
1	2	3	4	5	6	7	8		10	11	9													8
1	2	3	4	5	6	7	8	10		11	9													9
	2	3	4	5		7	8		10	11	9		1	6										10
	2	3	4	5		7	8		10	11	9		1	6										11
	2	3	4	5		7	8		10	11	9		1	6										12
	2	3	4	5		7	8		10		9		1	6	11									13
1		2	4	5		7		10	8					11	3	6	9							14
1		2	4	5		7	8		10					11	3	6	9							15
1		2	4	5		7	8		10					11	3	6	9							16
1	2		4	5		7	8		10					11	3	6	9							17
1	2		4	5		7	8		10					11	3	6	9							18
1		2	4	5		7	8		10					11	3	6	9							19
1		2	4	5		7	8		10					11	3	6	9							20
1		2	4	5		7	8		10					11	3	6	9							21
1		2		5		7	8		10			4		11	3	6	9							22
1		2		5		7	8		10			4		11	3	6	9							23
1	2	3		5		7	8		10	11		4				6	9							24
	2		4	5			8		10	11	9		1	6	3			7						25
1	2		4	5		7	8			11	9			6	3		10							26
1	2		4	5	6	7	8		10								3			9	11			27
1	2		4	5	6	7	8		10								3			9	11			28
1	2	3	4	5		7	8					6	10				9				11			29
1	3	2	4	5	6	7	8						10				9				11			30
1	2	3	4	5		7	8					6	10				9				11			31
1	2	3	4	5		7	8					6	10				9				11			32
1	2	3	4			7	8					6	10				9				11	5		33
1	2	3	4			7	8					6	10				9				11	5		34
1	2	3	4			7	8					6	10				9				11	5		35
1	2	3	4				8		7			6	10				9				11	5		36
1	2		4	9			8		7			6	10			3					11	5		37
1	2		4				8		7			6	10	3	5		9				11			38
1	2	3	4				8		7			6	10				9				11	5		39
1	2	3	4				8		7			6	10				9				11	5		40
	2	3	4				8		10		7		1	6			9				11	5		41
1	2		4			7	8			11		6	10			3	9					5		42
36	30	37	36	32	15	36	40	3	26	24	14	6	22	24	17	12	25	1		2	15	9		
		2		1	8	41			1	1	5		8	1	9		1				16	1	1		

2 own-goals

Bonetti P	Sillett J	Sillett P	Venables T	Evans R	Bradbury T	Brabrook P	Greaves J	Gibbs D	Brooks J	Blunstone F	Livesey C	Matthews R	Anderton S	Tambling R	Harris A	Mortimore J	Crowther S	Tindall R	Nicholas A	Block M	Bridges B	Harrison M	Scott M	
1		2	4	5		7	8			11		6	10				3				9			3
1		1	1	1		1	1			1		1	1				1				1			
										1														

Bonetti P	Sillett J	Sillett P	Venables T	Evans R	Bradbury T	Brabrook P	Greaves J	Gibbs D	Brooks J	Blunstone F	Livesey C	Matthews R	Anderton S	Tambling R	Harris A	Mortimore J	Crowther S	Tindall R	Nicholas A	Block M	Bridges B	Harrison M	Scott M	
	2	3	4	5		7	8		10	11	9		1	6										1
1		2		5		7			8						11	3	4	6		9	10			2
1	2		4	5		7	8		10						11	3	6			9				3
1		2	4	5		7	8		10						11	3	6	9						4
3	2	3	3	4		4	2		4	2	1	1	1	3	3	3	1	3		1	1			
	1	2		1		4	2		1	2				3	1		1				1			

1961-62

Manager: Ted Drake. Tommy Docherty from October.

1	Aug	19	(h)	Nottingham F	D	2-2	Brabrook, Tambling	20,857
2		23	(a)	Manchester U	L	2-3	Tambling 2	45,847
3		26	(a)	Aston Villa	L	1-3	Tambling	29,390
4		30	(h)	Manchester U	W	2-0	Tambling, Bridges	42,248
5	Sep	2	(h)	Fulham	D	0-0		37,998
6		6	(a)	Cardiff C	L	2-5	Venables, Bridges	20,883
7		9	(h)	Sheffield U	W	6-1	Brabrook, Tambling 3, Bridges 2	22,026
8		16	(a)	West Ham U	L	1-2	Bridges	27,530
9		20	(h)	Cardiff C	L	2-3	Harrison, Milne (og)	15,804
10		23	(h)	Blackburn R	D	1-1	Brabrook	23,301
11		30	(a)	Blackpool	L	0-4		24,191
12	Oct	7	(a)	Sheffield W	L	3-5	Tambling 3	25,217
13		14	(h)	Leicester C	L	1-3	Block	21,377
14		21	(a)	Birmingham C	L	2-3	Tambling (pen), Bridges	20,079
15		28	(h)	Everton	D	1-1	Brabrook	25,535
16	Nov	4	(a)	Arsenal	W	3-0	Blunstone, Bridges 2	37,604
17		11	(h)	Bolton W	W	1-0	Tambling	12,404
18		18	(a)	Manchester C	D	2-2	Tambling, Bridges	16,583
19		25	(h)	West Brom A	W	4-1	Tambling, Bridges 3	25,025
20	Dec	2	(a)	Ipswich T	L	2-5	Murray, Tambling	22,726
21		9	(h)	Burnley	L	1-2	Tambling	33,296
22		16	(a)	Nottingham F	L	0-3		17,419
23		23	(h)	Aston Villa	W	1-0	Bridges	20,538
24		26	(h)	Tottenham H	L	0-2		51,282
25		30	(a)	Tottenham H	L	2-5	Moore 2	44,630
26	Jan	13	(a)	Fulham	W	4-3	Brabrook, Tambling (pen), Malcolm, Mealand (og)	35,640
27		20	(h)	Sheffield U	L	1-3	Bridges	19,626
28	Feb	3	(h)	West Ham U	L	0-1		34,259
29		10	(a)	Blackburn R	L	0-3		12,206
30		16	(h)	Blackpool	W	1-0	Tambling	24,276
31		24	(h)	Sheffield W	W	1-0	Harrison	23,760
32	Mar	9	(h)	Birmingham C	D	1-1	Murray	23,959
33		17	(a)	Everton	L	0-4		37,215
34		24	(h)	Arsenal	L	2-3	Brabrook, Harrison	31,016
35		31	(a)	Bolton W	L	2-4	Murray, Bridges	15,495
36	Apr	7	(h)	Manchester C	D	1-1	Bridges	18,629
37		11	(a)	Leicester C	L	0-2		15,184
38		14	(a)	West Brom A	L	0-4		14,573
39		20	(h)	Wolves	L	4-5	Murray, Brabrook, Tambling (pen), Bridges	31,221
40		21	(h)	Ipswich T	D	2-2	Brabrook, Bridges	28,462
41		23	(a)	Wolves	D	1-1	Bridges	14,597
42		28	(a)	Burnley	D	1-1	Blunstone	29,078

FINAL LEAGUE POSITION: 22nd in Division One

Appearances
Goals

FA Cup

3	Jan	6	(a)	Liverpool	L	3-4	Tambling 2, Bridges	48,455

Appearances
Goals

Aggregate League attendances:
Home: 568,273 (average 27,060)
Away: 525,713 (average 25,033)

Bonetti P	Sillett J	Sillett P	Venables T	Scott M	Upton F	Murray A	Brabrook P	Tindall R	Tambling R	Blunstone F	Cliss D	Harrison M	Harris A	Mortimore J	Bridges B	Docherty T	Anderton S	Shellito K	Block M	Bradbury T	Malcolm A	Butler D	Bolland G	Young A	Moore G	Shaw C	Harris R	Sorrell D	McNally E	Pinner M	
1	2	3	4	5	6		7	9	10	11	8																				1
1	2	3	4	5	6		7	9	10	11	8																				2
1	2	3	4	5	6		7	9	10		8	11																			3
1	2		4	5			7		10		8	11	3	6	9																4
1	2		4	5			7		10		8	11	3	6	9																5
1	2		4	5			7		10		8	11	3	6	9																6
1	2			5			7		10		8	11	3	4	9	6															7
1	2			5			7		10		8	11	3	6	9	4															8
1	2			5			7	9	10		8	11	3	4	6																9
1	2			5			7		10		8	11	3	6	9	4															10
1	2		4	5			7		10		8	11	3	6	9																11
1	2		4	5			7		10		8	11	3	6	9																12
1			4	5			7	9	10		8	11	3				6	2													13
1				5			7	9			8	11	3				6	2		10	4										14
1				5			7	9			8	11	3				6	2		10	4										15
1				5			7	9			8	11	3				6	2		10	4										16
1				5			7	9			8	11	3				6	2		10	4										17
1				5			7	9			8	11					6	2		10	4	3									18
1				5			7	9			8	11	3				6	2		10	4										19
1				5			7	9			8	11	3				6	2		10	4										20
1				5			7		10	11					9		6	2		8	4	3									21
1				5		8	7		10	11					9		6	2			4	3									22
1							7		10	11			3				6	2		8	4			5	9						23
1				5			7				8	11	3				6	2		10	4				9						24
1					6		7		10			11	3					2		8	4			5	9						25
1					6		7		10			11	3					2		8	4			5	9						26
1					6		7		10			11	3					2		8	4			5	9						27
1				5			7		10	11							6	2			4	3		8	9						28
1			5				7					11					6	2	8	10	4	3			9						29
1				5		8	7		10			11					6	2			4	3			9						30
1				5		8	7		10			11						2			4	3	6		9						31
1				5		11	7		10		8							2			4	3	6		9						32
				5		8	7			11					9			2			4	3	6		10				1		33
1						8	7		10	11					9			2			4	3	5		6						34
						9	7					11	3	6	8			2		8	4			5	10				1		35
				5		9	7					11	3	6				2		8	4				10				1		36
				5		9	7					11	3	6				2		8	4				10				1		37
				5		9	7					11	3	6				2		8	4				10				1		38
				5		8	7		10	11			3	6	9			2			4	3						1			39
					6	8	7		10			11	3	5	9			2			4	3							1		40
					6		7		10	11			3	5	9			2			4				8				1		41
	8				6		7		10	11			3	5				2			4				9					1	42
33	12	3	12	36	10	18	37	5	34	26	8	22	27	14	32	4	6	26	1	14	27	16	2	6	17	1	3	1	8	1	
			1			4	8		20	2		3			19					1		1			2						

2 own-goals

Bonetti P	Sillett J	Sillett P	Venables T	Scott M	Upton F	Murray A	Brabrook P	Tindall R	Tambling R	Blunstone F	Cliss D	Harrison M	Harris A	Mortimore J	Bridges B	Docherty T	Anderton S	Shellito K	Block M	Bradbury T	Malcolm A	Butler D	Bolland G	Young A	Moore G	Shaw C	Harris R	Sorrell D	McNally E	Pinner M	
1			6		10	7		8	11		3		9		2		4		5												3
1			1		1	1		1	1		1		1		1		1		1												
						2							1																		

1962-63

Manager: Tommy Docherty

1	Aug	18	(a)	Rotherham U	W	1-0	Tambling	11,268
2		22	(h)	Scunthorpe U	W	3-0	Bridges 2, Moore	18,377
3		25	(h)	Charlton A	W	5-0	Upton, Bridges 2, Moore 2	24,683
4		28	(a)	Scunthorpe U	L	0-3		11,196
5	Sep	1	(a)	Stoke C	D	0-0		19,470
6		8	(h)	Sunderland	W	1-0	Upton	32,901
7		10	(h)	Southampton	W	2-0	Tambling, Moore	18,890
8		15	(a)	Leeds U	L	0-2		27,620
9		19	(a)	Southampton	L	1-2	Bridges	18,717
10		22	(h)	Swansea T	D	2-2	Murray, Tambling (pen)	22,693
11		29	(a)	Portsmouth	W	2-0	Tambling 2	22,627
12	Oct	6	(h)	Cardiff C	W	6-0	Venables, Upton, Murray, Tambling 2, Bridges	25,434
13		13	(a)	Huddersfield T	L	0-1		23,936
14		20	(h)	Middlesbrough	W	3-2	Tambling 2, Bridges	32,551
15		27	(a)	Derby C	W	3-1	Tambling 3	12,653
16	Nov	3	(h)	Newcastle U	W	4-2	Murray, Tambling, Bridges 2	34,428
17		10	(a)	Walsall	W	5-1	Tambling 2, Bridges, Moore, Dudley (og)	8,492
18		17	(h)	Norwich C	W	2-0	Tambling 2	28,816
19		24	(a)	Grimsby T	W	3-0	Tambling 2, Keeble (og)	10,823
20	Dec	1	(h)	Plymouth A	D	1-1	Blunstone	29,829
21		8	(a)	Preston NE	W	3-1	Tambling 2, Bridges	14,487
22		15	(h)	Rotherham U	W	3-0	Bridges, Blunstone 2	19,735
23		22	(a)	Charlton A	W	4-1	Tambling 4	21,307
24		26	(a)	Luton T	W	2-0	Moore 2	11,867
25	Feb	9	(a)	Swansea T	L	0-2		13,359
26		16	(a)	Cardiff C	L	0-1		16,108
27	Mar	2	(h)	Huddersfield T	L	1-2	Mulholland	32,427
28		9	(a)	Middlesbrough	L	0-1		24,781
29		23	(a)	Newcastle U	L	0-2		39,418
30		27	(h)	Derby C	W	3-1	Tambling, Blunstone 2	19,553
31		30	(h)	Walsall	L	0-1		19,625
32	Apr	1	(h)	Luton T	W	3-1	Tambling 2 (1 pen), Blunstone	21,211
33		6	(a)	Norwich C	L	1-4	Tambling	20,205
34		12	(h)	Bury	W	2-0	Tambling (pen), Bridges	45,069
35		13	(h)	Grimsby T	W	2-1	Tambling, Bridges	21,768
36		16	(a)	Bury	L	0-2		11,936
37		20	(a)	Plymouth A	L	1-2	Moore	17,027
38		27	(h)	Preston NE	W	2-0	Mortimore, Murray	23,770
39		30	(h)	Leeds U	D	2-2	Bridges, Blunstone	24,387
40	May	11	(h)	Stoke C	L	0-1		66,199
41		18	(a)	Sunderland	W	1-0	Harmer	47,918
42		21	(h)	Portsmouth	W	7-0	Venables (pen), Tambling 4, Blunstone, Kevan	54,558

FINAL LEAGUE POSITION: 2nd in Division Two

Appearances
Goals

FA Cup

3	Jan	5	(a)	Tranmere R	D	2-2	Tambling, Bridges	17,162
R		30	(h)	Tranmere R	W	3-1	Venables, Bridges, Moore	20,505
4	Mar	6	(a)	Charlton A	W	3-0	Murray, Tambling, Mulholland	37,907
5		16	(a)	Manchester U	L	1-2	Sorrell	48,298

Appearances
Goals

Aggregate League attendances:
Home: 616,904 (average 29,376)
Away: 405,215 (average 19,295)

Appearances and goals grid (player shirt numbers by match):

Bonetti P	Shellito K	Butler D	McCreadie E	Venables T	Mortimore J	Upton F	Murray A	Tambling R	Bridges B	Moore G	Blunstone F	Knox T	Harrison M	Harmer T	Harris A	Dunn J	Harris R	Mulholland J	Watson I	Sorrell D	Kevan D	#
1	2		3	4	5	6	7	8	9	10	11											1
1	2		3	4	5	6	7	8	9	10	11											2
1	2		3	4	5	6	7	8	9	10	11											3
1	2		3	4	5	6	7	8	9	10	11											4
1	2		3	4	5	6	7	8	9	10	11											5
1	2		3	4	5	6	7	8	9	10	11											6
1	2		3	4	5	6	7	8	9	10	11											7
1	2		3	4	5	6	7	8	9	10	11											8
1	2		3	4	5	6	7	8	9	10			11									9
1	2		3	4	5	6	7	8	9	10		11										10
1	2		3	4	5	6	7	8	9	10	11											11
1	2		3	4	5	6	7	8	9	10	11											12
1	2		3	4	5	6	7	8	9	10		11										13
1	2		3	4	5	6	7	8	9			11		10								14
1	2			4	5	6	7	8	9			11		10	3							15
1	2			4	5	6	7	8	9	10					3			11				16
1	2			4	5	6	7	8	9	10		11			3							17
1	2			4	5	6	7	8	9	10	11				3							18
1	2			4	5	6	7	8	9	10	11				3							19
1		2		4	5		7		8	10	11				3		6	9				20
1	2			4	5		7	8	9	10	11				3		6					21
1	2			4	5	6	7		9	10	11				3			8				22
1	2			4	5	6	7	8	9	10	11				3							23
1	2			4	5	6	7	8	9	10	11				3							24
1			3	4	5	6	7	8	9	10	11								2			25
1		2		4	5	6	7	8	9	10	11				3							26
1	2		3	4	5	6	7	8		10	11							9				27
1	2		3	4	5	6	7	8	9	10	11											28
1		2		4	5	6	7	8		9	11			3						10		29
		2	3	4	5	6	7	8			11			10		1				9		30
1			3	4	5	6	7	8	9		11				2					10		31
			3	4	5	6	7	8	9	10	11				2	1						32
			3	4	5	6	7	8	9	10		11			2	1						33
1	2		3	4	5	6	7	8	9	10	11											34
1	2		3	4	5	6	7	8	9	10	11											35
1	2		3	4	5	6		8	7	9	11									10		36
1	2		3	4	5	6	7	8		9	11									10		37
1	2		3	4	5		7	8	9	10	11						6					38
1	2		3	4	5		7	8	9	10	11						6					39
1	2		3	4	5		7	8	9	10	11						6					40
1	2		3	4	5	9		11			7			10			6			8		41
1	2		3	4	5	9		11			7			10			6			8		42
39	**34**	**2**	**32**	**42**	**42**	**37**	**39**	**40**	**36**	**36**	**34**	**6**	**1**	**5**	**15**	**3**	**7**	**4**	**1**	**7**		
				2	1	3	4	35	15	8	8			1				1		1		

2 own-goals

Cup appearances:

Bonetti P	Shellito K	Butler D	McCreadie E	Venables T	Mortimore J	Upton F	Murray A	Tambling R	Bridges B	Moore G	Blunstone F	Knox T	Harrison M	Harmer T	Harris A	Dunn J	Harris R	Mulholland J	Watson I	Sorrell D	Kevan D	#
1	2			4	5	6	7	8	9	10	11				3							3
1				4	5	6	7	8	9	10	11				3				2			R
1	2		3	4	5	6	7	8		10	11					9						4
1	2		3	4	5	6	7	8		9	11							10				5
4	**3**		**2**	**4**	**4**	**4**	**4**	**4**	**2**	**4**	**4**				**2**	**1**		**1**	**1**			
					1	1	2	2	1		1							1				

1963-64

Manager: Tommy Docherty

1	Aug	24	(h)	West Ham U	D 0-0		46,298
2		27	(a)	Burnley	D 0-0		19,674
3		31	(a)	Sheffield U	D 1-1	Murray	18,125
4	Sep	4	(h)	Burnley	W 2-0	Venables (pen), Blunstone	31,881
5		7	(h)	Liverpool	L 1-3	Mulholland	38,202
6		11	(h)	Blackburn R	W 1-0	Blunstone	27,384
7		14	(a)	Aston Villa	L 0-2		23,681
8		16	(a)	Blackburn R	D 2-2	Murray, Bridges	23,217
9		21	(h)	Tottenham H	L 0-3		57,401
10		28	(a)	Wolves	L 1-4	Bridges	20,762
11	Oct	2	(h)	Manchester U	D 1-1	Brown	45,351
12		5	(h)	Stoke C	D 3-3	Mortimore, Moore, Blunstone	29,204
13		12	(a)	Ipswich T	W 3-1	Venables (pen), Tambling 2	15,703
14		19	(h)	Sheffield W	L 1-2	Venables	31,948
15		26	(a)	Fulham	W 1-0	Tambling	32,945
16	Nov	2	(h)	Birmingham C	L 2-3	Moore 2	22,974
17		9	(a)	West Brom A	D 1-1	Murray	16,267
18		16	(h)	Arsenal	W 3-1	Murray, Bridges, Watson	47,050
19		23	(a)	Leicester C	W 4-2	Venables 2 (1 pen), Tambling, Bridges	23,175
20		30	(h)	Bolton W	W 4-0	Murray, Tambling, Blunstone 2	19,969
21	Dec	7	(a)	Everton	D 1-1	Bridges	39,328
22		14	(a)	West Ham U	D 2-2	Tambling, Blunstone	21,950
23		21	(h)	Sheffield U	W 3-2	Venables, Bridges, Hinton	19,505
24		26	(a)	Blackpool	W 5-1	Venables, Murray, Bridges 2, Houseman	17,563
25		28	(h)	Blackpool	W 1-0	Bridges	34,380
26	Jan	11	(a)	Liverpool	L 1-2	Bridges	46,460
27		18	(h)	Aston Villa	W 1-0	Bridges	23,968
28	Feb	1	(a)	Tottenham H	W 2-1	Tambling 2	51,007
29		8	(h)	Wolves	L 2-3	Murray, Tambling	26,131
30		22	(h)	Ipswich T	W 4-0	Murray, Tambling, Bridges 2	20,703
31		29	(a)	Sheffield W	L 2-3	R.Harris, Tambling	19,416
32	Mar	4	(a)	Stoke C	L 0-2		21,441
33		7	(h)	Fulham	L 1-2	Mortimore	26,249
34		14	(a)	Arsenal	W 4-2	Tambling 4	25,513
35		21	(h)	West Brom A	W 3-1	McCreadie, Venables (pen), Tambling	19,434
36		23	(a)	Manchester U	D 1-1	Murray	43,172
37		28	(a)	Birmingham C	W 4-3	Shellito, Murray, Tambling, Bridges	14,485
38		30	(h)	Nottingham F	W 1-0	Bridges	26,086
39		31	(a)	Nottingham F	W 1-0	Murray	16,453
40	Apr	6	(h)	Leicester C	W 1-0	R.Harris	25,315
41		11	(a)	Bolton W	L 0-1		18,868
42		18	(h)	Everton	W 1-0	Murray (pen)	37,963

FINAL LEAGUE POSITION: 5th in Division One

Appearances
Goals

FA Cup

3	Jan	4	(a)	Tottenham H	D 1-1	Murray	49,382
R		8	(h)	Tottenham H	W 2-0	Murray, Tambling	70,123
4		25	(h)	Huddersfield T	L 1-2	Tambling	39,036

Appearances
Goals

League Cup

2	Sep	25	(a)	Swindon T	L 0-3	17,916

Appearances
Goals

Aggregate League attendances:
Home: 657,351 (average 31,016)
Away: 528,824 (average 25,182)

Bonetti P	Shellito K	McCreadie E	Venables T	Mortimore J	Harris R	Murray A	Tambling R	Mulholland J	Moore G	Blunstone F	Knox T	Harris A	Bridges B	McNally E	Hollins J	Hinton M	Brown D	O'Rourke J	Harmer T	Sorrell D	Watson I	Upton F	Houseman P	Dunn J	No.
1	2	3	4	5	6	7	8	9	10	11															1
1	2	3	4	5	6	7	8	9	10	11															2
1	2	3	4	5	6	7		9	10	11			8												3
1	2	3	4	5	6	7	8	9	10	11															4
1	2	3	4	5	6	7	8	9	10	11															5
1	2	3	4	5	6	7	8		10	11			9												6
	2	3	4	5	6	7	8		10	11			9	1											7
1	2	3	4	5	6	7	8		10	11			9												8
1	2	3	4	5	6	7	8		10	11			9												9
1		2	4	5	6	7	8		10	11	3		9												10
1		3	4	5	6		8		10	11		2	9			7									11
1		3	4	5	6		8		10	11		2	9			7									12
1	2	3	4		6		8		10	11			9			5	7								13
1	2	3	8	5	6				10	11			9			4	7								14
1		3	8	5	2			9	10	11						4	7					6			15
1		3	8	5	2			9	10	11						4	7					6			16
1		3	4	5		7				11			9			2	8		10			6			17
1		3	10	5	4	7	8			11			9			2						6			18
1		3	10	5	4	7	8			11			9			2						6			19
1		3	10	5	4	7	8			11			9			2						6			20
1		3	10	5	4	7	8			11			9			2						6			21
1		3	10	5	4	7	8			11			9			2						6			22
1		3	10	5	4	7				11			9			2						6	8		23
1		3	10	5	4	7				11			9			2						6	8		24
1		3	10	5	4	7				11			9			2						6	8		25
			10	5	4	7	8			11		3	9			2						6		1	26
			10	5	4	7	8			11		3	9			2						6		1	27
		3		5	4	7	8			11			9			2			10			6		1	28
		3	10	5	4	7	8			11			9			2						6		1	29
			10	5	4	7	8			11		3	9			2						6		1	30
				5	4	7	8			11		3	9			2			10			6		1	31
1			10	5	6	7		9		11		3				2	4						8		32
1			10	5	6	7				11		3				2	4						8		33
1	2	3	10	5	4	7	8			11			9									6			34
1	2	3	10	5	4	7	8			11			9									6			35
1	2	3	10	5	4	7	8			11			9									6			36
1	2	3		5	4		8		10	11			9			7						6			37
1		3		5	4		8		10	11			9			2	7					6			38
1	2		10	5	4	7	8			11		3	9									6			39
1	2	3	10	5	4	7	8			11			9									6			40
1	2	3	10	5	4		8			11			9			7						6			41
1		3	10	5	4	7	8			11			9			2						6			42
35	18	35	38	41	41	37	35	7	15	41	1	10	33	1	2	21	10		3	2	2	24	4	6	
	1	1	8	2	2	12	17	1	3	6			15			1	1					1		1	

Bonetti P	Shellito K	McCreadie E	Venables T	Mortimore J	Harris R	Murray A	Tambling R	Mulholland J	Moore G	Blunstone F	Knox T	Harris A	Bridges B	McNally E	Hollins J	Hinton M	Brown D	O'Rourke J	Harmer T	Sorrell D	Watson I	Upton F	Houseman P	Dunn J	No.
		3	10	5	4	7				11			9			2	8					6		1	3
		3	10	5	4	7	8			11			9			2						6		1	R
		3	10	5	4	7	8			11			9			2						6		1	4
		3	3	3	3	3	2			3			3			3	1					3		3	
							2	2																	

Bonetti P	Shellito K	McCreadie E	Venables T	Mortimore J	Harris R	Murray A	Tambling R	Mulholland J	Moore G	Blunstone F	Knox T	Harris A	Bridges B	McNally E	Hollins J	Hinton M	Brown D	O'Rourke J	Harmer T	Sorrell D	Watson I	Upton F	Houseman P	Dunn J	No.
1		3			6		8			11		2			4	5	7	9	10						2
1		1			1		1			1		1			1	1	1	1	1						

1964-65

Manager: Tommy Docherty

1	Aug	22	(a)	Wolves	W	3-0	Tambling 2, Venables	25,181
2		26	(h)	Aston Villa	W	2-1	Tambling, Bridges	30,389
3		29	(h)	Sunderland	W	3-1	Shellito, Murray, Graham	46,710
4		31	(a)	Aston Villa	D	2-2	Murray, Tambling	19,757
5	Sep	5	(a)	Leicester C	D	1-1	Hollins	22,186
6		9	(h)	Sheffield W	D	1-1	Venables (pen)	31,973
7		12	(h)	Fulham	W	1-0	Bridges	41,472
8		16	(a)	Sheffield W	W	3-2	Murray 2, Graham	17,387
9		19	(h)	Leeds U	W	2-0	Hollins, Venables	38,006
10		26	(a)	Arsenal	W	3-1	Murray, Tambling, Venables	54,936
11		30	(h)	Manchester U	L	0-2		60,769
12	Oct	3	(h)	Blackburn R	W	5-1	R.Harris, Tambling, Bridges 3	34,913
13		10	(a)	Nottingham F	D	2-2	Bridges, Venables	35,320
14		17	(h)	Stoke C	W	4-0	Murray, Tambling, Graham 2	28,650
15		24	(a)	Tottenham H	D	1-1	Graham	52,927
16		31	(h)	Burnley	L	0-1		29,040
17	Nov	7	(a)	Sheffield U	W	2-0	Murray, Bridges	23,505
18		14	(h)	Everton	W	5-1	Murray, Tambling, Bridges, Graham 2	30,716
19		21	(a)	Birmingham C	W	6-1	Graham 3, Mortimore, McCalliog 2	19,803
20		28	(h)	West Ham U	L	0-3		44,204
21	Dec	5	(a)	West Brom A	W	2-0	Bridges, Graham	15,277
22		12	(h)	Wolves	W	2-1	Bridges 2	20,952
23		19	(a)	Sunderland	L	0-3		41,236
24		26	(h)	Blackpool	W	2-0	Bridges 2	30,581
25	Jan	2	(h)	Leicester C	W	4-1	McCreadie, Murray, Bridges, Graham	28,344
26		16	(a)	Fulham	W	2-1	Tambling, Graham	26,400
27		23	(a)	Leeds U	D	2-2	Bridges, Graham	47,109
28	Feb	6	(h)	Arsenal	W	2-1	Graham 2	46,798
29		13	(a)	Blackburn R	W	3-0	Murray, Tambling, Bridges	16,683
30		22	(h)	Nottingham F	L	0-1		29,038
31		27	(a)	Stoke C	W	2-0	Murray, Graham	28,005
32	Mar	10	(h)	Tottenham H	W	3-1	Tambling, Bridges, Venables	51,390
33		13	(a)	Manchester U	L	0-4		57,662
34		22	(h)	Sheffield U	W	3-0	Murray 2, Bridges	31,837
35		31	(a)	Everton	D	1-1	Murray	40,385
36	Apr	3	(h)	Birmingham C	W	3-1	Tambling, Bridges, Lynn (og)	28,975
37		12	(a)	West Ham U	L	2-3	Bridges, Venables	33,288
38		16	(h)	Liverpool	W	4-0	Hinton, Murray 2, Tambling	62,587
39		17	(h)	West Brom A	D	2-2	Murray, Tambling	30,792
40		19	(a)	Liverpool	L	0-2		41,847
41		24	(a)	Burnley	L	2-6	R.Harris, Houseman	15,213
42		26	(a)	Blackpool	L	2-3	Tambling, Mortimore	16,008

FINAL LEAGUE POSITION: 3rd in Division One

Appearances
Goals

FA Cup

3	Jan	9	(h)	Northampton T	W	4-1	Tambling, Bridges 2, Foley (og)	44,335
4		30	(a)	West Ham U	W	1-0	Tambling	37,000
5	Feb	20	(h)	Tottenham H	W	1-0	Bridges	63,205
6	Mar	6	(h)	Peterborough U	W	5-1	Hollins, Murray, Tambling 2, Bridges	63,635
SF		27	(n*)	Liverpool	L	0-2		67,686

*Played at Villa Park, Birmingham.

Appearances
Goals

League Cup

2	Sep	23	(a)	Birmingham C	W	3-0	Tambling 2, Graham	15,300
3	Oct	26	(h)	Notts C	W	4-0	Tambling 2, A.Harris, McCalliog	6,596
4	Nov	11	(h)	Swansea T	W	3-2	Graham 2, Brown	5,979
5		25	(a)	Workington	D	2-2	Bridges 2	18,000
R	Dec	16	(h)	Workington	W	2-0	Osgood 2	7,936
SF	Jan	20	(a)	Aston Villa	W	3-2	Tambling, Bridges, Boyle	12,000
	Feb	10	(h)	Aston Villa	D	1-1	Graham	17,425
F	Mar	15	(h)	Leicester C	W	3-2	McCreadie, Tambling, Venables (pen)	20,690
	Apr	5	(a)	Leicester C	D	0-0		26,957

Appearances
Goals

Aggregate League attendances:
Home: 778,136 (average 37,054)
Away: 650,115 (average 30,957)

Appearances
Goals

Bonetti P	Shellito K	McCreadie E	Hollins J	Hinton M	Harris R	Murray A	Tambling R	Bridges B	Venables T	Knox T	Graham G	Watson I	Houseman P	Harris A	Mortimore J	McCalliog J	Dunn J	Boyle J	Upton F	Sinclair W	Smart J	Fascione J	Brown D	Osgood P	Young A	
1	2	3	4	5	6	7	8	9	10	11																1
1	2	3	4	5	6	7	8	9	10	11																2
1	2	3	4	5	6	7		9	10	11	8															3
1	2	3	4	5	6	7	8	9	10	11																4
1	2	3	4	5	6	7	8		10	11	9															5
1	2	3	4	5	6	7	8	9	10	11																6
1		3	4	5	6	7	8	9	10	11		2														7
1	2	3	4	5	6	7		9	10	11	8															8
1		3	4	5	6	7		9	10	11	8	2														9
1	2	3	4	5	6	7	8	9	10				11													10
1	2	3	4	5	6	7	8	9	10				11													11
1	2	3	4	5	6	7	8	9	10				11													12
1	2		4	5	6	7	8	9	10				11	3												13
1	2	3	4		6	7	11	9	10		8				5											14
1		3	4	2	6	7	11	9	10		8				5											15
1		3	4	2	6	7	8	9	10	11					5											16
1		3	4	2	6	7	11	9	10		8				5											17
1		3	4	2	6	7	11	9	10		8				5											18
1		3	4	2	6		8	7			9		11		5	10										19
1		3	4	2	6	7	11	9	10		8				5											20
1		3	4	2	6	7		9	10		8		11		5											21
1		3	4	2	6	7		9	10		8		11		5											22
1		3	4	2	6	7		9	10	11	8				5											23
1		3	4	2	6	7		9	10	11	8				5											24
		3	4	2	6	7		9	10	11	8	1			5											25
1		3	4	2	6	7	11	9	10		8				5											26
1			4	2	3	7	11	9	10		8				5			6								27
1		3	4	2	6	7	11	9	10		8				5											28
1			4	2	3	7	11	9	10		8				5			6								29
1		3	4	2	6	7	11	9	10				8		5											30
1			4	2	3	7	11	9	10		8				5			6								31
1		3	4	2	6	7	11	9	10		8				5											32
1		3	4	2	6	7	11	9	10											5						33
1		3	4	2	6	7	11	9	10		8				5											34
1		3	4	2	6	7	11	9	10		8				5											35
1		3	4	2	6	7	11	9			8				5	10										36
1			4	2	3	7	11	9	10		8				5			6								37
1		3	4	2	6	7	11	9	10		8				5											38
1			4	2	3	7	11	9	10		8				5			6								39
1		3	4	2	6	7	11	9	10		8				5											40
1	2		3		8						11				5	10		6	9	4	7					41
1			4	2	3	7	11	9	10		8				5			6								42
41	13	34	41	40	42	40	33	41	39	13	30	2	9	1	28	3	1	6	3	1	1					
	1	1	2	1	2	17	15	20	7		17				1	2	2									

1 own-goal

Bonetti P	Shellito K	McCreadie E	Hollins J	Hinton M	Harris R	Murray A	Tambling R	Bridges B	Venables T	Knox T	Graham G	Watson I	Houseman P	Harris A	Mortimore J	McCalliog J	Dunn J	Boyle J	Upton F	Sinclair W	Smart J	Fascione J	Brown D	Osgood P	Young A	
1			4	2	3	7	11	9	10		8				5			6								3
1			4	2	3	7	11	9	10		8				5		6									4
1		3	4	2	6	7	11	9	10		8				5											5
1			4	2	3	7	11	9	10		8				5		6									6
1		3	4	2	6	7	11	9	10		8				5											SF
5		2	5	5	5	5	5	5		5					5		2	1								
		1				1	4	4																		

1 own-goal

Bonetti P	Shellito K	McCreadie E	Hollins J	Hinton M	Harris R	Murray A	Tambling R	Bridges B	Venables T	Knox T	Graham G	Watson I	Houseman P	Harris A	Mortimore J	McCalliog J	Dunn J	Boyle J	Upton F	Sinclair W	Smart J	Fascione J	Brown D	Osgood P	Young A	
1		3	4				8		9	2	11				5	10		6		7						2
1	2		4				8	9			11	3	5	10			6		7							3
1		4		6	7	11		10		9	2	3	5						8							4
1		3		2	6			9			8	4	11		5	10		7						9		5
1		3		2		7			4	11	8				5	10		6				9				R
1		4	2	3	7	11	9				8				5	10	6									SF
1	9	4	2	3	7	11		10			8						6						5			F
1		2	4	7	11	9	10					5			8	6										
9	1	5	6	6	6	6	7	5	5	1	7	3	3	2	8	5	4	4	3	1	1	1				
	1		6	3	1		4				1		1		1	1		1	2							

1965-66

Manager: Tommy Docherty

1	Aug	21	(h)	Burnley	D	1-1	Venables	34,067
2		25	(a)	Stoke C	D	2-2	Venables (pen), Tambling	28,549
3		28	(a)	Fulham	W	3-0	Murray, Graham, Bridges	34,027
4	Sep	1	(h)	Stoke C	L	1-2	Hollins	25,071
5		4	(a)	Arsenal	W	3-1	Graham, Bridges, Fascione	45,456
6		11	(h)	Everton	W	3-1	Graham, Bridges, Venables	29,816
7		15	(h)	Sheffield W	D	1-1	Venables	26,183
8		18	(a)	Manchester U	L	1-4	Venables	38,183
9		25	(h)	Newcastle U	D	1-1	Graham	30,856
10	Oct	2	(a)	West Brom A	W	2-1	Graham, Bridges	23,186
11		9	(h)	Blackpool	L	0-1		28,022
12		16	(a)	Blackburn R	W	1-0	Graham	16,167
13		23	(h)	Leicester C	L	0-2		30,400
14		30	(a)	Sheffield U	W	2-1	Graham, Osgood	20,795
15	Nov	6	(h)	Leeds U	W	1-0	Hollins	39,373
16		13	(a)	West Ham U	L	1-2	Tambling	31,551
17		27	(a)	Aston Villa	W	4-2	Graham, Tambling 2, Osgood	16,414
18	Dec	4	(h)	Liverpool	L	0-1		36,839
19		11	(a)	Tottenham H	L	2-4	Graham, Bridges	42,299
20		27	(a)	Northampton T	W	3-2	Graham, Tambling 2	23,325
21		28	(h)	Northampton T	W	1-0	Bridges	17,635
22	Jan	1	(a)	Blackpool	W	2-1	Graham, Tambling	14,065
23		8	(h)	Tottenham H	W	2-1	Graham, Osgood	48,529
24		29	(a)	Burnley	W	2-1	Osgood 2	23,825
25	Feb	5	(h)	Fulham	W	2-1	Tambling, Osgood	34,247
26		19	(h)	Arsenal	D	0-0		48,641
27		22	(h)	Sunderland	W	3-2	Graham, Bridges, Osgood	20,828
28		26	(a)	Everton	L	1-2	Bridges	52,752
29	Mar	12	(h)	Manchester U	W	2-0	Graham, Tambling	60,269
30		19	(a)	Newcastle U	W	1-0	Venables	35,118
31		21	(a)	Leicester C	D	1-1	Bridges	25,363
32	Apr	4	(a)	Leeds U	L	0-2		37,786
33		9	(h)	West Ham U	W	6-2	Harris, Graham 2, Venables (pen), Tambling 2	35,958
34		11	(h)	Nottingham F	W	1-0	Tambling	39,380
35		12	(a)	Nottingham F	W	2-1	Tambling 2	29,569
36		16	(a)	Sunderland	L	0-2		32,880
37		25	(h)	West Brom A	L	2-3	Venables (pen), Tambling	22,804
38		30	(a)	Liverpool	L	1-2	Murray	53,754
39	May	2	(a)	Sheffield W	D	1-1	Harris	26,777
40		4	(h)	Blackburn R	W	1-0	Kirkup	10,024
41		7	(h)	Sheffield U	W	2-0	Graham, Tambling	23,072
42		16	(h)	Aston Villa	L	0-2		16,232

FINAL LEAGUE POSITION: 5th in Division One

Appearances
Sub Appearances
Goals

FA Cup

3	Jan	22	(a)	Liverpool	W	2-1	Tambling, Osgood	54,097
4	Feb	12	(h)	Leeds U	W	1-0	Tambling	57,847
5	Mar	5	(h)	Shrewsbury T	W	3-2	Graham, Bridges 2	51,144
6		26	(h)	Hull C	D	2-2	Graham, Tambling	46,924
R		31	(a)	Hull C	W	3-1	Graham, Tambling 2	45,328
SF	Apr	23	(n*)	Sheffield W	L	0-2		61,321

* Played at Villa Park, Birmingham.

Aggregate League attendances:
Home: 658,246 (average 31,344)
Away: 651,841 (average 31,040)

Appearances
Goals

Appearance and shirt-number grid (Chelsea FC). Player columns left to right; match numbers in right-hand column.

Bonetti P	Shellito K	McCreadie E	Boyle J	Hinton M	Harris R	Murray A	Graham G	Bridges B	Venables T	Tambling R	Hollins J	McCalliog J	Osgood P	Houseman P	Young A	Barron J	Fascione J	Dunn J	Robson T	Kirkup J	Thomson J	
1	2		6	5	3		9	7	10	11	4	8										1
1	2		6	5	3	7	8	9	10	11	4											2
1	2	3	12	5	6	7	8•	9	10	11	4											3
	2	3	7	5	6		9	10		4	8			11		1						4
1	2	3		5	6	7	8	9	10		4						11					5
1	2	3		5	6	7	8	9	10		4						11					6
1	2	3	12	5•	6	7	8	9	10		4						11					7
1	2	3			6	7	8	9	10		4			5			11					8
1	2	3			6		8	7	10		4		9	5			11					9
1		6	2	3	7	8	9	10	11	4•				5			12					10
	2	3	6•		7	8	9	10		4			12	5		1	11					11
1	2	3	6		7	8	9	4	10					5			11					12
1	2	3•	4	6		7		12	10		8	9		5			11					13
1	2		6	3		12	8	7	10•		4		9	5			11					14
1	2		6	3		7	8	9		11	4		10	5								15
1	2		6	3		10	8			11	4		9	5			7					16
1	2	3	6	5		7	8		10	11	4		9									17
1		3	6	5	2		8		10		4		9		7				11			18
1		3	6	5	2		8	7	10		4		9						11			19
1		3	6	5	2		8	7	10	11	4		9									20
1		3	6	5	2		8	7	10		4		9						11			21
1		3	7	2	6		8	12	10	11	4		9•	5								22
1		3		2	6		8	7	10	11	4		9	5								23
1		3	6	5	2	7	8		10	11	4		9									24
1		3	6	5	2		8	7	10	11	4		9									25
1		3	6	5	2		8	7	10	11•	4		9				12					26
1		3	6	5	2		8	7	10	11	4		9									27
1		3	6	5	2	12	8	7	10	11	4•		9									28
1		3		5	6		8	7	10	11	4		9							2		29
1		3	8	5	6			7	10	11	4		9							2		30
1		3	8	5	6			7	10	11	4		9							2		31
1		10•	6	3	7	8					4		9	11	5			12		2		32
1		3		5	6		8	7	10	11	4		9							2		33
1		3		5	6	12	8	7•	10	11	4		9							2		34
1		3		5	6	7			10	11	4		9	8						2		35
1	3•		5	6	12	8			10	11	4		9	7						2		36
1		6	5	3	7				10	11	4		9	8						2		37
		6	5	3	10		8				4		9	7		1		11		2		38
		8	3	6	10				4		9	7	5•		12	1		11		2		39
1		6	5	3	10						9	8			7			11		2	4	40
1			5	3	10	8			11	4	9	7								2	6	41
1	3•	12	5	6	10	8			11	4	9	7								2		42
38	16	30	27	38	36	22	33	27	34	26	39	4	31	10	13	1	12	3	6	14	2	—
		3		4		2					1				3		1					—
			2	2	17	9	8	16	2		7				1		1					—

Bonetti P	Shellito K	McCreadie E	Boyle J	Hinton M	Harris R	Murray A	Graham G	Bridges B	Venables T	Tambling R	Hollins J	McCalliog J	Osgood P	Houseman P	Young A	Barron J	Fascione J	Dunn J	Robson T	Kirkup J	Thomson J	
1		3	6	5	2		8	7	10	11	4		9									3
1		3	6	5	2		8	7	10	11	4		9									4
1		3	6	5	2	10	8	7	4	11			9									5
1		3	7	5	6		8	9	10	11	4									2		6
1		3		5	6		8	7	10	11	4		9							2		R
1			6	5	3		8	7	10	11	4		9							2		SF
6		5	5	6	6	1	6	6	6	6	5		5							3		—
			3	2				5									1					—

1966-67

Manager: Tommy Docherty

1	Aug	20	(a)	West Ham U	W	2-1	Hollins, Cooke	36,122
2		24	(h)	Nottingham F	W	2-1	Osgood 2	27,501
3		27	(h)	Sheffield W	D	0-0		33,489
4		30	(a)	Nottingham F	D	0-0		22,199
5	Sep	3	(a)	Southampton	W	3-0	Graham, Osgood, Tambling	29,479
6		7	(h)	Leicester C	D	2-2	Osgood, Cooke	29,760
7		10	(h)	Sunderland	D	1-1	Boyle	31,766
8		17	(a)	Aston Villa	W	6-2	Tambling 5, Boyle	18,259
9		24	(h)	Arsenal	W	3-1	Osgood, Tambling 2	48,001
10	Oct	1	(a)	Manchester C	W	4-1	Kirkup, Osgood, Tambling, Baldwin	31,989
11		8	(h)	Burnley	L	1-3	Baldwin	42,573
12		15	(a)	Manchester U	D	1-1	Crerand (og)	52,717
13		26	(h)	Tottenham H	W	3-0	Tambling (pen), Baldwin 2	54,191
14		29	(a)	Fulham	W	3-1	Boyle, Hateley 2	42,159
15	Nov	5	(h)	Manchester U	L	1-3	Hollins	56,452
16		12	(a)	West Brom A	W	1-0	Tambling	28,151
17		19	(h)	Sheffield U	D	1-1	Tambling	25,976
18		26	(a)	Stoke C	D	1-1	Hateley	28,447
19	Dec	3	(h)	Everton	D	1-1	Hateley	35,495
20		10	(a)	Newcastle U	D	2-2	Tambling, Baldwin	32,529
21		17	(h)	West Ham U	D	5-5	Cooke, Tambling 2, Baldwin, Hateley	47,805
22		24	(h)	Liverpool	L	1-2	Boyle	36,921
23		26	(a)	Liverpool	L	1-2	Tambling (pen)	51,920
24		31	(a)	Sheffield W	L	1-6	Tambling	30,866
25	Jan	7	(h)	Southampton	W	4-1	Tambling, Boyle, Baldwin 2	27,719
26		14	(a)	Sunderland	L	0-2		35,839
27		21	(h)	Aston Villa	W	3-1	Tambling, Baldwin, Hateley	30,922
28	Feb	4	(a)	Arsenal	L	1-2	Tambling	52,467
29		11	(h)	Manchester C	D	0-0		28,633
30		25	(a)	Burnley	W	2-1	Thomson, Baldwin	20,379
31	Mar	4	(h)	Fulham	D	0-0		46,784
32		18	(a)	Tottenham H	D	1-1	Hamilton	49,553
33		24	(h)	Blackpool	L	0-2		37,852
34		25	(h)	Newcastle U	W	2-1	Tambling, Baldwin	26,388
35		27	(a)	Blackpool	W	2-0	Baldwin 2	16,186
36	Apr	1	(a)	Leeds U	L	0-1		39,728
37		10	(h)	West Brom A	L	0-2		18,448
38		17	(a)	Sheffield U	L	0-3		18,003
39		19	(a)	Everton	L	1-3	Baldwin	39,316
40		22	(h)	Stoke C	W	1-0	Baldwin	24,853
41	May	6	(h)	Leeds U	D	2-2	McCreadie, Baldwin	35,882
42		9	(a)	Leicester C	L	2-3	Houseman, Hamilton	17,142

FINAL LEAGUE POSITION: 9th in Division One

Appearances
Sub Appearances
Goals

FA Cup

3	Jan	28	(a)	Huddersfield T	W	2-1	Houseman, Tambling	36,407
4	Feb	18	(a)	Brighton & HA	D	1-1	Tambling	35,000
R		22	(h)	Brighton & HA	W	4-0	Tambling 2, Young, Hateley	54,852
5	Mar	11	(h)	Sheffield U	W	2-0	Tambling, Hateley	40,730
6	Apr	8	(h)	Sheffield W	W	1-0	Baldwin	52,481
SF		29	(a*)	Leeds U	W	1-0	Hateley	62,378
F	May	20	(a†)	Tottenham H	L	1-2	Tambling	100,000

*Played at Villa Park, Birmingham.   †Played at Wembley Stadium.

Appearances
Sub Appearances
Goals

League Cup

2	Sep	14	(h)	Charlton A	W	5-2	Hollins, Houseman, Graham, Tambling, King (og)	14,262
3	Oct	5	(a)	Blackpool	D	1-1	Houseman	13,520
R		17	(h)	Blackpool	L	1-3	Houseman	20,240

Aggregate League attendances:
Home: 747,421 (average 35,591)
Away: 693,450 (average 33,021)

Appearances
Sub Appearances
Goals

Appearance and goal grid (shirt numbers per match; asterisk = substitute used / came on, "12" = substitute).

Stepney A	Kirkup J	McCreadie E	Harris A	Hollins J	Hinton M	Harris R	Houseman P	Graham G	Osgood P	Cooke C	Tambling R	Boyle J	Bonetti P	Young A	Thomson J	Baldwin T	Hateley T	Hughes T	Hamilton I	Fascione J	Lloyd B	Wosahlo R	Whiffen K	Luke G	No.
	2	3		4	5	6	8	9	10	11	7		1												1
	2	3		4	5	7	8	9	10	11	6		1												2
	2	3		4	5	7	8	9	10	11	6		1												3
	2	3		4	5	6	12	8	9	10*	11	7	1												4
1	2	3		4	5	6	8	9		11	11				12				7*						5
	2	3		4		6	8	9	10	11	7		1	5											6
	2	3		4	5	6	8	9	10	11	7		1												7
	2	3	12	4	5	6	8	9	10	11*	7		1												8
	2	3		4	5	6	8	9	10*	11	7		1		12										9
	2	3		4	5	6		9	10	11	7		1			8									10
	2	3		4	5	6	8		10	11	7		1				9								11
	2	3*	12	4	5	6	8		10	11	7		1				9								12
	2	3		4	5	6	8*		10	11	7		1		12		9								13
	2	3		4	5	6			10	11	7		1			8	9								14
	2	3		4	5	6	12		10	11*	7		1			8	9								15
	2	3			5	6	12		10*	11	7		1		4	8	9								16
		3		4	5	6				10	11	7			2	8	9	1							17
		3		4	5	6				10	11	7	1		2	8	9								18
		3		4	5	6				10	11	7	1		2	8	9								19
		3		4	5	6				10	11	7	1		2	8	9								20
	2	3		4	5	6				10	11	7	1			8	9								21
		3		4	5	6	12			10	11	7	1		2	8	9*								22
		3		4	5	6				10	11	7	1		2	8	9								23
		3		4	5	6	12			10	11*	7			2	8	9	1							24
		3		4	5	6				10	11	7	1		2	8	9								25
		3	2	4	5*	6				10	11	7	1		12	8	9								26
	2	3		4	5	6	11				7	10	1			8	9								27
		3		4	5	6	11			7		8	1		2	10	9								28
		3		4	5	6	11			7*	8	10	1		2		9	12							29
	2	3		4	5	6	10*			7	8		1		11	12	9								30
	2	3		4	5	6				7	8		1		11	10	9								31
		3	2	4	5	6					7		1		11	8	9		10						32
		3	2		5	6				10	11		1		4	8	9		7						33
		3	2*	4	5	6				10	7		1		12	8	9	11							34
		3	2	4		6				10*	11		1		5	8	9	12	7						35
	12	3	2*	4	5	6				10		11	1		7	8	9								36
	2		3	4	5	6					7		1		11	8	9*		12		10				37
	2		3	4	5	6	9				7		1		11	8					10				38
		3	2	4	5	6	9				7*		1		11	8				12	10				39
	2		3	4	5	6	9						1		11*	8			7	10	12				40
	12	3	2	4	5	6			7	10	11		1			8*	9								41
	2		3		5	6	11			10	7				9	8						1	4		42
1	24	38	12	39	38	42	13	9	10	33	36	36	38	1	21	30	26	2	3	4	4	1	1		
	2	2		5											4	2	1	2	1	1		1			
	1	1		2	1	1	6	3	21	5					1	16	6		2						

1 own-goal

Stepney A	Kirkup J	McCreadie E	Harris A	Hollins J	Hinton M	Harris R	Houseman P	Graham G	Osgood P	Cooke C	Tambling R	Boyle J	Bonetti P	Young A	Thomson J	Baldwin T	Hateley T	Hughes T	Hamilton I	Fascione J	Lloyd B	Wosahlo R	Whiffen K	Luke G	No.
		3		4	5	6	11			7	8	10	1		2		9								3
	2	3		4	5	6			7	8	11	1			10	9									4
			4		6	2	7			12	11	8	1	5	3	9*	10								R
	2	3	12	4	5	6			7	10*	11	1			8	9									5
	12	3	2	4	5	6			7	10*		1		11	8	9									6
		3	2	4	5	6			7	10	11	1			8	9									SF
		3	2	4	5	6			7	10	11	1			8	9									F
	2	7	3	7	7	7	1			6	7	6	7	1	3	7	6								
		1	1							1					1										
		1								6					1	1	3								

1 own-goal

Stepney A	Kirkup J	McCreadie E	Harris A	Hollins J	Hinton M	Harris R	Houseman P	Graham G	Osgood P	Cooke C	Tambling R	Boyle J	Bonetti P	Young A	Thomson J	Baldwin T	Hateley T	Hughes T	Hamilton I	Fascione J	Lloyd B	Wosahlo R	Whiffen K	Luke G	No.
	2	3		4	5	6	12	8	9*	10	11	7	1												2
	2	3	12	4	5	6	8	9*	10	11	7		1												3
	2		3	4	5	6	11			10	9	8	1		7										R
	3	2	1	3	3	3	2	1	2	3	3	3	3		1										
			1					1																	
								1		3		1			1										

1 own-goal

1967-68

Manager: Tommy Docherty. Dave Sexton from October.

1	Aug	19	(a)	West Brom A	W	1-0	Tambling	33,283
2		23	(h)	Newcastle U	D	1-1	Baldwin	33,634
3		26	(h)	Fulham	D	1-1	Baldwin	38,404
4		30	(a)	Newcastle U	L	1-5	Tambling	34,809
5	Sep	2	(h)	Southampton	L	2-6	Osgood 2	32,726
6		6	(h)	Sheffield U	W	4-2	Tambling 2, Houseman, Mallender (og)	22,742
7		9	(a)	Liverpool	L	1-3	Houseman	53,839
8		16	(h)	Stoke C	D	2-2	Tambling (pen), Osgood	26,614
9		23	(a)	Nottingham F	L	0-3		34,871
10		30	(h)	Coventry C	D	1-1	Boyle	29,800
11	Oct	7	(a)	Leeds U	L	0-7		40,460
12		14	(h)	Everton	D	1-1	Baldwin	34,206
13		25	(a)	Leicester C	D	2-2	Boyle, Bell (og)	24,171
14		28	(h)	West Ham U	L	1-3	Osgood	40,303
15	Nov	4	(a)	Burnley	D	1-1	Osgood	17,651
16		11	(h)	Sheffield W	W	3-0	Hollins, Osgood, Boyle	29,569
17		18	(a)	Tottenham H	L	0-2		53,981
18		25	(h)	Manchester U	D	1-1	Baldwin	54,712
19	Dec	2	(a)	Sunderland	W	3-2	Cooke, Baldwin, Birchenall	26,274
20		16	(h)	West Brom A	L	0-3		27,739
21		23	(a)	Fulham	D	2-2	Cooke, Baldwin	33,492
22		26	(h)	Arsenal	W	2-1	Birchenall 2	51,672
23		30	(a)	Arsenal	D	1-1	Osgood (pen)	47,157
24	Jan	6	(a)	Southampton	W	5-3	Cooke, Tambling, Osgood, Baldwin, Boyle	27,132
25		20	(a)	Stoke C	W	1-0	Birchenall	21,861
26	Feb	3	(h)	Nottingham F	W	1-0	Osgood	33,483
27		10	(a)	Coventry C	L	1-2	Tambling	36,646
28		12	(h)	Liverpool	W	3-1	Tambling 2, Baldwin	40,670
29	Mar	2	(a)	Manchester U	W	3-1	Tambling, Osgood, Baldwin	62,471
30		16	(h)	Leicester C	W	4-1	Tambling 2, Osgood (pen), Baldwin	35,990
31		20	(h)	Leeds U	D	0-0		47,470
32		23	(a)	West Ham U	W	1-0	Osgood	36,301
33	Apr	6	(a)	Sheffield W	D	2-2	Hollins, Baldwin	27,004
34		12	(a)	Manchester C	L	0-1		47,132
35		13	(h)	Tottenham H	W	2-0	Baldwin, Houseman	53,049
36		16	(h)	Manchester C	W	1-0	Birchenall	36,466
37		20	(a)	Everton	L	1-2	Osgood (pen)	47,370
38		22	(h)	Burnley	W	2-1	Baldwin 2	23,494
39		27	(h)	Sunderland	W	1-0	Osgood	33,086
40		29	(h)	Wolves	W	1-0	Osgood	29,730
41	May	4	(a)	Wolves	L	0-3		35,600
42		11	(a)	Sheffield U	W	2-1	Osgood, Baldwin	28,680

FINAL LEAGUE POSITION: 6th in Division One

Appearances
Sub Appearances
Goals

FA Cup

3	Jan	27	(h)	Ipswich T	W	3-0	Tambling, Birchenall 2	42,986
4	Feb	17	(h)	Norwich C	W	1-0	Cooke	57,987
5	Mar	9	(a)	Sheffield W	D	2-2	Tambling, Baldwin	49,186
R		12	(h)	Sheffield W	W	2-0	Tambling, Osgood	55,013
6		30	(a)	Birmingham C	L	0-1		52,500

Appearances
Sub Appearances
Goals

League Cup

2	Sep	13	(a)	Middlesbrough	L	1-2	Cooke	30,425

Aggregate League attendances:
Home: 755,559 (average 35,979)
Away: 770,380 (average 36,684)

Appearances
Sub Appearances
Goals

Appearance and goalscoring grid (shirt numbers by match). Players across the top; match numbers down the right-hand side.

Bonetti P	Hinton M	Thomson J	Hollins J	Waldron C	Harris R	Cooke C	Tambling R	Osgood P	Baldwin T	Boyle J	Hughes T	McCreadie E	Houseman P	Lloyd B	Fascione J	McMillan J	Butler G	Kirkup J	Birchenall A	Houston S	Webb D	#
1	2	3	6	4	5	9	11	7	10	8												1
1	2	3	6	4	5	9*	11	7	10	8					12							2
1	2	3	6	4	5	9	11	7*	10	8			12									3
1	2		4	5	6		8	9	10	7		3		11								4
1	2		4	5	6	7	11	9	8			3				10						5
1	2		4	5	6	7	8	9	10			3	11									6
1	2		4	5	6	7	8	9	10			3	11									7
1	5	2	4		6	7	8	9	10			3	11									8
1	6	2		5	8	7	11*	9				4	10				3	12				9
1		2	4	5	6	7	11*	9	8	12		3	10									10
1	3	2	6		4		8	9	10	7			11				5					11
1	5				6	7	10	9	8	4		3	11				2					12
1	5		4		6	11		9	8	10		3			7		2					13
1	5		4		6	11		9	8	10		3			7		2					14
1	5		4		6	11		9	8	10		3			7			2				15
1	5		4		6	11		9	8	10		3			7			2				16
1	5		4		6	11		9	8	10		3			7			2				17
1	5		4		6	11		9	8	10		3			7			2				18
1			4		6	7		9	8	11		3					2	5	10			19
1			4		6	7		9	8	11		3					2	5	10			20
1	5		4*		6	7		9	8	11		3					12	2	10			21
1	5				6	7	11	9	8	4		3						2	10			22
1	5				6	7	11	9	8	4		3						2	10			23
	5				6	7	11	9	8	4	1	3						2	10			24
1	5	2			6	7	11	9	8	4		3							10			25
1	5	2			6	7	11	9	8	4		3					12		10*			26
1	5	2			6	7	10	9	8	4		3	11*				12					27
1		2			6	7	10	9	8	4		3	11					5				28
1	3				6	4	11	9	8	2			7					10			5	29
1		2			6	7	11	9	8	4		3						10			5	30
1	2	8			6	7	11	9		4		3						10			5	31
1	5		6		2	7	8	9		4		3	11					10				32
1	6		4		2	7	11	9	8			3						10			5	33
1	6	3	4		2	7	10*	9	8				11			12					5	34
1	6		4		2	7		9	8			3	11					10			5	35
1	6		4		2	7		9	8			3	11					10			5	36
1	6		4		2	7		9	8			3	11					10			5	37
1	12		4		2	7		9*	8	6		3	11					10			5	38
1			4		2	7		9	8	6		3	11					10			5	39
1	2	12	4			7		9	8	6		3	11					10			5	40
1	2	12	4			7		9	8*	6		3	11					10			5	41
			4		2	7		9	8	6	1	3	11					10			5	42
40	32	10	36	9	40	41	24	42	39	31	2	36	19	1	6	1	8	10	21	1	13	
	1	2									1		1			2		1	3			
		2			3	12	16	15	4			3							5			

2 own-goals

Bonetti P	Hinton M	Thomson J	Hollins J	Waldron C	Harris R	Cooke C	Tambling R	Osgood P	Baldwin T	Boyle J	Hughes T	McCreadie E	Houseman P	Lloyd B	Fascione J	McMillan J	Butler G	Kirkup J	Birchenall A	Houston S	Webb D	#
1		2			6	7	11	9	8	4		3						5	10			3
1	5	2*			6	7	11	9	8	4		3					12		10			4
1	5	2			6	7	11	9	8	4		3							10			5
1	5	2			6	7	8	9		4		3	11						10			R
1	5	12	2		6	4	11	9	8			3	7*						10			6
5	2	2	5		5	5	5	5	4	4		5	2				1		5			
		1															1					
					1		3	1	1										2			

Bonetti P	Hinton M	Thomson J	Hollins J	Waldron C	Harris R	Cooke C	Tambling R	Osgood P	Baldwin T	Boyle J	Hughes T	McCreadie E	Houseman P	Lloyd B	Fascione J	McMillan J	Butler G	Kirkup J	Birchenall A	Houston S	Webb D	#
1	12	2	4	5*	6	7	8	9	10			3	11									2
1		1	1	1	1	1	1	1	1			1	1									
	1																					
						1																

1968-69

Manager: Dave Sexton

1	Aug	14	(h)	Nottingham F	D	1-1	Tambling	36,515
2		17	(a)	West Brom A	W	3-1	Tambling, Baldwin 2	33,766
3		21	(a)	Newcastle U	L	2-3	Tambling, Birchenall	39,048
4		24	(a)	Manchester U	W	4-0	Tambling, Baldwin 2, Birchenall	55,114
5		28	(h)	Sheffield W	W	1-0	Tambling	33,402
6		31	(h)	Tottenham H	D	2-2	Osgood (pen), Birchenall	48,412
7	Sep	7	(h)	Everton	D	1-1	Osgood (pen)	42,017
8		10	(a)	Coventry C	W	1-0	Osgood	36,217
9		14	(a)	Queen's Park R	W	4-0	Osgood (pen), Baldwin 2, Birchenall	26,358
10		21	(h)	West Ham U	D	1-1	Tambling	58,062
11		28	(a)	Burnley	L	1-2	Tambling	14,762
12	Oct	5	(h)	Ipswich T	W	3-1	Hollins, Birchenall, Baxter (og)	31,625
13		9	(a)	Sheffield W	D	1-1	Baldwin	30,445
14		12	(a)	Wolves	D	1-1	Tambling	27,810
15		19	(h)	Leicester C	W	3-0	Baldwin 3	33,462
16		26	(a)	Stoke C	L	0-2		16,799
17	Nov	2	(h)	Manchester C	W	2-0	Osgood, Baldwin	40,700
18		9	(a)	Liverpool	L	1-2	Birchenall	47,248
19		16	(h)	Southampton	L	2-3	Baldwin, Birchenall	31,325
20		23	(a)	Arsenal	W	1-0	Houseman	45,588
21		30	(h)	Leeds U	D	1-1	Osgood	43,286
22	Dec	7	(a)	Sunderland	L	2-3	Baldwin, Birchenall	21,976
23		14	(h)	Wolves	D	1-1	Osgood (pen)	26,194
24		21	(a)	Leicester C	W	4-1	Tambling, Osgood 2, Birchenall	23,597
25		26	(a)	Ipswich T	W	3-1	Webb 3	24,083
26	Jan	11	(a)	Manchester C	L	1-4	Houseman	35,605
27		18	(h)	Liverpool	L	1-2	Tambling	52,295
28	Feb	1	(a)	Southampton	L	0-5		28,147
29		15	(a)	Leeds U	L	0-1		35,789
30		22	(h)	Sunderland	W	5-1	Tambling 4, Birchenall	29,381
31	Mar	5	(h)	Stoke C	W	1-0	Webb	19,856
32		8	(a)	West Brom A	W	3-0	Boyle, Houseman, Hutchinson	25,137
33		10	(a)	Coventry C	W	2-1	Tambling, Hutchinson	17,639
34		15	(h)	Manchester U	W	3-2	Tambling, Webb, Hutchinson	60,436
35		22	(a)	Tottenham H	L	0-1		47,349
36		29	(a)	Everton	W	2-1	Birchenall, Hutchinson	42,190
37	Apr	4	(h)	Newcastle U	D	1-1	Hutchinson	42,078
38		5	(h)	Burnley	L	2-3	Hollins, Tambling	30,266
39		8	(a)	Nottingham F	W	2-1	Birchenall, Hutchinson	30,413
40		12	(a)	West Ham U	D	0-0		32,322
41		14	(h)	Arsenal	W	2-1	Baldwin, Webb	37,890
42		19	(h)	Queen's Park R	W	2-1	Baldwin 2	41,263

FINAL LEAGUE POSITION: 5th in Division One

Appearances
Sub Appearances
Goals

FA Cup

3	Jan	4	(h)	Carlisle U	W	2-0	Tambling, Osgood	37,322
4		25	(a)	Preston NE	D	0-0		31,875
R	Feb	3	(h)	Preston NE *	W	2-1	Webb, Cooke	36,522
5		12	(h)	Stoke C	W	3-2	Osgood 2, Birchenall	39,191
6	Mar	1	(h)	West Brom A	L	1-2	Webb	52,285

* The match on 29 January was abandoned after the floodlights failed with Chelsea leading 2-0.

Appearances
Sub Appearances
Goals

League Cup

2	Sep	3	(a)	Birmingham C	W	1-0	Foster (og)	31,560
3		25	(h)	Derby C	D	0-0		26,975
R	Oct	2	(a)	Derby C	L	1-3	Birchenall	34,346

Aggregate League attendances:
Home: 789,870 (average 37,612)
Away: 685,997 (average 32,666)

Appearances
Sub Appearances
Goals

Football season appearance & goalscorers grid. Jersey (shirt) numbers are shown per match; `*` denotes a substitute used / substituted, and match numbers / round references appear in the right-hand column.

Bonetti P	McCreadie E	Hinton M	Hollins J	Harris R	Tambling R	Osgood P	Baldwin T	Boyle J	Birchenall A	Houseman P	Fascione J	Webb D	Hughes T	Cooke C	Hutchinson I	Lloyd B	Houston S	Dempsey J	Hudson A	#
1	3		4	2	8	9	7	6	10	11		5								1
1	3		4	2	8	9	7	6	10			5		11						2
1	3		4	2	8	9	7	6	10			5		11						3
1	3		4	2	8	9	7	6	10	11		5								4
1	3		4	2	8	9	7	6	10			5		11						5
1	3		4	2	8*	9	7	6	11	12		5		10						6
1	3	2	4		8	9*	7	6	10	12		5		11						7
1	3	2	4		8	9	7	6	10			5		11						8
1	3		4	2	11	9	7	6	10			5		8						9
1	3		4	2	11	9	7	6	10			5		8						10
1	3	12	4	2	8	9	7	6*	10	11		5								11
1	3	2	4	6	8	9*			10	11		5		7	12					12
1	3	2	4	6	8		7		10	11		5			9					13
1	3	2	4	6	8			9	10	11		5		7						14
1	3		4	6	8		9	2	10	11		5		7						15
1	3			6	8	9	7	2	10	11		5		4						16
1	3	12		6	8	4*	9	2	10	11		5		7						17
1	3			6	8	4		2	9	11		5		7		10				18
1	3*	2		6	8	4	9	12	10	11		5		7						19
1		2	3		4	7	6	9	11			5		8		10				20
1	3	2		6		4	7	10	9*	11		5		8		12				21
1	3	2		6	12	4	9	10	7	11		5				8*				22
1	3	2		6	8	4	9	10	7			5		11						23
1	3	2		6	8	4	9	10	7			5		11						24
1		2		6	8	4	9*	10	7	12		5		11			3			25
1	3	2		6	8	4		10	9	11		5		7						26
	3	2		6	8	4		10	9	11		5	1	7						27
1	2		7	6	11			10				12		4	9*	3	5	8		28
1		2	3	10	4		8	9	11			6		7			5			29
1	3		8	2	10	4		9	11			6		7			5			30
1	3		8	6	10	4*		9	11			2		7	12		5			31
1	3		4	6	8		7	10	11			2		9			5			32
1	3		4	6	8		7	10	11			2		9			5			33
1	3		4	6	8	10	7		11			2		9			5			34
1	3		4	10	8	6	7		11			2		9			5			35
1	3		4	10		6	7	8	11			2		9			5			36
1	3		4	10		6	7	8	11			2		9			5			37
1	3	12	4	6	8*		7		11			2		10	9		5			38
1	3		4	10	11	6	7	8				2		9			5			39
1	3		4	10	12	6	7*	8	11			2		9			5			40
1		4	3	8	6	7		10	11			2		9			5			41
1	3		4	10	6*	7		8	11			2		12	9		5			42
41	38	6	37	40	36	35	25	33	39	29		42	1	25	14	3	2	15	1	app
	3		2						1		3	1			1	1	2			sub
		2		17	9	16	1	12	3		6			6						gls

1 own-goal

Bonetti P	McCreadie E	Hinton M	Hollins J	Harris R	Tambling R	Osgood P	Baldwin T	Boyle J	Birchenall A	Houseman P	Fascione J	Webb D	Hughes T	Cooke C	Hutchinson I	Lloyd B	Houston S	Dempsey J	Hudson A	#
1	3	2		6	8*	4*		10	9	11		5		7						3
1	2		7	6	10	4		8	9			5		11		3				4
1	2		7	6	10	4		8	9			5		11		3				R
1	2		7	6	10	4		8	9			5		11		3				5
1	3*		8	2	10	4		12	9	11		6		7			5			6
5	5		5	5	5	5		4	5	2		5		5		3	1			app
								1												sub
				1	3			1				2		1						gls

Bonetti P	McCreadie E	Hinton M	Hollins J	Harris R	Tambling R	Osgood P	Baldwin T	Boyle J	Birchenall A	Houseman P	Fascione J	Webb D	Hughes T	Cooke C	Hutchinson I	Lloyd B	Houston S	Dempsey J	Hudson A	#
1	3		4	2	8	9	7	6	10			5		11						2
1	3	12	4	2	11	9	7	6	10			5		8*						3
1	3	2	4	6	8		7		10	11		5		9						R
3	3	1	3	3	3	3	3	2	2	3		3		2	1					app
		1																		sub
									1											gls

1 own-goal

1969-70

Manager: Dave Sexton

1	Aug	9	(a)	Liverpool	L 1-4	Hutchinson	48,383
2		11	(a)	West Ham U	L 0-2		39,003
3		16	(h)	Ipswich T	W 1-0	Hutchinson	29,613
4		20	(h)	West Ham U	D 0-0		43,346
5		23	(a)	Southampton	D 2-2	Osgood 2	25,935
6		27	(a)	Tottenham H	D 1-1	Webb	47,395
7		30	(h)	Crystal P	D 1-1	Osgood	41,908
8	Sep	6	(a)	Manchester C	D 0-0		35,995
9		13	(h)	Wolves	D 2-2	Osgood, Dempsey	38,599
10		17	(h)	Burnley	W 2-0	Houseman, Birchenall	24,904
11		20	(a)	Leeds U	L 0-2		33,130
12		27	(h)	Arsenal	W 3-0	Baldwin, Birchenall 2	46,370
13	Oct	4	(a)	Sunderland	D 0-0		24,216
14		11	(h)	Derby C	D 2-2	Hollins, Houseman	51,421
15		18	(h)	West Brom A	W 2-0	Osgood, Cooke	34,810
16		25	(a)	Newcastle U	W 1-0	Osgood	38,860
17	Nov	1	(h)	Coventry C	W 1-0	Cooke	38,899
18		8	(a)	Sheffield W	W 3-1	Osgood, Hutchinson 2	18,044
19		15	(h)	Everton	D 1-1	Osgood	49,895
20		18	(a)	Ipswich T	W 4-1	Hollins, Osgood 2, Hutchinson	20,935
21		22	(a)	Nottingham F	D 1-1	Cooke	23,808
22	Dec	6	(a)	Manchester U	W 2-0	Hutchinson 2	49,344
23		13	(a)	Wolves	L 0-3		26,775
24		20	(h)	Manchester C	W 3-1	Webb 2, Hutchinson	34,791
25		26	(h)	Southampton	W 3-1	Hollins, Hutchinson 2	41,489
26		27	(a)	Crystal P	W 5-1	Osgood 4, Houseman	49,498
27	Jan	10	(a)	Leeds U	L 2-5	Hollins, Osgood	57,221
28		17	(a)	Arsenal	W 3-0	Hollins, Baldwin, Hutchinson	51,338
29		31	(h)	Sunderland	W 3-1	Osgood 3	38,775
30	Feb	11	(a)	Derby C	D 2-2	Osgood, Hudson	35,109
31		25	(h)	Newcastle U	D 0-0		35,341
32		28	(a)	Coventry C	W 3-0	Baldwin, Webb, Hudson	37,448
33	Mar	7	(h)	Nottingham F	D 1-1	Baldwin	38,280
34		17	(h)	Stoke C	W 1-0	Cooke	28,996
35		21	(h)	Manchester U	W 2-1	Hutchinson	61,479
36		25	(h)	Sheffield W	W 3-1	Osgood (pen), Hutchinson, Hudson	29,590
37		28	(a)	Everton	L 2-5	Osgood, Dempsey	57,828
38		30	(a)	West Brom A	L 1-3	Hutchinson	32,000
39	Apr	4	(h)	Tottenham H	W 1-0	Baldwin	44,925
40		13	(a)	Stoke C	W 2-1	Hutchinson, Skeels (og)	22,707
41		15	(a)	Burnley	L 1-3	Hollins	12,030
42		18	(h)	Liverpool	W 2-1	Osgood 2 (1 pen)	36,521

FINAL LEAGUE POSITION: 3rd in Division One

Appearances
Sub Appearances
Goals

FA Cup

3	Jan	3	(h)	Birmingham C	W 3-0	Osgood, Hutchinson 2	45,088
4		24	(h)	Burnley	D 2-2	Hollins, Osgood	42,282
R		27	(a)	Burnley	W 3-1§	Baldwin, Houseman 2	32,000
5	Feb	7	(a)	Crystal P	W 4-1	Osgood, Dempsey, Houseman, Hutchinson	48,479
6		21	(a)	Queen's Park R	W 4-2	Osgood 3, Webb	33,572
SF	Mar	14	(n*)	Watford	W 5-1	Osgood, Houseman 2, Webb, Hutchinson	55,209
F	Apr	11	(n†)	Leeds U	D 2-2§	Houseman, Hutchinson	100,000
R		29	(n‡)	Leeds U	W 2-1§	Osgood, Webb	62,078

*Played at White Hart Lane, London. †Played at Wembley Stadium.
‡Played at Old Trafford, Manchester. §After extra-time.

Appearances
Sub Appearances
Goals

League Cup

2	Sep	2	(a)	Coventry C	W 1-0	Hutchinson	24,790
3		24	(a)	Leeds U	D 1-1	Birchenall	21,933
R	Oct	6	(h)	Leeds U	W 2-0	Cooke, Birchenall	38,485
4		15	(a)	Carlisle U	L 0-1		18,513

Aggregate League attendances:
Home: 847,174 (average 40,341)
Away: 730,488 (average 34,785)

Appearances
Sub Appearances
Goals

Appearance and goalscoring grid (player columns across, match rows down). Player shirt numbers shown per match; `*` denotes a substitute appearance.

Bonetti P	Hollins J	Houston S	Osgood P	Dempsey J	Harris R	Cooke C	Tambling R	Baldwin T	Houseman P	Birchenall A	Webb D	Hutchinson I	Boyle J	McCreadie E	Hinton M	Hudson A	Mulligan P	Hughes T	
1	2	3	4	5	6	7	11	8	10			9							1
1	4		6	5	2	7	11	12	10		9*	3	8						2
1	4	3	12	5		8	11	7*	10		9	2	6						3
1	4	3	7	5		11	8*		10	12	9	2	6						4
1	4	12	7*		11		9	10	8	3		2	6						5
1	4	12	7	5		11*		10	8	2		3	6	9					6
1	4		7	5	11			10	9	2		3	6	8					7
1	8		7	5	6			10	11	2	9	3	4						8
1	4		7	5	6			11	10	2	9	3		8					9
1	4		7	5	6		9	11	10	2		3		8					10
1	4	12		5	6*	11	9	8	10	2		7	3						11
1	4	11	5		7	9	8	10			2	3	6						12
1	4	11	5	2	7	9	8*	10			12	3	6						13
1	4	12	5*	3	11		8	9	2		7		6	10					14
1	4	9		2	7		11	10	5		3	6	8						15
1	4	9		2	11		10		5	7	3	6	8						16
1	4	9		2	11		10		5	12	7*	3	6	8					17
1	4	9	5	3	7		11		2	10			6	8					18
1	4	9	5	3	7		11		2	10			6	8					19
1	4	9	5	3	7		11		2	10			6	8					20
1	4	9	5	3	7		11		2	10*		12	6	8					21
1	4	9	5	6	7		11		2	10		3		8					22
1	4	9	5	6	7		11		2	10		3		8					23
1	4	9	5	6	7		11		2	10*		3		8	12				24
1	4	9	5	6	7		11		2	10		3		8					25
1	4	9	5	6	7		11		2	10		3		8					26
	4	9	5	6	7		11		2	10		3		8		1			27
1	4	9	5	6		7	11		2	10		3		8					28
1	4	9	5	6*	7	12	11		2	10		3		8					29
1	4	9		7	11		2	10		3	6	8	5						30
	4		5	6	7	9	11	10*	2		3		8	12	1				31
1	4	9	5	3	7	10	11		2			8	6						32
1	4	9		3	7	10	11		2		6	8	5						33
1	4		5	3	7	10		11	2	9		6	8						34
1	4	9	5	3	7		11		2	10		6	8						35
	4	9	5	3*	7	12	11		10			6	8	2	1				36
	4	9	5		7		11		2	10		6	8	3	1				37
1	4	9	5		12	7	11		2	10		3	6	8*					38
1	4	9	5		11	7	8	10	2		3	6							39
	4		5		8	7	11		2	10		6		3	1				40
	4		5		10	7	11	9	2		8	3	6		1				41
1	4	9	5		8	7	11		2	10		3	6						42
36	42	3	36	37	30	35	5	17	42	14	35	26	6	29	28	29	6	6	
	3	2			2	2		1		1	1	1		1	1	1		2	
	6	23	2		4		5	3	3	4	16					3			

1 own-goal

Bonetti P	Hollins J	Houston S	Osgood P	Dempsey J	Harris R	Cooke C	Tambling R	Baldwin T	Houseman P	Birchenall A	Webb D	Hutchinson I	Boyle J	McCreadie E	Hinton M	Hudson A	Mulligan P	Hughes T	
1	4	9	5	6	7		11		2	10		3		8					3
1	4	9	5	6		7	11		2	10		3		8					4
1	4		5	6	7	9	11		2	10		3		8					R
1	4	9	5	6		7	11		2	10		3		8					5
1	4	9	5	6	7		11		2	10		3		8					6
1	4	9	5	6	7		11		2	10		3		8					SF
1	4	9	5	6*	11		7	8		2	10		3	12					F
1	4	9*	5	2	8		7	11		6	10		3	12					R
8	8		7	8	8	6		5	8		8	8		8		6			
															2				
	1		8	1			1	6			3	5							

Bonetti P	Hollins J	Houston S	Osgood P	Dempsey J	Harris R	Cooke C	Tambling R	Baldwin T	Houseman P	Birchenall A	Webb D	Hutchinson I	Boyle J	McCreadie E	Hinton M	Hudson A	Mulligan P	Hughes T	
1	4		7	5	6			10	11	2	9	3	8						2
1	4	6	11	5		12		9	8	10*	7	3	2						3
1	4		5	3	11		8	9	2		7	6	10						R
1	4	9		3	7	11	10	5		2	6	8							4
4	4	1	3	3	3	2	1	4	4	3	1	3	2	4	2				
			1																
			2		1														

1970-71

Manager: Dave Sexton

1	Aug	15	(h)	Derby C	W 2-1	Hutchinson 2	46,969
2		19	(a)	Manchester U	D 0-0		50,979
3		22	(a)	West Ham U	D 2-2	Weller 2	39,240
4		26	(h)	Everton	D 2-2	Dempsey, Weller	48,195
5		29	(h)	Arsenal	W 2-1	Hollins, Mulligan	53,722
6	Sep	1	(a)	Burnley	D 0-0		14,543
7		5	(a)	Leeds U	L 0-1		47,662
8		12	(h)	Wolves	D 2-2	Harris, Hutchinson	34,889
9		19	(a)	Coventry C	W 1-0	Hollins	29,328
10		26	(h)	Ipswich T	W 2-1	Osgood, Hudson	38,541
11	Oct	3	(a)	Liverpool	L 0-1		46,196
12		10	(h)	Manchester C	D 1-1	Weller	51,903
13		17	(a)	Derby C	W 2-1	Weller 2	35,166
14		24	(a)	Blackpool	W 4-3	Webb, Weller 2, Hatton (og)	24,940
15		31	(h)	Southampton	D 2-2	Webb, Hollins	44,843
16	Nov	7	(a)	Huddersfield T	W 1-0	Baldwin	24,631
17		14	(h)	Tottenham H	L 0-2		61,277
18		21	(h)	Stoke C	W 2-1	Osgood, Bernard (og)	36,227
19		28	(a)	West Brom A	D 2-2	Weller, Cooke	29,760
20	Dec	5	(h)	Newcastle U	W 1-0	Weller	39,413
21		12	(a)	Nottingham F	D 1-1	Weller	20,080
22		19	(h)	West Ham U	W 2-1	Osgood 2	42,075
23	Jan	9	(h)	Manchester U	L 1-2	Hudson	53,482
24		13	(a)	Crystal P	D 0-0		40,489
25		16	(a)	Everton	L 0-3		43,648
26		30	(h)	West Brom A	W 4-1	Hollins 2 (1 pen), Hutchinson, Smethurst	26,874
27	Feb	6	(a)	Newcastle U	W 1-0	Hudson	34,320
28		13	(a)	Wolves	L 0-1		34,110
29		17	(h)	Nottingham F	W 2-0	Hollins, Kane (og)	19,339
30		20	(a)	Stoke C	W 2-1	Hutchinson, Smethurst	26,959
31		27	(a)	Southampton	D 0-0		29,937
32	Mar	6	(h)	Blackpool	W 2-0	Webb, Baldwin	26,530
33		13	(a)	Tottenham H	L 1-2	Weller	49,192
34		20	(a)	Huddersfield T	D 0-0		28,207
35		27	(h)	Leeds U	W 3-1	Osgood, Houseman 2	58,452
36	Apr	3	(a)	Arsenal	L 0-2		62,087
37		10	(h)	Crystal P	D 1-1	Webb	38,953
38		12	(h)	Liverpool	W 1-0	Smethurst	38,705
39		17	(a)	Manchester C	D 1-1	Weller	26,120
40		24	(h)	Coventry C	W 2-1	Feely, Smethurst	27,517
41		26	(h)	Burnley	L 0-1		14,356
42	May	1	(a)	Ipswich T	D 0-0		24,706

FINAL LEAGUE POSITION: 6th in Division One

Appearances
Sub Appearances
Goals

FA Cup

3	Jan	2	(a)	Crystal P	D 2-2	Osgood, Baldwin	42,123
R		6	(h)	Crystal P	W 2-0	Houseman, Baldwin	55,074
4		23	(h)	Manchester C	L 0-3		50,176

Appearances
Sub Appearances
Goals

League Cup

2	Sep	9	(a)	Sheffield W	D 1-1	Osgood	15,869
R		22	(h)	Sheffield W	W 2-1	Webb, Osgood (pen)	26,646
3	Oct	7	(h)	Middlesbrough	W 3-2	Hutchinson, Baldwin, Weller	28,597
4		28	(a)	Manchester U	L 1-2	Hollins	47,322

Aggregate League attendances:
Home: 830,469 (average 39,546)
Away: 734,093 (average 34,956)

Appearances
Sub Appearances
Goals

Chelsea player appearance & shirt-number grid (season).

Bonetti P	Harris R	Boyle J	Webb D	Dempsey J	Hollins J	Weller K	Cooke C	Osgood P	Hudson A	Hutchinson I	Houseman P	Feely P	Hinton M	Smethurst D	Mulligan P	Baldwin T	Houston S	Phillips J	McCreadie E	Droy M	Match
1	3			5	4	7	12	9*	8	10	11		6		2						1
1	3			5	4	7		9	8	10	11		6		2						2
1	3			5	4	7		9	8	10	11		6		2						3
1	3			5	4	7		9	8	10	11		6		2						4
1	3			5	4	7	12	9	8	10*	11		6		2						5
1	3			5	4	7		9	8		11		6	10	2						6
1	3	6		5	4	7		9	8	10	11				2						7
1	3	6		5	4	7	11	9	8	10					2						8
1	3	6		5	4	7	11*	9	8	10	12				2						9
1	3	6		5	4	7		9	8	10	11				2						10
1	3	6		5	4	7			8	10	11				2	9					11
1	3	6			4	7		9	8		11		5		2	10					12
1	3	6			4	7		9	8		11		5		2	10					13
	3	6			4	7	12	9	8		11		5		2	10*		1			14
1	3	6			4	7	8	9	10		11		5		2						15
1	3	2	6		4	7	8	9			11		5			10					16
1	3	2	6	12	4	7	8	9			11		5*			10					17
1	3	2	6		4	7	8	9			11		5			10					18
1	3	2	6		4	7	8	9	10		11		5								19
1	3	2	6		4	7	8	9	10		11		5								20
1	3	2	6	12	4	7	8	9	10*		11		5								21
1	3	2	6		4	7*	8	9	12		11		5			10					22
1	3	2	6		4	7	10				11	9	5			8					23
1	3	2		5	4	7		9	10		11		6			8					24
1	3	2		5	4	12	7	9	10		11		6			8*					25
1	2		6	5	4	7	8	9	10				11						3		26
	2		6	5	4	7	8	9	10				11					1	3		27
	2		5		4	7	8	9	10				11					1	3	6	28
	2		6	5	4	12	8	9	10*				11	7				1	3		29
	2		6	5	4	11	8	9	10					7				1	3		30
	2	12	6	5	4	11	8	9*	10					7				1	3		31
	2		6	5	4	11	8		10					7		9		1	3		32
	2		6	5	4	7	8		10				11			9		1	3		33
	2		6	5	4	7	8		10				11			9		1	3		34
	2		6	5	4		8	9	10				11	7				1	3		35
	2		6	5	4		8	9	10				11	7				1	3		36
	3	2	6	5	4	12	7	9*	10				11			8		1			37
1	3	2	9	5	4	12	8	7*					11			10				6	38
	2	10	6	5	4	7*		9					11	8				1	3	12	39
1	3	2	6	5	4*	7			10			9	11			8				12	40
	2	4	6			7		9*	10				11	8		12		1	3	5	41
1	3	10	6	5		7	8	9					11		2						42
28	**38**	**19**	**34**	**29**	**40**	**32**	**28**	**27**	**33**	**20**	**36**	**2**	**20**	**12**	**16**	**18**		**14**	**13**	**3**	
	1		2		4	3	1		1				1			1			1	1	
1		4	1	6	13	1	5	3	5	2	1		4	1	2						

3 own-goals

Bonetti P	Harris R	Boyle J	Webb D	Dempsey J	Hollins J	Weller K	Cooke C	Osgood P	Hudson A	Hutchinson I	Houseman P	Feely P	Hinton M	Smethurst D	Mulligan P	Baldwin T	Houston S	Phillips J	McCreadie E	Droy M	Rd
1	3	2	6		4	7	10	9			11		5			8					3
1	3	2	6		4	7	10	9			11		5			8					R
1	3	2	6	12	4	7	8	9*		10	11		5								4
3	**3**	**3**	**3**		**3**	**3**	**3**	**3**		**1**	**3**		**3**			**2**					
			1																		
							1				1					2					

Bonetti P	Harris R	Boyle J	Webb D	Dempsey J	Hollins J	Weller K	Cooke C	Osgood P	Hudson A	Hutchinson I	Houseman P	Feely P	Hinton M	Smethurst D	Mulligan P	Baldwin T	Houston S	Phillips J	McCreadie E	Droy M	Rd
1	3		6	5	4	7	8	9		10	11				2						2
1	3		6	5	4		9	8			11		10		2	7					R
1	3	2*	6		4	7	8		10		11		5			9	12				3
1	3		6		4	7	8	9	10		11		5		2						4
4	**4**	**1**	**4**	**2**	**4**	**3**	**3**	**3**	**1**	**3**	**4**		**2**	**1**	**3**	**2**					
			1													1					
		1		1	1		2		1						1						

305

1971-72

Manager: Dave Sexton

1	Aug	14	(a)	Arsenal	L	0-3		49,174
2		18	(h)	Manchester U	L	2-3	Osgood, Baldwin	54,763
3		21	(h)	Manchester C	D	2-2	Baldwin, Weller	38,425
4		25	(a)	Everton	L	0-2		38,994
5		28	(a)	Huddersfield T	W	2-1	Hollins (pen), Osgood	15,303
6	Sep	1	(h)	West Brom A	W	1-0	Hollins	29,931
7		4	(h)	Coventry C	D	3-3	Hollins, Osgood 2	35,459
8		11	(a)	West Ham U	L	1-2	Hollins	36,866
9		18	(h)	Derby C	D	1-1	Baldwin	42,872
10		25	(a)	Sheffield U	L	0-1		40,651
11	Oct	2	(h)	Wolves	W	3-1	Hollins, Baldwin, Houseman	42,706
12		9	(a)	Liverpool	D	0-0		48,464
13		16	(h)	Arsenal	L	1-2	Osgood	52,338
14		23	(h)	Southampton	W	3-0	Hollins (pen), Baldwin, Kember	38,940
15		30	(a)	Leicester C	D	1-1	Osgood	36,574
16	Nov	6	(h)	Nottingham F	W	2-0	Cooke, Osgood	25,812
17		13	(a)	Stoke C	W	1-0	Osgood	22,190
18		20	(a)	Crystal P	W	3-2	Hudson, Osgood, Baldwin	34,637
19		27	(h)	Tottenham H	W	1-0	Cooke	52,581
20	Dec	4	(a)	Newcastle U	D	0-0		37,562
21		11	(h)	Leeds U	D	0-0		45,867
22		17	(a)	Coventry C	D	1-1	Osgood	22,424
23		27	(h)	Ipswich T	W	2-0	Garland, Kember	43,896
24	Jan	1	(a)	Derby C	L	0-1		33,663
25		8	(h)	Huddersfield T	D	2-2	Hollins, Osgood	30,801
26		22	(a)	Manchester U	W	1-0	Osgood	55,927
27		29	(h)	Everton	W	4-0	Hollins (pen), Dempsey, Osgood 2	38,558
28	Feb	19	(h)	Leicester C	W	2-1	Osgood 2	38,783
29	Mar	11	(h)	Liverpool	D	0-0		38,691
30		14	(a)	Nottingham F	L	1-2	Hollins (pen)	13,346
31		18	(a)	Manchester C	L	0-1		53,322
32		25	(h)	West Ham U	W	3-1	Hollins, Osgood, Mulligan	45,137
33		29	(h)	Sheffield U	W	2-0	Webb 2	28,444
34	Apr	1	(a)	Ipswich T	W	2-1	Webb 2	24,325
35		8	(h)	Crystal P	W	2-1	Hollins, Garland	34,105
36		12	(a)	Wolves	W	2-0	Osgood, Garland	24,566
37		15	(a)	Tottenham H	L	0-3		45,799
38		18	(a)	Southampton	D	2-2	Baldwin 2	24,933
39		22	(h)	Newcastle U	D	3-3	Baldwin 2, Kember	33,000
40		24	(h)	Stoke C	W	2-0	Hudson, Garland	23,443
41		27	(a)	West Brom A	L	0-4		18,489
42	May	1	(a)	Leeds U	L	0-2		46,565

FINAL LEAGUE POSITION: 7th in Division One

Appearances
Sub Appearances
Goals

FA Cup

3	Jan	15	(a)	Blackpool	W	1-0	Dempsey	22,135
4	Feb	5	(h)	Bolton W	W	3-0	Hollins (pen), Cooke, Houseman	38,006
5		26	(a)	Orient	L	2-3	Webb, Osgood	30,329

Appearances
Sub Appearances
Goals

League Cup

2	Sep	8	(h)	Plymouth A	W	2-0	Hollins, Houseman	23,011
3	Oct	6	(a)	Nottingham F	D	1-1	Webb	16,811
R		11	(h)	Nottingham F	W	2-1	Osgood, Baldwin	24,817
4		27	(h)	Bolton W	D	1-1	Hudson	27,679
R	Nov	8	(a)	Bolton W	W	6-0	Hollins 2 (1 pen), Cooke, Baldwin 3	29,805
5		17	(a)	Norwich C	W	1-0	Osgood	35,927
SF	Dec	22	(h)	Tottenham H	W	3-2	Hollins (pen), Osgood, Garland	43,330
	Jan	5	(a)	Tottenham H	D	2-2	Hudson, Garland	52,755
F	Mar	4	(n*)	Stoke C	L	1-2	Osgood	100,000

*Played at Wembley Stadium.

Appearances

Aggregate League attendances:
Home: 814,542 (average 38,787)
Away: 723,774 (average 34,465)

Sub Appearances
Goals

Bonetti P	McCreadie E	Harris R	Hollins J	Dempsey J	Webb D	Cooke C	Hudson A	Osgood P	Baldwin T	Houseman P	Mulligan P	Weller K	Boyle J	Smethurst D	Phillips J	Garland C	Hinton M	Kember S	Droy M	Potrac A	Sherwood S	Feely P	
1	2	3	4	5	6		8	9	10	11			7										1
2	6	4	5			12	8	9	10	11*			3	7	1								2
	2	3	4	5	6	11		9	10			7	8		1								3
	2*	3	4	5	6	11		9	10	12		7	8		1								4
		3	4	5	6	7	8	9		10	2				1	11							5
		3	4	5	6	7	8	9		10	2				1	11							6
		3	4	5	6	7		9		10	2				1	11		8					7
		3	4	5	6		8	9		11	2				1	10							8
1		3	4		5	7	10	9	8	11			2				6						9
1		3	4		5		10	9	7	11			2				6	8					10
1		3	4		5	7	10	9	8	11			2				6						11
1		3	4		5	7		9	8	11			2				6	10					12
1		3	4		5	11	7	9	8				2				6	10					13
1		3	4	5	6	11	10	9	7		2							8					14
1		3	8	5	6	11	10	9			2			4				7					15
1		3	4	5	6	7	10	9		11	2							8					16
1		3	4	5	6	7	10	9	8	11	2							8					17
1		3	4	5	6	7	10	9	8*	11	2					12							18
1		3	4	5	6	7	10	9		11	2							8					19
1		3	4	5	6	7	10	9		11	2							8					20
1		3	4	5	6	7	10	9		11	2							8					21
1*		3	4	5	6	7	10	9		11	2					12		8					22
	2		4	5	1	12	10	9	11*	3	6		7					8*					23
		3	4	5	6	12	10	9		11	2					7	8*		1				24
1	2	3	10	5	6*			9		11	4					8				7	12		25
1		3	4	5	6	8	10	9			2					11		7					26
1		3	4	5	6	8	10	9			2					11		7					27
1		3	6	4		5	7	10	9		11	2						8					28
1	2		4	5	6	7	10	9	11	3						8							29
1	2		4	5	6	8		9*		11	3					7	12	10					30
		4	5	6	7	10	9		11*	2			3			8		12					31
1	6		4	5	8	11	10	9			2		3			7							32
1	6		4	5	7	11	10	9			2		3			8							33
1	6		4	5	8	11	10	9			2		3			7							34
1	6		4	5	8	11	10	9			2		3			7							35
1	6		4	5	8	11	10	9			2		3			7							36
1	6		4	5	8	11	10	9*			2		3			7		12					37
1		3	4	5	6	11	10		9		2					7		8					38
1		3	4	5	6	11	10		9		2					7		8					39
1		3	4		6	11	10		9		2					7		8	5				40
1		3	4	5	6	7	10		9	11	2							8					41
1	3	2	4	5	6	7	10	9		11						8							42
33	7	41	42	35	41	35	36	36	20	26	27	2	24	2	7	16	5	24	1	1	1		
						3			1							1	1	3			1		
		11	1		4		2	2	18	10	1	1	1			4		3					

Bonetti P	McCreadie E	Harris R	Hollins J	Dempsey J	Webb D	Cooke C	Hudson A	Osgood P	Baldwin T	Houseman P	Mulligan P	Weller K	Boyle J	Smethurst D	Phillips J	Garland C	Hinton M	Kember S	Droy M	Potrac A	Sherwood S	Feely P	
1		3	4	5	6	7	10*	9		11	2					8		12					3
1	3	6	4		5	7	10	9		11	2					8							4
1		3	4	5	6	7	10	9		11	2					8							5
3	1	3	3	2	3	3	3	3		3	3					1		2					
		1	1	1	1		1	1															

Bonetti P	McCreadie E	Harris R	Hollins J	Dempsey J	Webb D	Cooke C	Hudson A	Osgood P	Baldwin T	Houseman P	Mulligan P	Weller K	Boyle J	Smethurst D	Phillips J	Garland C	Hinton M	Kember S	Droy M	Potrac A	Sherwood S	Feely P	
1		3	4		5			8	9		11	2				7		10	6				2
1	2	3	4	12	5		7	9	8							10	11*	6					3
1	12	3	4		5	7	10	9	8	11*			2				6						R
1		3	8	12	5	11	10	9	7*		2		4				6						4
1		3	4	5	6	7	10	9	8	11	2												R
1		3	4	5	6	7	10	9	8	11	2												5
		3	4	5	6	8*	10	9	12	11	2				1	7							SF
1		3	4	5	6	7	10	9	12	11	2*					8							F
8	1	9	9	5	9	7	9	9	5	7	5		6		1	5	4						
	1			2				2															
		4		1	1	2	4	4	1							2							

1972-73

Manager: Dave Sexton

1	Aug	12	(h)	Leeds U	W	4-0	Garland 2, Osgood, Cooke	51,102
2		16	(a)	Leicester C	D	1-1	Garland	22,873
3		19	(a)	Derby C	W	2-1	Harris, Garland	31,868
4		23	(h)	Liverpool	L	1-2	Garland	35,375
5		26	(h)	Manchester C	W	2-1	Osgood, Houseman	30,845
6		30	(a)	Manchester U	D	0-0		44,482
7	Sep	2	(a)	Arsenal	D	1-1	Cooke	46,675
8		9	(h)	West Ham U	L	1-3	Garland	34,392
9		16	(a)	Sheffield U	L	1-2	Garland	24,458
10		23	(h)	Ipswich T	W	2-0	Osgood, Feely	29,647
11		30	(a)	Coventry C	W	3-1	Houseman, Garner, Blockley (og)	20,058
12	Oct	7	(a)	Birmingham C	D	2-2	Webb, Osgood	38,756
13		14	(h)	West Brom A	W	3-1	Webb, Garland, Osgood	28,998
14		21	(a)	Tottenham H	W	1-0	Hollins	47,429
15		28	(h)	Newcastle U	D	1-1	McCreadie	35,273
16	Nov	4	(a)	Liverpool	L	1-3	Baldwin	48,932
17		11	(h)	Leicester C	D	1-1	Garner	28,456
18		18	(a)	Southampton	L	1-3	Osgood	24,164
19		25	(h)	Crystal P	D	0-0		36,608
20	Dec	2	(a)	Stoke C	D	1-1	Osgood	21,274
21		9	(h)	Norwich C	W	3-1	Garner, Hutchinson 2	29,998
22		16	(a)	Wolves	L	0-1		20,799
23		23	(h)	Everton	D	1-1	Hutchinson	23,385
24		26	(a)	Ipswich T	L	0-3		26,243
25		30	(h)	Derby C	D	1-1	Osgood	29,794
26	Jan	20	(h)	Arsenal	L	0-1		36,292
27		27	(a)	West Ham U	L	1-3	Garner	35,336
28	Feb	10	(h)	Sheffield U	W	4-2	Garland 2, Garner 2	21,464
29		17	(a)	Leeds U	D	1-1	Osgood	41,781
30	Mar	3	(h)	Birmingham C	D	0-0		26,259
31		6	(h)	Wolves	L	0-2		18,868
32		10	(a)	West Brom A	D	1-1	Garland	21,820
33		24	(a)	Newcastle U	D	1-1	Garner	21,720
34		27	(a)	Manchester C	W	1-0	Osgood	23,973
35		31	(a)	Crystal P	L	0-2		39,325
36	Apr	3	(h)	Tottenham H	L	0-1		25,536
37		7	(h)	Stoke C	L	1-3	Ord	19,706
38		14	(a)	Norwich C	L	0-1		24,763
39		17	(a)	Everton	L	0-1		24,999
40		21	(h)	Southampton	W	2-1	Hollins, Brolly	19,699
41		23	(h)	Coventry C	W	2-0	Hollins (pen), Hinton	18,279
42		28	(h)	Manchester U	W	1-0	Osgood	44,184

FINAL LEAGUE POSITION: 12th in Division One

Appearances
Sub Appearances
Goals

FA Cup

3	Jan	13	(a)	Brighton & HA	W	2-0	Osgood 2	29,287
4	Feb	3	(h)	Ipswich T	W	2-0	Garner 2	36,491
5		24	(a)	Sheffield W	W	2-1	Osgood, Garner	46,410
6	Mar	17	(h)	Arsenal	D	2-2	Osgood, Hollins	36,992
R		20	(a)	Arsenal	L	1-2	Houseman	62,746

Appearances
Sub Appearances
Goals

League Cup

2	Sep	6	(a)	Southend U	W	1-0	Garland	24,160
3	Oct	4	(a)	Derby C	D	0-0		28,065
R		9	(h)	Derby C	W	3-2	Webb, Kember, Osgood	26,395
4		31	(a)	Bury	W	1-0	Garland	16,226
5	Nov	22	(h)	Notts C	W	3-1	Garland, Kember, Osgood	22,580
SF	Dec	13	(h)	Norwich C	L	0-2		34,316
	Jan	3	(a)	Norwich C *	L	0-1		34,265

* Semi-final second leg on 20 December was abandoned due to fog with Norwich leading 3-2.

Appearances
Sub Appearances
Goals

Aggregate League attendances:
Home: 624,520 (average 29,739)
Away: 651,728 (average 31,034)

Chelsea appearances & goals (shirt numbers worn per match). Each cell shows the number worn; `*` denotes substitute/substituted.

Bonetti P	Mulligan P	Harris R	Boyle J	Dempsey J	Webb D	Garland C	Kember S	Osgood P	Hudson A	Cooke C	Baldwin T	Houseman P	Phillips J	McCreadie E	Hollins J	Droy M	Garner W	Feely P	Bason B	Locke G	Hinton M	Sherwood S	Wilkins G	Hutchinson I	Britton I	Brolly M	Ord T	#
1		2	5		6	7	8	9	10	11				3	4													1
1		2	5		6	7	8	9	10	11				3	4													2
1		2			6	7	8	9	10	11				3	4	5												3
		2			6	7	8	9	10	11	12		1	3	4	5*												4
1		2	6		5	7	8	9	10	11*	12			3	4													5
1		2	6		5	7	8	9	10	12		11		3*	4													6
1		2	6		5	7	8*	9		11	10			3	4	12												7
1		2	6		5	7	8	9	10*	11				3	4	12											8
1		2	4	12	6*	11	8			3	10	5		9	7													9
1		2	6		7	8	9		11		3	4	5		10													10
1		6		5	7	8	9		11	3	4	10*		2	12													11
1		6	10	7	8	9		11	3	4	5		2															12
1		6	10	7	8	9		11	3	4	5		2															13
1		6	5	10	8	9		11	3	4		7	2															14
1		6	5		8	9		11	3	4	10	7	2															15
		6	5	10	8		7	11	3	4	9		2	1														16
		6	5	7	8	9		11	3	4	10		2	1														17
		6	5		8	9	10	11	3	4	7		2	1														18
		2		6		8	9	10	11	1	3	4	5	7														19
		2		6		8	9	10	11	1	3	4	5	7														20
		2		6			9	8	11	1	3	4	5	7					10									21
		6		5	7	10*	9	8	3	1	4		11	2	12													22
	3	12	5	6	11		8	7	10*	1	4		2	9														23
	2	10*	5	6	11	9	8	7	1	4		12	3															24
	3	11	5	2		9	8	7	1	4	6	10*	12															25
	3	5	6	10	9	8	7	1	4	11	2																	26
	3	5	6	10	9	8	7	1	4	11	2																	27
	6	12	5*	11	10	9	8	3	1	4	7	2																28
	3		7	6	9	8	11	1	4	10	2	5																29
	3	11	6	9	8		1	4	10	2	5		7															30
	3	7	6	9	8		1	4	10	2	5		11															31
	3	9	8	6	7	1	4	10	2	5	11																	32
	6	10	4	8	11*	1	3	2	9	12	5	7																33
1		6	7	4	9	8	3	2	10	5	11																	34
1		6	12	4	9	8	3	2	10*	7	5	11																35
1		2	5	10	7*	9	8	3	4	6	11	12																36
1		2	8	5	9	3	4	6	7	11	10																	37
1		2	10	9	8	3	4	6	5	7	11																	38
1		2	10*	9	8	3	4	6	5	12	11	7																39
1		2	10	9	8	3	4	6	5	12	11	7*																40
1		2	10	9*	8	3	4	6	12	5	7	11																41
1		2	10	9	8	3	4	6	5	7	11																	42
23	6	42	5	10	26	27	35	38	26	7	11	19	16	31	42	14	19	2	4	17	15	3	1	3	11	6	3	
	3	1									1	2		1	2		1	3			3	1							
	1		2	11		11			2	1	2		1	3		7	1			1			3	1	1			

1 own-goal

Bonetti P	Mulligan P	Harris R	Boyle J	Dempsey J	Webb D	Garland C	Kember S	Osgood P	Hudson A	Cooke C	Baldwin T	Houseman P	Phillips J	McCreadie E	Hollins J	Droy M	Garner W	Feely P	Bason B	Locke G	Hinton M	Sherwood S	Wilkins G	Hutchinson I	Britton I	Brolly M	Ord T	#
	3		5	6		10	9	8		7		1			4	11			2									3
	3		5	6*		10	9	8		11	1		4	7		2	12											4
	2			7	6	9	8		11	1	3	4	10		5												5
		5		7	10	9	8		11	1	3	4		2	6													6
		5		7	4	9	8		11	1	3	2	10		6													R
	3	4	2	3	5	5	5	1	4	5	3	5		4	3	3				1								
			4					1			1	1	3															

Bonetti P	Mulligan P	Harris R	Boyle J	Dempsey J	Webb D	Garland C	Kember S	Osgood P	Hudson A	Cooke C	Baldwin T	Houseman P	Phillips J	McCreadie E	Hollins J	Droy M	Garner W	Feely P	Bason B	Locke G	Hinton M	Sherwood S	Wilkins G	Hutchinson I	Britton I	Brolly M	Ord T	#
1		2	6	10		5	7	8	9		11		3	4					2									2
1		6		10	7	8	9		11	3	4	5		2														3
1		6	7		10	8	9		11	3	4		2	5														R
1		6		5	7	8	9*	10	11	3	4		2	12														4
		6		5	7	8	9	10	11	1	3	4	2															5
		6		5	7		9	8	11	1	3	4	2						10									SF
1		3		5	6	11	10	9	8	7		4		2														
5	1	7	2	1	7	6	6	7	3		2	6	2	6	7	1			6	1			1					
					1	3	2	2												1									

309

1973-74

Manager: Dave Sexton

1	Aug	25	(a)	Derby C	L	0-1	30,666
2		28	(a)	Burnley	L	0-1	23,818
3	Sep	1	(h)	Sheffield U	L	1-2	Hollins (pen)	27,972
4		5	(h)	Birmingham C	W	3-1	Hollins, Kember, Hutchinson	25,660
5		8	(a)	Liverpool	L	0-1	47,016
6		11	(a)	Birmingham C	W	4-2	Hudson, Osgood, Baldwin 2	30,252
7		15	(h)	Coventry C	W	1-0	Osgood	30,593
8		22	(a)	Manchester C	L	2-3	Baldwin 2	32,118
9		29	(h)	Wolves	D	2-2	Osgood, Garner	27,846
10	Oct	6	(a)	Queen's Park R	D	1-1	Mancini (og)	31,009
11		13	(h)	Ipswich T	L	2-3	Hollins, Baldwin	25,111
12		20	(a)	Newcastle U	L	0-2	32,154
13		26	(h)	Norwich C	W	3-0	Kember, Baldwin 2	21,953
14	Nov	3	(a)	Manchester U	D	2-2	Osgood, Baldwin	48,036
15		10	(h)	Everton	W	3-1	Osgood 2, Baldwin	26,398
16		17	(a)	Arsenal	D	0-0	38,677
17		24	(h)	Southampton	W	4-0	Britton, Kember 2, Garland	22,596
18	Dec	8	(h)	Leicester C	W	3-2	Hollins 2 (2 pens), Osgood	20,676
19		15	(h)	Leeds U	L	1-2	Osgood	40,768
20		22	(a)	Wolves	L	0-2	20,837
21		26	(h)	West Ham U	L	2-4	Britton, Hudson	26,982
22		29	(h)	Liverpool	L	0-1	32,901
23	Jan	1	(a)	Sheffield U	W	2-1	Hollins, Kember	32,575
24		12	(a)	Coventry C	D	2-2	Harris, Garland	20,813
25		19	(h)	Derby C	D	1-1	Garner	27,185
26		27	(a)	Stoke C	L	0-1	31,985
27	Feb	2	(a)	Leeds U	D	1-1	Garner	41,510
28		9	(h)	Manchester C	W	1-0	Webb	20,206
29		23	(h)	Queen's Park R	D	3-3	Garner 2, Cooke	34,264
30		26	(a)	Ipswich T	D	1-1	Garland	22,415
31	Mar	2	(a)	West Ham U	L	0-3	34,043
32		9	(a)	Norwich C	D	2-2	Houseman, Kember	19,866
33		13	(h)	Burnley	W	3-0	Houseman, Kember, Hutchinson	8,171
34		16	(h)	Newcastle U	W	1-0	Hutchinson	24,207
35		23	(a)	Everton	D	1-1	Garner	29,542
36		30	(h)	Manchester U	L	1-3	Garner	29,602
37	Apr	3	(a)	Tottenham H	W	2-1	Harris, Droy	23,646
38		6	(a)	Southampton	D	0-0	27,268
39		13	(h)	Arsenal	L	1-3	Swain	29,152
40		15	(h)	Tottenham H	D	0-0	26,258
41		20	(a)	Leicester C	L	0-3	22,828
42		27	(h)	Stoke C	L	0-1	17,150

FINAL LEAGUE POSITION: 17th in Division One

Appearances
Sub Appearances
Goals

FA Cup

3	Jan	5	(h)	Queen's Park R	D	0-0	31,540
R		15	(a)	Queen's Park R	L	0-1	28,573

Appearances
Sub Appearances
Goals

League Cup

2	Oct	8	(a)	Stoke C	L	0-1	17,281

Appearances
Sub Appearances
Goals

Aggregate League attendances:
Home: 545,651 (average 25,983)
Away: 641,074 (average 30,527)

Appearance / scoring grid (Chelsea FC season record).

Bonetti P	Harris R	McCreadie E	Locke G	Hollins J	Webb D	Droy M	Britton I	Hudson A	Osgood P	Garner W	Houseman P	Boyle J	Hinton M	Kember S	Hutchinson I	Phillips J	Garland C	Baldwin T	Wilkins G	Wilkins R	Sparrow J	Brolly M	Cooke C	Swain K	#
1	6	3		2	5			9		11	4			8	10		7								1
1	6	3		2	5	12		8	9	10	11			4			7								2
1	6	3		2	5	12		8	9	7	11			4	10*										3
1	3		2	4	6	5		8	9		11				10		7								4
1	3		2	4	6	5		8	9		11				10		7								5
1	3	12	2	4	6	5		8	9		11			7*			10								6
1	3		2	4	6	5		8	9		11				10		7								7
1	3		2	4	6	5		8	9		11				10		7								8
1	3		2	4	6	5		8	9		11				10*		7	12							9
1	3		2	4	6	5		8	9		11			10			7								10
1	3	12	2*	4	6	5	7				11				10		9	8							11
	6	3	2		5			8	9		10			4		1	11	7							12
1	6		2		5*			8	9		11			4			7	10	3	12					13
1			2	4		5		8	9		11			6			7*	10	3	12					14
1			2	3	6		7	10	9		11		5	4			8								15
1	6		2	3	5		8		9		11			4			7	10							16
1	3		2	4	5		7	10	9				6				11	8							17
	3		2	4	5		7	10	9				6			1	11	8							18
1	3		2	4	5			10	9		11		6				7	8							19
1	6		2	4	5		7	10	9		3			11			8								20
1	3		2	4	5		7	10	9		11		6				8								21
1	3		2	4	6	5	7	10	9		11						8								22
	3		2	4	6	5	8		9*		11			10		1	7	12							23
	3		2	4	6	5	7				8					1	10	9		11					24
	3		2	4	6	5	7			10				9		1		8					11		25
	3		2	4	6	5	7			10				9		1		8					11		26
	3		2	4	6	5	7			10				9		1		8					11		27
	3		2	4	6	5	7			10				9		1		8					11		28
	3		2	4	6	5	7			10				9		1		8					11		29
	3		2	4	6	5	7			10				9		1		8					11		30
	3		2	4	6	5	7			10				9		1		8					11		31
	3		2	4	6	5				10	11			9		1		8					7		32
			2	4	6	5				10*	11			9	12	1		8			3		7		33
	3		2	4	6	5		8						9	10	1	7*						11	12	34
			2	4	6	5				11	8			9	10	1					3		7		35
	3		2	4	6	5				11*	8			9	10	1							7	12	36
	2			4		5				10	9	6				1		8	3			11	7		37
	2			4		5				10*	9	6				12	1		8	3		11	7		38
	2			4		5				10	9	6				12	1		8	3		11*	7		39
	2			4	6	5					11			9	10	1		8			3		7		40
				4	6	5					11			9	10*	1		8	2		3		7	12	41
				4	6	5					11			10		1		8	2	9	3		7		42
20	36	4	31	42	39	29	17	19	21	23	25	1	4	37	10	22	26	18	4	4	8	1	17	4	
	2				1									4			1		2				3		
2			6	1	1	2	2	8	7	2				7	3		3	9					1	1	

1 own-goal

Bonetti P	Harris R	McCreadie E	Locke G	Hollins J	Webb D	Droy M	Britton I	Hudson A	Osgood P	Garner W	Houseman P	Boyle J	Hinton M	Kember S	Hutchinson I	Phillips J	Garland C	Baldwin T	Wilkins G	Wilkins R	Sparrow J	Brolly M	Cooke C	Swain K	#
	3		2	4	6	5	8				11			10		1	7	9	12						3
	3		2	4	9	5	7	6	8		10								11						R
	2		2	2	2	2	2		1		1		2	2	1	2			1						
																			1						

Bonetti P	Harris R	McCreadie E	Locke G	Hollins J	Webb D	Droy M	Britton I	Hudson A	Osgood P	Garner W	Houseman P	Boyle J	Hinton M	Kember S	Hutchinson I	Phillips J	Garland C	Baldwin T	Wilkins G	Wilkins R	Sparrow J	Brolly M	Cooke C	Swain K	#
1	3		2	4	6	5		8	9		10						11	7							2
1	1		1	1	1	1		1	1		1						1	1							

1974-75

Manager: Dave Sexton to October 1974, Ron Suart to April 1975 then Eddie McCreadie.

1	Aug	17	(h)	Carlisle U	L 0-2		31,268
2		21	(h)	Burnley	D 3-3	Cooke, Houseman, Garner	23,745
3		24	(a)	Coventry C	W 3-1	Locke, Cooke, Garner	21,251
4		27	(a)	Burnley	W 2-1	Hutchinson, Garner	17,154
5		31	(h)	Liverpool	L 0-3		39,461
6	Sep	7	(a)	Middlesbrough	D 1-1	Hutchinson	25,480
7		14	(h)	Arsenal	D 0-0		34,596
8		21	(a)	Ipswich T	L 0-2		23,121
9		25	(a)	Derby C	L 1-4	Hutchinson	22,036
10		28	(h)	Wolves	L 0-1		23,073
11	Oct	5	(a)	Manchester C	D 1-1	Hutchinson	32,412
12		12	(h)	Tottenham H	W 1-0	Hollins (pen)	32,660
13		19	(a)	Everton	D 1-1	Cooke	35,806
14		26	(h)	Stoke C	D 3-3	Droy, Garland, Hutchinson	24,718
15	Nov	2	(a)	Birmingham C	L 0-2		30,364
16		9	(h)	Leicester C	D 0-0		23,915
17		13	(h)	Coventry C	D 3-3	Garland, Cooke, Garner	11,048
18		16	(a)	Newcastle U	L 0-5		33,821
19		30	(a)	Leeds U	L 0-2		30,444
20	Dec	7	(h)	Luton T	W 2-0	Kember, Hutchinson	19,009
21		14	(a)	Carlisle U	W 2-1	Hollins 2	12,854
22		21	(h)	West Ham U	D 1-1	Hutchinson	34,969
23		26	(a)	Arsenal	W 2-1	Garland 2	33,784
24		28	(h)	Queen's Park R	L 0-3		38,917
25	Jan	11	(a)	Luton T	D 1-1	Kember	23,096
26		18	(h)	Leeds U	L 0-2		34,733
27	Feb	1	(a)	Leicester C	D 1-1	Kember	23,759
28		8	(h)	Birmingham C	W 2-1	R.Wilkins, Langley	18,144
29		15	(a)	Sheffield U	L 1-2	Garner	20,542
30		22	(h)	Newcastle U	W 3-2	Hollins (pen), Cooke, Finnieston	26,770
31	Mar	1	(a)	Liverpool	D 2-2	Britton, Finnieston	42,762
32		8	(h)	Derby C	L 1-2	Hollins	22,644
33		15	(a)	Wolves	L 1-7	Garner	21,649
34		18	(a)	Queen's Park R	L 0-1		25,324
35		22	(h)	Middlesbrough	L 1-2	Sparrow	22,240
36		29	(a)	West Ham U	W 1-0	Droy	31,025
37		31	(h)	Ipswich T	D 0-0		35,005
38	Apr	5	(a)	Stoke C	L 0-3		26,375
39		12	(h)	Manchester C	L 0-1		26,249
40		19	(a)	Tottenham H	L 0-2		51,064
41		23	(h)	Sheffield U	D 1-1	Maybank	23,380
42		26	(h)	Everton	D 1-1	R.Wilkins	28,432

FINAL LEAGUE POSITION: 21st in Division One

Appearances
Sub Appearances
Goals

FA Cup

3	Jan	4	(h)	Sheffield W	W 3-2	Droy 2, Garland	24,679
4		25	(h)	Birmingham C	L 0-1		35,450

Appearances
Sub Appearances
Goals

League Cup

2	Sep	11	(h)	Newport C	W 4-2	Garland 3, Cooke	13,322
3	Oct	9	(h)	Stoke C	D 2-2	Hutchinson 2	19,954
R		16	(a)	Stoke C	D 1-1*	Britton	24,377
2R		22	(a)	Stoke C	L 2-6	Hollins, Baldwin	26,712

*After extra-time

Aggregate League attendances:
Home: 575,323 (average 27,396)
Away: 584,123 (average 27,815)

Appearances
Sub Appearances
Goals

Football appearances / line-up grid (shirt numbers per player per match). Asterisks (*) denote substitutes.

	Bonetti P	Locke G	Sparrow J	Hollins J	Droy M	Harris R	Garland C	Hay D	Wilkins R	Kember S	Hutchinson I	Cooke C	Phillips J	Sissons J	Houseman P	Garner W	Dempsey J	Baldwin T	Britton I	Wicks S	Hinton M	Langley T	Wilkins G	Finnieston S	Maybank E	
1	1	2		4	5	6	9*	8		7		12			11	3	10									1
2	1	2		4	5	6		8		7		9			11	3	10									2
3	1	2		4	5	6		8		7		9			11	3	10									3
4		2		4	5	6		8		7	12	9*	1		11	3	10									4
5		2		4	5	6	12	8		7		9	1		11	3	10*									5
6		2		4	5	6	9	8	10	7			1		11	3										6
7		2		4		6		8		7	10	9	1		11	3	5									7
8		2		4		6		8		7	10	9	1		11	3	5									8
9		2		4	5	6		8	10	7		9	1		11	3										9
10		2		4	6	9		7	8			11	1			3	10				5					10
11		2	4*	5	3		12	7				10	9	1	11						8	6				11
12		2		4	5	3		7				10	9	1	11						6	8				12
13		2		4	5	3						9	1		11	10		6	8	7						13
14		2		4	5	3	8				11	10	9	1				6	7							14
15	1	2		4	5	3	8				11	9		12		6	10	7*								15
16	1	2		4	5	3				7		11	10			8			6	9						16
17	1	2		5	3	9	4			7		11	10	8		12	6*									17
18	1	2		5	3	9	4			7		11	10	8	6											18
19	1	2		5	3		4	8	10	11		12	9		7*		6									19
20		2		5	9	4	6	8	10	7		1	11		3											20
21		2		4	5	3	9	6	8	7		10	11	1												21
22		2		4	5	3	9	6	8	7*		10	11	1		12										22
23		2		4	5	3	9	6	8			10	7	1	11											23
24		2		4	5	3	9	6	8	7	10*	11	1			12										24
25		2		4		3	9	6	8	7		10	11	1		12	5*									25
26		2		4		3	9	6	8	7		10	11	1					5							26
27		2	3	4		5		6	8	7		11	1			10								9		27
28		2*	3	4		5		6	8	7	10	11	1									12		9		28
29		2	3	4	5*	6	12	7	8			11	1			10								9		29
30		2	3	4*	5	10	6	8				11	1			12			7					9		30
31		2	3*	4	5	10	6	8	12			11	1						7					9		31
32		2	3	4	5	10	6	8				11	1						7					9		32
33		2	3	4		6		8	12			11	1			10	5*		7					9*		33
34		2	3	4		6		8	7			11	1				10		11	5		12		9*		34
35		2	3	4	5			6	8	10		11	1						7			9				35
36		2		4	5	3		8		7		11	1		10				6	9						36
37		2		4		3		8		7		11	1		10	5			6	9						37
38		3		4	5	2		8		7		1	11	12					6	9		10*				38
39		2		4	5	3		8		7	10	9	1		11				6*	12						39
40		2	3		5	6		7	8			10	11	1				4						9		40
41		2*	3		5	6		7	8			10	11	1				4						9		41
42		3			6	2		8	7			10	11	1				4	5					9		42
	8	41	12	34	26	42	20	34	20	29	21	38	34	10	20	15	11	4	14	1	10	5	1	9	3	
								2		1	2	1	1			1	4	2	1		1		3			
	1	1	5	2		4			2	3	7	5			1	6		1			1		2	1		

	Bonetti P	Locke G	Sparrow J	Hollins J	Droy M	Harris R	Garland C	Hay D	Wilkins R	Kember S	Hutchinson I	Cooke C	Phillips J	Sissons J	Houseman P	Garner W	Dempsey J	Baldwin T	Britton I	Wicks S	Hinton M	Langley T	Wilkins G	Finnieston S	Maybank E	
		2		4	5	3	9	6	8			7	1		11	10										3
		2		4	5	3	9	6	8	7	10		1	11												4
		2		2	2	2	2	2	2	1	1	1	2	1	1	1										
				2		1																				

	Bonetti P	Locke G	Sparrow J	Hollins J	Droy M	Harris R	Garland C	Hay D	Wilkins R	Kember S	Hutchinson I	Cooke C	Phillips J	Sissons J	Houseman P	Garner W	Dempsey J	Baldwin T	Britton I	Wicks S	Hinton M	Langley T	Wilkins G	Finnieston S	Maybank E	
		2		4	5	6		8		7		10	9	1	11	3										2
		2		4	5	3	8*		12	7	10	9	1		11		6									3
		2		4	5	3	8*				10	9	1		11	12	6		7							R
		2		4	5	3					10	9	1		11*	8	6	12	7							2R
		4		4	4	4	3		2	4	4	4	1		4	1	3	2								
				1					3			2	1					1	1							

313

1975-76

Manager: Eddie McCreadie

1	Aug	16	(a)	Sunderland	L	1-2	Garner	28,689
2		20	(a)	West Brom A	D	0-0		18,014
3		23	(h)	Carlisle U	W	3-1	Maybank 2, Bason	19,165
4		27	(h)	Oxford U	W	3-1	R.Wilkins 2, Swain	22,841
5		30	(a)	Luton T	L	0-3		19,024
6	Sep	6	(h)	Nottingham F	D	0-0		21,023
7		13	(a)	Oldham A	L	1-2	R.Wilkins	10,406
8		20	(h)	Bristol C	D	1-1	Garner	17,661
9		23	(a)	Portsmouth	D	1-1	Garner	16,144
10		27	(a)	Fulham	L	0-2		22,986
11	Oct	4	(h)	York C	D	0-0		15,323
12		11	(a)	Southampton	L	1-4	R.Wilkins	21,227
13		18	(h)	Blackpool	W	2-0	R.Wilkins, Langley	16,974
14		25	(a)	Blackburn R	D	1-1	Hutchinson	12,128
15	Nov	1	(h)	Plymouth A	D	2-2	Britton, R.Wilkins	20,096
16		8	(a)	Hull C	W	2-1	Britton, Hutchinson	9,097
17		15	(h)	Notts C	W	2-0	R.Wilkins (pen), Garner	18,229
18		22	(a)	Blackpool	W	2-0	Droy, Maybank	8,595
19		29	(a)	Bristol R	W	2-1	Maybank, Hutchinson	16,227
20	Dec	6	(h)	Bolton W	L	0-1		20,896
21		13	(a)	Carlisle U	L	1-2	R.Wilkins	8,096
22		20	(h)	Sunderland	W	1-0	Britton	22,806
23		26	(a)	Orient	L	1-3	Maybank	15,509
24		27	(h)	Charlton A	L	2-3	Britton, Swain	25,367
25	Jan	10	(h)	Oldham A	L	0-3		16,464
26		17	(a)	Nottingham F	W	3-1	R.Wilkins, Garner, Hutchinson	14,172
27		31	(a)	West Brom A	L	1-2	Britton	15,896
28	Feb	7	(a)	Oxford U	D	1-1	Garner	11,162
29		18	(h)	Hull C	D	0-0		10,254
30		21	(a)	Notts C	L	2-3	Stanley, Finnieston	14,528
31		25	(h)	Portsmouth	W	2-0	Cooke, Locke	12,709
32		28	(h)	Blackburn R	W	3-1	R.Wilkins 2, Finnieston	14,855
33	Mar	6	(a)	Plymouth A	W	3-0	Britton, Swain, Stanley	20,638
34		13	(h)	Southampton	D	1-1	Finnieston	29,011
35		20	(h)	Bristol R	D	0-0		16,132
36		27	(a)	Bolton W	L	1-2	Britton	20,817
37	Apr	6	(h)	Fulham	D	0-0		23,605
38		10	(a)	Bristol C	D	2-2	Swain, Stanley	24,710
39		16	(h)	Luton T	D	2-2	Hay, Finnieston	19,878
40		17	(h)	Orient	L	0-2		17,679
41		19	(a)	Charlton A	D	1-1	Berry (og)	23,263
42		24	(a)	York C	D	2-2	Britton (pen), Finnieston	4,914

FINAL LEAGUE POSITION: 11th in Division Two

Appearances
Sub Appearances
Goals

FA Cup

3	Jan	1	(h)	Bristol R	D	1-1	Garner	35,226
R		3	(a)	Bristol R	W	1-0	Swain	13,939
4		24	(a)	York C	W	2-0	Garner, Hutchinson	9,591
5	Feb	14	(h)	Crystal P	L	2-3	R.Wilkins, Wicks	54,407

Appearances
Sub Appearances
Goals

League Cup

2	Sep	10	(a)	Crewe A	L	0-1	6,723

Aggregate League attendances:
Home: 398,088 (average 18,956)
Away: 340,300 (average 16,204)

Appearances
Sub Appearances
Goals

Football season appearances/line-up grid (shirt numbers by player and match).

	Sherwood S	Harris R	Wilkins G	Cooke C	Droy M	Dempsey J	Britton I	Wilkins R	Maybank E	Garner W	Swain K	Stanley G	Wicks S	Hutchinson I	Bason B	Sparrow J	Hay D	Langley T	Locke G	Bonetti P	Lewington R	Finnieston S	Phillips J	
1	1	2	11	5	6	7	8	9	10		4						3							1
2	1	2	11	5	6	7	8	9	10*	12	4						3							2
3	1	12	2	11	5	6	7*	8	9		10				4		3							3
4	1	7	2	11	5	6		8	9		10				4		3							4
5	1	12	2	11	5	6	7*	8	9		10				4		3							5
6	1	7		11	5	6		8	9		10	4					3	2						6
7	1	2			5	6	7	8		11	10	4					3	9						7
8	1	2			5	6	7	8		11		4		10	9		3							8
9	1	2			5	6	7	8		11		4		10	9		3							9
10	1	2			5	6	7	8				4		10	12	9*	3	11						10
11	1	2			5	6	7	8						10	9		3	4	11					11
12	1	3			5	6	7	8		11				10	9*		4	12	2					12
13		3			5	6	7	8	9*	11	10						4	12	2	1				13
14		3			5	6	7	8	9	11	10						4	12	2*	1				14
15		3			5	6	7	8	9	11	4			10					2	1				15
16		3			5	6	7	8	9	11	4			10					2	1				16
17		3			5	6	7	8	9	10	4			11					2	1				17
18		3			5	6	7	8	9	11*	4			10	12				2	1				18
19		3			5	6	7	8	9	11	4			10					2	1				19
20		3	11	5	6	7	8	9			4			10					2	1				20
21		3	11	5	6	7	8	9				4		10					2	1				21
22		3			5	6	7	8	9	11	4			10*			12		2	1				22
23		3			5	6	7	8	9	11	4	12		10*					2	1				23
24		3	10	5	6*	7	8	9	11	4							12		2	1				24
25		3	12	5		7	8	9	11		6*	10			4				2	1				25
26		3	4			7	8	9	11			5	10				6		2	1				26
27		3	4			7	8	9	11			5	10				6		2	1				27
28		6	3	4			7	8	9	11	10	5							2	1				28
29		3	4			7	8		11	10		5					6		2	1		9		29
30		3	11			7	8		10	4*		5					6		2	1	12	9		30
31		3	11			7	8		10	4		5					6		2	1		9		31
32		3	11			7	8*		10	4		5					6	12	2	1		9		32
33		3				7	8		10	4		5					6		2	1	11	9		33
34		3				7	8		12	10	4	5					6		2*	1	11	9		34
35		2				7	8		12	10*	4	5		3	6					1	11	9		35
36		3	2			7	8		9	10	4	5					6			1	11			36
37		2	3			7	8		9	10	4	5					6			1	11			37
38		3	2			7	8			10	4	5					6			1	11	9		38
39		2	3			7	8		12	10	4	5					6		1*		11	9		39
40		2	3			7	8		11	10	4	5					6				11*	9	1	40
41		2	3			7	8		11	10	4	5					6					9	1	41
42		2	3*			7	8		11	10	4	5		12			6					9	1	42
	12	38	13	16	25	24	40	42	22	21	24	29	18	18	8	8	27	4	23	27	8	12	3	—
	2	1							4	1		1		1	1	1	6		1					—
			1	1		8	11	5	6	4	3		4	1		1	1	1				5		—

1 own-goal

	Sherwood S	Harris R	Wilkins G	Cooke C	Droy M	Dempsey J	Britton I	Wilkins R	Maybank E	Garner W	Swain K	Stanley G	Wicks S	Hutchinson I	Bason B	Sparrow J	Hay D	Langley T	Locke G	Bonetti P	Lewington R	Finnieston S	Phillips J	
3		3		12	5		7	8	9*	10	11	4	6						2	1				3
R		3			5		7	8	9	12	11	4*	6			10			2	1				R
4		3	4			7	8	9	11		5	10				6			2	1				4
5		3	4	5*		7	8	9	11	10		6				12			2	1				5
		4	2	3	4	4	4	3	3	2	4	1		2					4	4				—
								1						1										—
			1		2	1		1	1															—

	Sherwood S	Harris R	Wilkins G	Cooke C	Droy M	Dempsey J	Britton I	Wilkins R	Maybank E	Garner W	Swain K	Stanley G	Wicks S	Hutchinson I	Bason B	Sparrow J	Hay D	Langley T	Locke G	Bonetti P	Lewington R	Finnieston S	Phillips J	
2	1	2			5	6	7	8		11	10*	9		12	3	4								2
	1	1			1	1	1	1		1	1	1			1	1								—
											1													—

1976-77

Manager: Eddie McCreadie

1	Aug	21	(a)	Orient	W	1-0	Finnieston	11,456
2		25	(h)	Notts C	D	1-1	Britton	17,426
3		28	(h)	Carlisle U	W	2-1	Finnieston, Swain	18,681
4	Sep	4	(a)	Millwall	L	0-3		21,002
5		11	(a)	Plymouth A	W	3-2	Britton (pen), Finnieston, Swain	18,356
6		18	(h)	Bolton W	W	2-1	Stanley, Hay	24,835
7		25	(a)	Blackpool	W	1-0	Finnieston	19,041
8	Oct	2	(h)	Cardiff C	W	2-1	Swain, Lewington	28,409
9		5	(a)	Bristol R	L	1-2	Finnieston	13,199
10		16	(h)	Oldham A	W	4-3	R.Wilkins, Finnieston, Wicks, Swain	25,825
11		23	(a)	Blackburn R	W	2-0	Finnieston 2	15,039
12		30	(h)	Southampton	W	3-1	R.Wilkins, Finnieston, Swain	42,654
13	Nov	6	(a)	Hereford U	D	2-2	Finnieston 2 (1 pen)	12,858
14		10	(h)	Charlton A	W	2-1	Stanley, Swain	38,879
15		20	(a)	Nottingham F	D	1-1	Britton	27,089
16		27	(h)	Burnley	W	2-1	Britton, Finnieston (pen)	28,595
17	Dec	3	(a)	Sheffield U	L	0-1		23,393
18		7	(a)	Southampton	D	1-1	Finnieston	19,909
19		11	(h)	Wolves	D	3-3	Britton, R.Wilkins, Finnieston	36,137
20		18	(a)	Hull C	D	1-1	Britton	11,774
21		27	(h)	Fulham	W	2-0	Droy, Swain	55,003
22		29	(a)	Luton T	L	0-4		17,102
23	Jan	1	(h)	Hereford U	W	5-1	Stanley, R.Wilkins, Finnieston, Swain, Galley (og)	27,720
24		22	(h)	Orient	D	1-1	Stanley	25,744
25	Feb	5	(a)	Carlisle U	W	1-0	Swain	11,356
26		12	(h)	Millwall	D	1-1	Stanley	34,857
27		15	(a)	Notts C	L	1-2	R.Wilkins	11,902
28		19	(h)	Plymouth A	D	2-2	Britton (pen), Swain	22,154
29		26	(a)	Bolton W	D	2-2	Finnieston, Swain	31,600
30	Mar	5	(h)	Blackpool	D	2-2	Wicks, Swain	27,412
31		12	(a)	Cardiff C	W	3-1	Stanley, Britton, Swain	20,194
32		19	(h)	Bristol R	W	2-0	Wicks, Aitken (og)	26,196
33	Apr	2	(h)	Blackburn R	W	3-1	Wicks, Finnieston 2	20,769
34		8	(a)	Fulham	L	1-3	R.Wilkins	29,690
35		9	(h)	Luton T	W	2-0	Finnieston, Sparrow	31,911
36		11	(a)	Charlton A	L	0-4		25,757
37		16	(h)	Nottingham F	W	2-1	Britton, Finnieston	36,499
38		19	(a)	Oldham A	D	0-0		10,074
39		23	(a)	Burnley	L	0-1		14,927
40		30	(h)	Sheffield U	W	4-0	R.Wilkins, Finnieston, Lewington, Langley	28,158
41	May	7	(a)	Wolves	D	1-1	Langley	33,465
42		14	(h)	Hull C	W	4-0	Britton, Finnieston 3 (1 pen)	43,718

FINAL LEAGUE POSITION: 2nd in Division Two

Appearances
Sub Appearances
Goals

FA Cup

3	Jan	8	(a)	Southampton	D	1-1	Locke	26,041
R		12	(h)	Southampton	L	0-3		42,868

Appearances
Sub Appearances
Goals

League Cup

2	Sep	1	(h)	Sheffield U	W	3-1	R.Wilkins 2, Swain	16,883
3		20	(h)	Huddersfield T	W	2-0	Finnieston 2	19,860
4	Oct	26	(a)	Arsenal	L	1-2	Hay	52,305

Aggregate League attendances:
Home: 643,302 (average 30,633)
Away: 399,183 (average 33,465)

Appearances
Sub Appearances
Goals

Bonetti P	Locke G	Wilkins G	Stanley G	Wicks S	Hay D	Droy M	Britton I	Wilkins R	Finnieston S	Swain K	Lewington R	Phillips J	Harris R	Bason B	Maybank E	Cooke C	Langley T	Walker C	Sparrow J	#
1	2	3	4	5	6		7	8	9	11	10									**1**
1	2	3		5	6		7	8	9	11	10			4						**2**
1	2	3	4	5	6		7	8	9	11	10									**3**
1	2	3	4		6	5	7	8	9*	11	10		12							**4**
1	2	3	4	5	6		7	8	9	11	10									**5**
1	2	3	4	5	6		7*	8	9	11	10		12							**6**
1	2	3	4	5	6			8	9	11	10		7							**7**
1	2	3		5	6			8	9	11	10		7			4				**8**
1	2	3		5*	6			8	9	11	10	12	7			4				**9**
1	2	3	4	5	6			8	9	11	10		7							**10**
1	2	3	4	5				8	9	11	10		6	7						**11**
	2	3	4	5	6		7	8	9	11	10	1								**12**
1	2	3	4	5	6		7	8	9	11	10									**13**
1	2	3	4	5*	6		7	8	9	11	10		12							**14**
1	2	3	4	5	6		7	8	9	11	10									**15**
1	2	3	4	5	6		7	8	9	11	10									**16**
1	2	3	4	5	6		7	8	9	11	10									**17**
1	2	3	4	5	6		7	8	9	11	10									**18**
1	2	3	4	5	6		7	8	9	11	10									**19**
1	2	3	4	5	6		7	8	9	11	10									**20**
1	2	3	4		6	5	7	8	9	11	10									**21**
	2	3	4		6	5	7	8	9	11	10	1								**22**
	2		4*		6	5	7	8	9	11	10	1		3					12	**23**
	2		4		6	5	7	8	9	11	10	1		3						**24**
	2		4		6	5	7	8	9*	11	10	1		3					12	**25**
	2		4		6	5	7	8		11	10	1		3	9					**26**
	2	3	4		6	5	7	8		11	10	1			9					**27**
	2	3	4	5	6		7	8		11	10	1			9					**28**
	2	3	4	5	6		7	8	9	11	10	1								**29**
	2	3	4	5	6		7	8	9	11	10	1								**30**
1	2		4	5	6		7	8	9	11	10								3	**31**
1	2		4	5	6		7	8	9	11	10								3	**32**
1	2		4	5			7	8	9	11	10		6						3	**33**
1	2		4	5			7	8	9	11	10		6						3	**34**
1	2		4	5			7	8	9	11	10		6						3	**35**
	2		4	5			7	8	9	11	10	1	6						3	**36**
1	2			5			7	8	9		10		6			4	11		3	**37**
1	2			5			7	8	9		10		6			4	11*	12	3	**38**
1	2			5			7	8	9		10		6			4	11		3	**39**
1	2			5			7	8	9		10		6			4	11		3	**40**
1	2			5			7	8	9		10		6			4	11		3	**41**
1	2			5			7	8	9		10		6			4	11		3	**42**
31	42	26	33	34	31	8	37	42	39	36	42	11	15	6	3	8	6		12	
													4					1	2	
		6	4	1	1		10	7	24	13	2						2		1	

2 own-goals

Bonetti P	Locke G	Wilkins G	Stanley G	Wicks S	Hay D	Droy M	Britton I	Wilkins R	Finnieston S	Swain K	Lewington R	Phillips J	Harris R	Bason B	Maybank E	Cooke C	Langley T	Walker C	Sparrow J	#
	2		4		6	5	7	8	9	11	10	1		3						**3**
	2		4		6	5	7	8	9	11	10	1		3						**R**
	2		2		2	2	2	2	2	2	2	2		2						
	1																			

Bonetti P	Locke G	Wilkins G	Stanley G	Wicks S	Hay D	Droy M	Britton I	Wilkins R	Finnieston S	Swain K	Lewington R	Phillips J	Harris R	Bason B	Maybank E	Cooke C	Langley T	Walker C	Sparrow J	#
1	2	3	4		6	5	7	8	9	11	10									**2**
1	2	3	4	5	6			8	9	11	10		7							**3**
	2	3	4	5	6			8	9	11	10	1	12	7*						**4**
2	3	3	3	3	2	3	1	1	3	3	3	3	1		2					
													1							
						1		2	2	1										

1977-78

Manager: Ken Shellito

1	Aug	20	(a)	West Brom A	L 0-3	20,145
2		24	(h)	Birmingham C	W 2-0 Stanley, Lewington	18,008
3		27	(h)	Coventry C	L 1-2 Langley	25,432
4	Sep	3	(a)	Ipswich T	L 0-1	20,835
5		10	(h)	Derby C	D 1-1 Langley	25,759
6		17	(a)	Manchester U	W 1-0 Garner	54,764
7		24	(a)	Queen's Park R	D 1-1 Swain	26,267
8	Oct	1	(h)	Leeds U	L 1-2 R.Wilkins	35,427
9		5	(h)	Leicester C	D 0-0	19,575
10		8	(a)	Liverpool	L 0-2	40,499
11		15	(h)	Middlesbrough	D 0-0	21,091
12		22	(a)	Newcastle U	L 0-1	23,683
13		29	(h)	Bristol C	W 1-0 Aylott	22,313
14	Nov	5	(h)	Nottingham F	W 1-0 Aylott	36,116
15		12	(a)	Norwich C	D 0-0	19,566
16		19	(h)	Aston Villa	D 0-0	31,764
17		26	(a)	Manchester C	L 2-6 Britton (pen), R.Wilkins	34,354
18	Dec	3	(h)	Everton	L 0-1	33,899
19		10	(a)	Wolves	W 3-1 Langley, Walker 2	16,400
20		17	(h)	Norwich C	D 1-1 R.Wilkins	22,751
21		26	(a)	Arsenal	L 0-3	46,074
22		27	(h)	West Ham U	W 2-1 Langley, Garner	44,093
23		31	(a)	Birmingham C	W 5-4 Langley 3, Garner, Walker	19,876
24	Jan	2	(h)	West Brom A	D 2-2 Garner, Walker	29,540
25		14	(a)	Coventry C	L 1-5 R.Wilkins	21,155
26		21	(h)	Ipswich T	W 5-3 R.Wilkins, Langley, Swain 2, Finnieston	26,044
27	Feb	11	(h)	Manchester U	D 2-2 R.Wilkins, Walker	32,238
28		25	(a)	Leeds U	L 0-2	25,263
29	Mar	4	(h)	Liverpool	W 3-1 Langley, Finnieston 2	35,550
30		11	(a)	Derby C	D 1-1 Walker	21,504
31		18	(h)	Newcastle U	D 2-2 Harris, Swain (pen)	22,777
32		21	(a)	Bristol C	L 0-3	19,961
33		25	(a)	West Ham U	L 1-3 Garner	24,987
34		27	(h)	Arsenal	D 0-0	40,764
35	Apr	1	(a)	Nottingham F	L 1-3 Langley	31,262
36		4	(a)	Middlesbrough	L 0-2	15,288
37		15	(a)	Aston Villa	L 0-2	27,375
38		22	(h)	Wolves	D 1-1 Langley	31,637
39		26	(a)	Leicester C	W 2-0 R.Wilkins, Walker	12,970
40		29	(a)	Everton	L 0-6	39,504
41	May	2	(h)	Queen's Park R	W 3-1 Droy, Lewington, Hollins (og)	21,201
42		5	(h)	Manchester C	D 0-0	18,782

FINAL LEAGUE POSITION: 16th in Division One

Appearances
Sub Appearances
Goals

FA Cup

3	Jan	7	(h)	Liverpool	W 4-2 Langley, Walker 2, Finnieston	45,449
4		31	(h)	Burnley	W 6-2 Droy, Wicks, R.Wilkins, Langley, Walker, Swain	32,168
5	Feb	18	(a)	Orient	D 0-0	25,123
R		27	(h)	Orient	L 1-2 Roffey (og)	36,379

Appearances
Sub Appearances
Goals

League Cup

2	Aug	30	(a)	Liverpool	L 0-2	33,170

Aggregate League attendances:
Home: 603,420 (average 28,734)
Away: 561,732 (average 26,749)

Appearances
Sub Appearances
Goals

Bonetti P	Wilkins G	Locke G	Harris R	Sparrow J	Britton I	Droy M	Wicks S	Stanley G	Wilkins R	Langley T	Lewington R	Garner W	Phillips J	Walker C	Frost L	Swain K	Finnieston S	Aylott T	Cooke C	Hay D	
	2	6	3		7	5	4	8	11	10			1			9					1
	2	6	3		7	5	4	8	11	10			1			9					2
	2	6	3		7	5	4	8	11	10			1			9					3
			3	2	4	5	6	7	8	11		12	1			10	9*				4
			3	2	4	5	6	11	8	9		7	1			10					5
		12	3	2	4	5	6	11	8	9		7*	1			10					6
			3	2	4	5	6	11	8	9		7	1			10					7
			3	2	4	5	6	11	8	9		7	1			10					8
			3	2	4	5	6	11	8	9		10	1			7					9
		12	3	2	4	5	6	11*	8	9		7	1			10					10
1			3	2	4	5	6	11*	8	9		7		12		10					11
1			3	2	4	5	6		8	9*		7			11	10		12			12
1			3	2	4	5	6		8	9		12				10	7*	11			13
1	2			3	4	5	6		8	9						10	7	11			14
1	2			3	4	5	6		8	9						10	7	11			15
1	2			3	4	5	6		8	9						10	7	11			16
1	2			3	4	5	6		8	9	12					10	7	11*			17
1		2	3		4	5	6		8	9	12					10	7	11*			18
1		2	3		4	5	6		8	9					11	10	7				19
1		2	3		4	5	6		8	9					11	10	7				20
1		2	3		4	5	6		8	9	12					10	7*				21
1	3			2	4	5	6			9		8*	7			11	10	12			22
1	3			2	4	5	6			9		8	7			11	10				23
1	3*	12		2	4	5	6			9		8	7			11	10				24
1		2	5	3	4			6		10	9	8	7			11					25
1		2	3		4	5	6		8	9		7*			11	10	12				26
1		2	3		4	5	6		8	9					11	10	7				27
1	3	2	6		4	5			8		12	11*		10		7	9				28
1		2	3		4	5	6		8	9	10					11	7				29
1		2	3		4	5	6		8	9	10					11	7				30
1		2	3		4	5	6		8*	9	10					11	12	7			31
1		2	3		4	5	6			9	10	12				8	7*		11		32
	2	3		4		6			12	10	9*	1	11			8	7		5		33
1		2	3		4	5	6			9	10					8	7		11		34
1		2	3		4	5	6			9	10					8	7	11			35
1		2	3		4		6			9	10					8	7		5		36
1	2		3		4		6			9	10	12	11*			8	7		5		37
1	3	2		4	5	6			10	9		11				8	7				38
1		2	3			5	6		8	9						11	7	10	4		39
1		2	3			5	6		8	9	4					11	7	10			40
1		2	3		4	5	6		10	12	7	9*				11	8				41
1			3		4	5	6			10	9	7				11	8			2	42
31	21	18	37	12	40	35	41	11	33	39	20	15	11	21	1	35	18	10	6	7	
		3									2	4	3		2		1	2	1		
		1		1	1		1		7	11	2	5		7		4	3	2			

1 own-goal

Bonetti P	Wilkins G	Locke G	Harris R	Sparrow J	Britton I	Droy M	Wicks S	Stanley G	Wilkins R	Langley T	Lewington R	Garner W	Phillips J	Walker C	Frost L	Swain K	Finnieston S	Aylott T	Cooke C	Hay D	
1	2		5	3	4		6			9	8	7			11			12	10*		3
1		2	3		4	5	6		8	9					11	10	7				4
1	3	2	6		4	5			8	9					11	10	7				5
1	3	2	6		4	5			8	9	10				11		12	7*			R
4	3	3	4	1	4	3	2		3	4	2	1		4		2	2	1	1		
												2									
						1	1			1	2			3		1	1				

1 own-goal

Bonetti P	Wilkins G	Locke G	Harris R	Sparrow J	Britton I	Droy M	Wicks S	Stanley G	Wilkins R	Langley T	Lewington R	Garner W	Phillips J	Walker C	Frost L	Swain K	Finnieston S	Aylott T	Cooke C	Hay D	
	2	6	3	4	5		7	8	11		12	1			10	9*					2
	1	1	1	1	1		1	1	1		1	1			1	1					
										1											

1978-79

Manager: Ken Shellito to December 1978 then Danny Blanchflower

1	Aug	19	(h)	Everton	L	0-1	31,755
2		22	(a)	Wolves	W	1-0 Langley	22,041
3		26	(a)	Tottenham H	D	2-2 Swain 2	40,632
4	Sep	2	(h)	Leeds U	L	0-3	30,099
5		9	(a)	Coventry C	L	2-3 Langley, McKenzie	24,920
6		16	(h)	Manchester C	L	1-4 Stanley	28,980
7		23	(a)	Birmingham C	D	1-1 McKenzie	18,458
8		30	(h)	West Brom A	L	1-3 Wicks	20,186
9	Oct	7	(a)	Derby C	L	0-1	20,251
10		14	(h)	Bolton W	W	4-3 Swain, Langley, Walker, Allardyce (og)	19,879
11		21	(a)	Liverpool	L	0-2	45,775
12		28	(h)	Norwich C	D	3-3 Swain, Stanley (pen), Walker	23,941
13	Nov	4	(a)	Queen's Park R	D	0-0	22,876
14		11	(a)	Everton	L	2-3 Langley, McKenzie	38,694
15		18	(h)	Tottenham H	L	1-3 Langley	41,594
16		22	(a)	Leeds U	L	1-2 Langley	24,088
17		25	(h)	Manchester U	L	0-1	27,156
18	Dec	9	(h)	Aston Villa	L	0-1	19,080
19		16	(a)	Middlesbrough	L	2-7 Bumstead, Osgood	15,107
20		23	(h)	Bristol C	D	0-0	19,093
21		26	(a)	Southampton	D	0-0	20,770
22		30	(a)	Ipswich T	L	1-5 Langley	21,439
23	Jan	21	(a)	Manchester C	W	3-2 Walker, McKenzie, Osgood	31,876
24	Feb	3	(h)	Birmingham C	W	2-1 R.Wilkins 2	22,129
25		21	(h)	Coventry C	L	1-3 Langley	15,282
26		24	(a)	Bolton W	L	1-2 Bannon	19,457
27	Mar	3	(h)	Liverpool	D	0-0	40,594
28		10	(a)	Norwich C	L	0-2	19,071
29		14	(a)	West Brom A	L	0-1	20,425
30		17	(h)	Queen's Park R	L	1-3 Shanks (og)	25,871
31		24	(h)	Wolves	L	1-2 Langley	20,502
32		28	(a)	Nottingham F	L	0-6	24,514
33	Apr	4	(h)	Derby C	D	1-1 Langley	10,682
34		7	(h)	Nottingham F	L	1-3 R.Wilkins	29,213
35		10	(a)	Bristol C	L	1-3 Langley (pen)	18,645
36		14	(h)	Southampton	L	1-2 Stanley	18,243
37		16	(a)	Arsenal	L	2-5 Langley, Walker	37,232
38		21	(h)	Middlesbrough	W	2-1 G.Wilkins, Stanley	12,007
39		28	(a)	Aston Villa	L	1-2 Langley	29,219
40	May	5	(h)	Ipswich T	L	2-3 Langley 2	15,462
41		14	(h)	Arsenal	D	1-1 Stanley	28,386
42		16	(a)	Manchester U	D	1-1 Johnson	38,116

FINAL LEAGUE POSITION: 22nd in Division One

Appearances
Sub Appearances
Goals

FA Cup

3	Jan	5	(a)	Manchester U	L	0-3	38,500

Appearances
Sub Appearances
Goals

League Cup

2	Aug	29	(a)	Bolton W	L	1-2 Langley	10,449

Aggregate League attendances:
Home: 520,426 (average 24,782)
Away: 553,609 (average 26,362)

Appearances
Sub Appearances
Goals

Player appearance and shirt-number grid (numbers indicate shirt worn; * denotes substitute used).

#	Bonetti P	Wilkins G	Nutton M	Hay D	Harris R	Droy M	Wicks S	Swain K	Wilkins R	Langley T	Stanley G	Walker C	Britton I	Phillips J	Lewington R	Garner W	Aylott T	Locke G	Frost L	McKenzie D	Stride D	Iles R	Johnson G	Bumstead J	Fillery M	Osgood P	Bannon E	Sitton J	Borota P	Docherty J	Chivers G
1	1			4	3	5	6	7	8	9*	10	11	12					2													
2	1			4	3	5	6	7	8	9	10	11						2													
3	1			4	3	5	6	7	8	9	10	11						2													
4	1			4	3	5	6	7	8	9	10	11						2													
5	1		5		3		6	7	8	9	10*		12			4		2		11											
6	1		5		3		6	7	8*	9	10		12			4		2		11											
7	1			6		5	7	8	9	4							10	2		11	3										
8	1			6		5	7	8	9	4	12						10	2		11*	3										
9			2	6		5	7	8	9						10	4	11				3	1									
10			2	6		5	7	8	9	11*	12	10			4						3	1									
11		2		6		5	10	8*	9	4	11	12	1							7	3										
12		2		6		5	10	8	9	4	11		1							7	3										
13		2		6		5	10	8	9	4	11		1							7	3										
14		2		6		5	10	8	9	4	11		1							7	3										
15		2		6		5	10	8	9	4	11		1							7	3										
16		2		6		5		8	9	4	12				11					7*	3	1	10								
17		2		6		5		8	9	4	11				10					7	3	1									
18		2		6		5		8		4	12	11				9				7*	3	1	10								
19		2		6		5		8	11	12	7					10				3	1	4	9*								
20		4		2		5	10	7	11								8	3	1	6	9										
21		4		2		5	10	7*	11	1	6	12					8	3			9										
22		4		2		5	10	7*	12	11	1	8	9							3		6									
23	1	2		4	5	6	10	7	11								8	3				9									
24	1	2	6	12	5*		8	10	7	11								3				9	4								
25	1	2	6	5*		8	10	7	11								9	3				4	12								
26	1	2	6		8	10	7	11									3				9	4*	5								
27		2	6	9	8	10	7*	11									3				4	5	1	12							
28		2	6	9	8	10	11				7						3	12			4	5	1*								
29		2	6	9	8	10	11									3*		12				4	5	1	7						
30		2	6	9	8	12	10	11									3					4	5	1	7*						
31		2	6	7	8	10	12	11								9	3*					4	5	1							
32	2*	6		7	8	10	12				11					9	3					4	5	1							
33		2	6	7	5	8	10		11*							9	3			12		4	1								
34		2	6	7	5	8	10	12								9	11*			3		4	1								
35		2	6	7	5	8	10									9	3				11	4	1								
36		2		7	8	10	12									9	3				11	6*	4	5	1						
37		2	5	8	10	11	12									9*	3				7	4	6	1							
38	1	2	12	5	8	10	7	11								3*	9	4	6												
39	1	2	3	5	8	10	7	11						12		9*	4	6													
40	1	2	3	5	8	10	7				12					11*	9	4	6												
41	1		3	5	10	7	11					8				9	4	6	2												
42		2	3		10	11	8					9		7	4	5	1	6													
App	16	28	15	8	38	14	23	15	35	40	32	23	9	7	10	1	13	8	2	15	32	7	1	6	6	6	9	19	11	12	2
Sub			2					1	4	7	4				2	1						2	1			1	1				
Gls	1				1	4	3	15	5	4						4				1	1		2	1							

2 own-goals

	Bonetti P	Wilkins G	Nutton M	Hay D	Harris R	Droy M	Wicks S	Swain K	Wilkins R	Langley T	Stanley G	Walker C	Britton I	Phillips J	Lewington R	Garner W	Aylott T	Locke G	Frost L	McKenzie D	Stride D	Iles R	Johnson G	Bumstead J	Fillery M	Osgood P	Bannon E	Sitton J	Borota P	Docherty J	Chivers G	
	1	2			6	5			4	12	11	7					8*	3		10			9									3
	1	1			1	1			1		1	1					1	1		1			1									
										1																						

	Bonetti P	Wilkins G	Nutton M	Hay D	Harris R	Droy M	Wicks S	Swain K	Wilkins R	Langley T	Stanley G	Walker C	Britton I	Phillips J	Lewington R	Garner W	Aylott T	Locke G	Frost L	McKenzie D	Stride D	Iles R	Johnson G	Bumstead J	Fillery M	Osgood P	Bannon E	Sitton J	Borota P	Docherty J	Chivers G	
	1			4	3	5	6	7	8	9	10	11					2															2
	1			1	1	1	1	1	1	1	1	1					1															
										1																						

321

1979-80

Manager: Geoff Hurst

1	Aug	18	(h)	Sunderland	D 0-0		23,636
2		20	(a)	West Ham U	W 1-0	Johnson	31,627
3		25	(h)	Wrexham	W 3-1	Harris, Britton, Bumstead	18,732
4	Sep	1	(a)	Newcastle U	L 1-2	Fillery	25,320
5		8	(h)	Birmingham C	L 1-2	Walker	17,182
6		15	(h)	Shrewsbury T	L 0-3		9,271
7		22	(h)	Watford	W 2-0	Johnson 2	21,480
8		29	(a)	Cambridge U	W 1-0	Johnson	8,792
9	Oct	6	(a)	Burnley	W 1-0	Langley	8,341
10		13	(h)	Bristol R	W 1-0	Chivers	18,236
11		20	(a)	Cardiff C	W 2-1	Fillery, Frost	16,328
12		27	(h)	Fulham	L 0-2		30,567
13	Nov	3	(a)	Sunderland	L 1-2	Johnson	24,988
14		10	(a)	Orient	W 7-3	Fillery, Britton, Frost 3 (1 pen), Walker 2	13,005
15		14	(h)	West Ham U	W 2-1	Fillery, Frost	30,859
16		17	(h)	Charlton A	W 3-1	Fillery, Britton 2 (2 pens)	23,035
17		24	(a)	Notts C	W 3-2	Britton, Walker 2	12,646
18	Dec	1	(h)	Preston NE	W 2-0	Droy, Britton	21,192
19		8	(a)	Oldham A	L 0-1		10,201
20		15	(h)	Swansea C	W 3-0	Langley, Johnson, Bumstead	18,065
21		18	(a)	Queen's Park R	D 2-2	Langley, Bumstead	26,568
22		26	(h)	Leicester C	W 1-0	Fillery	25,320
23		29	(a)	Wrexham	L 0-2		15,641
24	Jan	1	(a)	Luton T	D 3-3	Fillery, Britton, Walker	19,717
25		12	(h)	Newcastle U	W 4-0	Langley, Fillery, Walker, Barton (og)	32,281
26	Feb	2	(h)	Shrewsbury T	L 2-4	Langley 2	18,120
27		9	(a)	Watford	W 3-2	Johnson, Britton, Walker	24,716
28		16	(h)	Cambridge U	D 1-1	Fillery	17,112
29		23	(a)	Bristol R	L 0-3		14,176
30	Mar	1	(h)	Cardiff C	W 1-0	Walker	18,449
31		8	(a)	Fulham	W 2-1	Walker 2	22,348
32		11	(a)	Birmingham C	L 1-5	Langley	27,297
33		15	(h)	Burnley	W 2-1	Harris, Langley	16,188
34		22	(h)	Orient	W 1-0	Britton	19,706
35		29	(a)	Charlton A	W 2-1	Langley, Britton	16,425
36	Apr	2	(h)	Queen's Park R	L 0-2		31,035
37		5	(a)	Leicester C	L 0-1		25,826
38		7	(h)	Luton T	D 1-1	Lee	28,078
39		12	(a)	Preston NE	D 1-1	Fillery	13,069
40		17	(h)	Notts C	W 1-0	Chivers	24,002
41		26	(a)	Swansea C	D 1-1	Langley	18,016
42	May	3	(h)	Oldham A	W 3-0	Fillery, Walker	28,253

FINAL LEAGUE POSITION: 4th in Division Two

Appearances
Sub Appearances
Goals

FA Cup

3	Jan	14	(h)	Wigan A	L 0-1	22,300

Appearances
Sub Appearances
Goals

League Cup

2	Aug	28	(a)	Plymouth A	D 2-2	Fillery 2	10,802
	Sep	4	(h)	Plymouth A	L 1-2	Droy	14,112

Aggregate League attendances:
Home: 481,528 (average 22,929)
Away: 384,348 (average 18,302)

Appearances
Sub Appearances
Goals

Borota P	Locke G	Wilkins G	Nutton M	Droy M	Harris R	Bannon E	Langley T	Johnson G	Fillery M	Stride D	Chivers G	Britton I	Osgood P	Iles R	Sparrow J	Bumstead J	Rhoades-Brown P	Sitton J	Frost L	Aylott T	Walker C	Hales K	Pates C	Rofe D	Lee C	Viljoen C	
1	2	3	4	5	6		8	9	10	11		7															1
1	2		4	5	6		8	9	10	11		3	7														2
1	2	4		5	6		8	9		11		3	7		12				10*								3
1		3		5	6		8	9		11		2	7		4			12	10*								4
1	2	3	6	5				9		11	12	8*		4					10	7							5
1	2	3	6	5		8*	9	10	11			7		4					12								6
1	2	3*	6	5	12		9	10	8			7		4					11								7
1	2	3	6*	5	11		9	10	8			7		4					12								8
1	2		5	11		9	10	8		6	7		4*					12									9
1	2		5	11		9	10	8	3	6	7		4														10
1	2	3		5	11			10	8		6	7		4		9											11
1	2	3		5	11	6*	9	10	8		7		4					12									12
1	2	3		5*	11	9	10	8			7		4					12									13
1	2	3		11		8		6	7		4*		9		10	12	5										14
1	2		5	11		8		6	7	3	4		9		10												15
1	2		5	11	12	8		6	7	3*	4		9		10												16
1	2	3	5	11		8		6	7		4		9		10												17
1	2	3	5	11		8		6	7		4		9		10												18
1	2	3	5	11		8		6	7		4		9		10*	5											19
1	2		11		9	12	8		6	7		3	4		10*	5											20
1	2		11	9		8		6	7		3	4		10	5												21
1	2		5	11	9		8		6	7		3	4		10												22
1	2		5	11*	9		8		6	7		3	4	12		10											23
1	2		11	9		8		4	7		3	6		10	5												24
1	2		5	11	9		8		6	7		3	4		10												25
1	2		5	11	9	12	8		6	7		3	4*		10												26
1	2		5	11	9	4	8		6	7		3			10												27
1	2		11	9	4	8		6	7		3*			12	10	5											28
	2		11	4		8		6	7	1				9	10	5	3										29
1	2	6		11	9		8		7						12	4*	5	3	10								30
1		2	6	5	11	9		8		7					4	12	3	10*									31
1		2	6	5	11	9	12	8		7					10	4*		3									32
1		2	6		11	9		8		7					10		5	3		4							33
1	2		6	5	11	9*		8		7				12	10			3		4							34
1	2		6		11	9			12	7			8*		10	4	5	3									35
1	2		6		11	9		8		7			12		10	4*	5	3									36
1		6			9		8	2	7			12		10	4*	5	3		11								37
1		6		11	9		12	2	7					10		5	3*	8	4								38
1		6		11	9		8	2	7			4		12		5	3	10*									39
1		6		11	9		8	2	7			4		10*		5	3	12									40
1		6	12	11*	9		8	2	7			4		10		5	3										41
1		6	12	11	9		8	2	7			4*		10		5	3										42
41	32	18	19	26	38	6	35	12	40	3	27	41	1	1	11	27	1		8	3	29	5	16	14	4	4	
		2	1		1	3	1		2						1	3	1	2		7	2			1			
		1	2		10	7	11		2	10				2	10				3			5	13			1		

1 own-goal

Borota P	Locke G	Wilkins G	Nutton M	Droy M	Harris R	Bannon E	Langley T	Johnson G	Fillery M	Stride D	Chivers G	Britton I	Osgood P	Iles R	Sparrow J	Bumstead J	Rhoades-Brown P	Sitton J	Frost L	Aylott T	Walker C	Hales K	Pates C	Rofe D	Lee C	Viljoen C	
1	2			11		9	12	8		6	7		3						10	4*	5						3
1	1			1		1	1	1		1	1		1						1	1	1						
					1																						

Borota P	Locke G	Wilkins G	Nutton M	Droy M	Harris R	Bannon E	Langley T	Johnson G	Fillery M	Stride D	Chivers G	Britton I	Osgood P	Iles R	Sparrow J	Bumstead J	Rhoades-Brown P	Sitton J	Frost L	Aylott T	Walker C	Hales K	Pates C	Rofe D	Lee C	Viljoen C	
1	2	4		5	6	8	9		11	3		7			12					10*							2
1				5	12	8	9			2	7*		3	4		6		10	11								
2	1	1		2	1	2	2		1	1	1	2		1	1		1		2	1							
					1							2			1												

1980-81

Manager: Geoff Hurst

1	Aug	16	(h)	Wrexham	D	2-2	Fillery, Rhoades-Brown	20,001
2		20	(a)	Derby C	L	2-3	Johnson, Walker	20,353
3		23	(a)	Shrewsbury T	D	2-2	Fillery, Walker	7,370
4		30	(h)	Queen's Park R	D	1-1	Chivers	23,381
5	Sep	6	(h)	West Ham U	L	0-1		32,669
6		13	(a)	Cambridge U	W	1-0		9,474
7		20	(h)	Preston NE	D	1-1	Lee	13,775
8		27	(a)	Watford	W	3-2	Walker 2, Lee	19,802
9	Oct	4	(a)	Bolton W	W	3-2	Fillery, Lee 2	11,888
10		8	(h)	Bristol R	W	2-0	Walker, R.Lee (og)	13,108
11		11	(h)	Grimsby T	W	3-0	Walker, Lee 2	16,206
12		18	(a)	Blackburn R	D	1-1	Walker	15,503
13		21	(a)	Orient	W	1-0	Fillery	11,950
14		25	(h)	Newcastle U	W	6-0	Chivers, Fillery, Walker, Lee 3	22,916
15		31	(a)	Cardiff C	W	1-0	Hutchings	8,489
16	Nov	8	(h)	Oldham A	W	1-0	Lee	19,327
17		12	(h)	Derby C	L	1-3	Lee	19,449
18		15	(a)	Wrexham	W	4-0	Britton, Walker, Lee, Driver	7,953
19		22	(h)	Sheffield W	W	2-0	Walker, Lee	24,947
20		30	(a)	Notts C	D	1-1	Bumstead	14,459
21	Dec	6	(h)	Swansea C	D	0-0		20,067
22		13	(a)	Grimsby T	L	0-2		14,708
23		20	(h)	Orient	L	0-1		15,940
24		26	(a)	Luton T	L	0-2		16,006
25		27	(h)	Bristol C	D	0-0		18,514
26	Jan	10	(a)	Sheffield W	D	0-0		25,113
27		17	(a)	Queen's Park R	L	0-1		22,873
28		31	(h)	Shrewsbury T	W	3-0	Fillery, Lee (pen), Mayes	14,673
29	Feb	7	(h)	Cambridge U	W	3-0	Droy, Mayes 2	16,704
30		14	(a)	West Ham U	L	0-4		35,164
31		21	(h)	Watford	L	0-1		19,153
32		28	(a)	Preston NE	L	0-1		8,129
33	Mar	7	(h)	Bolton W	W	2-0	Walker, Mayes	12,948
34		14	(a)	Bristol R	L	0-1		7,565
35		21	(h)	Blackburn R	D	0-0		14,314
36		28	(a)	Newcastle U	L	0-1		17,392
37	Apr	4	(h)	Cardiff C	L	0-1		11,569
38		11	(a)	Oldham A	D	0-0		6,740
39		18	(a)	Bristol C	D	0-0		9,764
40		20	(h)	Luton T	L	0-2		12,868
41		25	(a)	Swansea C	L	0-3		16,063
42	May	2	(h)	Notts C	L	0-2		13,324

FINAL LEAGUE POSITION: 12th in Division Two

Appearances
Sub Appearances
Goals

FA Cup

3	Jan	3	(a)	Southampton	L	1-3	Lee	23,694

Appearances
Sub Appearances
Goals

League Cup

2	Aug	27	(a)	Cardiff C	L	0-1		6,549
	Sep	3	(h)	Cardiff C	D	1-1	Droy	12,959

Aggregate League attendances:
Home: 373,833 (average 17,896)
Away: 306,020 (average 14,572)

Appearances
Sub Appearances
Goals

Appearance grid — columns left to right: Borota P, Wilkins G, Rofe D, Bumstead J, Droy M, Chivers G, Britton I, Fillery M, Johnson G, Walker C, Rhoades-Brown P, Nutton M, Viljoen C, Elmes T, Lee C, Pates C, Frost L, Clare J, Driver P, Hutchings C, Locke G, Mayes A.

Borota P	Wilkins G	Rofe D	Bumstead J	Droy M	Chivers G	Britton I	Fillery M	Johnson G	Walker C	Rhoades-Brown P	Nutton M	Viljoen C	Elmes T	Lee C	Pates C	Frost L	Clare J	Driver P	Hutchings C	Locke G	Mayes A	No.
1	2	3	4	5	6	7	8	9*	10	11		12										1
1	2	3	4	5	6	7	8	9	10	11												2
1	2	3	4	5	6	7	8	9*	10	12	11											3
1	2	3	12		6	7	8		10*	11		4		9	5							4
1	2	3	4*		12	7	8		10		5	11		9	6							5
1	2	3	4	5	11	7	8		10		6			9								6
1	2	3	4	5	11	7	8*		10	12	6			9								7
1	2	3	4	5	6	7	8		10	11				9								8
1	2	3	4		6	7	8		10*	11				9	5		12					9
1	2	3	4		6	7*	8		10	11				9	5		12					10
1	2	3	4		6	7	8		10	11				9	5*		12					11
1		3	4	2		7*	8		10	11	6			9	5		12					12
1		3	4		6		8		10	11	2			9	5			7				13
1		3	4	5	2	12	8		10*	11	6			9				7				14
1		3	4	5	6		8*		10	11	2			9				7	12			15
1		3	4	5	6				10	11	2			9				7	8			16
1		3	4	5	6*		8		10	11	2			9				7	12			17
1	2	3	4	5			7		10	11	6*			9			12	8				18
1		3	4	5	6	7			10	11	2*			9			12	8				19
1		3	4	5	6	8			10	11				9				7	2			20
1		3	4	5	6	8			10	11				9				7	2			21
1		3	4	5	6	7	8		10	11*				9			12		2			22
1	3*		4	5	6	7	8		10	11				9			12		2			23
1		3	4				8			6*		12		9	5			7	11	2	10	24
1		3	4		6		8				12	11		9	5			7*		2	10	25
1		3		5	6	7	8		10	11*		4		9			12		2			26
1		3	4	5	6	7	8		10	11*		12							2	9		27
1		3	4	5	6		8		10			7		9					2	11		28
1		3	4	5	6		8		10			7		9					2	11		29
1		3	4	5	6		8			11		7*		9			12		2	10		30
1		3	4*	5	6		8		12	11		7		9					2	10		31
1		3	4	5	6	7	8		10	9		11*					12		2			32
1		3	4	5	6	7*	8		10	11							12		2	9		33
1		3	4	5	6	7	8		10	11*							12		2	9		34
1		3	4	5	6	7	8		10	11*		12							2	9		35
1		3	4	5	6		8*		10	11				9			7	12	2			36
1		3	4	5	6		8		10	11				9			7		2			37
1			4	5	6		8			2				9	3		7	11		10		38
1			4	5*	6		8			2				9	3		7	11	12	10		39
1		3	4		6		8			12	5			9	2				11	7	10*	40
1	3		4		6	8	12		10	11	5*			9	2			7				41
1	3		4		6	7	8		10	12		11		9	5			2*				42
42	14	38	40	30	39	27	35	3	35	30	18	6	2	34	15		12	8	21	13		
		1		1	1	1			2	4		1	2	1			1	11	4	1		
		1	1	2	1	6	1	11	1			15					1	1		4		

1 own-goal

Borota P	Wilkins G	Rofe D	Bumstead J	Droy M	Chivers G	Britton I	Fillery M	Johnson G	Walker C	Rhoades-Brown P	Nutton M	Viljoen C	Elmes T	Lee C	Pates C	Frost L	Clare J	Driver P	Hutchings C	Locke G	Mayes A	No.
1		3	4*	5	6	7	8		10	11				9				12		2		3
1		1	1	1	1	1	1		1	1				1				1				
																	1					
														1								

Borota P	Wilkins G	Rofe D	Bumstead J	Droy M	Chivers G	Britton I	Fillery M	Johnson G	Walker C	Rhoades-Brown P	Nutton M	Viljoen C	Elmes T	Lee C	Pates C	Frost L	Clare J	Driver P	Hutchings C	Locke G	Mayes A	No.
1	2	3	4	5	6	7	8	9*	10		11			12								2
1	2	3	4	5*	6	7	8		12			11		9	10							
2	2	2	2	2	2	2	2	1	1		1	1		1	1							
				1										1								
			1																			

1981-82

Manager: John Neal

1	Aug	29	(h)	Bolton W	W 2-0	Droy, Lee	16,606
2	Sep	5	(a)	Cardiff C	W 2-1	Mayes 2	8,898
3		12	(h)	Watford	L 1-3	Walker	20,036
4		19	(a)	Shrewsbury T	L 0-1		5,616
5		23	(h)	Charlton A	D 2-2	Driver 2	15,329
6		26	(h)	Norwich C	W 2-1	Bumstead (pen), Driver	14,509
7		28	(a)	Orient	W 2-0	Mayes, Fillery	9,698
8	Oct	3	(a)	Cambridge U	L 0-1		8,806
9		10	(h)	Wrexham	W 2-0	Lee, Fillery	14,710
10		16	(a)	Leicester C	D 1-1	Fillery	18,358
11		24	(h)	Barnsley	L 1-2	Mayes	15,236
12		31	(a)	Rotherham U	L 0-6		10,145
13	Nov	7	(h)	Newcastle U	W 2-1	Lee, Fillery	16,059
14		14	(a)	Oldham A	L 0-1		9,773
15		21	(h)	Grimsby T	D 1-1	Lee	11,931
16		24	(a)	Charlton A	W 4-3	Walker 2, Bumstead 2	11,082
17		28	(a)	Derby C	D 1-1	Walker	13,963
18	Dec	5	(h)	Sheffield W	W 2-1	Lee, Hales	17,033
19		19	(h)	Blackburn R	D 1-1	Lee	11,768
20		26	(a)	Queen's Park R	W 2-0	Walker, Mayes	22,022
21	Jan	16	(h)	Bolton W	D 2-2	Bumstead, Mayes	7,278
22		30	(h)	Shrewsbury T	W 3-1	Walker 3	11,446
23	Feb	6	(a)	Watford	L 0-1		17,001
24		17	(h)	Cardiff C	W 1-0	Walker	9,710
25		20	(a)	Norwich C	L 1-2	Walker	16,018
26		27	(a)	Wrexham	L 0-1		3,935
27	Mar	9	(h)	Leicester C	W 4-1	Locke, Mayes 2, Hales	10,586
28		12	(a)	Barnsley	L 1-2	Lee	12,706
29		16	(h)	Crystal P	L 1-2	Mayes	13,894
30		19	(h)	Rotherham U	L 1-4	Rhoades-Brown	11,900
31		26	(a)	Newcastle U	L 0-1		26,887
32	Apr	3	(h)	Oldham A	D 2-2	Mayes 2	8,938
33		7	(h)	Cambridge U	W 4-1	Lee 2, Fillery, Hutchings	6,196
34		10	(h)	Queen's Park R	W 2-1	Droy, Lee	18,365
35		12	(a)	Crystal P	W 1-0	Walker	17,189
36		17	(a)	Grimsby T	D 3-3	Walker 3	9,164
37		20	(a)	Luton T	D 2-2	Walker, Fillery	16,185
38		24	(h)	Derby C	L 0-2		11,005
39	May	1	(a)	Sheffield W	D 0-0		19,259
40		5	(h)	Orient	D 2-2	Lee, Mayes	6,009
41		8	(h)	Luton T	L 1-2	Walker	15,044
42		15	(a)	Blackburn R	D 1-1	Pates	6,133

FINAL LEAGUE POSITION: 12th in Division Two

Appearances
Sub Appearances
Goals

FA Cup

3	Jan	18	(h)	Hull C	D 0-0		14,899
R		21	(a)	Hull C	W 2-0	Bumstead, Mayes	13,238
4		23	(h)	Wrexham	D 0-0		17,226
R		26	(a)	Wrexham	D 1-1*	Mayes	8,655
2R	Feb	1	(a)	Wrexham	W 2-1	Droy, Mayes	10,647
5		13	(h)	Liverpool	W 2-0	Lee, Rhoades-Brown	41,412
6	Mar	6	(h)	Tottenham H	L 2-3	Mayes, Fillery	42,557

*After extra-time

Appearances
Sub Appearances
Goals

League Cup

2	Oct	6	(a)	Southampton	D 1-1	Fillery	16,901
		28	(h)	Southampton	W 2-1	Walker, Fillery	27,370
3	Nov	11	(a)	Wigan A	L 2-4	Bumstead, Fillery	12,068

Aggregate League attendances:
Home: 275,802 (average 13,133)
Away: 270,206 (average 12,866)

Appearances
Sub Appearances
Goals

Borota P	Locke G	Rofe D	Viljoen C	Droy M	Pates C	Walker C	Bumstead J	Lee C	Mayes A	Fillery M	Driver P	Chivers G	Iles R	Wilkins G	Hutchings C	Nutton M	Britton I	Hales K	Rhoades-Brown P	Francis S	Canoville P	
1	2	3	4	5	6	7	8*	9	10	11	12											1
1	2	3	4	5*	6	7	8	9	10	11	12											2
1	2	3	4		5*	7	8	9	10	11	12	6										3
1	2	3	4		5	7	8	9	10*	11	12	6										4
	2	3*	4		5		8	9	10	11	7	6	1						12			5
1	2				5		8	9	10	11	7	6			3				4			6
1	2				5		8	9	10	11	7	6			3				4			7
1	2				5	12	8	9	10	11	7*	6			3				4			8
1	2		4		5			9	10	11		6			3		8		7			9
1	2		4	12	5			9	10*	11		6			3		8		7			10
1	2			12	5		4	9	10	11		6			3		8*		7			11
1			4	5	6	10	8	9	12	11		2			3				7*			12
1					5	10	8	9		11		6		2	3	4			7			13
				12	5	10	8	9		11		6		2	3	4*			7	1		14
				5	6	10	8	9	12	11		2			3	4*			7	1		15
				5	6	10	8	9	7	11		2			3	4				1		16
				5	6	10	8	9	7	11		2			3	4				1		17
				5	6	10	8	9	7	11		2*			3	4	12			1		18
				5	6	10	8	9	7	11		2			3	4				1		19
				5	6	10	8	9	7	11		2			3	4				1		20
				5	6	10	8	9	7	11		2			3	4				1		21
	2			5	6	10	8		7	11*					3	12	4		9	1		22
	2			5	6	10	8*	9	7	12					3	4			11	1		23
	2			5	6	10		9		11					3	4	8		7	1		24
	2			5*	6	10		9	12	11					3	4	8		7	1		25
	2				6	10		9	12	11		5			3	4	8*		7	1		26
	2				6	10		9		11		5			3	4	8		7	1		27
	2				6	12		9	10	11		5			3	4	8*		7	1		28
	2				6*	12		9	10	11		5			3	4	8		7	1		29
	2				6	12		9	10	11		5			3	4	8*		7	1		30
	2		8		6	12		9	10	11		5			3	4			7*	1		31
	2				6	8		9	10	11		5			3	4			7	1		32
				5	6	9*	2		10	11		8			3	4	12		7	1		33
	3			5	6	9	2		10			8		12		4	11		7*	1		34
	2				6	8*		9	10	11		5			3	4	7			1	12	35
	2				6	9	5		10	11		8			3	4	7			1		36
	2				6	9	5		10	11		8			3	4	7			1		37
	2				8	9	5		10	11		6*			3	4	7		12	1		38
	2			12	5	6		9	10	11		8			3	4*			7	1		39
	2		3*	5	6	7		9	10	11		12				4	8					40
	2			5	6	9	4		10	11		8			3				7*	1	12	41
	2			5	4	8*		9	10	11		6			3		12			1	7	42
12	31	6	9	20	42	31	21	40	35	39	4	28	1	10	35	17	17	10	24	29	1	—
	1		3		5				4	1	4	1		1			2	1	3		2	—
1		2	1		16	4	11	12	6	3					1				2	1		—

Borota P	Locke G	Rofe D	Viljoen C	Droy M	Pates C	Walker C	Bumstead J	Lee C	Mayes A	Fillery M	Driver P	Chivers G	Iles R	Wilkins G	Hutchings C	Nutton M	Britton I	Hales K	Rhoades-Brown P	Francis S	Canoville P	
				5	6	10	8	9	7*	11		2			3	4	12			1		3
	2				6	10	8	9	7	11		5			3	4				1		R
	2				6	10	8	9	7	11		5			3	4				1		4
	2			5	6	10	8	9	7	11					3	4*	12			1		R
	2			5	6	10	8	9	7						3	4			11	1		2R
	2			5	6	10		9				3			4		8		7	1		5
	2		12		6	10*	8	9		11		5			3	4			7	1		6
	6			4	7	7	6	6	6	6		3			1	7	3		5	3	7	—
	1								1	1		1			4	1				2		—
				1											1					1		—

Borota P	Locke G	Rofe D	Viljoen C	Droy M	Pates C	Walker C	Bumstead J	Lee C	Mayes A	Fillery M	Driver P	Chivers G	Iles R	Wilkins G	Hutchings C	Nutton M	Britton I	Hales K	Rhoades-Brown P	Francis S	Canoville P	
	2		4		5			9	10	11		6			3		8		7	1		2
1	2*		4	12	5	10	8	9		11		6			3				7			—
				12	5	10	8	9		11		6		2*	3	4			7	1		3
1	2		2		3	2	2	3	1	3		3		1	3	2			3	2		—
			2																			—
				1	1				3													—

327

1982-83

Manager: John Neal

1	Aug	28	(a)	Cambridge U	W 1-0	Robson	8,124
2		31	(h)	Wolves	D 0-0		14,192
3	Sep	4	(h)	Leicester C	D 1-1	Droy	14,127
4		8	(a)	Derby C	L 0-1		8,075
5		11	(a)	Newcastle U	D 1-1	Lee	29,084
6		18	(h)	Oldham A	W 2-0	Speedie 2	10,263
7		25	(a)	Sheffield W	L 2-3	Lee, Fillery (pen)	18,833
8	Oct	2	(h)	Grimsby T	W 5-2	Droy, Bumstead, Fillery, Speedie 2	10,019
9		9	(h)	Leeds U	D 0-0		25,358
10		16	(a)	Blackburn R	L 0-3		6,062
11		23	(h)	Charlton A	W 3-1	Pates, Bumstead, Robson	14,492
12		30	(a)	Carlisle U	L 1-2	Lee	7,141
13	Nov	6	(h)	Crystal P	D 0-0		15,169
14		13	(a)	Barnsley	D 1-1	Fillery	13,286
15		20	(h)	Shrewsbury T	L 1-2	Lee	8,690
16		27	(a)	Rotherham U	L 0-1		8,793
17	Dec	4	(h)	Burnley	W 2-1	Droy, Speedie	8,184
18		11	(a)	Middlesbrough	L 1-3	Fillery (pen)	8,836
19		18	(h)	Bolton W	W 2-1	Pates, Deakin (og)	6,903
20		27	(a)	Queen's Park R	W 2-1	Walker, Speedie	23,744
21		28	(h)	Fulham	D 0-0		29,797
22	Jan	1	(a)	Shrewsbury T	L 0-2		7,545
23		3	(a)	Leicester C	L 0-3		13,745
24		15	(h)	Cambridge U	W 6-0	Bumstead, Fillery 2, Mayes, Jones, Murray (og)	7,808
25		22	(a)	Wolves	L 1-2	Pates	19,533
26	Feb	5	(h)	Derby C	L 1-3	Pates	8,661
27		12	(a)	Grimsby T	L 1-2	Mayes	6,711
28		19	(a)	Leeds U	D 3-3	Walker, Fillery (pen), E.Gray (og)	19,365
29		26	(h)	Blackburn R	W 2-0	Walker, Rhoades-Brown	6,982
30	Mar	5	(a)	Charlton A	L 2-5	Lee, Robson	11,211
31		12	(h)	Carlisle U	W 4-2	Walker, Bumstead, Canoville 2	6,667
32		19	(a)	Crystal P	D 0-0		13,437
33		26	(h)	Barnsley	L 0-3		7,223
34	Apr	2	(a)	Fulham	D 1-1	Canoville	15,249
35		4	(h)	Queen's Park R	L 0-2		20,821
36		9	(a)	Oldham A	D 2-2	Fillery 2 (1 pen)	4,923
37		16	(h)	Newcastle U	L 0-2		13,446
38		23	(a)	Burnley	L 0-3		7,393
39		30	(h)	Rotherham U	D 1-1	Walker	8,674
40	May	2	(h)	Sheffield W	D 1-1	Speedie	10,462
41		7	(a)	Bolton W	W 1-0	Walker	8,687
42		14	(h)	Middlesbrough	D 0-0		19,340

FINAL LEAGUE POSITION: 18th in Division Two

Appearances
Sub Appearances
Goals

FA Cup

3	Jan	8	(a)	Huddersfield T	D 1-1	Mayes	17,064
R		12	(h)	Huddersfield T	W 2-0	Bumstead, Fillery	14,417
4		29	(a)	Derby C	L 1-2	Fillery	23,383

Appearances
Sub Appearances
Goals

League Cup

2	Oct	6	(h)	Tranmere R	W 3-1	Fillery (pen), Speedie 2	7,982
		28	(a)	Tranmere R	W 2-1	Robson 2	4,579
3	Nov	9	(a)	Notts C	L 0-2		8,852

Aggregate League attendances:
Home: 267,488 (average 12,737)
Away: 259,827 (average 12,372)

Appearances
Sub Appearances
Goals

Francis S	Nutton M	Hutchings C	Chivers G	Droy M	Pates C	Walker C	Bumstead J	Lee C	Robson B	Fillery M	Canoville P	McAndrew A	Speedie D	Driver P	Locke G	Rhoades-Brown P	Mayes A	Iles R	Hales K	Jones J	Falco M	Jones K	Williams P	
1	2	3	4	5	6	7*	8	9	10	11	12													1
1	2	3	4	5	6	7	8	9	10	11														2
1	2	3	4	5	6		8	9	10	11		7												3
1	2	3	4	5	6*		8	9	10	11	12	7												4
1	2	3	4	5			8	9	10*	11	7	6		12										5
1	2	3	4	5			8	9	12	11	7*	6	10											6
1	2	3	4	5			8	9	12	11	7*	6	10											7
1		3	4	5		9	8	2		11	7	6	10											8
1		3		5	4	9*	8		12	11	7	6	10		2									9
1	3			5	4		8		12	11			10	7	2	6*	9							10
1		3	6	5	4	7	8		9	11			10		2									11
1		3		5	4	7	8	12	9*				10		2	11				6				12
1		3	6	5	4	7	8	12	9*	11			10							2				13
1		3	6	5	4			9	8	11			10		2	7								14
1			6	5	4		8	9		11			10	12	2*	7				3				15
1		3		5		12	4	6		11			9*	7		8				2	10			16
1		3		5		12	4	6		11			9	7		8*				2	10			17
1		3		5		12	4	6		11			9	7		8*				2	10			18
1		3	4	5	6	12	8						9	7*		11	10			2				19
1		3	4	5	6	7	8						9			11	10			2				20
1		3	4	5	6	7	8			12			9			11	10*			2				21
1		3	4	5	6	7*	8	12		10			9			11				2				22
1		3	4	5	6	7	8	12		10			9			11*				2				23
1			4		5	12	8*	2		7			9			11	10		6	3				24
1			6		5	12	4	2		7			9*			11	10		8	3				25
1			6		5	10	4	2	8	7			9	12		11*				3				26
1		3			6	8		5		7			9	4		11	10			2				27
1		5	12		6	8		2		7			9	4*		11	10			3				28
1		3	2		6	8		5		7			9	4		11	10							29
1		3			6	8	12	5*	10	7	11		9	4						2				30
		3	5		6	8	4			7	11		9				10	1		2				31
1		3	5		6	8		4		7	11		9			10				2				32
1		3	5		6	8*	4	2			11		9			10			7			12		33
		3		5	6		8	4		7	11		9			10		1		2				34
		3		5	6		8	4		7	11		9			10*	12	1		2				35
		3			6			4		7	10		9			11	8	1		2			5	36
		3		5	6		8	4		7	11*					10	9	1		2		12		37
1			3	5	6		8	4			11		7	12		10	9*			2				38
1		3	4	5	6	11	10	9		7	12		8							2*				39
1		3	4	5	6	11	10	9		7			8							2				40
1		3	4	5	6	11	8	9		7	10									2				41
1		3	4	5	6	11	8	9		7	10									2				42
37	8	36	29	31	35	23	35	31	11	36	16	7	34	9	6	25	13	5	3	28	3		1	
			1			6	1	4	4	1	3			4			1					2		
				3	4	6	4	5	3	9	3		7			1	3			1				

3 own-goals

1			4	5	6	12	8	2		7			9*			11	10			3				3
1			4	5	6		8	2		7			9			11	10			3				R
1				5*	6	12	4	2		8			9			11	10		7	3				4
3			2	3	3		3	3		3			3			3	3		1	3				
						2																		
							1			2							1							

1		3	4	5		9	8	2*		11	7	6	10	12										2
1		3		5	4	7	8		9	11		6	10		2									
1		3	6	5	4		8	9	12	11	7		10*		2									3
3		3	2	3	2	2	3	2	1	3	2	2	3		2									
									1					1										
									2	1			2											

1983-84

Manager: John Neal

1	Aug	27	(h)	Derby C	W 5-0	Hutchings, Walker, Spackman, Dixon 2	17,338
2	Sep	3	(a)	Brighton & HA	W 2-1	Dixon 2 (1 pen)	20,874
3		7	(a)	Blackburn R	D 0-0		5,873
4		10	(h)	Cambridge U	W 2-1	Bumstead, Walker	14,425
5		17	(a)	Sheffield W	L 1-2	Walker	20,596
6		24	(h)	Middlesbrough	D 0-0		15,822
7	Oct	1	(a)	Huddersfield T	W 3-2	Dixon, Canoville	13,280
8		8	(a)	Fulham	W 5-3	Dixon 2, Lee, Jones, Nevin	24,787
9		15	(h)	Cardiff C	W 2-0	Lee, Nevin	15,459
10		22	(a)	Carlisle U	D 0-0		6,774
11		29	(h)	Charlton A	W 3-2	Dixon, Speedie 2	17,789
12	Nov	5	(a)	Oldham A	D 1-1	Bumstead	5,807
13		12	(h)	Newcastle U	W 4-0	Spackman, Speedie 2, Rhoades-Brown	30,628
14		15	(a)	Charlton A	D 1-1	Nevin	14,393
15		19	(h)	Crystal P	D 2-2	Hollins, Speedie	19,060
16		22	(a)	Swansea C	W 3-1	Bumstead, Dixon, Nevin	7,848
17		26	(a)	Leeds U	D 1-1	Dixon	20,680
18	Dec	3	(h)	Manchester C	L 0-1		29,142
19		6	(h)	Swansea C	W 6-1	Bumstead, Dixon, Canoville 3, Nevin	12,389
20		10	(a)	Barnsley	D 0-0		10,300
21		17	(h)	Grimsby T	L 2-3	Bumstead, Dixon (pen)	13,151
22		26	(a)	Shrewsbury T	W 4-2	Bumstead 2, Dixon (pen), Speedie	7,582
23		27	(h)	Portsmouth	D 2-2	Dixon, Canoville	25,409
24		31	(h)	Brighton & HA	W 1-0	Speedie	18,542
25	Jan	2	(a)	Middlesbrough	L 1-2	McAndrew	11,579
26		14	(a)	Derby C	W 2-1	McAndrew (pen), Cherry (og)	16,727
27		21	(h)	Sheffield W	W 3-2	Nevin, Thomas 2	35,147
28	Feb	4	(h)	Huddersfield T	W 3-1	Dixon 2, Speedie	17,922
29		11	(a)	Cambridge U	W 1-0	McAndrew	10,602
30		25	(h)	Carlisle U	D 0-0		16,543
31	Mar	3	(h)	Oldham A	W 3-0	Dixon, Speedie, McAndrew (pen)	12,736
32		10	(a)	Newcastle U	D 1-1	Speedie	36,506
33		16	(h)	Blackburn R	W 2-1	Speedie, Nevin	18,905
34		31	(a)	Cardiff C	D 3-3	Spackman (pen), Dixon, Lee	11,060
35	Apr	7	(h)	Fulham	W 4-0	Dixon 2, Speedie, Nevin	31,947
36		14	(a)	Crystal P	W 1-0	Nevin	20,540
37		21	(h)	Shrewsbury T	W 3-0	Dixon 2, Nevin	17,295
38		24	(a)	Portsmouth	D 2-2	Nevin (pen), Thomas	19,267
39		28	(h)	Leeds U	W 5-0	Dixon 3, Canoville, Thomas	33,447
40	May	4	(a)	Manchester C	W 2-0	Dixon, Nevin	21,713
41		7	(h)	Barnsley	W 3-1	Speedie, Nevin 2	29,541
42		12	(a)	Grimsby T	W 1-0	Dixon	13,995

FINAL LEAGUE POSITION: 1st in Division Two

Appearances
Sub Appearances
Goals

FA Cup

3	Jan	7	(a)	Blackburn R	L 0-1	10,994

Appearances
Sub Appearances
Goals

League Cup

1	Aug	30	(a)	Gillingham	W 2-1	Walker, Dixon	8,633
	Sep	13	(h)	Gillingham	W 4-0	Dixon 4	9,704
2	Oct	5	(a)	Leicester C	W 2-0	Dixon, Canoville	7,825
		25	(h)	Leicester C	L 0-2*		15,646
3	Nov	9	(h)	West Brom A	L 0-1		22,932

*After extra-time, Chelsea won 4-3 on penalties.

Aggregate League attendances:
Home: 442,668 (average 21,079)
Away: 320,783 (average 15,275)

Appearances
Sub Appearances
Goals

Appearances and goals grid (shirt numbers by match):

#	Niedzwieckie E	Hollins J	Hutchings C	Pates C	McLaughlin J	Bumstead J	Walker C	Speackman N	Dixon KM	Lee C	Canoville P	Speedie D	Jones J	Nevin P	Rhoades-Brown P	McAndrew A	Thomas M	Johnstone D	Jasper D	Dublin K
1	1	2	3	4	5	6	7	8	9	10	11									
2	1	2	3	4	5	6	7	8	9	10	11									
3	1	2	3	6	5	4	7*	8	9	10	11	12								
4	1	2		4	5	6	7	8	9	10	11			3						
5	1	2		4	5	6	7	8	9	10		12	3	11*						
6	1	2		4	5	6	7	8	9	10*		12	3	11						
7	1	2		4	5	6		8	9	10	7		3	11						
8	1	2		4	5	6		8	9	10	11	12	3	7*						
9	1	2		4	5	6		8	9	10	11		3	7						
10	1	2		4	5	6		8	9	10*	11	12	3	7						
11	1	2		4	5	6		8	9		7	10	3	11						
12	1	2		4	5	6		8	9	12	7	10*	3	11						
13	1	2		4	5	6		8	9	12		10	3	7	11*					
14	1	2	3	4	5	6		8	9			10	7	11						
15	1	2		4	5	6*		8	9	12		10	3	7	11					
16	1	2		4	5	6		8	9			10	3	7	11					
17	1	2		4	5	6		8	9	12		10	3	7	11*					
18	1	2		4	5	6		8	9	12		10	3	7	11*					
19	1	2		4	5	6		8	9		11	10	3	7						
20	1	2		4	5	6		8	9		11	10	3	7						
21	1	2		4	5	6		8	9	12	11	10*	3	7						
22	1	2		4	5	6			9		11	10	3	7		8				
23	1	2		4	5	6*			9	12	11	10	3	7		8				
24	1	2		4	5			8	9		11	10	3	7		6				
25	1	2		4	5			8	9	12	11*	10	3	7		6				
26	1			4	5			8	9	2		10	3	7		6	11			
27	1			4	5			8	9	2		10	3	7		6	11			
28	1			4	5			8	9	2		10	3	7		6	11			
29	1			4	5			8	9	2		10	3	7		6	11			
30	1	3		4	5			8	9	2		10		7		6*	11	12		
31	1	3		4	5			8	9	2		10		7		6	11			
32	1			4	5			8	9	2		10	3	7		6	11			
33	1			4	5			8	9	2		10	3	7		6	11*	12		
34	1			4		12		8	9	2		10	3	7		6*	11	5		
35	1			4	5	6		3	9	2		10	3	7			11			
36	1			4	5	6		8	9	2	12	10	3	7			11*			
37	1			4	5	6		8	9	2		10	3	7			11			
38	1			4	5	6		8	9	2		10	3	7			11			
39	1			4	5	6*		8	9	2	12	10	3	7			11			
40	1			4	5	6		8	9	2	12	10	3*	7			11			
41	1	2		4	5			8	9			10		7			11	6	3	
42	1	2		4	5	6		8	9			10		7			11	3		
	42	29	4	42	41	30	6	40	42	25	17	32	34	38	6	13	17	3	1	
					1							8	3	5		2				
		1	1			7	3	3	28	3	6	13	1	14	1	4	4			

1 own-goal

#	Niedzwieckie E	Hollins J	Hutchings C	Pates C	McLaughlin J	Bumstead J	Walker C	Speackman N	Dixon KM	Lee C	Canoville P	Speedie D	Jones J	Nevin P	Rhoades-Brown P	McAndrew A	Thomas M
3	1	2		4	5			8	9		11	10	3	7		6	
	1	1		1	1			1	1		1	1	1	1		1	

#	Niedzwieckie E	Hollins J	Hutchings C	Pates C	McLaughlin J	Bumstead J	Walker C	Speackman N	Dixon KM	Lee C	Canoville P	Speedie D	Jones J	Nevin P	Rhoades-Brown P
1	1	2	3	4	5	6		8	7	9	10	11			
	1	2		4	5	6	7	8	9	10		12	3		11*
2	1	2		4	5	6		8	9	10	7*	12	3	11	
	1	2		4	5			8	9	10	7	6	3	11	
3	1	2		4	5	6		8	9	12	7*	10	3	11	
	5	5	1	5	5	4	2	5	5	4	4	2	4	3	1
										1			1	1	
					1			6		1					

1984-85

Manager: John Neal

#	Date			Venue	Opponent	Result		Scorers	Attendance
1	Aug	25	(a)	Arsenal		D	1-1	Dixon	45,329
2		27	(h)	Sunderland		W	1-0	Canoville	25,554
3		31	(h)	Everton		L	0-1		17,734
4	Sep	5	(a)	Manchester U		D	1-1	Thomas	48,398
5		8	(a)	Aston Villa		L	2-4	Bumstead 2	21,494
6		15	(h)	West Ham U		W	3-0	Lee, Nevin, Speedie	32,411
7		22	(a)	Luton T		D	0-0		16,066
8		29	(h)	Leicester C		W	3-0	Nevin, Dixon 2	18,521
9	Oct	6	(a)	Norwich C		D	0-0		18,272
10		13	(h)	Watford		L	2-3	Dixon 2	25,340
11		20	(a)	Southampton		L	0-1		20,212
12		27	(h)	Ipswich T		W	2-0	Dixon 2	19,213
13	Nov	3	(h)	Coventry C		W	6-2	Dixon 3, Speedie, K.Jones 2	17,306
14		10	(a)	Newcastle U		L	1-2	Dixon	23,723
15		17	(h)	West Brom A		W	3-1	Rougvie, Speedie 2	17,573
16		24	(a)	Tottenham H		D	1-1	Dixon	31,197
17	Dec	1	(h)	Liverpool		W	3-1	McLaughlin, Dixon, Speedie	40,972
18		8	(a)	Sheffield W		D	1-1	Davies	29,373
19		15	(h)	Stoke C		D	1-1	Dixon	20,534
20		22	(a)	Everton		W	4-3	Pates, Davies 3	29,887
21		26	(a)	Queen's Park R		D	2-2	Dixon 2 (2 pens)	26,610
22		29	(h)	Manchester U		L	1-3	Davies	42,197
23	Jan	1	(h)	Nottingham F		W	1-0	Thomas	21,552
24		19	(h)	Arsenal		D	1-1	Speedie	34,752
25	Feb	2	(a)	Leicester C		D	1-1	Speedie (pen)	15,657
26		16	(h)	Newcastle U		W	1-0	Wood	21,806
27		23	(a)	Coventry C		L	0-1		11,430
28	Mar	2	(a)	Ipswich T		L	0-2		17,735
29		9	(h)	Southampton		L	0-2		15,202
30		16	(a)	Watford		W	3-1	Dixon, Speedie, McClelland (og)	16,316
31		30	(a)	Sunderland		W	2-0	Dixon, Thomas (pen)	13,489
32	Apr	6	(h)	Queen's Park R		W	1-0	Dixon	20,340
33		10	(a)	Nottingham F		L	0-2		14,666
34		13	(h)	West Ham U		D	1-1	Speedie	19,003
35		16	(h)	Aston Villa		W	3-1	Thomas (pen), Bumstead, Evans (og)	13,267
36		20	(a)	West Brom A		W	1-0	Dixon	11,196
37		27	(h)	Tottenham H		D	1-1	Nevin	26,310
38	May	4	(a)	Liverpool		L	3-4	Spackman (pen), Dixon, Davies	33,733
39		6	(h)	Sheffield W		W	2-1	Dixon 2	17,085
40		8	(h)	Luton T		W	2-0	Nevin, Dixon	13,789
41		11	(a)	Stoke C		W	1-0	Speedie	8,905
42		14	(h)	Norwich C		L	1-2	Thomas	22,882

FINAL LEAGUE POSITION: 6th in Division One

Appearances
Sub Appearances
Goals

FA Cup

3	Jan	5	(h)	Wigan A		D	2-2	Nevin, Speedie	16,220
R		26	(a)	Wigan A		W	5-0	Dixon 4 (1 pen), Speedie	9,708
4	Feb	4	(h)	Millwall		L	2-3	Spackman, Canoville	25,148

Appearances
Sub Appearances
Goals

League Cup

2	Sep	26	(h)	Millwall		W	3-1	Dixon 2, Nutton (og)	19,912
	Oct	9	(a)	Millwall		D	1-1	Dixon	11,157
3		30	(a)	Walsall		D	2-2	Lee, Nevin	11,102
R	Nov	6	(h)	Walsall		W	3-0	Dixon, Speedie, K.Jones	19,502
4		21	(h)	Manchester C		W	4-1	Dixon 3, K.Jones	26,364
5	Jan	28	(h)	Sheffield W		D	1-1	Speedie	36,038
R		30	(a)	Sheffield W		D	4-4*	Dixon, Canoville 2, Thomas	36,505
2R	Feb	6	(h)	Sheffield W		W	2-1	Speedie, Thomas	36,395
SF		13	(a)	Sunderland		L	0-2		32,440
	Mar	4	(h)	Sunderland		L	2-3	Nevin, Speedie	38,440

*After extra-time

Aggregate League attendances:
Home: 484,300 (average 23,061)
Away: 472,691 (average 22,509)

Appearances
Sub Appearances
Goals

Football appearance and scoring grid.

Niedzwieckie E	Lee C	Rougvie D	Pates C	McLaughlin J	Jasper D	Nevin P	Speckman N	Dixon KM	Speedie D	Canoville P	Jones K	Thomas M	Bumstead J	Wood D	Davies G	Johnstone D	Jones J	Francis S	Droy M	Dublin K	Isaac R	Howard T	No
1	2	3	4	5	6	7	8	9	10	11													1
1	2	3	4	5	6	7	8	9	10	11*				12									2
1	2	3	4	5	6*	7	8	9	10	11		12											3
1	2	3	4	5		7	8	9	10	12	11*	6											4
1	2	3	4	5		7	8	9*	10	12		11	6										5
1	2	3	4	5		7	8	9	10			11	6										6
1	2	3	4	5		7	8	9	10			11	6										7
1	2	3	4	5		7	8	9	10		6	11											8
1	2	3	4	5			8	9	10		6	11	7										9
1	2	3	4*	5		7	8	9	10		6	11	12										10
1	2*	3	4	5		7	8	9	10	11	12		6										11
1		3	4	5		7	8*	9	10	11	12		6	2									12
1	2	3	4	5		7	8	9	10	11		6											13
1	2	3	4	5*		7	8	9	10	11		6			12								14
1	2	3	4	5*		7	8	9	10	11		6			12								15
1	2	3	4	5		7	8	9	10	11		6											16
1		3	4	5		7	8	9*	10	11		6	12	2									17
1		3	4	5		7	8			11	6*		12	2	9	10							18
1		3	4	5		7	8	9		11*	6		2	10	12								19
1	12		4	5		7	8	9			6	11	2	10*		3							20
1	4			5		7*	8	9	12		6	11	2	10		3							21
1			4	5		7	8	9	12		6*	11	2	10		3							22
1		3	4	5		7	8	9	10			11	2	6									23
1	12	3	4	5		7*	8	9	10	11	6		2										24
1		3	4	5		7	8	9*	10	12		11	6		2								25
1		2	4		5	7	8	9			6		11	10*		3	12						26
1			4			7	8	9	10	12	6*		11	2		3	5						27
1		4			5	7	8	9	10	11		6	2			3*	12						28
1	5	4				7	8	9	10	6*		11	12	2			3						29
1						7	8	9	10			11	6	2			5			3	4		30
1		4				7	8	9		10	6	2	11				5			3			31
1		4	5			7	8	9	10		6	11	2				3						32
		4	5			7	8	9	10			11*	6	2	12	1	3						33
		4	5		11	7	8	9	10			6		2		1	3						34
1		4	5			7	8	9	10			11	6*		12		3			2			35
1		4*	5			7	8	9	10	12		11	6				3			2			36
1		4	5			7	8	9				11	6		10		3			2			37
1		4	5			7	8	9				11	6		10		12			3	2*		38
1	2	3		5		7	8	9	10	12		11*	6				4						39
1	2	3		5		7	8	9	10	12		11	6*				4						40
1	2		4	5		7	8	9	10*	12		11	6				3						41
1	2		4	5		7	8	9	10	12		11*	6				3						42
40	20	27	36	36	7	41	42	41	33	15	17	26	21	17	10	1	14	2	1	10	1	4	
2										2	9	2	1	4	2	2	1	2		1	1		
	1	1	1	1		4	1	24	10	1	2	5	3	1	6								

2 own-goals

Niedzwieckie E	Lee C	Rougvie D	Pates C	McLaughlin J	Jasper D	Nevin P	Speckman N	Dixon KM	Speedie D	Canoville P	Jones K	Thomas M	Bumstead J	Wood D	Davies G	Johnstone D	Jones J	Francis S	Droy M	Dublin K	Isaac R	Howard T	No
1		3	4	5		7	8	9	10			11	12	2	6*								3
1	2	3	4	5		7	8	9	10*	12		11	6										R
1			4	5		7	8		10	6		11		2	9	3							4
3	1	2	3	3		3	3	2	3	1		3		3	2	1							
												1			1								
	1			1		4		2	1														

Niedzwieckie E	Lee C	Rougvie D	Pates C	McLaughlin J	Jasper D	Nevin P	Speckman N	Dixon KM	Speedie D	Canoville P	Jones K	Thomas M	Bumstead J	Wood D	Davies G	Johnstone D	Jones J	Francis S	Droy M	Dublin K	Isaac R	Howard T	No
	2	3	4	5		7*	8	9	10	12		11	6				1						2
1	2	3	4	5			8	9	10			6	11	7									
1	2	3	4	5		7	8	9	10	11	12		6*										3
1	2	3	4	5		7	8	9	10	11		6											R
1	2	3	4	5		7	8	9	10	11*		6			12								4
1	2	3	4	5		7	8	9	10	12	6*	11											5
1	4*	3		5	6	7	8	9	10	12		11			2								R
1	2		4	5		7	8	9		6		11			3								2R
1	2		4	5*	12	7	8	9		6		11	10		3								SF
		3	4		5*	7	8	9	10	12		11	6		2								
9	9	8	9	9	2	9	10	10	9	5	4	7	5		4	1							
					1							4	1		1								
1				2		8	4	2	2	2													

1 own-goal

333

1985-86

Manager: John Hollins

1	Aug	17	(a)	Sheffield W	D	1-1	Speedie	26,164
2		20	(h)	Coventry C	W	1-0	Speedie	15,679
3		24	(h)	Birmingham C	W	2-0	Rougvie, Jones	16,534
4		28	(a)	Leicester C	D	0-0		11,248
5		31	(h)	West Brom A	W	3-0	Spackman (pen), Speedie 2	15,376
6	Sep	4	(a)	Tottenham H	L	1-4	Dixon	23,692
7		7	(a)	Luton T	D	1-1	Dixon	10,720
8		14	(h)	Southampton	W	2-0	Dixon, Canoville	15,711
9		21	(h)	Arsenal	W	2-1	Nevin, Spackman (pen)	33,241
10		28	(a)	Watford	L	1-3	Rougvie	16,035
11	Oct	5	(a)	Manchester C	W	1-0	Dixon	20,104
12		12	(h)	Everton	W	2-1	Dixon, Speedie	27,634
13		19	(a)	Oxford U	L	1-2	Dixon	12,072
14		26	(h)	Manchester U	L	1-2	McLaughlin	42,485
15	Nov	2	(a)	Ipswich T	W	2-0	Dixon, Speedie	15,324
16		9	(h)	Nottingham F	W	4-2	Dixon 2, Speedie, Hazard (pen)	17,743
17		16	(a)	Newcastle U	W	3-1	Spackman, Dixon, Speedie	22,355
18		23	(h)	Aston Villa	W	2-1	Dixon, Speedie	17,509
19		30	(a)	Liverpool	D	1-1	Nevin	38,382
20	Dec	7	(a)	Coventry C	D	1-1	Murphy	8,721
21		14	(h)	Sheffield W	W	2-1	Spackman, Speedie	19,658
22		21	(a)	Birmingham C	W	2-1	Nevin, Hagan (og)	10,594
23		28	(h)	Tottenham H	W	2-0	Spackman (pen), Dixon	37,115
24	Jan	11	(h)	Luton T	W	1-0	Speedie	21,102
25		18	(a)	West Brom A	W	3-0	Nevin, Speedie, Murphy	10,300
26	Feb	1	(h)	Leicester C	D	2-2	Jones, Shearer	12,372
27		8	(h)	Oxford U	L	1-4	Bumstead	16,182
28	Mar	8	(h)	Manchester C	W	1-0	Reid (og)	17,573
29		16	(a)	Everton	D	1-1	Murphy	30,145
30		19	(h)	Queen's Park R	D	1-1	Nevin	17,871
31		22	(a)	Southampton	W	1-0	Pates	15,509
32		29	(h)	West Ham U	L	0-4		29,955
33		31	(a)	Queen's Park R	L	0-6		18,584
34	Apr	5	(h)	Ipswich T	D	1-1	Speedie	13,072
35		9	(a)	Manchester U	W	2-1	Dixon 2	45,355
36		12	(a)	Nottingham F	D	0-0		18,055
37		15	(a)	West Ham U	W	2-1	Nevin, Spackman	29,361
38		19	(h)	Newcastle U	D	1-1	Nevin	18,970
39		26	(a)	Aston Villa	L	1-3	Spackman (pen)	17,770
40		29	(a)	Arsenal	L	0-2		24,025
41	May	3	(h)	Liverpool	L	0-1		43,900
42		5	(h)	Watford	L	1-5	Speedie	12,017

FINAL LEAGUE POSITION: 6th in Division One

Appearances
Sub Appearances
Goals

FA Cup

3	Jan	4	(a)	Shrewsbury T	W	1-0	Speedie	8,100
4		26	(h)	Liverpool	L	1-2	Speedie	33,625

Appearances
Sub Appearances
Goals

League Cup

2	Sep	25	(a)	Mansfield T	D	2-2	Nevin, Speedie	6,018
	Oct	9	(h)	Mansfield T	W	2-0	Dixon 2	11,664
3		29	(h)	Fulham	D	1-1	Hazard	19,699
R	Nov	6	(a)	Fulham	W	1-0	Dixon	20,190
4		26	(h)	Everton	D	2-2	Nevin, Dixon	27,544
R	Dec	11	(a)	Everton	W	2-1	McLaughlin, Dixon	26,373
5	Jan	22	(a)	Queen's Park R	D	1-1	Nevin	27,000
R		29	(h)	Queen's Park R	L	0-2*		27,937

*After extra-time

Appearances
Sub Appearances
Goals

Aggregate League attendances:
Home: 461,699 (average 21,985)
Away: 424,695 (average 20,233)

334

Niedzwieki E	Lee C	Rougvie D	Pates C	McLaughlin J	Bumstead J	Nevin P	Spackman N	Dixon KM	Speedie D	Murphy J	Jones K	Wood D	Dublin K	Isaac R	Davies G	McAllister K	Jasper D	Howard T	Canoville P	Hazard M	Shearer D	Millar J	Francis S	Godden A	Fridge L	Durie G	McNaught J	#
1	2	3	4	5	6	7	8*	9	10	11	12																	1
1	2	3	4	5	6	7		9	10	11	8																	2
1	2	3	4	5	6	7		9	10	11	8																	3
1	2	3	4	5	6	7	8	9	10	11																		4
1	2	3	4	5	6	7	8	9	10	11																		5
1	2	3	4	5	6	7	8	9	10	11*										12								6
1	2	3	4	5	6	7	8	9	10	11																		7
1		3	4	5	6*	7	8	9				2			10	12				11								8
1		3		5	6	7	12	9				2			4	10				11	8*							9
1		3	4	5	6	7*	11	9	10			2				12				8								10
1		3	4	5	6	7	11	9	10			2				12				8*								11
1		3	4	5	6	7	11	9	10			2								8								12
1	3*	4	5	6	7			9	10	11		2				12				8								13
1		3	4	5	6*	7	8	9	10		12			2						11								14
1			4	5	6	7	8	9	10			2			3					11								15
1			4	5		7	8	9	10		6	2		3						11								16
1			4	5	6	7	8	9	10			2		3						11								17
1			4	5	6	7	8	9	10			2		3						11*								18
1			4	5		7	8	9		11	6	2	3			10*			12									19
1			4	5		7	8	9	10	11*	6	2	3			12												20
1		3	4	5		7*	8	9	10		6	2				11			12									21
1		3	4	5	6*	7	8	9		11		2				10			12									22
1	2		4	5		7	8	9	10		6		3			11*			12									23
1	2		4	5	6	7	8	9	10				3							11								24
1	2		4	5	6	7	8	9	10*	11			3						12									25
1			5	4		6	7	8			12	2	3			10*				11	9							26
1			5	4		6	7	8	10			2								11	9	3						27
1	2*	3	4	5	6		12	9	10	11	8					7												28
1		3	4	5	6	7	8	9	10	11		2																29
1*	12	3	4	5	6	7	8	9	10	11		2																30
		3	4	5	6	7	8	9	10			2				11							1					31
	9	3	4	5	6*	7	8		10			2				11				12			1					32
	2	3	4	5		7*	8	9	10							11				12	6		1					33
			4	5	6	7	8	9	10	11			3					2						1				34
		3	4	5		7	8	9	10	11		2									6			1				35
			4	5		7	8	9	10	11		2									6		3	1				36
			4	5	6*	7	8	9		11						12					10		3	1				37
	3*	4	5	6	7	8	9			11		2				12					10	11		1				38
			4	5	6	12	8	9	10	11			3								7*		1					39
		3	4*	5	6	7	8	9	10	11	12	2											1					40
			4	5		7	8	9	10		6	2				12			11			3*	1			9	12	41
			4	5			8		10		6	2*				7			11			3			1	9	12	42
30	12	34	35	40	32	39	37	38	34	21	10	28	11	3	1	13		1	4	17	2	7	3	8	1	1		—
	1									1	2			4						7						1		—
		2	1	1	1	7	7	14	14	3	2									1	1	1						—

2 own-goals

League Cup

Niedzwieki E	Lee C	Rougvie D	Pates C	McLaughlin J	Bumstead J	Nevin P	Spackman N	Dixon KM	Speedie D	Murphy J	Jones K	Wood D	Dublin K	Isaac R	Davies G	McAllister K	Jasper D	Howard T	Canoville P	Hazard M	Shearer D	Millar J	Francis S	Godden A	Fridge L	Durie G	McNaught J	#
1		2	4	5		7	8	9	10		6		3						12	11*								3
1	2	5	4		6	7	8	9*	10	11			3						12									4
2	1	2	2	1	1	2	2	2	2	1	1		2						1	1								—
																			2									—
							2																					—

FA Cup

Niedzwieki E	Lee C	Rougvie D	Pates C	McLaughlin J	Bumstead J	Nevin P	Spackman N	Dixon KM	Speedie D	Murphy J	Jones K	Wood D	Dublin K	Isaac R	Davies G	McAllister K	Jasper D	Howard T	Canoville P	Hazard M	Shearer D	Millar J	Francis S	Godden A	Fridge L	Durie G	McNaught J	#
1		3	4	5	6	7	12	9	10			2								11*	8							2
1		3	4	5		7	11	9	10		6	2								8								3
1			4	5	6	7	8	9	10				3		2	11*			12									3
1			4			7	8	9	10		6	2	3		5	11*			12									R
1			4*	5	6	7	8	9	10			2	3			12	11											4
1		3	4	5		7	8	9	10	11	6	2																R
1	2	5	4		6	7*	8	9	10	11		3				12												5
1		5	4		6	7	8		10	11		2	3*			9			12									R
8	1	5	8	5	5	8	7	7	8	3	3	6	5	2		3	1		1	2								—
				1					1							1				2	2							—
			1		3							5	1			1												—

1986-87

Manager: John Hollins

1	Aug	23	(h)	Norwich C	D 0-0		19,887
2		25	(a)	Oxford U	D 1-1	Speedie	11,238
3		30	(a)	Sheffield W	L 0-2		25,853
4	Sep	2	(h)	Coventry C	D 0-0		11,839
5		6	(h)	Luton T	L 1-3	Dixon	13,040
6		13	(a)	Tottenham H	W 3-1	Dixon, Hazard 2 (1 pen)	28,202
7		20	(h)	Nottingham F	L 2-6	Bumstead, Nevin	20,171
8		28	(a)	Manchester U	W 1-0	Dixon	33,340
9	Oct	4	(h)	Charlton A	L 0-1		15,243
10		11	(a)	West Ham U	L 3-5	Bumstead, Dixon, Jones (pen)	26,859
11		18	(h)	Manchester C	W 2-1	Bumstead, Hazard	12,990
12		25	(a)	Arsenal	L 1-3	Bumstead	32,990
13	Nov	1	(h)	Watford	D 0-0		13,334
14		8	(a)	Everton	D 2-2	Pates, Jones	29,727
15		15	(a)	Aston Villa	D 0-0		17,739
16		22	(h)	Newcastle U	L 1-3	Durie	14,544
17		29	(a)	Leicester C	D 2-2	Bumstead, Speedie	10,047
18	Dec	6	(h)	Wimbledon	L 0-4		15,446
19		14	(a)	Liverpool	L 0-3		25,856
20		20	(h)	Tottenham H	L 0-2		21,576
21		26	(a)	Southampton	W 2-1	Bumstead, Mclaughlin	12,709
22		27	(h)	Aston Villa	W 4-1	Pates, Spackman (pen), Dixon 2	14,637
23	Jan	1	(h)	Queen's Park R	W 3-1	McNaught 2, Wegerle	20,982
24		3	(a)	Luton T	L 0-1		10,956
25		24	(a)	Norwich C	D 2-2	Bumstead, Wicks	16,562
26	Feb	7	(h)	Sheffield W	W 2-0	Hazard (pen), Madden (og)	12,493
27		10	(h)	Oxford U	W 4-0	Durie, Dixon, Nevin, Hazard (pen)	9,546
28		14	(a)	Coventry C	L 0-3		12,906
29		21	(h)	Manchester U	D 1-1	Hazard	26,516
30		28	(a)	Nottingham F	W 1-0	Nevin	18,317
31	Mar	7	(h)	Arsenal	W 1-0	West	29,301
32		14	(a)	Manchester C	W 2-1	McLaughlin, Durie	19,819
33		21	(h)	West Ham U	W 1-0	Nevin	25,386
34	Apr	4	(h)	Everton	L 1-2	Dixon	21,914
35		7	(a)	Charlton A	D 0-0		11,530
36		14	(a)	Watford	L 1-3	Jones	14,108
37		18	(a)	Queen's Park R	D 1-1	Coady	18,081
38		20	(h)	Southampton	D 1-1	Nevin	11,512
39		25	(a)	Newcastle U	L 0-1		21,962
40	May	2	(h)	Leicester C	W 3-1	Durie, Dixon 2	11,975
41		5	(a)	Wimbledon	L 1-2	Wegerle	9,572
42		9	(h)	Liverpool	D 3-3	Bumstead, Durie, Speedie	29,245

FINAL LEAGUE POSITION: 14th in Division One

Appearances
Sub Appearances
Goals

FA Cup

3	Jan	10	(a)	Aston Villa	D 2-2	Bumstead, Speedie	21,997
R		21	(h)	Aston Villa	W 2-1*	Durie, Hazard (pen)	13,473
4	Feb	1	(a)	Watford	L 0-1		18,832

*After extra-time

Appearances
Sub Appearances
Goals

League Cup

2	Sep	3	(a)	York C	L 0-1		7,448
	Oct	8	(h)	York C	W 3-0	Dixon, McAllister, Sbragia (og)	9,927
3		28	(a)	Cardiff C	L 1-2	Jones (pen)	8,018

Aggregate League attendances:
Home: 371,577 (average 17,694)
Away: 407,973 (average 19,427)

Appearances
Sub Appearances
Goals

Football appearance grid (shirt numbers per match; * = substitute, † = as marked). Player columns read left to right; match numbers appear at the right.

Godden A	Wood D	Pates C	Bumstead J	McLaughlin J	Wicks S	Durie G	Spackman N	Dixon KM	Speedie D	Murphy J	Nevin P	Millar J	Hazard M	Howard T	Jones K	Rougvie D	McNaught J	McAllister K	Dublin K	Isaac R	Wegerle R	Niedwiecki E	Clarke S	Lee C	West C	Dodds W	Freestone R	Coady J	Hall G	No.
1	2	3	4	5	6	7	8	9	10	11																				1
1	2	3	4	5	6	7*	8	9	10	11	12																			2
1	2	3	4	5	6	7	8	9	10	11																				3
1	2		4	6	5			8	9	10	11	7	3																	4
1	2	6	4*	5			12	8	9	10	11	7	3																	5
1	2		4	5			12	8	9	10	7	3	6*																	6
1		4	8	5			12	9	10		7	3	6	2	11*															7
1	2	4	8	5	6			9	10*		7		12		3	11														8
1	2	4	8*	5	6			9	10		7				3	11	12													9
1	2	4	6	5				9			7				8	3	11	10												10
1	2	4	6	5				9			7		12		8	3	11*	10												11
1	2	4*	6	5				9		11	7				8	3		10						12						12
1	11	6		5	4			9			7				8	2		10	3											13
1	11	6		5				9			7				8*	2		10	3		4	12								14
	11	6		5			12	9			7*				8	2		10	3		4	1								15
	11	6		5			10	9			7				8*	2			3		4	1	12							16
	12	6	11	5				8	9		10*				7	2			3		4	1								17
	12	6		5			8	9	10		7		11			2			3		4*	1								18
	12	4	6	5				9	8		10	11				2			7*		3	1								19
	2	4	6	5				8	9	10	7							11*	3			1	12							20
	2	4	6	5				8	9	10	7								3		11	1								21
	2	4	6	5*			12	8	9	10	7								3		11	1								22
	2	4		5			12	8	9	10	7					6			3		11*	1								23
	2	4		5			12	8	9	10	7					6			3		11*	1								24
1	2	4	6		5			9	8		10*		7		11				3				12							25
1	2*	8	6		5	9	11				10		7		12				3				4							26
1	12	4	6		5	9*	8	10			7				11				3				2							27
1	12	4	6*		5	9		10			7		8				11		3				2							28
1	12	4		5		9	8	10		11	7		6*						3				2							29
1	12	4	6	5		9*		10	11		7		8						3				2							30
1	6	4		5							7				8				3		11		2	9*	10	12				31
1	6	4		5	9						7		8		11				3				2	10						32
1	6			5	4	9		12			7		8		11				3				2	10*						33
1	6	4		5	9			10			7		8		11				3				2							34
1	6			5	4			9			7		8		11				3		12		2	10*						35
1	6	4*		5				9			7		8		11				3		12		2	10						36
	2		6	5				9			7		8		10				3				4				1	11		37
	6	4		5				10			9		7		8*	11							2	12		1	3			38
	11	4	6	5				10			9		7		8*			3					2	12		1	12			39
	8		6	5	4			10			9		7*								11		2	12		1	3			40
	8		6	5	4			9	10							2		3*			7					1	11	12		41
	2		6	5	4	7		9	10	8									3							1	11			42
26	34	33	29	36	15	18	20	35	22	11	36	4	16	1	16	13	8	7	28	5	7	10	15	1	5	6	5			
7				7						1			2		1			1					5	1	1	2	1		1	1	
	2	8	2	1	5	1	10	3		5			6		3		2						2			1			1	

1 own-goal

Godden A	Wood D	Pates C	Bumstead J	McLaughlin J	Wicks S	Durie G	Spackman N	Dixon KM	Speedie D	Murphy J	Nevin P	Millar J	Hazard M	Howard T	Jones K	Rougvie D	McNaught J	McAllister K	Dublin K	Isaac R	Wegerle R	Niedwiecki E	Clarke S	Lee C	West C	Dodds W	Freestone R	Coady J	Hall G	No.
	2	4	6	5		7		9	10				8						3		11	1								3
	2	4	6		5	11	8	9*	10		7		12						3			1								R
1	2		6		5	9*	8	12	10		7		11						3				4							4
1	3	2	3	1	2	3	2	2	3		2		2						3		1	2	1							
								1					1										1							

Godden A	Wood D	Pates C	Bumstead J	McLaughlin J	Wicks S	Durie G	Spackman N	Dixon KM	Speedie D	Murphy J	Nevin P	Millar J	Hazard M	Howard T	Jones K	Rougvie D	McNaught J	McAllister K	Dublin K	Isaac R	Wegerle R	Niedwiecki E	Clarke S	Lee C	West C	Dodds W	Freestone R	Coady J	Hall G	No.
	2	4	6	5				9	10		7		8*		12	3	11						1							2
1	2	4	6		5			9			7*		14		8†	3	11	10						12						
	2		6	5				9			7		8		4	11*	10	3						12						3
1	3	2	3	2	1			3	1		3		1		2	3	3	2				1		1						
									1				1		1	1		1						2						

1 own-goal

1987-88

Manager: John Hollins until March 1988 then Bobby Campbell acting manager; manager from May.

1	Aug	15	(h)	Sheffield W	W	2-1	Dixon, Durie (pen)	21,929
2		18	(a)	Portsmouth	W	3-0	Nevin, Dixon, C.Wilson	16,917
3		22	(a)	Tottenham H	L	0-1		37,079
4		29	(h)	Luton T	W	3-0	Nevin, Dixon, Coady	16,075
5		31	(a)	Manchester U	L	1-3	Walsh (og)	46,478
6	Sep	5	(h)	Nottingham F	W	4-3	Clarke, Durie 2, C.Wilson	18,414
7		12	(a)	Queen's Park R	L	1-3	Durie	22,583
8		19	(h)	Norwich C	W	1-0	Dixon	15,242
9		26	(a)	Watford	W	3-0	Dixon, Durie 2 (1 pen)	16,213
10	Oct	3	(h)	Newcastle U	D	2-2	Dixon, McCreery (og)	22,071
11		10	(a)	Everton	L	1-4	Dixon	32,004
12		17	(h)	Coventry C	W	1-0	Dixon	16,699
13		24	(a)	Southampton	L	0-3		11,890
14		31	(h)	Oxford U	W	2-1	Nevin, Wegerle	15,027
15	Nov	3	(a)	Arsenal	L	1-3	Nevin	40,230
16		22	(a)	Derby C	L	0-2		18,644
17		28	(h)	Wimbledon	D	1-1	Durie (pen)	15,608
18	Dec	6	(a)	Liverpool	L	1-2	Durie (pen)	31,211
19		12	(h)	West Ham U	D	1-1	K.Wilson	22,850
20		20	(a)	Charlton A	D	2-2	Wood (pen), Bodley	10,893
21		26	(h)	Queen's Park R	D	1-1	McLaughlin	18,020
22		28	(a)	Norwich C	L	0-3		19,668
23	Jan	1	(a)	Luton T	L	0-3		8,018
24		2	(h)	Tottenham H	D	0-0		29,317
25		16	(a)	Sheffield W	L	0-3		19,859
26		23	(h)	Portsmouth	D	0-0		15,856
27	Feb	6	(a)	Nottingham F	L	2-3	Dixon, K.Wilson	18,203
28		13	(h)	Manchester U	L	1-2	West	25,014
29		27	(a)	Newcastle U	L	1-3	K.Wilson	17,858
30	Mar	5	(a)	Coventry C	D	3-3	Nevin, K.Wilson 2	16,816
31		12	(h)	Everton	D	0-0		17,390
32		19	(a)	Oxford U	D	4-4	Nevin, Dixon 2, Bumstead	8,468
33		26	(h)	Southampton	L	0-1		15,380
34		29	(h)	Watford	D	1-1	West	11,240
35	Apr	2	(h)	Arsenal	D	1-1	Hazard	26,084
36		9	(h)	Derby C	W	1-0	Hazard	16,996
37		23	(a)	Wimbledon	D	2-2	Durie 2 (1 pen)	15,128
38		30	(h)	Liverpool	D	1-1	Durie (pen)	35,625
39	May	2	(a)	West Ham U	L	1-4	West	28,521
40		7	(h)	Charlton A	D	1-1	Durie (pen)	33,701

FINAL LEAGUE POSITION: 18th in Division One

Appearances
Sub Appearances
Goals

Play-offs

SF	May	15	(a)	Blackburn R	W	2-0	Nevin, Durie	16,568
		18	(h)	Blackburn R	W	4-1	Dixon, Durie, K.Wilson 2	22,757
F		25	(a)	Middlesbrough	L	0-2		25,531
		28	(h)	Middlesbrough	W	1-0	Durie	40,550

Appearances
Sub Appearances
Goals

FA Cup

3	Jan	9	(a)	Derby C	W	3-1	McAllister, Dixon, Wegerle	18,753
4		30	(a)	Manchester U	L	0-2		50,816

Appearances
Sub Appearances
Goals

League Cup

2	Sep	23	(a)	Reading	L	1-3	Durie (pen)	11,034
	Oct	7	(h)	Reading	W	3-2	Durie 3 (1 pen)	15,469

Appearances
Sub Appearances
Goals

Aggregate League attendances:
Home: 408,538 (average 20,426)
Away: 436,681 (average 21,834)

Niedzwiecki E	Clarke S	Dorigo A	Wicks S	McLaughlin J	Wood D	Nevin P	Hazard M	Dixon KM	Durie G	Wilson C	Wilson KJ	McNaught J	Coady J	Bodley M	West C	Pates C	Wegerle R	Freestone R	Hall G	Murphy J	McAllister K	Bumstead J	Digweed P	Hitchcock K	
1	2	3	4	5	6	7	8*	9	10	11	12														1
1	2	3	4	5	6	7	8	9	10	11															2
1	2	3	4	5	6	7	8	9	10*	11	12														3
1	2	3	4	5	6	7		9	10	8					11										4
1		3	4	5	2	7		9	10	8	12			6	11*										5
1	2	3	4	5	6	7	8	9*	10	11	12														6
1	2	3	4	5	6	7	8		10	11	9														7
1	2†	3		5	6	7	8*	9		11	10		14		12	4									8
1	2	3		5	6	7	8*	9	10	11			12			4									9
1	2	3		5	6	7	8	9	10	11						4									10
1	2	3		5	6	7*	8†	9	10	11	12		14			4									11†
1	2	3		5	6	7	8	9*		11	10		12			4									12
1	2	3		5	6	7	8		9	11	10					4									13
1*	2	3		5	6	7			10	11	9		12			4	8								14
	2	3		5	6	7			10	11	12		9*			4	8*	1							15
	2	3		5	6	7	8†		10	11	14		9*			4	12	1							16
	2*	3		5	6	7		9	10	11						4	12	1	8						17
	2	3		5	6	7		9	10	11						4		1	8						18
	2	3		5	6	7*	8	9		11	10					4	12	1							19
		3		5	6	7*		9		11	10		14			4	8†	1	2		12				20
	4	3		5	6	7		9	10	11	8							1	2						21
	4	3*		5	6	7			10	11	9		12				8	1	2						22
	4	3		5	2		8	9	10	11								1	6		7				23
	4	3		5	2		8	9	10	11							12	1	6		7*				24
	4	3		5	2		8	9	10	11*							12	1	6		7				25
	2	3		5	11		8	9†	10		14					4	12	1	6*		7				26
	2	3*		5		7	8	9	10		12					4		1	6			11			27
	2	3		5		7	8*	9	10		12					4		1	6			11			28
	2*	3		5	6	7	8	9	10		14					4	12	1				11†			29
	5	3			6	7	8	9	10							4			2			11		1	30
	2	3	5		6	7	8	9								4			2			11		1	31
	2	3	5		6	7	8*	9		12	10*					4			12			11		1	32
	2	3	5		6	7	8	9		14	10†					4*			12			11	1		33
	2	3	4	5	6	7	8	9								10						11	1		34
	2	3	4	5	6	7	8	9†	10*							14			12			11	1		35
	2	3	4	5	6	7	8	10*		12						9						11	1		36
	6	3	4	5		7	8	9	10										2			11	1		37
	6	3	4	5		7	8	9	10										2			11	1		38
	6	3	4	5		7	8*	9	10		12						6			2			8	1		39
	2	3	4	5		7		9	10	11*			12		6				8				1		40
14	38	40	17	36	34	36	28	33	26	27	16	1	4	6	3	16	8	15	8	2	4	17	3	8	
							1		4	9	6		6	1		3		5			1				
1			1	1	6	2	11	12	2	5			1	1	3		1					1			

2 own-goals

Niedzwiecki E	Clarke S	Dorigo A	Wicks S	McLaughlin J	Wood D	Nevin P	Hazard M	Dixon KM	Durie G	Wilson C	Wilson KJ	McNaught J	Coady J	Bodley M	West C	Pates C	Wegerle R	Freestone R	Hall G	Murphy J	McAllister K	Bumstead J	Digweed P	Hitchcock K	
	2	3*		5		7		9	10	11	14			6			4		12		8†			1	SF
	2			5		7		9	10	3	11			4			6		12		8*			1	
	2	3	4	5		7		9	10	11				6					8					1	F
	2	3	4	5		7		9	10	11†				6*			12		14		8			1	
	4	3	2	4		4		4	4	3	2			4			2		4		4			4	
								1											1		3				
								1		1	3			2											

Niedzwiecki E	Clarke S	Dorigo A	Wicks S	McLaughlin J	Wood D	Nevin P	Hazard M	Dixon KM	Durie G	Wilson C	Wilson KJ	McNaught J	Coady J	Bodley M	West C	Pates C	Wegerle R	Freestone R	Hall G	Murphy J	McAllister K	Bumstead J	Digweed P	Hitchcock K	
	4	3		5	2		8	9	10*	11						12	1		7		6				3
	2	3		5	6	14	12	9		11	10					4	1		7†		8*				4
	2	2		2	2	1	1	2	1	2	1					2	2		2		2				
				1	1					1						1					1				

Niedzwiecki E	Clarke S	Dorigo A	Wicks S	McLaughlin J	Wood D	Nevin P	Hazard M	Dixon KM	Durie G	Wilson C	Wilson KJ	McNaught J	Coady J	Bodley M	West C	Pates C	Wegerle R	Freestone R	Hall G	Murphy J	McAllister K	Bumstead J	Digweed P	Hitchcock K	
1	2	3		5	6	7	8	9	10	11				4											
1	2	3		5	6	7	8	9	10*	11†	12		14	4											2
2	2	2		2	2	2	2	2	2	2	1		1	1											
									1		1														
								4																	

339

1988-89

Manager: Bobby Campbell

1	Aug	27	(h)	Blackburn R	L 1-2	K.Wilson	* 8,722
2		30	(a)	Crystal P	D 1-1	K.Wilson	17,490
3	Sep	3	(a)	Bournemouth	L 0-1		8,763
4		10	(h)	Oxford U	D 1-1	McAllister	* 7,587
5		17	(a)	Barnsley	D 1-1	Roberts (pen)	6,942
6		20	(h)	Manchester C	L 1-3	Pates	* 8,858
7		24	(a)	Leeds U	W 2-0	Bumstead, Durie	26,080
8	Oct	1	(h)	Leicester C	W 2-1	Lee, Roberts (pen)	* 7,050
9		4	(h)	Walsall	W 2-0	Dixon, Dorigo	* 6,747
10		9	(a)	Swindon T	D 1-1	Dixon	11,347
11		15	(a)	Oldham A	W 4-1	K.Wilson, Nicholas, McAllister, Wood	7,817
12		22	(h)	Plymouth A	W 5-0	Dixon, Durie 2, Roberts (pen), Dorigo	12,658
13		25	(a)	Hull C	L 0-3		6,953
14		29	(h)	Brighton & HA	W 2-0	K.Wilson, Dixon	15,406
15	Nov	5	(a)	Watford	W 2-1	Durie, Dixon	17,631
16		12	(h)	Sunderland	D 1-1	K.Wilson	19,210
17		19	(a)	Bradford C	D 2-2	Lee, K.Wilson	11,442
18		26	(h)	Shrewsbury T	W 2-0	Dorigo, Dixon	11,595
19	Dec	3	(a)	Stoke C	W 3-0	Roberts (pen), C.Wilson, McAllister	12,288
20		10	(h)	Portsmouth	D 3-3	Dixon, Durie, K.Wilson	20,221
21		16	(a)	Birmingham C	W 4-1	Durie 2, Dixon 2	7,897
22		26	(h)	Ipswich T	W 3-0	Durie, Lee, Dixon	17,621
23		31	(h)	West Brom A	D 1-1	Roberts (pen)	25,906
24	Jan	2	(a)	Oxford U	W 3-2	Dixon 2, C.Wilson	11,427
25		14	(h)	Crystal P	W 1-0	Dorigo	24,184
26		21	(a)	Blackburn R	D 1-1	Dixon	11,713
27	Feb	4	(a)	Walsall	W 7-0	Durie 5, K.Wilson, Roberts (pen)	6,860
28		11	(h)	Swindon T	W 3-2	Durie, Gittens (og), MacLaren (og)	17,829
29		18	(a)	Plymouth A	W 1-0	Dixon	13,180
30		25	(h)	Oldham A	D 2-2	Roberts 2 (1 pen)	13,261
31		28	(h)	Hull C	W 2-1	Dixon, K.Wilson	11,407
32	Mar	11	(h)	Watford	D 2-2	Dorigo, Roberts (pen)	22,188
33		15	(a)	Brighton & HA	W 1-0	K.Wilson	12,600
34		18	(a)	Manchester C	W 3-2	Dixon, K.Wilson, Dorigo	40,070
35		21	(a)	Sunderland	W 2-1	Roberts, K.Wilson	14,714
36		25	(h)	Bournemouth	W 2-0	Durie, Roberts (pen)	22,467
37		28	(a)	Ipswich T	W 1-0	Durie	22,950
38	Apr	1	(h)	Barnsley	W 5-3	Dixon 4, Durie	16,023
39		4	(h)	Birmingham C	W 3-1	K.Wilson, Roberts, Dixon	14,796
40		8	(a)	West Brom A	W 3-2	Roberts (pen), Lee, McAllister	22,858
41		15	(a)	Leicester C	L 0-2		19,468
42		22	(h)	Leeds U	W 1-0	Bumstead	30,337
43		29	(a)	Shrewsbury T	D 1-1	Dixon	5,588
44	May	1	(h)	Stoke C	W 2-1	Dixon, Roberts (pen)	14,946
45		6	(h)	Bradford C	W 3-1	Robets, (pen), Dixon 2	18,003
46		13	(a)	Portsmouth	W 3-2	McAllister 2, C.Wilson	12,051

FINAL LEAGUE POSITION: 1st in Division Two   *Stamford Bridge terraces closed

Appearances
Sub Appearances
Goals

FA Cup

3	Jan	7	(a)	Barnsley	L 0-4		13,241

Appearances
Sub Appearances
Goals

League Cup

2	Sep	27	(a)	Scunthorpe U	L 1-4	Lister (og)	5,061
	Oct	12	(h)	Scunthorpe U	D 2-2	K.Wilson, Dixon	5,814

Aggregate League attendances:
Home: 367,022 (average 15,957)
Away: 328,129 (average 14,266)

Appearances
Sub Appearances
Goals

Player appearance / goals grid (shirt numbers worn, by match). An asterisk (*) or dagger (†) beside a number denotes a substitution.

Match	Hitchcock K	Clarke S	Wilson C	Roberts G	McLaughlin J	Pates C	McAllister K	Nicholas P	Wilson KJ	Durie G	Bumstead J	Wood D	Freestone R	Hall G	Dodds W	Dorigo A	Dixon KM	Lee D	Beasant D	Mitchell D	Hazard M	Monkou K	Le Saux G
1	1	2	3	4*	5	6	7	8	9	10	11	12											
2		2	3	4	5		8	9	10	11	6		1	7									
3	1	2	3	4	5		11	8	9	10	6	12		7*									
4		2	3	4	5		11	8	9	10	6	12	1	7*									
5		2	3	4	5		7	8	9	10*	11	6	1	12									
6	1	2	11	4	5		7	8	12	10	6*					3	9						
7		2	6	4	5		7	8	12	10*	11		1			3	9						
8		2		4	5		7	8*	10	11	6†	12	1			3	9	14					
9		2		4	5		7	8	10	11			1			3	9	6					
10		2		4	5		8		10	11			1	7		3	9	6					
11		2	11	4	5		7	8	10		6		1			3	9						
12		2	12	4	5		7*	8	10	11	6		1			3	9						
13		2	12	4	5		7†	8	10	11	6*		1			3	9	14					
14		2	11	4	5		7	8	10		6	12	1			3	9*						
15		2	11	4	5		7	8	10		6		1			3	9*	12					
16		2†	11	4	5		7	8	10		6*	12	1			3	9	14					
17		2	11	4		5	7	8	10		6*	12	1			3	9						
18		2	11	4		5	7	8	10		6		1			3	9						
19		2	11	4		5	7	8		10	6		1			3	9						
20		2	11	4		5	7	8	10*		6	12	1			3	9						
21		2	11	4		5	7	8	10		6		1			3	9						
22		2	11	4	5		7	8†	10		6	12	1			3*	9	14					
23		2	11	4	5		7	8*	10		6	12	1			3	9						
24		2	11	4	5		7	8*	10†		6	12	1			3	9	14					
25		2	11	4*	5		7				6	12				3	9	10	1	8			
26		2	11	4	5		7				6					3	9	10	1	8			
27		2	3	4	5		8	7	10		6						9	11	1				
28		2		4	5		8	7	10		6					3	9	11	1				
29		2		4	5		8		10†		6	12				3	9	14	1	7	11*		
30		2		4	5		8		10		6	12				3	9		1	7*	11		
31		2	11	4	5		7	8	10		6					3	9		1				
32		2	11	4	5		7	8	10		6					3	9		1				
33		2	11	4	5		7	8	10		6					3	9		1				
34		2	12	4	5		7	8	10*	11	6					3	9		1				
35		2		4	5		7	8	10	11	6					3	9		1				
36		2		4	5		7	8	10	11	6					3	9		1				
37		2		4	5		7	8	10	11	6					3	9		1				
38		2		4*	5		7	8	10	11	6					3	9	12	1				
39		2		4	5*		7	8	10	11	6					3	9	12	1				
40		2		4	5		7	8*	10	11	6	12				3	9	5	1				
41		2		4	5		7	8	10	11	6*					3	9	12	1				
42		2		4	5		7	8	10	11	6					3	9		1				
43		2	8	4	5		7		10*	11	6	12				3	9		1				
44		2	8	4	5*		7		10	11	6					3	9		1			12	
45		2	10	4	5		7	8		11	6					3	9		1				
46		2†	6	4	5		7	8	10	11						3	9*		1			12	14
Apps	3	36	29	46	31	10	28	39	43	32	27	21	21	17		40	39	12	22	6	4		
Sub		3				8			3		2	1				5	2	8		2	1		
Goals		3	15		1		6	1	13	17	2	1				6	25	4					

2 own-goals

	Hitchcock K	Clarke S	Wilson C	Roberts G	McLaughlin J	Pates C	McAllister K	Nicholas P	Wilson KJ	Durie G	Bumstead J	Wood D	Freestone R	Hall G	Dodds W	Dorigo A	Dixon KM	Lee D	Beasant D	Mitchell D	Hazard M	Monkou K	Le Saux G	Matches
		2†	11*	4	5		7	8	10		6	12	1	14		3	9							3
Sub		1	1	1			1	1	1		1	1		1		1	1							
Goals		1							1								1							

3

	Hitchcock K	Clarke S	Wilson C	Roberts G	McLaughlin J	Pates C	McAllister K	Nicholas P	Wilson KJ	Durie G	Bumstead J	Wood D	Freestone R	Hall G	Dodds W	Dorigo A	Dixon KM	Lee D	Beasant D	Mitchell D	Hazard M	Monkou K	Le Saux G	Matches
		2	6	4	5		7	8	10		11		1			3	9							2
			12	4	5		7*	8	6	10	11†		1	2		3	9	14						
Sub		1	1	2	2		2	2	1	2	2		2	1		2	2							
Goals			1						1							1								

1 own-goal

1989-90

Manager: Bobby Campbell

1	Aug	19	(a)	Wimbledon	W	1-0	K.Wilson	14,625
2		22	(h)	Queen's Park R	D	1-1	Dorigo	24,354
3		26	(h)	Sheffield W	W	4-0	Roberts (pen), Harper (og), Dixon, McAllister	16,265
4		29	(a)	Charlton A	L	0-3		17,221
5	Sep	9	(h)	Nottingham F	D	2-2	Durie, Dixon	21,523
6		16	(a)	Tottenham H	W	4-1	Dixon, K.Wilson 2, Clarke	16,260
7		23	(h)	Coventry C	W	1-0	K.Wilson	18,247
8		30	(h)	Arsenal	D	0-0		31,833
9	Oct	14	(a)	Norwich C	L	0-2		19,042
10		21	(a)	Derby C	W	1-0	Dixon	17,279
11		28	(h)	Manchester C	D	1-1	Dixon	21,917
12	Nov	4	(h)	Millwall	W	4-0	K.Wilson 2, Dixon 2	24,969
13		11	(a)	Everton	W	1-0	Clarke	33,737
14		18	(h)	Southampton	D	2-2	Monkou, K.Wilson	23,093
15		25	(a)	Manchester U	D	0-0		47,106
16	Dec	2	(h)	Wimbledon	L	2-5	Dixon, Roberts (pen)	19,976
17		9	(a)	Queen's Park R	L	2-4	Dickens, Clarke	17,935
18		16	(h)	Liverpool	L	2-5	Durie, Dixon	31,005
19		26	(a)	Crystal P	D	2-2	Dixon, Le Saux	24,002
20		30	(a)	Luton T	W	3-0	K.Wilson 2, Dixon	10,068
21	Jan	1	(a)	Aston Villa	L	0-3		23,990
22		14	(a)	Sheffield W	D	1-1	Lee	18,042
23		20	(h)	Charlton A	W	3-1	K.Wilson 2, Dixon	15,667
24	Feb	3	(a)	Coventry C	L	2-3	Dorigo, Dixon	15,243
25		10	(h)	Tottenham H	L	1-2	Bumstead	28,130
26		17	(a)	Nottingham F	D	1-1	Roberts	22,500
27		24	(h)	Manchester U	W	1-0	Hall	29,979
28	Mar	3	(a)	Southampton	W	3-2	K.Wilson, Dorigo, Dixon	16,526
29		10	(h)	Norwich C	D	0-0		18,796
30		17	(a)	Arsenal	W	1-0	Bumstead	33,805
31		21	(a)	Manchester C	D	1-1	Durie	24,670
32		31	(h)	Derby C	D	1-1	K.Wilson	14,265
33	Apr	7	(h)	Luton T	W	1-0	Durie	15,221
34		14	(a)	Aston Villa	L	0-1		28,361
35		16	(h)	Crystal P	W	3-0	Dixon, K.Wilson, Stuart	16,132
36		21	(a)	Liverpool	L	1-4	Dixon	38,481
37		28	(h)	Everton	W	2-1	Dixon 2	18,879
38	May	5	(a)	Millwall	W	3-1	Dixon 3	12,230

FINAL LEAGUE POSITION: 5th in Divison One

Appearances
Sub Appearances
Goals

FA Cup

3	Jan	6	(h)	Crewe A	D	1-1	Clarke	18,066
R		10	(a)	Crewe A	W	2-0	Dixon 2	6,944
4		27	(a)	Bristol C	L	1-3	K.Wilson	24,535

Appearances
Sub Appearances
Goals

League Cup

2	Sep	19	(h)	Scarborough	D	1-1	Roberts	10,349
	Oct	4	(a)	Scarborough	L	2-3	Clarke, K.Wilson	5,086

Appearances
Sub Appearances
Goals

Aggregate League attendances:
Home: 414,241 (average 21,802)
Away: 427,083 (average 22,478)

Football appearance grid — Beasant D, Clarke S, Dorigo A, Roberts G, Lee D, Monkou K, Dickens A, Nicholas P, Dixon KM, Durie G, McAllister K, Bumstead J, Wilson KJ, Hazard M, Johnsen E, Le Saux G, Hall G, Matthew D, Stuart G

Bea	Cla	Dor	Rob	Lee	Mon	Dic	Nic	Dix	Dur	McA	Bum	Wil	Haz	Joh	LeS	Hal	Mat	Stu	No.
1	2	3	4	5	6	7	8	9	10*	11†	12	14							1
1	2	3	4	5	6	7	8	9	10			11							2
1	2	3	4	5	6	7	8	9		11		10							3
1	2	3	4	5	6	7	8	9	10	11*		12							4
1	2		4	5	6	7*	8	9	10†		12	14	3	11					5
1	2		4	5	6	7*	8	9			12	10	3	11					6
1	2*	3	4	5	6	7	8	9			12	10		11					7
1	2	3	4*	5	6	7	8	9			12	10		11					8
1	2	3		5	6	7*	8	9	14	4	10	12	11†						9
1	2*	3	4	5	6	7	8	9			12	10		11					10
1	2*	3	4	5	6	7	8	9			12	10		11					11
1	2	3	4	5	6	7	8	9				10		11					12
1	2	3	4	5	6	7	8	9				10		11					13
1	2	3	4	5	6	7	8	9				10		11					14
1	2	3	4	5	6	7	8	9				10		11					15
1		3	4	5	6*	7	8†	9	14	2	10	12	11						16
1	2	3	4	5		7		9	14	8	10	12	11*	6†					17
1	2	3	4	5	6	7		9	10		8		11						18
1	2	3	4	5	6			9		7	8*	10	11		12				19
1	2	3	4	5	6			9		7	8	10	11						20
1	2	3	4	5	6	12		9		7	8*	10	11†		14				21
1	2		4	8	6			9		11	7	10		5	3				22
1	2	3	4*	6	8			9		7		10	12	5	11				23
1	2	3	4	12		8*		9		7	6	10	11	5					24
1	2	3	4				8	9		7	6	10	11	5					25
1		3	4				8	9		7	6	10	11*	5	12	2			26
1		3		12	6			8	9	7	4	10	11	5		2*			27
1		3		12	6			8	9	14	7	4	10	11†	5	2*			28
1		3			6			8	9	10	7	4	11	5	2				29
1		3			6			8	9	10	7	4	11	5	2				30
1		3			6			8	9	10	7	4	11	5	2				31
1		3			6			8	9	10	7	4	11	5	2				32
1		3		12	6			8	9	10	7	4*	11†	14	5	2			33
1		3			6			8	9	10	7	4	11	5	2				34
1		3		12	6			8	9	10†			14	5	11	2	4	7*	35
1		3		12	6			8	9	10	7	4*	11†	14	5	2			36
1		3			6			8	9	10	7	4	8	11	5	2			37
1		3		12	6	14	8†	9			10			5	11	2*	4	7	38
38	24	35	24	23	34	20	29	38	14	21	21	33	12	13	18	4	13	2	2
			7		2				1	3	7	4	6			3			
3	3	3	1	1	1			20	5	1	2	14				1	1	1	

1 own-goal

Bea	Cla	Dor	Rob	Lee	Mon	Dic	Nic	Dix	Dur	McA	Bum	Wil	Haz	Joh	LeS	Hal	Mat	Stu	No.
1	2		4	7	6			9		12	8	10	3*		5	11			3
1	2		4	12	6		8	9	10*		7	11			5	3			R
1	2	3	4	12	6*			9		7	8	10			5	11			4
3	3	1	3	1	3		1	3	1	1	3	3	1		3	3			
				2									1						
	1								2				1						

Bea	Cla	Dor	Rob	Lee	Mon	Dic	Nic	Dix	Dur	McA	Bum	Wil	Haz	Joh	LeS	Hal	Mat	Stu	No.
1	2	3	4	5	6	7*	8	9				10	12	11					2
1	2	3			5	6	7*	8	9	14	4	10	12	11†					
2	2	2	1	2	2	2	2	2		1	2		2		2				
													1						
	1		1										1	2					

1990-91

Manager: Bobby Campbell

1	Aug	25	(h)	Derby C	W	2-1	Lee, Nicholas	25,835
2		28	(a)	Crystal P	L	1-2	Dorigo	27,101
3	Sep	1	(a)	Queen's Park R	L	0-1		19,813
4		8	(h)	Sunderland	W	3-2	Dixon, Wilson, Wise (pen)	19,424
5		15	(a)	Arsenal	L	1-4	Wilson	41,516
6		22	(h)	Manchester C	D	1-1	Wilson	20,924
7		29	(h)	Sheffield U	D	2-2	Wilson 2	19,873
8	Oct	6	(a)	Southampton	D	3-3	Clarke, Wilson, Wise (pen)	16,911
9		20	(h)	Nottingham F	D	0-0		22,403
10		27	(a)	Liverpool	L	0-2		38,463
11	Nov	3	(h)	Aston Villa	W	1-0	Le Saux	23,555
12		10	(h)	Norwich C	D	1-1	Wise (pen)	16,925
13		17	(a)	Wimbledon	L	0-1	Durie	10,773
14		25	(a)	Manchester U	W	3-2	Pallister (og), Townsend, Wise (pen)	37,836
15	Dec	1	(h)	Tottenham H	W	3-2	Dixon, Bumstead, Durie	33,478
16		8	(h)	Crystal P	W	2-1	Stuart, Durie	21,558
17		15	(a)	Derby C	W	6-4	Dixon 2, Durie 2, Wise, Le Saux	15,057
18		22	(h)	Coventry C	W	2-1	Townsend, Wise	16,317
19		26	(a)	Leeds U	L	1-4	Dixon	30,893
20		29	(a)	Luton T	L	0-2		11,050
21	Jan	1	(h)	Everton	L	1-2		18,351
22		12	(h)	Queen's Park R	W	2-0	Durie 2	19,255
23		19	(a)	Sunderland	L	0-1		20,038
24	Feb	2	(h)	Arsenal	W	2-1	Stuart, Dixon	29,094
25		9	(a)	Manchester C	L	1-2	Wise	25,116
26		16	(h)	Wimbledon	D	0-0		13,378
27	Mar	2	(a)	Tottenham H	D	1-1	Durie	26,168
28		9	(h)	Manchester U	W	3-2	Durie, Dorigo, Monkou	22,818
29		16	(a)	Sheffield U	L	0-1		20,581
30		23	(h)	Southampton	L	0-2		13,391
31		30	(h)	Leeds U	L	1-2	Le Saux	17,585
32	Apr	1	(a)	Coventry C	L	0-1		14,272
33		6	(h)	Luton T	D	3-3	Le Saux, Stuart, Wise	12,603
34		13	(a)	Everton	D	2-2	Dixon 2	19,526
35		17	(a)	Norwich C	W	3-1	Wise, Durie 2	12,301
36		20	(a)	Nottingham F	L	0-7		20,305
37	May	4	(h)	Liverpool	W	4-2	Dixon 2, Wise (pen), Durie	32,266
38		11	(a)	Aston Villa	D	2-2	Cundy, Stuart	27,866

FINAL LEAGUE POSITION: 11th in Division One

Appearances
Sub Appearances
Goals

FA Cup

3	Jan	5	(h)	Oxford U	L	1-3	Dixon	14,586

Appearances
Sub Appearances
Goals

League Cup

2	Sep	26	(a)	Walsall	W	5-0	Townsend 2, Wilson, McAllister, Dixon	5,666
	Oct	10	(h)	Walsall	W	4-1	Durie, Dixon 2, Le Saux	10,037
3		31	(h)	Portsmouth	D	0-0		16,699
R	Nov	6	(a)	Portsmouth	W	3-2	Lee, Wise (pen), Wilson	16,085
4		28	(a)	Oxford U	W	2-1	Durie 2	9,789
5	Jan	16	(h)	Tottenham H	D	0-0		34,178
R		23	(a)	Tottenham H	W	3-0	Townsend, Dixon, Wise (pen)	33,681
SF	Feb	24	(h)	Sheffield W	L	0-2		34,074
		27	(a)	Sheffield W	L	1-3	Stuart	34,669

Appearances
Sub Appearances
Goals

Aggregate League attendances:
Home: 399,035 (average 21,001)
Away: 435,586 (average 22,925)

Beasant D	Hall G	Dorigo A	Townsend A	Johnsen E	Lee D	Wise D	Nicholas P	Dixon K	Wilson K	Le Saux G	McAllister K	Cundy J	Bumstead J	Monkou K	Dickens A	Clarke S	Stuart G	Durie G	Hitchcock K	Matthew D	Mitchell D	Sinclair F	Myers A	Burley C	Pearce I	
1	2	3	4	5	6	7	8	9	10	11*	12															1
1	2	3	4	5	6	7	8	9	10	11*	12															2
1	2	3	4		6	7	8	9	10	11			5													3
1	2	3	4		6	7	8*	9	10	11†	14		5	12												4
1	2	3	7		6		8*	9	10			12	5	11†	4	14										5
1		3	4	5*	12		8	9	10	11	7			6		2										6
1		3	4	5	7		8	9	10	11				6		2										7
1		3	4	5	7		8	9		11		12		6		2		10*								8
1		3	4	5	7		8*	9†		11		12	14	6		2		10								9
1		3	4	5	11		8*	9				12	7	14		6	2†	10								10
	2	3	4	5	7		9			11	12			8	6*			10	1							11
	2	3	4	6	7		9			11	12			5	8*			10	1							12
	2	3	4	6	7	8†	9			11	12			5				10	1							13
1	2		4		11		9	12	3				5	6			7	10*	8							14
1	2	3	4		11		9	7					5	8	6			10								15
1	2		4		11		9	3					5	8	6		7	10								16
1	2	3		8	11*	14	9	12	7				5			6†	4	10								17
1	2	3	4	8	11		9	7					5	6*		12		10								18
1	2	3*	4	6	11		9	12	7				5			8		10								19
1	2			6	4†	11	9	10	3	14			5	8*		12	7									20
1	2			6	11		9	10	7*	12			5	8		3	4									21
1	2	3	4		9			11					5	6			7	10	8							22
1	2	3	4	14	9		11†						5	12	6		7	10	8*							23
1	2	3	4		11		9†	14	7*	12				6		5	10		8							24
1	2*	3	4		11		10†		7	5			6	14	12	9			8							25
1		3		11	9		7				5	8*	6	4	2		12	10								26
1		3	4	14	11*		9	12			5		6	8	2	7†	10									27
1		3	4		11		9				7	5	6	8	2		10									28
1		3	4		11		9*				7	5	6	8	2	12	10									29
1		3	4		11		9*				5	6	8	2	7	10	12									30
1		3	4		11		9				7	5	6	8	2	10										31
1		3	4		11		9				7	5	6	8	2	10										32
1	2		4	6	11			7				5	8	9		10*	3	12								33
1	2		4	12	11		9	7				5	6	8		10*	3									34
1	2		4		11		9	7				5	6	8		10	3									35
1	2	11	4	5		9†						8	6	7	10	3*	12	14								36
1		3	4		11		9	12				5	6	8	2	7*	10									37
1		3	4		11		9				5*	6	8†	2	7	10	14	12								38
35	24	31	34	6	17	33	11	33	17	24	5	28	8	27	13	17	17	24	3	6	1	4				
				4	1			5	4	8	1	5		3	1	2			2			3	1	1		
	2	2		1	10	1	10	7	4			1	1	1		1	4	12								

1 own-goal

Beasant D	Hall G	Dorigo A	Townsend A	Johnsen E	Lee D	Wise D	Nicholas P	Dixon K	Wilson K	Le Saux G	McAllister K	Cundy J	Bumstead J	Monkou K	Dickens A	Clarke S	Stuart G	Durie G	Hitchcock K	Matthew D	Mitchell D	Sinclair F	Myers A	Burley C	Pearce I	
1	2		4	6†	14	11		9	10	12		5	8*			3	7									3
1	1		1	1		1		1	1			1	1			1	1									
					1					1																
									1																	

Beasant D	Hall G	Dorigo A	Townsend A	Johnsen E	Lee D	Wise D	Nicholas P	Dixon K	Wilson K	Le Saux G	McAllister K	Cundy J	Bumstead J	Monkou K	Dickens A	Clarke S	Stuart G	Durie G	Hitchcock K	Matthew D	Mitchell D	Sinclair F	Myers A	Burley C	Pearce I	
1		3	4		5		8	9	10	11	7			6		2										2
1		3	4		5	7	8*	9	11†	14				12	6	2		10								3
1	2	3	4		5	11	8*	9		14	7†			12	6			10								R
	2	3	4		6	7		12	9	11*		5	8					10	1							4
1	2		4	14	11		9	12	3			5		6		7*	10	8†								5
1	2	3	4			9				11		5		6		7*	10	8								R
1	2	3	4			11	9		12			5		6		7	10	8*								SF
1		3	4			11	9				5		6	8	2	7	10									
8	6	8	9		4	7	3	7	4	4	2	6	1	8	1	3	5	8	1	4						
					1			1	1	3				3												
		3			1	2		4	2	1	1						1	3								

345

Chelsea in Wartime

URING the two world wars, football inevitably took on an atmosphere of unreality. Yet, undoubtedly, it fulfilled an important role in helping to maintain morale among the civilian population by providing some measure of entertainment (as cricket did during the summer months), in dark and often dangerous times.

In 1914, refusing to face facts and with the flimsiest of excuses, the football authorities decided to carry on with normal competitions, despite the fact that many players were already away on 'active service'. Not until August 1915, and under an ever-growing barrage of criticism, were the peacetime competitions suspended.

In the south-east, a London Combination league was formed, made up of the 11 leading clubs in the metropolis, along with Southern League champions, Watford. At first the competition was launched for a four-month period, with a firm understanding that 'all footballers are amateurs' and that 'no man shall earn even as much as a shilling by the playing of football'.

On this basis it was well received, as indeed it was in 1939, and spectators, many of them men in uniform on leave, often came through the turnstiles in surprisingly large numbers.

Club programmes listed players with their service rank attached. Chelsea stalwarts included Gunner Hampton (MMG), Corporal Croal, Airman Halse and, in World War Two, Sergeant Payne (RAF), and Lance Corporals Bidewell and Spence.

Most intriguing of all was a certain Cyclist Murphy, who, apparently, spent the four years from 1914 to 1918 pedalling his way around London in his country's cause, apart from Saturday afternoons during the football season when he was allowed to dismount from his machine to play football.

News about players abroad on active service continually crept into the columns of the *Chelsea FC Chronicle*. Captain V.J.Woodward was reported 'severely wounded' in January 1916; two months later, Tommy McDermott was said to have lost both legs (a report subsequently and happily proved to be inaccurate); Tom Logan was awarded the Military Medal; and, sadly, Arthur Wileman lost his life in action in 1918.

Twenty-five years later it was a similar story. Private Jack Sherborne was wounded in France, his football career over; young David Alexander injured in a motor-cycle accident was invalided out of the Army, also never to play again; George Mills was commissioned in the RAF and reached the rank of Flight Lieutenant; LAC Doug Smale saw service in India, and Sergeant Alex White with the BLA in Europe.

With playing contracts suspended, players flitted from club to club as war service carried them to different parts of the country. Or clubs, trying desperately to complete their teams, took advantage of neighbours with a surplus of talent. Harry Deverall, a winger registered with Reading, played for his club against Chelsea one weekend, only to change his allegiance seven days later. And he scored a goal on each occasion!

London, obviously, was better favoured than most places in the country because of its size and location. Aldershot, too, muscled in to include many famous names stationed in the military barracks in the town. At times the scramble to 'sign up' star players, albeit on a temporary basis only, almost resembled peacetime transfer market activity.

Charles Buchan was Chelsea's 'prize capture' in World War One. The famous international inside-forward from the north-east was a regular at Stamford Bridge in the first season of the London Combination and was tremendously popular with

346

the Chelsea faithful, his great skill and artistry swelling the 'gate' wherever the club played.

A quarter of a century on, considerably more 'guest' stars appeared in the blue shirts and again household names flocked down the Fulham Road. Matt Busby (briefly), Arsenal and England full-back Eddie Hapgood, Scottish international Alex Herd and George Hardwick, England captain of the future, were prominent on a long list. Another, and more permanent, spin-off sometimes led to the signing of players on a permanent basis when 'it was all over'. In this way Chelsea acquired John Harris, Danny Winter, Bobby Russell and, not least, Tommy Walker, Scotland's 'Ace of Hearts' from Edinburgh.

Vic Woodley collects a high ball from an Aldershot forward during a friendly game at the Recreation Ground in September 1939. Football had just resumed with a limit of 8,000 on attendances.

347

Curious memories of those days abide. Of the ARP 'spotter', perilously stationed on the roof of the old Stamford Bridge East Stand, binoculars at the ready. Of trainer Charlie Freeman waiting anxiously at railway station ticket-barriers taking his roll-call before the guard waved his green flag. Or the tall, gaunt figure of assistant secretary Harold Palmer, peering anxiously through his office window at Stamford Bridge overlooking the main entrance to see who had managed to extract a 'leave-pass' from a sympathetic CO.

On one occasion an enemy air-raid caused the abandonment of a match at The Bridge with nearly a quarter of an hour still to play. The 'result' was allowed to stand and no replay took place. Another game never even started due to enemy action and proved impossible to rearrange.

If all else failed there was always that somewhat decrepit notice-board which was frequently trailed round the ground asking for a volunteer to make up a team. The name 'Friend' appeared on many a team-sheet. Sometimes, too, a player would

'jump barracks' and play under an assumed name, lest his CO should spot his identity in a newspaper report. On one occasion, a journalist was tactless enough to remark in print on the likeness of a tall defender to a certain Jack Harrow!

Against such a backcloth of improvisation, Chelsea emerged from both wars with considerable credit. They were twice champions of the London Combination in World War One, as well as winning the London Victory Cup in April 1919. And next time, they made their first-ever appearance at Wembley Stadium, losing to Charlton Athletic in the 1944 South Cup Final before beating Millwall in that competition 12 months later, with two 'intruders' making their debut, one of whom — Leslie Smith of Brentford and England — never played for Chelsea again.

More important than such trivial details was the fact that wartime football was immensely enjoyable, and relaxing, to watch. However artificial its mechanics may have been at times, it seldom failed its customers, or lost its sense of proportion in difficult days.

General Eisenhower meets the Chelsea team before the 1944 South Cup Final against Charlton Athletic at Wembley. He shakes hands with Bobby Russell as Jimmy Bowie, Len Ashcroft and Dick Foss wait in line.

1915-16

Manager: David Calderhead

1	Sep	4	(h)	Clapton O	W	3-1	Buchan 3	12,000
2		11	(a)	West Ham U	D	0-0		5,000
3		18	(h)	Watford	W	1-0	Ford	10,000
4		25	(a)	Tottenham H	W	3-1	Buchan 2, Halse	8,653
5	Oct	2	(h)	Millwall A	D	2-2	Logan (pen), Halse	8,000
6		9	(a)	Crystal P	W	5-1	Middelboe, Buchan 3, Steer	4,000
7		16	(h)	Croydon Comm	W	3-1	Bridgeman, Thomson, Halse	4,000
8		23	(a)	Queen's Park R	L	0-1		4,000
9		30	(h)	Arsenal	W	3-1	Croal 2, Thomson	12,500
10	Nov	6	(a)	Fulham	W	3-0	Ford, Buchan, Croal	14,000
11		13	(a)	Clapton O	W	6-1	Buchan 5, Croal	5,000
12		20	(h)	West Ham U	W	5-2	Ford, Buchan, Croal, Thomson 2	8,000
13		27	(a)	Watford	W	3-0	Ford, Croal, Thomson	4,000
14	Dec	4	(h)	Tottenham H	W	8-1	Taylor, Ford, Croal 2, Thomson 2, Freeman, Baker	8,000
15		11	(a)	Millwall A	L	0-1		4,000
16		18	(h)	Crystal P	W	6-1	Buchan 3, Brittan, Croal, Thomson	4,000
17		25	(a)	Brentford	W	2-1	Buchan, Moores	3,000
18		27	(h)	Brentford	W	4-1	Moores, Thomson 2, Freeman	2,000
19	Jan	1	(a)	Croydon Comm	W	2-0	Thomson, Brown	5,000
20		8	(h)	Queen's Park R	W	5-1	Buchan 2 (1 pen), Croal, Thomson, Bridgeman	4,000
21		15	(a)	Arsenal	W	6-0	Ford 3, Buchan 2, Thomson	15,000
22		22	(h)	Fulham	D	1-1	Middelboe	4,000

FINAL LEAGUE POSITION: 1st in London Combination, 1st Competition   Appearances
Goals

23	Feb	5	(a)	Queen's Park R	W	3-0	Ford, Buchan 2	3,000
24		12	(h)	Crystal P	L	0-1		5,000
25		19	(a)	West Ham U	L	0-2		3,000
26	Mar	4	(a)	Fulham	W	1-0	Thomson	4,000
27		11	(h)	Luton T	W	11-1	Buchan 4, Thomson 7	8,000
28		18	(a)	Crystal P	L	2-4	Thomson, Harrow	5,000
29		25	(h)	West Ham U	W	4-0	Thomson 2, Harrow, Nicholls	6,000
30	Apr	1	(a)	Croydon Comm	W	4-1	Croal, Thomson 3	4,000
31		8	(h)	Fulham	W	6-3	Buchan 2, Thomson 4	20,000
32		15	(a)	Luton T	D	1-1	Buchan	4,000
33		21	(h)	Arsenal	W	9-0	Buchan 4, Thomson 5	26,000
34		22	(h)	Croydon Comm	W	3-1	Buchan 2, Croal	3,000
35		24	(a)	Arsenal	W	3-1	Buchan, Thomson 2	4,000
36		29	(h)	Queen's Park R	W	3-0	Ford, Buchan, Freeman	12,000

FINAL LEAGUE POSITION: 1st in London Combination, Subsidiary Competition   Appearances
Goals

Hampton C	Walker A	Marshall O	Taylor F	Logan T	Middelboe N	Ford H	Buchan C	Brittan H	Croal J	Bridgeman W	Moores	Thomson R	Harrow J	Spratt W	Hale H	Haviland	Butterworth H	Steer W	Denoon J	Macfarlane A	Walker J	Bettridge W	Freeman C	Baker W	Brown W	Calderhead D	Nicholls G	McNeil R	Whitley J	
1	2	3	4	5	6	7	8	9	10	11																				1
1	2	3	4	5	6	7	8	9	10		11																			2
1		2	4	5	6	7	8	11	10			9	3																	3
1		3	6	5	4	11	10		8			7		2	9															4
1			4	5	6	7	8		10	11			3	2	9															5
1			4	5			8		10	11		7		3	2	6	9													6
1		2	4	5		7			10	11		9	3	8	6															7
			4	5		7		9	10			8		3	6				2	1	11									8
1		2	4	5		7	8		10	11		9	3		6															9
1		3	6	5		11	10		7			9	2	4			8													10
1			4	5		7	8			11		9	3	2	6		10	6												11
1		3	4	5		7	8		10	11		9			6							2								12
1		3	4	5		7			10			9			6							2	8	11						13
1		3	4	5		7			10			9			6							2	8	11						14
		3	4	5		7			10			9			6		11		1			2	8							15
		6	4	5			8	9		11		7	3						1			2	10							16
			4	5	9	7		11				8	3		6				1			2	10							17
			4	5		7	8	11				9	3		6				1			2	10							18
1		3	4	5		7		11				9			6				1			2	10		8					19
			4	5		7	8		10	11		9	3		6				1			2								20
			4	5		7	8			11		9	3		6			10	1			2								21
1			4	5	6	7	8		10	11		9	3									2								22
14	2	13	22	6	22	20	17	4	19	5	8	18	5	10	16	1	4	5	8	1	1	11	7	2	1					
	1	1	2	8	23	1	10	2	2			13		3			1					2	1	1						

Hampton C	Walker A	Marshall O	Taylor F	Logan T	Middelboe N	Ford H	Buchan C	Brittan H	Croal J	Bridgeman W	Moores	Thomson R	Harrow J	Spratt W	Hale H	Haviland	Butterworth H	Steer W	Denoon J	Macfarlane A	Walker J	Bettridge W	Freeman C	Baker W	Brown W	Calderhead D	Nicholls G	McNeil R	Whitley J	
1		3	4			7	8		10	11		9		2	6		5														23
1		3	4	5		7	8		10			9		2	6											11				24
1		2	4	5		7	8		10			9	3													6	11			25
1			4	5			8			11		9	3		6							2	10				7			26
1			4	5		7	8			11		9	3		6							2	10							27
1			4	5					10	11		9	3	2			8									6	7			28
1			4	5			8		10	11		9	3	2												6	7			29
			4	5			8		10	11		9	3	2	6												7		1	30
			4	5			8		10	11		9	3	2	6												7		1	31
1			4	5		7	8		10			9	3	2												6	11			32
			4	5		7	8		10	11		9	3	2	6													1		33
1		2	4	5			8		10	11		9	3													6	7			34
		2	4				8		10	11		9	3		6							5					7	1		35
1			4	5		7	8			11		9	3	2	6								10							36
10		5	14	12		7	13	1	13	7	1	13	10	9	13		1	1	2			4	3			4	8	1	2	
			2	17			2					25	2				1									1		1		

1916-17

Manager: David Calderhead

1	Sep	2	(a)	Tottenham H	W	2-0	Taylor, Thomson	4,000
2		9	(h)	Crystal P	W	4-1	Croal, Freeman 2, Mosscrop	4,500
3		16	(a)	Brentford	W	3-0	Mosscrop, Halse 2	4,000
4		23	(h)	Southampton	W	3-0	Thomson, Halse, Steer	10,000
5		30	(h)	Arsenal	W	3-0	Thomson, Middelboe, Freeman	6,000
6	Oct	7	(a)	Luton T	W	4-1	Thomson 2, Croal 2	5,000
7		14	(h)	Reading	W	6-0	Thomson 2, Croal, Middelboe, Halse 2	4,000
8		21	(a)	Millwall A	D	0-0		14,000
9		28	(h)	Watford	W	3-2	Croal 3	7,000
10	Nov	4	(a)	Clapton O	W	2-0	Thomson, Bridgeman	4,000
11		11	(h)	Fulham	W	4-0	Thomson, Middelboe, Ford, Freeman	15,000
12		18	(a)	Queen's Park R	W	2-1	Thomson 2	6,000
13		25	(h)	Tottenham H	L	2-4	Croal, Dodd	10,000
14	Dec	2	(a)	Crystal P	D	1-1	Harrow	7,000
15		9	(h)	Brentford	W	7-2	Harrow 2, Spratt, Freeman 2, Halse 2	6,000
16		16	(a)	Southampton	L	0-2		5,000
17		23	(a)	Arsenal	L	1-2	Spratt	8,000
18		25	(h)	West Ham U	D	1-1	Thomson	15,000
19		26	(a)	West Ham U	L	0-2		5,000
20		30	(h)	Luton T	L	1-4	Thomson	5,000
21	Jan	6	(a)	Portsmouth	L	1-2	Steer	4,000
22		13	(h)	Millwall A	W	4-0	Taylor 2, Thomson 2	5,000
23		20	(a)	Watford	W	3-0	Thomson 3	4,000
24		27	(h)	Clapton O	W	1-0	Croal	1,000
25	Feb	3	(a)	Fulham	L	0-2		7,000
26		10	(h)	Queen's Park R	W	3-0	Thomson 2, Kelly	5,000
27		17	(a)	Arsenal	L	0-3		7,000
28		24	(h)	Millwall A	L	0-2		5,000
29	Mar	3	(a)	Brentford	L	0-3		3,000
30		10	(h)	Fulham	W	3-1	Thomson, Ford 2	5,000
31		17	(h)	Watford	D	2-2	Middelboe, Jaynes	5,000
32		24	(a)	Luton T	W	2-0	Thomson 2	6,000
33		31	(h)	Arsenal	W	2-0	Croal, Halse	6,000
34	Apr	6	(a)	Queen's Park R	D	2-2	Halse 2	7,000
35		7	(a)	Millwall A	L	1-2	Avelin	4,000
36		9	(h)	Queen's Park R	W	3-1	Croal 2, Halse	7,000
37		14	(h)	Brentford	W	3-2	Thomson, Croal, Halse	8,500
38		21	(a)	Fulham	W	4-0	Thomson 3, Vizard	5,000
39		26	(h)	Luton T	W	4-0	Thomson 2, Croal, Middelboe	2,000
40		28	(a)	Watford	W	6-3	Spratt, Halse 3, Bresname, Croal	5,000

FINAL LEAGUE POSITION: 3rd in London Combination

Appearances
Goals

Denoon J	Worrall E	Harrow J	Taylor F	Davidson S	Spratt W	Nicholl G	Taylor D	Thomson J	Croal J	Bridgeman W	Middelboe N	Ford H	Freeman C	Mosscrop E	Halse H	Hampton C	Steer W	Hughes J	Proudfoot P	Kelly H	Brown A	Coyle JWR	Calderhead D	Macdonald	Bresname C	Dodd G	Howell	Coaer J	Corke	Campbell J	Jackson H	Newman J	Lessons W	Dale G	Brown J	Avelin J	Rogers A	Vizard E	
1	2	3	4	5	6	7	8	9	10	11																													1
1		3	4	5			2	9	10			6	7	8	11																								2
1		3	4	5		7	2	9	10			6			11	8																							3
		3	4		6		2	9	10	5						8		1	7																				4
1		3	4				2	9	10	11	5	7	8		6																								5
			4		2	7	3	9	10	8					6			1	5	11																			6
		3	4		6	7	2	9	10						5	8		1		11																			7
		3	4	5		7	2	9	10						6	8		1		11																			8
		3	4			7	2	9	10	5					6			1		11	8																		9
	2							9	10	5					3			1		7		4	6	8	11														10
		3		5			2	9	10	4		7	8		6			1		11																			11
	2	3			6	7		9							5	8	4	1		11						10													12
		3			6		2	9	10	5					4			1		11						7	8												13
		3		5				9	10	4		7			6			1		11			8		2														14
		3		5	4	7	2	9							6	10	8	1		11																			15
	2	3			6		8	9	10						5			1		11						7				4									16
	2	3		5	4			9	10						6	8		1		11						7													17
		3			6		2	9	10	5					4			1		11						7	8												18
		3		5	6		2	9	10	11			4					1								7	8												19
	2	3			4			9		11	5	7	8					1								10													20
	2				4	5	3	9		11						8		1				6				7					10								21
	2	3	4	5			8	9	10						6			1		11						7													22
	2	3	4	5			8	9	10						6			1		11						7													23
	2	3		5	6			9	10	4		7				8		1		11																			24
	2	3	4	5	10	11		9						8	6			1								7													25
	2	3		5				9	11	8			4					1		10						7													26
		3		5			2	9	10	4								1		11						7					6	8							27
	2				4	5	3		10						8		9	1		11						7													28
					4	5	3	9	10							8		1		11						7						2	6						29
	2			5			3	9		4			8	10	6			1		11						7													30
							3	9		4			10		2	8		1		11		6				7					5								31
	2						3	9		5			8	10	4			1		11						7							6						32
	2				4		3	9	10	5					8			1		11						7													33
		3			4		2	9	11	5					8			1								7								6					34
		3		5											8	10	9	1		7					11											4	2		35
	2		4									10	11		5	8	9	1								7										6	3		36
					4		3	9	10	5					8			1								7										2	6	11	37
	6				4		3	9	10	5					8			1								7											2	11	38
							3	9	10	5					6			1								7	8									2	4	11	39
		3			6		2	9		8					10			1		7			5		11											4			40
4	20	26	16	10	27	9	33	37	30	12	33	9	10	2	25	8	4	28	1	27	2	4	2	1	16	5	1	1	1	6	4	2	1	4	2	4	3	3	
	3	1			3		2	29	15	1	5	3	6	2	15			2		1					1	1										1	1		

A.N.Other played number 6 in Matches 26, 28 and 33; T.Quinn played number 8 in Match 29; R.Jaynes played number 8 in Match 31 and scored one goal; A.Macfarlane played number 10 in Match 34; J.Smith played number 6 in Match 35.

1917-18

Manager: David Calderhead

1	Sep	1	(h)	Millwall A	L	3-4	Croal, Thomson, Smith	10,000
2		8	(a)	Tottenham H	W	4-0	Thomson 3, Vizard	12,000
3		15	(a)	Crystal P	W	3-0	Croal, Thomson 2	3,700
4		22	(h)	Brentford	W	3-1	Halse 3	10,000
5		29	(a)	Arsenal	W	1-0	Halse	9,000
6	Oct	6	(h)	West Ham U	W	4-3	Thomson 2, Ford, Freeman	12,000
7		13	(a)	Fulham	D	1-1	Thomson	8,000
8		20	(h)	Queen's Park R	L	1-2	Thomson	5,000
9		27	(a)	Millwall A	D	0-0		8,000
10	Nov	3	(h)	Tottenham H	D	0-0		8,000
11		10	(h)	Crystal P	L	0-1		5,000
12		17	(a)	Brentford	L	0-1		3,000
13		24	(h)	Arsenal	W	4-3	Croal, Thomson 2, Taylor	6,000
14	Dec	1	(a)	West Ham U	D	1-1	Croal	6,000
15		8	(h)	Fulham	D	2-2	Smith, Taylor	8,000
16		15	(a)	Queen's Park R	W	1-0	Nicholls	4,000
17		22	(h)	Millwall A	W	6-2	Thomson, Smith 2, Taylor, Rolls, Logan	6,000
18		25	(a)	Clapton O	W	4-1	Croal, Thomson, Ford 2	4,000
19		26	(h)	Clapton O	L	0-2		8,000
20		29	(a)	Tottenham H	L	0-2		8,000
21	Jan	5	(a)	Crystal P	D	0-0		6,000
22		12	(h)	Brentford	W	4-1	Thomson 2, Freeman, Casey	6,000
23		19	(a)	Arsenal	L	1-4	Abrams	7,000
24		26	(h)	West Ham U	D	2-2	Nicholson, Freeman	8,000
25	Feb	2	(a)	Fulham	W	2-0	Freeman 2	3,000
26		9	(h)	Clapton O	W	3-0	Thomson 2, Smith	5,000
27		16	(a)	Millwall A	W	4-0	Thomson 2, Smith, Jones	8,000
28		23	(h)	Tottenham H	W	3-0	Smith 3	20,000
29	Mar	2	(a)	Crystal P	W	2-0	Thomson, Barber	7,000
30		9	(a)	Brentford	W	1-0	Ford	5,000
31		16	(h)	Arsenal	W	4-2	Halse, Smith 2, Langford	4,000
32		23	(a)	West Ham U	D	2-2	Thomson, Freeman	14,000
33		29	(h)	Queen's Park R	W	1-0	Thomson	8,000
34		30	(h)	Fulham	W	7-0	Halse, Thomson, Smith, Rolls, Jackson, Woodward 2	7,000
35	Apr	1	(a)	Queen's Park R	W	2-1	Thomson, Smith	6,000
36		6	(a)	Clapton O	W	6-1	Thomson, Smith, Kelly, Langford 3	5,000

FINAL LEAGUE POSITION: 1st in London Combination, 1st Competition

Appearances
Goals

National War Fund Competition

37	Apr	13	(h)	Tottenham H	D	1-1	Smith	5,000
38		20	(a)	Tottenham H	W	1-0	Langford	5,000
39		27	(a)	West Ham U	D	3-3	Thomson 2, Harrow	3,000
40	May	4	(h)	West Ham U	W	4-1	Thomson, Smith 2, Freeman	3,000

Appearances
Goals

Hughes J	Spratt W	Halse H	Rogers	Dickie W	Nicholson J	Nicholls G	Croal J	Thomson R	Smith J	Vizard E	Taylor D	Avelin J	Ford H	Middelboe N	Skinner H	Kelly H	Cadman A	Freeman C	Bresname C	Bettridge W	Kimberley	Rolls A	Jackson C	Casey J	Burton	Bridgeman W	Barber T	Hargreaves R	Molyneux J	Harrow J	Rawlings J	Jones	Compton W	Steer W	Forsyth A	Woodward J	Langford T	Wilson W	#
1	2	3	4	5	6	7	8	9	10	11																													1
1	5	6	4				8	9	10	11	2	3	7																										2
1	6	4					8	9	3					2	5	7																							3
1	8			5			11	9	3					2	7	6	4	10																					4
1	8			5			11	9	3							6	4	10	7																				5
1	4						11	9	10		3			6		7		5	8		2																		6
1	4						8	9	10		3			5		11		6		7																			7
1	5	6						9	10		3					11		8		2																			8
1	4	6	5					9	8		2					3		10		7																			9
1	4	8		5				9			3	2		6								11	7				10												10
1	6	8	4	5			10	9			2			3								7	6	11															11
1	2	8	6	5			10	9			3											7			4														12
1				5			10	9			3			2		11						6	7				8	4											13
1		6		5			8	9	10	7	2			3		11																							14
1	6			4			10		9	11	3			5				8		2		7																	15
1	5			4		7	10	9			3			6		11		8		2																			16
1	6			4	8		11	9	10		3									2		7																	17
1	5			4			11	9	10		3		7	2				8								6													18
1	10	4	5				11	9			3			2		7		8								6													19
	6		5				10	9			3			4		11		8								6	1	2	7										20
1				5	4			9						2		7						11	8		5		3	10											21
1						10	9				3			2		7		8				11					4												22
				5	11		9				3			7		10						2		1			4												23
	4					10		9			3	2		11		8				7				1			6												24
1	6					11		10			3	7	2	8								4	9																25
1					6	8	9	10			3			2		11						7	5				4												26
1							4	9	8		2	3		5		11								6	7														27
1	6							9	10		2			11								7	5				4	8											28
1	5						10	9			3			2		11						7				6							4	8					29
1	9								3			7	6	11		8				5						10		2					4						30
1	9		6					10			3			2						5	11						4						4				8		31
1	6						9	10	11		2			8						5						4		3					4						32
1	7			6	8		9	10			3	2								5	11												4						33
1	4						6	9	10		3			2		11						7	5														8		34
1	6							9	10		3			2		11						7	5	11									4				8		35
1	6							9	10		3			2		11						7	5														8		36
33	5	25	10	5	18	6	23	31	22	5	32	7	6	27	1	17	4	16	2	5	3	12	10	6	1	3	5	4	3	3	2	2	12	2	1	3	2		
	6				1	1	5	26	14		3			4		1		6				2	1	1		1		1				1					2	4	

Hughes J	Spratt W	Halse H	Rogers	Dickie W	Nicholson J	Nicholls G	Croal J	Thomson R	Smith J	Vizard E	Taylor D	Avelin J	Ford H	Middelboe N	Skinner H	Kelly H	Cadman A	Freeman C	Bresname C	Bettridge W	Kimberley	Rolls A	Jackson C	Casey J	Burton	Bridgeman W	Barber T	Hargreaves R	Molyneux J	Harrow J	Rawlings J	Jones	Compton W	Steer W	Forsyth A	Woodward J	Langford T	Wilson W	#
1				5				9	10		2					11						7													4	8	6		37
1								9	10		3	2	7	5		11						4													6	8			38
		2			5			9	10		3					11								8		1	7								6		4		39
1		6			4			9	10		3	7	5	11		8							2														2		40
3		2		1	2			4	4		4	1	2	2		4		1				2	1	1		1	1								3	2	2		
								3	3					1										1															

T.Brown played number 10 in Match 3; F.Johnson played number 11 in Match 3; A.Hendon played number 2 in Match 5; W.Jenkins played number 2 in Match 7; J.Nicol played number 4 in Matches 8 and 36; Bunyan played number 7 in Matches 8 and 10; Ross played number 11 in Match 9; Barnfather played number 11 in Match 12; T.Logan played number 5 in Match 17 and scored one goal; W.White played number 6 in Matches 22 and 23; L.Abrams played number 8 in Match 23 and scored one goal; Manning played number 10 Match 27; T.Jones played number 3 in Match 28; J.Charles played number 7 in Matches 31 and 32; Brice played number 3 in Match 37; S.Dawson played number 5 in Matches 24 and 25.

1918-19

1	Sep	7	(a)	Millwall A	W	6-1	Ford 2, Freeman, Smith 3	7,000
2		14	(h)	Fulham	W	4-2	Ford, Halse 3	10,000
3		21	(a)	Brentford	D	0-0		5,996
4		28	(h)	West Ham U	W	3-1	Smith 2, Langford	12,000
5	Oct	5	(a)	Tottenham H	L	1-2	Smith	12,000
6		12	(h)	Clapton O	W	6-0	Kelly, Halse 4, Langford	8,000
7		19	(h)	Arsenal	W	4-1	Kelly 3, Rolyat	12,500
8		26	(a)	Queen's Park R	D	2-2	Smith 2	8,000
9	Nov	2	(h)	Millwall A	L	0-1		10,000
10		9	(a)	Fulham	W	2-1	Brittan	10,000
11		16	(h)	Brentford	D	2-2	Halse, Thomson	12,000
12		23	(a)	West Ham U	L	1-3	Goffin	11,000
13		30	(h)	Tottenham H	W	3-1	Bird 3	10,000
14	Dec	7	(a)	Clapton O	W	5-0	Taylor 2, Freeman 2, Brittan	5,000
15		14	(a)	Arsenal	L	0-3		4,000
16		21	(h)	Queen's Park R	W	2-0	Bettridge, Smith	15,000
17		25	(h)	Crystal P	L	0-2		10,000
18		26	(a)	Crystal P	D	0-0		12,000
19		28	(a)	Millwall A	D	1-1	Bird	20,000
20	Jan	4	(h)	Fulham	W	3-0	Smith 2, Woodward	25,000
21		11	(a)	Brentford	D	1-1	Ford	17,000
22		18	(h)	West Ham U	D	0-0		24,000
23		25	(a)	Tottenham H	D	1-1	Freeman	20,000
24	Feb	1	(h)	Clapton O	D	3-3	Smith 2, Halse	7,000
25		8	(h)	Arsenal	L	1-2	Ford	16,000
26		15	(a)	Crystal P	L	0-1		15,000
27		22	(h)	Millwall A	W	3-2	Freeman, Halse, Croal	17,000
28	Mar	1	(a)	Fulham	L	2-6	Halse, Croal	25,000
29		8	(h)	Brentford	L	1-4	Thomson	30,500
30		15	(a)	West Ham U	D	3-3	Ramsay, Wilding 2	25,300
31		22	(h)	Tottenham H	L	1-2	Woosnam	25,000
32		29	(a)	Clapton O	D	0-0		7,000
33	Apr	5	(a)	Arsenal	L	1-2	Wilding	35,000
34		12	(h)	Crystal P	W	3-0	Wilding, Whitehouse, Whittingham	12,000
35		18	(a)	Queen's Park R	L	2-3	Whitehouse, Whittingham	15,000
36		21	(h)	Queen's Park R	W	3-0	Smith, Wilding 2	20,000

FINAL LEAGUE POSITION: 6th in London Combination

Appearances
Goals

London Victory Cup

2	Mar	20	(h)	Queen's Park R	W	2-0	Smith, Wilding	
SF	Apr	19	(n*)	Crystal P	W	4-0	Smith 2, Davidson, Wilding	22,000
F		26	(n*)	Fulham	W	3-0	Wilding, Rutherford 2	36,000

*Played at Arsenal Stadium, Highbury, London.

Appearances
Goals

Hughes J	Bettridge W	Taylor D	Harrow J	Middelboe N	Ford H	Freeman C	Dickie W	Smith J	Kelly H	Adams J	Halse W	Casey J	Rolyat D	Nicholson J	Nicholls G	Langford T	Pacey H	Cadman A	Godson	Goffin J	Brittan H	Tillotson	Fazackerley S	Thomson J	Davidson S	Bird A	Buchanan R	Bridgeman W	Woodward VJ	Ramsay R	Molyneux J	Wilding H	Yorke R	Whitehouse B	Whittingham R	Henson	Croal J	Vizard E	
1	3	4	5	6	7	8	9	10	11																														1
1	2	3	6	4	7			5	10		8	9	11																										2
1				2				5	10	11		4	7	3	6	8	9																						3
1		3		2				10	11		8	6	7				9	4	5																				4
1	2	3	4				8	5	10			6	11				7	9																					5
1		3	5					10	11			9			7	8	6	4	2																				6
1		3		2				5	10	11		9	7		8	6		4																					7
1				2				10	11			5	3		4	8	6		7																				8
1		3		2				5	10	11	9				7	6																							9
1		3		2				5	8	7	9	11			6		4			10																			10
1		3	6					10				5	7		4					2	8	9	11																11
1			3					5	11			7			4	6		8		2	10	9																	12
1	3	2	4	5				10			8	7			6									9															13
1	2	8	3	4				10	5		11				7					6					9														14
1	2	9	3	4				10			11				6					8				5	7														15
1	2		3	5			8	10			11				4	6				9					7														16
1		3		2				10			4	11	5		6					8				7	9														17
1		3						10	11		7			5	4	6				8				9	2														18
1		3	5					4						7	6					8				9	2	11													19
1	2		3	5	7			10	11	4					6					9					8														20
1	2		3	5	7	8		10			4	11			6					9																			21
1	2		3	5			8	10			4				6					9				7													11		22
1	2		3	5	7	8		10			4				11					9				6															23
1	2		3	5	7	8		10			6				9					4				11															24
1	2		3	5	7	10		6			9				4					11																			25
1	2		3			7	10	6			4	5			9									11															26
1	2		3			8		9	7	5					4					11																	10		27
1	2		3	5		8		9	7						4					11	6																10		28
	2	3	6	4	7			10			8				9									1													11		29
	2		3			7	8		4			11			6									1	9					4	10						10		30
	2		3			7									6			1	9					4	10						8						8		31
	2		3			7	8								5						4				6	1	9										10		32
	2		3			7	10					4								6	1	9				8											11		33
	2		3	6	7			11			4										6	1			9	10	8												34
	2						10	3			11	6			4	1					7	9	5	8															35
	2		3	6			10				7				4					8				1	9					11	5								36
28	24	16	23	27	14	18	8	21	13	5	20	17	3	5	13	6	21	2	2	2	11	2	3	7	10	8	2	7	2	8	8	6	1	4	3	2	9		
1	2			5	5			17	1			11	1				2			1	3			2		4				1	1			6			2	2		

2		3				7			10					5										6	1	9	4								8			11	2
2		3	5	7					10												6					4				1	9			8					SF
2		3	6	7			5														4					1	9	8							11				F
3		3	2	3			1	2				1			1						2					1	3	3	1	2					1	2			
				3																	1						3												

Naylor played number 2 in Match 1; A.Fisher played number 9 in Match 8; B.Taylor played number 4 in Match 9; A.N.Other played number 8 in Match 9; H.Nisbet played number 11 in Match 13; W.Smith played number 10 in Match 19; W.Steer played number 8 in Match 26; Wright played number 5 in Matches 29 and 33; A.Ormiston played number 5 in Match 30; M.Woosnam played number 5 in Matches 31 and 34 and scored one goal; Davies played number 11 in Match 31; R.McNeil played number 11 in Match 32; C.Lewis played number 11 in the Semi-final of the Victory Cup; J.Rutherford played number 10 in the Final of the Victory Cup and scored 2 goals; D.Jack played number 8 in Match 25.

1939-40

Manager: William Birrell

1	Aug	27	(h)	Bolton W	W 3-2	J.F.Smith 2, James	33,902
2		31	(h)	Manchester U	D 1-1	Spence	15,157
3	Sep	2	(a)	Liverpool	L 0-1		18,386

Above matches played in Division One, abandoned upon outbreak of war. Appearances
Goals

Football League South Group 'B'

4	Oct	21	(a)	Brentford	D 2-2	Payne, Burgess	6,628
5		28	(h)	Southampton	W 6-2	Payne 3, Weaver, J.F.Smith, Buchanan	2,818
6	Nov	4	(a)	Brighton & HA	L 1-5	Payne	4,500
7		11	(h)	Reading	W 3-0	Buchanan, Payne, Spence	5,070
8		18	(a)	Fulham	W 3-1	Foss, Payne, Buchanan	8,000
9		25	(h)	Portsmouth	W 1-0	Foss	6,217
10	Dec	2	(a)	Queen's Park R	L 2-3	Payne 2	8,010
11		9	(h)	Aldershot	D 2-2	Mills, Spence	5,297
12		16	(a)	Bournemouth	D 2-2	Payne, J.F.Smith	4,000
13		25	(a)	Southampton	L 3-5	Strauss 2	3,000
14		26	(h)	Brighton & HA	W 3-2	Payne, Strauss, Sherbourne	3,000
15		30	(a)	Reading	W 5-1	Payne 4, Sherbourne	3,000
16	Jan	6	(h)	Fulham	D 1-1	J.F.Smith	6,240
17		13	(a)	Portsmouth	W 2-1	Payne, Mills	5,000
18		20	(h)	Queen's Park R	D 0-0		8,819
19		24	(h)	Brentford	W 3-2	Payne, Mills, Sherbourne	1,500
20	Feb	22	(h)	Bournemouth	W 4-3	Buchanan 2, Burgess, Spence	
21	Mar	6	(a)	Aldershot	L 1-5	Buchanan	

FINAL LEAGUE POSITION: 3rd in Group 'B' Appearances
Goals

Football League South Group 'C'

22	Feb	10	(a)	Charlton A	D 3-3	Payne, Spence 2	3,500
23		17	(h)	Southampton	W 5-1	Mills 2, Payne, Weaver, Alexander	2,500
24		24	(h)	Tottenham H	L 0-2		14,073
25	Mar	2	(a)	Brentford	D 1-1	Mills	7,110
26		9	(h)	Portsmouth	W 4-1	Mills, Payne 2, Alexander	8,091
27		16	(a)	Millwall	W 3-2	Payne 2, Alexander	13,981
28		22	(h)	Fulham	L 1-4	Payne	15,000
29		23	(a)	Arsenal	L 0-3		15,000
30		25	(a)	Fulham	L 3-4	Payne, Weaver 2	10,000
31		30	(h)	West Ham U	L 3-10	Payne 3	8,645
32	Apr	6	(h)	Charlton A	L 1-4	Payne	8,000
33		13	(a)	Southampton	L 0-3		
34		17	(a)	Arsenal	D 2-2	Weaver, Payne	8,500
35		24	(h)	Millwall	W 2-1	Kiernan, Payne	
36		29	(a)	West Ham U	L 2-4	Payne 2	5,000
37	May	4	(a)	Portsmouth	L 1-3	Payne	4,000
38		11	(h)	Brentford	L 0-2		3,000
39		25	(a)	Tottenham H	L 2-3	Mills, Brown	4,000

FINAL LEAGUE POSITION: 9th in Group 'C' Appearances
Goals

Football League War Cup

40	Apr	20	(a)	West Ham U	L 2-3	Hanson, Kiernan	15,200
41		27	(h)	West Ham U	L 0-2		14,755

Appearances
Goals

Appearance / line-up grid (numbers are shirt positions; final column is the match number).

Woodley V	Barber G	Smith AJ	Mitchell W	Salmond R	Weaver S	Spence R	Smith JF	Argue J	James D	Hanson A	Burgess H	Mayes AJ	Payne J	Jackson J	Busby M	Smale D	Buchanan P	Mills G	Foss SR	Alexander D	Griffiths R	Sherborne J	Strauss W	O'Hare J	Tennant A	Vaux E	Kiernan T	Lowe HP	Dickie M	Farmer A	Crook W	Butler MP	Pugh SJ	Reay EP	Ridyard A	Abel S	Bott W	Brown RAJ	White A	#
1	2	3	4	5	6	7	10	8	9	11																														1
1	2	3	4	5	6	7	10		9	11	8																													2
1	2	3		5	6	7	10		9	11		4	8																											3
3	3	3	2	3	3	3	3	1	3	3	1	1	1																											
								1	2	1																														

Woodley V	Barber G	Smith AJ	Mitchell W	Salmond R	Weaver S	Spence R	Smith JF	Argue J	James D	Hanson A	Burgess H	Mayes AJ	Payne J	Jackson J	Busby M	Smale D	Buchanan P	Mills G	Foss SR	Alexander D	Griffiths R	Sherborne J	Strauss W	O'Hare J	Tennant A	Vaux E	Kiernan T	Lowe HP	Dickie M	Farmer A	Crook W	Butler MP	Pugh SJ	Reay EP	Ridyard A	Abel S	Bott W	Brown RAJ	White A	#
	2	3		5	6		8			10	4	9	1			11			7																					4
	2	3		5	6		8					9	1	4		11		7	10																					5
	2	3		5	6	11	8					9	1	4				7	10																					6
	2	3		5	6	11	8					9	1	4				7	10																					7
1		3		5	6	11	8					9				7			10	4			2																	8
	2	3			6	11	8					9	1			7			10	4	5																			9
1	2	3			6	7	8					9				11			10	4	5																			10
1	2	3		5	6	7	8					9				11	10			4																				11
1	2	3		5	6	7	8					9				11	10			4																				12
1	2	3		5	6	7	8					9					4				10	11																		13
1	2	3		5	6	7	8					9					4				10	11																		14
		3		5	6	7	8					9	1			11				10			2	4																15
	3			5		7	8				6	9	1			11				10			2	4																16
1	2	3		5	6	7	8				4	9				11																								17
1	2	3		5	6		8				4	9				7	10		11																					18
		3		5	6						4	9	1			7	8	11	10				2																	19
	2			5	6	7	8			10	4	9	1			11							2																	20
	3			5	6	7	8					1				11	9	10		4					2															21
8	16	14		16	17	14	17			2	6	17	10	3	2	13	7	6	12	3	5	2	4	2	2															
					1	3	3				2	17				6	3	2			3	3																		

Woodley V	Barber G	Smith AJ	Mitchell W	Salmond R	Weaver S	Spence R	Smith JF	Argue J	James D	Hanson A	Burgess H	Mayes AJ	Payne J	Jackson J	Busby M	Smale D	Buchanan P	Mills G	Foss SR	Alexander D	Griffiths R	Sherborne J	Strauss W	O'Hare J	Tennant A	Vaux E	Kiernan T	Lowe HP	Dickie M	Farmer A	Crook W	Butler MP	Pugh SJ	Reay EP	Ridyard A	Abel S	Bott W	Brown RAJ	White A	#
	3			5		7	8				6	9	1			10		11	4				2																	22
	2			5	6	7	8				4	9	1			10		11					3																	23
1	3			5	6		8				4	7	9			11	10	2																						24
	3			5	6	7	8				4		1			9	10	11	2																					25
1	3			5	6	7					4	9				10		11	2							8														26
	3			5	6	7					4	9	1			10		11	2							8														27
1	3			5	6	7					4	9				10		11	2	8																				28
	3			5	6	7	10				4	9	1			11		2	8																					29
1	3			5	6	7					4	9				10		11	2	8																				30
	2	3		5		7					6	9	1			10		11	4				8																	31
1					10	7						9		4		8		11	5									2	3	6										32
	3				6	7						9	1			10		11	5				2			8														33
					6							9	1	7		10	11						2			8	4		3	5										34
					6	7				4		9	1			10	11						2			8		5		3										35
1	3				6	7				8		9				10	11						2				4	5												36
1	3			5	6	7				8						11	4		2																		10			37
1	3			5	6	7				8		9	10			11	4		2																				38
	3			5	6	7				8		9	11			4			2																		10		39
8	14	2		13	16	16	5			5	11	15	10	1		2	15	7	13	7	1		15		1	7	2	2	2	2	1	1	1	1	1	1	1	1	1	
				4	2							17				5	3						1														1			

Woodley V	Barber G	Smith AJ	Mitchell W	Salmond R	Weaver S	Spence R	Smith JF	Argue J	James D	Hanson A	Burgess H	Mayes AJ	Payne J	Jackson J	Busby M	Smale D	Buchanan P	Mills G	Foss SR	Alexander D	Griffiths R	Sherborne J	Strauss W	O'Hare J	Tennant A	Vaux E	Kiernan T	Lowe HP	Dickie M	Farmer A	Crook W	Butler MP	Pugh SJ	Reay EP	Ridyard A	Abel S	Bott W	Brown RAJ	White A	#
	3				6	7				11		9	1			10	4	5				2				8														40
	3				6	7				11		9	1			10	4	5								8													2	41
	2				2	2				2		2	2			2	2	2				1				2													1	
										1																1														

359

1940-41

Manager: William Birrell

1	Aug	31	(a)	Crystal P	L 3-6	Kiernan 2, Weaver	600
2	Sep	7	(h)	Brentford	W 2-1	Mills, Kiernan	3,500
3		14	(a)	Tottenham H	L 2-3	Spence 2	1,622
4		21	(h)	Tottenham H	W 4-1	Jones, Mills 2, Spence	1,756
5	Oct	5	(h)	West Ham U	D 1-1	Kilduff	1,874
6		12	(a)	Queen's Park R	W 3-2	Jones 2, Mills	1,500
7		19	(h)	Queen's Park R	W 3-1	Weaver, Kilduff 2	1,500
8		26	(a)	Millwall	L 1-3	Jones	600
9	Nov	2	(h)	Millwall	D 2-2	Kiernan, Kilduff	600
10		9	(a)	Aldershot	L 3-5	Tennant 2, Kiernan	2,000
11		16	(h)	Charlton A	D 2-2	Kilduff, Spence	300
12		23	(a)	Portsmouth	L 2-4	Spence 2	1,500
13		30	(a)	Portsmouth	L 0-5		1,500
14	Dec	7	(a)	West Ham U	L 2-6	Griffith, Smith	1,000
15		14	(h)	Crystal P	L 1-3	Galloway	940
16		21	(a)	Charlton A	W 3-1	Spence 2, Galloway	500
17		25	(h)	Fulham	W 5-2	Spence 2, Mills, Galloway, Macaulay	3,441
18		28	(h)	Aldershot	W 6-0	Spence, Foss 2, Smith, Mills, Jones	1,516
19	Apr	14	(h)	Arsenal	W 3-1	Mills, Smith, Smith	3,000
20		26	(a)	Reading	W 3-2	Kurz, Spence 2	6,000
21	May	10	(a)	Cardiff C	L 2-1	Kurz, Spence	4,000
22		17	(a)	Northampton T	L 1-4	Spence	3,000
23		24	(a)	West Ham U	D 3-3	Foss 3	2,500

FINAL LEAGUE POSITION: 21st in Football League South

Appearances
Goals

London Cup 'A' Competition

24	Jan	4	(a)	Aldershot	L 0-1		2,000
25		11	(h)	Aldershot	W 5-1	Spence 2, Hurley, Kurz, Galloway	2,000
26		25	(h)	Brentford	L 0-1		1,318
27	Feb	1	(a)	Queen's Park R	L 2-5	Tennant, Galloway	1,900
28		8	(a)	Crystal P	D 3-3	Galloway, Spence, Kurz	3,703
29	Mar	29	(a)	Brentford	D 2-2	Kiernan 2	1,654
30	Apr	5	(h)	Crystal P	L 1-3	Kurz	3,500
31		12	(a)	Fulham	L 0-4		5,000
32		19	(h)	Fulham	W 4-3	Opp own-goal, Kurz 2, Mills	2,712
33	May	3	(h)	Queen's Park R	L 2-3	Spence 2	4,000

FINAL LEAGUE POSITION: 6th in London Cup 'A' Competition

Appearances
Goals

Football League War Cup (South)

1	Feb	15	(h)	Portsmouth	W 3-1	Galloway 2, Kurz	4,284
		22	(a)	Portsmouth	W 4-1	Kurz 2, Foss 2	6,000
2	May	1	(a)	Brentford	D 2-2	Galloway 2	4,520
		8	(h)	Brentford	W 3-1	Galloway, Kurz 2	5,992
3		15	(a)	Queen's Park R	L 0-2		5,575
		22	(h)	Queen's Park R	L 2-4	Galloway, James	7,232

Appearances
Goals

Appearance and goal grid (shirt numbers worn by each player per match).

Woodley V	Barber G	Smith AJ	Griffiths R	Salmond R	Weaver S	Spence R	Kiernan T	Mills G	Foss SR	O'Hare J	Tennant A	Jackson J	Mercer J	Jones EN	Kilduff G	Lyon W	Macaulay J	Galloway J	Smith JF	Smith G	Hardwick GF	Kurz FJ	Clatworthy L	Cronk FJ	Milburn G	Friend A	March R	Alexander D	Greenwood R	Chalkley AG	Clifton H	Etherton RP	Molloy P	Hipkin RW	Milton GW	Bedford G	Hurley C	Ferguson W	Revell C	James D	#
1	2	3	4	5	6	7	8	9	11		10																														1
1	2	3	4	5	6	7	8	9	11		10																														2
1		3	4	5	6	7	8	9	11	2					10																										3
1		3	4	5	6	7	8	9	11	2					10																										4
		3		5	6	7		9		2		8		1	4	10	11																								5
		3		5	6	7		9		2		8		1	4	10	11																								6
		3			6	7		9		2		10		1	4	8	11											5													7
	2	3			6	7	8	9						1		10	11	5	4																						8
	2	3		5	6	7		10	9	1		8					11		4																						9
		3			6	7	8	9		2				1		10	11	5	4																						10
		3			6	7		9		2				1		10	11	5	4	8																					11
		3			6	7			11	2		9		1			10	5	4	8																					12
		3		5	6	7			11	2		9		1			10		4	8																					13
		3		5	6	7			11	2		9		1			10		4	8																					14
		3				7		9		2		10		1			11	5	4	8									6												15
	2	3			6	7			11			9		1			10	5	4	8																					16
		3		5		7		9	11	2		6		1			10		4	8																					17
1	2	3				7		9	10	6		11			4		8													5											18
1	2		3		6	7		9	11												4	8	5								10										19
1	2		4		6	7		10		8		11										5	3	9																	20
			4		11			10		1												5		9	2		3				6	7	8								21
		3		5		7		10	1															9	2										4	6	8	11			22
		3	4					10	11		1										8	7	5	6	9	2															23
7	**18**	**10**	**16**	**8**	**12**	**22**	**7**	**14**	**12**	**12**	**19**	**16**	**3**	**11**	**8**	**7**	**10**	**8**	**8**	**4**	**2**	**4**	**3**	**2**	**1**	**1**	**1**	**1**	**1**	**1**	**1**	**1**	**1**	**1**	**1**	**1**	**1**	**1**		
		1						2	15	5	7	5		2		5	5		1	3	3	1		2																	

Woodley V	Barber G	Smith AJ	Griffiths R	Salmond R	Weaver S	Spence R	Kiernan T	Mills G	Foss SR	O'Hare J	Tennant A	Jackson J	Mercer J	Jones EN	Kilduff G	Lyon W	Macaulay J	Galloway J	Smith JF	Smith G	Hardwick GF	Kurz FJ	Clatworthy L	Cronk FJ	Milburn G	Friend A	March R	Alexander D	Greenwood R	Chalkley AG	Clifton H	Etherton RP	Molloy P	Hipkin RW	Milton GW	Bedford G	Hurley C	Ferguson W	Revell C	James D	#
		3		5	6	7		10	11	2		8		1							4	9																			24
	2	3		5		7		10		1		8						4	8		6	9															11				25
1		3		5	6	7				2					4	8	10					9																11			26
					6	7				2		8		1	4		10				5	9	3															11			27
	2		11		6	7	8							1	4		10				5	9	3																		28
	2	3			6	7	8	10	11			4		1					5			9																			29
	2	3			6	7	8					4		1			10		5			9			10					11											30
1	2	3			6	7	8	9				4							5						10					11											31
1	2		4		6			10	11												8	5	3	9														7			32
	2		4		6	7		10				8		1			11					5	3	9																	33
3	**8**	**2**	**7**	**3**	**8**	**10**	**4**	**5**	**2**	**3**	**8**	**7**		**1**	**3**	**4**	**4**	**4**	**6**	**2**	**9**		**2**	**2**													**1**	**1**	**1**		
		5		2	1					1								3				5																			1 own-goal

Woodley V	Barber G	Smith AJ	Griffiths R	Salmond R	Weaver S	Spence R	Kiernan T	Mills G	Foss SR	O'Hare J	Tennant A	Jackson J	Mercer J	Jones EN	Kilduff G	Lyon W	Macaulay J	Galloway J	Smith JF	Smith G	Hardwick GF	Kurz FJ	Clatworthy L	Cronk FJ	Milburn G	Friend A	March R	Alexander D	Greenwood R	Chalkley AG	Clifton H	Etherton RP	Molloy P	Hipkin RW	Milton GW	Bedford G	Hurley C	Ferguson W	Revell C	James D	#
	2		3	5	6	7	8			11				1				4	10			9																			1
	2		3	5	6	7	8			11				1				4	10			9																			—
1	2		3	5	6	7	8			11								4	10			9																			2
	2	3	11	5	6	7	8							1				4	10			9																			—
1	2	3	11	5	6	7	8											4	10			9																			3
	2	3	5		6	7	8					4		1			10					9																	11		—
2	**6**	**3**	**6**	**5**	**6**	**6**	**6**			**3**		**1**		**4**			**5**	**6**	**6**			**6**																	**1**		
										2							6					5																	1		

1941-42

Manager: William Birrell

1	Aug	30	(a)	Charlton A	L 1-2	Spence	6.766
2	Sep	6	(h)	West Ham U	L 4-8	Payne, C.Smith, Kurz, Kiernan	6,427
3		13	(a)	Watford	W 3-1	Payne, Kurz, Spence	4,000
4		20	(h)	Aldershot	W 4-0	Galloway 2, J.F.Smith 2	6,000
5		27	(a)	Millwall	L 3-6	Galloway 3	5,500
6	Oct	4	(a)	Arsenal	L 0-3		7,747
7		11	(a)	Queen's Park R	L 1-2	Kurz	6,000
8		18	(h)	Reading	L 0-5		3,000
9		25	(h)	Brighton & HA	L 1-3	Galloway	3,000
10	Nov	1	(a)	Brentford	L 1-3	Tennant	6,000
11		8	(h)	Crystal P	W 1-0	Wrigglesworth	3,000
12		15	(a)	Fulham	W 4-1	J.F.Smith 2, Galloway, Weale	4,994
13		22	(h)	Tottenham H	D 1-1	Galloway	6,718
14		29	(a)	Portsmouth	W 3-2	Weaver, Weale, J.F.Smith	6,000
15	Dec	6	(h)	Clapton O	L 1-3	Galloway	2,718
16		13	(h)	Charlton A	L 2-4	Spence, Weale	3,000
17		20	(a)	West Ham U	L 0-5		3,800
18		25	(h)	Watford	D 2-2	Galloway, Weaver	
19		27	(a)	Aldershot	W 3-2	Weale, Galloway, Kurz	6,000
20	Jan	3	(h)	Millwall	D 3-3	Peacock, Kurz, Bearryman	3,442
21		10	(a)	Arsenal	L 1-5	Weale	12,260
22		17	(h)	Queen's Park R	W 3-1	Weale 2, Galloway	1,829
23		31	(a)	Brighton & HA	L 2-8	Thomas 2	2,500
24	Feb	7	(h)	Brentford	D 1-1	Gibbons	3,135
25		14	(a)	Crystal P	L 2-3	Galloway, Townsend	5,583
26		21	(h)	Fulham	L 1-5	Townsend	3,255
27		28	(a)	Tottenham H	L 0-2		6,558
28	Mar	7	(h)	Portsmouth	L 3-4	Townsend 3	3,258
29		14	(a)	Clapton O	W 3-0	Opp own-goal, Weaver 2	2,000
30	May	2	(a)	Reading	L 2-3	Weaver, Weale	3,000

FINAL LEAGUE POSITION: 13th in London War League

Appearances
Goals

War Cup (Group 4)

31	Mar	21	(h)	Crystal P	D 3-3	Spence, Weaver, Joyner	4,412
32		28	(a)	Fulham	L 0-1		5,886
33	Apr	4	(a)	Crystal P	W 3-0	Tennant 2, J.F.Smith	5,900
34		6	(h)	Fulham	D 2-2	Townsend, Foss	10,986
35		11	(a)	Portsmouth	L 0-2		10,000
36		18	(h)	Portsmotuh	D 0-0		7,721

FINAL LEAGUE POSITION: 3rd in War Cup (Group 4)

Appearances
Goals

Woodley V	Barber G	Griffiths R	Macaulay J	Salmond R	Weaver S	Smith C	Kiernan T	Kurz FJ	Payne J	Spence R	Mayes AJ	Hardwick GF	Johnson J	Tennant A	Vause PG	Smith JF	Galloway J	Clements BA	Smith AJ	Little G	Jackson J	Craig B	Wrigglesworth W	Griffiths M	Weale J	Clatworthy L	Bearryman HW	Peacock J	Joyner F	Townsend LF	Anderson D	Bacon CW	Winterbottom W	Dykes J	Foss SR	Kilpatrick W	Mills G	Mutitt E	
1	2	5	4		6	7	8	9		11		3			10																								1
1	2	3	4		6	7	8	9	10	11	5																												2
1		4			6	7	8	9	10	11	2	3			5																								3
1	3				6	7		9		11		2		4	5	8	10																						4
1	2				6	7		9		11		3		4	5	8	10																						5
1				5	6	7	8			11		2	3	4		10	9																						6
1				5	6	7	8	9				3		4					3					11												2	10		7
1	3			5	6	7	8	9		11				4			10																					2	8
				5	6	7	8	9				3		4			10				1	2		11															9
		4		5	6	7	8					3					10	9			1	2		11															10
				5	6		8					3		4			10				1	2		11	7														11
				5	6			9				3		4		8	10				1	2		11	7														12
				5	6							3		4		8	10				1	2			7														13
				5	6			9		7		3		4		8	10				1			11		10	2	6											14
				5						7				4		8	9				1		11			10	2	6											15
				5	6		8	9		7		3		4			10				1	2		11															16
				5	6		8	9		7		3		4			10				1	2		11															17
				5	6		8	9		7		3		4			10				1			11	2														18
				5	6			9		7				4		8		3			1	2		11		10													19
					6			9		7						5		3			1	2		11	4	10													20
		5			6			9		7				4			10				1	2		11		10													21
		3		5	6		8	9		7				4			10				1	2		11	2														22
		3		5	6					7											1			11	2	4													23
				5						7	2					8					1			11		6	10												24
		3		5	6					7						8	10				1	2		11	4			9											25
				5						7	2					8	10	3			1			11	4			9											26
				5	6					11							8								10	2	4		9	3									27
					6					7	3			4		8					1			11	5			9		10									28
					10					7	2			8							1			11	4			10	6	5									29
					6					7	2			8							1			11	3	4		10		5									30
8	4	10	2	19	25	10	13	16	2	23	5	20	2	25	4	6	21	2	4	3	21	10	2	19	8	10	4		4	1	3	1	2		1	1	1		
				5			1	1		5	2	3				1					5	13					1		8		1	1			5				

1 own-goal

Woodley V	Barber G	Griffiths R	Macaulay J	Salmond R	Weaver S	Smith C	Kiernan T	Kurz FJ	Payne J	Spence R	Mayes AJ	Hardwick GF	Johnson J	Tennant A	Vause PG	Smith JF	Galloway J	Clements BA	Smith AJ	Little G	Jackson J	Craig B	Wrigglesworth W	Griffiths M	Weale J	Clatworthy L	Bearryman HW	Peacock J	Joyner F	Townsend LF	Anderson D	Bacon CW	Winterbottom W	Dykes J	Foss SR	Kilpatrick W	Mills G	Mutitt E	
				9						7	3			4		8					1			11		10	2	6							5				31
				9						11	3			6		8					1			7		4						2	10	5					32
				6						7				9		8					1			2		11			3	10	4	5							33
1				6						7	3			4		8					2			9						10	5			11					34
				6						7	3			9		8					1			11	2	4							5		10				35
			8							7	3			9							1			11	2						10	4	5	6					36
1		1		5						6	5			6		5					4			4	5	3		2	1	2	4	6	2	3					
				1							1			2		1					1			1							1								

W.Croom played number 9 in Match 11; D.McCulloch played number 9 in Match 13; D.Smale played number 11 in Match 13; S.T.Malpass played number 3 in Match 15; Finch played number 8 in Match 23; D.Thomas played number 9 in Match 23 and scored 2 goals; Attwell played number 10 in Match 23; A.Jefferson played number 3 in Match 24; H.Goslin played number 4 in Match 24; A.H.Gibbons played number 9 in Match 24 and scored one goal; A.V.Aicken played number 6 in Match 26; F.P.Boulton played number 1 in Match 27; A.Sibley played number 7 in Match 27; L.H.Compton played number 2 in Match 28; F.A.Lewis played number 3 in Match 29; W.H.Dixon played number 9 in Match 30; G.Tweedy played number 1 in Match 32.

1942-43

Manager: William Birrell

#	Date			Opponent	Result	Scorers	Attendance
1	Aug	29	(h)	Queen's Park R	D 1-1	McKennan	6,787
2	Sep	5	(a)	Brighton & HA	W 2-1	Payne 2	3,000
3		12	(h)	Portsmouth	W 2-1	Airlie, Tennant	8,760
4		19	(a)	Brentford	W 2-0	Foss, McKennan	8,480
5		26	(h)	Fulham	W 4-2	Foss, McKennan 2, Payne	10,635
6	Oct	3	(a)	West Ham U	W 1-0	Payne	10,200
7		10	(h)	Aldershot	L 1-3	Payne	6,299
8		17	(a)	Southampton	W 2-1	Spence 2	8,000
9		24	(h)	Crystal P	W 4-1	McKennan 3, Spence	7,824
10		31	(a)	Tottenham H	D 1-1	Foss	12,625
11	Nov	7	(h)	Clapton O	L 0-2		4,564
12		14	(a)	Reading	W 4-1	Foss, Bryant 3	5,000
13		21	(h)	Millwall	W 4-2	Bryant 2, Mills, Foss	7,000
14		28	(a)	Queen's Park R	L 1-4	Spence	8,900
15	Dec	5	(h)	Brighton & HA	D 0-0		4,261
16		12	(a)	Portsmouth	L 0-3		7,500
17		19	(h)	Brentford	L 2-4	Liddell, Hardwick	8,154
18		25	(h)	Arsenal	W 5-2	Bryant 4, Liddell	17,000
19		26	(a)	Arsenal	W 5-1	McKennan 3, Spence 2	18,253
20	Jan	2	(a)	Fulham	L 1-3	Foss	8,900
21		9	(h)	West Ham U	L 1-3	McKennan	8,580
22		16	(a)	Aldershot	D 1-1	Mills	5,000
23		23	(h)	Southampton	W 3-1	McKennan 2, Foss	6,321
24		30	(a)	Crystal P	W 2-0	Foss 2	4,172
25	Feb	6	(h)	Tottenham H	L 0-1		12,125
26		13	(a)	Clapton O	L 1-3	Spence	2,000
27		20	(h)	Reading	W 2-0	Mills, Bidewell	2,832
28		27	(a)	Millwall	L 0-3		4,000

FINAL LEAGUE POSITION: 7th in Football League South

Appearances
Goals

Football League South Cup (Group 3)

#	Date			Opponent	Result	Scorers	Attendance
29	Mar	6	(a)	Tottenham H	L 0-2		13,438
30		13	(h)	Millwall	W 5-2	Foss, Mathie, Spence 2, Soo	7,152
31		20	(a)	Reading	L 2-7	Mills, Foss	6,000
32		27	(h)	Tottenham H	L 0-2		11,107
33	Apr	3	(a)	Millwall	W 2-1	Deverall, Bryant	4,000
34		10	(h)	Reading	L 0-4		10,897

FINAL LEAGUE POSITION: 3rd in Football League South Cup (Group 3)

Appearances
Goals

The table below records the shirt number worn by each player in each match.

Woodley V	White A	Hardwick GF	Brown WH	Allen JP	Tennant A	McKennan P	Airlie S	Payne J	Foss SR	Weaver S	Spence R	Mountford RC	Winterbottom W	Birkett R	Bearryman HW	Palmer RW	Bryant BL	Bidewell S	Buchanan P	Liddell W	Farmer A	Mills G	Soo F	Campbell J	Whittaker W	Mathie D	Greenwood R	Muttit E	Smith L	Butt L	Jones L	Jefferson A	Abel S	Hold O	Kurz FJ	Duke GE	Moseley W	Davies E	Match
1	2	3	4	5	6	8	9	10	11																				7										1
1	2	3	4	5	6	8	9	10	11																						10								2
1	2	3		5	4		8	9	11	6	7																			10									3
1		3		5	6	8	9	10	11		7	2	4																										4
1	2			5		10	8	9	11	6		3	4	7																									5
1	2	3		5		10	8	9	11	6			4	7																									6
1	2	3		5		8	9	11		6	7		4															10											7
1		3		5		8	9	11		7	2	4	6	10																								8
1				5		8	9	10	11		2	4	7	6																		3							9
1		3		5		9	8	10	11		2	4	7	6																									10
1		3		5		9	8	11		7	2	4	6	10																								11
1		3		5		8		11		7	2	4	6	9	10																							12
1				5			10	11	2	4	7	6	9	8																		3						13
1		3		5		8	10	11	2	4	6	9	7																									14
1				5	2	8	10	11	3	6	9	4	7																									15
1		3		5	2	8	10	7	4	6	9	11																										16
1		3	4	8	7	2	6	5	9	11																								10				17
1		5	8	10	7	2	6	9	4	11	3																											18
1		5	8	10	7	2	6	9	4	11	3																											19
1		5	8	10	7	3	2	6	9	4	11																											20
1		3	5	8	10	7	2	6	9	4	11																											21
1		3	5	8	10	7	2	6	9	4	11																											22
1		3	5	8	10	11	2	4	9	6	7																											23
1		5	8	10	3	2	7	6	4	11	9																											24
1		3	8	10	11	2	7	5	9	4	6																											25
	2	8	10	7	3	6	4	11	1	5	9																						1	5	9		26
1		3	6	10	7	2	4	11	8	5	9																											27
1		5	9	10	7	2	6		4	11																												28

Totals (Matches 1–28): Woodley 27, White 6, Hardwick 18, Brown 2, Allen 24, Tennant 16, McKennan 22, Airlie 5, Payne 8, Foss 27, Weaver 4, Spence 24, Mountford 18, Winterbottom 18, Birkett 7, Bearryman 20, Palmer 2, Bryant 12, Bidewell 14, Buchanan 2, Liddell 5, Farmer 2, Mills 6, Soo 3, Campbell 2, Whittaker 1, Mathie 1, Greenwood 1, Muttit 1, Smith 1, Butt 1, Jones 1, Jefferson 1, Abel 1, Hold 1, Kurz 1, Duke 1, Moseley 1.

Goals: Allen 1, Tennant 1, McKennan 13, Airlie 1, Spence 5, Mountford 9, Bearryman 7, Bryant 9, Bidewell 1, Liddell 2, Soo 3.

Woodley V	White A	Hardwick GF	Brown WH	Allen JP	Tennant A	McKennan P	Airlie S	Payne J	Foss SR	Weaver S	Spence R	Mountford RC	Winterbottom W	Birkett R	Bearryman HW	Palmer RW	Bryant BL	Bidewell S	Buchanan P	Liddell W	Farmer A	Mills G	Soo F	Campbell J	Whittaker W	Mathie D	Greenwood R	...	Match
1									10	8	3	4	7	6				9						5					29
1		3			6				10	7	2		4	11	8									5	9				30
1	2		5				8		10	7				11	6									4	9				31
1				6	8				10	7	2				9	4								11		5	3		32
1		3							10	7	2			6	9	8									7	9	5	4	33
1								8		11					7											9	5	4	34

Totals (Matches 29–34): Woodley 6, Hardwick 3, Brown 1, Allen 2, Tennant 3, Foss 6, Weaver 5, Spence 4, Winterbottom 1, Birkett 1, Bearryman 2, Palmer 2, Bidewell 4, Campbell 4, Whittaker 2, Mathie 3, Greenwood 3, ... (Goals: 2, 2, 1, 1, 1).

A.Fitzgerald played number 3 in Match 28; A.E.Hall played number 8 in Match 28; R.E.Savage played number 2 in Match 29; J.Mahon played number 11 in Match 29; A.Sinclair played number 3 in Match 31; H.T.Cothliff played number 4 in Match 33; H.R.Deverall played number 11 in Match 33 and scored one goal; A.J.Smith played number 2 in Match 34; E.Hapgood played number 3 in Match 34; E.Collett played number 6 in Match 34; J.Fiddes played number 10 in Match 34.

365

1943-44

Manager: William Birrell

1	Aug	28	(h)	Queen's Park R	L 1-3 Whittingham	9,469
2	Sep	4	(a)	Brighton & HA	W 3-1 Payne 3	3,000
3		11	(h)	Portsmouth	W 6-2 Mitten, Whittingham, Payne 3, Fagan	9,572
4		18	(a)	Brentford	L 1-3 Payne	9,580
5		25	(h)	Fulham	W 3-0 Payne, Whittingham, Fagan	11,717
6	Oct	2	(a)	Charlton A	W 1-0 Fagan	10,000
7		9	(a)	Aldershot	W 3-1 Mitten, Payne, Spence	7,500
8		16	(h)	Luton T	W 6-0 Milton, Mitten 2, Payne 3	8,082
9		23	(h)	Crystal P	W 2-1 Payne 2	8,373
10		30	(a)	Tottenham H	L 1-5 Payne	10,375
11	Nov	6	(a)	Arsenal	L 0-6	16,007
12		13	(a)	Reading	L 2-3 Payne, Spence	7,000
13		20	(h)	Millwall *	L 0-1	6,000
14		27	(a)	Queen's Park R	W 11-2 Russell, Payne 4, Ashcroft 2, Fagan 4	6,000
15	Dec	4	(h)	Brighton & HA	L 0-1	7,224
16		11	(a)	Portsmouth	W 5-1 Spence, Opp own-goal, Payne, Tennant 2	5,000
17		18	(a)	Watford	L 0-1	2,229
18		25	(h)	West Ham U	D 3-3 Payne 2, Sperrin	16,000
19		27	(a)	West Ham U	L 0-3	19,137
20	Jan	1	(h)	Brentford	L 0-3	12,000
21		8	(h)	Arsenal	W 2-0 Payne 2	19,310
22		22	(h)	Charlton A	W 5-2 Payne 2, Ashcroft 2, Effern	7,629
23		29	(h)	Aldershot	W 8-0 Effern 2, Payne 4, Mitten, Spence	11,752
24	Feb	5	(a)	Luton T	W 5-3 Spence 2, Payne 3	3,500
25		12	(a)	Crystal P	L 0-1	10,602
26	Apr	8	(h)	Tottenham H	D 1-1 Payne	25,000
27		10	(a)	Fulham	W 3-2 Foss, Spence 2	
28		22	(h)	Watford	W 2-1 Foss, Payne	5,586
29		29	(h†)	Reading	W 3-1 Weaver, Russell, Payne	4,000
30	May	6	(a)	Millwall	L 2-4 Payne 2	4,710

FINAL LEAGUE POSITION: 8th in Football League South. *Match abandoned after 60 minutes
due to an air raid. Result allowed to stand. †Home fixture played at Reading.

Appearances
Goals

Football League South Cup (Group B)

31	Feb	19	(h)	Southampton	W 3-2 Payne, Mitten, Tennant	5,343
32		26	(a)	Watford	W 3-0 Payne, Mitten, Bowie	5,282
33	Mar	4	(h)	West Ham U	W 4-0 Payne, Mitten 2, Harris	15,520
34		11	(a)	Southampton	W 5-1 Payne 3, Barlow, Spence	13,000
35		18	(h)	Watford	D 1-1 Payne	14,440
36		25	(a)	West Ham U	L 1-6 Payne	11,500
37	Apr	1	(n‡)	Reading	W 3-2# Russell, Payne 2	23,312
38		15	(n§)	Charlton A	L 1-3 Payne (pen)	85,000

FINAL LEAGUE POSITION: 1st in Football League South Cup (Group B). ‡Semi-final played at
White Hart Lane, London. #After extra-time. § Final played at Wembley Stadium.

Appearances
Goals

366

Woodley V	Mountford RC	Hardwick GF	Harris J	Spence R	Whittingham A	Fagan W	Mitten C	Westwood E	Wales H	Foss SR	Payne J	Russell W	Jackson J	Millar J	Greenwood R	Dyer JB	Bentley G	Curtis GF	Ashcroft L	Tennant A	Sperrin W	Bacon CW	Martin JD	Effern A	Bowie J	Latimer JE	James D	Humphreys JV	Mayes AJ	McKennan P	Law J	Campbell A	Milton GW	Sinclair MJ	Jefferson A	Devlin J	Lloyd C	Malpass ST	
1	2	3		5	7	9	10	11																				4	6	8									1
1	2	3		5	7	9		11	4	6	10																			8									2
1	2			5		9	8	11	3	4	6	10																			7								3
	2			5	7	10		11	3		6	9	4	1						8																			4
1				5	7	10	8	11	3		6	9	4	2																									5
	2			5	7	10	8	11	3		6	9	4	1																									6
				5	7		8	11	3		6	9	4	1	2																		10						7
				5	7		8	11	3		6	9	4	1		2																		10					8
	2			5	7		8	11			6	9	4	1	4																				3	10			9
		3		5	7		8	11			6	9	1																								2	4	10
				5	7		8	11	3		6	9	4	1	2																								11
	2			5	7		8	11	3		6	9	4																										12
	2			5	7		8	11	3		6	9	4			1	10																						13
	2			5		11	8		3		6	9	4			1	10	7																					14
				5		8					6		4			1	11	7																					15
	2			5	7		8	11	3		6	9	4						1	10																			16
	2			5	7		10		3		6	9	4						1	8																			17
	2			5			11		3		6	9	4						1	8	7	10																	18
	2			5			11		3		6	9	4						1	8	7	10																	19
1		3		5			11				6	9	4								7	10																	20
1	2			5			11	3			10	9	4						7	8			6																21
1				5			11				6	9							7	2				4	10														22
1	2			5	7		11				6	9								8				4	10														23
				5	7		8	11	3		6	9	4							2						10	1												24
1	2			5	7		10	11	3		6	9	4							8																			25
1	2			5	7		8		3		6	9	4							10																			26
1	2			7			11				9	4			5					10																			27
1				5			11	8			6	9	4		3				7	2					10														28
1				5	7						6	9	8		3					2						10													29
1	2			5			11				6	9								2						10													30
13	**3**	**19**	**29**	**26**	**6**	**17**	**22**	**18**	**2**	**29**	**27**	**22**	**7**	**2**	**4**	**2**	**7**	**3**	**5**	**13**	**3**	**3**	**3**	**2**	**4**	**2**	**2**	**1**	**1**	**1**	**1**	**1**	**1**	**1**	**1**	**1**	**1**	**1**	Totals
		8	3	7	5					2	39	2								4	2	1			3							1							Goals

1 own-goal

Woodley V	Mountford RC	Hardwick GF	Harris J	Spence R	Whittingham A	Fagan W	Mitten C	Westwood E	Wales H	Foss SR	Payne J	Russell W	Jackson J	Millar J	Greenwood R	Dyer JB	Bentley G	Curtis GF	Ashcroft L	Tennant A	Sperrin W	Bacon CW	Martin JD	Effern A	Bowie J	Latimer JE	James D	Humphreys JV	Mayes AJ	McKennan P	Law J	Campbell A	Milton GW	Sinclair MJ	Jefferson A	Devlin J	Lloyd C	Malpass ST	
1				5	7		10	11	3		6	9	4							2												8							31
	2			5	7		10	11	3		6	9	4																			8							32
1	2			5			11		3		6	9	4						7	10												8							33
1				5			11				6	9	4		3				7	2					10														34
	2			5	7		11		3		6	9	4							10												8							35
1	2			5	7		10		3		6	9	4																			8							36
1				5			10	11	3		6	9	4						7													8							37
1	2			5			10	11	3		6	9	4						7													8							38
7	**5**		**8**	**4**		**5**	**7**	**7**		**8**	**8**	**8**			**1**				**4**	**4**												**8**							Totals
			1	1		1	4				11				1					1												1							Goals

A.R.Lowes played number 10 in Match 10; G.Stewart played number 4 in Match 11; T.Hinchliffe played number 8 in Match 11; G.H.Swindin played number 1 in Match 12; S.Dimond played number 10 in Match 12; A.E.Young played number 2 in Match 15; E.Muttitt played number 3 in Match 15; J.R.Smith played number 10 in Match 15; G.Ludford played number 9 in Match 15; A.Friend played number 11 in Match 17; F.Marsden played number 2 in Match 20; J.F.Smith played number 8 in Match 20; J.Fullwood played number 3 in Match 22; C.Williams played number 8 in Match 22; E.Hapgood played number 3 in Match 23; S.H.Bidewell played number 11 in Match 26; L.Morgan played number 3 in Match 27; J.Newbold played number 6 in Match 27; H.Gilberg played number 8 in Match 27; S.Weaver played number 4 in Match 29 and scored one goal; V.A.Dagley played number 11 in Match 29; B.Purvis played number 3 in Match 30; J.Mackay played number 4 in Match 30; A.H.Machin played number 8 in Match 30; J.A.Sanders played number 1 in Match 32; H.Barlow played number 8 in Match 34 and scored one goal; E.R.Riley played number 11 in Match 36; A.White played number 2 in Match 37.

1944-45

Manager: William Birrell

						Attendance
1	Aug	26	(a)	Fulham	L 4-7 Walker 2, Payne, Hapgood	8,000
2	Sep	2	(h)	Aldershot	D 1-1 Buchanan	4,500
3		9	(a)	Brentford	W 5-0 Walker 3, Payne, Russell	16,100
4		16	(h)	Crystal P	W 8-2 Payne 3, Foss, Mitten 3, Walker	20,000
5		23	(a)	Charlton A	W 3-0 Payne 2, Walker	13,500
6		30	(h)	Clapton O	W 5-0 Tennant, Payne 2, Mitten 2	12,000
7	Oct	7	(a)	Portsmouth	W 5-1 Payne 2, Buchanan 2, Machin	14,000
8		14	(a)	Tottenham H	W 5-1 Payne, Whittingham, Machin, Wardle 2	21,087
9		21	(h)	Millwall	W 7-0 Payne, Wardle 2, Walker 2, Russell, Buchanan	16,000
10		28	(a)	Watford	W 6-1 Payne 4, Wardle, Machin	7,730
11	Nov	4	(a)	Southampton	D 3-3 Payne, Wardle 2	16,000
12		11	(h)	Luton T	W 7-1 Bacon, Payne 5, Wardle	8,000
13		18	(a)	Brighton & HA	W 5-3 Payne 4, Hardwick	6,000
14		25	(h)	Arsenal	W 2-1 Payne, Machin	37,753
15	Dec	2	(h)	Fulham	W 2-0 Bacon, Mitten	18,000
16		9	(a)	Aldershot	W 4-3 Mitten, Machin, Payne 2	8,000
17		16	(h)	Brentford	L 0-2	24,492
18		30	(a)	Crystal P	D 3-3 Mitten, Payne 2	10,106
19	Jan	6	(a)	Charlton A	W 4-0 Hurrell 2, Payne 2	11,812
20		13	(a)	Clapton O	W 6-2 Payne 2, Hurrell, Buchanan 2, Russell	3,000
21		20	(h)	Portsmouth	D 1-1 Mitten	11,404
22		27	(h)	Tottenham H	L 1-2 Wardle	20,540
23	Mar	31	(a)	Southampton	L 3-4 Payne 2, McDonald	16,434
24	Apr	2	(h)	West Ham U	L 3-4 Hassell, Machin, Hurrell	23,327
25		14	(a)	Luton T	D 1-1 Payne	6,400
26		21	(h)	Brighton & HA	L 0-2	9,176
27		28	(a)	Arsenal	L 0-3	10,349
28	May	5	(h)	Watford	L 3-4 Bacon, Roper, Wardle	1,896
29		19	(a)	West Ham U	L 1-2 Hurrell	10,000
30		26	(a)	Millwall	W 2-1 Foss, Roper	5,000

FINAL LEAGUE POSITION: 4th in Football League South

Appearances

Goals

Football League (South) Cup

						Attendance
31	Feb	3	(a)	Luton T	W 1-0 Spence	8,881
32		10	(h)	Watford	W 3-1 Hurrell, Wardle, Payne	12,622
33		17	(a)	Crystal P	D 1-1 McDonald	12,000
34		24	(h)	Luton T	W 4-1 Herd 2, McDonald, Wardle	12,611
35	Mar	3	(a)	Watford	W 2-0 Machin, Herd	5,992
36		10	(h)	Crystal P	W 2-0 Spence, Wardle	20,960
37		17	(n*)	West Ham U	W 2-1 Wardle, Whittingham	35,109
38	Apr	7	(n†)	Millwall	W 2-0 McDonald, Wardle	90,000

FINAL LEAGUE POSITION: 1st in Football League South Cup (Group 4)

Appearances

*Played at White Hart Lane, London.   †Played at Wembley Stadium.

Goals

Appearance and scorers grid (players as columns, match number at right):

Woodley V	Purvis B	Hapgood E	Tennant A	Harris J	Foss SR	Buchanan P	Walker T	Payne J	Mitten C	Winter DT	Russell R	Hardwick GF	Anderson A	Bacon CW	Machin AH	Whittingham A	Wardle G	Hurrell W	Spence R	Black I	McDonald J	Cowan RM	Bidewell S	Hassell TW	Franks D	Roper DG	Herd A	McDonald P	Mills G	Bearryman H	Muttit E	Toop RW	Williams EC	Prentice JW	Wallis J	Stevens J	Evans C	Gillies R	Match
1	2	3	4	5	6	7	8	9		11																			10										1
1	4	3	8	5	10	7		9	11	2																				6									2
1	3		2	5	6	7	8	9	11			4																				10							3
		3	10	5	6	7	8	9	11	2		4																						1					4
1			10	5	6	7	8	9	11	2		4		3																									5
1	2	3	10	5	6	7	8	9	11			4																											6
		3		5	6	7		9	11			4	1	8	10																				2				7
		3		5	6		9	11	2	4			1		10	7	8																						8
1		3		5	6	11	8	9		2		4				7	10																						9
1		3		5	6		9	11	2	4					10	7	8																						10
		3	8	5	6		9		4	2	1			10	11	7																							11
		3	10	5	6		9	2	4	1	11				8																					7			12
		3	4	5	6	7	9	11	2	1				10			8																						13
		3		5	6		9	11	2	4	1			10			7	8																					14
		3	10	5	6		9	11	2	4	1		8				7																						15
1		3	4	5			9	11	2	6				10			8	7																					16
		3	8	5	6		9	11	2	4	1			10			7																						17
1				5	6	7	9	11	2	4	3			10			8																						18
1			10	5	6	7	9		2	4	3			11	8																							19
1				5	6	7	9		4	2				11	8																			3	10				20
1	3			5	6	7	9	11	2	4				10	8																								21
1				5	6		9	11	2	4	3			8			7																			10			22
			5		6		9		2	4	3			10			8	7	1	11																			23
1					6	7				3				9			10				2	4	11															5	24
1	3				6	7			4					9			11	10			2	8																	25
	3				6	7		9						10					1	11	2	4		5															26
				8		6				4				7	10			1	11	2	9		5																27
	3		4		6									10			8		7	1		2	11		9														28
				5	6					4				8	10	7	1			2					9														29
			9	5	6					8				11	10	1			2						7														30
15	**8**	**15**	**17**	**24**	**29**	**16**	**6**	**24**	**17**	**16**	**24**	**9**	**8**	**4**	**13**	**4**	**20**	**10**	**5**	**6**	**3**	**7**	**4**	**2**	**2**	**3**				1	1	1	1	1	1	1	1	1	
	1	1		2	6	9	39	9		3	1		3	6	1	10	5		1			1		2															

Woodley V	Purvis B	Hapgood E	Tennant A	Harris J	Foss SR	Buchanan P	Walker T	Payne J	Mitten C	Winter DT	Russell R	Hardwick GF	Anderson A	Bacon CW	Machin AH	Whittingham A	Wardle G	Hurrell W	Spence R	Black I	McDonald J	Cowan RM	Bidewell S	Hassell TW	Franks D	Roper DG	Herd A	McDonald P	Mills G	Bearryman H	Muttit E	Toop RW	Williams EC	Prentice JW	Wallis J	Stevens J	Evans C	Gillies R	Match
1	3		8	5	6		9			4				11			7				2															10			31
1			5	6			9		2	4	3				7	8					11																		32
	3		5	6	7		9		4				10							1	11	2									8								33
			5	6			2	4					9	8	7	1	11	3													10								34
			5	6			2	4				10	7			1	11														8	3					9		35
		9	5	6			2	4				8	7	1	11															10	3								36
			5	6			4	3				10	9	7		1	11	2													8								37
			5	6		9	2	4	3				7			1	11																						38
2	**2**		**2**	**8**	**8**	**1**	**4**	**5**	**8**	**3**	**3**		**3**	**1**	**7**	**2**	**3**	**6**	**7**	**4**											**5**	**2**				**2**			
				1		1	5	1	2			3			3																								

L.Jones played number 8 in Match 24; J.Hickman played number 5 in Match 25; D.Saunders played number 8 in Match 26; F.Dawes played number 3 in Match 27; W.Dodgin played number 5 in Match 28; F.T.Fisher played number 3 in Match 29; J.Bain played number 11 in Match 29; C.Gingell played number 3 in Match 30; R.Williams played number 4 in Match 30; J.D.Bowie played number 10 in Match 32; G.Smith played number 8 in Match 38; L.A.Goulden played number 10 in Match 38.

1945-46

Manager: William Birrell

1	Aug	25	(h)	Nottingham F	L 0-4		21,299
2	Sep	1	(a)	Nottingham F	W 1-0	James	23,444
3		8	(a)	Newport C	W 3-1	James, Goulden 2	11,677
4		12	(h)	Southampton	W 1-0	Goulden	11,729
5		15	(h)	Newport C	W 2-0	Bain, Opp own-goal	20,685
6		19	(a)	Derby C	W 3-0	Machini 2, Williams	17,514
7		22	(h)	Wolves	D 1-1	Machin	35,580
8		29	(a)	Wolves	L 0-1		33,313
9	Oct	6	(a)	West Ham U	W 4-2	Williams, Goulden 2, Machin	26,078
10		13	(h)	West Ham U	L 1-2	Bain	44,626
11		20	(h)	West Brom A	W 7-4	Bain, Opp own-goal, Brown, McCall, Williams 3	31,532
12		27	(a)	West Brom A	L 1-8	Williams	18,179
13	Nov	3	(a)	Birmingham C	L 2-5	McCall, Williams	26,306
14		10	(h)	Birmingham C	L 2-3	Lawton 2	53,813
15		17	(h)	Tottenham H	L 1-2	Buchanan	35,343
16		24	(a)	Tottenham H	L 2-3	Lawton, Goulden	43,000
17	Dec	1	(a)	Brentford	D 4-4	Lawton 2, Buchanan, Hanson	28,200
18		8	(h)	Brentford	W 4-2	Lawton 2, Foss, Goulden	38,497
19		15	(a)	Swansea T	L 3-5	Dolding 2, Williams	19,651
20		22	(h)	Swansea T	L 3-4	Lawton 3	23,024
21		25	(h)	Millwall	W 3-0	Lawton 2, Goulden	27,765
22		26	(a)	Millwall	W 8-0	Spence 2, Goulden, Lawton 3, Payne 2	30,493
23		29	(a)	Southampton	L 0-7		23,339
24	Jan	12	(a)	Leicester C	W 7-1	Williams 3, Payne 2, Foss, Dolding	15,894
25		19	(h)	Leicester C	W 4-0	Williams 3, Payne	14,349
26	Feb	2	(a)	Coventry C	L 0-2		19,289
27		16	(h)	Luton T	W 2-1	Lawton, Williams	19,510
28		23	(h)	Aston Villa	D 2-2	Williams, Lawton	37,069
29	Mar	9	(a)	Arsenal	W 2-1	Lawton, Spence	30,554
30		16	(h)	Arsenal	L 1-2	Brindle	45,000
31		23	(a)	Luton T	L 1-3	Foss	14,000
32		27	(a)	Aston Villa	W 3-0	James 2, Goulden	25,000
33		30	(a)	Charlton A	D 0-0		46,658
34	Apr	3	(h)	Charlton A	L 0-1		25,000
35		6	(a)	Fulham	L 2-3	Chisholm, Dolding	35,000
36		10	(h)	Coventry C	W 2-1	Goulden, Galloway	10,000
37		13	(h)	Fulham	D 0-0		35,000
38		19	(h)	Plymouth A	W 2-0	Goulden, Galloway	30,000
39		20	(a)	Portsmouth	L 0-3		26,000
40		22	(a)	Plymouth A	W 4-1	Goulden 2, Argue, Machin	27,000
41		27	(h)	Portsmouth	W 3-0	Goulden 2, Dolding	30,000
42	May	4	(a)	Derby C	D 1-1	Lawton	27,000

FINAL LEAGUE POSITION: 10th in Football League South

Appearances
Goals

FA Cup

3	Jan	5	(h)	Leicester C	D 1-1	Lawton	39,678
		10	(a)	Leicester C	W 2-0	Goulden, Williams	25,368
4		26	(h)	West Ham U	W 2-0	Machin, Spence	65,726
		30	(a)	West Ham U	L 0-1		35,000
5	Feb	9	(h)	Aston Villa	L 0-1		65,307
		12	(a)	Aston Villa	L 0-1		55,000

Appearances
Goals

Winter DT	Hardwick GF	Russell R	Williams R	Foss SR	Buchanan P	Goulden LA	Bain JA	Williams B	Gingell C	Harris J	Ashcroft LL	James D	Woodley V	Tennant A	Spence R	Woodward T	Machin AH	McCall W	Robertson WH	Dolding DL	White A	Lawton T	Hanson A	Payne J	Lewis FA	Armstrong K	Brindle J	Galloway J	Argue J	Dickie M	Brown R	Bowie JD	Bidewell S	Scott L	Smith G	Phipps HJ	Brown, Hugh	Dawes FW	Match
2	3	4	5	6	7	10	11																							1	8	9							1
2		4	8	6		10	11	1	3	5	7	9																											2
2		4	8	6		10	11	1	3	5	7	9																											3
2		4	8	6		10	11			5		9	1	3	7																								4
2		4	8	6		10	11			5		9	1	3		7																							5
2		4	8	6		10	11			5			1				7	9															3						6
2		4	8	6		10	11			5			1	3			9	7																					7
2			8	6		10	11			5			1	3			9	7																4					8
2		4	8	6		10	11			5			1	3			9	7																					9
		4	8	6		10	11			5			1	3			9	7																	2				10
2		4	9	6			11			5				3			7		1			10														8			11
		4	8	6		10	11			5				3			9	7	1																		2		12
2		4	9	6		10	11			5			1	3			8	7																					13
		4	8	6		10	11			5			1	3			7				2	9																	14
2		4	9		7	10	11			5			1	3																									15
2		4		6	7	10	11			5			1	3								9		8															16
2		6	4		7	10				5				3					1	11		9		8															17
2		4	8	6	7	10				5				3					1	11		9																	18
2		4	5									10			8				1			6		7		9													19
2		4	8	6		10	11							3			7					9																	20
2		4	8	6		10	11			5				3			7		1			9																	21
2		4		6		10	11			5				3			7		1			9		8															22
2		4		6		10	11			5				3			7		1			9		8															23
2			8	6	7	10				5				3					1	11		9																	24
2		4	8	6		10	11			5				3			7		1			9																	25
		4								5				3			7		1	11	10	9		8	2	6													26
2			8	6						5				3			7		1	11	10	9				4													27
2			8	6						5				3			7		1	11	10	9				4													28
2		10		6						5				3			7		1	11		9					4	8											29
		10		6						5				3			7		1	11	2	9					4	8											30
2			8	6		10				5				3			7		1	11		9							4										31
2			8	6		10	11			5				3	9		7		1										4										32
2			8	6		10				5				3	9		7		1	11									4										33
2			8	6		10	11			5				3	9		7		1										4										34
2				6		10				5				3	9		7		1	11									4										35
2		4		6		10				5				3			7		1	11									8										36
2		4		6		10				5				3			7		1	11		9							8										37
2		4		6		10				5							7		1	11		9							8										38
2		4		6		10				5				3					1	11		9			7	8													39
2				6		10				5				3					1			9				8	4	7											40
2				6		10				5				3					1	11		9				8	4	7											41
2				6		10				5				3			7		1	11		9				8			4										42
36		**22**	**42**	**31**	**8**	**35**	**25**	**2**	**2**	**39**	**2**	**10**	**11**	**38**	**15**	**2**	**17**	**6**	**27**	**19**	**3**	**20**	**3**	**7**	**6**	**5**	**2**	**2**	**4**	**3**	**1**	**1**	**1**	**1**	**1**	**1**	**1**	**1**	
			16	3	2	16	3					4		3			5	2		5		19	1	5		1	2	1								1			

2 own-goals

Winter DT	Hardwick GF	Russell R	Williams R	Foss SR	Buchanan P	Goulden LA	Bain JA	Williams B	Gingell C	Harris J	Ashcroft LL	James D	Woodley V	Tennant A	Spence R	Woodward T	Machin AH	McCall W	Robertson WH	Dolding DL	White A	Lawton T	Hanson A	Payne J	Lewis FA	Armstrong K	Brindle J	Galloway J	Argue J										Match
2		4		6		10	11			5				3			7		1			9		8															3
2		4	8	6		10	11			5				3			7		1			9																	
2		4		6			11			5				3			7		1		10	9		8															4
2		4		6		10	11			5				3			7		1			9		8															
2		4		6			11			5				3			7		1		10	9		8															5
2		4		6			11			5				3			7		1	11	10	9																	
6		**6**	**2**	**6**		**5**	**3**			**6**				**6**			**6**		**6**	**1**	**3**	**6**		**5**															
														1								1		1															

D.Ridley played number 6 in Match 15; A.P.Robson played number 8 in Match 15; H.Ferrier played number 3 in Match 19; Harry Brown played number 1 in Match 20; F.W.Hall played number 5 in Match 20; J.V.Humphreys played number 4 in Match 24; K.Chisholm played number 8 in Match 35 and scored one goal; W.Hanlon played number 11 in Match 40.

Chelsea in Europe

Inter-Cities Fairs Cup

1958-9
Round 1 (1st leg)
Sep 30 v BK Frem (Denmark) (a) 3-1
Harrison, Greaves, Nicholas
Matthews; P.Sillett, J.Sillett, Huxford, Scott,
Saunders, Court, Greaves, Tindall, Nicholas, Harrison.
Round 1 (2nd leg)
Nov 4 v BK Frem (Denmark) (h) 4-1 (agg 7-2)
Greaves 2, P.Sillett, Lees (og)
Matthews; P.Sillett, J.Sillett, Mortimore, Scott,
Saunders, Brabrook, Greaves, Allen, Tindall, Block.
Att: 13,104
Round 2 (1st leg)
Apr 29 v Ville de Belgrade (Yugoslavia) (h) 1-0
Brabrook
Matthews; P.Sillett, Whittaker, Anderton, Mortimore,
Crowther, Brabrook, Greaves, Allen, Blunstone,
Harrison.
Att: 25,771
Round 2 (2nd leg)
May 13 v Ville de Belgrade (Yugoslavia) (a) 1-4 (agg 2-4)
Brabrook
Robertson; P.Sillett, Whittaker, Anderton,
Mortimore, Crowther, Brabrook, Nicholas, Allen,
Blunstone, Harrison.

1965-6
Round 1 (1st leg)
Sep 22 v AS Roma (Italy) (h) 4-1

Venables 3, Graham
Bonetti; Shellito, McCreadie, Hollins, Young,
R.Harris, Bridges, Graham, Osgood, Venables,
Fascione.
Att: 32,753
Round 1 (2nd leg)
Oct 6 v AS Roma (Italy) (a) 0-0 (agg 4-1)
Bonetti; Shellito, McCreadie, Hollins, Hinton,
R.Harris, Murray, Graham, Bridges, Venables, Boyle.
Att: 40,000
Round 2 (1st leg)
Nov 17 v Wiener Sport-Club (Austria) (a) 0-1
Bonetti; Shellito, McCreadie, Hollins, Young, Hinton,
Fascione, Graham, Osgood, Boyle, Tambling.
Att: 4,000
Round 2 (2nd leg)
Dec 1 v Wiener Sport-Club (Austria) (h) 2-0 (agg 2-1)
Murray, Osgood
Bonetti; Shellito, McCreadie, Hollins, Hinton, Boyle,
Murray, Graham, Osgood, Venables, Tambling.
Att: 28,254
Round 3 (1st leg)
Feb 9 v AC Milan (Italy) (a) 1-2
Graham
Bonetti; R.Harris, McCreadie, Hollins, Hinton, Boyle,
Bridges, Graham, Osgood, Venables, Tambling.
Att: 11,411

*Peter Bonetti gets his hand to the ball during Chelsea's
Inter-Cities Fairs Cup third-round first-leg tie in Milan
in February 1966.*

Manager Tommy Docherty (extreme left), skipper Ron Harris and trainer Harry Medhurst celebrate the fact that Chelsea have just moved through to the fourth round on the toss of a coin.

Round 3 (2nd leg)
Feb 16 v AC Milan (Italy) (h) 2-1 (agg 3-3)
Graham, Osgood
Bonetti; R.Harris, McCreadie, Hollins, Hinton, Boyle, Bridges, Graham, Osgood, Venables, Tambling.
Att: 59,541

Round 3 (play-off)
Mar 2 v AC Milan (Italy) (a) 1-1 a.e.t.
Chelsea won on toss of a coin.
Bridges
Bonetti; R.Harris, McCreadie, Hollins, Hinton, Boyle, Bridges, Graham, Osgood, Murray, Tambling.
Att: 30,620

Round 4 (1st leg)
Mar 15 v TSV München 1860 (West Germany) (a) 2-2
Tambling 2
Bonetti; Kirkup, McCreadie, Hollins, Hinton, R.Harris, Bridges, Graham, Osgood, Venables, Tambling.
Att: 11,000

Round 4 (2nd leg)
Mar 29 v TSV München 1860 (West Germany) (h) 1-0 (agg 3-2)
Osgood
Bonetti; Kirkup, McCreadie, Hollins, Hinton, R.Harris, Bridges, Graham, Osgood, Venables, Tambling.
Att: 42,224

Semi-final (1st leg)
Apr 27 v FC Barcelona (Spain) (a) 0-2
Bonetti; Kirkup, R.Harris, Hollins, Hinton, Young, Houseman, Boyle, Osgood, Venables, Tambling.
Att: 70,000

Semi-final (2nd leg)
May 11 v FC Barcelona (Spain) (h) 2-0 (agg 2-2)
Torres (og), Reina (og)
Bonetti; Kirkup, A.Harris, Hollins, Hinton, R.Harris, Houseman, Graham, Osgood, Cooke, Tambling.
Att: 40,073

Semi-final (play-off)
May 25 v FC Barcelona (Spain) (a) 0-5
Bonetti; Kirkup, A.Harris, Hollins, Hinton, R.Harris, Boyle, Graham, Osgood, Cooke, Tambling.
Att: 45,000

1968-9
Round 1 (1st leg)
Sep 18 v Greenock Morton (Scotland) (h) 5-0
Osgood, Birchenall, Cooke, Boyle, Hollins
Bonetti; R.Harris, McCreadie, Hollins, Webb, Boyle, Baldwin, Cooke, Osgood, Birchenall, Tambling.
Att: 28,736

Round 1 (2nd leg)
Sep 30 v Greenock Morton (Scotland) (a) 4-3 (agg 9-3)
Baldwin, Birchenall, Houseman, Tambling
Bonetti; Hinton, McCreadie, Hollins, Webb, R.Harris, Baldwin, Tambling, Osgood, Birchenall, Houseman.
Att: 8,000

Round 2 (1st leg)
Oct 23 v DWS Amsterdam (Holland) (h) 0-0
Bonetti; Boyle, McCreadie, Hollins, Webb, R.Harris, Cooke, Tambling(Osgood), Baldwin, Birchenall, Houseman.
Att: 28,428

Round 2 (2nd leg)
Oct 30 v DWS Amsterdam (Holland) (a) 0-0 a.e.t. (agg 0-0)
DWS won tie on toss of a coin.
Bonetti; Hinton, McCreadie, Boyle, Webb, R.Harris, Cooke, Baldwin, Osgood, Birchenall, Tambling.
Att: 14,000

European Cup-winners' Cup

1970-71
Round 1 (1st leg)
Sep 16 v Aris Thessalonikis (Greece) (a) 1-1
Hutchinson
Bonetti; Mulligan, Harris, Hollins, Dempsey, Webb,
Weller, Hudson, Osgood, Hutchinson, Cooke.
Att: 50,000
Round 1 (2nd leg)
Sep 30 v Aris Thessalonikis (Greece) (h) 5-1 (agg 6-2)
Hollins 2, Hutchinson 2, Hinton
Bonetti; Mulligan, Harris, Hollins, Hinton, Webb,
Weller, Hudson, Osgood(Baldwin), Hutchinson,
Houseman.
Att: 40,425
Round 2 (1st leg)
Oct 21 v CFKA Sredets (Bulgaria) (a) 1-0
Baldwin
Bonetti; Mulligan, Harris, Hollins, Hinton, Webb,
Weller, Hudson, Osgood, Baldwin, Houseman.
Att: 45,000

Round 2 (2nd leg)
Nov 4 v CFKA Sredets (Bulgaria) (h) 1-0 (agg 2-0)
Webb
Bonetti; Mulligan(Boyle), Harris, Hollins, Hinton,
Webb, Weller, Cooke, Osgood, Hutchinson,
Houseman.
Att: 41,613
Round 3 (1st leg)
Mar 10 v RFC Bruges (Belgium) (a) 0-2
Phillips; Boyle, McCreadie, Hollins, Dempsey, Webb,
Smethurst, Cooke, Baldwin, Hudson, Weller.
Att: 23,000
Round 3 (2nd leg)
Mar 24 v RFC Bruges (Belgium) (h) 4-0 a.e.t. (agg 4-2)
Houseman, Osgood 2, Baldwin
Phillips; Harris, McCreadie, Hollins, Dempsey(Boyle),
Webb, Baldwin, Cooke, Osgood, Hudson, Houseman.
Att: 45,558
Semi-final (1st leg)
Apr 14 v Manchester City (England) (h) 1-0
Smethurst
Phillips; Boyle, Harris, Hollins, Dempsey, Droy,
Hudson, Smethurst(Baldwin), Webb, Cooke(Weller),
Houseman.
Att: 45,595

Chelsea embark on a lap of honour after their Cup-winners' Cup triumph over Real Madrid in Athens.

374

Semi-final (2nd leg)
Apr 28 v Manchester City (England) 1-0 (agg 2-0)
Healey (og)
Phillips; Mulligan, Harris, Cooke, Dempsey, Webb,
Weller, Hudson, Smethurst, Boyle, Houseman.
Att: 43,633
Final
May 19 v Real Madrid (Spain) (in Athens) 1-1 a.e.t.
Osgood
Bonetti; Boyle, Harris, Hollins(Mulligan), Dempsey,
Webb, Weller, Hudson, Osgood(Baldwin), Cooke,
Houseman.
Att: 41,000
Replay
May 21 v Real Madrid (Spain) (in Athens) 2-1
Dempsey, Osgood
Bonetti; Boyle, Harris, Cooke, Dempsey, Webb,
Weller, Baldwin, Osgood(Smethurst), Hudson,
Houseman.
Att: 24,000

*Peter Bonetti does not seem to mind the close attentions
of Alan Hudson (left) and Tommy Boyle. After all,
Chelsea have just lifted a European trophy.*

1971-2
Round 1 (1st leg)
**Sep 15 v Jeunesse Hautcharage (Luxembourg)
  (a) 8-0**
Osgood 3, Houseman 2, Hollins, Webb, Baldwin
Bonetti; Boyle, Harris, Hollins, Dempsey(Hinton),
Webb, Cooke, Hudson, Osgood, Baldwin, Houseman.
Att: 13,000
Round 1 (2nd leg)
**Sep 29 v Jeunesse Hautcharage (Luxembourg)
  (h) 13-0 (agg 21-0)**
*Osgood 5, Hudson, Hollins (pen), Webb, Harris,
Baldwin 3, Houseman*
Bonetti; Boyle, Harris, Hollins, Webb, Hinton, Cooke,
Baldwin, Osgood, Hudson, Houseman.
Att: 27,621
Round 2 (1st leg)
Oct 20 v Åtvidaberg (Sweden) (a) 0-0
Bonetti; McCreadie(Mulligan), Harris, Boyle, Webb,
Hinton, Baldwin, Hollins, Osgood, Hudson, Cooke.
Att: 10,212
Round 2 (2nd leg)
Nov 3 v Åtvidaberg (Sweden) (h) 1-1 (agg 1-1)
Åtvidaberg won on away-goals rule.
Hudson
Bonetti; Mulligan(Hinton), Harris, Boyle, Dempsey,
Webb, Cooke, Hollins, Osgood, Hudson, Houseman.
Att: 28,071

The victorious Blues with the Cup-winners' Cup in 1971.

Chelsea
in Other Competitions

Full Members' Cup
(Later the Simod Cup and Zenith Data Systems Cup)

1985-6
Group Matches
Oct 2 v Portsmouth (h) 3-0
Bumstead, Hazard, Dixon
Niedzwiecki; Wood, Rougvie, Pates, McLaughlin, Bumstead, Nevin, Hazard(Canoville), Dixon, Speedie, Spackman.
Att: 6,833
Oct 23 v Charlton Athletic (a) 3-1
Nevin 2, Speedie
Niedzwiecki; Wood, Dublin, Pates, McLaughlin, Bumstead(McAllister), Nevin, Hazard, Dixon, Speedie, Spackman(K.Jones).
Att: 3,714
Semi-final
Nov 13 v West Bromwich Albion (a) 2-2 a.e.t.
Chelsea won 5-4 on penalties
Speedie, McAllister

Niedzwiecki; Wood, Dublin, Pates, Isaac, K.Jones (Jasper), Nevin, Spackman(Lee), McAllister, Speedie, Hazard.
Att: 4,070
Southern Final (1st leg)
Dec 4 v Oxford United (a) 4-1
Slatter (og), Dixon 3
Niedzwiecki; Wood, Dublin, Rougvie, McLaughlin, K.Jones, Nevin, Spackman, Dixon, McAllister, Murphy.
Att: 6,018
Southern Final (2nd leg)
Dec 17 v Oxford United (h) 0-1 (agg 4-2)
Niedzwiecki; Wood, Rougvie, Pates, McLaughlin, K.Jones, Nevin, Spackman, Dixon, Speedie (McAllister), Bumstead(Dublin).
Att: 8,528
Final
Mar 23 v Manchester City (Wembley) 5-4
Speedie 3, Lee 2
Francis; Wood, Rougvie, Pates, McLaughlin, Bumstead, Nevin, Spackman, Lee, Speedie, McAllister.
Att: 67,236

Hat-trick hero David Speedie celebrates one of his goals in the 5-4 thriller against Manchester City at Wembley.

Two-goal Colin Lee (left) and David Speedie, who hit three, with the Full Members' Cup in 1986.

1986-7
Round 3
Nov 25 v West Ham United (a) 2-1
Dixon, Spackman (pen)
Niedzwiecki; Rougvie, Dublin, Isaac, McLaughlin, Pates, Nevin, Spackman(Wood), Dixon, Speedie, Bumstead.
Att: 12,140
Quarter-final
Mar 3 v Blackburn Rovers (a) 0-3
Godden; Clarke, Dublin(Coady), Pates, McLaughlin, Rougvie, Nevin, Wood, Wegerle, Speedie(Dodds), K.Jones.
Att: 7,298

1987-8
Round 1
Nov 18 v Barnsley (h) 2-1
Durie, Coady
Freestone; Clarke, Dorigo, Pates, McLaughlin, Wood, Nevin, C.Wilson, K.Wilson(Hazard), Durie, Coady.
Att: 8,501
Round 2
Dec 16 v Manchester City (a) 2-0
K.Wilson, Dixon
Freestone; Hall, Dorigo, Bodley, McLaughlin, Wood, Nevin, Wegerle, Dixon, K.Wilson, C.Wilson.
Att: 6,406
Round 3
Jan 19 v Swindon Town (a) 0-4
Freestone; Clarke, Dorigo, Pates, McLaughlin, Bumstead(C.Wilson), McAllister(Wegerle), Hazard, Dixon, K.Wilson, Wood.
Att: 12,317

1988-9
Round 1
Nov 9 v Plymouth Argyle (h) 6-2
K.Wilson, McAllister 2, Roberts, Clarke, McLaughlin
Freestone; Clarke(Hall), Dorigo, Roberts, McLaughlin, Wood, K.Wilson(Dodds), Lee, McAllister, Durie, C.Wilson.
Att: 4,767
Round 2
Nov 30 v Bradford City (a) 3-2
Dixon, Roberts (pen), Wood
Freestone; Hall, Dorigo, Roberts, Lee, Wood, K.Wilson, Nicholas, Dixon, Durie(McAllister), C.Wilson
Att: 5,341
Round 3
Jan 10 v Nottingham Forest (h) 1-4 a.e.t.
Dixon
Freestone; Clarke, Dorigo, Roberts, McLaughlin, Wood, McAllister, Mitchell(K.Wilson), Dixon, Durie(Lee), C.Wilson.
Att: 8,475

1989-90
Round 2
Nov 2 v AFC Bournemouth (a) 3-2 a.e.t.
Dickens 3
Beasant; Clarke, Dorigo, Roberts, Lee, Monkou, Dickens, Bumstead(C.Wilson), Dixon, K.Wilson, Hazard(McAllister).
Att: 6,214

Round 3
Dec 22 v West Ham United (h) 4-3
Dixon, Roberts (pen) Lee, K.Wilson
Beasant; Clarke, Le Saux, Roberts, Lee, Monkou, McAllister, Bumstead, Dixon, Durie(K.Wilson), C.Wilson.

Southern Semi-final
Jan 23 v Ipswich Town (a) 3-2
Dixon, K.Wilson 2
Beasant; Clarke, Dorigo, Bumstead, Johnsen, Monkou, McAllister, Dickens, Dixon, K.Wilson, Le Saux.
Att: 13,365
Southern Final (1st leg)
Feb 21 v Crystal Palace (a) 2-0
Dixon, K.Wilson
Beasant; Hall, Dorigo, Roberts, Johnsen, Bumstead, McAllister, Nicholas, Dixon, K.Wilson, C.Wilson.
Att: 14,839
Southern Final (2nd leg)
Mar 12 v Crystal Palace (h) 2-0 (agg 4-0)
Bumstead, Hall
Beasant; Hall, Dorigo, Bumstead, Johnsen, Monkou, McAllister, Nicholas, Dixon, Durie, K.Wilson.
Att: 15,061
Final
Mar 25 v Middlesbrough (Wembley) 1-0
Dorigo
Beasant; Hall, Dorigo, Bumstead, Johnsen, Monkou, McAllister, Nicholas, Dixon, Durie, K.Wilson.
Att: 76,369

1990-91
Round 2
Dec 12 v Swindon Town (h) 1-0
Wise (pen)
Beasant; Hall, Dorigo, Townsend(Stuart), Cundy, Monkou, Le Saux, Lee, Dixon, Durie, Wise.
Att: 5,888
Round 2
Feb 18 v Luton T (h) 1-1 a.e.t.
Luton won 4-1 on penalties
Stuart
Beasant; Clarke, Dorigo, Dickens, Cundy, Monkou, Stuart(Wilson), Matthew, Dixon, Durie, Le Saux(Hall).
Att: 3,849

FA Charity Shield

1955
Sep 14 v Newcastle United (h) 3-0
Bentley, Blunstone, McMichael (og)
Robertson; P.Sillett, Willemse, Armstrong, Wicks, Saunders, Parsons, Brabrook, Bentley, Stubbs, Blunstone.
Att: 12,802

1970
Aug 8 v Everton (h) 1-2
Hutchinson
Bonetti; Webb, Harris, Hollins, Mulligan, Hinton, Weller, Hudson, Osgood, Hutchinson, Houseman.
Att: 43,547

The Stamford Bridge Trophy

Although the regular series of games between Chelsea and Heart of Midlothian was inaugurated in 1947, it was not until 1951 that the Chelsea FC chairman, Joe Mears, provided the trophy. There is no evidence that the 1980 pre-season friendly was for the trophy, but it is included here for the sake of completeness.

1946-7
Apr 21 v Heart of Midlothian (a) 4-1
Walker 3, Machin
Medhurst; Winter, Bathgate, Machin, Harris, Macaulay, Spence, Walker, Lawton, Goulden, Paton.

1947-8
Apr 26 v Heart of Midlothian (h) 4-1
Campbell, Bentley 2, Billington
Medhurst; Lewis, Bathgate, Armstrong, Harris, Macaulay, Dyke, Bentley, Billington, Walker, Campbell.

1948-9
Apr 27 v Heart of Midlothian (a) 1-1
Bentley
Medhurst; Winter, Hughes, Armstrong, Harris, Macaulay, Campbell, Billington, Bentley, Goulden, McInnes.

1949-50
Apr 26 v Heart of Midlothian (h) 3-2
Billington, Bentley 2
Medhurst; Bathgate, Hughes, Armstrong, Harris, Mitchell, Gray, Williams, Bentley, Billington, Jones.
Att: 10,228

1950-51
May 12 v Heart of Midlothian (a) 2-0
R.Smith 2
Robertson; Bathgate, Tickridge, Allister, Saunders, Mitchell, Parsons, Campbell, R.Smith, Armstrong, Gray.
Att: 20,000

1951-2
Apr 23 v Heart of Midlothian (h) 3-2
D'Arcy 2, Armstrong
Robertson; Tickridge, Willemse, Armstrong, Harris, Dickson, Gray, D'Arcy, R.Smith, Campbell, J.Smith.
Att: 7,471

1953-4
Mar 31 v Heart of Midlothian (a) 3-1
Bentley, Willemse, McNichol
Robertson; Harris, P.Sillett, McKnight, Greenwood, Saunders, Parsons, McNichol, Bentley, Stubbs, Willemse.
Att: 10,000

1963-4
Apr 24 v Heart of Midlothian (a) 0-2
Bonetti; Hinton, McCreadie, Hollins, Mortimore, R.Harris, Murray, Tambling, Mulholland, McCalliog, Knox.
Att: 7,000

1980-81
Jul 26 v Heart of Midlothian (a) 1-0
Viljoen
Borota; Rofe, Sulley, Elmes, Droy, Chivers, Viljoen, Fillery, Lee, Walker, Langley.
Att: 6,126

Southern Floodlight Cup

1956-7
Sep 26 v Luton Town (a) 2-4
Stubbs, Owen (og)
Robertson; MacFarlane, Livingstone, Armstrong, Dicks, Casey, Baker, McNichol, Stubbs, Brabrook, Block.

1951 Festival of Britain Matches

May 8 v Floriana (Malta) (h) 5-1
Gray, Bentley, Armstrong, Smith 2
Robertson; Bathgate, Tickridge, McKnight, Saunders, Allister, Parsons, Bentley, R.Smith, Armstrong, Gray.
Att: 11,436
May 15 v KB Copenhagen (Denmark) (h) 1-0
Armstrong
Robertson; Bathgate, Tickridge, Dickson, Saunders, Mitchell, Campbell, Bentley, R.Smith, Armstrong, Gray.
Att: 11,905

Anglo-Scottish Cup

1975-6
Group Matches
Aug 2 v Bristol City (h) 1-0
Swain
Sherwood; Harris, G.Wilkins, Cooke, Droy, Dempsey, Britton, R.Wilkins(Stanley), Maybank, Garner, Swain.
Att: 7,515

Aug 6 v Norwich City (h) 1-1
Garner
Sherwood; Harris, G.Wilkins, Stanley, Wicks, Dempsey, Britton, R.Wilkins, Maybank(Garner), Hutchinson, Bason.
Att: 7,886
Aug 9 v Fulham (a) 0-1
Sherwood; Harris, G.Wilkins, Cooke, Wicks, Dempsey, Britton, R.Wilkins, Stanley, Garner (Maybank), Bason.
Att: 13,080

1976-7
Group Matches
Aug 7 v Fulham (h) 0-0
Bonetti; Locke, G.Wilkins, Stanley, Wicks, Hay (Droy), Britton, R.Wilkins, Finnieston, Swain, Lewington.
Att: 12,001
Aug 11 v Norwich City (h) 1-1
Finnieston
Bonetti; Locke, G.Wilkins, Bason, Wicks, Harris,

Chelsea training on board the boat to South America at the end of the 1928-9 season.

Action from Chelsea's game against Independiente during their South American tour in May 1929.

Britton, R.Wilkins, Finnieston, Lewington, Swain.
Att: 7,130
Aug 14 v Orient (a) 1-2
Droy
Phillips; Locke, G.Wilkins, Stanley, Droy, Hay (Dempsey), Britton, R.Wilkins, Finnieston, Lewington, Swain.
Att: 6,591

1977-8
Group Matches
Aug 6 v Fulham (a) 0-1
Bonetti; Locke, Harris, Britton, Droy, Wicks, Stanley, R.Wilkins, Langley, Lewington, Garner.
Att: 9,821
Aug 9 v Orient (h) 2-0
Langley, Finnieston

Bonetti; G.Wilkins, Sparrow, Stanley, Droy(Harris), Wicks, Swain, R.Wilkins, Finnieston, Lewington, Langley.
Att: 5,702
Aug 13 v Norwich City (h) 2-2
Finnieston, R.Wilkins
Bonetti(Phillips); Locke, Sparrow, Stanley, Wicks, Harris, Swain, R.Wilkins, Finnieston, Lewington, Garner.
Att: 6,858

Coronation Festival

1952-3
May 4 v Fulham (a) 1-1
McNichol
Robertson; Harris, Willemse, Rule, Greenwood, Mitchell, Gray, McNichol, Stubbs, Edwards, Blunstone.
Att: 9,000

Glasgow Charity Cup

1965-6
Aug 11 v Glasgow Select XI (Hampden Park) 3-0
Tambling 2, Graham
Bonetti; Shellito, R.Harris, Hollins, Hinton, Boyle, Bridges, McCalliog, Graham, Venables, Tambling.
Att: 36,641

Prince Philip Cup

1975-6
Oct 27 v Italy Under-23s (h) 0-0
Bonetti; Harris, Sparrow, Stanley, Droy, Dempsey (Wicks), Britton(Lewington), R.Wilkins, Maybank, Hutchinson, Garner.
Att: 9,061

Former Chelsea players at the 1967 FA Cup Final banquet. Standing (from left to right): Andy Wilson, George Mills and Billy Russell. Seated (from second left): Nils Middleboe, Bob Thomson and B.Howard Baker.

Norfolk Invitation Cup

1979-80
Mar 18 v Norwich City (a) 0-2
Borota; G.Wilkins(Chivers), Rofe, Viljoen, Pates,
Nutton, Britton, Sulley, Langley, Walker(Rhoades-
Brown), Hales(Johnson).
Att: 2,209

*Chelsea's 1980 squad. Back row (left to right): Tommy
Langley, Gary Johnson, Colin Lee, Gary Chivers, Peter
Rhoades-Brown. Middle row: Geoff Hurst (manager),
Dennis Rofe, John Sparrow, Colin Pates, Petar
Borota, Bob Iles, Micky Nutton, Gary Locke, Mike
Fillery, Bobby Gould (assistant manager). Front row:
Ian Britton, Colin Viljoen, Clive Walker, John
Bumstead, Kevin Hales.*

The Chelsea Reserves

Before World War One (1914-1918) Chelsea were members of the South-Eastern League
and (for four seasons) the London League. Both these competitions were open to clubs
in the South of England to provide football for reserve teams.

South Eastern League

Season	Teams	P	W	D	L	F	A	Pts	Pos
1905-06	13	24	8	1	15	55	60	17	10th
1906-07	13	24	7	4	13	50	52	18	10th
1907-08	18	34	19	6	9	84	37	44	4th
1908-09	20	38	21	8	9	75	41	50	3rd
1909-10	18	34	23	6	5	86	30	52	1st
1910-11	19	36	25	8	3	89	36	58	2nd
1911-12	20	38	24	9	5	87	32	57	1st
1912-13	19	36	25	4	7	97	28	54	1st
1913-14	21	40	18	8	14	65	44	44	8th
1914-15		No details available.							

London League

Season	Teams	P	W	D	L	F	A	Pts	Pos
1905-06	8	14	9	1	4	46	20	19	2nd
1906-07	10	18	4	5	9	35	44	13	7th
1907-08		Did not enter competition.							
1908-09		Did not enter competition.							
1909-10	10	18	13	3	2	58	18	29	1st
1910-11	8	14	9	2	3	33	14	20	3rd

The London (Football) Combination

The London Combination League started at the beginning of season 1915-16 to provide competitive football for teams in the London area after the Football League, bowing to external pressure, had decided to suspend activities during World War One. For four seasons it operated in this way until 'normal' League football was resumed in September 1919. Since then it has continued as a competition for reserve teams in London and surrounding areas, at one time embracing a total of 32 Football League clubs.

Season	Teams	P	W	D	L	F	A	Pts	Pos
1919-20	10	36	12	9	15	43	53	33	7th
1920-21	10	36	12	11	13	51	51	35	6th
1921-22	11	40	12	13	15	47	43	37	7th
1922-23	11	40	16	13	11	58	57	45	5th
1923-24	12	44	21	12	11	74	61	54	3rd
1924-25	12	44	18	12	14	74	53	48	5th
1925-26	12	44	16	12	16	64	72	44	6th
1926-27	22	42	17	3	22	66	73	37	17th
1927-28	22	42	22	8	12	102	72	52	5th
1928-29	22	42	20	10	12	92	63	50	4th
1929-30	22	42	18	7	17	89	81	43	9th
1930-31	22*	42	26	7	9	101	48	59	2nd
1931-32	22*	42	20	9	13	85	74	49	5th
1932-33	24*	46	20	6	20	77	98	46	10th
1933-34	24	46	18	11	17	75	85	47	11th
1934-35	24	46	18	14	14	87	81	50	7th
1935-36	24	46	22	9	15	100	81	52	5th
1936-37	24	46	23	9	14	91	64	54	5th
1937-38	24	46	19	11	16	88	73	49	7th
1938-39	24	46	21	11	14	88	71	53	6th
Competition suspended during World War Two									
1946-47	16§	30	12	3	15	66	63	27	10th
1947-48	16§	30	18	5	7	71	33	41	2nd
1948-49	16‡	30	21	5	4	74	24	47	#1st
1949-50	16§	30	18	5	7	61	31	41	3rd
1950-51	16§	30	20	6	4	64	33	46	#1st
1951-52	16‡	30	20	3	7	63	35	43	2nd
1952-53	16*	30	11	6	13	41	48	28	10th
1953-54	16*	30	15	6	9	68	36	36	3rd
1954-55	16*	30	18	4	8	72	37	40	1st
1955-56	32	42	28	7	7	116	49	63	2nd
1956-57	32	42	28	8	6	110	55	64	2nd
1957-58	32	42	33	4	5	131	36	70	1st
1958-59	18*	34	23	4	7	88	42	50	2nd
1959-60	18*	34	23	5	6	80	36	51	1st
1960-61	18*	34	24	5	5	111	45	53	1st
1961-62	18•	34	17	5	12	84	59	39	5th
1962-63	18•	34	19	10	5	67	33	48	1st
1963-64	18†	34	21	6	7	74	27	48	1st
1964-65	18*	34	24	5	5	100	32	53	1st
1965-66	18*	34	12	7	15	72	77	31	11th
1966-67	17*	32	11	6	15	58	77	28	11th
1967-68	15*	28	13	5	10	43	40	31	5th
1968-69	26	25	9	4	12	33	46	22	15th
1969-70	26	25	8	5	12	36	40	21	18th
1970-71	22	42	14	8	20	54	62	36	15th
1971-72	21	40	12	12	16	51	51	36	16th
1972-73	21	40	17	11	12	36	38	45	7th

Season	Teams	P	W	D	L	F	A	Pts	Pos
1973-74	22	42	17	9	16	63	53	43	12th
1974-75	21	40	26	11	3	76	33	63	1st
1975-76	22	42	20	10	12	81	51	60	6th
1976-77	22	42	26	12	4	96	32	64	1st
1977-78	22	42	18	12	12	68	42	48	8th
1978-79	22	42	18	14	10	74	54	50	7th
1979-80	22	42	23	9	10	66	43	55	4th
1980-81	22	42	21	7	14	80	64	49	8th
1981-82	20	38	11	9	18	42	58	31	14th
1982-83	22	42	19	7	16	80	61	45	7th
1983-84	22	42	25	5	12	84	38	55	3rd
1984-85	22	42	30	5	7	97	38	65	1st
1985-86	22	42	26	5	11	107	40	57	4th
1986-87	20	38	24	8	6	87	33	56	2nd
1987-88	20	38	16	8	14	60	54	40	10th
1988-89	20	38	20	9	9	74	52	49	5th
1989-90	20	38	22	6	10	78	47	72	3rd
1990-91	20	38	24	7	7	93	43	79	1st

* Division One.   § Section 'B'.
† Division Two.   • Midweek Section.
‡ Section 'A'.

\# Championship 'play-offs'
1948-49   Chelsea 3 Arsenal 1
1950-51   Arsenal 5 Chelsea 0

Kevin Hales, pictured in 1979.

Chelsea Reserves' line-up in 1979-80. Back row (left to right): John Sitton, Micky Nutton, Bob Iles, Colin Pates, Timmy Elmes, Jimmy Clare, Gary Johnson. Front row: Gary Donnellian, Peter Rhoades-Brown, Chris Sulley, Kevin Hales, Tommy Langley.

Football Combination Cup

Season	Teams	P	W	D	L	F	A	Pts	Pos	Season	Teams	P	W	D	L	F	A	Pts	Pos
1946-47	8*	14	12	0	2	28	16	24	#1st	1953-54	8†	14	7	6	1	27	15	20	2nd
1947-48	8*	14	8	2	4	27	18	18	2nd	1954-55	8†	14	8	3	3	31	13	19	2nd
1948-49	8†	14	9	2	3	30	15	21	2nd		No competition from 1955-56 to 1965-66								
1948-50	8†	14	7	6	1	20	13	20	3rd	1966-67	3‡	4	2	1	1	6	5	5	2nd
1950-51	8†	14	7	2	5	24	16	16	2nd	1967-68	5‡	8	2	4	2	14	18	8	3rd
1951-52	8†	14	11	1	2	38	21	23	2nd	1968-69	6§	10	6	2	2	17	9	14	2nd
1952-53	8†	14	6	2	6	16	15	14	4th	1969-70	6•	9	1	3	5	10	17	5	°5th

Competition discontinued from season 1970-71

* Section Four.   § Group A.   # Cup semi-final.
† Section Two.   • Group B.   1946-47   Swansea Town 3 Chelsea 1
‡ Group Two.   ° Final fixture cancelled

A pre-war Chelsea squad of the early 1920s. Back row (left to right): J.Hutchinson, J.Priestley, T.Grey, W.Marsh, C.Hampton, F.Barrett, F.Linfoot, W.Bennett. Third row: T.Meehan, G.Dale, W.Harrison, J.Frew, A.Thain, W.Ferguson, I.Holling. Second row: H.Ford, J.Lee, J.Armstrong, H.Wilding, B.Howard Baker, H.Sillito, G.Alsop, T.Langton, S.Smith. Front row: W.Haywood, B.Sharp, J.Ashford, J.Cock, J.Harrow, D.Cameron, J.Duncan, G.Smith, R.McNeil.

The London Challenge Cup

1908-09
Round 1
Brentford (h) 4-1
Round 2
Millwall Athletic (a) 1-2

1909-10
Round 1
Brentford (h) 6-0
Round 2
Queen's Park Rangers (h) 0-1

1910-11
Round 1
Clapton (h) 5-0
Round 2
Tottenham Hotspur (a) 0-3

1911-12
Round 1
Crystal Palace (h) 2-1
Round 2
Woolwich Arsenal (a) 3-2
Semi-final
Clapton Orient (at Craven Cottage) 1-5

1912-13
Round 1
Dulwich Hamlet (a) 3-0
Round 2
Barking (a) 0-0
Replay
Barking (h) 7-0
Semi-final
West Ham United (at The Den) 0-4

1913-14
Round 1
Bromley (a) 2-2
Replay
Bromley (h) 6-0
Round 2
Woolwich Arsenal (h) 0-1

1914-15
Round 1
Queen's Park Rangers (a) 0-1

1915-16 to 1918-19
No competition owing to war.

1919-20
Round 1
Clapton Orient (h) 2-1
Round 2
Nunhead (a) 6-0
Semi-final
Queen's Park Rangers (at Highbury) 1-0
Final
Crystal Palace (at Highbury) 1-0

1920-21
Round 1
Ilford (h) 2-1
Round 2
Clapton Orient (h) 0-1

1921-22
Round 1
Millwall Athletic (h) 0-3

1922-23
Round 1
West Ham United (h) 1-3

1923-24
Round 1
Clapton Orient (a) 1-3

1924-25
Round 1
Arsenal (a) 0-2

1925-26
Round 1
Crystal Palace (h) 4-0
Round 2
Brentford (a) 1-3

1926-27
Round 1
Fulham (a) 3-3
Replay
Fulham (h) 1-0
Round 2
Millwall (h) 1-0
Semi-final
Crystal Palace (at The Den) 3-2
Final
Clapton Orient (at Highbury) 2-1

1927-28
Round 1
Clapton (h) 4-5

1928-29
Round 1
West Ham United (a) 1-4

1929-30
Round 1
Dulwich Hamlet (h) 4-0
Round 2
Clapton Orient (h) 3-0
Semi-final
Brentford (at Craven Cottage) 0-1

1930-31
Round 1
West Ham United (a) 2-1
Round 2
Tottenham Hotspur (h) 1-2

1931-32
Round 1
Thames (h) 4-2
Round 2
Fulham (h) 0-2

1932-33
Round 1
Queen's Park Rangers (a) 1-2

1933-34
Round 1
Queen's Park Rangers (a) 2-1
Round 2
Millwall (h) 4-1
Semi-final
Arsenal (at Highbury) 2-3

1934-35
Round 1
Wimbledon (a) 2-1
Round 2
Charlton Athletic (h) 2-0
Semi-final
Brentford (h) 0-1

1935-36
Round 1
Millwall (a) 2-1
Round 2
Tottenham Hotspur (h) 0-1

1936-37
Round 1
Millwall (a) 0-2

1937-38
Round 1
Charlton Athletic (a) 2-2
Replay
Charlton Athletic (h) 0-3

1938-39
Round 1
West Ham United (a) 2-2
Replay
West Ham United (h) 2-1
Round 2
Queen's Park Rangers (a) 3-3
Replay
Queen's Park Rangers (h) 2-2*
Second Replay
Queen's Park Rangers (h) 1-3

1939-40 to 1945-46
No competition owing to war.

1946-47
Round 1
Charlton Athletic (h) 1-1
Replay
Charlton Athletic (a) 0-5

1947-48
Round 1
Charlton Athletic (a) 3-1
Round 2
Queen's Park Rangers (h) 2-1
Semi-final
Tottenham Hotspur (a) 1-1*
Replay
Tottenham Hotspur (h) 1-2

1948-49
Round 1
Crystal Palace (h) 3-2*
Round 2
Arsenal (h) 4-1
Semi-final
Charlton Athletic (h) 5-1
Final
West Ham United (at White Hart Lane) 1-1*

Replay
West Ham United (at White Hart Lane) 1-2

1949-50
Round 1
Tooting & Mitcham (a) 7-1
Round 2
Millwall (a) 3-1
Semi-final
Fulham (h) 1-1
Replay
Fulham (a) 5-2
Final
Brentford (at Highbury) 4-4
Replay
Brentford (at Highbury) 3-0

1950-51
Round 1
Millwall (a) 1-2

1951-52
Round 1
West Ham United (a) 0-2

1952-53
Round 1
Millwall (a) 3-3
Replay
Millwall (h) 2-0
Round 2
Finchley (h) 5-3*
Semi-final
West Ham United (a) 1-5

1953-54
Round 1
Crystal Palace (h) 3-0
Round 2
Tottenham Hotspur (h) 7-2
Semi-final
West Ham United (h) 1-0
Final
Arsenal (h) 1-1
Replay
Arsenal (a) 2-3

1954-55
Round 1
Crystal Palace (a) 2-1
Round 2
Tottenham Hotspur (h) 2-0
Semi-final
Arsenal (a) 1-4

1955-56
Round 1
Hendon (h) 6-3
Round 2
Crystal Palace (h) 8-0
Semi-final
Brentford (a) 2-6

1956-57
Round 1
Tottenham Hotspur (h) 1-2

1957-58
Round 1
Charlton Athletic (a) 1-3

1958-59
Round 1
Crystal Palace (a) 1-3

1959-60
Round 1
Wembley (h) 16-0
Round 2
Arsenal (a) 2-1
Semi-final
Tottenham Hotspur (a) 4-1
Final
Tooting & Mitcham (h) 2-1

1960-61
Round 1
Bexleyheath (h) 2-1
Round 2
Queen's Park Rangers (h) 4-0
Semi-final
Leyton Orient (h) 1-0
Arsenal (h) 3-1

1961-62
Round 1
Charlton Athletic (a) 1-1
Replay
Charlton Athletic (h) 4-0
Round 2
West Ham United (a) 2-1
Semi-final
Millwall (h) 3-3
Replay
Millwall (a) 0-2

1962-63
Round 1
Leyton Orient (h) 3-1

Round 2
Brentford (a) 5-0
Semi-final
Wimbledon (a) 0-0
Replay
Wimbledon (h) 2-1
Final
Arsenal (a) 1-4

1963-64
Round 1
Finchley (h) 4-0
Round 2
Arsenal (h) 3-0
Semi-final
Barnet (a) 6-2
Final
Tottenham Hotspur (a) 0-2

1964-65
Round 1
Fulham (a) 3-0
Round 2
Tottenham Hotspur (a) 2-1
Semi-final
Leyton Orient (h) 6-3
Final
Brentford (a) 1-2

1965-66
Round 1
Queen's Park Rangers (a) 0-1

1966-67
Round 1
Barnet (a) 2-3

1967-68
Round 1
Brentford (a) 2-0
Round 2
Millwall (a) 1-1
Replay
Millwall (h) 3-2
Semi-final
Dagenham (a) 0-1

1968-69
Round 1
West Ham United (h) 1-1
Replay
West Ham United (a) 3-3*
Second Replay
West Ham United (a) 2-4

1969-70
Round 1
Queen's Park Rangers (h) 0-1

1970-71
Round 1
Fulham (a) 1-1
Replay
Fulham (h) 3-2
Round 2
West Ham United (a) 1-6

1971-72
Round 1
West Ham United (a) 0-1

1972-73
Round 1
Charlton Athletic (h) 1-1
Replay
Charlton Athletic (a) 2-1
Round 2
Orient (h) 1-2

1973-74
Round 1
West Ham United (a) 0-0
Replay
West Ham United (h) 0-2

Competition discontinued from 1974-75.

Middlesex Senior Charity Cup

1988-89
Round 4
Staines Town (a) 1-0
Round 5
Feltham (a) 6-2
Semi-final
Hounslow (a) 4-2
Final
Kingsbury Town (h) 4-0

1989-90
Round 3
Kingsbury Town (a) 5-2
Round 4
Ruislip Manor (a) 5-0
Semi-final
Wembley (a) 2-0
Final
Hampton (a) 2-1

1990-91
Round 3
Brook House (a) 6-0
Round 4
Wembley (a) 3-2
Semi-final
Hayes (a) 1-2

Jimmy Greaves poaches another goal for Chelsea, this time against Spurs, the club he later joined and also served with great distinction.

Roy Bentley gets the better of the Blackpool defence at Stamford Bridge during the 1949-50 season. Centre-half Hayward is well beaten as Johnston and Suart (number-two) look on.

The Chelsea Juniors

The South East Counties League

Season	Teams	P	W	D	L	F	A	Pts	Pos
1954-55	11	20	18	1	1	93	16	37	1st
1955-56	11	20	13	5	2	84	30	31	2nd
1956-57	13	24	23	0	1	159	19	46	1st
1957-58	15	28	23	2	3	151	21	48	1st
1958-59	16	30	25	4	1	149	21	54	1st
1959-60	14	26	17	3	6	102	29	37	1st
1960-61	15	28	24	1	3	117	27	49	1st
1961-62	14	26	21	1	4	96	31	43	1st
1962-63	16	30	24	3	3	96	22	51	1st
1963-64	16	30	22	4	4	121	34	48	2nd
1964-65	16	30	20	3	7	107	51	43	3rd
1965-66	16	30	20	2	8	93	46	42	3rd
1966-67	16	30	16	6	8	86	51	38	4th
1967-68	16	30	20	5	5	90	45	45	2nd
1968-69	17	32	13	4	15	79	65	30	8th
1969-70	16	30	9	7	14	47	63	25	11th
1970-71	16	30	19	2	9	73	36	40	4th
1971-72	16	30	15	8	7	54	30	38	4th
1972-73	17	32	21	5	6	94	43	47	3rd
1973-74	17	32	26	3	3	86	19	55	1st
1974-75	16	30	13	7	10	64	46	33	7th
1975-76	16	30	19	3	8	63	26	41	3rd
1976-77	16	30	20	6	4	67	30	46	2nd
1977-78	16	30	20	2	8	73	33	42	3rd
1978-79	16	30	14	4	12	65	59	*28	9th
1979-80	16	30	4	9	17	34	58	17	15th
1980-81	16	30	11	7	12	38	39	29	9th
1981-82	16	30	11	4	15	30	47	26	12th
1982-83	15	28	10	9	9	53	53	29	6th
1983-84	16	30	23	5	2	87	29	51	1st
1984-85	16	30	17	8	5	76	40	42	4th
1985-86	16	30	22	3	5	93	41	47	2nd
1986-87	16	30	19	4	7	65	35	42	3rd
1987-88	16	30	16	5	9	65	42	37	5th
1988-89	16	30	13	5	12	60	50	31	7th
1989-90	16	30	17	8	5	59	22	42	2nd
1990-91	16	30	11	5	14	47	49	27	9th

* points deducted for fielding ineligible player.

FA Youth Cup

1952-53
Round 2
Oxford City (h) 6-0
Round 3
Queen's Park Rangers (a) 1-3

1953-54
Round 1
Headington United (a) 1-0
Round 2
Queen's Park Rangers (h) 3-0
Round 3
Brentford (a) 2-1
Round 4
Bexleyheath & W (a) 2-4

1954-55
Round 1
Queen's Park Rangers (h) 8-0
Round 2
Fulham (h) 6-2
Round 3
Crystal Palace (a) 8-0
Round 4
West Ham United (h) 3-0
Round 5
Portsmouth (a) 5-1
Semi-final (1st leg)
Manchester United (h) 1-2
Semi-final (2nd leg)
Manchester United (a) 1-2
(Lost 2-4 on aggregate)

1955-56
Round 2
Hendon (a) 9-0
Round 3
Tottenham (h) 2-0
Round 4
West Ham United (a) 3-1
Round 5
Chesterfield (h) 0-1

1956-57
Round 1
Fulham (h) 10-1
Round 2
Southend United (a) 8-0
Round 3
Peterborough (h) 10-1
Round 4
Arsenal (a) 0-3

1957-58
Preliminary Round
Grays Athletic (h) 12-0
Round 1
Woodford YC ((h) 14-0
Round 2
Queen's Park Rangers (h) 4-0
Round 3
West Ham United (a) 3-1
Round 4
Bexleyheath & W (a) 11-0

Round 5
Southampton (h) 4-1
Semi-final (1st leg)
Arsenal (h) 3-1
Semi-final (2nd leg)
Arsenal (a) 3-1
Won 6-2 on aggregate.
Final (1st leg)
Wolverhampton Wanderers (h) 5-1
Final (2nd leg)
Wolverhampton Wanderers (a) 1-6
Lost 6-7 on aggregate.

1958-59
Round 2
Briggs Sports (a) 13-0
Round 3
Charlton Athletic (a) 3-4

1959-60
Round 1
West Thurrock (h) 10-0
Round 2
Colchester United (a) 9-1
Round 3
Ford United (a) 0-0
Replay
Ford United (h) 11-0
Round 4
Portsmouth (a) 2-1
Round 5
Aston Villa (h) 3-0

Semi-final (1st leg)
Bristol City (a) 3-0
Semi-final (2nd leg)
Bristol City (h) 3-0
Won 6-0 on aggregate.
Final (1st leg)
Preston North End (h) 1-1
Final (2nd leg)
Preston North End (a) 4-1
Won 5-2 on aggregate.

1960-61
Round 1
Ipswich Town (h) 7-0
Round 2
Fulham (h) 9-0
Round 3
Tottenham (h) 4-0
Round 4
Oxford United (h) 7-0
Round 5
Swindon Town (a) 3-0
Semi-final (1st leg)
Arsenal (h) 2-0
Semi-final (2nd leg)
Arsenal (a) 2-0
Won 4-0 on aggregate.
Final (1st leg)
Everton (h) 4-1
Final (2nd leg)
Everton (a) 1-2
Won 5-3 on aggregate.

1961-62
Preliminary Round
Gorleston (h) 10-0
Round 1
Cator Rovers (a) 8-0
Round 2
Ipswich Town (h) 3-0
Round 3
Arsenal (a) 2-1
Round 4
Cambridge United (a) 3-0
Round 5
West Ham United (h) 2-1
Semi-final (1st leg)
Wolverhampton Wanderers (h) 0-1
Semi-final (2nd leg)
Wolverhampton Wanderers (a) 0-3
Lost 0-4 on aggregate.

1962-63
Round 2
Tottenham (h) 1-0
Round 3
Cambridge United (h) 4-0
Round 4
Wolverhampton Wanderers (h) 0-1

1963-64
Round 2
Eton Manor (a) 8-1
Round 3
Arsenal (a) 1-3

1964-65
Round 2
Queen's Park Rangers (a) 4-1

Round 3
Swindon Town (a) 8-1
Round 4
Charlton Athletic (h) 2-0
Round 5
Wolverhampton Wanderers (a) 3-1
Semi-final (1st leg)
Arsenal (a) 1-4
Semi-final (2nd leg)
Arsenal (h) 2-0
Lost 3-4 on aggregate.

1965-66
Round 2
Crystal Palace (h) 4-0
Round 3
Charlton Athletic (a) 1-3

1966-67
Round 2
Queen's Park Rangers (a) 4-3
Round 3
Millwall (a) 0-2

1967-68
Round 2
Limbury Old Boys (h) 12-0
Round 3
Arsenal (h) 3-1
Round 4
Ipswich Town (a) 3-0
Round 5
Crystal Palace (h) 3-5

1968-69
Round 2
Oxford United (a) 6-0
Round 3
Queen's Park Rangers (a) 1-0
Round 4
Arsenal (h) 2-1
Round 5
West Bromwich Albion (h) 1-2

1969-70
Round 2
Fulham (h) 3-2
Round 3
Millwall (h) 0-3

1970-71
Round 2
Orient (h) 2-0
Round 3
Tottenham (h) 1-2

1971-72
Round 2
Orient (a) 0-0
Replay
Orient (h) 3-0
Round 3
Millwall (h) 3-2
Round 4
Crystal Palace (h) 3-0
Round 5
Aston Villa (h) 1-1

Replay
Aston Villa (a) 0-3

1972-73
Round 2
Fulham (h) 2-0
Round 3
Queen's Park Rangers (h) 4-0
Round 4
Stoke City (a) 5-0
Round 5
Sunderland (a) 1-1
Replay
Sunderland (h) 3-2
Semi-final (1st leg)
Ipswich (a) 0-1
Semi-final (2nd leg)
Ipswich (h) 0-0
Lost 0-1 on aggregate.

1973-74
Round 2
Slough Town (h) 1-0
Round 3
Derby County (h) 1-1
Replay
Derby County (a) 1-2

1974-75
Round 2
Gillingham (h) 5-1
Round 3
Newport County (h) 2-0
Round 4
Rotherham United (a) 1-0
Round 5
West Ham United (a) 2-2
Replay
West Ham United (h) 1-2

1975-76
Round 2
Charlton Athletic (a) 1-2

1976-77
Round 2
Queen's Park Rangers (a) 3-3
Replay
Queen's Park Rangers (h) 1-0
Round 3
Ipswich Town (a) 2-2
Replay
Ipswich Town (h) 3-0
Round 4
Crystal Palace (h) 2-3

1977-78
Round 2
Queen's Park Rangers (h) 5-1
Round 3
Crystal Palace (h) 0-3

1978-79
Round 2
Oxford United (a) 3-0
Round 3
Southampton (h) 0-1

1979-80
Round 2
West Ham United (a) 1-3

1980-81
Round 2
Ipswich Town (h) 3-2
Round 3
Tottenham Hotspur (h) 1-1
Replay
Tottenham Hotspur (a) 0-1

1981-82
Round 2
Crystal Palace (a) 1-0
Round 3
Cardiff City (h) 1-1
Replay
Cardiff City (a) 0-2

1982-83
Round 2
Leatherhead (a) 2-0
Round 3
Southampton (h) 3-0
Round 4
Sunderland (a) 1-0
Round 5
Sheffield Wednesday (a) 2-4

1983-84
Round 2
Charlton Athletic (h) 5-1
Round 3
Portsmouth (h) 1-0

Round 4
Brentford (h) 5-0
Round 5
Stoke City (h) 1-2

1984-85
Round 2
Fulham (h) 0-1

1985-86
Round 2
Bristol Rovers (h) 2-4

1986-87
Round 1
Aldershot (a) 4-0
Round 2
Cardiff City (a) 1-1
Replay
Cardiff City (h) 6-0
Round 3
Southend United (a) 1-1
Replay
Southend United (h) 2-0
Round 4
Wimbledon (a) 3-1
Round 5
Leicester City (h) 1-1
Replay
Leicester City (a) 1-2

1987-88
Round 2
West Ham United (a) 2-0

Round 3
Watford (a) 3-2
Round 4
Tottenham Hotspur (a) 0-6

1988-89
Round 2
Wimbledon (a) 4-0
Round 3
Ipswich Town (h) 2-2
Replay
Ipswich Town (a) 1-2

1989-90
Round 2
Maidenhead United (h) 5-1
Round 3
Ipswich Town (a) 0-1

1990-91
Round 2
Brentford (a) 2-2
Replay
Brentford (h) 1-1
Second Replay
Brentford (a) 7-4
Round 3
Crystal Palace (h) 4-0
Round 4
Wimbledon (h) 2-2
Replay
Wimbledon (a) 0-2

Southern Junior Floodlit Cup

1955-56
Round 1
Reading (a) 11-1
Round 2
Crystal Palace (a) 6-0
Semi-final
Portsmouth (a) 8-0
Final
West Ham United (a) 2-1

1956-57
Round 1
Queen's Park Rangers (a) 6-1
Round 2
Luton Town (a) 5-0
Semi-final
Tottenham Hotspur (a) 3-2
Final
West Ham United (h) 1-2

1957-58
Round 1
Crystal Palace (a) 10-0
Round 2
Tottenham Hotspur (h) 4-0
Semi-final
West Ham United (a) 0-3

1958-59
Round 1
Queen's Park Rangers (a) 3-1
Round 2
Bexleyheath (h) 7-1
Semi-final
Southampton (h) 3-0
Final
West Ham United (h) 0-1

1959-60
Round 1
Brentford (a) 2-0
Round 2
Southend United (h) 5-0
Semi-final
West Ham United (h) 3-2*
Final
Reading (a) 3-0

1960-61
Round 1
Leyton Orient (a) 7-1
Round 2
Tottenham Hotspur (h) 2-1
Semi-final
Fulham (h) 5-1

Final
Portsmouth (a) 3-1

1961-62
Round 1
Luton Town (h) 2-1
Round 2
Fulham (h) 5-0
Semi-final
Tottenham Hotspur (h) 1-0
Final
Portsmouth (a) 1-1
Replay
Portsmouth (h) 3-1

1962-63
Round 1
Bexleyheath (h) 5-0
Round 2
Fulham (h) 3-1
Semi-final
Tottenham Hotspur (a) 0-1

1963-64
Round 1
Brentford (a) 3-1
Round 2
Charlton Athletic (h) 4-2

Semi-final
Portsmouth (a) 3-0
Final (1st leg)
West Ham United (h) 2-0
Final (2nd leg)
West Ham United (a) 3-1
Won 5-1 on aggregate.

1964-65
Round 1
Arsenal (h) 3-1
Round 2
Charlton Athletic (h) 0-1*

1965-66
Round 1
Brentford (h) 0-1

1966-67
Round 1
Reading (h) 6-1
Round 2
Southampton (h) 8-0
Semi-final
West Ham United (a) 2-7

1967-68
Round 1
Romford (a) 5-1
Round 2
Bristol City (h) 1-1
Replay
Bristol City (a) 2-1
Semi-final
Arsenal (h) 2-3

1968-69
Round 1
Brighton & Hove Albion (a) 1-0
Round 2
Orient (h) 3-2
Semi-final
Ipswich Town (a) 0-4

1969-70
Round 1
Cambridge United (h) 4-0
Round 2
Arsenal (a) 1-0
Round 3
Coventry City (h) 1-1
Replay
Coventry City (a) 0-2

1970-71
Round 1
Bournemouth & Boscombe Athletic
(a) 2-1
Round 2
Southampton (a) 0-0
Replay
Southampton (h) 5-2
Round 3
Bristol City (h) 2-2
Replay
Bristol City (a) 3-4

1971-72
Round 1
Brentford (a) 3-2
Round 2
Swindon Town (a) 1-1
Replay
Swindon Town (h) 2-0
Round 3
Southampton (a) 2-1*
Semi-final
Aston Villa (h) 1-0
Final 1
Coventry City (h) 1-0
Final 2
Coventry City (a) 1-3
Lost 2-3 on aggregate.

1972-73
Round 1
West Bromwich Albion (h) 2-2
Replay
West Bromwich Albion (a) 0-2

1973-74
Round 1
Brentford (a) 2-1
Competition suspended owing to
floodlighting ban in fuel crisis.

1974-75
Round 1
Gillingham (h) 3-0
Round 2
Tottenham Hotspur (h) 0-3

1975-76
Results for this season have never
been made available.

1976-77
Round 1
Bye
Round 2
Derby County (a) 0-2

1977-78
Round 1
Fulham (a) 2-2
Replay
Fulham (h) 0-3

1978-79
Round 1
Portsmouth (a) 1-0
Round 2
Southampton (h) 1-0
Round 3
Leicester City (h) 1-4

1979-80
Round 1
Bye
Round 2
Aston Villa (a) 1-2

1980-81
Preliminary Round
Leicester City (a) 0-0

Replay
Leicester City (h) 1-2

1981-82
Round 1
Ipswich Town (a) 3-1
Round 2
Queen's Park Rangers (h) 3-0
Round 3
Aston Villa (a) 1-2

1982-83
Round 1
Leicester City (a) 0-3

1983-84
Round 1
Queen's Park Rangers (a) 1-2

1984-85
Round 1
Fulham (h) 1-0
Round 2
Charlton Athletic (h) 4-3*
Round 3
Southampton (h) 3-1
Round 4
Ipswich Town (a) 0-1

1985-86
Round 1
Oxford United (h) 5-2
Round 2
Arsenal (a) 0-1

1986-87
Round 1
Brighton & Hove Albion (a) 2-2
Replay
Brighton & Hove Albion (h) 3-1*
Round 2
Southampton (a) 1-0
Round 3
Crystal Palace (a) 3-0
Semi-final
Arsenal (h) 1-0
Final (1st leg)
Luton Town (h) 1-2
Final (2nd leg)
Luton Town (a) 0-4
Lost 1-6 on aggregate.

1987-88
Preliminary Round
Wimbledon (h) 2-1
Round 1
Millwall (a) 2-0
Round 2
Southampton (a) 4-4
Replay
Southampton (h) 1-4

1988-89
Round 1
Charlton Athletic (h) 2-3

1989-90
Round 1
Fulham (a) 4-0
Round 2
Luton Town (h) 0-1

1990-91
Round 1
Charlton Athletic (a) 1-1
Replay
Charlton Athletic (h) 2-0

Round 2
Cambridge United (a) 5-2
Round 3
Millwall (a) 0-2

South-East Counties League Cup

1955-56
Round 1 (1st leg)
Arsenal (a) 0-6
Round 1 (2nd leg)
Arsenal (h) 4-2
Lost 4-8 on aggregate.

1956-57
Round 1 (1st leg)
Bexleyheath (h) 9-0
Round 1 (2nd leg)
Bexleyheath (a) 6-0
Won 15-0 on aggregate.
Round 2 (1st leg)
Arsenal (h) 6-0
Round 2 (2nd leg)
Arsenal (a) 6-1
Won 12-1 on aggregate.
Semi-final
West Ham United (h) 6-0
Final
Charlton Athletic (h) 3-2

1957-58
Round 1
Charlton Athletic (a) 4-1
Round 2
Watford (h) 4-0
Semi-final
Queen's Park Rangers (h) 2-0
Final (1st leg)
Portsmouth (h) 5-1
Final (2nd leg)
Portsmouth (a) 8-1
Won 13-2 on aggregate.

1958-59
Round 1
Crystal Palace (h) 6-0
Round 2
Luton Town (h) 9-0
Semi-final
Arsenal (h) 4-1
Final (1st leg)
Portsmouth (h) 4-1
Final (2nd leg)
Portsmouth (a) 4-1
Won 8-2 on aggregate.

1959-60
Round 1
Millwall (a) 2-1
Round 2
Portsmouth (h) 3-2
Semi-final
West Ham United (a) 0-1

1960-61
Round 1
Portsmouth (a) 1-2

1961-62
Round 1
Charlton Athletic (h) 3-0
Round 2
Luton Town (a) 5-1
Semi-final
Arsenal (h) 0-3

1962-63
Round 1
Watford (a) 3-2
Round 2
Arsenal (h) 1-0
Semi-final
Fulham (a) 2-0
Final 1
Brighton & Hove Albion (a) 5-1
Final 2
Brighton & Hove Albion (h) 1-0
Won 6-1 on aggregate.

1963-64
Round 1
Fulham (h) 1-5

1964-65
Round 1
Crystal Palace (h) 4-1
Round 2
Arsenal (h) 2-1
Semi-final
Queen's Park Rangers (h) 2-1
Final (1st leg)
Millwall (h) 2-1
Final (2nd leg)
Millwall (a) 2-0
Won 4-1 on aggregate.

1965-66
Round 1
Brentford (a) 0-1

1966-67
Round 1
Charlton Athletic (h) 1-4

1967-68
Round 1
Ipswich Town (h) 1-4

1968-69
Round 1
West Ham United (h) 2-3

1969-70
Round 1
Reading (a) 2-1
Match awarded to Reading — Chelsea fielded an ineligible player.
1970-71
Round 1
Crystal Palace (h) 1-4

1971-72
Round 1
Reading (a) 3-3
Replay
Reading (h) 4-0
Round 2
Ipswich Town (a) 2-1
Semi-final
Arsenal (h) 0-0
Replay
Arsenal (a) 0-0*
Second Replay
Arsenal (h) 0-1*

1972-73
Round 1
West Ham United (a) 5-0
Round 2
Luton Town (h) 3-0
Semi-final
Tottenham Hotspur (a) 3-2
Final (1st leg)
Watford (h) 3-0
Final (2nd leg)
Watford (a) 2-0
Won 5-0 on aggregate.

1973-74
Round 1
Millwall (a) 2-1
Round 2
Charlton Athletic (h) 1-1*
Replay
Charlton Athletic (a) 2-0
Semi-final
Arsenal (h) 0-0*
Replay
Arsenal (a) 1-0
Final (1st leg)
Ipswich Town (h) 1-0
Final (2nd leg)
Ipswich Town (a) 0-0
Won 1-0 on aggregate.

1974-75
Round 1
Reading (h) 3-1

Round 2
Orient (h) 1-0
Semi-final
Tottenham Hotspur (a) 2-0
Final (1st leg)
West Ham United (h) 3-0
Final (2nd leg)
West Ham United (a) 2-6
Lost 5-6 on aggregate.

1975-76
Round 1
Watford (a) 0-1

1976-77
Round 1
Ipswich Town (a) 1-2

1977-78
Round 1
West Ham United (h) 0-0*
Replay
West Ham United (a) 4-0
Round 2
Orient (a) 5-0
Semi-final
Portsmouth (a) 1-2

1978-79
Round 1
Norwich City (a) 1-6

1979-80
Round 1
Crystal Palace (h) 2-2*
Replay
Crystal Palace (a) 0-2

1980-81
Round 1
Crystal Palace (h) 2-0
Round 2
Queen's Park Rangers (a) 1-0

Semi-final
Norwich City (h) 1-2

1981-82
Round 1
Watford (a) 0-0*
Replay
Watford (h) 3-1
Round 2
Orient (a) 4-4*
Replay
Orient (h) 0-1

1982-83
Round 1
Southend United (h) 2-3

1983-84
Round 1
Ipswich Town (h) 2-0
Round 2
Orient (a) 6-1
Semi-final
Arsenal (h) 4-1
Final (1st leg)
West Ham United (a) 5-0
Final (2nd leg)
West Ham United (h) 1-2
Won 6-2 on aggregate.

1984-85
Round 1
Charlton Athletic (a) 6-0
Round 2
Arsenal (h) 0-4

1985-86
Round 1
Charlton Athletic (a) 3-1
Round 2
Watford (h) 0-0*
Replay
Watford (a) 1-3

1986-87
Round 1
Fulham (h) 1-0
Round 2
Wimbledon (h) 2-2*
Replay
Wimbledon (a) 3-2
Round 3
Luton Town (a) 2-2*
Replay
Luton Town (h) 4-0
Semi-final
Brighton & Hove Albion (h) 2-1
Final (1st leg)
Ipswich Town (h) 7-1
Final (2nd leg)
Ipswich Town (a) 3-1
Won 10-2 on aggregate.

1987-88
Round 1
Fulham (a) 3-0
Round 2
Wimbledon (h) 1-1*
Replay
Wimbledon (a) 1-3

1988-89
Round 1
Cambridge United (h) 2-0
Round 2
Portsmouth (a) 0-2

1989-90
Round 1
Bournemouth (h) 4-0
Round 2
Brighton & Hove Albion (h) 0-2

1990-91
Round 1
Queen's Park Rangers (h) 3-1
Round 2
Bournemouth (h) 0-1

London FA Youth Cup
London Minor Cup (Under 18)

1955-56
Round 1
Arsenal (a) 9-0
Semi-final
Tottenham Hotspur (a) 0-3

1956-57
Round 1
Eton Manor (h) 15-0
Round 2
Woodford (h) 4-6

1957-58
Round 1
West Ham United (h) 5-1
Round 2
Eton Manor (h) 15-1

Semi-final
Tottenham Hotspur (h) 6-3
Final
Bexleyheath (a) 2-3

1958-59
Round 1
West Ham United (a) 2-1
Round 2
Fulham (a) 4-1
Semi-final
Tottenham Hotspur (a) 1-1
Replay
Tottenham Hotspur (h) 3-0
Final
Queen's Park Rangers (a) 4-2

1959-60
Round 1
Bexleyheath (h) 3-0
Round 2
Tottenham Hotspur (h) 4-2
Semi-final
West Ham United (h) 0-2

1960-61
Round 1
Queen's Park Rangers (h) 5-0
Round 2
Barking (a) 10-0
Semi-final
Tottenham Hotspur (a) 3-2
Final
Arsenal (a) 6-1

1961-62
Semi-final
Fulham (a) 3-2
Final
Arsenal (h) 4-2

1962-63
Round 1
Brentford (h) 4-0
Round 2
Arsenal (h) 3-1
Semi-final
Bexleyheath (a) 3-1
Final
West Ham United (a) 0-2

1963-64
Round 1
Queen's Park Rangers (h) 4-2
Round 2
Crystal Palace (a) 0-2

1964-65
Round 1
Leyton Orient (h) 2-1
Round 2
Queen's Park Rangers (h) 1-2

1965-66
Round 2
Millwall (a) 2-1
Semi-final
Fulham (a) 2-0
Final
Charlton Athletic (a) 0-3

1966-67
Round 1
Fulham (a) 3-2
Round 2
Queen's Park Rangers (h) 3-1
Semi-final
Crystal Palace (a) 0-1

1967-68
Round 2
Tottenham Hotspur (a) 1-4

1968-69
Round 1
Crystal Palace (a) 2-1
Semi-final
Orient (a) 1-0*
Final
Tottenham Hotspur (a) 2-1

1969-70
Round 2
Fulham (a) 0-2

1970-71
Round 1
Millwall (a) 3-1
Round 2
Fulham (a) 3-1
Semi-final
Tottenham Hotspur (a) 1-2

1971-72
Round 1
West Ham United (h) 1-0
Semi-final
Millwall (h) 4-1
Final
Crystal Palace (a) 0-1*

Competition discontinued from 1972-73.

* denotes after extra time.

Former England Schoolboy international centre-forward Barry Bridges is welcomed to Stamford Bridge by coach Albert Tennant in May 1958.

Chelsea Internationals

A TOTAL of 71 players have won full international honours whilst in the service of Chelsea. Dates given are for the second half of the season (*ie* 1984 refers to season 1983-4). The figure in brackets behind each set of appearances is the total number of caps won whilst with Chelsea only. Before 1925 there was only one Ireland team. Ray Wilkins, honoured 24 times by England, won more caps whilst with Chelsea than any other player.

England

Ken Armstrong 1955 v Scotland. (1)
B.Howard Baker 1921 v Belgium; 1926 v Ireland. (2)
Dave Beasant 1990 v Italy(sub), v Yugoslavia(sub). (2)
Roy Bentley 1949 v Sweden; 1950 v Scotland, Portugal, Belgium, Chile, USA; 1953 v Wales, Belgium; 1955 v Wales, West Germany, Spain, Portugal. (12)
Frank Blunstone 1955 v Wales, Scotland, France, Portugal; 1957 v Yugoslavia. (5)
Peter Bonetti 1966 v Denmark; 1967 v Spain, Austria; 1968 v Spain; 1970 v Holland, Portugal, West Germany. (7)
Peter Brabrook 1958 v Russia; 1959 v Northern Ireland; 1960 v Spain. (3)
Barry Bridges 1965 v Scotland, Hungary, Yugoslavia; 1966 v Austria. (4)
Jack Cock 1920 v Scotland, Ireland. (2)
Jackie Crawford 1931 v Scotland. (1)
Kerry Dixon 1985 v Mexico(sub), West Germany, USA; 1986 v Northern Ireland, Israel, Mexico(sub), Poland(sub); 1987 v Sweden. (8)
Tony Dorigo 1990 v Yugoslavia(sub), v Czechoslovakia(sub) v Denmark(sub), v Italy; 1991 v Hungary(sub). (5)
Jimmy Greaves 1959 v Peru, Mexico, USA; 1960 v Wales, Sweden, Yugoslavia, Spain; 1961 v Northern Ireland, Luxembourg, Spain, Wales, Scotland, Portugal, Italy, Austria. (15)
Jack Harrow 1923 v Ireland, Sweden. (2)
George Hilsdon 1907 v Ireland; 1908 v Ireland, Scotland, Wales, Austria, Hungary, Bohemia; 1909 v Ireland. (8)
John Hollins 1967 v Spain. (1)
Tommy Lawton 1947 v Northern Ireland, Wales, Scotland, Republic of Ireland, Holland, France, Switzerland, Portugal; 1948 v Wales, Northern Ireland, Belgium. (11)
Tommy Meehan 1924 v Ireland. (1)
George Mills 1938 v Wales, Northern Ireland, Czechoslovakia. (3)
Peter O'Dowd 1932 v Scotland; 1933 v Northern Ireland, Switzerland. (3)
Peter Osgood 1970 v Belgium, Rumania(sub), Czechoslovakia(sub); 1974 v Italy. (4)
Ken Shellito 1963 v Czechoslovakia. (1)
Peter Sillett 1955 v France, Spain, Portugal. (3)
Dick Spence 1938 v Austria, Belgium. (2)
Bobby Tambling 1963 v Wales, France; 1966 v Yugoslavia. (3)
Terry Venables 1965 v Belgium, Holland. (2)
Ben Warren 1909 v Scotland, Ireland, Wales, Hungary (twice), Austria; 1911 v Scotland, Ireland, Wales. (9).
Ray Wilkins 1976 v Italy; 1977 v Republic of Ireland, Finland, Northern Ireland, Brazil, Argentina, Uruguay; 1978 v Switzerland(sub), Luxembourg, Italy, West

Germany, Wales, Northern Ireland, Scotland, Hungary; 1979 v Denmark, Republic of Ireland, Czechoslovakia, Northern Ireland, Wales, Scotland, Bulgaria, Sweden(sub), Austria. (24)
Jimmy Windridge 1908 v Scotland, Wales, Ireland, Austria (twice), Hungary, Bohemia; 1909 v Ireland. (8)
Dennis Wise 1991 v Turkey. (1)
Vic Woodley 1937 v Scotland, Norway, Sweden, Finland; 1938 v Scotland, Wales, Northern Ireland, Czechoslovakia, Germany, Switzerland, France; 1939 v Scotland, Wales, Northern Ireland, Rest of Europe, Norway, Italy, Rumania, Yugoslavia. (19)
Vivian Woodward 1910 v Ireland; 1911 v Wales. (2)

Scotland
Peter Buchanan 1938 v Czechoslovakia. (1)
Jack Cameron 1909 v England. (1)
Bobby Campbell 1950 v Switzerland, Portugal, France. (3)
Steve Clarke 1987 v Hungary, Belgium, Bulgaria; 1988 v Saudi Arabia, Malta. (5)
Charlie Cooke 1966 v Portugal, Brazil; 1968 v England, Holland; 1969 v Wales, Northern Ireland, Austria, West Germany(sub), Cyprus (twice); 1970 v Austria; 1971 v Spain, Portugal. (14)
Angus Douglas 1911 v Ireland. (1)
Gordon Durie 1988 v Bulgaria(sub); 1989 Italy(sub), Cyprus; 1990 v Yugoslavia, East Germany, Egypt, Sweden; 1991 v Switzerland, Bulgaria (twice), Russia(sub), v San Marino. (12)
Bobby Evans 1960 v Austria, Hungary, Turkey. (3)
Hughie Gallacher 1934 v England. (1)
Johnny Jackson 1934 v England; 1935 v England; 1936 v Wales, Northern Ireland. (4)
Tommy Law 1928 v England; 1930 v England. (2)
Eddie McCreadie 1965 v England, Spain, Poland, Finland; 1966 v Northern Ireland, Poland, Wales, Italy, Portugal; 1967 v England, Russia; 1968 v Northern Ireland, Wales, England, Holland; 1969 v Austria, Denmark, Cyprus (twice), West Germany, Wales, Northern Ireland, England. (23)
Pat Nevin 1986 v Rumania(sub), England(sub); 1987 v Luxembourg, v Republic of Ireland, v Belgium(sub); 1988 v Luxembourg (6).
David Speedie 1985 v England; 1986 v Wales, E.Germany(sub), Austria, England. (5)

Wales
Gordon Davies 1985 v Norway. (1)
Gareth Hall 1988 v Yugoslavia(sub), Malta, Italy; 1989 v Holland, Finland, Israel; 1990 v Republic of Ireland. (7)
Tom Hewitt 1913 v England, Scotland, Ireland. (3)
Evan Jones 1910 v Scotland, Ireland. (2)
Joey Jones 1983 v Yugoslavia, England, Bulgaria, Scotland, Northern Ireland, Brazil; 1984 v England, Northern Ireland v Norway (twice), Rumania, Scotland, Bulgaria, Israel, Yugoslavia; 1985 v Iceland, Norway (twice), Scotland. (19)
Graham Moore 1962 v Brazil; 1963 Hungary, Northern Ireland. (3)
Peter Nicholas 1989 v Holland, Finland, Israel, Sweden, West Germany; 1990 v Finland, Holland, West Germany, Republic of Ireland, Sweden, Costa Rica, Denmark(sub), Belgium, Luxembourg; 1991 v Republic of Ireland. (15)
Eddie Niedzwiecki 1985 v Norway(sub); 1988 v Denmark. (2)
John Phillips 1973 v England; 1974 v England; 1975 v Hungary(sub); 1978 v Kuwait. (4)
Mickey Thomas 1984 v Scotland, England; 1985 v Iceland (twice), Spain (twice), Scotland, Norway; 1986 v Scotland. (9)

Northern Ireland

Joe Bambrick 1935 v Wales; 1936 v England, Scotland; 1938 v Wales. (4)
Seamus (Jimmy) D'Arcy 1952 v Wales; 1953 v England. (2)
Bill Dickson 1951 v Wales, France; 1952 v Scotland, England, Wales; 1953 v England, Scotland, France, Wales. (9)
Jim Ferris 1921 v England, Scotland. (2)
Sam Irving 1929 v England; 1931 v Wales. (2)
Johnny Kirwan 1906 v England, Scotland, Wales; 1907 v Wales. (4)
Billy Mitchell 1934 v Wales, Scotland; 1935 v Scotland, England; 1936 v Scotland, England; 1937 v England, Scotland, Wales; 1938 v England, Scotland. (11)
Tom Priestley 1934 v England. (1)
Kevin Wilson 1988 v Yugoslavia, Turkey; v Greece(sub), Poland(sub), Hungary, France(sub), Spain (twice), Malta, Chile; 1990 v Republic of Ireland(sub), Norway, Uruguay; 1991 v Yugoslavia (twice), Austria, Poland, Faroe Islands. (18)

Republic of Ireland

John Dempsey 1969 v Czechoslovakia, Denmark; 1970 v Hungary, West Germany; 1971 v Poland, Sweden (twice), Italy; 1972 v Iran, Ecuador, Chile, Portugal. (12)
Paddy Mulligan 1970 v Hungary, Poland, West Germany; 1971 v Poland, Sweden, Italy; 1972 v Austria, Iran, Ecuador, Chile, Portugal. (11)
Andy Townsend 1991 v Morocco, Turkey, England (twice), Wales, Poland. (6)
Dick Whittaker 1959 v Czechoslovakia. (1)

Australia

Dave Mitchell 1989 v Israel. (1)

Norway

Erland Johnsen 1990 v Korea, Northern Ireland, Sweden. (3)

Great Britain v Rest of Europe

Tommy Lawton 1947. (1)

Wartime and Victory Internationals
(No caps were awarded for these games)

England

Alf Hanson 1941 v Scotland. (1)
Vic Woodley 1940 v Wales, Scotland. (2)

Wales

Jack Smith 1940 v England. (1)

'B' Internationals

England

Ken Armstrong 1953 v Scotland, West Germany, Yugoslavia. (3)
Dave Beasant 1989 v Italy(sub) v Republic of Ireland, Czechoslovakia(sub), Switzerland, Iceland(sub), Norway(sub); 1991 v Wales. (7)
Roy Bentley 1948 v Holland. (1)
Tony Dorigo 1989 v Italy, Switzerland, Iceland, Norway; 1991 v Iceland. (5)

Billy Gray 1949 v Switzerland. (1)
Peter Sillett 1956 v Scotland. (1)
Stan Willemse 1953 v Switzerland. (1)

Scotland
Steve Clarke 1989 v Yugoslavia. (1)
Gordon Durie 1989 v Yugoslavia. (1)

Under-23 Internationals

England
Tommy Baldwin 2, Alan Birchenall 2, Frank Blunstone 5, Peter Bonetti 12, Peter Brabrook 9, Jimmy Greaves 11, Ron Harris 4, Mike Harrison 3, John Hollins 12, Alan Hudson 5, Ian Hutchinson 2, Steve Kember 2, Bert Murray 6, Peter Osgood 6, Mel Scott 4, Ken Shellito 1, Peter Sillett 3, Bobby Tambling 13, Terry Venables 4, Ray Wilkins 2.

Scotland
George Graham 2, Tommy Hughes 2.

Wales
Graham Moore 3, John Phillips 4.

Under-21 Internationals

England
Jason Cundy 2, Kerry Dixon 1, Tony Dorigo 4, Tommy Langley 1, David Lee 6, Damien Matthew 4, Graham Le Saux 4, Graham Stuart 5, Ray Wilkins 1.

Scotland
Eamonn Bannon 2, Gordon Durie 4, Pat Nevin 5, David Speedie 1.

Wales
Roger Freestone 1, Gareth Hall 1.

Republic of Ireland
Leo Donnellan 1.

Youth Internationals

England
Glen Aitken, Mike Block, Barry Bridges, David Cliss, John Cowen, Bobby Evans, Mike Fillery, Steve Francis, Jimmy Greaves, Ian Hamilton, Allan Harris, Ron Harris, John Hollins, Cliff Huxford, Keith Jones, Tommy Langley, Bobby Laverick, David Lee, Barry Lloyd, Gary Locke, S.McDonald, Bert Murray, Andrew Myers, Tony Nicholas, Peter Osgood, Colin Pates, Phil Priest, Colin Shaw, Barry Smart, Graham Stuart, Terry Venables, Eric Whitington, Steve Wicks, Ray Wilkins, Ray Willis.

Football League Representative Appearances

Ken Armstrong 1955 v Scottish League. (1)
Benjamin Howard Baker 1925 v Irish League. (1)
Roy Bentley 1949 v League of Ireland; 1953 v League of Ireland; 1955 v Scottish League. (3)
Sid Bishop 1928 v Scottish League. (1)
Frank Blunstone 1955 v Scottish League; 1960 v League of Ireland. (2)
Peter Bonetti 1966 v Irish League; 1967 v Scottish League; 1969 v Scottish League, League of Ireland. (4)
Peter Brabrook 1957 v Irish League; 1960 v League of Ireland; 1961 v Scottish League. (3)
Steve Clarke 1987 v Rest of the World. (1)
Jack Cock 1920 v Scottish League. (1)
Jimmy Greaves 1958 v Scottish League, 1960 v Scottish League, League of Ireland; 1961 v Scottish League. (4)
Harold Halse 1913 v Scottish League; 1914 v Southern League. (2)
Jack Harrow 1914 v Southern League (1).
George Hilsdon 1906 v Irish League. (1)
John Hollins 1967 v Scottish League; 1967 v Belgian League; 1971 v Scottish League. (3)
Tommy Lawton 1947 v Irish League. (1)
Tommy Meehan 1922 v Irish League. (1)
George Mills 1937 v Irish League. (1)
Pat Nevin 1987 v Rest of the World. (1)
Peter O'Dowd 1932 v Irish League. (1)
Peter Osgood 1968 v Irish League; 1969 v Scottish League, 1971 v League of Ireland. (3)
John Sillett 1960 v League of Ireland. (1)
Peter Sillett 1957 v Scottish League. (1)
Bobby Tambling 1969 v Scottish League. (1)
Fred Taylor 1909 v Southern League. (1)
Ron Tindall 1957 v League of Ireland. (1)
Jack Townrow 1926 v The Army. (1)
Terry Venables 1964 v Irish League. (1)
Ben Warren 1908 v Scottish League. (1)
Stan Wicks 1956 v Irish League. (1)
Ray Wilkins 1976 v Scottish League. (1)
Stan Willemse 1954 v Scottish League. (1)
Vic Woodley 1937 v Scottish League, Irish League; 1938 v Irish League, Scottish League. (4)
Vivian Woodward (2) 1909 v Scottish League; 1913 v Scottish League.

Most Internationals in a Chelsea Team:

The most full international players in a single Chelsea team were the eight who lined up against Sunderland in a First Division match at Stamford Bridge on 13 December 1930. There were five Scots (Tommy Law, Alex Jackson, Alex Cheyne, Hughie Gallacher and Andy Wilson); two Englishmen (Jack Townrow and Sid Bishop); and one Irish cap (Sam Irving). Chelsea won the match 5-0.

Football League representatives George Hilsdon (above left); Terry Venables (above right); Ben Warren (below left); Bobby Tambling (below right).

Chelsea Records

Player-of-the-Year
Joe Mears Memorial Trophy Winners

1967	Peter Bonetti	1980	Petar Borota
1968	Charlie Cooke	1981	Petar Borota
1969	David Webb	1982	Mike Fillery
1970	John Hollins	1983	Joey Jones
1971	John Hollins	1984	Pat Nevin
1972	David Webb	1985	Kerry Dixon
1973	Peter Osgood	1986	David Speedie
1974	Gary Locke	1987	Pat Nevin
1975	Charlie Cooke	1988	Gordon Durie
1976	Ray Wilkins	1989	Graham Roberts
1977	Ray Wilkins	1990	Kevin Wilson
1978	Micky Droy	1991	Andy Townsend
1979	Tommy Langley		

Chelsea Official Supporters' Club Award

1978	Micky Droy	1985	David Speedie
1979	Tommy Langley	1986	Eddie Niedzwiecki
1980	Clive Walker	1987	Pat Nevin
1981	Petar Borota	1988	Tony Dorigo
1982	Mike Fillery	1989	Graham Roberts
1983	Joey Jones	1990	Kenneth Monkou
1984	Pat Nevin	1991	Andy Townsend

Ever-present in a Football League Season

Ken Armstrong 1947-8; Dave Beasant 1989-90; Peter Borota 1980-81; Allan Craig 1934-5; Kerry Dixon 1983-4, 1989-90; Tony Dorigo 1987-8; Willie Ferguson 1926-7; Billy Gray 1951-2; Jimmy Greaves 1958-9; Ron Harris 1964-5, 1966-7, 1972-3, 1974-5; John Hollins 1968-9, 1971-2, 1972-3, 1973-4; Peter Houseman 1969-70; Ray Lewington 1976-7; Gary Locke 1976-7; Reg Matthews 1957-8; Tommy Meehan 1922-3; Bobby McNeil 1921-2; Tommy Miller 1906-07; John Mortimore 1962-3; Eddie Niedzwiecki 1983-4; Peter Osgood 1967-8; Eric Parsons 1954-5; Colin Pates 1981-2, 1983-4; Graham Roberts 1988-9; Derek Saunders 1954-5; George Smith 1922-3, 1926-7; Terry Venables 1962-3; Dave Webb 1968-9; Bob Whittingham 1910-11; Stan Wicks 1955-6; Ray Wilkins 1975-6, 1976-7; Vic Woodley 1932-3.

Most Consecutive Appearances

John Hollins: 167 appearances (14 August 1971 to 25 September 1974 inclusive) comprising 135 Football League, 10 FA Cup, 18 Football League Cup, 4 European Cup-winners' Cup.

More Than 300 First-team Appearances

	Total	League	FA Cup	League Cup	Others	European
Ron Harris (1961-1979)	784(11)	646(9)	64	46(2)	1*	27
Peter Bonetti (1959-1978)	729	600	57	45	1*	26
John Hollins (1963-1983)	592	465	51	48	1*	27
Eddie McCreadie (1962-1973)	405(5)	327(4)	41	21(1)	-	16
John Bumstead (1978-1991)	379(30)	318(24)	20(1)	29(5)	12‡	-
Ken Armstrong (1947-1956)	402	362	39	-	1*	-
Peter Osgood (1964-1979)	376(4)	286(3)	34	30	1*	25(1)
Charlie Cooke (1965-1977)	360(13)	289(10)	32(2)	22(1)	-	17
Kerry Dixon (1983-1991)	372(2)	303(1)†	14(1)	38(1)	17‡	-
George Smith (1921-1931)	370	351	19	-	-	-
Bobby Tambling (1958-1969)	366(4)	298(4)	36	18	-	14
Roy Bentley (1947-1956)	367	324	42	-	1*	-
John Harris (1945-1955)	364	326	38	-	-	-
Harold Miller (1923-1937)	363	337	26	-	-	-
Frank Blunstone (1952-1963)	347	317	24	3	1*	2
Colin Pates (1979-1988)	345(1)	284(1)†	20	32	9‡	-
Marvin Hinton (1963-1974)	328(16)	257(8)	30(3)	22(3)	1*	18(2)
Peter Houseman (1963-1974)	325(18)	252(17)	25	32(1)	1*	15
Jack Harrow (1911-1925)	333	304	29	-	-	-
Tommy Law (1926-1937)	319	293	26	-	-	-
Gary Locke (1972-1982)	315(2)	270(2)	24	21	-	-
Jackie Crawford (1923-1932)	308	288	20	-	-	-
Robert McNeil (1914-1927)	307	279	28	-	-	-
Micky Droy (1970-1983)	302(11)	263(9)	21	17(2)	1*	-

(Substitute appearances in brackets). ‡Full Members' Cup. *Charity Shield. †Includes Play-off games.

Bobby Tambling (11) scores against Fulham in February 1966. Tambling tops the list of Chelsea's all-time scorers, with 202 goals, and is 11th in the club's overall appearances list with 366 full games to his name.

Transfer Milestones

October 1907. First £1,000 fee paid for Fred Rouse from Stoke.
May 1930. First £10,000 fee paid for Hughie Gallacher from Newcastle United.
October 1966. First £100,000 fee paid for Tony Hateley from Aston Villa.
May 1987. Club record fee of £475,000 paid for Tony Dorigo from Aston Villa.
January 1989. Club record fee of £725,000 paid for Dave Beasant from Newcastle United.
July 1990. Current club record fee of £1,600,000 paid for Dennis Wise from Wimbledon.

Incoming £100,000 + Transfers

£100,000	Tony Hateley	Aston Villa	October 1966
£100,000	Alan Birchenall	Sheffield United	November 1967
£100,000	Keith Weller	Millwall	May 1970
£100,000	Chris Garland	Bristol City	September 1971
£170,000	Steve Kember	Crystal Palace	September 1971
£225,000	David Hay	Glasgow Celtic	July 1974
£165,000	Duncan McKenzie	Everton	September 1978
£200,000	Eamonn Bannon	Heart of Midlothian	January 1979
£200,000	Colin Lee	Tottenham Hotspur	January 1980
£200,000	Alan Mayes	Swindon Town	December 1980
£175,000	Kerry Dixon	Reading	July 1983

Crystal Palace's Steve Kember (centre) was purchased by Chelsea for £170,000 in September 1971. Alan Hudson (right) was sold for £240,000 in January 1974.

£150,000	Doug Rougvie	Aberdeen	July 1984
£300,000	Mick Hazard	Tottenham Hotspur	September 1985
£381,000	Gordon Durie	Hibernian	April 1986
£450,000	Steve Wicks	Queen's Park Rangers	July 1986
£400,000	Steve Clarke	St Mirren	January 1987
£250,000	Clive Wilson	Manchester City	March 1987
£475,000	Tony Dorigo	Aston Villa	May 1987
£335,000	Kevin Wilson	Ipswich Town	June 1987
£250,000	Kevin Hitchcock	Mansfield Town	March 1988
£475,000	Graham Roberts	Glasgow Rangers	July 1988
£350,000	Peter Nicholas	Aberdeen	August 1988
£150,000	Dave Mitchell	Feyenoord	December 1988
£725,000	Dave Beasant	Newcastle United	January 1989
£100,000	Kenneth Monkou	Feyenoord	March 1989
£650,000	Alan Dickens	West Ham United	June 1989
£306,000	Erland Johnsen	Bayern Munich	November 1989
£1,200,000	Andy Townsend	Norwich City	July 1990
£1,600,000	Dennis Wise	Wimbledon	July 1990
£800,000	Tommy Boyd	Motherwell	May 1991

Outgoing £100,000 + Transfers

£100,000	Alan Birchenall	Crystal Palace	June 1970
£100,000	Keith Weller	Leicester City	September 1971
£240,000	Alan Hudson	Stoke City	January 1974
£275,000	Peter Osgood	Southampton	March 1974
£100,000	David Webb	Queen's Park Rangers	May 1974
£100,000	Kenny Swain	Aston Villa	December 1978
£275,000	Steve Wicks	Derby County	January 1979
£875,000	Ray Wilkins	Manchester United	April 1979
£300,000	Garry Stanley	Everton	August 1979
£170,000	Eamonn Bannon	Dundee United	October 1979
£425,000	Tommy Langley	Queen's Park Rangers	August 1980
£155,000	Mike Fillery	Queen's Park Rangers	August 1983
£100,000	Mickey Thomas	West Bromwich Albion	September 1985
£100,000	Gordon Davies	Manchester City	October 1985
£400,000	Nigel Spackman	Liverpool	February 1987
£750,000	David Speedie	Coventry City	July 1987
£925,000	Pat Nevin	Everton	July 1988
£430,000	Colin Pates	Charlton Athletic	October 1988
£350,000	Darren Wood	Sheffield Wednesday	January 1989
£100,000	Mick Hazard	Portsmouth	January 1990
£450,000	Clive Wilson	Queen's Park Rangers	June 1990
£105,000	Colin West	Dundee	July 1990
£250,000	Graham Roberts	West Bromwich Albion	November 1990
(Tribunal)	Tony Dorigo	Leeds United	May 1991

Youngest Player

Ian ('Chico') Hamilton became the youngest player to make a competitive first-team appearance for Chelsea when he made his Football League debut against Tottenham Hotspur at White Hart Lane on 18 March 1967, at the age of 16 years 4 months and 18 days. Hamilton headed Chelsea's goal in the 1-1 draw.

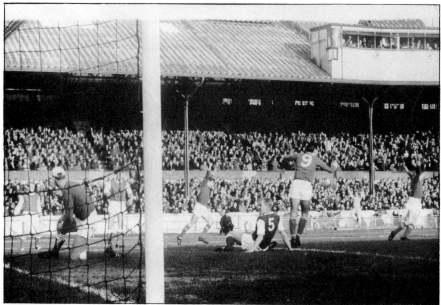

Barry Bridges (number-nine) scores Chelsea's first goal in their 3-1 win over Arsenal in November 1963. Altogether, Bridges scored 93 goals for Chelsea.

One that got away. Wolves' goalkeeper Alan Boswell saves Peter Osgood's penalty in 1968-9. Osgood scored 150 goals for Chelsea, level with the great Roy Bentley.

Oldest Player

Dick Spence became the oldest player to play in a senior competitive fixture for Chelsea when when he made his final Football League appearance against Bolton Wanderers, at Stamford Bridge, on 13 September 1947, at the age of 39 years 1 month and 26 days.

Goalscoring

Most Goals in a Season — 121 (56 matches) in 1964-65
(89 League: 11 FA Cup: 21 Football League Cup)
Most League Goals in a Season: Overall — 98 (Division One) in 1960-61
Home Games — 61 (Division One) in 1960-61
Away Games — 46 (Division Two) in 1988-89

More Than 80 First-team Goals in a Career

	Total	League	FA Cup	League Cup	Others	European
Bobby Tambling (1958-1969)	202	164	25	10	-	3
Kerry Dixon (1983-1991)	187	143†	8	25	11‡	-
Roy Bentley (1947-1956)	150	128	21	-	1*	-
Peter Osgood (1964-1979)	150	105	19	10	-	16
Jimmy Greaves (1957-1960)	132	124	3	2	-	3
George Mills (1929-1938)	123	116	7	-	-	-
George Hilsdon (1906-1911)	107	98	9	-	-	-
Barry Bridges (1958-1965)	93	80	9	3	-	1
Tommy Baldwin (1966-1974)	92	74	5	6	-	7
Hughie Gallacher (1930-1934)	81	72	9	-	-	-
Bob Whittingham (1909-1919)	80	71	9	-	-	-

† Includes one Play-off goal. ‡Full Members' Cup. * FA Charity Shield.

More Than 30 First-team Goals in a Season

	Total	League	FA Cup	League Cup	European
Jimmy Greaves (1960-1961)	43	41	-	2	-
Jimmy Greaves (1958-1959)	37	32	2	-	3
Bobby Tambling (1962-1963)	37	35	2	-	-
Kerry Dixon (1984-1985)	36	24	4	8	-
Bob Whittingham (1910-1911)	34	30	4	-	-
Peter Osgood (1969-1970)	31	23	8	-	-
Peter Osgood (1971-1972)	31	18	1	4	8
Hughie Gallacher (1931-1932)	30	24	6	-	-
Jimmy Greaves (1959-1960)	30	29	1	-	-
George Hilsdon (1907-1908)	30	24	6	-	-
Tommy Lawton (1946-1947)	30	26	4	-	-
Bob Turnbull (1925-1926)	30	29	1	-	-

Most Goals in a Match

George Hilsdon 6 v Worksop Town (h) *FA Cup, 1907-08*
George Hilsdon 5 v Glossop (h) *Division Two, 1906-07*
Jimmy Greaves 5 v Wolves (h) *Division One, 1958-9*
Jimmy Greaves 5 v Preston NE (a) *Division One, 1959-60*
Jimmy Greaves 5 v West Brom A (h) *Division One, 1960-61*
Bobby Tambling 5 v Aston Villa (a) *Division One, 1966-7*
Peter Osgood 5 v Jeunesse Hautcharage (h) *European Cup-winners' Cup, 1971-2*
Gordon Durie 5 v Walsall (a) *Division Two, 1988-9*

Miscellaneous Facts

Dick Spence's 19 League goals in 1934-5 are the most in a season by a Chelsea winger.

Peter Sillett's 34 goals between 1953-4 and 1961-2 are the most goals in a career by a Chelsea full-back.

Benjamin Howard Baker, from the penalty-spot, is the only Chelsea goalkeeper to score in a first-team match, against Bradford City in a Division One game on 19 November 1921.

Graham Roberts, with 13 successful penalty-kicks (12 in the League and one in the Full Members' Cup) in 1988-9 established a new club record for goals from spot-kicks.

Chelsea completed their last nine Division Two fixtures in 1980-81 without scoring a goal. The spell was finally broken in the 28th minute of the opening game of the 1981-2 season, 876 minutes of playing time having elapsed since the previous goal.

Best Scoring Sequence by a Player
Roy Bentley scored in eight consecutive Division One games from 10 September to 18 October 1952.

Best Goal-Average by a Player
(amongst leading scorers)
Jimmy Greaves 0.78 goals per-match

Fastest Recorded Goal
13 seconds by Ben Whitehouse v Blackburn Rovers at Stamford Bridge, *2 December 1907, Division Two.*

Paul Canoville scored a goal in 11 seconds at the start of the second half at Hillsborough on 30 January 1985 in a Football League Cup 5th-round replay.

Highest Aggregate Scores

13 Goals
Chelsea 13 Jeunesse Hautcharage (Luxembourg) 0 *European Cup-winners' Cup, 29 September 1971*
(Chelsea set up a new record for European competitions when they defeated Jeunesse Hautcharage 8-0 away and 13-0 at home for a 21-0 aggregate for the two legs).

11 Goals
Chelsea 9 Glossop 2 *Division Two, 1 September 1906.*
Liverpool 7 Chelsea 4 *Division One, 7 September 1946.*

Chelsea 5 Manchester United 6 *Division One, 16 October 1954.*
Chelsea 7 Portsmouth 4 *Division One, 25 December 1957.*
Chelsea 6 Newcastle United 5 *Division One, 10 September 1958.*

The Chelsea team which played at Villa Park on 27 March 1946, the transitional season before League soccer resumed. Back row (left to right): Albert Tennant, Danny Winter, Bill (H) Robertson, Freddie Lewis, Dick Foss. Front row: Alex Machin, Reg Williams, John Harris, Dai James, Len Goulden, Jimmy Bain.

10 Goals
Chelsea 9 Worksop Town 1 *FA Cup 1st round, 11 January 1908.*
Orient 3 Chelsea 7 *Division Two, 10 November 1979.*
Wolverhampton Wanderers 6 Chelsea 4 *Division One, 26 April 1947.*
Bolton Wanderers 5 Chelsea 5 *Division One, 30 October 1937.*
Chelsea 5 West Ham United 5 *Division One, 17 December 1966.*
Derby County 4 Chelsea 6 *Division One, 15 December 1990.*

Heaviest Defeats

Division One — 1-8 v Wolverhampton Wanderers (a) *26 September 1953.*
  — 0-7 v Leeds United (a) *7 October 1967.*
  — 0-7 v Nottingham Forest (a) *20 April 1991.*
Division Two — 0-6 v Rotherham United (a) *31 October 1981.*
FA Cup — 1-7 v Crystal Palace (a) *3rd qualifying round, 18 November 1905*
Football League Cup — 2-6 v Stoke City (a) *3rd round second replay, 22 October 1974.*
Full Members' Cup — 0-4 v Swindon Town (a) *3rd round, 19 January 1988*
European Competitions — 0-5 v CF Barcelona (a) *Fairs Cup semi-final play-off, 25 May 1966*

Heaviest Home Football League Defeats

0-6 v Notts County *Division One, 1923-4*
1-6 v Blackburn Rovers *Division One, 1912-13*
2-6 v Burnley *Division One, 1960-61*
2-6 v Southampton *Division One, 1967-8*

2-6 v Nottingham Forest *Division One, 1986-7*
3-6 v Aston Villa *Division One, 1931-2*
3-6 v Manchester United *Division One, 1959-60*
5-6 v Manchester United *Division One, 1954-5*

Points

Most In A Season

99 in 1988-9 (Division Two) Maximum possible 138; % obtained — 71
88 in 1983-4 (Division Two) Maximum possible 126; % obtained — 69
57 in 1906-07 (Division Two) Maximum possible 76; % obtained — 75
56 in 1964-5 (Division One) Maximum possible 84; % obtained — 66

In 1981-2, Chelsea also obtained 57 points, but this was out of a possible 126 and represented only 45%.

Best Points-Winning Sequence

1962-3 Division Two (20 October — 26 December) 21 points from 11 successive games

1988-9 Division Two (29 October — 15 April) 67 points from 27 successive games

Chelsea in 1965-6, the season they achieved their longest winning sequence in League and Cup combined. Back row (left to right): Hollins, Hinton, Bonetti, R.Harris, Boyle, McCreadie, Fascoine. Front row: Bridges, Graham, Osgood, Venables, Tambling.

Unbeaten Sequences

Longest in a Season (Football League)
27 matches (Division Two) 1988-9 (29 October to 8 April)
W,W,D,D,W,W,D,W,W,D,W,W,D,W,W,
W,D,W,D,W,W,W,W,W,W,W,W.

Longest Home Sequence in a Season (Football League)
21 matches (Division Two) 1976-7 (August 21 to end of season)
D,W,W,W,W,W,W,W,D,W,W,D,D,D,D,
W,W,W,W,W,W.

Longest Away Sequence in a Season (Football League)
13 (Division Two) 1988-9 (November 5 to April 8)
W,D,W,W,D,D,W,W,W,W,W,W,W.

Longest at Start of a Season
14   1925-6 (9 wins and 5 draws)   Division Two
10   1964-5 (7 wins and 3 draws)   Division One
10   1966-7 (6 wins and 4 draws)   Division One

Longest Winning League Sequence
8 Matches (Division Two) 1927-8 (4 October to 19 November)
8 Matches (Division Two) 1988-9 (15 March to 8 April)

Longest Winning Sequence in League and Cup Combined
8 Matches (6 League, 2 FA Cup) 1965-6 (27 December to 12 February)

Longest Home League Winning Sequence
10 Matches 1906-07 (1 September to 26 January)

Longest Away League Winning Sequence
7 Matches 1988-89 (4 February to 8 April)

Longest Sequence Without a League Win
21 Matches (Division One) 1987-8 (3 November to 2 April)

Most League Wins in a Season
29 (46 Matches) 1988-9

Most Home League Wins in a Season
18 (19 Matches) 1906-07

Most Away League Wins in a Season
14 (23 Matches) 1988-9

Biggest Wins

Division One
7-1 v Leeds United (h) 1934-5
7-1 v West Bromwich Albion (h) 1960-61
Division Two
9-2 v Glossop (h) 1906-07
7-0 v Portsmouth (h) 1962-3
7-0 v Burslem Port Vale (h) 1905-06
7-0 v Lincoln City (h) 1910-11
7-0 v Walsall (a) 1988-9
FA Cup
9-1 v Worksop (h) 1st round, 1907-08
Football League Cup
7-1 v Millwall (a) 1st round, 1960-61
7-0 v Doncaster Rovers (a) 3rd round, 1960-61
European Football
13-0 v Jeunesse Hautcharage, European Cup-winners' Cup 1st round 2nd leg, 1971-2.

Biggest Away Wins
8-0 v Jeunesse Hautcharage, European Cup-winners' Cup 1st round, 1st leg, 1971-2
6-1 v Newcastle United, Division One, 1960-61
6-1 v Birmingham City, Division One, 1964-5
6-2 v Aston Villa, Division One, 1966-7
6-0 v Port Vale, Division Two, 1925-6
7-3 v Orient, Division Two, 1979-80 (Chelsea's 1,000th League win)
7-1 v Millwall, League Cup 1st round, 1960-61
7-0 v Doncaster Rovers, League Cup 3rd round, 1960-61
7-0 v Walsall, Division Two, 1988-9

Chelsea Directors 1905-1991

Attenborough, Sir Richard, CBE	1969-1982	Mears, J.T.	1905-1935
Bates, Kenneth W.	1981- (*Chairman 1982-*)	Mears, H.A.	1905-1912
Bates, Robert M.	1985-1989	Mears, L.J. (Snr)	1946-1958
Bennett, J.G.	1952-1958	Mears, L.J.(Jnr)	1958-1964 & 1965-1978
Boyer, H.	1905-1922	Neal, John	1985-1986
Boyer, H.J.M.	1938-1948	Parker, F.W.	1907-1915
Budd, J.E.C.	1931-1952	Pratt, C.J. (Snr)	1922-1936 (*Chairman 1935-1936*)
Chelsea, Viscount	1964-1983 (*Chairman 1981-1982*)	Pratt, C.J. (Jnr)	1935-1968 (*Chairman 1966-1968*)
Crisp, Colonel C.D.	1926-1940 (*Chairman 1936-1940*)	Reed, Stanley G.	1981-1982
Dimbleby, Gordon	1983-1984	Schomberg, G.	1905-1913
Dobson, Major A.	1981-1982	Smith, Graham W.C.	1986-1989
Hutchinson, Colin	1989-	Spears, Barrie	1984-1986
Janes, A.F.	1905-1926	Spencer, Martin	1977-1978 & 1980-1983
Janes, E.H.	1905-1911	Thomson, G.M.	1968-1982
Kinton, T.L.	1905-1922	Thomson, Norman	1981-1982
Kinton, H.E.	1935-1940	Todd, Yvonne, S.	1989-
Kirby, W.Claude	1905-1935 (*Chairman 1905-1935*)	Tollman, Stanley S.	1982-
Maltby, J.H.	1905-1926	Webb, Gordon	1982-1984
Mears, David	1977-1983	Withey, L.R. 1948-1969 (*Chairman 1968-1969*)	
Mears, J.Brian	1958-1981 (*Chairman 1969-1981*)	Woodward, Vivian J.	1922-1930
Mears, J.H.	1931-1966 (*Chairman 1940-1966*)		

Chelsea Secretaries 1905-1991

Mr William Lewis*	1905-1907	Mr Tony Green	1971-1975
Mr Albert Palmer*	1907-1935	Miss Christine Mathews	1975-1979
Mr Harold Palmer*	1935-1947	Miss Sheila Marson	1979-1988
Mr C.E.Kemp*	1947-1948	Miss Janet Wayth	1988-1990
Mr John Battersby*	1949-1971	Miss Judy Nicholas (Match Secretary)	1990-1991

*Until the appointment of Mr Ted Drake as manager in May 1952, all previous managers had held the post of 'Secretary-manager', with the considerable help of an 'Assistant Secretary'. This latter title was therefore held by the first five incumbents above until Mr John Battersby officially became Chelsea's first 'Secretary' in May 1952.

Trainers 1905-1991

Jimmy Miller	1905-1907	Norman Smith	1946-1953
Harry Ransom	1907-1910	Jack Oxberry	1953-1960
Wright	1910-1914	Harry Medhurst	1960-1973
Jack Whitley	1919-1939	Norman Medhurst	*1973-1988
Arthur Stollery	1939-1946	Bob Ward	†1988-

*From October 1982 until the termination of his appointment, Norman Medhurst occupied the post of physiotherapist. †Physiotherapist.

SUBSCRIBERS

1 Chelsea Football Club
2 The Football League • 3 The Football Association

4 C S Cheshire	72 Benjamin Joseph Cooper	140 Leslie Kevin Turner
5 P J G Corn	73 Graham John Henderson	141 Tim Edwards
6 W H Corn	74 Carl McNeil	142 Ole Hall Olsen
7 T E Corn	75 Chris & Sarah Puddy	143 John Coates (JB)
8 Sir William Shakespeare	76 Bruce Bayliss	144 John Lathan
9 W Jacques	77 Alan Penfold	145 Alan Martin
10 J A Harris	78 Dr C J G Shaw	146 J A G Ford
11 Martin White	79 Jonathan Ivey	147 Andrew Harris
12 John Henry Hilton	80 Ralph Ogden	148 Caron Head
13 Gary Scott	81 Martin John Jackson	149 David Coughlan
14 G Columbine	82 Kevin Sayer	150 Mark Phillip Hulme
15 Barrie Coleman	83 Denis Smyth	151 Raymond Ludlow
16 Robert A Fennell	84 Antony Peck (4502)	152 John Edward Cox
17 Colin Franchi	85 N Chesterton	153 Ernest Arthur Lacey
18 Errick Peterson	86 John Coates	154 Trevor Fletcher
19 B H Standish	87 John & Sharon Balkman	155 Steven John Waite
20 Brian Spridgens	88 Albert Emons	156 Roy, Christine & Mark
21 Peter Sharp	89 Nicholas Jones	Sandom
22 Brian H Hobbs	90 Ian Thomas	157 A & J A Waterman
23 Raymond Shaw	91 Tony Banbury	158 Dave Harrison
24 John Motson	92 Steven Brett	159 S Burt
25 David Sullivan	93 Gary Riley	160 Richard Routledge
26 K P Wood	94 Gareth Campbell	161 Martin J Brooks
27 Mike Young	95 Ivan Lund	162 Neill Scott Macey
28 Harry Kay	96 John Edward Bell	163 Sgt Paul Gimson
29 David Coulson	97 Alan Wheatley	164 Hannah Harding
30 Roy K Shoesmith	98 Ross Green	165 Luke Harding
31 David Earnshaw	99 Douglas Lamming	166 Stephen Lane
32 D T Bryant	100 J M Moore	167 Doug Legge
33 Mark Southwell	101 Harald Landskroon	168 Peter Herriott
34 P Cogle	102 Alan Delaprelle	169 Peter Herriott
35 Ian Willott	103 Susan Smith	170 Frederick John Roll
36 Lars-Olof Wendler	104 R J Tickner	171 Roland Reeve
37 John Treleven	105 Lee David Carter	172 Howard Kallender
38 J A B Townsend	106 David J Clarke	173 M B Thompson
39 John Clancy	107 Andrew J P Bunyan	174 C E Thompson
40 David Keats	108 Mick Greenaway	175 Stephen Nelken
41 P J Cooke	109 Steve Frazer	176 John Henry Roberts
42 David Fisher	110 Ms Cathy McDonald	177 Sports Marketing
43 B White	111 Mark Turpin	178 J Ringrose
44 Anthony Jones	112 Gary Hearn	179 Fred Beale
45 Paul Bishop	113 Rob Harrison	180 Fred Lee
46 W D Phillips	114 J R Homes	181 Michael Patrick Palmer
47 David Downs	115 Michael Mostyn Davies	182 Michael Taylor
48 Per Norheim	116 Terence Dougan	183 Steven George Kinge
49 V I Pettitt	117 Joe Harvey	184 Michael John Whittaker
50 Colin Wood	118 Ken Keeble	185 Christopher Hawkins
51 Chris Hayes	119 Paul Woods	186 Sherry Golder
52 Brendan O'Leary	120 A N Davis	187 Anthony Ramos
53 Simon Lacey	121 A D Murrell	188 Robert Hanger
54 Lyn Bone	122 Dave Hillam	189 Philip Low
55 P A Dodman	123 John Harrison	190 David Harrington
56 Jonny Stokkeland	124 Graham David Newnham	191 Terry Last
57 Neal Lillis	125 David Terry	192 Barry Holland
58 Paul Baker	126 Mark Brian Morley	193 C J Morton
59 David John Sanders	127 Jason P Oliver	194 David J Godfrey
60 Colin J Guard	128 E C Carling	195 Gordon Small
61 Shaun Little	129 David J Radson	196 Peter A Cook
62 Nicholas John Martin	130 D A Neighbour	197 Mark Hudson
63 Paul R Southey	131 P B Clarke B.Eng, C.Eng, MICE	198 John Davies
64 Dean Burden	132 Paul Davis	199 Jonathan Brooks
65 Michael Edwards	133 John Senior	200 Andrew Roberts
66 Dermot James McCarthy	134 D J Stewart	201 Alan W Haden
67 Clifford J Hearne	135 Brian G Swan	202 Kelly Impett
68 Colin Palmer	136 Darren Floyd	203 Duncan Porter
69 Steven G Galloway	137 R L Finch	204 John Drewitt
70 David Kenyon	138 Paul Quero	205 Dennis Cotton
71 David Sparkes	139 Stephen Russell Pumfrey	206 Mark Killick

207	Robert Todd	279	David Gregg	350	A P J M Otten
208	Ove Fjellhøy	280	Rampton Hospital Library	351	Andrew Rose
209	Garth I Dykes	281	Michael Brett	352	Colin Hayes
210	Richard D N Wells	282	Allister Moore	353	Sanjit Kumar Teelock
211	Donald Noble	283	Tony Bentley	354	Carl A Magro (Malta)
212	Douglas Bidgood	284	Roy Sproule	355	Paul Moore
213	Simon Wheeler	285	Peter D Anderson	356	Christopher E C Hooker
214	Jeffrey Benham	286	Richard Reynolds		(Canada)
215	Howard Alan Inkin	287	Derek Banerji	357	Paul John Williams
216	Neil Jones	288	Arthur Karamouzis	358	Paul Anthony McAuliffe
217	Simon White	289	J Gardiner	359	M D Edroff
218	Rob Court	290	Leonard Watson	360	M R Pearce
219	Tim J Healy	291	Leonard Watson	361	Paul Vibert
220	Jim Munro	292	Ian Fear	362	Derry Good
221	Neil Turnham	293	Kevin Dodd	363	D M Siddall
222	Stephen George Durbridge	294	John L Beauchamp	364	Phil Edwards
223	Terry Sewell	295	Ernie McCluskey	365	Paul Jerome
224	Susan Cartwright	296	John McCluskey	366	Ivan Ponting
225	Göran Schönhult	297	Nigel Jessop	367	John Welsh
226	Phillip Hart	298	J D M Whitaker	368	C P Davies
227	Daniel Kerry Hyman	299	Mogens Hansen	369	R Dealey
228	James Henson	300	Tonny Pedersen	370	Sixten Ohman
229	Colin Turner	301	Mark Baker	371	John Reidy
230	Charles H Whalley	302	Alan Gardner	372	Ian Dumond
231	Natasha Creasy	303	Martin Bastick	373	Niall O'Rourke
232	Terry Frost	304	Gary Baglow	374	Graham Dunkerton
233	Peter Pickup	305	T D Culshaw	375	Matthew Landers
234	Keith Daniel	306	P Marks	376	E Kautonen
235	Gourlay Halley	307	Paul H Bannister	377	Diamant Yozef
236	Robert Briggs	308	Geoffrey Hall	378	W H Jackman
237	Maurice Curtin	309	Jim Walker	379	Gerald Hill
238	Paul Kelly	310	Stephen Dowdeswell	380	Dave Smith
239	Matthew Jackson	311	Stephen Warwick	381	Stanley A Robinson
240	Vince Balaam	312	Ian Petrie	382	Roger Wash
241	Geoffrey Wright	313	Mark A Whitmore	383	Duncan Cross
242	Trond Isaksen	314	Russell Kemp	384	Frank O'Farrell
243	Eric Woollard	315	Keith James Halliwell	385	Kieron Graham
244	Kevin A J Gee	316	Derek Wheatcroft	386	Gilbert Monnereau
245	John Stafford	317	Mike Purkiss	387	Juergen Hohmann
246	Stephen John Brooks	318	Mark Fifield	388	Ian Griffiths
247	Stephen Reilly	319	J R Hawkins	389	W R Mitchell
248	M P Waters	320	Robert Cowap	390	Alan Hindley
249	Bill Willmer	321	Ray Ellis	391	David Crawford
250	Tim Brackley	322	Angus W Rodger	392	Michael McConkey
251	Sune Ahlinder	323	Eric N Hayton	393	Pete Andrew
252	Keith Miller	324	John Van Den Elsen	394	Norman Green
253	Barry Rose	325	Ian Danks	395	P Baxter
254	Matthew Tobin	326	Derek Hyde	396	David Pease
255	Paul Leahy	327	Ingemar Stromberg	397	Dave Green
256	Reg Balch	328	Sharon Hurst	398	Theodoros Mantzouranis
257	Alexander Baldock	329	Souris Lamplighters FC	399	Patrick Gordon-Brown
258	Rick Vincent		PEI	400	Ulf Brennmo
259	Chris Eaves	330	Colin Cameron	401	Jonas Nilsson
260	L A Zammitt	331	Q C M Olsthoorn	402	Surapot Saengchote
261	David Chalk	332	David Lumb	403	Eric Heesom
262	Kim Holdaway	333	Martin Simons	404	George Mitchell
263	J S Pyke	334	M Swart	405	Jan Palsgaard
264	Michael Briggs	335	S P Tomlin	406	Roy Hinchcliffe
265	Michael Nicholas	336	Stephen Laski	407	Margaret Wittich
266	Paul Smith	337	Christopher Minchin	408	Tim Whittick
267	Riccardo Rossi	338	Rudolf Iseli	409	T W Stevenson
268	Christer Svensson	339	Harry Thompson	410	Jeff Spearing
269	Mario Antoine	340	Harald Lohr	411	Martin Humphrey
270	Maria Perrin	341	Anders Johansson	412	Duncan Pierce
271	Laurence Gething	342	Kåre M Torgrimsen	413	Andrew Anderson
272	Adrian John Davies	343	Andrew Tweddell	414	Steven F Thomas
273	D J Nelson	344	R G Woolman	415	Richard Stocken
274	Steve Welbourne	345	Richard Lane	416	David J Simmons
275	Nicholas Brown	346	John Knibbs	417	Roger G Waudby
276	Stephane Daugan	347	R J Prew	418	Paul Whetherly
277	Alan John Bannister	348	D Collett	419	Ian Harraden
278	Mark Allam	349	J W Cairns	420	Alan Jones